P9-AQE-252

Cities of the World

Cities of the World

World Regional Urban Development

THIRD EDITION

EDITED BY
STANLEY D. BRUNN, JACK F. WILLIAMS,
AND DONALD J. ZEIGLER

CARTOGRAPHY BY
ELLEN R. WHITE

ROWMAN & LITTLEFIELD PUBLISHERS, INC.
Lanham • Boulder • New York • Oxford

ROWMAN & LITTLEFIELD PUBLISHERS, INC.

Published in the United States of America
by Rowman & Littlefield Publishers, Inc.
A Member of the Rowman & Littlefield Publishing Group
4501 Forbes Blvd., Suite 200, Lanham, Maryland 20706
www.rowmanlittlefield.com

P.O. Box 317, Oxford OX2 9RU, United Kingdom

Cover photos, clockwise from top left, with location of photo, figure number, and photographer's name:

London (5.19) by Linda McCarthy; Sydney (12.6) by Jack Williams; Portland, Oregon (1.22) by Judy Walton; Moscow (6.13) by Donald Zeigler; Old Delhi (9.3) by Jack Williams; Bangkok (10.16) courtesy of Bangkok government; Dar Es Salaam (8.9) by Assefa Mehretu; Chicago (2.18) by Larry Ford; Huancayo, Peru (4.16) by Maureen Hays-Mitchell; Jerusalem (7.18) by Donald Zeigler; Macau (11.2) courtesy of Macau government; Mexico City (3.6) by Robert Smith

Earlier editions of this book were published by Pearson Education, Inc.

British Library Cataloguing in Publication Information Available

Library of Congress Cataloging-in-Publication Data

Cities of the world : world regional urban development / edited by
Stanley D. Brunn, Jack F. Williams, and Donald J. Zeigler.—3rd ed.
p. cm.
Includes bibliographical references and index.
ISBN 0-8476-9898-X (cloth : alk. paper)
1. Cities and towns. 2. City planning. 3. Urbanization. 4. Urban policy. I. Brunn, Stanley D. II. Williams, Jack F. III. Zeigler, Donald J., 1951–
HT151 .C569 2003
307.76—dc21 2002012872

Printed in the United States of America

∞ The paper used in this publication meets the minimum requirements of American National Standard for Information Sciences—Permanence of Paper for Printed Library Materials, ANSI/NISO Z39.48-1992.

Contents

Preface

Many changes have occurred in the urban scene on a global scale since the second edition of this book was published a decade ago. With nearly half the world's population now living in urban places and the daily lives of probably another third depending on decisions made in these agglomerations, it is an exciting time to study cities and related human issues. Cities are the origins of most news stories, the sites of major political and economic decisions, and the places associated with improvements in human well-being. Consider the reporting about stock markets, weather, disasters, sports, fashion, and conflicts. Most of it relates to cities.

A casual or keen observer of major global events during the past decade would associate most of them with some part of the urban realm. Political-military flash points have been associated with Sarajevo, Grozny, Freetown, and Kabul; immigrants and refugees with Los Angeles, Miami, Vienna, and Amsterdam; and terrorist attacks with New York, London, Belfast, Jerusalem, Bogotá, and Colombo. Global sports are dominated by cities competing to host major international events (the Olympics or the World Cup) and regional championships, while transnational corporations are associated with major centers of finance, telecommunications, fashion, and entertainment industries. The attributes of a mobile, fluid, and more globally conscious society are evident in the ways people identify with their places of work and residence.

Aside from these social changes, a number of technological changes have occurred that affect not only city businesses, cultures, and politics, but also the daily lives of residents. When the second edition of this book appeared in 1993, the Internet, the World Wide Web's development into a major reference source, and the use of geographic information systems in urban and regional planning all were in their infancy. Wireless communication was still a dream, the term *e-commerce* had not been coined, and cybercafes appeared only in science fiction material. Major companies, including Microsoft, America Online, and the dot.coms were not yet important in world markets. Emerging on the world urban scene is an entirely new and international mix of entrepreneurs who were not major players in regional economies and politics a decade ago. These new entrepreneurs are now just as likely to be in cities such as Moscow, Shanghai, Manila, Dubai, or Ho Chi Minh City as in the traditional capitals such as London, Paris, Rome, New York, Sydney, Tokyo, or San Francisco.

It is amid these urban dynamics that we embarked on the third edition of this book. Three changes were made in the organization. The former Latin America chapter was divided: an entire chapter is now devoted to Middle America and the Caribbean and another is devoted to South America. Second, the region of North Africa and the Middle East has been expanded to include Central Asia and retitled "The Greater Middle East."

Third, the two Europe chapters have been combined into one to reflect the forces of convergence and integration that are at work there in the post-Communist era. We made a conscious decision to include as authors some new, younger regional scholars with extensive field experience and active research agendas. Of the twenty-two authors, fifteen are new to this edition. As a result, a number of the chapters have been completely rewritten. Also, we strove to include more women authors; seven of the chapters now have been authored or coauthored by women. In any multiauthored volume on world regions, there are certain to be differences in the background, experience, research interests, and writing styles of the contributors. We consider these different experiences and approaches as assets in writing about cities and urban development in the regions covered in this volume. No two chapters are exactly alike, which adds to the appeal of the volume. Moreover, no one or two authors could possibly have the wealth of regional expertise on the entire world that our regional authors collectively bring to this volume. We believe this regional knowledge gives each of our chapters exceptional depth and accuracy, albeit within the constraints of space available to cover each of these large world culture realms.

Each region has been analyzed on the basis of some common themes:

- Evolution (history) of cities and urban development
- Settlement patterns and urban systems
- Internal structure and land-use patterns, including models
- Case studies of representative cities
- Daily life in cities
- Urban problems and solutions, including urban and regional planning initiatives

This volume also includes a number of significant changes and additions, including:

- A revision of chapter 1, an overview of "World Urban Development"
- An entirely new chapter 13, "Cities of the Future"
- A substantial number of new maps and graphs
- All-new boxes devoted to timely urban issues and problems
- More, and all-new, photographs
- More humanistic content, including that on the daily life of urban residents
- A listing of useful Web sites for urban study
- Updated appendixes using the latest United Nations data

This book is an outgrowth of a course that editors Brunn and Williams taught at Michigan State University during the 1970s. The course, Cities of the World, was a midlevel geography class that attracted students from a variety of disciplines. It is now taught as World Urban Systems in the university's Integrative Studies program. Many universities and colleges around the country have similar courses. Previous editions of this book have been used in classes on topics such as world urbanization, world cities, and cities and regions, and we believe these classes will be strong candidates for using this edition. Recognizing the changes that are occurring in entry-level geography courses in North America, especially in world regional geography and geographies of non-Western worlds, we consider this a perfect volume for teachers who choose to focus on urban issues in the context of regional geography. Whereas current world regional books focus on various themes, including economic development, culture, gender, environment, and human welfare, our book is the only one on the market with an urban focus. We believe that students will find use of an introductory- or intermediate-level book that examines cities and urban development a valuable and stimulating way to improve their knowledge of the world. The book could also be used in upper-division urban geography classes in which teachers wish to focus on world urbanism, especially to go beyond the common Eurocentric focus of many such classes currently taught. We also consider the book to be useful as supplemental reading in urban and regional planning courses; in regional courses, for example, on Europe, Asia, Latin America, Africa, or the Middle East; and in classes devoted to the developing countries, or third world.

We want to acknowledge the assistance of several individuals who were important in preparing this volume. A number of individuals at Rowman & Littlefield deserve our special thanks: executive editor Susan McEachern, who gave us valuable advice and support throughout the project; production editor Alden Perkins, who played the critical role of steering the book through the minefields of actual production and was superefficient and a pleasure to work with; copy editor Dave Compton, whose sharp eye and command of English caught errors and significantly improved the text; Piper Furbush, who designed the striking cover; and other staff who contributed to the project's completion. We thank Ellen White of Michigan State University for the cartography and graphics; she is recognized within the discipline for the quality of her craft. Thanks also to Dr. Kamesh Lullah, chief scientist at the NASA/Johnson Space Center in Houston, who provided the satellite images of cities used in the photo spread in the center of the book. We also greatly appreciate the kind words of Peter Hall in the foreword for the book. Lastly, we thank the talented team of regional experts who wrote the chapters and remained committed to the project through a long and sometimes difficult production process. Without them, there would be no book.

We, like the other authors, continue to find cities exciting to study. The combined travels of the editors include visits to cities on all six inhabited continents, while the combined travels of all twenty-two authors would likely include most of the world's countries. Even with scholars with such extensive teaching and research experience, we believe that geographers have only scratched the surface of what we know about cities. All the more reason for us to continue exploring, describing, recording, photographing, and mapping the geographies of our neighborhoods and cities.

Foreword
SIR PETER HALL

Cities of the World has become a staple of the urban geographical literature: a basic guide and compass, both for the beginning student in search of an overview of a vast territory, and for the advanced scholar seeking a particular reference point. Now, in this third edition, it has been comprehensively revised and updated to make it more essential than ever. Particularly valuable is the way it moves through three levels of analysis: from a broad synoptic and global treatment, through a regional analysis that seeks to present the essential features of the urban phenomenon as it manifests itself in the different continents and countries of the world, to a specific summary account of the great cities in each of these zones, each by local experts, isolating the key features that makes each of them unique.

Inevitably, these last are encapsulated digests: the advanced research scholar will have to dig below them—and, inspired by this book, will be enthusiastic to start the excavation. The point about *Cities of the World* is that it encourages, indeed enjoins its readers to fit the individual case into the more general context: to make comparisons and to generalize, sifting out what is common and shared, what is local and special. And this is the essence of what good geography is about.

1

World Urban Development

DONALD J. ZEIGLER, STANLEY D. BRUNN, AND JACK F. WILLIAMS

If one were to compare a map of the world as it was around the year 1900 with one of the world in 2000, two changes would be strikingly apparent: (1) the proliferation of nations and (2) the mushrooming numbers and sizes of cities. The basically simple division of the world of 1900 between the independent industrialized countries of Europe, North America, and Russia and the vast colonial empires controlled by them in Latin America, Africa, and Asia has been transformed into a far more complex mosaic of more than 190 independent nations of all sizes and levels of economic and political development. Likewise, the rather simple pattern exhibited by cities in 1900, when a relatively small number of major cities were concentrated in the industrial countries, has also been transformed, so that the greatest numbers of cities, and the largest cities, are increasingly found in the former colonial regions. Around the year 1800, perhaps 3% of the world's population lived in urban places of 5,000 people or more. The proportion had risen to more than 13% by 1900 and had skyrocketed to more than 47% by 2000. We are on the verge of becoming a majority-urbanized world.

The present phenomenon of worldwide urbanization is as dramatic in its revolutionary implications for the history of civilization as were the earlier agricultural and industrial revolutions. In the industrial countries of Europe and North America—the *more developed countries* (MDCs), as the UN calls them—urbanization accompanied and was the consequence of industrialization and economic development. Thus, cities in those regions, although far from utopias, brought previously undreamed of prosperity and longevity to the lives of millions. Industrial and economic growth combined with rapid urbanization to produce a demographic transformation that brought declining population growth and enabled the cities to expand apace with economic development. In the developing countries of Latin America, Africa, and Asia—the *less developed countries* (LDCs)—urbanization has occurred only partly as the result of industrial and economic growth and in many countries it has occurred primarily as the result of rising and unrealistic expectations of rural people who have flocked to the cities seeking escape from misery (and often not finding it). This march to the cities, unaccompanied until very recently by significant declines in natural population growth, has resulted in the explosion of urban places in the LDCs.

There is also the question of the relationship between the levels of urbanization and the degree of political and economic power. The most powerful nations of the world today are highly urbanized and have the highest standards of living, whether measured in per capita income or other standard indexes of economic and social well-being, are found in the countries with the highest percentages of urban population. A strong correlation thus exists between per capita income and percentage of urban population. But does it automatically follow that the LDCs will see corresponding rises in per capita incomes as their urban populations grow? The answer is probably that they will not, unless rates of urbanization are brought more closely in line with rates of economic growth. Otherwise, the problems of the cities multiply geometrically while the financial resources of cities and governments to deal with the problems grow only arithmetically at best. Indeed, this is exactly what is happening in many LDCs today.

However, even in the MDCs, where life for the vast majority of urban residents is incomparably better than for those living in the cities of the LDCs, there are serious concerns about the future of the city. What, for example, is the optimum size of a city? Are cities in general getting too large to permit effective administration and to ensure an adequate, let alone ideal and humane, urban environment to live in? Is the megalopolis, or superconurbation, to be the norm for the 21st century? What will be the impact of vast urban agglomerations on human society, on resource development, on environmental preservation, and on governments facing increased social disparities, cultural pluralism, and diversity of political expression?

These are not easy questions to answer. But these and many other questions are addressed in one way or another in the various regional chapters and in the concluding chapter, which looks at the future of the world's cities.

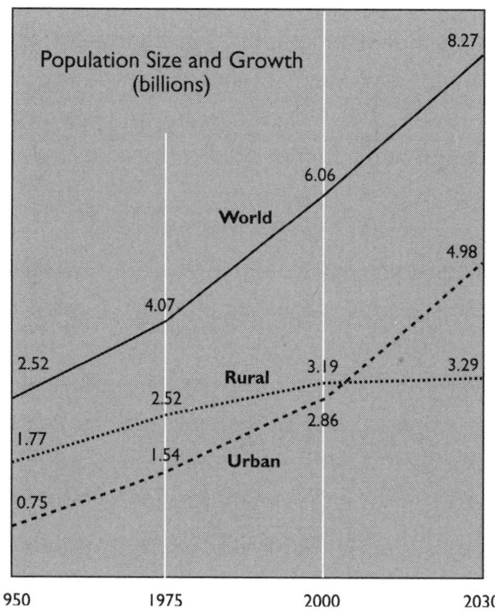

Figure 1.1 Growth of World and Urban Population, 1950–2030. *Source*: United Nations, *World Urbanization Prospects: 2001 Revision* (New York: United Nations Population Division, 2002), www.unpopulation.org.

THE WORLD URBAN SYSTEM

World population stood at 6.1 billion in 2000, having increased 2.5 times since 1950. The world's urban population, however, increased almost four times over that same period (fig. 1.1). Today, as noted above, almost half of the world's population lives in places defined as urban, up from less than one-third in 1950. Increases in urban populations have been felt worldwide, but the pace of urban change has been most dramatic in the world's developing regions. North and South America, Oceania, and Europe are the most urbanized, while the vast region stretching from Sub-Saharan Africa through South Asia, Southeast Asia, and China still is only about one-third urban, a reflection of their predominantly rural, agrarian economies (fig. 1.2).

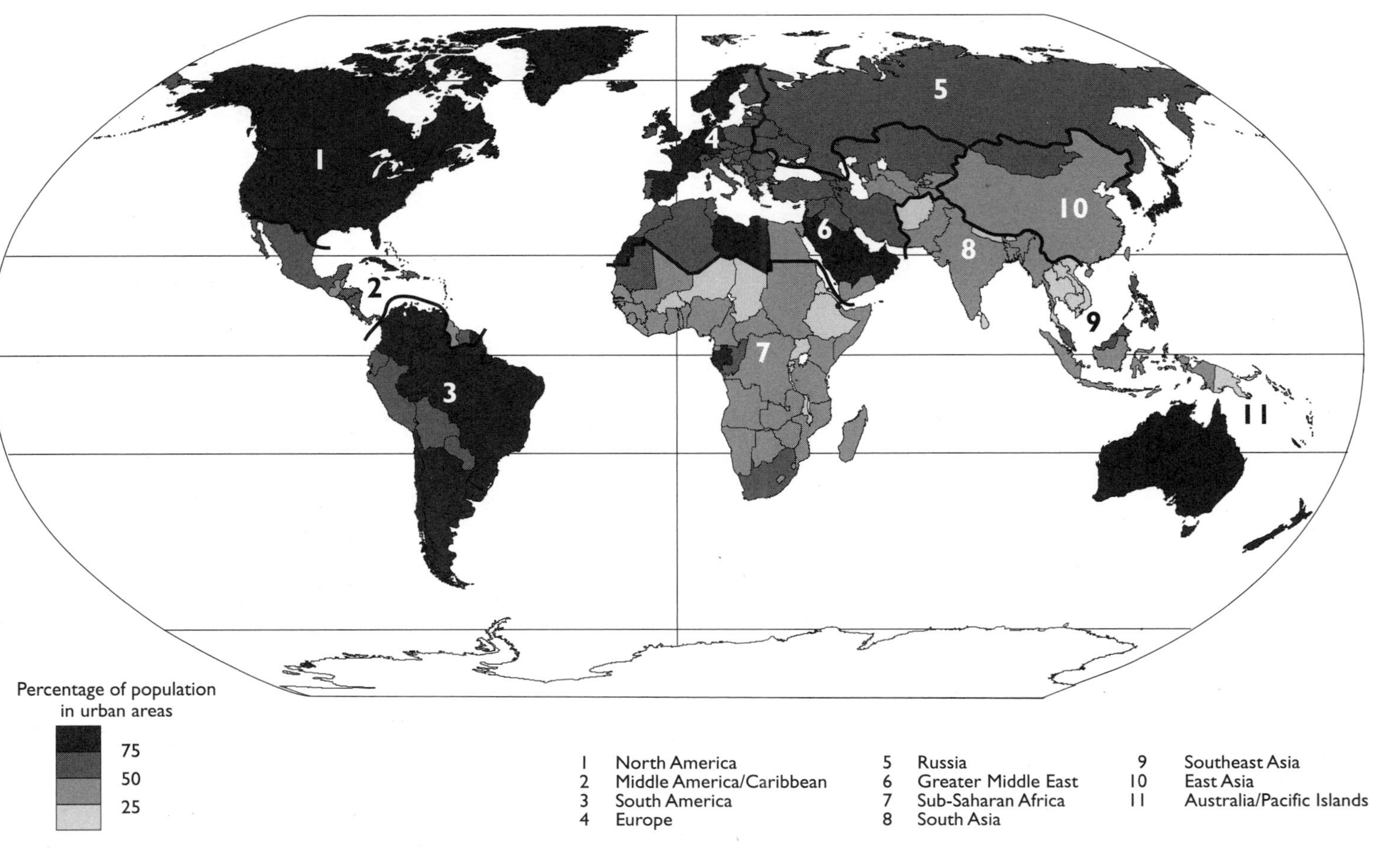

Figure 1.2 World Urbanization by Country, 2000. *Source*: Data from United Nations, *World Urbanization Prospects: 2001 Revision* (New York: United Nations Population Division, 2002), www.unpopulation.org.

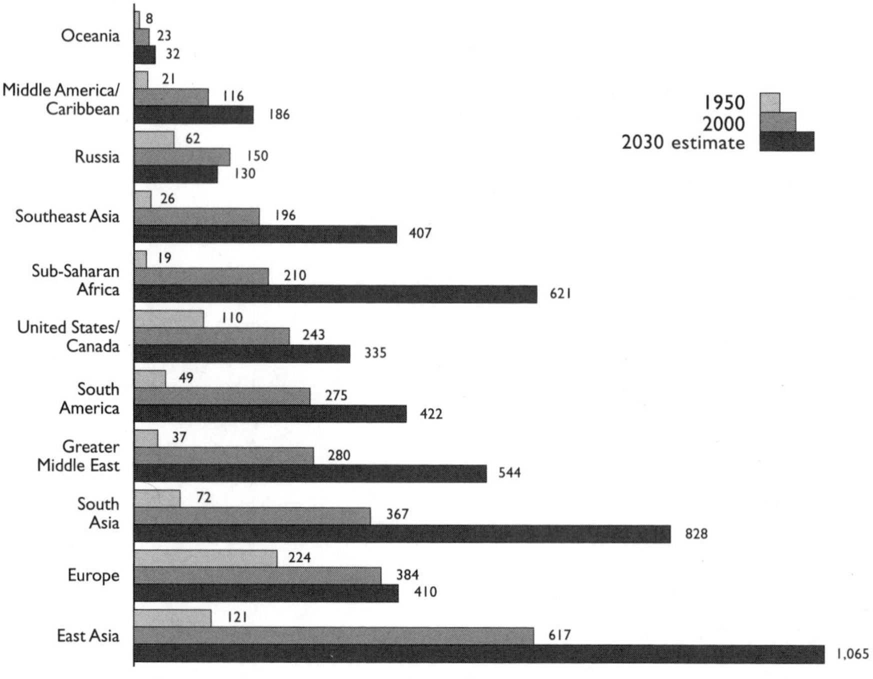

Figure 1.3 Urban Population of World Regions, 1950, 2000, 2030. *Source*: United Nations, *World Urbanization Prospects: 2001 Revision* (New York: United Nations Population Division, 2002), www.unpopulation.org.

While the MDCs of the world (now 75% urban) retained their lead over the LDCs (now 40% urban) in relative terms, more of the world's urban population in absolute numbers was accounted for by the LDCs in 2000 than in 1950, as shown in fig. 1.3 and tab. 1.1, and this imbalance will be far greater in 2030.

Unfortunately, throughout Middle and South America, Africa and the Middle East, and much of Asia, urban development has not kept up with urban growth. Latin America and the Caribbean, for instance, have caught up to the world's MDCs in level of urbanization (now 75% urban, about the same as the United States and Canada), but economic development, health care, and education continue to lag. Sub-Saharan Africa remains the least urbanized region in the world—and the least developed. Development challenges in the opening decade of the 21st century are increasingly *urban* development challenges, specifically, how to improve the lives of people living in cities while the cities of the LDCs grow ever larger. Latin America's urban explosion may be over, but in Africa, India, and China (among others), with only about one-third of their populations now living in cities, the urban population explosion continues.

For every city-dweller in the MDCs today, there are four city-dwellers in the LDCs. The greatest number of cities and the greatest number of large cities (3 million and above) are now found in LDCs (fig. 1.4). This can also be seen in a list of the world's largest urban areas, where those in the LDCs now outnumber those in the MDCs (tab. 1.2). Of the 20 largest urban ag-

Table 1.1 Urban Patterns in MDCs and LDCs: 1950 and 2000

	1950			2000		
	Total Population	*Urban Population*	*% Urban*	*Total Population*	*Urban Population*	*% Urban*
	(billions)			*(billions)*		
World	2.5	0.75	30	6.1	2.86	47
MDCs	0.8	0.45	55	1.2	0.90	75
LDCs	1.7	0.30	18	4.9	1.96	40

Source: United Nations, *World Urbanization Prospects: 2001 Revision* (New York: United Nations Population Division, 2002).

glomerations in 1950, 13 were in the MDCs and 7 were in the LDCs. The 20 largest urban agglomerations in 2000 included only five in the MDCs, and those five were located in only three countries: Japan (Tokyo and Osaka), the United States (New York and Los Angeles), and France (Paris). London fell from second place in 1950 to twenty-fifth place in 2000. Mexico City, now number two on the list with almost 20 million people, is larger than three-quarters of the world's independent states. By 2015, twenty-four of the thirty largest agglomerations will be in the LDCs. Moreover, the proportion of the people living in megacities has also increased. Today, eight out of every one hundred urban dwellers in the world live in one of the world's seventeen megacities. In 1975, more people lived in megacities in the MDCs than megacities in the LDCs. By 2000, the tables had turned: among people living in megacities, more than twice the number lived in the LDCs than lived in the MDCs.

A summary of the United Nation's findings on world urbanization trends is presented in box 1.1. Some of those trends are portrayed graphically in fig. 1.5, which demonstrates that less developed regions are urbanizing at much more rapid rates since 1975, compared to more developed regions, in terms of population class of urban settlements for the two periods, 1975–2000 and 2000–2015.

WORLD URBANISM: CONCEPTS AND DEFINITIONS

An understanding of some basic concepts and terms is necessary before proceeding further.

Urbanism

Urbanism is a broad concept that generally refers to all aspects—political, economic, social—of the urban way of life. Urbanism is not a process of urban growth, but rather the end result of urbanization. It suggests that the urban way of life is dramatically different in all respects from the rural way of life; as people leave the country and move to the city, their lifestyles and livelihoods change.

Urbanization

Urbanization is a process involving two phases: (1) the movement of people from rural to urban places, where they engage in primarily nonrural occupations, and (2) the change in lifestyle that results from living in cities. The important variables in the first phase are population density and economic functions. A place does not become urban in fact until its workforce is divorced from the soil; trade, manufacturing, and service provision dominate the economies of urban places. The im-

Table 1.2 The 30 Largest Urban Agglomerations, Ranked by Population Size, 1950–2015

1950			1975		
Rank	*Agglomeration and Country*	Population *(millions)*	*Rank*	*Agglomeration and Country*	Population *(millions)*
1	New York, USA	12.339	1	Tokyo, Japan	19.771
2	London, United Kingdom	8.733	2	New York, USA	15.880
3	Tokyo, Japan	6.920	3	Shanghai, China	11.443
4	Paris, France	5.441	4	Mexico City, Mexico	10.691
5	Moscow, USSR	5.356	5	São Paulo, Brazil	10.333
6	Shanghai, China	5.333	6	Osaka, Japan	9.844
7	Rhine-Ruhr North, Germany	5.296	7	Buenos Aires, Argentina	9.144
8	Buenos Aires, Argentina	5.042	8	Los Angeles, USA	8.926
9	Chicago, USA	4.945	9	Paris, France	8.885
10	Calcutta, India	4.446	10	Beijing, China	8.545
11	Osaka, Japan	4.147	11	London, United Kingdom	8.169
12	Los Angeles, USA	4.046	12	Rio de Janeiro, Brazil	7.963
13	Beijing, China	3.913	13	Calcutta, India	7.888
14	Milan, Italy	3.633	14	Moscow, USSR	7.623
15	Berlin, Germany	3.337	15	Bombay, India	7.347
16	Bombay, India	2.981	16	Seoul, South Korea	6.808
17	Rio de Janeiro, Brazil	2.965	17	Chicago, USA	6.749
18	Philadelphia, USA	2.939	18	Rhine-Ruhr North, Germany	6.448
19	Leningrad, USSR	2.903	19	Tianjin, China	6.160
20	Mexico City, Mexico	2.883	20	Cairo, Egypt	6.079
21	Detroit, USA	2.769	21	Milan, Italy	5.529
22	Naples, Italy	2.750	22	Manila, Philippines	5.000
23	Manchester, United Kingdom	2.537	23	Jakarta, Indonesia	4.814
24	São Paulo, Brazil	2.528	24	Delhi, India	4.426
25	Cairo, Egypt	2.410	25	Leningrad, USSR	4.326
26	Tianjin, China	2.374	26	Tehran, Iran	4.274
27	Birmingham, United Kingdom	2.314	27	Philadelphia, USA	4.069
28	Rhine-Main, Germany	2.295	28	Karachi, Pakistan	3.990
29	Boston, USA	2.238	29	Hong Kong	3.943
30	Hamburg, Germany	2.171	30	Detroit, USA	3.885

Source: United Nations, *World Urbanization Prospects: 2001 Revision* (New York: United Nations Population Division, 2002).

portant variables in the second phase are social, psychological, and behavioral. As a population becomes increasingly urban, family size becomes smaller because the value placed upon children changes.

Urban Place

As a place increases in population, it eventually becomes large enough to assume that its economy is no longer tied strictly to agriculture or other primary activities. At that point, a rural place becomes an *urban place.* Translating the dividing line between rural and urban into a minimum population size varies significantly from country to country. In Albania, for example, places with a population of 400 are considered urban; in Canada and New Zealand the figure is 1,000; in Ireland 1,500; in France, Israel, and Argentina 2,000;

Table 1.2 *(continued)*

2000			2015		
Rank	*Agglomeration and Country*	*Population (millions)*	*Rank*	*Agglomeration and Country*	*Population (millions)*
1	Tokyo, Japan	26.444	1	Tokyo, Japan	27.190
2	Mexico City, Mexico	18.066	2	Dhaka, Bangladesh	22.766
3	São Paulo, Brazil	17.962	3	Mumbai (Bombay), India	22.577
4	New York, USA	16.732	4	São Paulo, Brazil	21.229
5	Mumbai (Bombay), India	16.086	5	Delhi, India	20.884
6	Los Angeles, USA	13.213	6	Mexico City, Mexico	20.434
7	Kolkata (Calcutta), India	13.058	7	New York, USA	17.944
8	Shanghai, China	12.887	8	Jakarta, Indonesia	17.268
9	Dhaka, Bangladesh	12.519	9	Kolkata (Calcutta), India	16.747
10	Delhi, India	12.441	10	Karachi, Pakistan	16.197
11	Buenos Aires, Argentina	12.024	11	Lagos, Nigeria	15.966
12	Jakarta, Indonesia	11.018	12	Los Angeles, USA	14.494
13	Osaka, Japan	11.013	13	Shanghai, China	13.598
14	Beijing, China	10.839	14	Buenos Aires, Argentina	13.185
15	Rio de Janeiro, Brazil	10.652	15	Manila, Philippines	12.579
16	Karachi, Pakistan	10.032	16	Beijing, China	11.671
17	Manila, Philippines	9.950	17	Rio de Janeiro, Brazil	11.543
18	Seoul, South Korea	9.888	18	Cairo, Egypt	11.531
19	Paris, France	9.630	19	Istanbul, Turkey	11.362
20	Cairo, Egypt	9.462	20	Osaka, Japan	11.013
21	Tianjin, China	9.156	21	Tianjin, China	10.319
22	Istanbul, Turkey	8.953	22	Seoul, South Korea	9.918
23	Lagos, Nigeria	8.665	23	Kinshasa, Dem. Rep. Congo	9.883
24	Moscow, Russia	8.367	24	Paris, France	9.858
25	London, United Kingdom	7.640	25	Bangkok, Thailand	9.816
26	Lima, Peru	7.443	26	Lima, Peru	9.388
27	Bangkok, Thailand	7.372	27	Bogotá, Columbia	8.970
28	Chicago, USA	6.989	28	Lahore, Pakistan	8.721
29	Tehran, Iran	6.979	29	Bangalore, India	8.391
30	Hong Kong, China	6.860	30	Tehran, Iran	8.178

in Belgium and Ghana 5,000; and in Greece and Senegal 10,000. In Denmark and Sweden, only 200 people are required for a place to be classified as urban. In the United States, places are defined as urban by the Bureau of the Census if they have at least 2,500 people, the same minimum population used in Mexico and Venezuela. Smaller settlements are usually referred to as hamlets, villages, or small towns.

City

The term *city* is essentially a political designation referring to a place, generally larger than a town, that is legally incorporated as a municipality. However, a settlement of any size may call itself a city, whether it is large or small. Two colloquial terms that do equate cities with size are *millionaire city* and *megacity*. In the mid-20th century, it became fashionable to

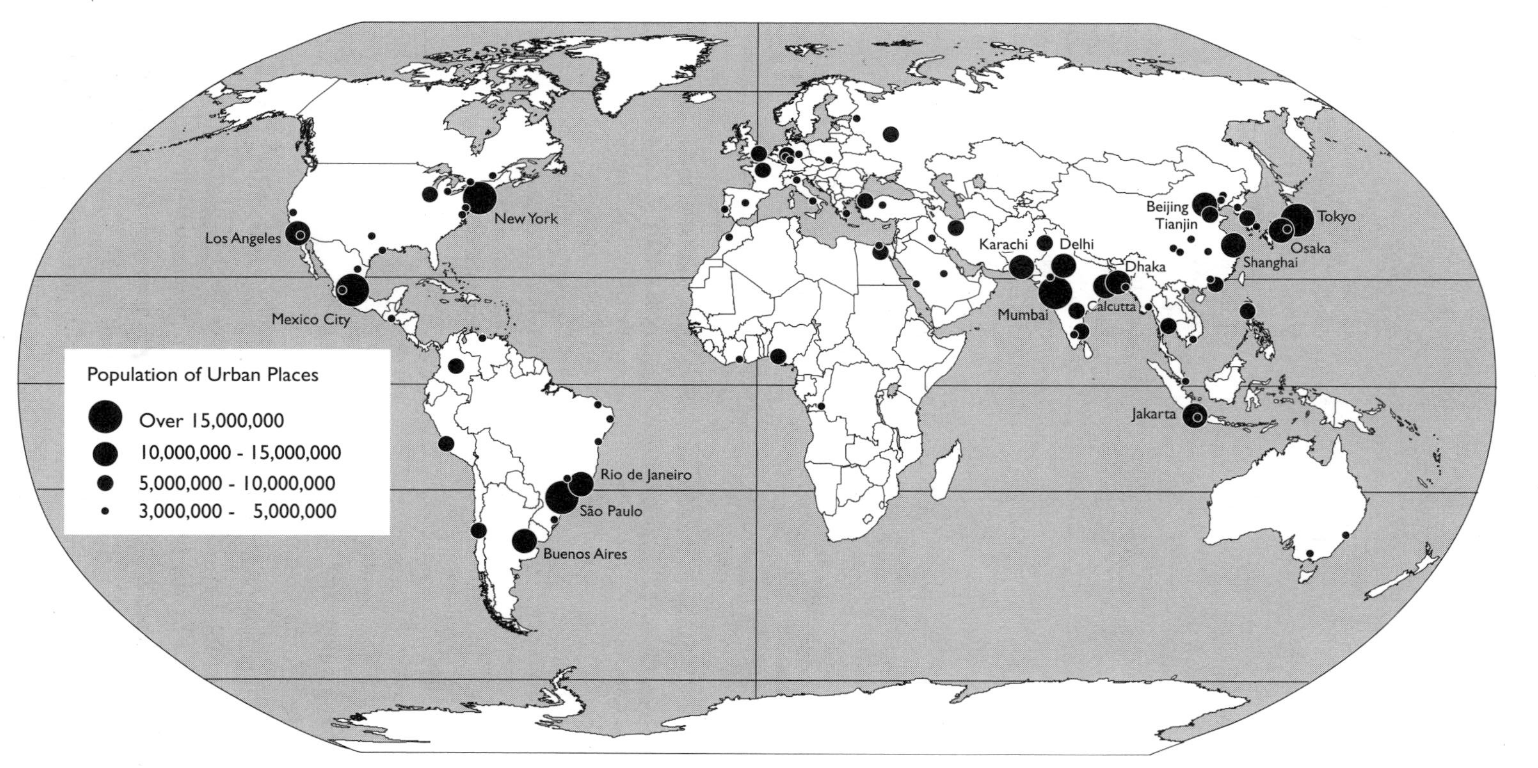

Figure 1.4 Major Cities of the World, 2000. *Source*: Data from United Nations, *World Urbanization Prospects: 2001 Revision* (New York: United Nations Population Division, 2002), www.unpopulation.org.

Box 1.1 World Urbanization Trends

World Urbanization Prospects: 2001 Revision, a report published by the United Nations Population Division, is a valuable data set on past, present, and future urbanization trends in regions and subregions. It also provides data on individual cities and urban agglomerations. The major findings of this most recent edition are as follows:

1. The world's urban population reached 2.9 billion in 2000 and is expected to increase to 5 billion by 2030. Whereas 40% of the world population lived in urban areas in 1950, that percentage increased to 47% by 2000 and will increase further, to 60%, by 2030. Based on current projections, the number of rural and urban dwellers will be about equal by 2007.
2. Almost all the projected population increases from 2000 to 2030 will be in urban areas. During this period, the numbers of those living in these areas will increase by 2.1 billion.
3. Nearly all the population increase in the 2000 to 2030 period will be in the LDCs, whose population will increase from approximately 2 billion to just under 4 billion. The urban population in the MDCs during these three decades will increase slowly, from 0.9 billion to 1 billion.
4. During the 2000–2030 period, the world's urban population is projected to grow at an average annual rate of 1.8%, which is nearly double the projected growth rate for the world (1.0%). Based on these rates, the urban population of the world will double in 38 years.
5. Urban population growth will be particularly acute in the LDCs, where it will average 2.4% per year during these three decades, compared to a rural growth rate of just less than 0.2% per year, and where the population will double in 29 years.
6. Both rural-urban migration and the transformation of rural settlements into cities will account for the high rate of population growth in the urban areas of LDCs, plus universal reduction in fertility levels and reduced rural population growth, in the next thirty years. Rural population numbers will peak around 2025 and then begin a steady decline, as has happened to the MDCs since 1950.
7. The level of urbanization, already high at 75% in MDCs, will continue to increase, to about 83% in 2030.
8. In 2000, the level of urbanization in the LDCs was about 40%, which was considerably higher than it was in 1950 (when it was only 18%), and it is expected to increase to 56% by 2030, about that of the MDCs in the 1950s.
9. Marked regional differences exist in the level and pace of urbanization. Latin America and the Caribbean had a level approximating 75% in 2000, which was higher than the level in Europe and almost twice that in Asia and Africa. By 2030, over half the populations of Asia and Africa will be living in urban areas, while the figure for

Latin America and the Caribbean will reach 84%, a level similar to North America, the most urbanized region by 2030.

10. In both Europe and the United States/Canada, the percentage of those living in urban areas is expected to increase, respectively, from 71% and 77% in 2000 to 81% and 85% in 2030. Oceania's increase will be somewhat smaller, from 74% to 77%.
11. Despite high levels of urbanization in Europe, North America, Latin America and the Caribbean, and Oceania, their combined urban populations in 2000 (1.2 billion) were less than that for Asia (1.4 billion). By 2030, both Africa and Asia will have more urban residents than any other world region, Asia's share of the world total rising to 54% from 48% in 2000.
12. Asia will retain its position as having the world's largest rural population (2.3 billion) in the 2000–2030 period. Africa, with nearly 500 million rural residents in 2000, will see an increase by 2030 to 702 million, the second largest share. Only Africa and Oceania among the world regions will experience increases in rural residents. Overall, the world's rural population will remain relatively stable from 2000 to 2030, at around 3.2 billion.
13. The number of people residing in the largest urban agglomerations will remain surprisingly small. In 2000, about 3.7% of humanity lived in places exceeding a population of 10 million, a percentage that will rise to 4.7% by 2015. The number living in urban centers of 5–10 million in 2015 will be about 3.7%.
14. The percentage of people living in urban agglomerations of over 5 million population in 2000 was 5.9% in LDC regions and 8.9% in MDC regions. By 2015, the figures will be 8.1% and 9.6%, respectively.
15. The numbers of those living in smaller cities is greater than that for those living in very large urban areas, though their increases are much slower. In 2000, about 25% of the world's population lived in areas with fewer than 0.5 million and by 2015 that number is expected to be about 27%. About half of all urban dwellers in both years will be living in areas with less than 0.5 million people.
16. In the MDC regions, the percentage of the population living in settlements of less than 0.5 million will rise slightly, from 42% in 2000 to 43% in 2015. In LDC regions, the percentage living in these smaller settlements will increase from 21% to 24% in the same period.
17. The largest cities not only account for a small percentage of the world's population, but also their share of the overall increases is likely to be moderate. From 2000 to 2015, cities over 5 million are expected to absorb about 21% of the annual growth in urban population, compared to 44% for those places with less than 0.5 million people. LDC regions are expected to see sharp increases in both categories.
18. Tokyo was the largest urban agglomeration in 2001 at 26.5 million residents; it was followed by São Paulo (18.3 million), Mexico City (18.3), New York (16.8), and Mumbai (Bombay, 16.5). In 2015, Tokyo will still be the largest (27.2) and it will be

followed by Dhaka, Mumbai, São Paulo, Delhi, and Mexico City, each with more than 20 million inhabitants.

19. The proportion of the population living in large urban agglomerations will increase due to an increase in the number of such places. Cities with more than 10 million residents will increase from 17 to 21 during this period. Most of these will be in LDCs. In 2001, nine of the forty cities exceeding 5 million were in MDCs, but by 2015 only 10 of the 58 will be there.
20. High urban population growth is not necessarily associated with population size. In fact, some of the highest growth rates are in cities with small populations, for as population size increases, the growth rate tends to decline. Megacities will experience low growth, with some growing less than 1% per year.

Source: United Nations, *World Urbanization Prospects: The 2001 Revision* (New York: United Nations Population Division, 2002), www.unpopulation.org.

compile lists of cities that had surpassed one million in population. Geographers and sociologists of that era called them "millionaire cities." Today, the term *millionaire city* has fallen into disfavor because of the connotation of wealth. Because of the proliferating number of ever-larger cities, those over 10 million in population are often referred to as megacities. In 1950, only New York City exceeded 10 million. Today, 17 cities worldwide fit that category and 1 out of every 27 people lives in one of those megacities.

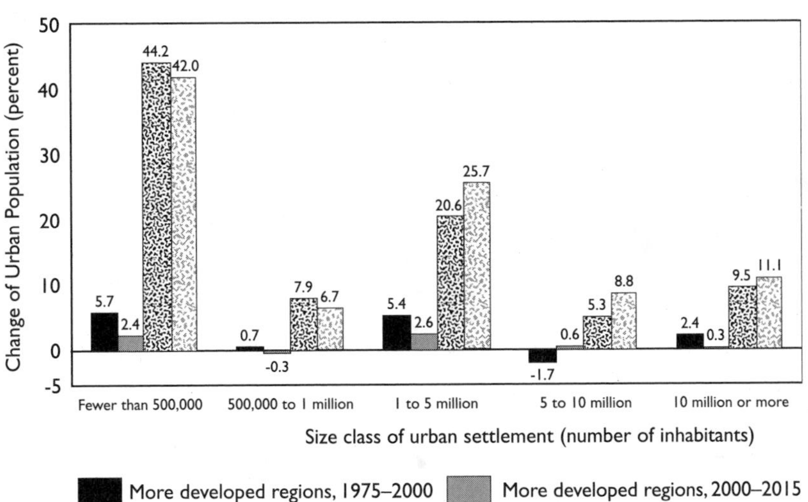

Figure 1.5 Urban Population in MDCs vs. LDCs by Size Class of Urban Settlement, 1975–2015. *Source:* United Nations, *World Urbanization Prospects: 2001 Revision* (New York: United Nations Population Division, 2002), www.unpopulation.org.

Figures 1.6, 1.7 Hong Kong is an excellent example of an economy that has evolved from industry to increasingly high-end services, and these two photos dramatically show the consequences of success. Both were shot from almost the same spot on the Peak on Hong Kong Island, the first in the mid-1970s, the second in the mid-1990s. (Photos by Jack Williams)

World Cities

A very few cities are in a class at the very top of the world economy. New York, London, and Tokyo are the only three in the top tier, known as *global cities.* These three dominate the global economy and the entire world feels their influence in finance, communications, and other sectors. These three cities are the key hubs of an increasingly interlinked globe. One rung lower on the urban pyramid are the second-tier *world cities:* Los Angeles, Paris, Hong Kong, Singapore, Sydney, and possibly others (figs. 1.6 and 1.7). Their economies are knowledge-based and tied to the provision of high-end services, especially producer services (accounting and advertising, for instance). Although they are large, it is not population but innovation that sets them apart as pacesetters in the information age (box 1.2).

Urbanized Area

As cities have expanded, the boundary between urban and rural has become increasingly blurred, especially in industrialized countries, such as the United States, where automobile transportation has fostered urban sprawl. Thus, the *urbanized area* is defined as the built-up area where buildings, roads, and essentially urban land uses predominate, even beyond the political boundaries of cities and towns. The urbanized area is basically a city and its suburbs.

Metropolis and Metropolitan Area

As cities have grown in size, territorially and demographically, a variety of terms have been coined to refer to ever-larger cities and city regions. One is *metropolis*—originally, the chief city of a country, state, or region. Today, this term is used loosely to refer to any large city. A metropolitan area is anchored by a large central city, but also includes all surrounding territory—urban or rural—that is integrated (a factor usually measured by commuting patterns) with the urban core. In the United States, they are officially termed *Metropolitan Areas* (MAs), of which there are three types: *Metropolitan Statistical Areas* (MSAs), *Primary Metropolitan Statistical Areas* (PMSAs), and *Consolidated Metropolitan Statistical Areas* (CMSAs). The U.S. Bureau of the Census has been designating metropolitan areas since 1950. While terminology and criteria have changed since that time, the core definition has remained the same in that metropolitan areas (1) have an urban core of at least 50,000 people, (2) include surrounding urban and rural territory that is socially and economically integrated with the core, and (3) are built from county (or county-equivalent) units. In Canada, their counterparts are officially termed *Census Metropolitan Areas* (CMAs), which must have an urban core of at least 100,000 people.

Conurbation and Super–Metropolitan Region

Conurbation is a 20th-century word of European origin that refers to a large urban region composed of a network of large cities. It is common to speak of the London conurbation or Paris conurbation. In essence, these are *super–metropolitan regions*. As a city grows, it engulfs smaller cities in its urban expansion

Box 1.2 Peter Hall's World Cities

Government and trade were invariably the original raison d'être of the world cities. But these places early became the centres where professional talents of all kinds congregated. Each of the world cities has its greatest hospitals, its distinct medical quarter, its legal profession gathered around the national courts of justice. Students and teachers are drawn to the world cities: they commonly contain great universities, as well as a host of specialized institutions for teaching and research in the sciences, the technologies and the arts. The great national libraries and museums are here. Inevitably, the world cities have become the places where information is gathered and disseminated: the book publishers are found here; so are the publishers of newspapers and periodicals, and with them their journalists and regular contributors. . . . [A]lso the world cities have become headquarters of the great national radio and television networks.

Source: Peter Hall, *The World Cities*, 3d ed. (New York: St. Martin's, 1984), 1–2.

zone, builds nearby towns into full-fledged cities, and often stimulates the development of new cities. These entities make up a single, interactive urban system.

Megalopolis and Ecumenopolis

Megalopolis is a 20th-century word of North American origin. It was first applied in 1961 by geographer Jean Gottmann to the urbanized northeastern seaboard of the United States from Boston to Washington (box 1.3). Its coinage focused attention on a new scale of urbanization. Today, megalopolis is used as a generic term referring to urban coalescence at the regional scale. That coalescence is channeled along transportation corridors connecting one city with another. It is evident in the magnitude of vehicle traffic, telephone calls, e-mail exchanges, and air transport among cities strung along a megalopolitan corridor. Beyond the megalopolis, some even see the emergence of an *ecumenopolis,* an urban network of communication threads that snake around the entire world. Metropolis, megalopolis, and ecumenopolis are all derived from the ancient Greek word for city, *polis.*

Site and Situation

Why are cities located where they are? How and why do they grow? Concepts used by urban geographers to answer these and related questions are site and situation. *Site* refers to the physical environment on which a city originated and evolved. Surface landforms, underlying geology, elevation, water features, coastline configuration, and other aspects of physical geography are considered site characteristics. Montreal's site, for instance, is defined by the Lachine Rapids, historically the upstream limit of ocean-going commerce. Paris's site is defined by an island in the Seine River, known as Île de la Cité, which gave the city defensive advantages and offered an easy bridging point. New York City's site is defined by a deepwater harbor. A city's origin is often wrapped up in its site.

Box 1.3 Jean Gottmann's Megalopolis

Some two thousand years before the first European settlers landed on the shores of the James River, Massachusetts Bay, and Manhattan Island, a group of ancient people, planning a new city-state in the Peloponnesus in Greece, called it Megalopolis, for they dreamed of a great future for it and hoped it would become the largest of the Greek cities. Their hopes did not materialize. Megalopolis still appears on modern maps of the Peloponnesus, but it is just a small town nestling in a small river basin. Through the centuries the word Megalopolis has been used in many senses by various people, and it has even found its way into Webster's dictionary, which defines it as 'a very large city.' Its use, however, has not become so common that it could not be applied in a new sense, as a geographical place name for the unique cluster of metropolitan areas of the northeastern seaboard of the United States. There if anywhere in our times, the dream of those ancient Greeks has come true.

Source: Jean Gottmann, *Megalopolis* (New York: Twentieth Century Fund, 1961), 4.

Situation, by contrast, refers to the relative location of a city (fig. 1.8). It connotes a city's connectedness with other places and the surrounding region. Some cities are centrally located at the junction of trade routes, while others are isolated, lacking good connections to markets and sources of raw materials. A city's growth and decline is more dependent on situation than it is on site characteristics. In fact, a good relative location can compensate for a poor site. Venice, for instance, triumphed as a center of the Renaissance not because of its site (so water saturated it is sinking), but because of its relative location at the head of the Adriatic Sea and its access to good passes through the Alps. New York City emerged as the United States' most populous city in the early 19th century, not because of a superior site, but because of a superior situation. After the opening of the Erie Canal in 1825, New York had easy access to the resource-rich interior of the United States via the Great Lakes.

Urban Morphology

When we refer to the *morphology* of urban settlements, we direct attention to their physical form. One city may be linear, for example, because of its location in a valley or along a river, while another may be compact. We also focus on the way in which some parts of an urban area support high-density populations and intensive land uses, while other parts support acre-and-a-half lots and open space. Urban form changes over time with population growth, improved transportation (especially the automobile), and new economic functions.

Urban Functions

Different cities serve different *functions.* Some come into being because a strategic location needs to be defended; others serve the needs of trade and commerce; others serve the needs of governmental administration or religious pilgrimage; and still others the need to turn pri-

Figure 1.8 Seattle grew initially on the basis of its site (superb harbor) and situation (jumping off point to Alaska and Asia), but its phenomenal growth after World War II was primarily due to businesses that had little directly to do with site and situation: Boeing Aircraft Company and Microsoft. (Photo by Larry Ford)

mary commodities into manufactured goods. These functions determine a city's economic orientation. Cities may serve primarily a single function—the "textile cities" of the southeastern United States, for instance—or (more often) a multitude of functions. Functional diversity is usually reflected in specialized districts within the city, from business districts, to office parks, to warehousing districts. As with form, functions are likely to change with new and improved technologies, population shifts, government priorities, and consumer demands for goods and services.

Urban Landscapes

Urban form and urban function work together to create *urban landscapes,* or the *built environment* of cities. Urban landscapes are the visible manifestations of the thoughts, deeds, and actions of human beings. They are charged with clues to the economic, cultural, and political values of the people who built them. At the macroscale, geographers may look at the vertical and horizontal dimensions of the landscape—at city skylines and urban sprawl. At the microscale, they may look at architectural styles, signage, or activity patterns near busy intersections. Interpreting, analyzing, and critiquing the landscape is one of the major themes of urban geography.

Capital City

"Capital" comes from the Latin word for "head," *caput. Capital cities* are literally "head cities," the headquarters of government functions. Every country has one (South Africa has

Box 1.4 Gideon Sjoberg's Preindustrial City

[T]he city's center is the hub of governmental and religious activity more than of commercial ventures. It is, besides, the prime focus of elite residence, while the lower class and outcaste groups are scattered centrifugally toward the city's periphery. Added to the strong ecological differentiation in terms of social class, occupational and ethnic distinctions are solemnly proclaimed in the land use patterns. It is usual for each occupational group to live and work in a particular street or quarter, one that generally bears the name of the trade in question. Ethnic groups are almost always isolated from the rest of the city, forming, so to speak, little worlds unto themselves. Yet, . . . a minimum of specialization exists in land use. Frequently a site serves multiple purposes—e.g., it may be devoted concurrently to religious, educational, and business activities; and residential and occupational facilities are apt to be contiguous.

Source: Gideon Sjoberg, *The Preindustrial City* (Glencoe, Ill: Free Press, 1960), 323–24.

three). Although not always the largest cities, their voices are often the loudest. Each is the seat of political power, the center of legislative decision making, and the locus of national sovereignty. Their landscapes are charged with the symbols of solidarity, real or imagined; their museums are the attics of the nation; their locations are symbolic of the central role they play in the national urban system. In some countries, national capitals share power with provincial capitals. As a class of cities, they are among the best known in the world.

Preindustrial City

The *preindustrial city*—sometimes referred to as the *traditional city*, sometimes inaccurately as the *non-Western city*—identifies a city that was founded and grew before the arrival of industrialization in the 19th and 20th centuries and thus typically had quite different characteristics from the modern industrial cities of today (box 1.4). Elements of the traditional city are still part of urban landscapes in the LDCs, although cities everywhere have been affected by industrialization (fig. 1.9). Most cities in the LDCs, therefore, exhibit simultaneously the characteristics of preindustrial and commercial-industrial cities.

Industrial City

The *industrial city* refers to those cities which have an economy based on the production of manufactured goods. These may be light industrial products, such as food, textiles, and footwear, or heavy industrial items, such as motor vehicles, appliances, ships, and agricultural machinery. Initially, the industrial city was a town or city that developed an industrial base during the industrial stage of urban growth. The thinking for a long time was that an industrial base was required for city formation. We know today that some cities have little industrial employment. Rather, their economies are based on services. We also know when we examine the growth of cities in LDCs that urban growth and industrial growth are not synonymous as was true in MDCs, which earlier experienced the Industrial Revolution.

Figure 1.9 The sun catches the top of the wall surrounding the old city of Fès, Morocco, one of the best-preserved traditional, or preindustrial, cities in the world. These cities were typically surrounded by walls, but the walls have disappeared from most cities around the world because they hinder urban "progress." (Photo by Jack Williams)

Postindustrial City

A relatively new type of city is emerging in the wealthy MDCs. The *postindustrial city*—whose economy is not tied to a manufacturing base—begins with high employment in the services sector. Cities that are mainly the headquarters for corporations or for governmental and intergovernmental organizations are examples, as are those specializing in research and development (R&D), health and medicine, and tourism/recreation. With an increase in the number of people employed in tertiary and quaternary occupations, especially in fields such as finance, health, leisure, R&D, education, and telecommunications and in various levels of government, the cities with concentrations of these activities have an economic base in sharp contrast to those cities that originated in industrial economies.

Primate City

A type of city defined by size and function is the *primate city* (fig. 1.10). The term was coined by geographer Mark Jefferson in the late 1930s to refer to the tendency for countries to have one city that is exceptionally large, economically dominant, and culturally expressive of national identity. A true primate city is at least twice as large as the second-largest city, but the gap is often much larger. Paris, for instance, is seven times larger than France's second-largest city, Lyon. In general, however, primacy is more typical of LDCs than MDCs. In a few instances, countries may be characterized by *dual primacy*, where two large cities share the dominant role, such as Rio de Janeiro and São Paulo in Brazil. The presence of a primate city in a country usually suggests an imbalance in development: a progressive core,

Figure 1.10 Mexico City, overwhelmingly the primate city of Mexico and one of the world's largest cities, seems to sprawl forever. With giant size come giant problems, too. (Photo by Robert Smith)

defined by the primate city and its environs, and a lagging periphery on which the primate city may depend for resources and migrant labor. Some see the relationship between core and periphery as a parasitic one. It is difficult for any country to overcome the dominance of a primate city that is many times larger than any other city in the national urban system.

Rank-Size Rule

One concept that represents an alternative to primacy is the *rank-size rule.* This concept evolved out of empirical research on the relationships between cities of different population size in a given region. Simply put, the rule states that, within a country, for a normal rank-size urban system the population of a particular city is equal to the population of the largest city divided by its rank. In other words, the fifth-largest city in a country should be one-fifth the size of the largest city. A deviation from this ranking means that the urban system is unbalanced. A more regionally balanced pattern of urban development tends to be found most often in MDCs. Rank-size relationships within a country are often presented in a series of rank-size curves portraying changes over time.

Colonial City

Although virtually gone from the face of the earth now, the *colonial city* had a profound impact on urban patterns throughout much of the world, starting around 1500 A.D. and culminating, with the global dominance of European imperial powers, in the 19th and early 20th centuries. The colonial city was unique because of its special focus on commercial functions, its peculiar situation requirements, and the odd blend of Western urban forms with traditional indigenous values and practices.

There were two distinct types of colonial city, depending on the age of the European or colonial enclave in relation to the age of the native or indigenous settlement. In one type, the European city was created virtually from scratch on a site where no other significant urban place had existed. This would then lead to in-migration of local peoples drawn by the economic opportunity created under colonial rule. Examples of this first type of colonial city include Mumbai (Bombay), Hong Kong, and Nairobi. In the other type, the European city was grafted onto an existing indigenous urban place and then became the dominant growth pole for that city, typically swallowing up or overwhelming in size and importance the original indigenous center. Examples of this second type of colonial city include Shanghai, Delhi, and Tunis.

Dual City

Either type of colonial city would eventually give rise to a *dual city* consisting of one modern, Western part and another more traditional, indigenous part. The European part, typically segregated along racial lines, would attempt to duplicate the urban culture of the mother country. The traditional part, usually much less developed and often only semiurbanized, would be primarily a residential area for workers (and their dependents) serving the colonial rulers. The dual city should not be confused with dual primacy, discussed earlier.

Socialist City

Cities that evolved under Communist/socialist regimes in the former Soviet Union, China, Eastern Europe, North Korea, Vietnam, and Cuba have given us the concept of the *socialist city.* Communism was characterized by massive government involvement in the economy, coupled with the absence of private landownership and free-market forces. Communism produced distinctly different cities in virtually all aspects of urbanism, including morphology and internal spatial structure (fig. 1.11). Although most Communist regimes collapsed in the late 20th century, central planning and the command economy have left a lasting, visible impression on urban landscapes. Now, however, most of the socialist cities of the world are experiencing rapid change. Even in China, still the province of Communist Party rule, competitive enterprise is transforming the urban landscape. Only North Korea and to some extent Cuba continue to maintain cities under the principles of communism.

New Town

The *new town,* narrowly interpreted, is a phenomenon of the 20th century and refers to a comprehensively planned urban community built from scratch with the intent of becoming as self-contained as possible by encouraging the development of a self-sufficient economic base and a full range of urban services and facilities. New towns have come into existence around the world to fulfill a number of functions: relieving overcrowding of large cities; providing an optimum living environment for residents; helping to control urban sprawl and preserve open land; and serving as foci, or *growth poles,* for the development of peripheral regions. The modern new-town movement began in Britain and later diffused to other European countries, the United States, the Soviet Union, and in the post–World War II era, to many other newly independent countries. The idealized form of the new town, in the West at least, tends to follow the Garden City concept of the British, with its emphasis on manageable population size, pod-like housing tracts, neighborhood service centers, mixed land uses, much green space, pedestrian walkways, and a self-contained employment base (akin to premodern villages). After a century of experimentation, however, most countries have found new towns to be extremely difficult to establish and sustain. Nevertheless, they have served as laboratories for urban planners, symbols of national aspirations, and stimulators of economic growth in frontier areas. Three types of new towns have been developed with some degree of success: (1) suburban-ring cities such as Reston, Virginia, in the United States; (2) new capitals such as Brasilia, Brazil; and (3) economic growth poles such as Ciudad Guayana, Venezuela. Growth poles, with their mixed industrial employment base, are typically an attempt to spark employment and economic development in less developed regions.

WORLD URBANIZATION: PAST TRENDS

The present urban pattern, although largely the product of the past two centuries, had its origins thousand of years ago in several of the very regions currently experiencing explosive urban growth. From these cradles of civilization, the concept of the city diffused to Europe and then tens of centuries later returned in the form of the colonial city, which was to have such a radical impact on the urban character of these ancient regions.

Early Urbanization (Antiquity to 5th Century A.D.)

The first cities in human history were located in agrarian Mesopotamia, probably about 4000 B.C. Cities were founded in the Nile Valley about 3000 B.C., in the Indus Valley (present-day Pakistan) by 2500 B.C., in the Yellow River Valley of China by 2000 B.C., and in Mexico and Peru by 500 A.D. Estimates of the size of these early cities suggest they were relatively small. The city of Ur in lower Mesopotamia may have had a population of 200,000, ca. 4000 B.C. Thebes, as the capital of Egypt, may have had 225,000 inhabitants in 1600 B.C. However, ancient cities on the average did not increase significantly in number and, in general, their populations remained in the range of 2,000 to 20,000 until well into the first thousand years of their existence. The largest ancient city was

Figure 1.11 These heroic statues in front of the opera house in Novosibirsk, Russia, are typical of former socialist cities. Statues, paintings, posters—all were designed to inspire the populace to sacrifice lives of personal comfort for the sake of national welfare. (Photo by Donald Zeigler)

Rome, which Peter Hall has called "the first great city in world history." In the 2nd century A.D., Rome may have had 1 million inhabitants, making it the first city of that size in history. But after the 2nd century, Rome's population began to decrease, declining below 200,000 by the 9th century. In fact, the world's largest cities in 100 A.D. were completely different from the largest cities in 1000 A.D. (fig. 1.12 and tab. 1.3)

The ancient cities appeared where nature and the state of technology enabled cultivators to produce more than they needed for themselves and their families. That surplus set the stage for a division of labor among specialized occupations and the beginning of commercial exchanges. Cities were the settlement form adopted by those members of society whose direct presence at the places of agricultural production was not necessary. They were religious, administrative, and political centers. These ancient cities represented a new social order, but one that was dynamically linked to rural society.

In these ancient cities were specialists working full-time, such as priests and service workers, as well as a population that appreciated the arts and the use of symbols for counting and writing. Other attributes of these early cities included taxation, external trade, social classes, and gender differences in the assignment of work. Each city was surrounded by a countryside of farms, villages, and even towns. Ancient cities demonstrated the emergence of specialization. Rural life limited the exchange of goods, ideas, and people, as well as the complexity of technology and the division of labor. Thus, trade was a basic function of ancient cities, which were linked to the surrounding rural areas and to other cities by a relatively complex system of production and distribution, as well as by religious, military, and economic institutions (fig. 1.13).

The Middle Period (5th–17th Century A.D.)

From the fall of the Roman Empire to the 17th century, cities in Europe grew only slowly or not at all. The few large cities declined in size and function. Thus, the Roman Empire's fall in the 5th century A.D. marked the effective end of urbanization in Western Europe for over six hundred years.

The important question is why urbanization ceased. The major reason was a decrease in spatial interaction. After the collapse of the Roman Empire, urban localities became isolated from one another and had to become self-sufficient in order to survive. From their very beginnings, cities have survived and increased in size because of trade with their rural hinterland and with other cities, near and far. The disruption of the Roman transportation system, the spread of Islam in the 7th and 8th centuries, and the pillaging raids of the Norse in the 9th century almost completely eliminated trade between cities. These events, plus periodic attacks by Germanic and other groups from the north, resulted in an almost complete disruption of urban and rural interaction. Both the rural and urban populations declined. With the loss of trade, entire regions became isolated, urban ideas experienced little diffusion, agricultural productivity declined, people became preoccupied with defense and survival, and transportation networks deteriorated, thus reinforcing the no-growth pattern.

Although urban revival did occur 600 years after the fall of the Roman Empire via fortified settlements and ecclesiastical centers, growth in population and production remained quite small. The reason is quite simply that exchange was limited, and was conducted largely with people of the immediate surrounding region.

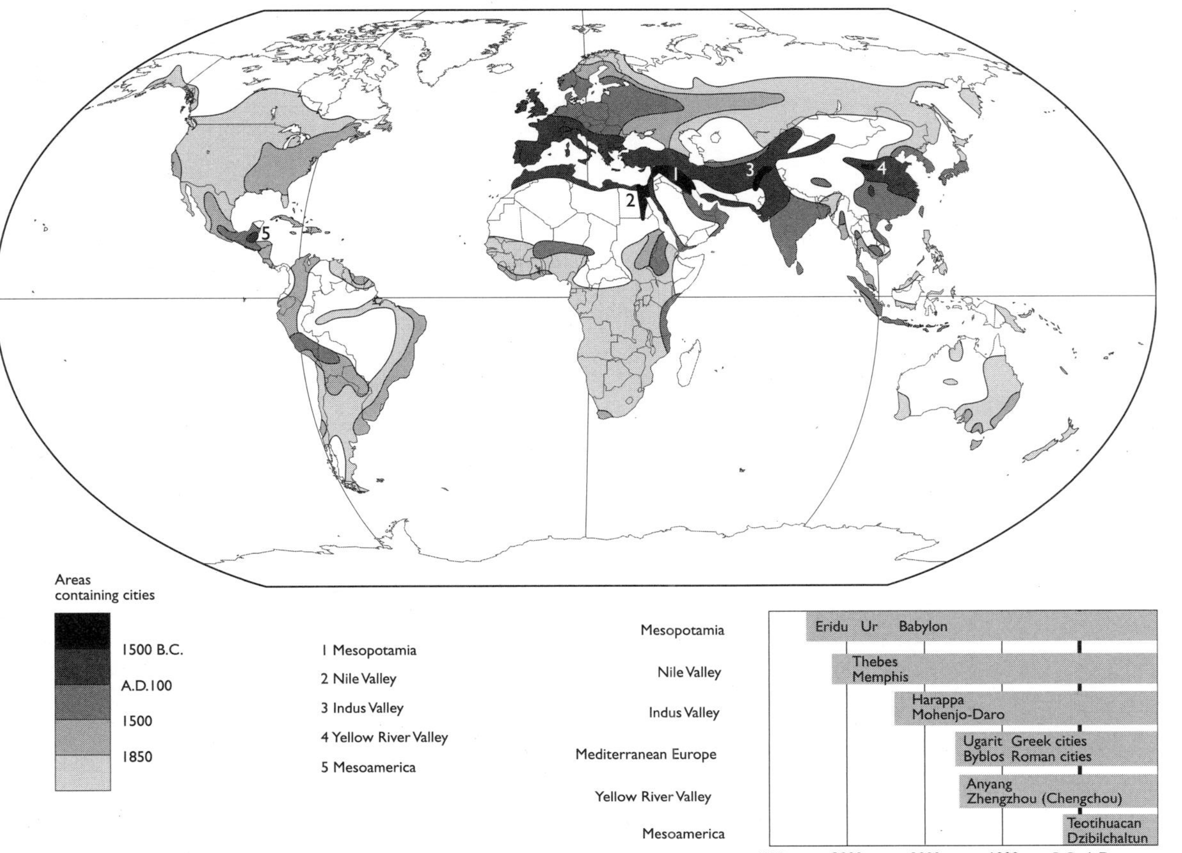

Figure 1.12 Spread of Urbanization, Antiquity to Modern Times. *Source*: Adapted from A. J. Rose, *Patterns of Cities* (Sydney: Thomas Nelson, 1967), 21. Used by permission.

Table 1.3 The Largest Cities in History

	Largest cities in the year 100			*Largest cities in the year 1000*	
1	Rome	450,000	1	Córdova, Spain	450,000
2	Luoyang, China	420,000	2	Kaifeng, China	400,000
3	Seleucia (on the Tigris), Iraq	250,000	3	Constantinople (Istanbul), Turkey	300,000
4	Alexandria, Egypt	250,000	4	Angkor, Cambodia	200,000
5	Antioch, Turkey	150,000	5	Kyoto, Japan	175,000
6	Anuradhapura, Sri Lanka	130,000	6	Cairo, Egypt	135,000
7	Peshawar, Pakistan	120,000	7	Baghdad, Iraq	125,000
8	Carthage, Tunisia	100,000	8	Nishapur (Neyshabur), Iran	125,000
9	Suzhou, China	n/a	9	Al-Hasa, Saudi Arabia	110,000
10	Smyra, Turkey	90,000	10	Pata (Anhilwara), India	100,000
	Largest cities in the year 1500			*Largest cities in the year 1900*	
1	Beijing, China	672,000	1	London, United Kingdom	6,480,000
2	Vijayanagar, India	500,000	2	New York, United States	4,242,000
3	Cairo, Egypt	400,000	3	Paris, France	3,330,000
4	Hangzhou, China	250,000	4	Berlin, Germany	2,707,000
5	Tabriz, Iran	250,000	5	Chicago, United States	1,717,000
6	Constantinople (Istanbul), Turkey	200,000	6	Vienna, Austria	1,698,000
7	Gaur, India	200,000	7	Tokyo, Japan	1,497,000
8	Paris, France	185,000	8	St. Petersburg, Russia	1,439,000
9	Guangzhou, China	150,000	9	Manchester, United Kingdom	1,435,000
10	Nanjing, China	147,000	10	Philadelphia, United States	1,418,000

Source: http://geography.about.com/library/weekly/aa01201a.htm

Figure 1.13 Countless ancient cities have ended up like these ruins of a former city in China's Xinjiang province. The city was once a thriving commercial center along the famous Silk Road, but once that economic base disappeared, the city withered and died also. (Photo by Stanley Brunn)

Most urban residents spent their lives within the walls of their cities. Thus, urban communities developed very close-knit social structures. Power was shared between feudal lords and religious leaders. The urban population was organized into guilds, with each craftsperson, artisan, and merchant belonging to a particular guild, according to their occupation. Within the social organization, each person had a clearly defined place. One's social status was determined by one's position in guild, family, church, and feudal administration. Gender roles were also well defined. Merchants and the guilds saw innovative possibilities in "free cities," where a person could reach his or her full potential within a community setting.

Over time, commerce expanded the function of the city and linked it to the expanding state power, resulting in a system called *mercantilism*. The purpose of mercantilism was the use of the power of the state to help the nation develop its economic potential and population. Mercantile policies protected merchant interests through the control of trade subsidies, the creation of trade monopolies, and the maintenance of a strong armed force to defend commercial interests. Cities were mercantilism's growth centers, and specialization and trade kept the system alive.

Mercantilism, though based on new economic practices, had one important element in common with the system of the previous period. It restrained and controlled individual merchants in favor of the needs of society. However, the rising new middle class of merchants and industrial capitalists were against any restrictions on their profits. They opposed economic regulation and used their growing power to demand freedom from state control. They desired an end to mercantilism. As the power of the capitalists increased, the goal of the economy became expansion, with economic profit the function of city growth. While the new market economy provided means to social recognition, the social costs were high. The greatest hardship fell on those receiving the fewest benefits—women, poor farmers, and members of the rising industrial working class. The new force of capitalism pushed aside the last vestiges of feudal life and created a new central function for the city—industrialization. It was capitalism that ushered in the Industrial Revolution and led to the emergence of the industrial city.

While Europe was going through this process of decline and then rebirth in its cities, areas of the non-Western world experienced quite different patterns. In East Asia, for example, the city did not suffer the decline it went through in medieval Europe. In China, numerous cities founded before the Christian era remained continuously occupied and economically viable down through the centuries. Moreover, long before any city in Europe again grew to a size to rival ancient Rome, very large cities were thriving in East Asia. Changan (present-day Xi'an), for example, reputedly had more than 1 million people when it was the capital of Tang China in the 7th century. Kyoto, the capital of Japan for over a thousand years (and modeled after ancient Changan), had a population exceeding 1 million by the middle of the 18th century. Although most of the ancient cities of Asia had populations of less than 1 million, they were still far larger than cities in Europe, until the commercial/industrial revolutions there (fig. 1.14). The principal explanation for this historical pattern of urban growth lies in the very different political/cultural systems and geographical environments of the great Asian civilizations. Although empires waxed and waned in Asia, just as in Europe, cities in premodern Asia continued to serve vital functions, as centers of political administration, cultural and religious centers, and commercial centers for Asia's highly developed traditional agrarian societies.

It was not until the arrival of Western colonialism that those societies and their cities began to be threatened. The several centuries of Western colonialism in Asia added a new kind of city to the region, a Western commercial city sometimes grafted onto a traditional city, sometimes created anew from virgin land. In either case, these new cities came eventually to dominate the urban landscape of most of Asia. That dominance has continued right into the contemporary period.

In the Greater Middle East, the traditional city also existed and thrived down through the centuries, long before Europeans began to claim pieces of the region as their colonial territories. But once colonialism was fully asserted in the region, the same process of grafting and creating new Western commercial cities occurred, with similar consequences to those experienced in Asia.

In Sub-Saharan Africa and Latin America, the urban experience varied somewhat from that of much of Asia and the Middle East. In the case of Latin America, the traditional city—and the societies that created that city, such as the Mayan, Incan, and Aztec—was obliterated by Spanish conquest and colonization. The Spanish, as well as the Portuguese, thus created new cities in the vast realm of Latin America, cities that reflected the cultures of Europe. In Sub-Saharan Africa, the indigenous cities of various African kingdoms, such as Mali, Songhay, Axum, and Zimbabwe, had existed for centuries, but they also felt the impact of European colonialism. By the 19th century, they were largely destroyed as viable urban centers. Thus, in that vast subcontinent the Europeans also carved out their colonial territories and created innumerable European commercial cities, usually coastal, that quickly grew to dominate the region.

Figure 1.14 Beijing, China's capital for many centuries, initially laid out along classical lines like those in Xi'an, has become a huge metropolis in the past fifty years. This bird's-eye view of Tiananmen Square reveals the majesty that has returned to Beijing as the political and cultural center of a vast nation (see chapter 11). (Photo courtesy *China Today*)

Hence, as it materialized in Europe and was exported with the creation of colonial empires after 1500 A.D., the European-created city became the model for urban growth and development worldwide. In some regions, it was imposed on indigenous societies that were exterminated or shoved aside (as in North and South America and Oceania). In regions with long histories of indigenous cultures and urban life, it existed alongside of and transformed indigenous cities (as in most of Asia, the Greater Middle East, and Africa).

Industrial and Postindustrial Urbanization (18th Century to the Present)

Only after the Industrial Revolution, which began around 1750, did significant urbanization occur. For the first time, a sizable proportion of the population in industrial countries came to live in cities. It was not until the 19th century, however, that cities emerged as important places of population concentration. By 1900, only one nation, Great Britain, could be regarded as an urbanized society in the sense that more than half of its inhabitants resided in urban places. During the 20th century, however, the number of urbanized nations increased dramatically. The United States became an urban nation in 1920. Only Africa and parts of Asia continue to lag behind the rest of the world in urbanization.

Most of the world's largest cities were produced by basically unregulated market and social forces. For the most part, the pricing mechanism operated to produce an economic city in which countless simultaneous and successive market-oriented decisions affected the allocation of resources. Even the emerging democracies of Eastern Europe and Central Asia are now adapting to market mechanisms.

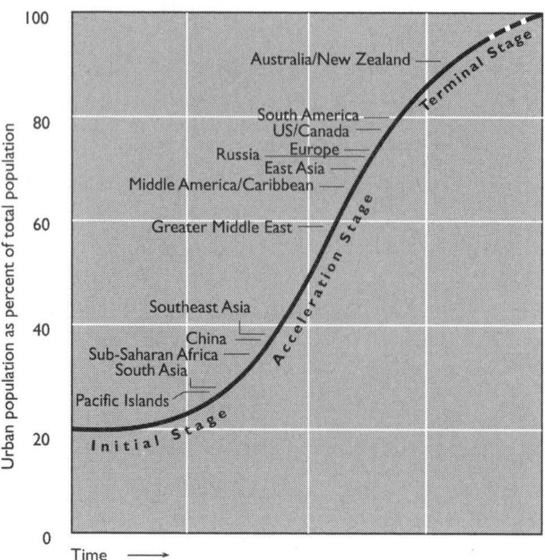

Figure 1.15 Urbanization Curve. *Source*: Adapted from Ray Northam, *Urban Geography* (New York: Wiley, 1979), 66.

The market system has channeled investment to produce a great variety of cities, specialized and diversified, large and small, growing and declining. The problems of the average citizen typically reflect the general prosperity of his/her city. The position and importance of a city (i.e., its rank in the international and national systems of cities) is a vital measure in an assessment of the problems of the residents.

The city is not a static entity, but a system in flux. Within the city, some sectors may decline and die as investment is withheld, while others may grow and prosper as investments increase. Every change in urban function has both positive and negative multiplier effects. Adjustment to the changed situation may occur slowly. If the change is a reduction in functions, poverty levels will usually rise as unemployment spreads through the city in a cumulative manner, which produces greater effects in some neighborhoods than in others. Whether the city is growing or declining, spatial change within it will occur as a result of the decline of older neighborhoods, an influx of poor rural families or of immigrants from foreign areas, labor-shedding as a result of automation, the development of new suburbs or satellite towns, and the migration of businesses and industries to the suburbs. Those without access to opportunities, skills, or transportation will be left out by the operation of the market system. Whenever and wherever the market system operates, it serves the affluent rather than the poor. Thus, the problems of urbanization are in a sense the problems of marginalized peoples and unheard voices.

At the national scale, the urbanization process may be divided into three stages (fig. 1.15). In the initial stage, the population lives mainly in rural areas and is engaged in primary-sector occupations. The growth of industries and mass rural-to-urban migration lead to the second stage, a period of accelerating urban growth. Eventually, the rate of urban increase begins to decline, as indicated toward the upper end of the curve. In the third, or terminal, stage, urban growth stabilizes, although individual urban areas may be growing or declining. Growth during the third stage is minimal, with the competition among cities in a national urban system intensifying: one city's gain is another city's loss.

CITY FUNCTIONS AND URBAN ECONOMIES

City Functions

Geographers have traditionally classified cities into three categories based on their dominant functions: (1) market centers (trade and commerce); (2) transportation centers (transport services); and (3) specialized service centers (such as government, recreation, or religious pilgrimage).

Cities categorized as market centers are also known as central places, because they perform a variety of retail functions for the surrounding area. Central places offer a variety of goods and services (from grocery stores and gas stations to schools and post offices). Small central places, or *market centers,* depend less on the characteristics of a particular site and more on being centrally located with respect to their market areas. These centers tend to be located within the trade areas of larger cities: people living in small cities must go to larger cities to buy certain goods and services for which there is not a sufficient market locally. There is thus a spatial order to the settlements and their functional organization. *Central place theory* is concerned with explaining the regular size, spacing, and functions of urban settlements as they might be distributed across a fertile agricultural region, for instance. Cities of a particular size or level in the urban hierarchy tend to be evenly distributed throughout a service area, at least according to theory. The largest cities, or highest-order centers, are surrounded by medium-sized cities that are in turn surrounded by small cities, all forming an integrated part of a spatially organized, nested hierarchy. The locational orientation of market centers is quite different from the locational orientation of transportation and specialized function cities.

Transportation cities perform break-of-bulk or break-in-transport functions along waterways, railroads, or highways. Where raw materials or semifinished products are transferred from one mode of transport to another—for example, from water to rail or rail to highway—cities emerge either as processing centers or as transshipment centers (fig. 1.16). Unlike central places, whose regularity in location is accounted for by marketing principles, transportation cities are located in linear patterns along rail lines, coastlines, or major rivers. Frequently, major transport cities are the focus of two or more modes of transportation, for example, the coastal city that is the hub of railways, highways, and shipping networks. Today, of course, almost all cities have multiple transportation linkages. Exceptions tend to be isolated towns, such as mining centers in Siberia that may have only air connections and perhaps primitive seasonal road linkages to the outside.

Cities that perform a single function, such as recreation, mining, administration, or manufacturing, are labeled specialized function cities. A very high percentage of the population participating in one or two related activities is evidence of specialization. Oxford, England, is a university town; Rochester, Minnesota, is a health-care town; Norfolk, Virginia, a military town; Canberra, Australia, a government town; and Cancún, Mexico, a tourist town. Specialization is also evident in cities where the extraction or processing of a resource is the major activity. Cities labeled as mining and manufacturing cities have much more specialization than those with diversified economic bases.

Sectors of the Economy

The economic functions of a city are reflected in the composition of its labor force. Preindustrial societies are associated with rural economies; these economies have the largest percentages of their labor force engaged in the primary sector. Primary economic activities are agriculture, fishing, forestry, and mining. Preindustrial cities have historically been commercial islands in seas of rural-oriented populations. The Industrial Revolution triggered the emergence of cities oriented to manufac-

Figure 1.16 Baltimore rose to prominence as a major East Coast port because of its superb harbor and rail and road links with the interior in the days of heavy industry. In recent decades, those advantages have become less important and the harbor has been revived into a recreation/tourism center in one of the most successful urban renewal programs of recent decades. (Photo by Larry Ford)

turing. The secondary sector of the economy, another name for manufacturing, expanded and so did the demand for labor to work in the factories. As larger percentages of the population began living in cities, retail trade, transportation, and all kinds of services began to flourish. The service sector, or tertiary economic activities, grew at the expense of the primary and secondary sectors, which declined in their proportions of the total labor force. The quaternary sector, a more advanced stage of the service sector, consists of information services, which are playing an increasingly important role in MDCs. The mix of primary, secondary, tertiary, and quaternary activities within urban regions, as it has changed over time, also helps us to identify specific stages in humanity's economic evolution (fig. 1.17).

The association between urbanization and industrialization has been characteristic of Europe, North America, Japan, Australia, and New Zealand. That is, cities and industries grew in synchronization with each other. In many parts of Africa, Asia, and Latin America, many countries that recently have been increasingly urban have not experienced a corresponding increase in the manufacturing, or secondary, sector of the economy. Rather, their service sectors have provided jobs for growing urban populations. Included in service-sector employment are small retailers, government servants, teachers, professionals, and bankers. Also included are many service workers in the *informal economy,* including those members willing to perform odd jobs (watching parked cars or cleaning houses) and those working in unskilled service

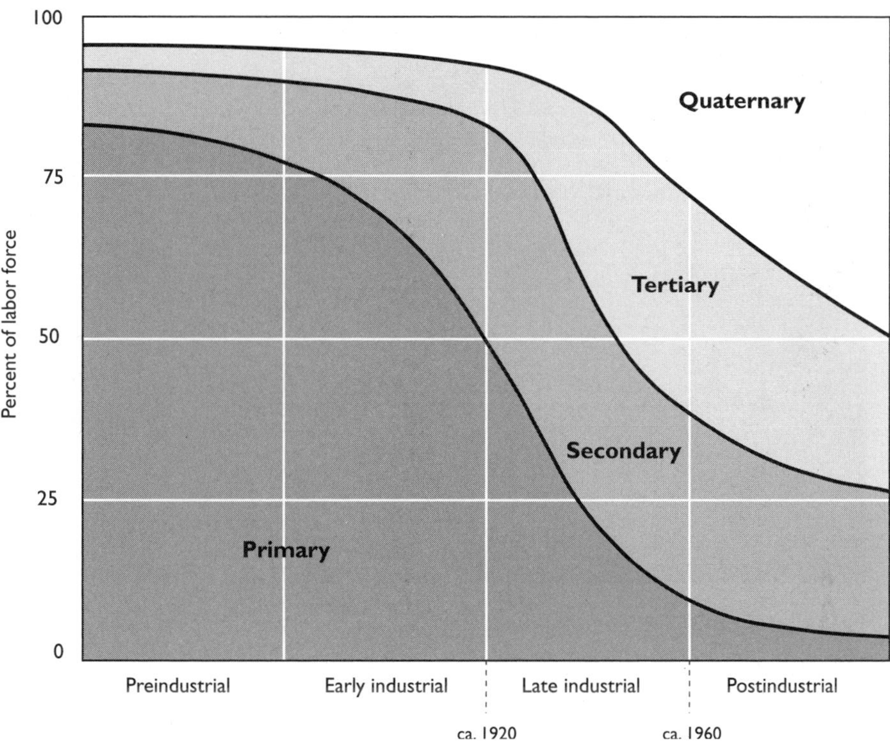

Figure 1.17 Labor Force Composition at Various Stages in Human History. *Source*: Adapted from Ronald Abler et al., *Human Geography in a Shrinking World* (Belmont, Calif.: Wadsworth, 1975), 49.

occupations, such as street vending, scavenging, and laboring at construction sites. In the informal sector, barter and the exchange of services often take the place of monetary exchanges, thus bypassing government accounting and taxation.

The Economic Base Concept

Economic functions are keys to the growth of cities. The *economic base concept* states that two types of activities or functions exist: those that are necessary for urban growth and those that exist primarily to supplement those necessary functions. The former are called *basic functions*, or city-forming activities. They involve the manufacturing, processing, or trading of goods or the providing of services for markets located outside the city's boundaries. Economic functions of a city-servicing nature are called *nonbasic functions.* Grocery stores, restaurants, beauty salons, and so forth are nonbasic economic activities because they cater primarily to residents within the city itself (fig. 1.18).

Of the two, the basic functions are the key to economic growth and prosperity. A city with a high percentage of its labor force in the production of such items as automobiles, furniture, and electronic equipment depends on sales beyond the city's boundaries to bring money into the community. Income generated by the sales of those industrial goods is channeled back into

Figure 1.18 This textile retailer in Kashgar, China, caters primarily to local residents, but tourist business helps, too. The cell phone, an increasingly visible sign of globalization around the world, helps the owner keep in touch and stay competitive. (Photo by Stanley Brunn)

the city, where employees in those industries spend it on groceries, gasoline, hardware, entertainment, and other everyday purchases.

The economic base of some cities is grounded in manufacturing industries, the secondary sector of the economy. Manchester, England, and Pittsburgh, Pennsylvania, are prime examples of older industrial cities whose growth and prosperity depended upon world markets, for cotton textiles and steel, respectively. Since World War II, both cities have lost their manufacturing base and have been challenged to find service industries for which there is a larger market. The economic base of postindustrial cities, in fact, is to be found in the tertiary and quaternary sectors of the economy (fig. 1.19). *Silicon valleys* developed around the world in the late 20th century to service the needs of the computer industry. In the early 21st century, *biotech valleys* are becoming the economic base of choice. Cities such as Geneva, Singapore, San Francisco, and Boston are competing to have biotechnology firms move into their regions. Money from biomedical and pharmaceutical research provides an economic base tied to high-level applications of technology and brainpower. Banking, accounting, architecture, and advertising are other service industries that some cities depend upon for their economic bases.

Urban Growth and the Principle of Circular and Cumulative Causation

The principle of *circular and cumulative causation* allows us to understand why some cities grow and others do not. Simply put, the principle states that changes in urban economic functions cause changes in population. As a city's economic base increases, it has a multiplier ef-

Figure 1.19 The Renaissance Center in downtown Detroit was an initiative to help Detroit make the transition from its original auto industry focus to a more service-based economy, a transition that has been fraught with all kinds of difficulties. (Photo by Larry Ford)

fect throughout the community. Growth (and conversely, decline) becomes a cumulative process. For instance, one of the major ways cities grew in the past was by attracting more manufacturing enterprises. Each new factory in an urban area stimulated general economic development and population growth. Business output increased due to a greater demand for products. Rising profits increased savings, causing investments to rise. Increased productivity resulted in greater wealth. The growing population then reached a new level, or threshold, resulting in a new round of demands. At each new level, cities were able to offer a greater number and variety of services than they could when there were fewer inhabitants. In sum, the growth of cities is cumulative and is strongly influenced by changes in the economy. Cities stagnate or die because they lose industries and population, conditions that create a negative circular and cumulative causation. Thus, it is easy to understand why city mayors and chambers of commerce work so hard to promote their respective cities as favorable sites for investment and new business locations. Competition for a particular type of business, such as Japanese automobile companies in the American Midwest, can be intense, as each city wants to benefit from the circular and cumulative effects of new jobs in new industries.

THEORIES ON THE INTERNAL SPATIAL STRUCTURE OF CITIES

In addition to the origin and growth of cities, geographers have long been intrigued by their internal spatial structure. Components of that structure, which varies from region to region around the world, include: the location of industry, commercial districts, transportation routes, and residences; the number and nature of parks and the amount of *green space;* and the direction in which a city is growing the fastest. Even with the increasing homogenization of urban life and the built environment—such as in the spread of skyscrapers, Western clothing styles, and transnational food habits and the widespread adoption of cars—distinctive differences remain in the internal arrangement of cities. Many factors account for those regional variations.

A variety of theories has been developed to describe and explain the pattern of land use and the distribution of population groups within cities. The four most widely accepted theories, or models, of city structure are the concentric zone theory, the sector theory, the multiple nuclei theory, and the inverse concentric zone theory (fig. 1.20). All evolved from observations of urban landscapes that suggested that land uses of different types were predictably, not randomly, distributed across the city.

The Concentric Zone Theory

The *concentric zone theory* was first conceptualized by Friedrich Engels (coauthor of the *Communist Manifesto*) in the mid-19th century. Engels observed that the population of Manchester, England, in 1844 was residentially segregated on the basis of class. He noted that the commercial district (offices plus retail and wholesale trade) was located in the center of Manchester and extended about half a mile in all directions. Besides the commercial district, Manchester consisted of unmixed working people's quarters, which extended a mile and a half (2.3 km) around the commercial district. Next, extending outward from the city, were the comfortable country homes of the upper bourgeoisie. Engels believed this general plan or pattern to be more or less common to all industrial cities.

Engels may have described the pattern first, but most social scientists consider E. W. Burgess, a University of Chicago sociologist, to be the father of the concentric zone model. According to Burgess, the growth of any city occurs through a radial expansion from the center so as to form a series of concentric rings, in essence, a set of nested circles that represent successive zones of urban expansion. The five zones Burgess observed and described during the 1920s, before the automobile transformed Chicago, were: (1) the central business district (CBD), with its retail and wholesale sectors; (2) the zone of transition, characterized by stagnation and social deterioration; (3) the zone of factory workers' homes; (4) the zone of better residential units, including single-family dwellings and apartments; and (5) the commuter zone, extending beyond the city limits and consisting of suburbs and satellite communities. The process Burgess used to explain these concentric rings was called *invasion and succession.* Each type of land use and each socioeconomic group in the inner zone tends to extend its zone by the invasion of the next outer zone. As the city grows or expands, there is a spatial redistribution of population groups by residence and occupation. Burgess further demonstrated that many social characteristics are spatially distributed in a series of gradients away from the central business district. Such characteristics include the percentage of foreign-born groups, poverty, and delinquency rates. Each tends to decrease outward from the city center.

The Sector Theory

The *sector theory* was developed in the 1930s by Homer Hoyt, an economist. Hoyt examined spatial variations in household rent in 142 American cities. He concluded that general patterns of housing values applied to all cities and that those patterns tended to appear as sectors, not concentric rings. According to Hoyt, residential land use seems to arrange itself along selected highways leading into the CBD, thus giving a land-use map a directional bias. High-

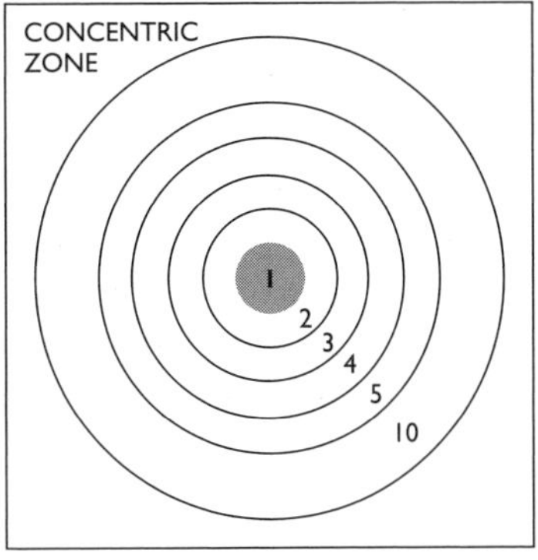

Figure 1.20 Generalized Patterns of Internal Urban Structure. *Source*: Adapted from various sources.

rent residences were the most important group in explaining city growth, because they tended to pull the entire city in the same direction. New residential areas did not encircle the city at its outer limits, but extended farther and farther outward along a few select transportation axes, giving the land-use map the appearance of a pie cut into many pieces. The sectoral pattern of city growth can be explained in part by a filtering process. When new housing is constructed, it is located primarily on the outer edges of the high-rent sector. The homes of community leaders, new offices, and stores are attracted to the same areas. As inner, middle-class areas are abandoned, lower-income groups filter into them. By this process, the city grows over time in the direction of the expanding high-rent residential sector.

The Multiple Nuclei Theory

In 1945, two geographers, Chauncy Harris and Edward Ullman, developed a third model to explain urban land-use patterns, the *multiple nuclei theory.* According to this theory, cities tend to grow around not one but several distinct nodes, thus forming a polynuclear (many-centered) pattern. The multiple nuclei pattern is explained by the following factors:

1. Certain activities are limited to particular sites because they have highly specialized needs. For example, the retail district needs accessibility, which can best be found in a central location, while the manufacturing district needs transportation facilities.
2. Certain related activities or economic functions tend to cluster in the same district because they can carry on their activities more efficiently as a cohesive unit. Automobile dealers, auto repair shops, tire shops, and auto glass shops are examples.
3. Certain related activities, by their very nature, repel each other. A high-class residential district will normally locate in a separate area from the heavy manufacturing district.
4. Certain activities, unable to generate enough income to pay the high rents of certain sites, may be relegated to more inaccessible locations. Examples may include some specialty shops.

The number of distinct nuclei occurring within a city is likely to be a function of city size and recentness of development. Auto-oriented cities, which often have a distinct horizontal as opposed to vertical appearance, include industrial parks, regional shopping centers, and suburbs layered by age of residents, income, and housing value. Rampant urban sprawl is likely to be reflected in a mixed pattern of industrial, commercial, and residential areas in peripheral locations. Geographer Peirce Lewis describes this sprawling urban landscape as the *galactic metropolis* because the nucleations resemble a galaxy of stars and planets. Some of those nucleations become cities in the suburbs, what some have called *edge cities.* These edge cities are, in effect, the CBDs of newly emerging urban centers scattered through the suburban ring surrounding older central cities. This pattern reinforces what has been described as the typical urban spatial model for most U.S. urban areas, the *doughnut model.* In this model, the hole in the doughnut is the central city (with poor, mostly nonwhite, blue collar/working class residents, large numbers of whom are on welfare, and a declining tax base and economy) and the ring of the doughnut is the suburbs (rich, mostly white middle and upper class, white-collar employment, and an expanding tax base and economy). Old, often declining manufacturing tends to be found in the hole; new, often high-tech manufacturing tends to be located in the suburbs, in the edge cities.

The Inverse Concentric Zone Theory

The preceding three theories of urban spatial structure apply primarily to cities of the MDCs and to American cities in particular. Many cities in the LDCs follow somewhat different patterns. A frequent one is the inverse concentric zone pattern, which is a reversal of the concentric zone model. Cities where this pattern exists have been called preindustrial; that is, they are primarily administrative and/or religious centers (or were at the time of their founding). In such cities, the central area is the place of residence of the elite class. The poor live on the periphery. Unlike most cities in the MDCs, social class in these places is inversely related to distance from the center of the city.

The reasons for this pattern are twofold: (1) the lack of an adequate and dependable transportation system, which thus restricts the elites to the center of the city so they can be close to their places of work, and (2) the functions of the city, which are primarily administrative and religious/cultural, functions controlled by the elite and concentrated in the center of the city (with its government buildings, cultural institutions, places of worship, etc.).

As many of the LDCs have begun to industrialize, especially in the past 30 years, growth industries have been primarily urban oriented, just as they were in the MDCs many decades ago. However, the newer and larger industrial establishments tend to locate not in city centers but on the periphery, often in industrial parks or *enterprise zones* established by the government for the purpose of attracting both domestic and foreign investors. The city centers tend to be far too congested for industrial plants of any considerable size. Moreover, the elites in the city centers often do not want large industrial plants near their place of work and residence. Hence, emerging gradually in many of the larger cities of the LDCs is the pattern of the multiple nuclei model, with new industrial parks serving as the nuclei. In other words, the inverse concentric zone pattern, while still valid in many LDCs, is merging with the multiple nuclei pattern.

As useful as these four theories of the internal spatial structure of cities are, they must be viewed with caution as generalizations of the extremely complex mix of factors that influence and determine the use of land within cities in any region or country. One can commonly find elements of more than one model present in a given city. Moreover, each of the models and the land uses associated with them must be viewed as dynamic. There are changes going on all the time in economic functions, social and administrative services, transportation, and population groups that will alter the size and shape of specific sectors or zones. Furthermore, the complexities of applying these theories multiply severalfold when working with non-Western cultures and economic systems. Nowhere is this more apparent than in China and the former Communist countries, where various forms of the so-called socialist city were being created and where internal spatial structures were quite unlike those described by any of the four theories mentioned. The legacy of those socialist patterns lingers on, as free-market forces transform those cities.

AN OVERVIEW OF URBAN PROBLEMS

Each of the regional chapters in this book deals extensively with urban problems and attempts being made to solve them. Some broad generalizations are made below about many problems that seem to be worldwide in scope.

Excessive Size

Excessive size of urban regions, both in population and in geographical area, might more properly be described as a cause of problems than a problem in itself. It presents a particularly severe challenge in the LDCs, where the economic base of cities is inadequate to cope with the stresses created by larger and larger numbers of people spread over ever more expansive realms. Better planning and urban design are the methods generally used to ameliorate problems of size before they get out of hand.

Overcrowding

An outgrowth of excessive size is overcrowding, meaning too many people occupying too little space. Overcrowding is a psychological concept that does not always equate to population density. It is particularly acute in the LDCs. For Americans or Europeans who have not traveled outside of their country or region, it is sometimes difficult to fully comprehend the magnitude and effects of really severe urban overcrowding. Seeing or being caught up in the tidal wave of humanity that one can find in the larger cities of the LDCs—Manila, Shanghai, Cairo—is a vivid lesson in the consequences of excessive urbanization that one never forgets.

Shortage of Urban Services

With so many people in urban settings, city governments are hard-pressed to provide all the human services that residents need—education, health care, clean water, sewage disposal, garbage pick-up, police and fire protection, public parks, mass transit, and numerous others. The provision of public services is difficult not just because of the large numbers of people involved, but also because of the rapid growth rates of cities, particularly in the LDCs. People may even look to the government to provide housing, particularly under socialist/communist regimes or when the private marketplace drives up property values to astronomical heights. Yet how can a city that is doubling in population every ten years or so maintain the economic growth needed to provide for so many new arrivals, particularly

Figure 1.21 Scavengers push their carts past squatter shacks in Smokey Mountain, a once-notorious slum of Manila that got its name from the continuously burning garbage. It has been the target of redevelopment efforts in recent years (see chapter 10). (Photo by James Tyner)

when those new residents are poor? While these problems exist around the world, MDCs are more likely to have the resources to deal with them in a rational manner.

Slums and Squatter Settlements

Most cities of the world have slums or squatter settlements, poorer communities that are not fully integrated, socially or economically, into the development process (fig. 1.21). Slums tend to be found in old, run-down areas of inner cities (sometimes, paradoxically, on very valuable land) in both LDCs and MDCs. Squatter settlements are typically new, but made up of makeshift dwellings erected without official permission on land that the squatters do not own. These settlements are usually located on the outskirts of cities in the LDCs, instead of near the center. The dwellings are constructed of any available materials, such as cardboard, tin, adobe bricks, mats, or sacks. Construction is generally uncontrolled and the areas tend to lack essential services, sometimes even electricity. Squatter settlements go by various names in different countries: *barriadas* in Peru, *geçekondu* in Turkey, *favelas* in Brazil, *bustees* in India, and *bidonvilles* in former French colonies of Africa. Some have existed for decades and are now integral parts of larger cities. Both slums and squatter settlements tend to be overcrowded and underserviced.

Traffic Congestion

Another obvious effect of overcrowding, produced in large part by the growing number of motor vehicles, is traffic congestion. Superficially, this might be viewed as merely a nuisance of urban life, an aggravation of much less consequence than survival-level problems such as employment, housing, and social services. Nonetheless, traffic congestion is a serious dilemma that is choking many cities to a

Figure 1.22 Portland, Oregon, offers a lesson in many aspects of successful urban development, including its trolley system to reduce reliance on private automobiles (see chapter 2). (Photo by Judy Walton)

standstill in terms of the movement of people and goods. Consequences include economic inefficiency (loss of time and waste of resources), social stress, and pollution, all of which diminish a city's development potential (fig. 1.22).

Lack of Social Responsibility

Perhaps one of the most insidious effects of urban overcrowding throughout the world is a reduction in people's sense of social responsibility. As more and more people compete for space and services, the competition tends to breed antisocial, even sociopathic, attitudes. City life can bring out the worst in human behavior: this is empirically obvious. People exhibit social pathologies when they resist waiting in line for services; think nothing of littering or despoiling public property (not to mention stealing property); disregard traffic regulations; exhibit *road rage;* and show a callous disregard for the rights of fellow citizens.

Unemployment and Underemployment

The issue of employment would probably top most lists of serious urban problems, since virtually everything else connected with the city is related in one way or another to the economic health of its population. Employment problems are certainly worldwide in scope, but again the magnitude varies. In the MDCs, the problem is primarily unemployment, with the greatest burden borne by the uneducated and unskilled. In the United States, for example, unemployment continues to be borne disproportionately by marginal labor force groups such as teenagers, older workers, women, racial minorities, unskilled workers in general, and non–English-speaking newcomers. In addition, large numbers of working persons earn so little that they remain essentially in poverty—the *working poor.* But the situation is not all that different in the cities of Europe, nor for that matter in the cities of the LDCs.

However, because the cities of the LDCs

tend to be far more overcrowded than those of the MDCs, and because high natural population growth rates continue in most of the LDCs, a huge proportion of the population is young, in the early employment period of 15–30 years of age. This creates tremendous strains on job markets. Unemployment rates of 30%–40% or more are not uncommon. Hundreds, even thousands, of young people may apply for a handful of job openings in a particular company. Even the lucky ones may end up with a job that is below their capabilities—in effect, underemployment. This is particularly true for college graduates, whose numbers each year in most of the LDCs are far greater than the number of available jobs equivalent to their skills. In the major cities of the LDCs, streets are cluttered with tens of thousands of workers in the informal sector who eke out marginal existences in jobs with long hours and no fringe benefits. Families barely manage to make ends meet by having all able-bodied members, including women and children, participating in such employment.

Especially in the LDCs, one effect of employment problems is the large proportion of people employed in the service sector, both by the government civil service and by private establishments that deal with the public. These include jobs in government offices, banks, post offices, department stores, construction, and restaurants. One commonly sees unusually large numbers of clerks and counter help in such establishments, where employees seem not to be expected to work hard, since their wages are usually very low. However, the hiring of more personnel than really needed is one way of absorbing some of the excess labor force.

Ethnic and Social Issues

Unemployment, underemployment, and other factors breed a variety of subsidiary problems related to ethnicity and class status. These vary from region to region, of course. For example, relative economic prosperity in the United States has produced a tidal wave of illegal immigrants, primarily from Mexico and other Latin American countries, who seek employment and a better life. These people, along with large numbers of legal immigrants and refugees, commonly settle in the cities. Cuban refugees dramatically transformed the population composition and economic base of Miami, Florida, for instance. The influx of these peoples becomes a problem when it breeds resentment and outright conflict with other groups, such as blacks or others of low income who normally are the major competitors for the jobs sought by immigrants. In Europe, a similar situation has developed, particularly in Germany, where large numbers of *guest workers* from Eastern Europe and the Mediterranean have been allowed entry in order to meet the labor demands in Germany's industrial economy. These temporary immigrants have spawned resentment and tensions on the basis of cultural differences rather than economic competition.

In South African cities, the legacy of *apartheid* (the governmentally enforced segregation of races, now outlawed) will not soon disappear. In Southeast Asian cities, the importation of millions of Chinese during the colonial era left the economy, after independence, with a distinct merchant class and a very divided racial structure. In short, throughout the world, many cities, especially where there are diverse and conflicting nationalities, face severe centrifugal forces that work against efforts aimed at solving many urban problems (fig 1.23). In LDCs one can also find sharp differences in employment and education levels between men and women, the able-bodied and disabled, and urban residents and rural residents.

Figure 1.23 This artwork in Aotea Square in Auckland, New Zealand, is reflective of the struggle by the Maori, the original inhabitants of New Zealand, for justice and rights in their homeland, a problem common to minorities in cities around the world. (Photo by Richard Le Heron)

Westernization vs. Modernization

One phenomenon that is sweeping the world's cities, especially the larger ones, is the dilemma of Westernization versus modernization. The problem facing the LDCs is how to raise standards of living without, at the same time, completely abandoning traditional cultural values and ways of life. Some might argue that tradition and modernization are incompatible, that modernization automatically entails change, and that change is likely to take the form of Westernization, since it is the West that took the lead in creating the modern city and the lifestyle that goes with it. To be sure, there are ample signs of this Westernization (some might wish to call it *homogenization* or *globalization*) of the world's major cities, in the forms of skyscrapers, modern architecture, the automobile society, advertising, the focus on high mass consumption, and so forth. Nonetheless, as anyone who has lived in cities of the LDCs for any length of time can attest, traditional cultural values and lifestyles do somehow manage to persist even in the middle of the most modern metropolis.

Environmental Degradation

Pollution of air and water, excessive noise levels, visual blight, and hillside clearance for urban expansion are among the many serious environmental problems in cities around the world. The chief difference between the MDCs and the LDCs is that the MDCs tend to have the wherewithal to do something about these problems. The LDCs, by and large, regard such concerns as less important in the face of more immediate life-and-death issues, such as job creation, food, housing, and control of infectious diseases. Thus, in general, the degree of urban degradation is most severe today in the cities of the LDCs. The cities with the greatest air pollution, for example, are no longer MDC cities such as Los Angeles, but rather cities such as Seoul, Shanghai, Mexico City, and São Paulo of the giant agglomerations or conurbations group. Levels of noise, ugliness, health hazards, and congestion in countless cities of the LDCs easily surpass the levels in the worst cities of the MDCs.

Urban Expansion and Loss of Agricultural Land

Part of the process of environmental degradation is the tremendous amount of land being gobbled up by the sprawl of cities, especially giant conurbations. In some countries, such as the United States, with its relative wealth of land resources, the problem is seen as unfortunate but not life threatening. In many other countries, however, where land resources in relation to population are less favorable, the loss of agricultural land to urban/industrial sprawl is of grave concern. Many countries in Asia particularly face this problem, perhaps none worse than Japan. On the one hand, these countries use land for industrial growth and economic advancement, while on the other they lose part of their ability to feed themselves. Food self-sufficiency ratios for Japan, South Korea, and a number of other rapidly urbanizing, industrializing states of Asia have been declining in real terms for several decades. Unfortunately, too, the best agricultural land is commonly found close to the major cities, since this was one of the initial site factors in their founding in the preindustrial era. Once lost, this prime land cannot be replaced and marginal land being reclaimed for agriculture does not begin to compensate in productivity for the land lost.

Urban Governance

Cities in the LDCs that are growing rapidly in population and area face problems of how to extend health care, education, water, sanitation, transportation, fire, police, and other services to inhabitants of fragmented suburbs and even to inhabitants of cities who have traditionally been excluded from governmental services. Problems arise over how to deliver human services without creating wide social and spatial disparities, how to prevent rampant and uncontrolled expansion, how to finance public services and allocate funds, and how to develop and implement a comprehensive urban plan. Conflicts occur over spending priorities and the location of new facilities (schools, hospitals, public housing projects, etc.). The task of governing or administering services to a mushrooming city is daunting. It is little wonder that portions of large cities in the LDCs may lack vital services, political representation, and hope. Government leaders faced with higher costs to provide human services may eventually have to select which cities or portions of cities can be saved with remedial and emergency care. Such a selection process may mean that some urban areas and residents will experience little relief from the many economic, social, and environmental ills they face.

Problems of governmental administration are not unique to the LDCs. In many MDCs, declining central city population and tax bases, politically balkanized suburbs, and population growth in fringe areas are current problems. Reorganization of school, park, health, fire, police, sanitation, and other districts is needed to provide effective and efficient delivery of services. Competing and conflicting jurisdictions, be they townships, counties, cities, or states, often jealously guard their political turf. The preservation of the status quo among the dozens or hundreds of administrative units within a metropolitan area stands in the way of effective, comprehensive planning efforts. The United States has a mixed record in metropolitan governments, city-county consolidations, and regional government structures. Reorganization seems to be much more popular and acceptable in the sunbelt than in the frostbelt states. In Canada, metropolitan reorganization efforts have been more successful than those in the United States. Wherever one finds declining populations, diminished tax bases, and higher costs for transportation, welfare, education, health, and police, it seems likely that a greater amount of administrative reorganization and region-wide planning is needed. Metropolitan planning schemes for future needs should be easier to accomplish in many MDCs than LDCs, in part because their populations will remain fairly stable.

Refugees and Resettlement

The world political map is marked by conflict. That conflict often generates massive flows of refugees, people uprooted from their homes who leave with few resources to support themselves. Some end up in the cities of surrounding countries. Others end up in the countryside, where city-size populations must make do in refugee camps bereft of urban infrastructure or services. Still others, many fewer in number, make their way to distant cities, perhaps in the United States. Displaced persons from Palestine, Afghanistan, Indochina (Vietnam and Cambodia), Rwanda, Kosovo, and many other areas have made headlines over the past three decades. At the beginning of the 21st century, the number of refugees in the world was equivalent to the population of the Los Angeles metropolitan area. Some of those refugees will return home, but others will remain in their cities of refuge.

Stagnation and No Growth

The rapid growth of urban agglomerations, as in many LDCs, is not the problem facing many older industrial cities in Europe and North America. These are places where the economies and populations are growing only slowly or not at all. Their population and economic growth is not being sustained; instead, there are pockets of stagnant economies and almost zero population growth. The problems of these cities are very similar, whether in Russia, Germany, France, or the United States. These include companies that have outdated technology, higher labor and production costs than those of newly industrialized countries, an aging labor force, and products with declining demand. Many of these cities were single-industry towns when the country was expanding industrially. With younger people and entire companies moving to attractive, new growth areas, the futures of some of these slowly growing or declining towns and cities are indeed bleak.

Consequences of Global Restructuring

Almost the entire world—rural and urban—is adjusting to changes in global economies. Globalization means the movement of products, money, information, and human talent around the world in ever-larger numbers at ever-lower costs and in ever less time. Mayors and governing councils must now think globally as well as locally. Companies produce items for world, not local or regional, markets. Money is transferred electronically from major financial centers in Europe to Asia and from North to South America. Trade barriers are being reduced between countries. The net result is an easier flow of people, money (including credit), and products across boundaries that once separated those with different ideologies and economies.

Transnational corporations and nongovernmental organizations (NGOs) have offices in major world capitals; their networks and offices also promote a "world without borders." Skilled workers are affected by these structural changes, as are those in the informal sector. Towns and cities around the world, but especially in the developed world, are competing for new businesses. The competition is no longer local and regional, but international. Decisions are made in corporate offices in North American, Asian, or European countries that affect the destinies and environments of workers and cities around the world.

The situation is not without hope. At least some countries among the LDCs and a great many among the MDCs are successfully attacking the problems of urban life and urban growth. The solutions tried or planned are far too numerous and complex to even attempt a summary of the panoply of approaches taken. There are pessimists who undoubtedly contend it is too late to solve the urban ills of humankind. Optimists hope this is not so. In the following chapters, we will observe both the problems and promises of urbanism in major world regions.

SUGGESTED READINGS

Amin, Ash, and Nigel Thrift. *Cities: Reimagining the Urban.* Cambridge, England: Polity, 2002. Challenges the notion that the contemporary city is separate from the country and offers a model of the New Urbanism.

Evans, Peter, ed. *Livable Cities? Urban Struggles for Livelihood and Sustainability.* Berkeley: University of California Press, 2002. A collection of articles, worldwide and interdisciplinary in scope, on urban livability.

Hall, Peter. *Cities in Civilization.* New York: Pantheon, 1998. Looks at the world's great cities during their golden ages, with an emphasis on culture, innovation, and the arts.

Hardoy, Jorge Enrique, Diana Mitlin, and David Satterthwaite. *Environmental Problems in an Urbanizing World: Finding Solutions for Cities in Africa, Asia, and Latin America.* London: Earthscan, 2001. Examines the critical issues of sustainable cities and of environmental policy and conditions in the LDCs.

Knox, Paul L., and Peter J. Taylor, eds. *World Cities in a World-System.* New York: Cambridge University Press, 1995. A set of original essays on world cities, including political and environmental issues and core-periphery relationships.

Lynch, Kevin. *The Image of the City.* Cambridge, Mass.: M.I.T Press, 1960. Seminal work on the "visual quality" of cities and how to read the urban landscape.

Pacione, Michael. "Modelling Cities." *Geography* (Geographical Association, United Kingdom) 86, nos. 2, 3, 4 (2001). A comprehensive critical analysis of the principal models of urban land use, in a three-part series (models of the developed world, models of the developing world, and models of future cities).

Sassen, Saskia. *The Global City: New York, London, Tokyo.* 2d ed. Princeton, N.J.: Princeton University Press, 2001. An exploration of the world's three leading centers for international transactions and their impact on the global urban hierarchy.

Stetler, Susan L., ed. *Cities of the World.* 4th ed. Detroit: Gale Research, 1993. Four volumes of city profiles based on the U.S. Department of State's "Post Reports."

Vance, James E., Jr. *The Continuing City: Urban Morphology in Western Civilization.* Baltimore, Md.: Johns Hopkins University Press, 1990. Explores the role of the city in Western society and its changing form through time.

WEBSITES

CIA Fact Book
http://www.odci.gov/cia/publicatons/factbook/rq.html
The Central Intelligence Agency's website for all kinds of information, including urban, about the countries of the world.

City Population
http://www.citypopulation.de
Presents population statistics and maps for cities around the world, including a list of urban agglomerations with more than 1 million inhabitants.

Cyburbia
http://www.cyburbia.org.
A large directory of Internet resources relevant to planning, architecture, urbanism, growth, sprawl, and other topics related to the built environment.

Degree Confluence Project
http://www.confluence.org
Visit each of the latitude and longitude integer degree intersections in the world, including some in cities.

GaWC—Globalization and World Cities
http://www.lboro.ac.uk/gawc/
Includes an inventory of world cities, data presentations, commentaries on specific cities, and articles of scholarly interest.

NASA "Search the Cities from Space" Collection
http://city.jsc.nasa.gov/cities/
Full color photographs of the world's cities taken by National Aeronautics and Space Administration (NASA) astronauts from the space shuttle and the International Space Station.

Population Reference Bureau
http://www.prb.org/
Includes data arranged by country and special reports on various topics, including urbanization; still the easiest way to find "percent urban" for any country or region.

Telegeography Project
http://www.telegeography.com/pubs/maps/index.html
A project that looks at various aspects of global linkages, such as the Internet, cable, and satellite; includes commercially available maps, viewable on the web page.

Thumbnail Sketches of Cities
http://www.cities.com
Brief synopses of cities around the world.

United Nations Population Division
http://www.un.org/esa/population/unpop.htm
Voluminous information on population, including the annual report on world urbanization prospects.

United Nations "Cities of Today, Cities of Tomorrow"
http://222.un.org/Pubs/CyberSchoolBus/habitat/index.asp
An interactive program of six units covering information and images of various aspects of urbanization of major cities around the world. Excellent for classes.

U.S. Bureau of the Census
http://www.census.gov/
Results of Census 2000 complete with copious data on towns and cities in the United States; includes tables from the U.S. *Statistical Abstract.*

The World Gazetteer
http://www.gazetteer.de/
A rich source of data on the world's countries, their administrative divisions, and their cities.

Figure 2.1 Major Cities of the United States and Canada, 2000. *Source*: Data from United Nations, *World Urbanization Prospects, 2001 Revision* (New York: United Nations Population Division, 2002), www.unpopulation.org.

2

Cities of the United States and Canada

JUDY WALTON AND LARRY FORD

KEY URBAN FACTS

Total Population	317 million
Percent Urban Population	78%
Total Urban Population	246 million
Most Urbanized Country	Canada (77%)
Least Urbanized Country	U.S. (75%)
Annual Urban Growth Rate	1.3%
Number of Megacities	2
Number of Cities of More than 1 Million	39
Three Largest Cities	New York, Los Angeles, Chicago
World Cities	New York, Los Angeles
Global Cities	New York

KEY CHAPTER THEMES

1. The United States/Canada is one of the most urbanized regions of the world, in terms of both percent urban population and numbers of major cities.
2. Cities of this region are unique in a number of ways, but especially in the way they have been shaped by capitalism and the homogeneity of their residential areas.
3. Cities in the United States/Canada developed largely within the past 200 years, in close association with advances in transportation and technology and the settling of a vast continent.
4. New York has dominated the United States since the very beginning because of its location, which enables connections with the interior as well as across the Atlantic.
5. Los Angeles came to dominate the West Coast, as America's no. 2 city, in the 20th century.
6. Although New York, Los Angeles, and Chicago are the giants, a multitude of smaller cities form the real base, and are more typical, of the American urban system.
7. U.S. cities are typified by a mix of land-use structures/models, but the most basic pattern is that of the "galactic" or multinuclei model, with its declining core and growing suburbs.

8. Canadian cities, by and large, have managed to sustain the vitality of the central city better than U.S. cities have, but cities in the two countries are becoming more alike.
9. The region's cities are renowned for their low population densities and enormous sprawl, due to their focus on the automobile, a problem of acute proportions and great complexity.
10. In the 21st century, the region's cities must deal with rapid change, economic restructuring, uneven development, sprawling growth, and a changing ethnic mosaic.

THE UNIQUENESS OF THE NORTH AMERICAN CITY

With over three-quarters of their combined population living in cities of over 5,000, Canada and the United States are among the most highly urbanized countries of the world (fig. 2.1). They are also among the most interesting. Yet few people understand much about them beyond a few popular myths, including the myths of youth, wealth, and a unique built environment. Many believe that cities of the United States and Canada (hereafter, "North America" in this chapter) lack the historic character of cities in other world regions. North American cities were not among the major large cities of the world as late as the 19th century. However, while cities in Europe, the Middle East, and China may have been around much longer, only a small portion of their built environment directly reflects this. In this respect, Boston and Montreal can be said to have maintained as strong a sense of place and heritage as, say, Barcelona. Similarly, some people explain the distinct character of North American cities as a function of the relative economic wealth of the region. Yet, Europe and Japan are also very wealthy, but have produced distinctly different urban landscapes. Finally, there is the myth of the built environment—do the ubiquitous skyscrapers, freeways, shopping malls, office parks, cookie-cutter subdivisions, and fast-food drive-thrus and even Disneyland set North American cites apart from their counterparts elsewhere? Here again, we argue "no." In an age of rapid globalization, these features can now be found throughout the world.

Once these myths are dispelled, can North American cities be seen as unique in any way? We argue that indeed they can. Two features in particular stand out—first, the degree to which they have been shaped by an ideology of laissez-faire capitalism and, second, the homogeneity of their residential areas.

Calvin Coolidge once remarked that "the business of America is business." This helps explain why North American city centers are generally filled with high-rise office towers, hotels, and department stores rather than grand central squares, boulevards, cathedrals, monuments, and palaces. Montreal and Washington, D.C., stand out as exceptions to the rule, having been planned as symbolic centers. The shaping of North American cities by a spirit of free enterprise and unfettered capitalism is a recurring theme in American literature, as evidenced in the classics *Babbitt* (1922) by Sinclair Lewis and *The Magnificent Ambersons* (1918) by Booth Tarkington. Typically, what determines the "highest and best" use of land in the city is who is willing to pay the most for it, its *exchange value,* rather than its symbolic, cultural, and emotional meaning, or *use value.* High order office and retail activities, which can afford rent at the center, tend to crowd out other potential activities.

The story of the special- or single-purpose building offers a good illustration of how this economic ideology (tied to individualism) has shaped the North American city. Historically, most cities of the Western world, aside from their unique and often monumental core areas, relied on a fairly narrow range of building types that housed many different activities. In the mid-19th century North American city, a new type of building arose, designed for efficiency to accommodate only one type of activity. This special-purpose building caught on and, by the early decades of the 20th century, North America had a far wider variety of building types than any other region of the world.

The special-purpose building led to a much higher level of sorting by activity, as entire buildings became exclusively devoted to a single function, such as office work or manufacturing. Residential uses were soon virtually excluded from downtown, leading to the peculiarly North American nine-to-five syndrome, in which downtowns become ghost towns after office workers head home. In hopes of recapturing middle- and upper-class residents and becoming twenty-four-hour cities again, U.S. and Canadian cities are starting to build luxury residential towers and other housing downtown.

Competition, closely associated with free-market ideology, has had a special imprint on the urban environment. From frontier days onward, North American cities have been in intense competition with each other. Urban boosterism, the grandiose promotion of one city over its rivals, is uniquely North American. Every city has a well-oiled *urban growth machine,* a loosely organized but powerful coalition of government, business, and real estate interests who stand to benefit from land development. Urban sociologists Logan and Molotch describe this growth machine in *Urban Fortunes* (1987). Typical actors include chambers of commerce, downtown associations, private business organizations, and even wealthy individuals. Most new skyscrapers, convention centers, stadiums, and shopping malls owe their existence to the workings of this growth machine. Cities copy the successes of other cities in order to avoid being left out of the competition for money and people. The whole process continues to have a tremendous impact on the North American landscape.

Another distinguishing feature of the North American city is its residential homogeneity. While market forces have played a role in this feature, zoning codes and discriminatory real estate practices have been far more influential. In the 1920s and 1930s, sociologists in the United States observed sharp, socioeconomic boundaries that divided relatively large areas of big cities. The names they applied to these areas—Gold Coast, Chinatown, Little Italy, slum, upper crust, working class, and ghetto—reflected very visible differences in class and ethnic composition. Although some scholars refer to this sifting and sorting as "social ecology," it was far from natural. Discriminatory real estate and loan practices, legal and illegal, overt and covert, played a prominent role and continue to do so. In both countries, ethnic and particularly racial discrimination against African Americans and Asians significantly shaped the city's residential landscape, from Chinatowns to ghettos to exclusive white enclaves. By itself, ability to pay for housing cannot account for the enormous degree of racial and social segregation still prevalent in North American cities.

Zoning ordinances also contributed to the shaping of a distinctive, homogeneous residential landscape. Since the first modern zoning ordinance was enacted in New York City in 1916, enthusiasm for zoning has made it the most popular form of land-use control in the United States and Canada. Huge tracts of land have been zoned as exclusively residential, commercial, industrial, or recreational, with very little mixing. Commercial businesses such as corner stores, dry cleaners, bars, and bakeries are prohibited in most neighborhoods due to zoning codes. Apartment buildings and duplexes are zoned out of single-family neighborhoods. This is beginning to change today, however, as urban planners and architects incorporate neotraditional designs, patterned after traditional neighborhoods and small towns that have a mix of housing types and neighborhood retail and commercial functions.

DEVELOPMENT OF THE URBAN SYSTEM

Normally, histories of urban development treat the evolution of the urban system (focusing on distribution and location and the broader network of cities) separately from the evolution of the internal structure of cities. One exception to this tendency is the work of geographer John Borchert, who identified various U.S. transportation/technology eras that shaped not only the sizes and relative locations of cities but their internal structures and landscapes as well. Cities that came into existence or experienced a growth spurt during the same era would tend to have similar spatial organizations and characters as well as similar types of locations. Over the years, Borchert's ideas have been adapted to accommodate a great number of societal changes, but for our purposes we require only four generalized epochs, although the fourth era blends directly into what could be called the "post–industrial capitalism" era of today.

Frontier Mercantilism (1790–1830)

The beginning of this period can be placed arbitrarily with the first U.S. census, which is about the time that the first substantial North American cities began to appear—sizable places with gradually increasing functional complexity. At the beginning of the 19th century, most important urban places were on or accessible to the Atlantic Coast. During this era, Philadelphia, New York City, Boston, Halifax, and Montreal became substantial urban centers (fig. 2.2).

During the early 1800s, North American cities were primarily commercial centers specializing in trade between their forested and agricultural hinterlands and Europe. Luxuries and manufactured goods were imported from Europe and natural resources were exported. There was little industry aside from traditional crafts. Buildings were small and undifferentiated and were almost all referred to as *houses,* as in banking house, warehouse, and schoolhouse. Most people lived and worked in the same district, if not the same building. Cities were true *walking cities* in the sense that they rarely covered more than 2 or 3 sq mi or had as many as 100,000 people; very little intraurban transportation existed except for a few carts and carriages. Since most cities were built along rivers or harbors, ferryboats offered the first opportunities for commuting. Some of the oldest North American cities, Quebec and Boston for example, still had many medieval characteristics, such as narrow, winding streets and defensible sites that made expansion awkward. By the 1820s, however, important changes were afoot.

Early Industrial Capitalism (1830–1870)

During the middle decades of the 19th century, the location, economic base, and internal

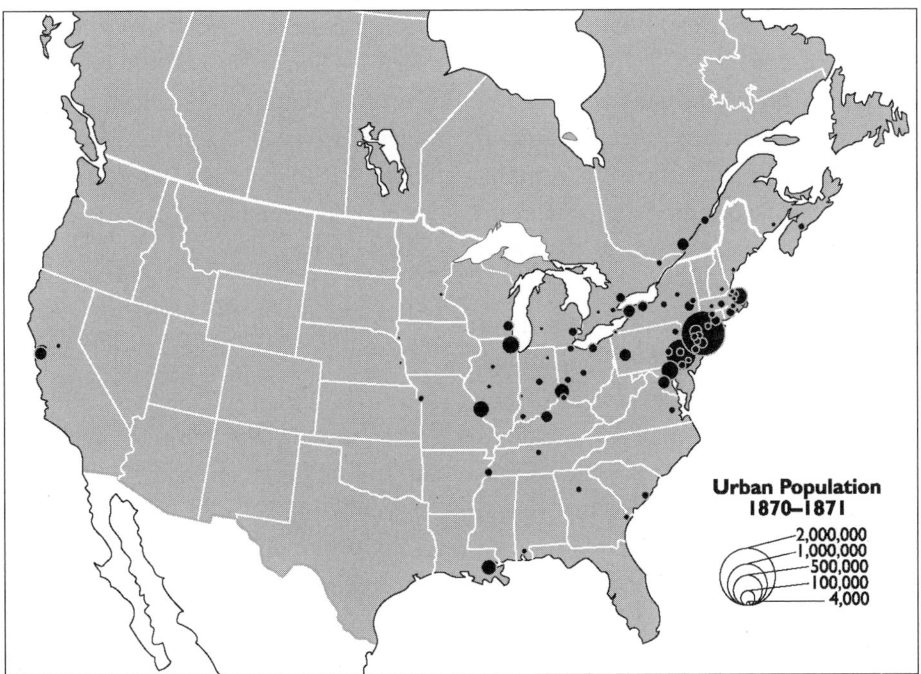

Figure 2.2 Urban Places of the United States and Canada, 1830–1831 and 1870–1871.
Source: Adapted from M. Yeates, *The North American City* (New York: Harper & Row, 1990).

structure of the typical North American city changed markedly. The advent of the steamboat made possible two-direction river trade and thus a better-connected urban system. Cities located along rivers, canals, and lakes in the interior of the continent boomed. Pittsburgh, Cincinnati, Louisville, St. Louis, and New Orleans, along the Ohio and Mississippi rivers, moved up the urban hierarchy. At the same time, many of the smaller Atlantic ports stagnated, as trade was increasingly concentrated in major cities such as New York and Boston. In Canada, Montreal and Toronto grew at the expense of smaller cities in the Maritime Provinces.

Toward the end of the era, cities in the U.S. South were hurt by the economic disruption of the Civil War, even as many northern cities benefited from the rapid industrialization that accompanied the war effort. Formerly dominant *border cities* such as Cincinnati and St. Louis began to experience stiff competition from northern centers such as Chicago and Cleveland, especially after the 1826 completion of the Erie Canal, connecting the Hudson River, and thus New York City, to the Great Lakes and the nation's agricultural interior. Many specialized industrial towns grew up in New England, New Jersey, and other locations, most of which were near waterfalls and thus sources of energy. As late as 1900, specialized industrial towns such as Lawrence and Lowell, Massachusetts, ranked high in the North American hierarchy of cities and helped to shape the new image of the city as a center of production.

The internal structure of cities changed during this period as well. In big cities such as New York and Cincinnati, ever-larger warehouses, port facilities, boat yards, breweries, and other commercial/industrial complexes began to appear. These helped define waterfront districts and emerging central business districts, or CBDs. Even though most cities were still very compact and characterized by a rich mix of land uses and activities, specialized office buildings for insurance, banking, and transportation companies began to appear, along with the equally novel department store. New waves of immigrants from Ireland and Germany began arriving during the 1840s and 1850s and they were housed mainly in peripheral *shantytowns* or improvised *tenements* near the docks.

At midcentury, most North American cities were still very small in area, although the first *carriage suburbs* had been pioneered. There were few innovations in intraurban transportation until the late 1850s, when the omnibus joined the profusion of carts and carriages on North American city streets. The omnibus was simply a large, stagecoach-like wheeled vehicle pulled by horses. Typically, there were many competing omnibus companies and no fixed routes. It served to loosen the urban fabric a little for the few who could afford a ride, but most neighborhoods remained dense and supported a variety of land uses.

National Industrial Capitalism (1870–1935)

During this era, North American cities joined the ranks of the largest, most complex cities in the world (fig. 2.3). By 1900, New York City vied with London to be the world's greatest metropolis. It was also during this era that the continent became fully urbanized, with cities located everywhere from Halifax to Los Angeles. Perhaps the seminal event defining the start of this epoch was the completion of the first transcontinental railroad. With the driving of the golden spike at Promontory, Utah, in 1869, the United States began to create a na-

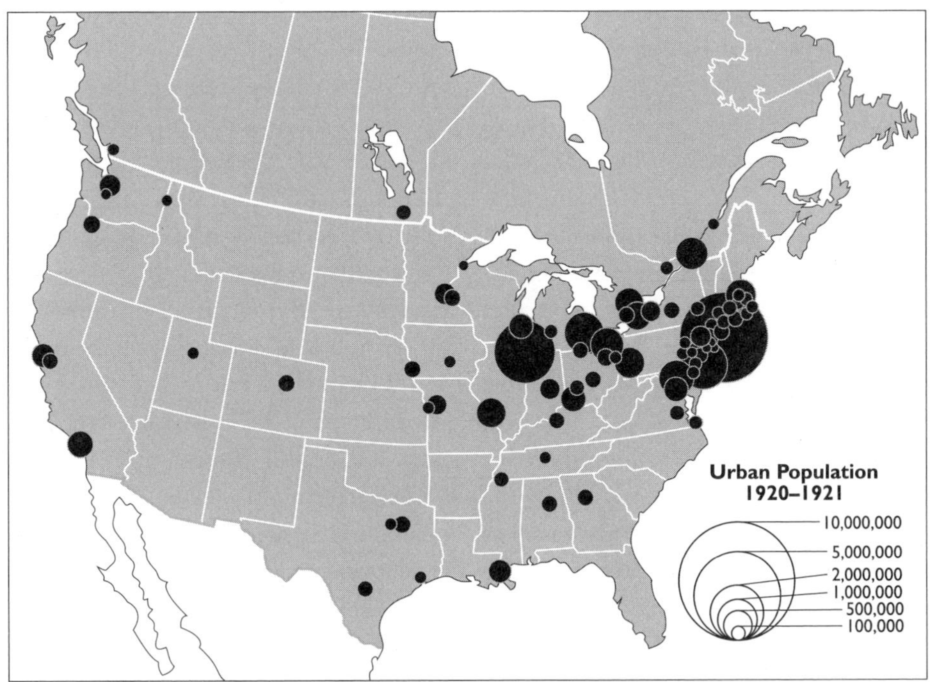

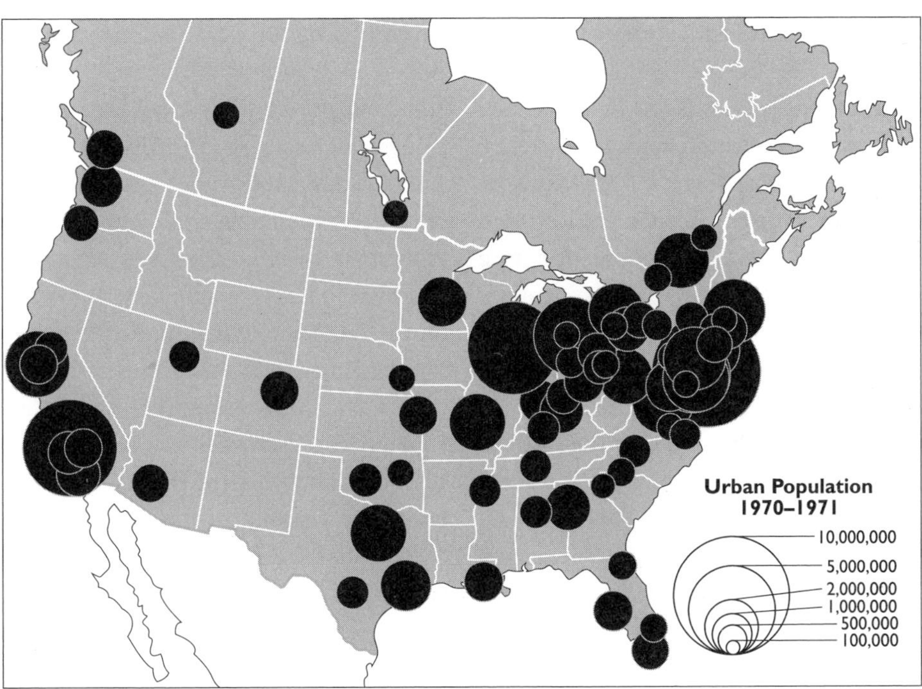

Figure 2.3 Urban Places of the United States and Canada, 1920–1921 and 1970–1971.
Source: Adapted from M. Yeates, *The North American City* (New York: Harper & Row, 1990).

tional urban network and Canada was not far behind. Much of the urban growth that occurred during this period was the result of an increased level of integration of the North American transport system, which created a continent-wide market. This was brought about by the standardization of rail gauges in the 1870s, an increased number of transcontinental lines, and a decrease in transport costs per mile.

At the start of the era, the biggest cities were still in the Northeast, but by 1900, Chicago, Detroit, Cleveland, and other cities in the industrial Midwest were moving rapidly up the urban hierarchy. New regional centers such as Denver, Seattle, and Vancouver were booming in parts of the continent that previously had been remote frontier areas. In addition, the development of a rail network fostered city specialization. By the early years of the 20th century, cities were becoming more functionally differentiated, since they no longer served primarily as service centers for a local region. For example, Youngstown, Ohio; Madison, Wisconsin; and Miami, Florida, each evolved to reflect a different dominant function (heavy industry, government, and recreation, respectively). These new functions were as important as traditional commercial activities in shaping the urban system.

It was during this period that the internal structure and spatial organization of most North American cities took on modern characteristics, with segregated land uses replacing the mixed landscapes of the traditional urban scene. Central business districts became filled with office towers, department stores, movie palaces, and other buildings serving businesses that could afford high-cost locations, while warehouses, factories, and especially housing occupied less desirable and more peripheral sites. By the 1920s, the classic North American city type was fully formed and new models of urban socioeconomic structure, such as the concentric zone and sectoral configuration, arose to describe it (see chapter 1). Of course, not all North American cities were alike, but since most were either built (e.g., Chicago) or largely rebuilt (e.g., New York) during this era, the classic concentric zone model of skyscraper center surrounded by industry and a suburban periphery works well as a descriptive device. City planning also developed during the early years of the 20th century and served to institutionalize existing social and economic tendencies. Large chunks of land were zoned commercial, industrial, or residential and developers had to abide by new restrictions.

Immigration has always been important in shaping the 20th-century metropolis, and it was a driving force behind many of the most important changes during this period. The trend toward segregated land uses in the 1920s came after a period of truly massive foreign immigration, almost exclusively from Europe, such that in many cities, especially in the Northeast, foreign-born or foreign-parentage residents became a majority. Between 1870 and 1920, about 30 million people entered the United States from Europe, and between 1901 and 1921, over 1 million people entered Canada from Europe. This continuous supply of cheap labor was the foundation of the urban and economic growth that occurred.

The major exception was the U.S. South, where low levels of industrialization and cheap African American labor acted as deterrents to immigration. Toward the end of the era, large numbers of southern blacks (and whites as well) migrated northward and added to the racial diversity, and division, of major U.S. industrial cities. Land-use segregation was soon overlain by class and ethnic segrega-

Figure 2.4 The Longaberger Basket Company headquarters in Newark, Ohio, illustrates the role of signature architecture in urban design. (Photo by Larry Ford)

tion that led to large, relatively isolated enclaves. African American *ghettos* coexisted with posh, exclusive suburbs in almost every industrial city in the United States (Canadian cities did not develop such ghettos, in large part due to very low numbers of African Canadians). All of these separate districts were tied together by transportation systems that included streetcars, buses, and sometimes elevated or underground rail lines.

A driving force behind the immigration streams of this period was the innovation of the industrial assembly line, often called the Fordist system, after Henry Ford's auto assembly line. The new system required a continuous supply of low-cost labor, and the arrival of large numbers of foreign and domestic immigrants to meet this need caused explosive growth in manufacturing cities in what would later become known as the *rust belt.* This period also witnessed the proliferation of architectural styles, especially in the United States, where rugged individualism was worshiped. The architectural exuberance of the early 20th century led to odd juxtapositions—Gothic skyscrapers rubbed shoulders with French Second Empire skyscrapers, while Romanesque churches were set amid English Tudor and Greek revival houses. Much specialized architecture was designed for the automobile. On the early commercial strips, gasoline stations adopted Dutch and Spanish-cottage styles, with massive neon signs plunked on top of the building or out front.

By the 1930s, with the automobile era in full swing, signature architecture appeared on the scene (fig. 2.4). Along the highway one might encounter drive-in restaurants in the shapes of giant donuts or ice-cream cones, drive-in theaters with towering cactus or palm tree themes, and motels with faux thatched roofs or Wild West themes. For almost every use there was a specialized building type. The standard plain box that signified commercial enterprise could be adorned with any of a thousand architectural themes, giving rise to the term "decorated shed." While the United States led the way in this practice, Canada soon fell in step, tending to concentrate on faux re-creations of European building types. Its string of major railroad hotels in French and Scottish Gothic styles offers a prime example. Architectural and functional diversity was eventually reined in by zoning and design regulations, since people in mock-Tudor cottages and Spanish haciendas generally did not want to be located next to a donut shop with screaming neon signs.

The Great Depression brought nearly all development to a screeching halt, with one notable exception in the field of urban planning—the appearance of the depression-era *new towns.* Greenbelt, Maryland; Greenhills, Ohio; and Greendale, Wisconsin, were developed by the federal government as part of a "New Deal" for the American people. They represented the continuation of a tradition in U.S. urban planning that had begun in the colonial era with such planned cities as Williamsburg, Virginia. This tradition continued through succeeding centuries with the utopian movements that begat Salt Lake City and two towns named Harmony in Pennsylvania and Ohio. In the late 1920s, it manifested itself in the innovative landscape of Radburn, New Jersey, which was built as "the town for the motor age," with a pedestrian-friendly environment. Neither the depression nor the war years, however, were kind to the new towns or old cities of the United States and Canada. Even the intensive industrial activity of the early 1940s was concentrated in existing facilities. By the late 1940s, however, a new round of expansion had begun.

Mature Industrial Capitalism to Post–Industrial Capitalism (1935–Present)

The general deconcentration and suburbanization of the population after World War II was directly related to the way the automobile, truck, and airplane shaped urban development. In particular, the widespread adoption of the automobile facilitated the decentralization of population in metropolitan areas. The rail hubs and streetcar systems that had shaped the compact North American central city gradually lost out to massive, multilane tollways and later "freeways" that enabled urban areas to spread outward to an unprecedented degree. Business travelers and tourists, rather than staying at downtown hotels close to the train station, could now rent cars at the airport and drive off to suburban resorts for meetings, golf, or other recreation.

The construction of federally financed highways in the 1930s, turnpikes in the 1950s, and high-capacity, limited-access interstate highways beginning in the 1960s resulted in a new network of surface transportation that allowed trucks to compete with trains and created a continental market that could be served from a number of different locations. As a consequence, metropolitan areas spread out and grew.

A notable feature of this era was the extensive concentration of urban population in a 500-mi (800-km) corridor along the northeastern coast of the United States, extending from Boston to Washington. This region was labeled *Megalopolis* (Greek for "great city") by geographer Jean Gottmann. Signaling a turning point in the history of human settlement, Megalopolis represented a whole new form of urban organization. Other megalopolises have since been recognized. They include "San–San"

Figure 2.5 This three-car garage in the Seattle suburbs is probably larger than most homes in cities of the developing countries. (Photo by Judy Walton)

(San Francisco–San Diego) and "Chipitts" (Chicago–Pittsburgh). Smaller megalopolitan belts stretch across central Florida from the Atlantic to the Gulf, across the Carolina piedmont, along the front range of the Rocky Mountains in Colorado, and around the Puget Sound from Portland to Vancouver, British Columbia.

The automobile also changed the internal structure of cities. While older cities such as New York, Boston, and Montreal, with their vast building stocks and complex infrastructures, were slower to change, newer centers such as Houston; Orange County, California; and Orlando, Florida, quickly adapted to the highway and became *galactic cities*—urban places with galaxy-like patterns of multiple nodes or realms but little sense of center or periphery, commonly referred to in older literature as a multiple nuclei pattern (see chapter 1). Commuters in these cities drive in all directions, often as much as 35–50 mi (56–80 km) per trip. Land set aside for parking consumes huge amounts of urban space. A multistory garage can be more expensive to construct, and have a larger foot print, than the buildings it serves. In residential areas, garages and off-street parking areas take up an increasing proportion of the neighborhood. In the United States, nearly a fifth of new homes now feature three-car garages (fig. 2.5). Long, auto-oriented commercial strips, a North American invention, continue to spread across the countryside, evolving into new forms to accommodate new features, such as big-box stores and outlet malls.

Just as the railroad tied the various regions of the continent together decades earlier, commercial airlines compressed the urban hierarchy still further. With the advent of jet travel in the late 1950s, it was possible to have a breakfast meeting in New York or Toronto and a dinner meeting in Los Angeles. This gave an advantage to cities in formerly remote but attractive locations such as Miami, San Diego, and Vancouver, since they were now better connected to the still dominant control cen-

Figure 2.6 Upscale apartment buildings on Vancouver's waterfront illustrate the economic vitality of Toronto's West Coast competitor. (Photo by Larry Ford)

ters in the East (fig. 2.6). This period witnessed the growth of metropolitan urban developments across the continent.

In the United States, by the later decades of the 20th century, a distinct contrast had developed between the older, slow-growing or declining urban areas of the Northeast (the *Rustbelt* or *Snowbelt*) and the newer, faster-growing cities of the West and South (the *Sunbelt*). Some of this was a result of the search for warm, amenity-laden locations by individuals and firms. Certainly, warmth was a key pull factor in Florida, where four major metropolitan areas grew up in response to the warmer weather, recreational facilities, and retirement amenities. This also explains why one of the authors of this chapter happened to grow up in San Diego instead of Bangor, Maine—her father moved the family "out West" in 1960 because he was tired of shoveling snow and because there were job opportunities.

Other factors behind the rise of the sunbelt included the decline of heavy industry in the face of foreign competition; government policies, including defense spending, that favored investment in the South and West; new streams of foreign immigration from Latin America and Asia rather than Europe; and the growth of new regional *headquarters cities* such as Atlanta and Phoenix. Urban areas along the Gulf Coast, in Texas, and in Oklahoma grew in population due to the development of oil fields and petrochemicals and, later, because of the electronics and aerospace industries. Houston, for instance, greatly benefited from the decision by the National Aeronautics and Space Administration to locate its Manned Spacecraft Center in the metropolis.

The most dramatic case study of growth during this era is provided by Los Angeles, which grew from a metropolitan area of nearly a million people in 1930 to the second-largest metropolis in North America today. Its diverse economic activities—deriving from oil and petrochemicals, food processing, recreation, film and television, electronics, and aerospace—underpin a super–metropolitan area extending over 250 mi (400 km), from Santa Barbara to San Diego.

Census data from the 1970s in the United States suggested a reversal of the long-standing trend toward population concentration, or urbanization. The process of population deconcentration was termed *counterurbanization,* a somewhat ambiguous term coined to describe a movement out of metropolitan counties that some people thought heralded the beginning of a "rural renaissance." Evidence from following censuses, however, indicates this was just a blip, as the bulk of the nation's growth continues to take place in metropolitan areas, despite certain counterurbanization streams.

Overall, this period witnessed the spectacular growth of urban areas beyond the old central cities that contained most of the urban population in 1930. The word *sprawl* entered the urban lexicon. The greatest volume of suburbanization occurred after World War II, when the supply of new housing was low due to limited wartime construction and the demand for housing was high as the population returned to peacetime activities. This need was met by the expansion of federal housing programs to provide low-interest, low-down-payment, federally insured mortgages for new housing. As new housing invariably requires the development of rural land at the urban periphery, governments in effect helped to promote rapid suburbanization and also subsidized middle-class white homeowners.

Between 1950 and 1970, suburban areas throughout the United States increased in population by 60%, whereas the central cities increased by only 32% (and this was largely attributable to an increase in the nonwhite population, which by 1970 composed almost 23% of the population of the central cities). During the 1960s and early 1970s, a number of these central cities became arenas for the expression of black rage over lack of employment opportunities, housing discrimination, and a wide array of socioeconomic inequalities. By then, the degree of segregation in many cities was such that many whites had little understanding of the severity of the situation that led to riots.

The past two hundred years of North American urbanization have featured often-frenzied searches for ideal locations for industry, business, and retirement. Today, the urban pattern has evened out and, to some extent, stabilized. There are few new frontier regions that are likely to house large metropolitan areas in the near future. The older, industrial cities are not declining so rapidly. Meanwhile, many amenity cities, from Atlanta to Los Angeles, have become at least as congested and expensive as the older cities they replaced in the urban hierarchy. As always, the North American system of cities is in a state of flux. One thing is certain, however: the type of growth and development that has occurred in the 20th century will be very difficult to maintain in the 21st. There must be change, but what kind?

PROBLEMS, CHALLENGES, AND FORCES AFFECTING THE NORTH AMERICAN CITY

Too often, we blame the problems encountered in cities on the nature of urbanism itself. But problems associated with sprawling, segregated, polluted, politically balkanized, and blighted settlements are actually the result of a failure to create truly urban places. They are also the result of larger forces, including globalization and immigration, beyond the control of cities. In addition, many so-called urban problems—for example, crime, homelessness, unemployment—are actually societal problems that are simply more evident in cities because of their concentrated populations (box 2.1). Moreover, these types of problems fluctuate greatly in importance across time and space—a high-profile issue one decade is low profile the next. With these caveats in mind, we can begin to examine some of the problems and challenges facing North American cities in the 21st century.

Globalization and the New Economy

The transition to a new urban economy, characterized by increasing global interdependence, an expanded service sector, and a shrinking manufacturing sector as blue collar jobs go overseas, is causing major reshuffling in the employment base of the typical North American city. Quaternary activities such as research and development, brokerage services, banking, and entertainment are gradually replacing old steel mills, shoe factories, and assembly-line manufacturing. Closed factories are being converted to themed shopping centers, loft apartments, and corporate offices. Waterfront promenades and festival marketplaces have largely replaced former port facilities and warehouses.

North American metropolitan areas continue to undergo the uneven transition from centers of manufacturing and production to centers of consumption and services. The cities that dominate the urban system today are home to large numbers of financial, insurance, legal, management, advertising, computing, and engineering firms. Perhaps not surprisingly, many of today's leading cities—such as New York, Chicago, and Toronto—were also atop the urban hierarchy during the earlier manufacturing era. They managed to use their competitive advantages of size, location, and connectedness to reinvent themselves as leading electronic-age cities.

Boston is another older city that has successfully made the transition to the new economy, while smaller, more specialized cities, such as Youngstown, Ohio, and Sudbury, Ontario, have had a tougher time diversifying—but diversify they must. Diversification has become a mantra among North American cities as they compete to lure footloose firms from across the country and even around the globe. This usually translates into adding high-tech, biotech, and other light industries to a city's economic portfolio, as frequently huge real estate and tax subsidies are handed to desirable firms.

To compete globally, North American cities must sell themselves as delightful places to live and work, with attractive sets of amenities. Efforts to achieve this image are a driving force behind the emergence of downtowns as centers of spectacle, with themed shopping and entertainment zones, waterfront parks, cultural districts, and sports stadiums (figs. 2.7 and 2.8). In a way, this development represents a return to the Renaissance period, as the city center becomes a place for promenades and gentility rather than production and distribution. North American cities may soon be joining Paris and Florence as centers for celebration, display, and upscale consumption, while most ordinary economic activities occur on the outer edges and beyond. Las Vegas and Orlando, with central city landscapes dominated by consumption and fun rather than

Box 2.1 Homelessness

The United States and Canada have seen sharp rises in homelessness since the 1980s. Between 700,000 and 2,000,000 people are homeless on any given night in the United States and, conservatively, over 200,000 are homeless in Canada. Of even greater concern are the number of people only one paycheck away from the streets.

The new face of homelessness shatters the stereotype of the middle-aged male "bum," as the homeless include increasing numbers of women and youth. Families with children make up nearly 40%, while single women are about 15% of urban homeless. Youth under age eighteen constitute over a quarter of the homeless population, including children in homeless families, runaways who have mental or drug-related problems or a history of abuse, and a small number who are homeless by choice and are living out nomadic, "hippie" lifestyles.

The reason for the rise in homelessness is complex, but can generally be linked to two major causes: increasing poverty and a shortage of affordable housing. While the number of poor has not changed much, the number of people living in extreme poverty has risen, and well over 40% of persons in poverty are children. The two main factors behind increases in poverty are eroding employment opportunities, including declining real wages for large segments of the workforce, and declines in public assistance. Even Canada, once considered generous with health, education, and employment programs, has been whittling away at social spending since the 1980s. Rising numbers of homeless are yet another way in which Canada's cities are beginning to resemble the ugly side of America.

The second major cause of homelessness—a shortage of affordable housing—is largely a result of sharp spikes in urban real-estate markets. Exacerbating this, however, is the loss of single room occupancy (SRO) units, which in the past housed many of the down and out. SRO residential hotels were largely destroyed in the 1970s and 1980s, as downtowns experienced a building boom. In some large cities, up to 80–90% of SRO units were demolished. While many list "deinstitutionalization" of the mentally ill as a major cause of the rise in homelessness, it is the loss of affordable housing, including SROs, that has put so many mentally ill people on the street. While 20–25% of the single adult homeless population suffer from mental illness, only 5–7% require institutionalization.

Cities have not coped well with the homeless crisis. Some have enacted a spate of ordinances, hoping to push the problem elsewhere. Benches have been "bum-proofed," lights have been installed, and parks have been reclaimed for more upscale clientele. Other cities have attempted to "contain" the homeless in skid row areas, where cardboard shelters are allowed on sidewalks and services are concentrated. Self-help tent cities and dome villages have sprung up as both a temporary solution and a visible way to bring recognition to the problem. In the end, numerous studies show that any long-term solution will have to involve a commitment by all levels of government to provide permanent, supportive housing (including rehabilitation, counseling, and welfare services) to all who need it.

Figure 2.7 Ghirardelli Square in San Francisco is one of the country's most successful festival marketplaces. (Photo by Judy Walton)

production and distribution, epitomize this trend. Larry Ford has modeled the typical American central city as a sort of Disneyland, in which the city is divided into districts, or "lands," devoted to specific functions (fig. 2.9).

Corporatization, Placelessness, and the Loss of Public Space

Concomitant with globalization is the growing corporatization of the urban landscape. Although many people complain about the homogenization of cities, this is nothing new. Most late-19th-century downtowns, for example, looked very similar, with standard architecture and building types. One Main Street looked much like another. The real difference since about the 1970s is the extent of corporate ownership of the city (and the size of the corporations). Few cities in North America are without a Starbucks, McDonalds, Borders Books, Gap, or Cineplex Odeon. This has exaggerated the sense of placelessness that people feel in a typical North American city. One of the authors of this chapter noted on a recent trip to Vancouver, British Columbia, that in many places she could not even determine whether she was in a Canadian or U.S. city. Locally owned shops and restaurants have left most downtowns of significant size. It is no wonder that citizens in smaller towns such as Arcata, California, or Bainbridge Island, Washington, have chosen to fight the forces of globalization by trying to limit the number of chain stores and restaurants.

Among the most striking features of the North American urban landscape are the master-planned, corporate megadevelopments that stand out from the surrounding city, such as Bunker Hill in Los Angeles or Battery Park City in Manhattan (fig. 2.10). Such specialized, large-scale developments affirm the accuracy of the multiple nuclei model of urban land use as applied to the 21st-century city. No

Figure 2.8 The use of sports facilities, such as Busch Stadium in St. Louis, as a way to stimulate downtown renewal has been popular for several decades. (Photo by Larry Ford)

other region in the world has completed so many truly massive urban projects over such a prolonged time period. Suburban housing tracts with thousands of units can also be considered corporate megadevelopments. Office parks, corporate campuses, and convention complexes form large areas of homogeneous design in the city. Many of these exclusionary buildings have limited public access and fortress-like architecture.

In fact, this is the dark side of the corporate dream—the city of fear as described by Mike Davis in *City of Quartz.* It is a city characterized by increasing surveillance, privatized public spaces, defensive architecture, and an enormous social and geographic gulf between the rich and poor (box 2.2). Corporations, in their search for safety and security in the inner city, have often created "cities within cities" for their employees, with malls, garages, and offices connected by elevators and skywalks. Huge developments adjacent to yet insulated from surrounding areas remain quintessential parts of the American urban scene.

Uneven Development

Uneven development results from the unequal distribution of resources in a capitalist economy. In the North American urban context, uneven development is worsened by forces of globalization, political fragmentation, racial discrimination, and government policies that encourage suburbanization.

Among the most disturbing manifestations of uneven development in North America are the vacant lots and boarded-up or crumbling buildings in the shadows of downtown financial centers. In Chicago, for example, some of the most valuable land in the world is just blocks away from buildings with almost no value at all. While such images are most typi-

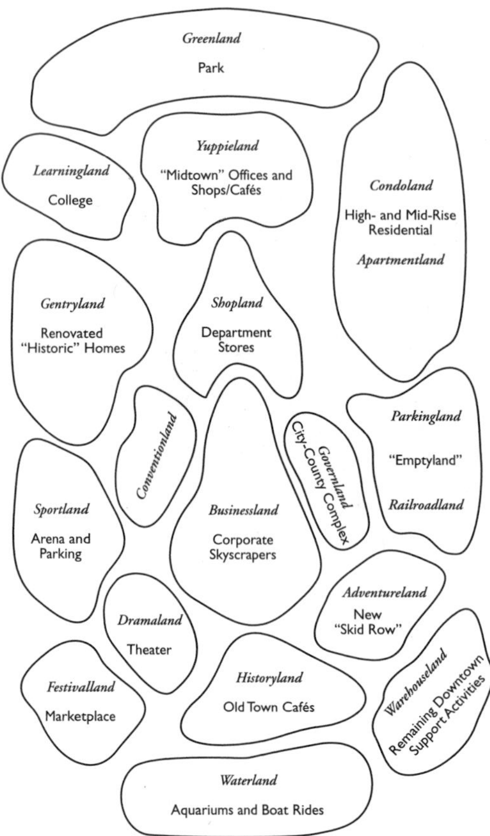

Figure 2.9 The Central City as Disneyland. *Source*: Larry Ford, *Cities and Buildings: Skyscrapers, Skid Rows, and Suburbs* (Baltimore: Johns Hopkins University Press, 1994), 91. Reprinted with permission.

cally associated with U.S. cities, they are by no means absent in Canada. Vancouver's skid row stands in marked contrast to luxury towers nearby.

While uneven development is most evident in the inner city, it is also found in the outer city, or suburbia, where new *edge city* landscapes of office towers, corporate parks, shopping malls, golf resorts, and mansions abut poor areas with remnant rural cottages or mobile homes and virtually no commerce. Contrasts certainly exist everywhere in the world, but the nature and scale of uneven development in wealthy North America is shocking to outsiders (fig. 2.11).

The Internet, Telecommuting, and the Digital Divide

Economic changes are rapidly appearing that could make traditional cities less necessary as more people recreate, shop, communicate, and even work from home. The digital age is contributing to the rapid population growth of peripheral towns, such as Boise, Idaho, and Missoula, Montana, especially by affluent elites and retirees seeking to flee the city. Through Internet connections, they are able to take advantage of high amenity areas without being disadvantaged by their relative remoteness.

In the early 1990s, as Internet use was becoming widespread, many thought it would renew the 1970s trend toward counterurbanization. However, the pace of change has been much slower than predicted. Ambitious young professionals are still moving to cities in droves. Likewise, with telecommuting: early predictions that significant numbers of people would work from home using the Internet and satellite hookups—thereby reducing freeway congestion and pollution—have turned out to be exaggerated. Centrality and face-to-face contact are still powerful centripetal forces.

A more important and pressing concern about the impact of information technology is the growing digital divide separating rich and poor, particularly in central cities. The rise of *electronic ghettos* parallels the evolution of real-world ghettos in the inner cities of past centuries. Place still matters, even in an electronic age.

Figure 2.10 Bunker Hill in Los Angeles was a major, but controversial, effort to revitalize the city's downtown. (Photo by Judy Walton)

Sprawl

It can be said that North Americans, but especially U.S. Americans, hate two things—density and sprawl. The fact that one is the converse of the other is the crux of the North American urban dilemma. To a degree unseen in most other cities of the world, North American urban areas are characterized by low-density development oriented around the automobile. Some metropolitan areas sprawl over more than 1,000 sq mi. Phoenix, one of the most rapidly growing cities, has been spreading outward at about an acre per hour. Farmland and other open spaces are disappearing by about two million acres a year. In 1990, the United States became the world's first "suburban nation," as the number of people living in the suburbs surpassed the 50% mark.

Average urban population densities of about 2,000 to 3,000 people per sq mi (770–1150 per sq km) are common in North America, whereas they often exceed ten times that in other regions of the world. Moreover, densities continue to decrease: in the United States in 1940, nine of the ten largest cities had over 10,000 people per sq mi (3,800 per sq km); today only three of the ten largest have over 7,500 people per sq mi (2,880 per sq km). The escape from the city, and the further escape to newer, more distant suburbs, has led to urban sprawl on such a scale that it is considered one of the key societal problems of our age.

Nothing affects land-use decisions as much

Box 2.2 Third Places

Cities need to have good *third places* in order to function well, argues Ray Oldenburg in *The Great Good Place.* A third place is a public or semipublic space, such as a plaza, coffee shop, or bar, where people gather for general conviviality and conversation. Importantly, it's neither home (which Oldenburg calls *first place*) nor work (which he calls *second place*). In the past, civic spaces offered the main opportunity for chance encounters and lively debate. From the agora in ancient Athens to the *plaza mayor* and courthouse square in more recent times, citizens have hung out in such spaces in order to keep abreast of news and debate issues of the day.

In recent years, however, civic space seems to have disappeared from most North American towns and cities, especially suburbs. Parks and public spaces, if they exist, are likely to be large and special purpose, such as soccer fields or boating facilities, rather than the small neighborhood *piazzas* so common in older European cities. Few residents are within walking distance of civic spaces designed as town centers. To make matters worse, many people spend long hours at work or driving alone in cars. As a result, most North Americans have come to rely almost exclusively on home and work to provide the social sustenance so vital to our species. The toll for all this is often high levels of stress and frustration. Furthermore, both sprawl-induced driving and "cocooning" at home have been tied to rising levels of obesity among Americans.

Oldenburg suggests that we try to reestablish some of the traditional third places that helped make cities work over the centuries. Among these are neighborhood coffeehouses and pubs or taverns, convivial places where "everybody knows your name" when you drop by for a bit of refreshment and conversation, places where you are known but not necessarily intimately. In such places, discussions and debates can take place that may take some of the demands for social interaction off family and coworkers.

Such places need not be oriented around liquid consumption, since laundry facilities, corner stores, barbershops, and even places to walk the dog can suffice. But we have zoned nearly all of these places out of our residential neighborhoods. The corner pub, so common in Britain, is largely absent from American neighborhoods. Zoning and urban design for the most part work to discourage casual interaction. If we go out socially, it is likely to be for a specialized gathering, such as for sports, hobbies, or church, where we meet people similar to ourselves, narrowing our social world rather than broadening it.

Oldenburg notes that our cities are becoming lonelier as they grow larger but argues that this is primarily a function of collective political decisions (such as single-use zoning). Specialty coffee shops, big-box bookstores, and video arcades have been heralded as new third places, but are they adequate substitutes for more traditional space? And what about truly public, civic space? Perhaps the most important question to ask is if we build such spaces, will Americans come?

Source: Ray Oldenburg, *The Great Good Place* (New York: Paragon House, 1991).

as a city's transportation system. If we must blame any one factor for encouraging sprawl, it would have to be the auto-dependent design of North American cities, with features ranging from multilane highways to drive-in banks to parking lots. Nearly every North American city is bisected by highways that divide neighborhoods and confound pedestrians. New highways promise to relieve congestion, but end up paving the way for yet more development and traffic.

The phenomenon of the *beltway* or *ring road* provides a good example of highway-induced development. Beltways provide a way around the congested centers of major metropolitan areas. But they often open the door for a surge of new development. Atlanta's outer belt has become so lined with edge cities along its northern section that congestion is often worse there than downtown. The beltways around Washington, D.C., Boston, and Chicago are no better off. There is considerable discussion about building ever-newer outer belts to get around the congestion of the older ring roads.

Figure 2.11 Bellevue, Washington, a major edge city in the eastern suburbs of Seattle, is a center for high-tech industry and corporate headquarters. (Photo by Judy Walton)

Ironically, the more a city sprawls, and the more time people spend in their vehicles getting from one point to another, the more likely people will be to vote for a new expressway to speed up their trip. Most North Americans seem quite accepting of the landscape of sprawl, with its big boxes, megaplexes, supermalls, corporate campuses, and clogged highways, perhaps because for so many who grew up in the past few decades, this is all they know.

Nevertheless, several cities have revolted against these dominating autoscapes. San Francisco and Portland (Oregon) have removed freeways from their downtowns, while Boston is undergrounding its central interstate highway. Milwaukee fought off a federally funded highway construction project. Rapid transit is gaining ground in cities from San Diego to Calgary. A number of popular books—for example, *Asphalt Nation,* by Jane Holtz Kay, and *Crossing the Expendable Landscape,* by Bettina Drew—have made the public more aware of the environmental, social, and economic costs of the burgeoning sprawlscapes. Even *National Geographic* featured a special article (July 2001) on sprawl and its alternatives.

The distinctive, sprawling character of North American cities is not solely the result of automobile dependency. Much of it has to do with cultural factors and the availability of land and capital for the mass production of housing subdivisions. Although home owner-

Figure 2.12 Levittown, on Long Island, New York, was on the forefront of suburbanization after World War II. (Photo by Larry Ford)

ship had long been the aspiration of the typical American, it was only after World War II that the first really huge housing tracts took form. Begun on a potato field in 1947, Levittown, Long Island (the first of three new communities to bear the name Levittown), is perhaps one of the best-known examples. By 1951, it had 17,450 housing units. Low-interest Federal Housing Administration and Veterans Administration loans (as low as 2%), especially for returning veterans on the GI bill, also facilitated home ownership (fig. 2.12). The American dream of owning a detached, single-family home with a grass lawn became possible for the majority of middle-class U.S. residents. While Canada lagged behind (especially French Canada, which had a different housing tradition), it too soon joined in constructing large suburban housing tracts.

New Urbanism and Smart Growth

One of the most important new philosophies in suburban design—New Urbanism—springs directly from frustration with the existing forms of residential development and is an attempt to rein in sprawl. Spearheading the New Urbanist "movement" is a husband-wife team of architects/town planners, Andres Duany and Elizabeth Plater-Zyberk. Since 1981, they have designed a few dozen towns around the United States, starting with the resort community of Seaside, Florida. All of their new towns hark back to a traditional, mixed-use neighborhood design with its gridded streets, pedestrian scale, front porches, sidewalks, and village-like atmosphere. Duany and Plater-Zyberk's radical intention was to create places where one could conduct most daily business without a car. In their book, *Suburban Nation: The Rise of Sprawl and the Decline of the American Dream,* they compare the towns they design to a Mazda Miata, "a car that looks, sounds, and handles like a British roadster but maintains the rate-of-repair record of a Honda Civic." In other words, it looks like the old, but works like the new.

While several hundred new developments have been built in the name of New Urbanism in the United States and Canada (and many more have borrowed a few features) (fig. 2.13), there are some serious critiques of the movement. Some see it as simply the acceptable face of sprawl, given that most projects are developed on greenfields and are actually just cute suburbs with picket fences and front porches. From this point of view, it is perhaps more properly called *new suburbanism,* offer-

Figure 2.13 Celebration, Florida, built by the Disney Corporation, is one of the most famous private new towns of recent years. (Photo by Larry Ford)

ing only a slightly more compact version of the contemporary suburb. Another criticism surrounds New Urbanist claims of fostering community by physical design. This perhaps overemphasizes architecture's power to influence behavior. Furthermore, New Urbanist neighborhoods have done very little to address social inequity in urban areas. Few urban infill projects have been built, although there are some model redevelopments of grayfields, or old shopping mall sites. New Urbanism has also changed the look of public housing in the United States, as mixed-income developments replace old tower blocks and barracks-like compounds. The social costs of this change in appearance, however, have not been fully measured. Displacement of residents and disruption of small businesses are among these costs.

Other solutions to sprawl fall under the rubric of *smart growth*, a new movement among planners and local governments to combine growth-management techniques, including urban infill, New Urbanist ideas, and open-space acquisitions, to control growth. Several metropolitan areas have passed smart growth legislation, but the movement has had little effect to date, other than to foster growing awareness of the costs of sprawl.

In recent years, a small percentage of North Americans has begun to accept higher-density apartment and condominium living in both central city and suburban locations, but it is too late to drastically alter the sprawling shape of the cities. It will take many decades of social and racial integration, changes in zoning codes and highway and home ownership subsidies, mass transit development, and architectural restraint before the excesses of sprawl can be ameliorated. But it is not at all clear that this is the direction in which North American cities are moving. Despite a number of efforts to follow smart growth principles and build more compact cities, there are many countervailing trends. The increasing number of gated and walled communities appearing on the fringes of cities in fortress-like isolation is perhaps the most glaring evidence of this.

Central City Decline

Suburbs are claiming an increasing proportion of metropolitan wealth and population and they are reluctant to share resources with their central cities. The continued decline of central cities remains one of the biggest challenges facing North American cities. In the United States, decline is worsened by anti-urban attitudes that have dominated intellectual and popular thought since the country's founding. From movies, literature, politics, and the media, it is evident that Americans love to hate their cities and see them as corrupt, immoral, dangerous, unhealthy, and ugly places, in contrast to the serenity, simplicity, and natural harmony of the countryside, free from the corrupting influence of commerce. This goes a long way toward explaining why so few people in the United States want to live in a central city.

Other factors exacerbating central city decline include steady decreases in central city tax revenues caused by post–World War II suburbanization, decentralization and "devolution" of federal government responsibilities, and the increasingly fragmented nature of metropolitan government. The number of governmental entities found in many metropolitan areas is overwhelming. Complex webs of local government agencies and authorities effectively prevent cooperation between municipalities and sharing of resources. David Rusk, former mayor of Albuquerque, found that the poorest and most racially segregated cities in the United States were those that were most "inelastic," that is, without power to annex their suburbs and share in the larger tax base. Elastic cities that could annex surrounding areas and become "cities without suburbs" were more successful at reversing patterns of racial and economic segregation. Regional governments have been proposed as a remedy, but to date Portland and Toronto are among the few successful examples. Other remedies include metropolitan-wide tax-base sharing, but this has been tried in only one place, the Minneapolis–St. Paul region. Overall, the move toward political integration and tax-base equity is slow. The Canadian situation is a good deal better than that in the United States, which may be one reason why Canadian inner cities are generally in a healthier condition.

To counter decline, cities have tried everything from making their centers more like European cities to making them more like suburbs. It is surprising that there could be so many developments leading us in the wrong direction. For example, new projects often lack human-scaled exteriors; this works against urban vitality and walkability. Convention center/hotel complexes, with their long, blank walls and multiple garage and delivery entrances, discourage pedestrians (fig. 2.14). Add to that the limited access to these buildings and their insular design—with shops and restaurants on the inside—and the life of a part of downtown can easily be killed.

Immigration

Immigration has always been a significant force fueling the growth of North American cities. At the same time, it has presented many challenges to social relations in the city. The post–World War II era witnessed a change in migration streams, with Latin America and Asia replacing Europe as the most important migrant source

Figure 2.14 Many cities construct convention centers, such as this one in San Jose, California, to promote business and tourism, especially in the downtown areas. (Photo by Judy Walton)

areas. This has had several significant effects on cities. For one, it has changed the ethnic makeup of many cities, as percentages of Latinos and Asians rose rapidly starting in the 1980s (fig. 2.15; also box 2.3). Los Angeles, a major recipient city, became the first big city to have no white majority. Canadian cities such as Vancouver began experiencing significant racial tensions as Asian immigration increased, especially with the reversion of Hong Kong to Chinese control.

Second, immigration in recent years has in some cases reversed central city population decline, particularly in large cities. In New York and Los Angeles, foreign immigration more than made up for out-migration during the 1990s. By contrast, cities that do not attract as many foreign immigrants, such as Pittsburgh, St. Louis, or Cleveland, lost population over the 1990s. A word of caution: while in general, central cities with a high percent of foreign-born population grew faster than others, some of the fastest-growing cities in North America—Phoenix and Las Vegas, for example—were fueled more by domestic rather than foreign migration.

Immigration is also changing the face of the North American suburb, as new immigrants increasingly move directly to the suburbs rather than to *incubator ghettos* in the central city. Commercial strips are always a good place to look for signs of change in the social fabric. In the suburbs of Los Angeles and Vancouver, for example, one can find entire strip malls with signs exclusively in Spanish, Chinese, Vietnamese, Laotian, or Cambodian and with full ranges of shops and services for the local immigrant population. Hillsboro, Oregon, a Portland suburb, is a major recipient of Latino immigrants to the metro area.

Ghettoization

Processes of *ghettoization*—the involuntary clustering of minority groups—exaggerate uneven development and lead to vast, racially

Figure 2.15 Ethnic islands, such as this one in Los Angeles, are part of the urban landscape of major cities across the United States and Canada. (Photo by Larry Ford)

segregated areas of the city. This is a problem mainly in the United States. In Canada, with the exception of a few traditionally segregated cities such as Anglo-French Montreal, most cities have smaller, more heterogeneous ethnic communities.

The scope and intensity of ghettoization in the United States is due largely to *racial steering* and the manipulation of housing markets. It can be said that the main color associated with ghettos in the United States is not black, white, brown, or yellow, but green, that is, the color of cash. Beginning in New York's Harlem in the late 19th century, real estate agents learned they could increase turnover and thus profits by scaring one group away with another. The practice, known as *blockbusting,* became common by the 20th century. Real estate agents would buy one house on a block and surreptitiously move a minority family in, thus "busting" the block. Then they would advertise in minority neighborhoods that bargains were to be had on that block. When large numbers of minority home-seekers arrived, alarmist flyers playing on racial fears were sent out to current residents to induce panic selling. The more panic the better, since it meant low prices. Some unscrupulous entrepreneurs bought up as many buildings as they could and charged high rents to a captive minority market until new blocks were opened up.

Thus, changing neighborhoods meant potentially big profits, and there were usually plenty of ethnic groups available for steering, including Asians, African Americans, Jews, Italians, and Latinos. The process fed on itself until vast areas of the central city were dominated by a single racial or ethnic group. Today, cities such as Los Angeles, Chicago, Detroit, and Atlanta have African American ghettos that occupy more land than many cities do. At the same time, wealthy, predominantly white suburbs occupy hundreds of square miles sur-

Box 2.3 Tropicalizing Cold Urban Space

Latinos are bringing redemptive energies to the neglected, worn-out cores and inner suburbs of many metropolitan areas. The process is most vivid in cities, especially in the Southwest, where immigrants have access to homeownership, even if that involves the leveraging of mortgages through the combination of three or even four low-wage adult incomes. A remarkable case is the belt of old (circa 1920) bungalow neighborhoods directly south and southeast of Downtown Los Angeles. Here, in the aftermath of the 1965 Watts riot, bank "redlining," civic indifference and absentee landlordism accelerated the decay of an aging, poorly built housing stock. Yet today, even in the historically poorest census tracts, including most of the Central-Vernon, Florence-Firestone, and Watts-Willowbrook districts, there is not a street that has not been dramatically brightened by new immigrants. Tired, sad little homes undergo miraculous revivifications: their peeling facades repainted, sagging roofs and porches rebuilt, and yellowing lawns replanted in cacti and azaleas. Cumulatively, the sweat equity of 75,000 or so Mexican and Salvadorean homeowners has become an unexcelled constructive force (the opposite of white flight) working to restore debilitated neighborhoods to trim respectability. Moreover, the insatiable immigrant demand for family housing has allowed older African-American residents to reap unexpected gains in home sales: a serendipitous aspect of "ethnic succession" that has been ignored by analysts who focus only on the rough edges of Black/Latino relations.

Source: Mike Davis, "Tropicalizing Cold Urban Space," chapter 6 in *Magical Urbanism: Latinos Reinvent the U.S. City,* rev. ed. (New York: Verso, 2001), 61–62. Originally published in 2000.

rounding the central city. The result is uneven development on a monumental scale.

While overt discriminatory real estate techniques are illegal today, covert practices still exist. To a large degree, school quality has replaced race/ethnicity as a tool for scare tactics. When a neighborhood school develops a bad reputation, whether deserved or not, a middle-class exodus generally results. Increasingly, middle-class African Americans are joining the search for neighborhoods with better schools, although they are often steered to largely black middle-class neighborhoods.

The image of master-planned communities with excellent schools and amenities such as parks and golf courses is the new suburban middle-class ideal. It is a carefully cultivated and marketed image, largely for white consumption. Master planned, however, generally means a fairly narrow range of house prices that offers little opportunity for low-income families to buy in. Huge, single-class housing tracts result and now dominate the residential scene, both product and producer of uneven development.

REPRESENTATIVE CITIES

New York, Los Angeles, and Chicago are among the best-known cities in the world. As first-order regional centers at the top of the urban hierarchy, they are often the first cities that come to mind when thinking about the United States; thus, an understanding of them is essential to mastering the urban geography of North America. Far more typical of the diversity of the United States and Canada, however, are the smaller cities that anchor their regions and typify the forces shaping the urban landscapes of the 21st century. The regional metropolises highlighted here, as examples of a type, are the struggling industrial cities of Cleveland and Pittsburgh, the booming regional metropolises of Atlanta and Phoenix, and the emerging *sustainable cities* of Toronto and Portland.

New York City, Los Angeles, and Chicago: Epitome Cities or Unique Icons?

New York and Los Angeles are actually atypical North American cities, but they dominate the media and provide many of the images that people use to construct ideas about the ways in which North Americans live. Chicago is perhaps a bit more typical, but its sheer size and functional importance as a headquarters city make even Chicago very unusual. What are the innovative roles that these three cities have played in creating both the myth and reality of North American urban society?

New York City

New York City started out during the 17th and 18th centuries as just another important seaport competing with Boston, Philadelphia, and Charleston for Atlantic trade. After the American Revolution, it served briefly as the national capital, but its political role soon waned. Still, by the mid-19th century, New York had become the largest city in the United States, with over half the nation's foreign trade going in and out of its vast, protected harbor. Its population exploded over the next century as it served as the main entryway for immigrants and as the country's main manufacturing center. The Hudson River and the Erie Canal gave it unparalleled access to the interior (fig. 2.16). By the 1840s that access was enhanced by a dense network of railroads. By 1900, New York City was one of the largest cities in the world. Manhattan, unlike any other major urban place in North America, is an island, thus making expansion into nearby suburbs more difficult. Partly as a result of this, New York City (which was synonymous with Manhattan until 1898, when the Five Boroughs merged to form a vast urban agglomeration of 300 sq mi, or 480 sq km) retained a dense urban fabric more reminiscent of Paris or Vienna than of other North American cities. For much of the 19th century, New York vied with cities such as Tokyo and Cairo for the "honor" of having the highest population density in the world. This concentration of population, coupled with its dominant economic and cultural role, meant that New York City was a pioneer in the making of the North American urban landscape.

When one examines the evolution of the American urban landscape, the New York City story always stands out. All sorts of ideas and inventions are associated with New York, including department stores, electric lights, skyscrapers, apartment buildings, luxury hotels, subway systems, the grid system, a central park, television networks, burlesque shows, musical comedies, symphony orchestras, public housing projects, and beatniks. True, many of these were not actually invented in New York, but they quickly came to be more important there than anyplace else. The biggest and most important office towers, train stations, department stores, nightclubs, factories, port facilities, and residential complexes were all in

Figure 2.16 The Erie Canal, running through downtown Syracuse, New York, was critical in helping to establish New York City as the leading port and city in the United States.

the "Big Apple." New York City thus invented both the North American urban reality and the North American urban image (fig. 2.17).

New York remained America's role-model city, for better and for worse, until sometime in the early 1950s. Glittering images of Broadway shows and Christmas pageants at Rockefeller Center defined what was best about American popular culture. At the same time, scenes of life in slums and in projects were also set in New York, as in the *Dead End Kids* movies. New York was home to the Mafia and street gangs as well as media tycoons and dazzling socialites. Everything was writ large in New York. Movies such as *An Affair to Remember* and *Miracle on 34th Street* stood alongside *On the Waterfront* and *West Side Story* in the telling of the American urban story. Even King Kong visited the Empire State Building. New York City, like London, Paris, and Mexico City, came to epitomize a national urban stereotype. The fact that most Americans had never seen a tenement, a mobster, an ocean liner, or even a notable skyscraper in 1950 scarcely mattered. New York City was the cultural hearth, while the rest of urban America selectively adopted bits and pieces of its identity over time. By the 1950s, however, a new urban role model was emerging in Los Angeles.

Los Angeles

Los Angeles was a small town as late as the 1880s, but with the arrival of railroads from the east, a boom began. To a very real degree, this initial boom period presaged the future roles of myth and romance as major factors in the growth of the urban region. For a decade or so, much of the region's growth consisted of people selling real estate to each other, as booms were periodically punctuated by busts. Advertisements showing orange trees in the foreground with snow-capped mountains be-

Figure 2.17 Crowded streets in midtown Manhattan during the Christmas shopping season typify the vitality of New York City. (Photo by Larry Ford)

hind were used to lure residents from the East. As the 20th century dawned, these images were joined by scenes of exotic architecture, such as that of Grumman's Chinese Theater, and movie stars lounging around bougainvillea-adorned tennis courts. It was not until midcentury, with its war-related industrialization, that the Los Angeles urban economy became truly diverse and resilient.

As an urban place, Los Angeles did not spring into the limelight all at once. For a long time, it was a stealth city. Its streets, mountains, parks, and beaches had been used in thousands of Hollywood movies, from the silent comedies of the 1920s to the dramas of the 1940s, but they were often utilized as generic city settings rather than as new and different types of places. It was not until later that Los Angeles became more than a handy backdrop, as it was in the escapades of Laurel and Hardy. By the 1950s, Los Angeles had joined New York as a city with star quality—a place to be emulated wherever possible. As in New York, the good qualities of the place coexisted with the bad. Both *Rebel without a Cause* and *Beach Blanket Bingo* depicted teenage life in the sunny metropolis, while the giant ants of *Them* terrorized the city much like King Kong had done in New York. Gradually, each city's icons took shape.

The image of Los Angeles as the quintessential American city evolved from the 1950s through the 1970s with a barrage of movies, television programs, advertisements, auto-related architecture, and leisure activities such as surfing and volleyball. Unlike with New York, images of Los Angeles rarely focused on downtown or anything very urban. Good guys and bad guys alike lived in sprawling es-

Figure 2.18 Chicago has one of America's most recognizable skylines, dominated by the Hancock Tower in the background. (Photo by Larry Ford)

tates in the hills above the city. Everyone drove around endlessly between Pasadena, Beverly Hills, and the beaches. Famous landmarks included places like Disneyland that were not even in Los Angeles County, let alone the city. People did not live in the city, they lived in the San Fernando Valley (or "the Valley"), the Santa Monica Mountains, or Malibu. Reyner Banham's *Los Angeles: The Architecture of Four Ecologies* (1971) was an attempt to describe the character of the city. Los Angeles was different. It was a noncity. It was California Crazy.

Chicago

With both New York City and Los Angeles being so atypical of American urban lifestyles, it is no wonder that many scholars rejected them in the search for models of city structure. For these endeavors, there was Chicago (fig. 2.18). Unlike New York City, Chicago was not topographically challenged by rivers, valleys, bays, and harbors. Unlike Los Angeles, it was not focused on mountains and beaches. Chicago was not only flat, it was everything a large, typically American city could hope to be. It had a downtown, an elite sector, inner-city immigrant districts, industrial zones along the railroad tracks, and leafy suburbs. It had all the right concentric zones, sectors, and multiple nuclei of the typical American city. While New York City had financiers and immigrants and Los Angeles had movie stars and surfers, Chicago had regular Americans living in modest neighborhoods close to the steel mills and stockyards. Chicago had rich and poor, white and black, native and foreign in all the right places and proportions.

Convergence and Divergence

In many ways, the three cities have today converged toward a new American urban norm. All three have huge metropolitan populations ranging from around 8 million for Chicago to 17 million for New York, depending on where the boundaries are drawn. They each sprawl over thousands of square miles. In all three cities, most people live in suburban tract homes, small apartment complexes, or some variation on the theme of planned unit developments. Relatively few live in the types of places that gave the cities their stereotypical identities. Similarly, all three urban areas are multicentered, with edge cities, office parks, vast and sprawling neighborhoods filled with recent immigrants, suburban shopping malls, huge university and medical complexes, airport-centered warehouse districts, and beltway industrial zones. All three cities have skyscrapers, subways, tract houses, and commercial strips lined with the same fast-food outlets and Wal-Marts. Population densities have also converged. Los Angeles is no longer particularly low-density, as low-, mid-, and even high-rise apartments have sprung up throughout the region. It has even joined the other two cities in adopting a sophisticated rapid transit system that, at least on some lines, is very heavily used. New York, by contrast, has experienced a great deal of low-density fringe development extending to northern New Jersey and southern Connecticut.

On the one hand, all three cities have converged in positive ways. All three have world-class centers for the visual and performing arts, major universities and research centers, excellent park systems, an increasingly diverse range of recreational opportunities, a plethora of sophisticated architectural and urban design achievements, and a full range of high-level business and professional service establishments. New York is still the Big Apple when it comes to theater, but Chicago and Los Angeles have a growing number of professional offerings as well.

On the other hand, all three cities have increasingly similar problems. They have vast and isolated ghettos and barrios, congested freeways, long-distance commuting, a lack of affordable housing close to employment centers, dreary, big-box retail strips, and political fragmentation. All three have had their share of riots, crime, and air pollution. The movie *Boyz in the Hood* delivered as powerful an image of L.A.'s urban woes as *West Side Story* did of New York's.

While the trend toward convergence, we believe, is dominant, there are also a few indicators of a trend in the opposite direction. After years of seeming decline, bankruptcy, and even abandonment, New York City now faces the problem of too much demand and skyrocketing prices. Even Harlem is being gentrified as people seek space in the center of the city. Sidewalks from the Upper West Side to Greenwich Village are crowded with cafes. Jokes about muggings in Central Park have been largely replaced by horror stories about the cost of a studio apartment. It remains to be seen if the events of September 11, 2001, will have an effect on the city's urbanity, but in the short run they seem to have pulled people together and contributed to a sense of esprit de corps.

In contrast, Los Angeles has become less idyllic than past imagery would suggest, with its teeming barrios separated by long distances from remote, suburban, gated communities (fig. 2.19). In spite of its benign climate, it has probably fewer sidewalk cafes than does Manhattan. The auto still reigns supreme. We can

Figure 2.19 Skid row in Los Angeles exists in the shadow of Bunker Hill. (Photo by Larry Ford)

learn a lot about urbanization in America by examining not only the hard data that exists for these three cities but also the roles they have played in developing our notions of the American city.

Pittsburgh and Cleveland: Struggling Industrial Cities

The classic industrial cities of North America boomed during the late 19th and early 20th centuries. While cities from Montreal to San Francisco industrialized during this era, those that specialized in heavy industry—places such as Youngstown, Ohio; Hamilton, Ontario; and Detroit, Michigan—epitomized the period. As recently as 1950, heavy industrial cities dominated the list of large, metropolitan areas, with Cleveland and Pittsburgh near the top. Unable to adjust to changing economic times, however, many of these cities declined rapidly during the 1960s and 1970s. Today they are characterized by very slow growth or even population decline. Most have attempted to reinvent themselves, with varying degrees of success. Two of the best examples of still-struggling cities are Pittsburgh and Cleveland; as jobs in steel mills and oil refineries plummeted, local governments worked to create new jobs in research and development, finance, and even tourism (fig. 2.20).

While other American cities are surrounded by upscale suburbs, shopping malls, and edge cities, Cleveland, Pittsburgh, and most struggling industrial cities are ringed by declining industrial suburbs that are often in worse shape than the central cities. They lack the booming periphery of, say, a San Francisco. While pleasant residential areas do exist, often in the form of elegant streetcar suburbs such as Cleveland's Shaker Heights, the fringe is more likely to be occupied by such humble, working-class suburbs as McKeesport (outside Pittsburgh) and Akron (outside Cleve-

Figure 2.20 Smokestack Park in Pittsburgh illustrates the transition of older heavy-industrial cities to postindustrial economies, and the desire to save relics of the past such as this. (Photo by Judy Walton)

land) than new office parks, resorts, or country clubs.

Older industrial cities also have a difficult hurdle to leap when it comes to inner-ring neighborhood revitalization. The housing stock tends to be old, poorly maintained, and so low in value that repairs are not feasible. Unlike Boston, where the housing is old but very expensive and well maintained, or San Diego, where the majority of the housing stock is postwar suburban development, Cleveland and Pittsburgh have very old working-class neighborhoods that were often redlined and ghettoized in the past. In addition, both central cities have been unable to annex new territory and so neither ranks among the 25 largest in North America. Both are trying to make lemonade out of these lemons, however, by advertising their housing affordability compared to cities in the sunbelt. A large suburban estate may cost the same as a tiny condominium in San Francisco, and there is evidence that both individuals and companies are beginning to pay some attention to this fact.

At present, economic success in Pittsburgh and Cleveland is heavily dependent on downtown revitalization. Fortunately, both downtowns house major corporations that maintain commitments to the success of the urban region. In Pittsburgh, Mellon Bank, Pittsburgh Paint and Glass, US Steel (and its parent USX Corporation), and Alcoa all have their names on major downtown towers, while US Airways adds to the city's status as a headquarters city. In Cleveland, the towers of Key Bank, National City Bank, and British Petroleum dominate the skyline, but also visible are traditional headquarters of railroad companies and manufacturing corporations. Both cities have major research universities and medical centers, such as Carnegie-Mellon University (Pittsburgh) and Case-Western Reserve University (Cleveland), that have played important roles in shifting employment away from heavy industry and toward R&D (re-

Figure 2.21 The Golden Triangle of Pittsburgh, where the Allegheny and Monongahela rivers join to form the Ohio River, is a classic story of urban renewal in America. (Photo by Larry Ford)

search and development) and services. The urban regions are growing very slowly, if at all, because job growth in the new sectors has barely balanced job losses in heavy industry.

As part of their development strategy, Cleveland and Pittsburgh have been busy sprucing up their images in an effort to create major tourist destinations in the midst of abandoned smokestack industries. Pittsburgh in the early 1950s became the first U.S. city to transform its image through urban renewal. Downtown's "Golden Triangle" (formed by the merging of the Allegheny and Monongahela rivers into the Ohio) emerged from the smoke and grime of earlier decades to become the centerpiece for the city's new look (fig. 2.21). Today, the Golden Triangle is an urban park, while new stadiums, excursion boats, museums, restaurants, luxury hotels, research facilities, corporate towers, and a new convention center have replaced steel mills along Pittsburgh's riverfronts.

In Cleveland, the Cuyahoga River (famous for catching fire in 1969 when surface pollution suddenly ignited) is now lined with parks, cafes, condominiums, harbor excursion slips, and entertainment centers. Nearby, the Rock and Roll Hall of Fame and the Great Lakes Science Center are helping to reinvent the city's Lake Erie waterfront. Cleveland, Pittsburgh, and a few other gritty cities have been dubbed *comeback cities*—former industrial cities that are weathering the transition to the new economy. The main challenge remains reinvigorating the surrounding neighborhoods and suburbs the way downtowns have been revitalized.

Atlanta and Phoenix: Regional Growth Magnets

While rustbelt cities such as Pittsburgh have been facing shrinking populations, sunbelt cities have been experiencing some of the highest growth rates ever. Sunbelt migration has played an enormous role in reconfiguring the North American urban system. A few regional centers in the sunbelt have acted as giant growth magnets, attracting people and capital from all over the continent and even internationally. These regional "capitals" generally began their ascendancy after World War II and are still growing rapidly. Atlanta and Phoenix are typical examples. Examining these two cities can help explain what is happening in other booming metropolitan areas, such as Los Angeles, Houston, and Denver. It has often been said that "American cities form in a blink," and nowhere does this seem truer than in the sunbelt.

Atlanta's emergence as the new poster child for sprawl has been chronicled in Bullard et al.'s *Sprawl City* (2000). Typical of other sunbelt regional capitals, Atlanta's accelerated growth began after World War II (averaging nearly 3% annually). By the late 1960s, the city was often called the "Mecca of the Southeast." In the 1990s, Atlanta experienced record growth, adding more people than any other metropolitan region in North America and doubling its area. It now boasts a metropolitan area larger than the entire state of Delaware.

Phoenix, the capital of Arizona, arose from an arid plain to become the fastest-growing large city in North America in the 1990s, experiencing nearly a 25% population increase over the decade. While the central city itself gained thousands of new residents, the major growth remained out in the suburbs, in places like Mesa, Scottsdale, and Chandler. Scottsdale, for example, grew from fewer than 2,000 residents in 1950, in one square mile, to over 175,000 people in 2000, in an area three times as large as San Francisco. Entirely new, master-planned communities, with names like Citrus Creek, Arrowhead Valley, and Anthem (which on opening day was 20 mi, or 32 km, from the nearest grocery store), keep sprouting from the desert floor north of Phoenix.

Like many other sunbelt cities, population growth in Atlanta and Phoenix did not happen purely by chance; it took constant, aggressive promotion by each city's network of elites who stood to profit from land and real estate development. This network is appropriately called an *urban growth machine.* In Atlanta, its gears have been grinding since the end of the 19th century, when it first created the "capital of the New South." Novelist Tom Wolfe depicts the inner workings of Atlanta's contemporary growth machine in *A Man in Full,* holding it largely responsible for the bland built environment that sprawls for miles in all directions.

Phoenix has been helped by a state growth machine that has been aggressively luring businesses to Arizona since the 1950s. Massive dams and irrigation projects, and policies of limited government and few regulations, have all enticed employers. The state has witnessed spectacular growth, with Phoenix at the core of it, far outstripping second-place Tucson. "New economy" industries—tourism, telecommunications, trade, and computer technology (with firms such as Honeywell, Intel, and Motorola)—have attracted thousands of employees. This job migration, in fact, has kept Phoenix's population relatively young, despite the city's image as a retirement haven. Retirement moves actually account for a much smaller proportion of population growth in Arizona than, say, in Florida. Many of the new, sprawling subdivisions, especially to the north of town, are aimed at young families and professionals.

Since the 1960s, a familiar refrain in Phoenix has been "We don't want to become another

Los Angeles!" One antisprawl group even named itself "Not L.A." But as the city continues to thrive economically, few realize that Phoenix surpassed Los Angeles a long time ago in terms of sprawl. With one-third of L.A.'s population, Phoenix spreads out over an area roughly the same size. (Los Angeles today, in fact, is one of the most densely populated "urbanized areas" in the United States.) Phoenix, with some of the dirtiest air in North America, also rivals Los Angeles in air quality. A sad irony is that many people originally moved to Phoenix seeking good health and are now warned to stay indoors on certain days.

As in many North American cities, most of Atlanta's population growth (the population has doubled since 1970) has been in the suburbs; the city itself has accounted for only a small fraction of this increase. The metropolitan area, with more than 3 million people, contains four of the fastest-growing counties in the United States and spans well over 100 mi north to south. Not surprisingly, Atlantans have longer commutes than virtually anyone else in the country, averaging about 35 mi a day. Like Phoenix, Atlanta is one of the least densely populated metro areas in the United States, at about one-fourth the density of Los Angeles. Concentric rings of low-density development have imposed themselves on formerly rural hinterlands. Each new "outer belt" highway stimulates another ring of development, and soon the new highway is as congested as an inner belt.

Atlanta's expansion, however, cannot be blamed on road-building decisions alone. Such decisions have been made in the context of a booming regional economy, widespread disinvestment in the central city, and a suburban house-building juggernaut. Complicating all these factors are issues of racism and political fragmentation. With no fewer than 20 counties in its extended metro area, all vigorously defending their political autonomy, Atlanta has been unable to plan regionally. Most of the whiter counties have resisted anything that might make them more accessible to the central city, which is nearly 70% African American. This has greatly hampered mass-transit efforts, and only recently did the Georgia legislature approve a regional transportation authority. In Atlanta, transportation planning means highway planning. Atlanta, with the most elaborate system in North America to track and control traffic and well over 50 mi (80 km) of highway under constant surveillance, rivals Los Angeles for high-tech highways. The project was supported by the federal government, which was worried over potential gridlock during the 1996 Olympics.

With Atlantans remaining firmly wedded to their cars, air quality has significantly deteriorated. As in Phoenix, Houston, and other "bad smog" cities, parents are warned to keep small children inside on some days, and asthma is on the rise. Atlanta has had record numbers of smog-alert days and violations of the Clean Air Act, causing the federal government at one point to cut off highway funds. This jolted Atlanta into action and it has suddenly become a leading promoter of alternative transportation, such as light rail and smart growth. Atlanta's visible sprawl is dramatically underscored by housing-market statistics. In the 1990s, the city was known as "Hotlanta" in building circles because it was one of the busiest housing construction markets in the nation. During that decade, as subdivisions sprawled across Atlanta's farms and forests, nearly 25% more housing units (mostly single family) were added to the stock. The social and environmental costs of this type of development have begun to register in many high-growth cities. In 1998, the Sierra Club rated Atlanta as the most sprawl-threatened large city (over one million population) in the United States. Atlanta's horrendous traffic congestion and escalating environmental problems are causing businesses to think twice about locating there. Media publicity about Atlanta's "heat island effect"(made worse by vegetation loss and paved surface area increase) sparked new calls for action.

Meanwhile, as in numerous other regional growth magnets, Atlanta's globally connected economy, particularly its high-technology and information sectors, continues to boom. Many firms choose to locate not in the center, but on the periphery of town, in sleek, corporate-looking edge cities (which generally have more jobs than bedrooms) with names such as Buckhead and Perimeter. Edge city growth has also created a huge demand for low-wage jobs in construction and services on the outer fringes, and many new immigrants, seeking better access to employment, have moved there rather than the central city. This has led to greater social diversification of Atlanta's suburban communities and institutions, a process being repeated in the suburbs of other regional growth capitals as well. Of course, with change comes resistance, and this is being played out in various Atlanta suburbs.

Phoenix and Atlanta, both flat and landlocked, with no major bodies of water or mountain ranges to constrain outward growth, have had few checks on their sprawling pattern of development. Fueled by booming economies, their rates of sprawl nevertheless outstrip those of their population growth. Sprawl is popularly measured in acres per day, although in the case of Phoenix growth has been measured at "an acre an hour." Environmental and quality-of-life concerns have only recently begun to be translated into policies, such as smart growth legislation and regional planning initiatives, but how effective these will be at alleviating the worst problems remains to be seen. For now, economic prosperity continues to fuel regional capitals in the South and West.

Toronto and Portland: Sustainable Cities

The sustainable city discourse took hold in North America soon after the concept of sustainability emerged on the global scene in the early 1990s. City governments realized that a "green" image could translate into jobs, dollars, and growth for the region. Leading the way were cities as diverse as Toronto (Ontario), Portland (Oregon), Boulder (Colorado), Chattanooga (Tennessee), and Vancouver (British Columbia).

Historically, concern over the ecological impacts of the industrial North American city mostly surrounded issues of human health. In the 1960s, the environmental movement shifted people's attention to urban impacts on natural surroundings, but few people thought about the internal ecology of cities. Ian McHarg's *Design with Nature* (1969) was an early attempt to suggest environmentally sustainable forms for North American cities. From the 1970s through the 1990s, a number of scholars and other writers turned their attention to ecologically sound urban designs. In addition to an environmental focus, the concept of sustainability also implies a healthy economy and a sound and just community. Therefore, issues of social equity, environmental justice, and local control over the economy are also a big part of the sustainable city agenda.

Strictly speaking, no city today is truly sustainable. It would take a wholesale remaking of the global economy and society to approach something even close to long-term sustainability. Nevertheless, North American cities of every size have joined the sustainability bandwagon in an effort to cope with many of the problems discussed earlier. This has given rise to an entirely new vocabulary, with phrases such as smart growth and transit-oriented development. New Urbanism and other efforts to create livable cities also fall under the sustainability umbrella. A number of local governments have developed official sustainability plans and promote themselves as livable and green. Many of these places look to European towns for their models, and for good reason. On most scales, European urban design is far less land-consumptive than North American design and experimentation in European cities has produced a number of innovative, practical ideas—such as cohousing, car-free cities, and eco-industrial parks. Chattanooga, Tennessee, is experimenting with an eco-industrial park. Chattanooga is an example of a once-declining, polluted, industrial town (dubbed "the dirtiest city in America" by the U.S. Environmental Protection Agency) that has cleaned up its act and is now championed as a model *green city.* Toronto and Portland are representative of the most common type of sustainable city—high-growth, postindustrial cities, typically seeking to curb sprawl.

With a population of about 5 million, the Toronto metropolitan area is Canada's largest. It comprises the cities of Toronto and North York and four contiguous boroughs: York, East York, Scarborough, and Etobicoke. Toronto, once called York, has been the capital of Ontario since 1867 and anchors an urban conurbation known as the "Golden Horseshoe," which curves around the western end of Lake Ontario and includes the cities of Mississauga and Hamilton. Toronto has become Canada's leading industrial, commercial, and financial center and is home to one out of every seven Canadians.

In the aftermath of World War II, Toronto was not without the same problems facing other cities: blight and decay (in some older areas near downtown); traffic congestion on expressways and on old, narrow streets; pollution; and assorted land-use conflicts. A major decision to resolve these at the metropolitan level was made by provincial legislation in 1953, when the Municipality of Metropolitan Toronto was created.

Portland is a medium-sized city of more than 2.2 million in its metro area and more than 500,000 in the central city. Unlike many industrial cities that experience severe boom-bust cycles, Portland's resource-based economy, based on a combination of timber and agriculture, helped insulate it from the dramatic downturns that have occurred in other places. It was left with a fairly intact downtown as well as a growing metropolitan fringe. Unlike Toronto, it was mainly concern over the future of farmland that led residents to try to rein in urban growth. Where Toronto fretted about its center, Portland initially worried about its fringe. (It was only subsequently that attention focused on the core.)

Both Toronto and Portland gained fame for innovative planning practices aimed at improving environmental and economic health as well as social equity. Toronto offers one of the best North American examples of using rail transit to shape and contain the city. Portland offers one of the best examples of using an *urban growth boundary* to control growth. Both cities also pioneered the establishment of a metropolitan (or regional) government, a key tenet of sustainable urban planning. The idea behind regional planning is to use resources and capital efficiently by achieving new economies of scale, being better able to manage externalities such as traffic congestion, and reducing competition and inequities between cities in a metropolitan region.

Toronto's Metro (short for Metropolitan Corporation) was the first regional government in North America, formed in the early 1950s and later encompassing six local governments. It is held up as a model internationally and was instrumental in Toronto's nickname, "the city that works." Portland is also called a "city that works"; it, too, has a regional government called Metro that is looked to as a model by other American cities. Established in the 1970s, Portland's Metro was the first (and it is still the only) popularly elected regional government in a U.S. metropolitan area. It currently serves three counties and frequently collaborates with the neighboring city of Vancouver, Washington.

One of the primary goals of a sustainable city is to achieve a compact urban form and a vital center. Both Toronto and Portland have traditions of genuine urbanism. From the 1960s to 1980s, Toronto avoided the redlining of inner-city areas that exacerbated much of the decline in U.S. downtowns. Rather than parking lots and garages, Toronto filled its downtown with human-scale development and encouraged rehabilitation over demolition wherever possible. Many of its inner-ring neighborhoods feature gridded street patterns, high density, mixed use, mixed-income units, public spaces, community facilities, public transit, and viable commercial districts—all the elements of a good neighborhood, according to New Urbanists. Even today, as author Roberta Brandes Gratz points out in *Cities Back from the Edge* (1998),

> Traditional urbanism is part of Toronto's soul. . . . Toronto builders are more willing than those in the United States to accept a genuine urban, rather than suburban standard. More New Urbanist projects seem to be advancing faster there than in the United States, gaining wide and enthusiastic acceptance, and exhibiting at least twice or three times the density of their U.S. counterparts. (332)

Although getting a later start, Portland has implemented many of these same ideas—compact urban design, vibrant core, healthy urban environment, and abundant open space, with one of the highest percentages of land devoted to urban green space of any city. Portland, like Toronto, has focused on human-scale development, creating an interesting, walkable (and bikable) downtown. Mixed-use buildings and neighborhoods, mixed-income housing, rehabilitated historic neighborhoods, and a variety of transit options help make Portland's downtown a place where people actually want to live, shop, work, or simply hang out. Portland is also pioneering the field of "green building," recycling or reusing building materials wherever possible and building with energy efficiency and resource conservation in mind.

Toronto is world famous for its transportation system, an efficient network of streetcars, historic trams, buses, trolleys, subways, and bicycle routes. The number of people using transit in Toronto is the highest in North America, equivalent to levels in Europe. Toronto's streetcars run past a series of distinct communities, each with its own commercial node. Because Canada's tax laws do not offer special homeowner deductions, more Canadians live in multifamily housing, making transit-oriented development easier to implement. Reduced car use combined with compact urban form has helped to minimize Toronto's environmental footprint.

Portland is also a leader in light-rail transit,

with its showpiece MAX (Metropolitan Area Express) system. New transit stops along MAX extensions in the 1990s became hubs of compact, high-density development. In addition, Portland is known for a variety of innovative programs aimed at reducing car use. Car sharing, for example, is being tested there. For a reasonable charge, car-share members can borrow a car from a nearby lot whenever they need one. Residents of Portland tend to get into the sustainable-city spirit. One building owner, for example, provides tenants with electric vehicles during the day to encourage them to leave their cars at home.

Toronto and Portland have also received high marks in social and economic sustainability, with diverse economies and programs that address inequality. However, forces beyond both cities' control can easily and suddenly reverse their successes. Toronto's ability to operate at the regional level is now being challenged, for example. In 1998, Metro was abolished and its six municipalities were incorporated into an expanded City of Toronto. But the City of Toronto is just one element of a larger, provincial association called the Office of Greater Toronto Area, which coordinates activities of a six-region area. Combined with other governance-related changes in Canadian cities, this arrangement seems to be fostering increased competition between cities, political fragmentation, job decentralization, and sprawl. Central Toronto is already jokingly referred to as "Vienna surrounded by Phoenix." Some fear Toronto will soon look like its U.S. counterparts.

Ironically, as Toronto sprawls, Portland, unlike other U.S. cities, is achieving relative success with its urban growth boundary (UGB), which marks the outer limit of urban development. Looking to imitate European *greenbelt cities*, a number of American cities (including Boulder, Colorado) have adopted this planning tool, but with mixed success. Compact development sits uneasy with many Americans, and even Portland has not enjoyed the unwavering support of its citizens. Opponents argue that a UGB creates a scarcity of developable land, thus causing home prices to soar. They also claim that densification denies people the choice to live at lower densities.

Portland's progressive growth management is struggling against some very powerful market and progrowth forces. When the first UGB was drawn in the 1970s, it encompassed plenty of undeveloped land meant to accommodate 20 years of growth. But since the 1990s, with the area almost entirely built out, there has been constant pressure to expand the UGB. The decision over where and how much to expand the boundary is rife with debate. Unfortunately, as in Toronto, Portland is facing a changing political climate, one less disposed toward centralized, regional planning. Whether Portland can continue its impressive sustainable land-use planning efforts in the face of rising population pressures and a new political landscape remains to be seen.

NORTH AMERICAN URBAN FUTURES

As North American cities enter the 21st century, they face a number of complex challenges. For one, there is the legacy of past planning practices. In many instances, as the saying goes, yesterday's solutions have become part of today's problems. For another, there is the problem of dealing with a period of very rapid change, marked by economic restructuring, uneven development, sprawling growth, and a changing ethnic mosaic. There are also on-going societal issues revolving around race, gender, and ethnicity. Finally, there is the fall-out from the events of September 11, which have caused new preoccupations with the safety, security, and vulnerability of large concentrations of people. Some have even suggested that the age of the really tall skyscraper is over. While it is unlikely that Canadian and U.S. cities will depart radically from past trajectories, there are several trends afoot that will simultaneously be shaping the cities of the future. The first of these is demographic.

The North American city has always been subject to demographic shifts through changes in migration and the life cycle stage of the "baby boom" generation. We can predict two possible outcomes. First, there is what can be termed the "browning of North America." Each year about a million people, predominantly Latin American and Asian in origin, arrive in the United States, settling mostly in urban areas. Already, several large multiethnic metropolitan areas house "majority minorities" in their cities and some may soon do so in their suburbs as well. The changes are most likely to affect the urban political landscape, as Asians and Latinos achieve greater political clout. Latino and Asian mayors will be increasingly common in big cities.

Migration is also changing those metropolitan areas where white-black racial dynamics have been an historically important demographic dimension. In the Southeast, metropolitan areas have been attracting back significant numbers of African Americans, especially in the suburbs, thus shifting these areas' racial profiles.

Another demographic trend is the aging of the baby boomers, the nation's first suburban generation. The number of households made of people in their 50s and 60s is already beginning to increase and most of these households will "age in place" in the suburbs. Thus, as central cities become sites for younger immigrant populations, the suburbs should be getting grayer, leading to differential demands for schools, hospitals, retirement facilities, and urban infrastructure among populations in the inner and outer cities. Dealing with the social services, health care, and transportation needs of a rapidly growing senior population will present challenges to both cities and suburbs alike. Meanwhile, retirement migration to high-amenity areas will likely continue as a minor flow.

Economic factors are also changing the cities of the United States and Canada. As a result of changing global economic forces, many cities are left with shaky economic bases (fig. 2.22). While diversification has been the response, it turns out that even jobs in the high-paying technology sector are no guarantee of success. California's Silicon Valley, for example, has continually had to reinvent itself to weather economic fluctuations, switching from R&D to electronic assembly and hardware manufacturing to software development and the *dot.com economy.* After the dot.com bomb in 2001, the silicon valleys, forests, glades, and gulches are all drying up and laying off massive numbers of workers. In one year alone, office vacancy rates in places like San Francisco, Silicon Valley, Seattle, and Vancouver catapulted from close to zero to roughly 20 percent. We can only speculate what will be the driving engine of the next boom-bust cycle to hit the urban economy.

What of cities unable to tap into global circuits of capital, such as the still-declining industrial cities of Flint, Michigan, and Youngstown, Ohio? Will they be left behind in a sort of urban Darwinism? Given the North American context and its history of boom-bust cycles, it is impossible to tell; one

Figure 2.22 The waterfront in Halifax, Nova Scotia, has been turned back to the people and developed to promote tourism. (Photo by Larry Ford)

never knows when a city will be rediscovered or reinvented.

Based on current trends, the tension between the inner cities and outer cities will likely continue. Recessions and economic downturns will most severely impact the inner cities, with a rise in numbers of homeless, unemployed, and marginalized populations. This will place increasing demands on cities and states to provide for their needs. Unless the trend toward regional governance intensifies, it is unlikely that future cities will see much of a wealth transfer from the suburbs to the central city.

Environmental factors are also transforming the urban landscape. One of the most promising directions cities are moving in today is toward a reduced environmental impact and a higher quality of life. Many cities are beginning to adopt sustainable practices. But it is hard to predict which way the North American city will go in terms of sustainability. One of the biggest environmental challenges is how to manage and reduce North American–style urban sprawl. Cities could continue morphing into 100-mi (160-km) cities, with their attendant low densities, or continue experimenting with growth-management techniques, including greenbelts, urban infill and density incentives, urban growth boundaries, and regional governance. There are bound to be more success stories that will be emulated by other cities. Already a number of cities have implemented some sort of metropolitan-wide governance, albeit not as strong as Portland or Toronto. Of course, once metropolitan governments are in place, the same problems of geographic unevenness and inequity might manifest themselves at the next larger scale—the super–metropolitan or megalopolitan scale.

Another encouraging direction North American cities seem to be taking is addressing the need for better mass transit. Rail systems are becoming more popular, especially light rail. The San Diego Trolley, San Francisco's BART, Portland's MAX, and Toronto's transit system are among the most successful systems. On the horizon are magnetic levitation networks. Yet despite these and other efforts, the number of miles driven per person continues to rise steadily and car ownership is higher than ever. It is hard to imagine a future without the private car, although due to rising gasoline costs we may see more alternative fuel vehicles.

While many people remain pessimistic about the future of North American cities—positing grim scenarios of growing social and spatial inequities—one should remain hopeful that the cities can address the challenges before them in a timely manner. Rapid reinvention is, after all, a hallmark of the North American city.

SUGGESTED READINGS

Banham, Reyner. *Los Angeles: The Architecture of Four Ecologies.* New York: Harper & Row, 1971.

Bourne, Larry S. *The Changing Social Geography of Canadian Cities.* Canadian Association of Geographers Series in Canadian Geography, edited by David F. Ley. Montreal: McGill-Queens University Press, 1993.

Bullard, Robert D., Glen S. Johnson, and Angel O. Torres, eds. *Sprawl City: Race, Politics, and Planning in Atlanta.* Washington, D.C.: Island Press, 2000.

Bunting, Trudi, and Pierre Filion, eds. *Canadian Cities in Transition: The Twenty-First Century.* 2d ed. New York: Oxford University Press, 1999. Edited collection offers overview of recent trends and issues in Canadian cities.

Clay, Grady. *Real Places: An Unconventional Guide to America's Generic Landscape.* Chicago: University of Chicago Press, 1994. A journalist presents a layperson's guide to the basic components of the urban landscape.

Davis, Mike. *City of Quartz.* New York: Random House, 1992.

Drew, Bettina. *Crossing the Expendable Landscape.* Saint Paul, Minn.: Graywolf, 1998.

Duany, Andres, Elizabeth Plater-Zyberk, and Jeff Speck. *Suburban Nation: The Rise of Sprawl and the Decline of the American Dream.* New York: North Point, 2000.

Ford, Larry R. *Cities and Buildings: Skyscrapers, Skid Rows, and Suburbs.* Baltimore: Johns Hopkins University Press, 1994. A detailed look at parts of the American city, from the CBD to the suburbs, and how they evolved historically and architecturally, by one of the authors of this chapter.

Garreau, Joel. *Edge City: Life on the New Frontier.* New York: Doubleday, 1991. A stimulating analysis by a newspaper writer of the edge cities that increasingly dominate our major urban centers.

Gratz, Roberta Brandes. *Cities Back from the Edge: New Life for Downtown.* New York: Wiley, 1998.

Hannigan, John. *Fantasy City: Pleasure and Profit in the Postmodern Metropolis.* New York: Routledge, 1998. The history of urban entertainment in North America and the development of casinos, malls, heritage developments, theme parks, and "urban entertainment destinations."

Jacobs, Jane. *The Death and Life of Great American Cities.* New York: Random House, 1961. A classic work that makes the case for high-density, 24-hour activity cycles, mixed land use, and human-scale development.

Kay, Jane Holtz. *Asphalt Nation: How the Automobile Took over America and How We Can Take It Back.* New York: Basic, 1997. An indictment of the American love affair with the automobile, highlighting its destruction of cities over the past one hundred years.

Kotkin, Joel. *The New Geography: How the Digital Revolution Is Reshaping the American Landscape.* New York: Random House, 2000. Explores American urbanism in a digital age, focusing on landscape changes and winners and losers.

Kunstler, James Howard. *The Geography of Nowhere: The Rise and Decline of America's Man-Made Landscape.* New York: Touchstone, 1993. Settlement history of the United States from vibrant Main Streets to soulless suburbs and auto-oriented sprawlscapes.

Logan, John R., and Harvey L. Molotch. *Urban Fortunes: The Political Economy of Space.* Berkeley: University of California Press, 1987.

Lynch, Kevin. *The Image of the City.* Cambridge: M. I. T. Press, 1960. A classic study of imageability and legibility as components of good urban design with case studies of Boston, Jersey City, and Los Angeles.

Marshall, Alex. *How Cities Work: Suburbs, Sprawl, and the Roads Not Taken.* Austin: University of Texas Press, 2000. Identifies the "real" forces that shape American cities—transportation systems, industry, and political decision making—and the need for change.

McHarg, Ian. *Design with Nature.* Garden City, N.Y.: Natural History, 1969.

Rusk, David. *Cities without Suburbs.* 2d ed. Washington, D.C.: Woodrow Wilson Center Press, 1995.

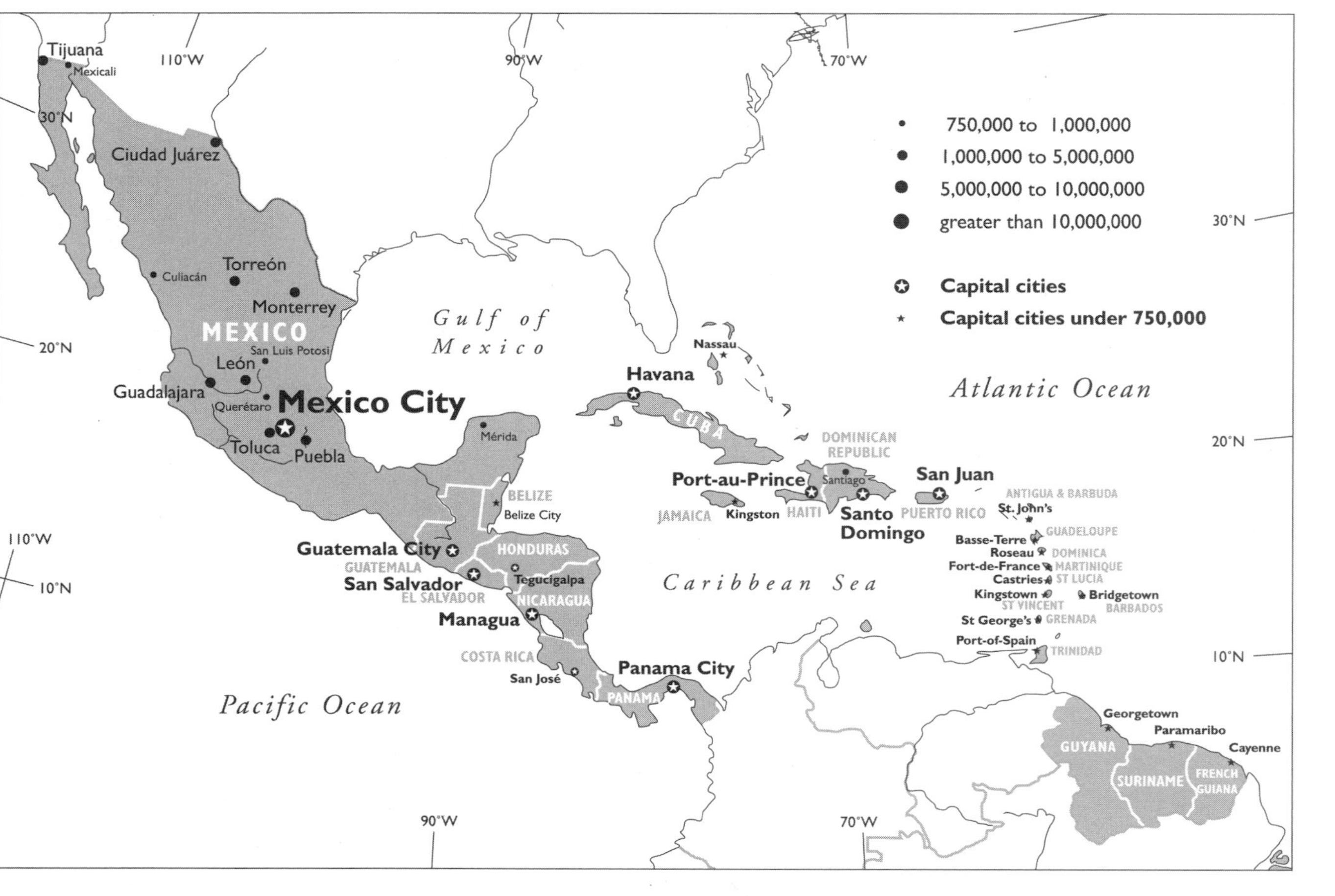

Figure 3.1 Major Cities of Middle America and the Caribbean. *Source*: Data from United Nations, *World Urbanization Prospects, 2001 Revision* (New York: United Nations Population Division, 2002), www.unpopulation.org.

3

Cities of Middle America and the Caribbean

GARY S. ELBOW AND LYDIA M. PULSIPHER

KEY URBAN FACTS

Total Population	176 million
Percent Urban Population	67%
Total Urban Population	118 million
Most Urbanized Country	Bahamas (89%)
Least Urbanized Country	Haiti (36%)
Annual Urban Growth Rate	2.0%
Number of Megacities	1
Number of Cities of More than 1 Million	17
Three Largest Cities	Mexico City, Guadalajara, Monterrey
World Cities	None

KEY CHAPTER THEMES

1. The cities of Middle America and the Caribbean emerged from different prehistorical contexts and were molded by different colonial and postcolonial forces.
2. The Spanish colonial influence largely shaped Middle America, whereas the Caribbean was developed under various European powers.
3. The original high Indian culture and cities of Middle America were obliterated by the Spanish.
4. Middle America has long been dominated by a single megacity and primate city—Mexico City, built on the site of the former Aztec capital city.
5. The Caribbean is a subregion of islands with more modest-sized urban centers, but also dominated by urban primacy.
6. Middle American cities tended to be in upland (highland) locations in both precolonial and colonial eras, and those cities are still the most important today, but coastal trading ports established by the European colonialists are also important.
7. Caribbean cities tend to be coastal ports and the modern incarnations of old colonial administrative and trade centers.

8. With few exceptions, industrialization continues to play a minor role in most Caribbean cities, whereas tourism has come to assume dominant importance.
9. Mexico has the most established urban system in the region, one in which Mexico City is playing a less dominating role as northern border industrial cities grow in importance.
10. Cuba has taken the most divergent path to urban and national development in the past half century, with its variant form of socialist cities.

The vast sprawl and seemingly hopeless congestion of giant Mexico City. Picturesque Spanish colonial buildings surrounding a large plaza bustling with street life. Quaint seaside island towns in the Caribbean with cruise ships docked along the shore, disgorging hordes of tourists for shopping and sight-seeing. These are some of the popular images evoked by this complex region, divided into two distinct parts: Middle America (composed of Mexico and the Central American states), and the many islands of the Caribbean (fig. 3.1).

The cities of Middle America and the Caribbean emerged from very different prehistorical contexts and were molded by different colonial and postcolonial forces. In the Caribbean, cities did not exist until the European colonial period, when port cities were founded to facilitate extraregional trade (fig. 3.2). Most Caribbean cities lie in lowland coastal locations, although in the interior lowlands and uplands of the larger islands, old trading towns that once served as the transfer points for cash crops and incoming merchandise still serve a commercial function. On the mainland, before the European era, principal cities were in highland locations, probably because the climate there was perceived to be salubrious and the land productive. Europeans sometimes established their colonial cities on or near the ruins of conquered indigenous highland cities. Coastal port cities were added shortly after the conquest, because the colonial economy was focused on the export of extracted resources and the import of European manufactured goods. Caribbean cities are by comparison much smaller than those on the mainland and less complicated by extremes in wealth disparity; hence they are also somewhat less likely to be characterized by the development of squatter settlements, though some do exist.

CITIES OF THE CARIBBEAN

Location and Structure

Major Caribbean cities are, with few exceptions, the modern incarnations of old colonial administrative and trade centers. They lie in coastal zones, having been founded as trading towns for plantation economies in the days when sea transport was the only avenue of commerce. But today the sea is less and less the primary point of entry for these cities. Heavy imported products like cars, refrigerators, and food still arrive via container ship, and cruise passengers debark by the thousands for a few hours of touring and souvenir shopping (fig. 3.3), but many Caribbean cities have spatially reoriented away from the waterfront, expanding along the urban periphery in the direction of their airport (box 3.1)

Other than cruise passengers, most people now arrive on Caribbean islands by airplane, from which most get their first impressions of the cities. For the most part, Caribbean cities

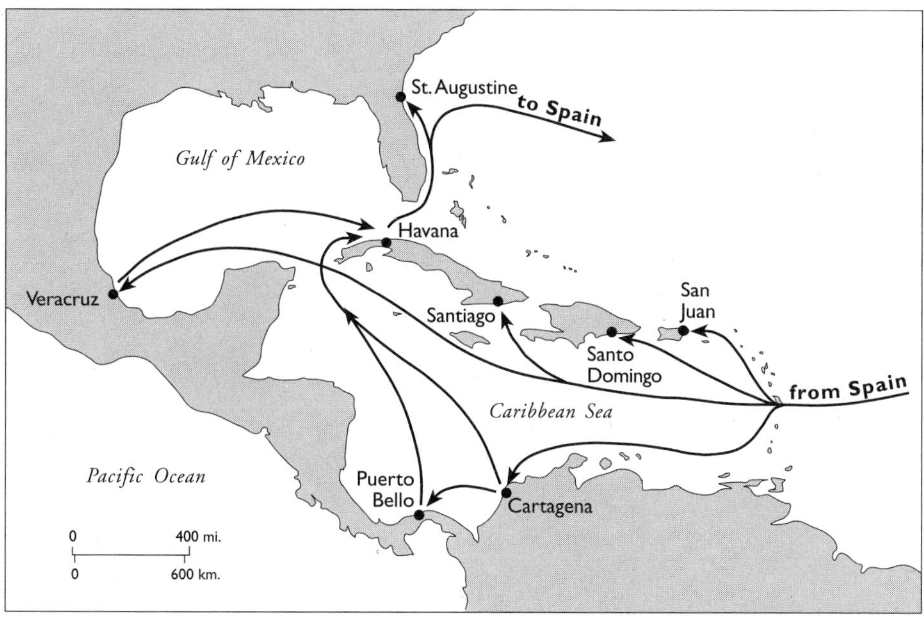

Figure 3.2 Spanish Ports and Convoy Routes in the Colonial Era. *Source*: Adapted from Robert C. West and John P. Augelli, *Middle America: Its Lands and Peoples,* 2d ed. (Englewood Cliffs, N.J.: Prentice Hall, 1976), 64.

are not high-rise affairs. The few buildings that soar above two or three stories are frequently resort hotels, often located along beaches that may be quite distant from the city. Whether one is flying over St. Johns, Antigua; San Juan, Puerto Rico; Havana, Cuba; Port of Spain, Trinidad; Paramaribo, Suriname; or Georgetown, Guyana, one will observe a low-slung city, characterized by a dense mixture of small one- and two-story dwellings grouped in fenced yards and compounds. There will also be medium-sized homes and business places and occasional industrial sites and roadside shopping centers. One may even spot remnants of earlier rural landscapes in the interior spaces set back from the main roads: an occasional windmill tower, once the heart of a sugar plantation; perhaps a still-occupied chicken coop; some lush vegetable gardens; and, occasionally, grazing goats.

In most cases, the hearts of old colonial Caribbean cities are arranged along a grid of streets at harbor side. Along these usually narrow streets, old and often architecturally significant two-story residences, business places, and government buildings are still to be found in many cities. Fanning out from this center will be hundreds, and in some cities thousands, of dwellings and business places arranged along streets that may eventually abandon the grid pattern and snake out into the countryside in a meandering manner. In Georgetown, Grenada, the large U-shaped harbor and surrounding hills have given the city a bowl form. In the case of Port of Spain, Trinidad, where mountains impede development to the north, a linear urban corridor stretches east into the hinterland, forming a conurbation with several smaller cities (fig. 3.4). In the Guianas, Antigua, Ja-

Figure 3.3 Nassau, Bahamas, is the center of the Caribbean cruise routes; here cruise ships line up side by side to disgorge thousands of tourists onto the streets. (Photo by Jack Williams)

maica, Puerto Rico, or Havana, where the landforms are less restrictive, a fan-shaped urban sprawl is evident. True shantytowns, where dwellings are built of the flimsiest materials and the occupants live in destitution, are not prominent in Caribbean cities. Housing that is built by the occupants themselves, comfortable but nonetheless substandard, is to be found in many cities, mostly in the Spanish-speaking Caribbean (but also see the case study of Kingston, Jamaica, page 102). In the former eastern Caribbean colonies of Britain, France, and the Netherlands, informal occupation of urban fringes has been discouraged by late-20th-century metropolitan urban planners.

On some of the smaller islands, such as Antigua, Guadeloupe, and Barbados, despite only moderate official rates of urbanization, even the countryside, with an ever-growing number of houses and businesses interspersed with agricultural land that is now idle or used mostly for grazing, has an urban feel to it. Roads are busy with traffic, as residents and business people commute to work in the city or service their customers in the hinterland. Relatively affluent Barbados, for example, has one of the highest population densities on earth, with more than 1,600 people per sq mi (618 per sq km), yet only 38% of the population actually lives in cities. In larger islands, such as Jamaica and the Dominican Republic, the urban landscapes are distinctly different from the rural. Here, because the technology of rural life and the organization of space and services vary noticeably from urban situations, one has the distinct feeling of traveling back in time, when driving, for example, from Kingston, Jamaica's capital and largest city, to the villages of Mavis Bank or Ramble, only a few miles away in the Blue Mountains.

The Historical Roots of Caribbean Urbanization

The antecedents of Caribbean urbanization lie in the plantation era. On nearly all islands, the importation of large labor forces—first indentured laborers from Europe, then slaves from Africa, and later indentured laborers from Asia—to work on colonial sugar, tobacco, and cotton plantations resulted in high rural popu-

Box 3.1 Middle American Transportation Patterns

During the colonial period, communication among Spain's colonies was discouraged—trade was limited to the mother country. Similar conditions prevailed within British, French, and Dutch colonies. Connections between Spanish, British, French, or Dutch colonies were even less evolved, since there was no need for communication among territories of competing colonizing powers. These patterns persisted after independence and still exist today. Middle American communication patterns are still designed more to carry people into and out of the region than to move them within it; Miami, which lies just outside the region, in south Florida, has become the primary gateway to Middle America and the Caribbean.

As a result, most travel between the mainland and the Caribbean islands requires a stop in Miami. In Middle America, only Panama offers connections to destinations in the Greater Antilles (Havana, Kingston, Port-au-Prince, Santo Domingo, and San Juan), while it is also possible to fly from San José to Havana. Caracas offers connections to Aruba, Bonaire, and Curaçao as well as to destinations in the Dominican Republic, Puerto Rico, and Martinique.

Even from Mexico City, with its millions of inhabitants, only Havana, of all Caribbean destinations, is accessible without a stop in Miami or some other intermediate point. Yet it is possible to fly nonstop from Mexico City to more distant cities in the United States, as well as to London, Paris, Amsterdam, Frankfurt, and Madrid in Europe.

Within the Lesser Antilles, a number of small airlines maintain daily scheduled connections between islands. Georgetown and Paramaribo are accessed from the Caribbean via Barbados and Trinidad, but have nonstop flights to New York and European gateway cities. In Central America, regional airlines link capital cities, but while service is better than in the Caribbean, access to air travel to places outside of the region is still better than it is within it.

lation densities. For example, the tiny island of Montserrat went from no more than a few hundred Native American inhabitants in 1630 to 2,000 mostly European inhabitants in the 1650s, to more than 10,000 by the end of the next century, at which time Africans and their progeny outnumbered Europeans ten to one. Other islands in the eastern Caribbean went through similar population explosions, due to labor importation. Because of the extractive and exploitative nature of plantation systems, these workers and their descendents were kept in poverty. Nonetheless, the laborers managed to feed themselves and others quite well, through the cultivation of elaborate gardens on plantation fringes, even providing the bulk of fresh produce for urban populations. Urbanization increased after the plantation system failed. After emancipation in the 19th century, despite the fact that they were now paid for their work, rural Caribbean people entered a long period of underemployment, extremely low wages, political oppression, and increasing poverty as the plantation system died a long, slow death. During this period of stagnation, which lasted to the mid-20th century, many Caribbean people chose to migrate. For most, the first move was to a nearby town or to an agricultural job on a larger island; later, if possible, they moved to more distant urban locales.

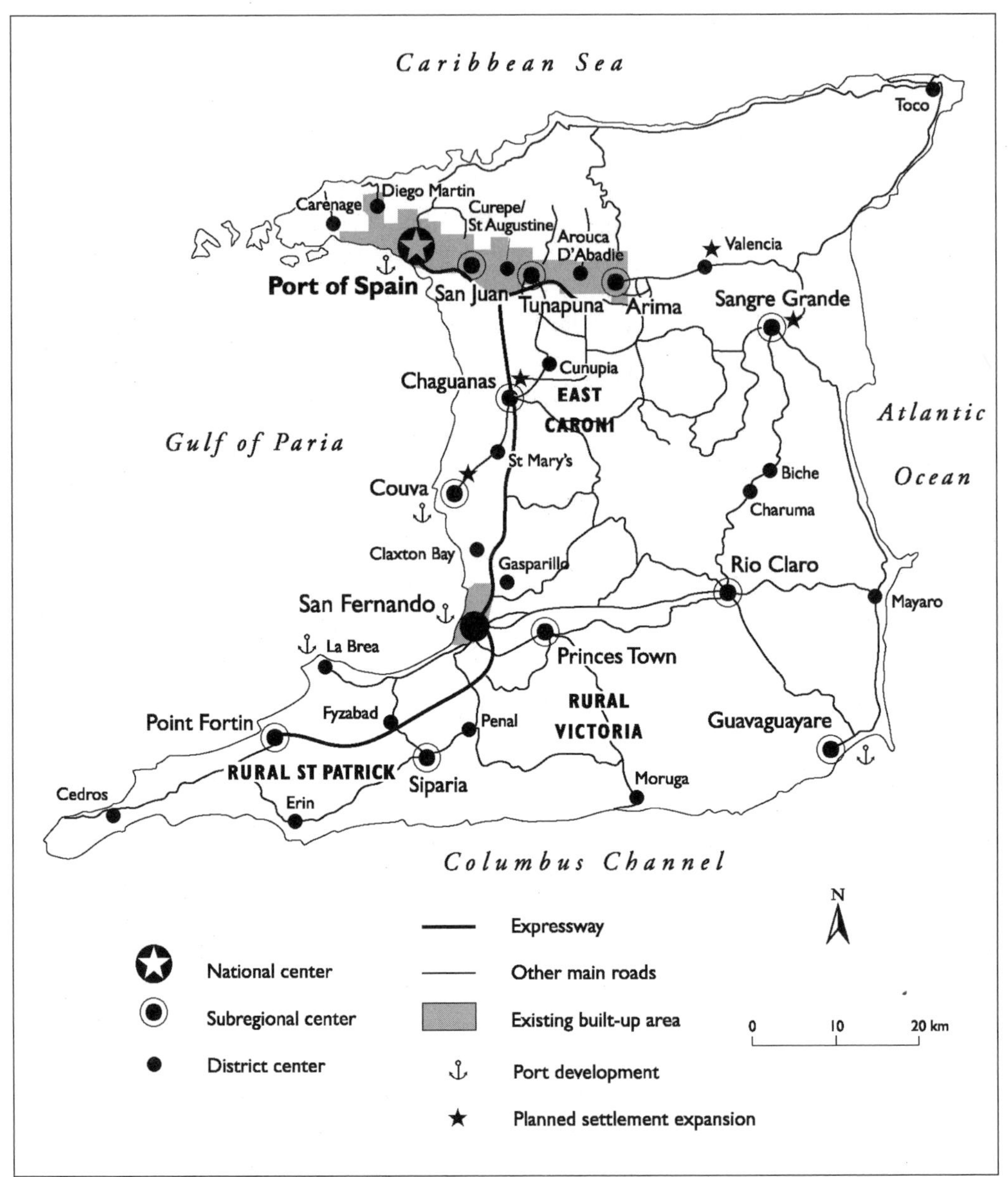

Figure 3.4 Urban Sprawl in Trinidad from Port of Spain to Arima. *Source*: Adapted from Robert Potter, "The Port of Spain Urban Corridor, Trinidad," in *A Reader in Caribbean Geography,* ed. David Barker, Carol Newby, and Mike Morrissey (Kingston, Jamaica: Ian Randle, 1998), 98.

World War II brought important changes in Caribbean fortunes and in rural-urban relationships. Many Caribbean men fought in the armed forces of the United States, Canada, and Britain. Some returned to their home islands with social and political change on their minds and founded labor movements that led to the establishment of political parties. These labor parties then began agitating for the end of colonial status and the beginning of nonagricultural development. Others went into business in towns and cities; only a few returned to the countryside. An ever-increasing number returned to the northern lands that they had served as soldiers, now to work in postwar industries. As before, these migrants retained close ties with home, sending money regularly, buying island land, fronting the cash for small family businesses, and building substantial family homes to which they retired in the 1980s and 1990s. All of these migrants, through their own efforts or through the money they sent home to relatives, transformed the options for rural youth, thereby adding to the stream of urban migration within the Caribbean.

Recent Urbanization Processes

The post–World War II strategy of extra-regional migration coupled with remittances to family members left behind was eventually supplemented by development within the islands: light manufacturing, offshore banking and related services, and tourism—all of which have resulted in significant rural to urban migration.

In the 1960s, the urban portion of the Caribbean population was 38%; by 1970 it was 45%; and by 2000 it was well in excess of 50% in half of the countries. In all cases, the capital city contained 20% or more of the population. Generally speaking, the most recent data show a slowing of urbanization in the 1980s and 1990s. In comparison to mainland Middle America, urban population growth rates were quite low in several islands: Antigua/Barbuda, Barbados, Cuba, Dominica, Grenada, St. Kitts/Nevis, Suriname, and Trinidad/Tobago.

Despite apparently slowing rates of urbanization, the character of urbanization in the Caribbean per se is fundamentally disturbing—a salient and signifying feature of the overall colonial history of the region. Today's Caribbean cities, with substantial numbers of underemployed, are but a link in the chain of extractive and exploitive relationships that have historically displaced surplus wealth from Caribbean countrysides and placed it ultimately in European and North American centers of consumption—a pattern of wealth transfer that is now recognized as part of globalization.

Rather than functioning primarily to service their hinterlands, island primate market towns and cities are midpoints in the transference of wealth from island hinterlands to distant developed metropolitan centers (primarily in Europe and North America) where people enjoy abundant and artificially cheap tropical commodities (first sugar and now bananas or even tourism). Two current examples come to mind. For one, the underpaid banana producer in St. Lucia subsidizes not only cheap bananas on the tables of Europe, but also the consumption levels of the island urban middle classes, who directly or indirectly make money off the banana trade—more money per capita than the producers make. Similarly, island natural resources such as beaches and wetlands are appropriated for hotel construction, at far below their innate value as natural areas for the local people who once relied on them for sustenance and now might view them as recreational green spaces. The income generated from these natural resources goes not to local people, but to investors far away in developed economies. A second example is tourism profits, which filter through island cities and into the pockets of merchants, supermarket retailers, and professionals who may or may not be local people, while the vast majority of island people subsidize the tourism economy with their low wages. Caribbean cities continue to grow, primarily because low rural wages and lack of access to adequate land and upward mobility ultimately drive people to migrate, pulled by the (often false) hope of a better life in the city.

In a pattern common to former colonies around the world, the Caribbean islands still exhibit the legacy of that mercantile system, in that these islands competed with each other in the colonial past in production of agricultural products and still compete today in the tourism business. Moreover, the outside linkages of these islands were with European powers, or the United States, while ties to neighboring islands were very limited. This still tends to be the case.

But will Caribbean cities forever continue as dreary links in the extraction of wealth for the benefit of outsiders so typical of the colonial era? Is colonialism merely being replaced by the neocolonialism of the banana trade, tourism, or low-wage-seeking light industry? Or perhaps is the Caribbean already undergoing a sea change that will see a new socioeconomic order, a new social psychology, and different settlement patterns materialize? Recent demographic data reveal some emerging patterns.

Compared to the rest of Latin America, Caribbean islands are experiencing lower population growth rates, slowing rates of urbanization, the spreading of urban amenities to the countryside, and improvement in indicators of well-being, which now rival urban populations in developed countries. Caribbean societies are also experiencing high rates of civic participation in volunteer and service organizations, both religious and secular. Many people eventually acquire advanced training or higher education at one or more regional universities; foreign leisure travel is in the plans of most adults; and earnings from investments accumulated while working abroad are available for local investment. All these factors are changing the dynamics of Caribbean societies, the character of Caribbean cities, and patterns of urbanization.

For some time now, several Caribbean states have made good showings on the United Nations Human Development Index (HDI), which ranks 174 of the world's countries on how well they are providing for their citizens. Barbados, for example, ranks just 30th from the top. Careful observation of life in Barbados confirms the societal context for this high rank, and it could be argued that urban attributes have been extended to the entire country. Serious poverty exists, but as in most prosperous countries, it is the affliction of only a few who are largely hidden from view. Moreover, what may look like poverty to affluent outsiders often is not. Women hold a higher percentage of administrative and managerial positions in Barbados than in most Western European countries and constitute a majority of professional technical workers.

Although Barbados is perhaps an extreme example of an island exhibiting urban (or suburban) qualities throughout, many other islands—Antigua/Barbuda, Cuba, Guadeloupe, Martinique, St. Kitts/Nevis, Puerto Rico, Trinidad/Tobago—share similar attributes. It can be argued that as rural poverty disappears, Caribbean islands increasingly face issues similar to those faced by urbanized communities worldwide. With already high levels of literacy and well-being, the islands need to complete the modernization of their economies by bringing the citizenry to yet higher levels of technological skills so they can capture jobs that now circulate from place to place in the global economy.

Manufacturing as an Option

Industrial development in the Caribbean lacks a comparative advantage. Local markets are small and raw materials are in short supply and expensive to import. Transportation to external markets is equally expensive and, by the time the products reach their destinations, they are likely to be undercut by competitors, even if they are going no further than the next island. Almost all manufacturing in the region has to take place under special agreements with investors from North America, Europe, or Asia, called "industrialization by invitation," that artificially alleviate the disadvantages of remote location, smallness, and wage rates that are too high to compete with poorer parts of the Americas, Asia, and Africa. Typically, these agreements are characterized by duty-free concessions on imported capital equipment and periods during which the new industries have their normal income and profit taxes suspended.

Puerto Rico, as a Commonwealth territory of the United States, is a classic example of a place that has been able to make special arrangements fostering industrialization and, by extension, urbanization. San Juan, Puerto Rico's capital, is now one of the most industrialized cities in the Caribbean, producing petrochemicals, pharmaceuticals, plastic, rubber and metal items, electronic components, appliances, and machinery. San Juan's inhabitants enjoy one of the highest per capita incomes in the region, but the long-term viability of industry in Puerto Rico remains questionable. Beginning as a site for the labor-intensive production of nondurable consumer goods by multinational firms that were attracted with tax incentives and low wages, over time San Juan and its environs have moved to production of durable goods such as household appliances. One result is that fewer jobs have been created than anticipated.

Puerto Rico's location close to the United States and the fact that it is linked to the United States, which facilitates both orders and transport from the mainland, have placed it in the position to take over as the entrepôt for goods entering the Caribbean market. The container ships that bring all manner of goods and food into the Caribbean often come from Puerto Rico, which has become a break-in-bulk center, with the attendant warehouses and services. All of these trade- and manufacturing-related activities have created jobs in the San Juan metropolitan area, which now contains well over one third of the island population. Job creation elsewhere in Puerto Rico has lagged.

Nonetheless, Puerto Rico's high wages are beginning to price it out of the market. Increasingly, companies that received tax incentives and other government assistance to locate in Puerto Rico are moving to even lower-wage locations in the region, such as the Dominican Republic and Haiti, or sites in Asia. When one shops for appliances in the Caribbean these days, the best made and most attractively priced come from China and Southeast Asia. Local Caribbean theoreticians now think that for any industrialization to succeed in the region, investors will have to have higher motives than just profit to keep them in the islands.

Tourism and Urbanization

Tourism and cities have a complex and often indirect relationship in the Caribbean. Urban

Figure 3.5 In Fort de France, Martinique, many of the businesses on the street cater to crowds from cruise ships. (Photo by Gary Elbow)

hotels exist—for example, there are several high-rise facilities in Kingston and Ocho Rios in Jamaica, while Puerto Rico's hotels lie adjacent to the city, but are functionally separated from it. But most tourist resorts lie away from the main cities, on beaches and former wetlands. In fact, except for cruise passengers who often move on foot through old central cities because these places lie close to docking facilities, many tourists make only one or two forays into the primate cities of the islands they visit (fig. 3.5). Such trips are often tightly organized by the hotel staff and circumscribe the amount of money tourists spend in Caribbean cities. Nonetheless, the impact of tourism on cities and on patterns of Caribbean urbanization is significant. Industries that serve tourism are often located in cities—import companies; ground transport companies; clerical, technical, and legal services; and travel services are usually located in cities, though some may have branch offices close to the hotels. More importantly, the wages of employees are spent in the cities on rent and on a wide range of services and consumer products. It is in this capacity that tourism has its greatest impact on urbanization in the Caribbean.

Representative Cities

Kingston (Jamaica) and Havana (Cuba) are two major cities of the Caribbean region that illustrate in many ways widely divergent paths of urban development, especially in the past 40 years.

Kingston: From Squatters to Scheme Houses

Kingston, Jamaica, is a classic primate city, roughly 12 times larger than the next largest city, Montego Bay. Kingston developed from a south coast trading town and has spread into the surrounding countryside. Efforts at urban planning in and around Kingston have been thwarted by lack of administrative authority and funds. One result is that the urban landscape is highly mixed.

Older, declining neighborhoods, built over the past 100 years near the colonial inner city, are now much more densely occupied than originally. They are said to have been *tenementized,* because original one-family houses have been subdivided many times over and rented to very poor rural migrants who share cooking and bathing facilities. Life in these now lower-class neighborhoods tends to take place on the streets and in the yard because interior spaces are too crowded (box 3.2).

Box 3.2 Jamaican Ghetto

The ghetto, Jamaican-style, is an enclave, whose ethnicity is its poverty. The typical urban ghetto is a criss-crossing and interweaving of access streets, lanes, and footpaths to yards separated from the outside view by zinc fences. The yards are called tenement yards. Some . . . were built by the government for poor people. Most, however, are the results of the spatial reconfiguration of the city when the affluent people moved out, taking with them their status symbols of residence and social class, and the poor people moved in, bringing with them their rural but changing work view. Inside a small tenement yard will live ten to fifteen people; inside a large one over forty. Over time they pay no rent, as rent collection is sometimes hazardous for the landlord who, if he/she has not already migrated, now lives in the hills—Red Hills, Beverly Hills, Jacks Hill, Stony Hill, looking down.

The two most socially significant characteristics of the tenement yard are its ritualized privacy and its cooperation. As private space, the yard is enclosed from public view and commerce. Its gate is always closed, and none but the most familiar may push and enter without calling or knocking, seeking permission. Entering this private space, the stranger is made to feel unwelcome until his or her *bona fides* is established. Then there is also the privacy of the occupants. Each apartment is secured from the intruding eyes and familiarity of the other occupants. Meals are usually served and eaten inside. From a functionalist point of view it hides the time of shame when a "lot of people have no supper tonight." . . . Your shame is your own. So also is your pride. As Harry Belafonte's mother drilled into him, "Poverty is no excuse for lack of class."

Second, the urban yard is a shared space of cooperation. They cooperate in the use of the domestic facilities, the kitchen, bathroom, and standpipe, and in common security against strangers. They cooperate, too, for mutual security against the state, the police. The yard . . . is also a problem-solving space for its occupants, particularly the women who cooperate in dealing with the problems of children. Such cooperation, however, assumes respect for each other. People who cannot get along with others are usually forced out by protracted quarreling, body language, singing.

Source: Barry Chevannes, "Jamaican Diasporic Identity: The Metaphor of the Yard," in Patrick Taylor, ed., *Nation Dance: Religion, Identity, and Cultural Difference in the Caribbean* (Bloomington: Indiana University Press, 2001), 131–32.

Newer neighborhoods, lying especially on the western periphery of Kingston, contain so-called "scheme houses," planned "affordable" communities built in the 1970s and 1980s with government money and consisting of standardized, box-like concrete houses that contain plumbed kitchens and baths, a small porch, a living room, and several bedrooms. These scheme houses, all nearly alike at the outset, now bear little resemblance to each other. In many cases, second stories have been added or the tiny yards have been filled in with additions to the house. Upkeep of the scheme houses varies greatly because some of the original low-income owners have since prospered, while others have foundered in the long-standing Jamaican recession.

Kingston also contains squatters. The city is situated on uneven land crossed by many gullies that carry intermittent rainfall south to the sea. Rural migrants now occupy the gully interstices that separate more formal neighborhoods. These squatters fence their spaces and raise gardens and animals, much to the annoyance of their middle-class neighbors. Some manage to tap into electricity illegally and even gain access to piped water, but they rarely have sufficient sanitary plumbing facilities. As a result, urban groundwater pollution is a serious problem. In the Kingston periphery, squatter shantytowns are occupied by people who have gathered enough personal and material resources to flee inner-city slums. Shantytowns actually afford their residents greater potential for social and spatial mobility than does more formal inner-city housing. Their location near the sea or agricultural land makes fishing and small gardens possible, thus the cost of living is lower and saving and investment in self-improvement are possible for those who have steady jobs. Also, community relations can be strong and supportive, while, surprisingly, the shanty housing stock turns over fairly rapidly, with old structures built out of scrap being soon replaced with more substantial concrete block and wood structures.

Economists estimate that, due to high inflation and the loss of jobs in Jamaica, 44% of the labor force create their own forms of employment. The Caribbean urban informal economy got its start during slavery, when slaves, legally blocked from working for wages, devised ways to supply high-demand products and services for cash. The range of informal jobs is now vast, including the provision of transport; procuring and delivering home-grown produce to urban households; preserving food for sale in market stalls; sewing; and producing crafts for gift-buying tourists (fig. 3.6). The flourishing Jamaican informal economy serves a host of positive social functions, but also, these small-scale enterprises retain inefficiencies that inhibit overall economic growth. Few informal businesses grow into larger firms that create jobs and pay taxes. There is rarely money left over for reinvestment, while entrepreneurial innovation can be stifled by cronyism and reciprocal obligations.

Life for most people in Kingston is circumscribed by low income, poor housing, high crime rates, and lack of adequate transportation to jobs, schools, and shopping. Yet most who have studied urban life there seem to concur that sense of community is strong. People survive by constantly exchanging favors: surveillance of each other's property, shared care of children and elderly, shared food, the lending of small amounts of money, and personal support during times of triumph or sadness.

Havana: The Socialist Dream Lives On

Havana, Cuba, has been a prominent city in the region over the past 500 years, but during the Castro administration (1959–onward), development has been so tightly controlled that many very old buildings are still standing. The city has become a kind of living museum. By 1950, Havana was an unusually large and opulent city in an underdeveloped poor island—a high-fashion international tourist mecca, famous for gambling and freely available commercial sex, as well as the transshipment point for agricultural export luxuries, chiefly sugar and fine cigars. The city's size, then, was not the result of its role within the country, but

Figure 3.6 The informal sector is a vital part of every city's economy in Middle America and the Caribbean, as in this street scene from Mexico City. (Photo by Robert Smith)

rather of its long history as a major colonial city with connections to the global economy.

Prior to the revolution, although one in five Cubans lived and worked in Havana, there was no government involvement in planning. Transport linkages were poor between sections of the city and most jobs were far from housing that was affordable to workers. Already sharp disparities of wealth were increasing, as the wealthy moved out of the old residences of Habana Vieja (Old Havana) and into the fashionable districts along the coast to the west. Havana's built environment was particularly rich: the city contained, as it does now, a valuable stock of architecturally important historic buildings of early colonial, baroque, art nouveau, neoclassical as well as art deco styles. In 1982, UNESCO named Havana's old city a world heritage site. But for the vast majority of residents there were few green spaces or other affordable urban amenities, and housing was expensive and far below acceptable standards; indeed, in the 1950s, several hundred thousand of Havana's 1.6 million people lived in shantytowns.

After the revolution, Cuba's economy became increasingly linked to that of the USSR, as the Soviets sought the propaganda value of a well-off socialist Cuba in America's backyard. In 1989, more than 85% of Cuba's trade and 22% of Cuba's national income were connected with the Soviet bloc and much of this trade was based on special prices and subsidies to Cuba. Cuba sold its sugar and other tropical crops at premium prices to Soviet bloc countries and purchased petroleum at subsidized rates. With this rather unsocialist economic base for his revolution, Castro decided to make Havana a demonstration project for social reform. To reverse Havana's prerevolutionary trajectory toward extreme primacy and wealth disparity, the government strictly limited residential construction and used work permits and controls on residency to manage who would live in the city. Havana was not to exceed 2 million people (it now has 2.2 million).

The transformation of Havana into a Cuban variation of a socialist city took many years. Class differences were explicitly discouraged; conspicuous consumption and other antisocialist behavior was controlled (often tyrannically) by neighborhood Committees for the Defense of the Revolution, which reported dissidents to the government. Lack of maintenance and unaesthetic renovation of historic structures for denser occupation resulted in a major degeneration of the built environment. As the revolution gained momentum and the elite and middle classes left for exile in Miami and elsewhere, old mansions were turned over to workers and students. These new residents used strictly rationed building materials to crudely partition spacious dining rooms or parlors into multiple dwellings. Often, government efforts to improve life in Havana ran out of money and energy or ideological direction—for example, entrepreneurial food production was alternately discouraged and encouraged as worries about the dangers of petty capitalism alternated with worries about food shortages. Nonetheless, despite the decline in the built environment and the scarcity of even the smallest luxuries, wealth disparity in Havana and in Cuba as a whole declined dramatically and the average quality of life improved. Literacy rates rose, infant mortality declined, life expectancy increased, and Cuba now outshines most Latin American countries on the United Nations' HDI, and this despite serious retrenchment during the 1980s and 1990s.

With the collapse of the Soviet empire at the end of the 1980s, it became apparent that Cuba's extreme economic dependence had serious drawbacks. A reconsideration of the island's economic prospects began in the late 1980s and the government soon settled on the old solution of tourism—but tourism with a difference (fig. 3.7). Cuba would earn foreign currency by promoting primarily Havana and its environs as a package-tour destination for Central European (and Russian) middle classes, emphasizing such activities as sports and medical tourism, but eventually also sex tourism.

By the mid-1990s, when it was apparent that Cuba's long association with the Soviet bloc was over, Castro sarcastically designated the disastrous economic downturn as the "Special Period in a Time of Peace." The reforms of the Special Period (which were still in place in 2002) bore close resemblance to neoliberal reforms implemented elsewhere in the developing world: downsizing of the labor force, encouragement of the informal economy, a shift away from government ownership of agricultural and industrial production, and encouragement for foreign investors (especially from Spain and Italy). In Havana, these policies have translated into a revived concern for how the city appears to foreigners, with an emphasis on repair and restoration and the revitalization of all aspects of the urban infrastructure. Small businesses and restaurants, especially those that serve tourism, are encouraged, though the level of encouragement fluctuates according to government perceptions of the effects of petty capitalism on Cuba's long-term goal of protecting the revolution against capitalism. Retrenchment in the use of petroleum has resulted in a transformation of traffic in the city. Hundreds of thousands of bicycles, some high-tech varieties

Figure 3.7 In Havana, Cuba, these stilt walkers in colorful costumes pose for tourists to take pictures, and they expect payment! (Photo by Jack Williams)

imported from Asia, are the vehicle of choice for Habaneras, and the Havana landscape is increasingly marked by accommodations for cyclists. Urban planning has been revitalized in that efforts are made to locate new jobs close to where people live, there is a notable increase in popular participation in urban design through neighborhood workshops, traditional building styles and materials are being reintroduced, and appropriate technology, recycling, and even sustainability are emphasized (fig. 3.8).

The emphasis in the Special Period on marketization is bringing change to Havana in ways that suggest its role as a demonstration of socialist reforms and its potential as an inadvertently preserved mecca of historic sites may be quickly dissipating. Real estate investment has been limited to large, foreign-financed projects related to tourism and the physical design of these projects is often outrageously mismatched with the existing historic structures. The service jobs created do not meet the egalitarian goals of the revolution—once again, Cubans are serving outsiders. Foreign managers (mostly Europeans) have reintroduced racist policies—often refusing to hire dark-skinned people—long illegal under Castro-led social reforms, and there is little doubt that sex tourism, which uses Cuban young women as a disposable resource, is a major focus of the European clientele.

Havana, once known as the pearl of the Caribbean, could reclaim this designation should the political climate change. Indeed, given all the international interest in the city—the money waiting to be invested by Americans and Europeans, the interest in its historic buildings, and the revival of Cuban jazz music begun by Ry Cooder's documentary, *The Buena Vista Social Club*—Havana could conceivably soon give Miami some competition as the unofficial capital of the Caribbean.

Figure 3.8 In socialist Havana, Cuba, the introduction of the dollar economy in recent years has increased the opportunity for some to have relatively upscale homes, as seen here. (Photo by Jack Williams)

CITIES OF MIDDLE AMERICA

Cities in former Spanish colonies of Middle America are quite different from cities that developed in other European colonies in the Americas (box 3.3). In large part, this stems from rules of colonization and city formation that were promulgated by the Spanish crown in the early 16th century. These laws, known as the Royal Ordinances concerning the Laying Out of New Towns, stipulated that cities must be built on a square grid and oriented to the cardinal points of the compass. In the center of the town, there was to be a public square or plaza. Around the plaza would be a church, the city hall, and other government buildings, stores, and homes of the wealthiest residents (fig. 3.9). Away from the plaza, lots were allocated according to status, with the most important families receiving land closest to the plaza and the poorest living in the outskirts. In towns that had an Indian population, the Indians were relegated to the edge of town or even forced to live beyond the city limits. These patterns established nearly 500 years ago are still reflected in the spatial organization of cities founded by Spanish colonists.

In the 21st century, a typical Spanish-speaking city is still likely to have a central square, or plaza, dominated by a large Catholic church (fig. 3.10). In small cities, the central plaza serves as a gathering place and market center. In larger cities, it is a public park and also a location for public ceremonies. Extending out from the square is a grid-pattern street network. Around the square are two- or three-story buildings with shops on the ground floor and, often, residences above. In national or provincial capitals, public buildings also front the square, along with shops and restaurants. Near the city center, one finds old mansions, reminders of the wealthy families who once occupied the most central part of the city. Now these large homes are often broken up into apartments or converted for commercial use. Interspersed

Box 3.3 Ancient Cities of Middle America

In the fall of 1519, a small army of Spaniards led by Hernando Cortés and accompanied by thousands of Indian allies came over a pass on the side of the volcano Popocatépetl and saw for the first time the Valley of Mexico and the city of Tenochtitlán, the center of the Aztec Empire. The valley was intensively cultivated and the city was, by European standards of the day, huge, with possibly between 200,000 and 300,000 inhabitants. The center of the city was occupied by a huge plaza, beside which were located temples and the palaces of the ruler. The market had thousands of vendors who sold goods that ranged from food to textiles, feathers, precious gems and metals, and more. The wealth and sophistication of the city astonished the would-be Spanish conquistadors.

Tenochtitlán was the product of an urban tradition that began about 1000 B.C., but the first large cities emerged after the beginning of the Christian era. Also in the Valley of Mexico, the city of Teotihuacán began to develop about 2,300 years ago. By the 7th century A.D. (900 years before Columbus's voyages), this city had grown to be one of the largest in the world, with a population as high as 200,000. Contemporaneous with Teotihuacán were a number of cities built by the Maya in the lowlands of what are now Guatemala, Yucatán, and Belize. There are hundreds of sites scattered through the tropical forests of this area, but only a few dominant centers such as Tikal and Mirador in Guatemala and Caracol in Belize reached populations of as much as 50,000. The Mayan cities were dominated by religious structures—tall pyramids, plazas, and residences for rulers, priests, and the people who served them. The bulk of the population lived in relatively low-density settlements scattered outside the city center, where they survived largely by farming and handicrafts.

Whereas the Maya lowland cities were abandoned and lay in ruins at the time of the Spanish conquest, urban life still flourished in the Valley of Mexico in 1519, when the Spanish arrived. Mexico City lies on the ruins of several cities that were thriving at the time of the conquest, including Tenochtitlán.

The Spanish conquest marked the end of the indigenous urban tradition. Pre-Columbian cities were destroyed during or after the conquest. A few, such as Tenochtitlán, became the sites of new cities built to Spanish specifications, but most were abandoned, their inhabitants killed or moved to sites that allowed the Spaniards to control their land and labor. In terms of urban development, the Spanish conquest represents an abrupt shift from indigenous to Hispanic urban ideas of city building.

with the older buildings may be modern high-rise office towers and hotels.

Beyond the older city are residential neighborhoods. The wealthy have large, stylish houses, often surrounded by high walls for privacy and security. Modern shopping centers with specialty stores and supermarkets selling name-brand goods that would be familiar to North Americans or Europeans occupy choice sites with access to major streets.

Figure 3.9 Flag raising on the Zócalo, the large plaza in the heart of old Mexico City, part of the classical Spanish colonial city design laid out for Latin America's largest city. (Photo by Gary Elbow)

As in the past, the poor often occupy land on the periphery of the city, where they are able to settle without permission in shantytowns. Building codes are not followed and shantytown residents usually cannot obtain municipal services such as running water, sewers, or electricity. They shop in tiny home-owned storefront shops or in public markets. Middle-class neighborhoods may be scattered in both wealthy and poor areas, but economic realities make the middle-class lifestyle closer to the poor than to the wealthy.

Quality of Life Issues

As a group, the mainland countries generally rank lower on the HDI than do the Caribbean countries. El Salvador, Guatemala, Honduras, and Nicaragua all rank below any Caribbean country except for Haiti. However, Mexico, Costa Rica, Panama, and Belize all are on a par with most Caribbean countries. Nonetheless, in the case of Mexico, the HDI fails to reflect a wide division between wealthy and poor. Because of this disparity, millions of Mexicans struggle to survive on less than a living wage. The presence of such a high level of poverty in Mexico, as well as in most of Central America, means that the cities of the region are characterized by extensive squatter settlements, poorly developed municipal services, and other signs of lack of well-being among the population.

Locational Patterns

Major cities in Mexico and Central America tend to be located in the highlands and away from the coast. The reasons for this are several. The Aztec Empire, with its vast wealth and population, was a strong attraction for the Spaniards, who chose the Aztec capital as their administrative center for both pragmatic and symbolic reasons. Also, highland areas were relatively free from tropical diseases. An additional factor was labor supply. The Indian population that would keep the Spanish colonial enterprise functioning lived primarily in the highlands. Finally, the Spanish colonial economy was geared to the export of precious metals and other raw materials that were found mainly in highland areas. Ports were transit points or locations to be visited mainly when the Spanish ships made their annual visit bringing trade goods and returning home with treasure from the American colonies.

Many of the largest cities in Mexico and Central America are still in the highlands. In addition to Mexico City, Guadalajara, Puebla, and a number of smaller but locally important cities are in the central Mexican highland core. The capitals of Guatemala, Honduras, El Salvador, and Costa Rica are also in highland locations. Today, more than 15% of Mexico's population lives within Mexico City's limits and the percentage goes much higher when the suburbs and other cities of the central highlands are included. Similar conditions are found in Guatemala, El Salvador, and Costa Rica, where highland population concentrations have dominated at least since the conquest.

In Mexico, despite the historic importance of the old highland core, in the second half of the 20th century the North has emerged as the most urbanized area of the country. About 75% of the population of the North is now urban. Monterrey is the industrial giant of the North, with its economy based on iron and steel, cement, glass making, and beverages. Some smaller northern industrial centers, such as Durango, Saltillo, and Monclova, also depend on heavy manufacturing and mining, but none approach the scale of Monterrey.

Along the U.S. border, Tijuana, Juárez, Matamoros, Nuevo Laredo, and other cities began to emerge during the first decades of the 20th century. In a situation that may be unique, each Mexican border city is paired with a border city in the United States. The largest such pairs are Tijuana-San Diego, Mexicali-Calexico, Juárez-El Paso, Nuevo Laredo-Laredo, and Matamoros-Brownsville. Each of these city pairs forms a common economic and cultural zone that is, nonetheless, separated by the international boundary. Efforts to deal with common economic, social, health, and environmental problems are complicated by the presence of the border and its dual national jurisdictions.

Figure 3.10 The oldest church in Mexico still stands in the Zócalo, the heart of Mexico City. (Photo by Robert Smith)

These northern Mexican cities developed initially as trade and tourist centers, but took on an additional function as industrial centers after 1965, when the United States and Mexico created the Border Industrialization Program. This program provided for the development of assembly plants on the Mexican side of the border that would utilize low-cost Mexican labor in clothing manufacture, electronics, and other industries in which hand labor was im-

Figure 3.11 The Japanese are important players in the *maquiladora* program in Mexico's northern border cities, as seen in this view of the Matsushita plant in Tijuana. (Photo by Robert Smith)

portant. These plants came to be known as *maquiladoras* (after the Spanish word *maquilar,* "to perform a task for another"). *Maquiladora* products could not be sold in Mexico, rather they were intended to be shipped across the border without import or export taxes. By March 2000, there were nearly 3,400 *maquiladora* plants operating in Mexico. About two-thirds of all *maquiladora* employment is located in or near the border cities, with nearly half in the three cities of Tijuana, Juárez, and Matamoros. Collectively, *maquiladora* plants account for well over one million jobs in Mexico (fig. 3.11).

The long-term impact of the Border Industrialization Program is clear. Since 1980, the northern border, led by Baja California, has displaced the Mexico City metropolitan area as the most rapidly growing part of Mexico. The border states (Baja California, Sonora, Chihuahua, Coahuila, Nuevo León, and Tamaulipas) grew at an annual rate of 2.5% in 1980–1990, while the Mexico City metropolitan area grew by only 0.7%.

The advent of free trade under the North American Free Trade Agreement (NAFTA) has added even more to the pressures for growth in the border cities. For example, Juárez and Tijuana both grew by more than 50% in the past decade and now have populations of about 1.2 million each. Nuevo Laredo increased its population by more than 40%, while Mexicali and Matamoros each recorded growth rates of more than 30%. Much of that growth was NAFTA related.

Lowland coastal cities, though many were initially founded by the colonists, experienced major development mostly in the latter half of the 20th century. The discovery of vast new oil deposits in the southern Gulf coastal lowlands and offshore during the 1960s and 1970s set off a boom within Mexico. A portion of the oil income was diverted to economic development and tourism was selected as one of the target

Figure 3.12 Posh hotels and resorts are the backbone of the economy of Cancún, one of Mexico's leading tourism playgrounds. (Photo by Robert Smith)

industries. In 1967, the government identified five areas that had great development potential. All are coastal areas and four of the five are on the Pacific side of the country. The first location to be developed, the only Caribbean site, and the most successful, was Cancún. On the strength of the tourism economy on nearby Cancún Island, Cancún City grew from a tiny Indian village in 1970 to a city of more than 300,000 in just 25 years. The Cancún Island resorts receive more than 1.2 million visitors yearly (fig. 3.12). Nearly as successful was the Pacific Coast city of Zihuatanejo, which along with the nearby community of Iztapa grew from sleepy ports into international tourist destinations, also in a matter of two decades. Cabo San Lucas, at the tip of the Baja California peninsula, and Huatulco, in southern Oaxaca, were slower to develop but are now doing well. Of the planned tourism centers, only Loreto, on the east coast of the Baja California peninsula, has yet to develop.

Models of Middle American City Structure

There is no one model of city structure that fits universally in this region. Griffin and Ford, in a 1980 article in the *Geographical Review*, developed a simple model of Latin American city structure that was derived, in part, from examples in Mexico and Central America (fig. 3.13). The Griffin-Ford model was based on a traditional, plaza-centered city as described earlier in this chapter, which then expands in certain ways. The model consists of a series of concentric circles of declining housing value radiating out from the traditional city center. On one side of the center, a primary traffic artery (or arteries) led into the new, upscale residential areas. Commercial activities were located along the arteries, termed the "spine." In its simplest form, the model looks a bit like an old-fashioned key hole with the plaza-centered concentric zones forming the round part of the

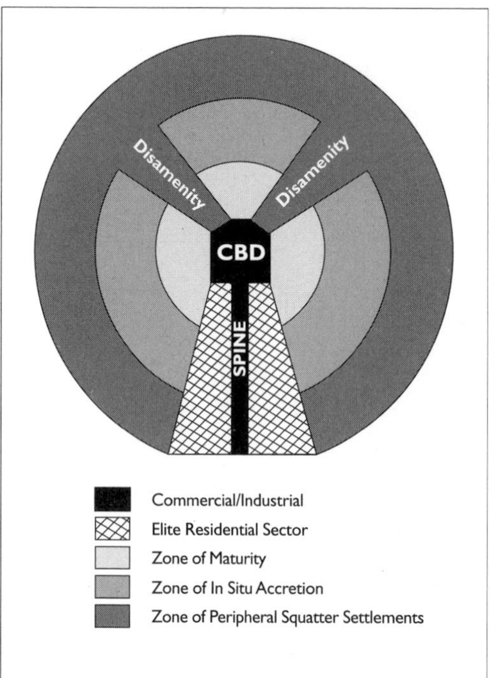

Figure 3.13 Griffin/Ford Model of Latin American City Structure. *Source*: E. Griffin and L. Ford, "A Model of Latin American Urban Land Use," *Geographical Review* 70 (1980): 397–422. Used by permission.

hole and the spine represented by the slot where the keyed plate fits.

This model is widely used in introductory geography texts. As such, it is part of the informal canon of geography. The simplicity of the Griffin-Ford model is surely one of the factors that accounts for its acceptance among textbook authors. However, its very simplicity also leaves the Griffin-Ford model open to criticism. Crowley, in his 1995 "Order and Disorder," has noted that the Griffin-Ford model does not take into account the chaotic mix of residential, commercial, and industrial land uses that characterizes Latin American cities. He proposes a model that is far less simple and orderly but that he believes better represents the reality of these cities (fig. 3.14). Anyone who has visited Mexico or Central America recently will agree that cities there are characterized by an almost bewildering array of activities that are widely distributed across the entire urbanized area.

Crowley's model reflects the lack of government control over land use that characterizes Mexican and Central American cities. To the North American observer, used to seeing cities where land uses are regulated by zoning laws, these cities do appear to be disorganized and chaotic. However, there is an underlying order that reflects their historical development and contemporary social and economic structure. Crowley recognizes the emergence of commercial zones of differing ages, residential differentiation, and manufacturing and other specialized areas of the city. The Crowley model appears to be a good fit with Mexican and Central American cities.

Representative Cities of Middle America

Mexico City and Tijuana are two key cities of modern-day Mexico that illustrate the widely divergent paths and complex mix of forces that have shaped this country's urban development.

Mexico City: Big, Bigger . . . Biggest?

A place of superlatives, Mexico City impresses with its sheer magnitude (fig. 3.15). One of the world's megacities, it is probably the most populous urban area in Latin America, with a metropolitan area population of about 18 million, according to the 2000 Mexican census. Mexico City is also reputed to be one of the world's most polluted cities and it has one of the largest shantytowns in the world (Ciudad Netzahualcóyotl). In addition, Mexico City copes with a variety of environmental hazards: it has the misfortune of having been built in one of the world's most earthquake-prone areas and

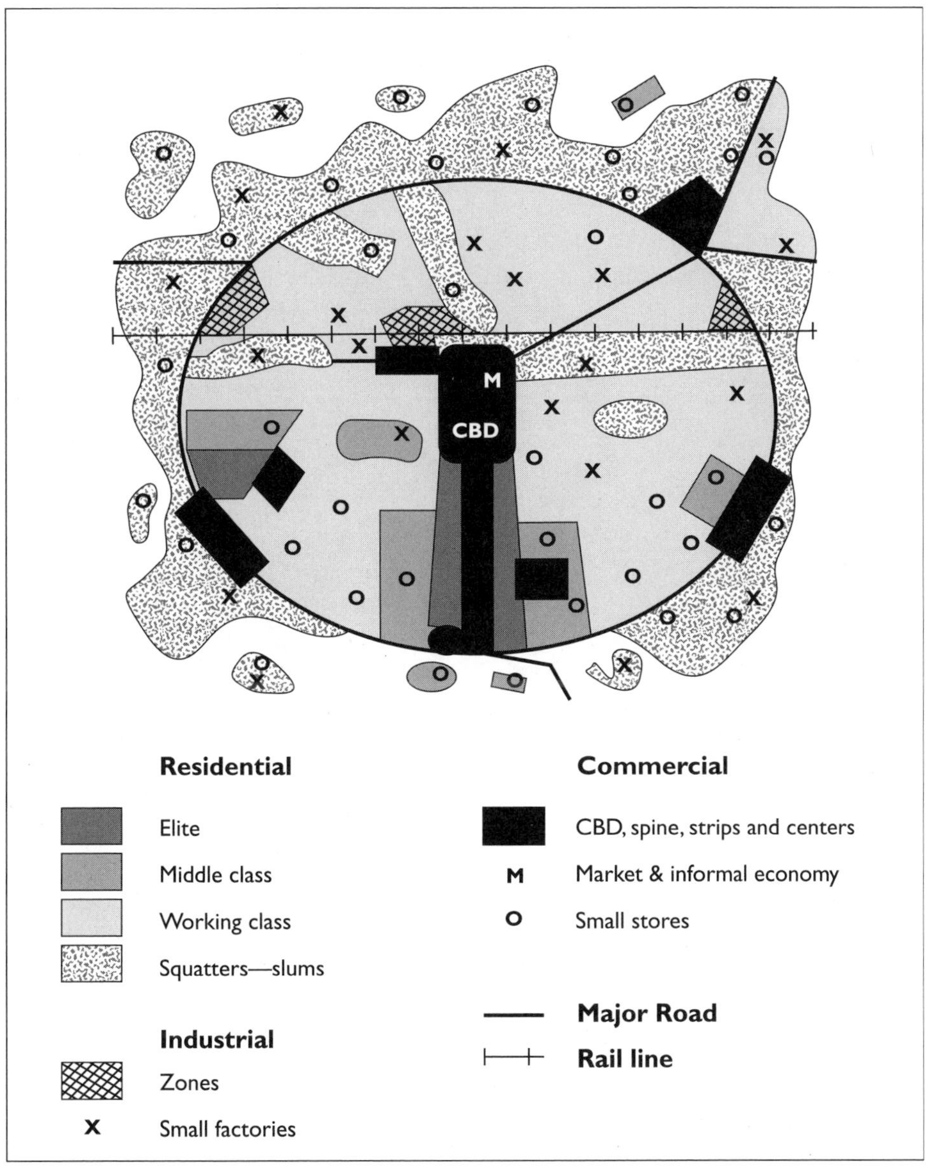

Figure 3.14 Crowley Model of Latin American City Structure. *Source:* William K. Crowley, "Order and Disorder—A Model of Latin American Urban Land Use," *Yearbook of the Association of Pacific Coast Geographers* 57 (1995): 28. Reprinted with permission.

in the shadow of an active volcano. Because of its high valley location, it suffers from frequent temperature inversions that contribute materially to air pollution problems; also, it is built on sediments of a former lake that covered much of the basin, sediments that are settling rapidly as groundwater supplies are drawn down to provide the city residents with freshwater. With such a litany of problems, it is small wonder that the city center has been losing population

Figure 3.15 This bird's-eye view of sprawling Mexico City shows Chapultepec Park and castle in the lower left. The view looks east northeast along Avenida Reforma, which has many high-rise buildings. (Photo by Gary Elbow)

for the past several decades and that net migration has been negative since the 1980s. Perhaps less understandable is that the metropolitan area continues to grow at all.

Politically, Mexico City is within the Federal District, the smallest of Mexico's 31 internal political divisions. Mexico City long ago outgrew the legal spatial limits of the Federal District and spread into 50 surrounding self-governing municipalities *(municipios)* in the State of Mexico and one in Hidalgo (fig. 3.16). As of 2000, more than half the metropolitan area population lived outside of the Federal District in these 51 *municipios.* Because the metropolitan area is divided among so many government units, control is fragmented and coordinated planning is difficult. Nevertheless, there has been some effort to provide for coordinated action between the head of government of the Federal District and the governor of the State of Mexico.

The 1940s saw the beginning of the modern period of growth of Mexico City. Favorable national government policies attracted many industries to Mexico City, and the government expanded as well, providing incentives for migration from rural areas to the city. In 1930, Mexico City claimed 7% of the country's manufacturing establishments; by 1980, it claimed 30%. For manufactured products, Mexico City's share was 29% in 1930 and 48% by 1980. Likewise, the city's share of Mexico's manufacturing employment rose from 19% in 1930 to 47% in 1980.

These patterns of growth through the mid-20th century seemed to indicate that Mexico

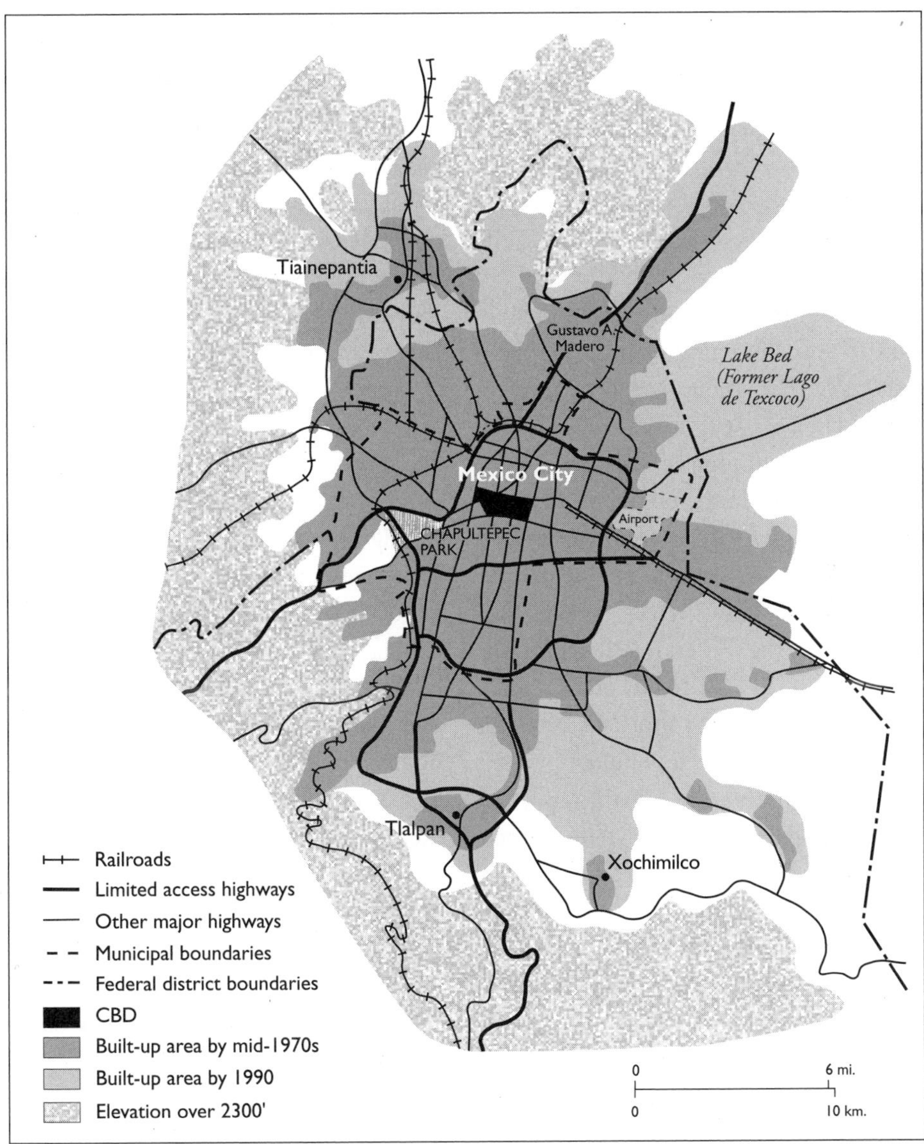

Figure 3.16 Mexico City. *Source*: Compiled by the authors.

City would grow to a size unprecedented on the globe. United Nations' projections made in the 1970s were that the greater Mexico City area would have a total population of more than 30 million by the end of the century, but it actually fell short of this estimate. The 2000 figure was 18 million. In fact, the city's relative position in the country has declined. The Mexico City metropolitan area presently accounts for a little more than 18% of Mexico's population, down from the peak of about 21% in 1980.

The reduction in Mexico City's rate of urban growth is attributed to declining fertility and a drop in net migration. The annual rate of natural increase dropped from 3.2% in the 1950–1960 period to 1.8% by 2001. Migration went from a high of 1.6% per year in the 1960–1970 decade to a rate of –2.8% by 2000. These figures show that the city's growth now depends on natural increase within the city, while more people leave than move to the city each year.

For most of the 20th century, the growth of Mexico City was concentrated in the northern *delegaciones* (civil divisions, roughly comparable to wards in a U.S. city) of the Federal District. However, beginning in the 1960s, there was a major change in the population growth patterns. The older city center *delegaciones* consistently lost population, while the peripheral *delegaciones* and, especially, several *municipios* outside the Federal District in the surrounding State of Mexico saw their populations double and triple, or more. In 2000, for the first time, the combined population of the 50 *municipios* of the State of Mexico was larger than that of the Federal District of Mexico. This pattern undoubtedly reflects the increasing scarcity of housing in the city center as older housing stock deteriorates and is not rebuilt because of the decreasing quality of life in the crowded and polluted central *delegaciones.*

Latin American cities are notorious for not being able to deal with demand for low-cost housing, and Mexico City is no exception. For decades, most of the migrants to the city were housed in *vecindades,* or tenements, which consisted of older houses subdivided into multifamily dwellings with shared services or collections of single-room residences built around a central patio where shared services were located. The latter are graphically described in Oscar Lewis's best-selling books, such as *The Children of Sanchez* (1961), in which he notes that in the early 1950s he visited hundreds of *vecindades* in Mexico City as he interviewed migrants from a particular rural village he was studying.

If Lewis were to return today, he would find a much different situation. There are still *vecindades* and rural migrants still come to them as a way to survive as they adjust to the city, but far more urban poor live in shantytowns on the outskirts of Mexico City, where they build their own homes on appropriated land using whatever materials they can find. In contrast with the past, many of these shantytown dwellers are migrants from inner-city *vecindades* and other residences in the older parts of metropolitan Mexico City, not recent immigrants from rural areas or small towns. The largest of the shantytowns associated with Mexico City, and probably the best known, is Ciudad Netzahualcóyotl. By the 1970s, Ciudad Netzahualcóyotl had a population of well over one million, the vast majority of whom were housed in dwellings they built themselves. This process has continued, as similar settlements have sprung up at increasingly greater distances from the city center.

Tijuana: Living on Uncle Sam's Doorstep

When most people in the United States think of Tijuana, they think of honky-tonk bars, cheap souvenirs, horse and dog races, and drug gangs. As with most urban stereotypes, the image is not entirely wrong, but it disguises a far more complex metropolitan area than most tourists ever see. A large part of this complexity is a product of Tijuana's border location. For nearly all of its history, the city has been shaped by its proximity to the United States. This impact intensified as San Diego emerged as a major metropolitan center and, especially, since the ratification of NAFTA in 1993.

After its founding in the late 19th century, Tijuana quickly developed as an attraction for tourists, mainly from nearby California. The growth of large California metropolitan areas within a few hours drive, as well as San Diego's emergence as a major military center, contributed to the importance of tourism in the city. Legalization of gambling in Baja California state further contributed to the city's attraction. Tijuana's location in Mexico, at the far northwest corner of the country and quite isolated from other large urban centers, limits its communication with the rest of Mexico and also helps to account for the high level of dependence on tourists and other trade with the United States.

The city's landscape reflects its orientation. The layout of the city, which was planned by a Mexican engineer, varies from the standard square grid system of Mexican cities in that avenues lie on the diagonal, though they still focus on plazas. The plaza that was planned to be central in the city turned out to be functionally secondary. Principal urban activities developed around a smaller plaza, closer to the border. This is due largely to the fact that much of the capital for the city's tourism businesses came from the United States. Investors apparently desired locations closest to the United States.

In 1940, the population of Tijuana was more than 16,000. By 1990 it had reached nearly 750,000 and in 2000 it was a little more than 1.2 million. This remarkable spurt in growth is linked to events north of the border. In 1942, the United States signed an agreement with Mexico that legalized the importation of temporary labor. In this program, known as the Bracero Program, thousands of workers from the interior of the country were attracted to border cities such as Tijuana. Upon their return, the *braceros* spent money, thus contributing to the local economy. Furthermore, some *braceros* remained in Tijuana or one of the other border cities rather than return home.

The Bracero Program ended in 1964. In its place, the United States and Mexico entered into the Border Industrialization Program, which was intended to provide work for former *braceros* and low-cost labor for U.S. industries. The Border Industries Program created the *maquiladoras,* and Tijuana, with its close proximity to the largest metropolitan area on the U.S. side of the border, soon became one of the major centers of *maquiladora* development. At the same time, the demand for labor north of the border continued unabated, and what had been legal, temporary migration for work soon was transformed into a burgeoning traffic in illegal migrants coming north for work. The combination of *maquiladora* labor opportunities and cross-border traffic, both legal and illegal, contributed substantially to Tijuana's rapid population growth between 1940 and the present.

One of the most striking things about Tijuana, especially evident on maps, is the abrupt truncation of urban development on the north, where the city meets the international border. It seems almost as if the border has split the city in two and the northern half has drifted away. Of course, what has really happened is that economic activity has focused south of the border, because this is where the economic advantages of cheaper labor, lower taxes, and fewer constraining regulations are located.

As in Mexico City, most of the poor housing in Tijuana is self-help housing—dwellings constructed by their owners on marginal lands and improved as funds for building materials become available. Generally, poorer housing is constructed in the least-suitable areas, along the sides of canyons and river courses, on the steep sides of mesas, and elsewhere where land has not been previously appropriated for other purposes. The old concentric distribution of housing quality, with the best in the center and grading lower with distance from there, has been modified by the addition of middle- and upper-income housing near the periphery. Newer middle income areas generally occupy the intermediate areas between the coast and the tourism-oriented old city.

Tijuana is in many ways typical of Mexican border cities. The border is its raison d'etre and strongly influences the urban landscape and economy. Proximity to the United States means that cultural influences from the north are evident in tourist-oriented activities and in the use of English for signs and by sales people in stores and restaurants. Influences from the United States are also evident in the large number of green card (work permit) holders who cross the border each day to work legally in San Diego or one of the other towns of the metropolitan area. *Maquiladoras* are another reflection of the linkages that exist across the border.

Drug trafficking oriented toward markets in California and elsewhere in the United States is a reflection of undesirable aspects of Tijuana's proximity to the border. Drug-related killings are frequent, as are assassinations of police and government officials who refuse to accept bribes offered by the drug gangs.

Border city pairs such as Tijuana–San Diego are to some extent integrated metropolitan areas. Nonetheless, the presence of the border makes it difficult to deal with many joint urban problems. Air pollution, for example, does not recognize international boundaries. Thus, when California enacts regulations to control automobile and factory emissions and Mexico does not, San Diegans may suffer from pollution that floats across the border. Likewise, problems of access to water, sewage treatment, and a wide range of public health issues affect people on both sides of the border. To be effective, responses must involve governments and citizens on both sides.

PROSPECTS

The cities of Middle America and the Caribbean present some interesting contrasts and similarities. Those in Middle America are notably larger and poorer and growing more rapidly than cities in the Caribbean, where, on several islands, cities can exhibit quite prosperous aspects. In both subregions, urban growth is slowing and rural areas are either already suburbanized (as in many Caribbean islands) or beginning to show signs of significant modernization (especially in Mexico), perhaps to a degree that will keep potential migrants home. The phenomenon of migrants demonstrating retained loyalty to home villages by sending regular remittances, and then by returning after decades to build family homes and fund civic improvement projects, suggests that migration and rapid urbanization may be only a stage in the life course of countries in this region. Slowing birthrates and the resultant aging of populations also portend a change in urbanization patterns throughout both subregions. Although these countries have been preoccupied with the effects of recent rapid population growth, increasing numbers of aged living well beyond their productive years will necessitate significant social reorganization in the future. As in Europe and North America, a decreasing corps of working-age people will have to support and care for an increasing population of elderly. Will families with several aged members continue to choose to live in urban areas or might more rural locations, even ancestral villages, regain popularity? Future trends may already be visible in some eastern Caribbean islands, where assisted living facilities and nursing homes for elderly returned migrants are now increasingly common in countryside locations.

SUGGESTED READINGS

Arreola, Daniel D., and James R. Curtis. *The Mexican Border Cities: Landscape Anatomy and Place Personality.* Tucson: University of Arizona Press, 1993.

Barker, David, Carol Newby, and Mike Morrissey, eds. *A Reader in Caribbean Geography.* Kingston, Jamaica: Ian Randle, 1998. Twenty-six short, readable articles on physical and human geography, such as urban patterns, agriculture, and tourism.

Crowley, William K. "Order and Disorder—A Model of Latin American Urban Land Use." *Yearbook of the Association of Pacific Coast Geographers* 57 (1995): 9–31.

Griffin, Ernst, and Larry R. Ford. "A Model of Latin American City Structure." *Geographical Review* 70 (1980): 397–422.

Herzog, Lawrence A. *Where North Meets South: Cities, Space, and Politics on the U.S.-Mexico Border.* Austin: University of Texas Press, 1990.

Kandel, Jonathan. *La Capital: A Biography of Mexico City.* New York: Random House, 1988.

Klak, Thomas, ed. *Globalization and Neoliberalism: The Caribbean Context.* Lanham, Md.: Rowman and Littlefield, 1998. A selection of articles that provide a broad critique of the effect that neoliberal policies have had in the Caribbean and of the ways that Caribbean people and policy makers have resisted pressure to conform to the global economy.

Lewis, Oscar. *The Children of Sanchez.* New York: Vintage, 1961.

Portes, Alejandro, Carlos Dore-Cabral, and Patricia Landolt. *The Urban Caribbean: Transition to the New Global Economy.* Baltimore: Johns Hopkins University Press, 1997.

Potter, Robert B., and Sally Lloyd-Evans. "Sun, Fun and a Rum Deal: Perspectives on Development in the Commonwealth Caribbean," *Focus* (Winter 1997).

Richardson, Bonham C. *The Caribbean in the Wider World, 1492–1992: A Regional Geography.* Cambridge: Cambridge University Press, 1992. The author examines the Caribbean as it was colonized by Europe, populated from the outside, and forced into a set of economic relationships with external seats of power that have consistently placed the region at a disadvantage.

Segre, Roberto, Mario Coyula, and Joseph L. Scarpaci. *Havana: Two Faces of the Antillean Metropolis.* New York: Wiley, 1997. The book traces the evolution of Havana's urban geography and built environment from before the revolution to the present.

Figure 4.1 Major Cities of South America. *Source*: Data from United Nations, *World Urbanization Prospects: 2001 Revision* (New York: United Nations Population Division, 2002), www.unpopulation.org.

4

Cities of South America

MAUREEN HAYS-MITCHELL AND BRIAN J. GODFREY

KEY URBAN FACTS

Total Population	351 million
Percent Urban Population	80%
Total Urban Population	281 million
Most Urbanized Country	Uruguay (92%)
Least Urbanized Country	Paraguay (57%)
Annual Urban Growth Rate	2.1%
Number of Megacities	3
Number of Cities of More than 1 Million	33
Three Largest Cities	São Paulo, Buenos Aires, Rio de Janeiro
World Cities	None

KEY CHAPTER THEMES

1. South America is highly urbanized, but its rate of urban growth has declined in recent years.
2. The region contains three of the world's largest megacities and a large number of cities of more than 1 million.
3. While South America was colonized starting in the 16th century, the region was transformed from a predominantly rural to an overwhelmingly urban society only in the 20th century.
4. Cities of Andean America reveal large indigenous and mestizo populations sharing urban space with small elite groups of European heritage.
5. Southern Cone cities are generally heavily European in ethnic composition as well as in urban planning traditions.
6. Brazil's cities have a Portuguese colonial heritage and urban forms distinct from their Hispanic counterparts.
7. South America's cities are poised on the global semiperiphery at present, somewhere between the more developed "core" nations and the less developed countries of the periphery.
8. Every country in South America, except for Brazil and Ecuador, is dominated by a primate city, which is in each case the national capital.

9. The cities (and countries) of South America exhibit extreme disparities in wealth, which is directly reflected in the land-use patterns and structures of the cities.
10. In recent decades, self-help movements have proliferated to try to overcome the severe imbalances and other problems within the cities, but so too have urban protest, social tension, and political violence.

South America's cities (fig. 4.1) evoke dramatic, if conflicting, mental images. The mere mention of Rio de Janeiro, Buenos Aires, Bogotá, Caracas, Lima, Quito, or Santiago conjures up scenes of spectacular natural settings, breathtaking vistas, cosmopolitan populations, exquisite colonial architecture, charming market streets, and modern amenities. By contrast, their mention also evokes images of decaying urban centers, sprawling squatter settlements, overwhelming poverty, random violence, hapless street children, congested motorways, filthy air, and polluted waterways. To be sure, both images accurately portray different aspects of contemporary urban life in South America. Just as the continent is a land of great extremes, so are its cities. Despite many outward similarities, South American cities are quite diverse in urban form, physical setting, culture, economic function, political governance, and quality of life.

South America's urban centers have long been part of a worldwide economic system. Since the colonial era, urban societies throughout the region have served as important producers and consumers within a global economy. Today, the region's major cities openly compete for the opportunity to serve as international centers for financial, manufacturing, and service-oriented multinational enterprises. Cultural currents from around the world—art, architecture, music, cuisine, athletic events—flow across South America's urban landscapes. Both advocates and critics of globalization agree that societies are being propelled in broadly similar socioeconomic, political, and cultural directions. Is it inevitable, then, that the particular places caught up in this process are destined to look and feel alike? South America's cities suggest otherwise.

Collectively, the region's cities contrast with cities of other world regions in many ways. Various factors account for their shared characteristics: a common colonial experience with Iberian urban planning; similar paths of historical development; recent internationalization of tastes, production, and technology; and ongoing conditions of economic recession and widespread informal-sector employment. Nonetheless, while similar processes have shaped urban development throughout the South American continent in many analogous ways, the diversity of national and local experiences also stands out. South America features some cities that originate with the Spanish conquest and others that derive their identity from the Portuguese. Many in both categories are laminated with the presence of indigenous cultures, European cultures such as German and Italian, and African cultures that date from the slavery era. These cities exhibit widely disparate urban forms, contrasting levels of economic development, and varying forms of political governance, all spread across some of the most diverse natural environments on earth.

South America's cities may be grouped into three major cultural-ecological regions: (1) Andean America (Colombia, Venezuela, Ecuador, Peru, and Bolivia), (2) the Southern Cone (Chile, Argentina, Uruguay, and Paraguay), and (3) Portuguese America (Brazil). The cities of Guyana, Suriname, and French Guiana are more appropriately understood in the context of the Caribbean region. Despite a general adherence to many broad continental trends, there are also significant regional differences:

- The cities of Andean America reveal a greater indigenous presence than do those of the Southern Cone and Brazil. Andean cities are divided by ethnicity, as large indigenous and mestizo masses share urban space with small elite groups of European heritage. The rapidly growing Andean cities also are dominated by an "alternative economy" of the informal sector and popular markets.
- Southern Cone cities, with the exception of Paraguay, are heavily European in ethnic composition as well as in urban planning traditions. Although most human development indicators suggest relative prosperity, these cities contend with longstanding problems of economic stagnation and a restive middle class. Despite its geographic location in the Southern Cone, Paraguay is similar to Andean countries in its strong indigenous presence, along with its generally low socioeconomic indicators and high rates of urbanization.
- Brazil's cities have a Portuguese colonial heritage and language, a unique popular culture, and various urban forms entirely distinct from their Hispanic counterparts. The Roman name for Portugal was Lusitania, hence we speak of the Luso-American cities of Brazil, which have displayed distinctive spatial patterns in their siting and internal organization of space since colonial times. In sociocultural terms, the important African admixture makes patterns of black-white stratification a key urban issue in many Brazilian cities.

TRENDS AND ISSUES IN SOUTH AMERICAN URBANIZATION

Contemporary Trends

A century ago, fewer than 10% of South Americans resided in urban centers. By the middle of the 20th century, only the national populations of Argentina, Chile, and Uruguay were predominantly urban. Today, every country is more than 50% urbanized, with Chile, Argentina, Uruguay, and Venezuela approaching, if not surpassing, 90%. It is expected that by 2015 the portion of national populations residing in urban areas will be more than 80% across the entire continent. With more than three-quarters of the region's population residing in urban areas, cityward migration and natural increase have declined in recent years, thus slowing urban growth rates (tab. 4.1). Still, South America continues to face problems associated with what arguably has been the world's most rapid and large-scale urban transformation.

The urban transformation of Latin America is characterized by urban primacy. At present, more than 30 South American urban centers contain at least one million people. South America contains four of the world's 25 largest cities: São Paulo, Buenos Aires, Rio de Janeiro, and Lima. Much of the region's urban population resides in metropolitan megacities. Yet South America's largest cities are unevenly distributed, suggesting significant spatial differences in the urban experience. Of

Table 4.1 Urban Indicators in South American Countries

Country	*Urban population (% of total) 1970*	*Urban population (% of total) 1995*	*Urban population (% of total) 2015*	*Urban growth rate (%) 1970–1995*	*Urban growth rate (%) 1995–2015*	*Cities of more than 750,000 as % of total population*	*Cities of more than 750,000 as % of urban population*
Argentina	78.4	88.1	91.9	1.97	1.34	43.44	49.31
Bolivia	40.7	60.5	73.7	3.92	3.11	28.33	46.81
Brazil	55.8	78.4	86.5	3.43	1.64	34.23	43.70
Chile	75.2	83.9	86.9	2.07	1.34	34.42	41.02
Colombia	57.2	72.6	80.0	3.07	1.92	36.80	50.68
Ecuador	39.5	58.9	70.6	4.29	2.59	27.31	46.35
Guyana	29.5	35.4	48.0	1.37	2.58	—	—
Paraguay	37.1	52.4	65.0	4.36	3.51	22.39	42.71
Peru	57.4	70.9	77.9	3.21	2.01	28.33	39.98
Suriname	46.0	49.2	60.8	0.83	2.27	—	—
Uruguay	82.1	90.3	93.2	0.89	0.68	41.59	46.07
Venezuela	71.6	85.8	90.4	3.64	2.01	35.86	41.80
Developing Countries (world)	24.7	37.4	49.3	3.80	2.88	15.60	41.20
Industrial Countries (world)	67.1	73.7	78.7	1.05	0.57	29.80	40.00
World	36.8	45.4	54.6	2.59	2.17	18.70	40.80

Source: United Nations, *Human Development Report,* 1998, http://www.undp.org/hdro/urban.htm.

the continent's 20 largest cities, ten are located in Brazil, eight are located in Andean America, and two are located in the Southern Cone (tab. 4.2; fig. 4.2). These data reflect notable variations in regional urbanization:

- The Southern Cone (except for Paraguay) underwent its urban and demographic transitions by the mid-20th century. Urbanization rates in these relatively high-income countries peaked long ago. The large cities—such as Buenos Aires and Montevideo—are growing slowly vis-à-vis the cities of Brazil and Andean America.
- Brazil is now just emerging from an exceedingly rapid and recent urban transition. The growth of Brazil's largest cities—São Paulo and Rio de Janeiro—is currently slowing, as the focus of urban growth shifts to smaller and peripheral cities.
- Andean America is at present the most rapidly urbanizing region of South America. Its cities are operating in an environment of extreme fiscal constraint and hence are experiencing severe social, political, environmental, and logistical crises.

Due primarily to urban-based industrial development, South American countries began their urban transition earlier than other regions of the developing world. Its cities today appear poised on the global semiperiphery, somewhere between the more developed "core" nations and the less developed worlds of the "periphery." While the developing countries of Africa and Asia are beginning to urbanize rapidly, South America's current urban levels already approximate those of North America and Europe. Yet South American cities are less affluent and less open socially and politically than their northern counterparts. Sadly, urbanization and economic growth have not necessarily been synonymous in South America. North American and European cities grew over decades of relative affluence, while the urbanization of these countries involved relatively small contingents of people. In contrast, South American cities have grown more rapidly and within a highly competitive and constraining global context, as well as a regional context of poorly distributed wealth and endemic poverty.

Critical Issues

South America's cities are confronted with a host of pressing social, economic, political, and environmental issues, many of which reflect the continent's distinctive regional and local experiences.

Urban Primacy and the Growth of Large Cities

Every country in South America, except for Brazil and Ecuador, is dominated by a primate city, invariably the national capital. Brazil is dominated by a huge megalopolis anchored by two large cities, São Paulo and Rio de Janeiro. The disproportionate growth of primate and other large cities emerged historically, as early colonial centers became modern *gateway cities*, attracting foreign investments, immigrants and internal in-migrants, transportation innovations, and infrastructural subsidies from governments. The concentration of population, economic activity, and political influence generates far-ranging problems, including the stagnation of smaller cities as resources concentrate in the primate city.

Urban Poverty and Survival Strategies

Although South America's megacities are centers of great wealth, this wealth is poorly distributed, a lingering impact of the hierarchical

Table 4.2 The 20 Largest Metropolitan Areas of South America, 1996

Regional Rank	*Metropolitan Area*	*Country*	*Population in millions*	*Worldwide Rank*
1	São Paulo	Brazil	16.8	3
2	Buenos Aires	Argentina	11.9	9
3	Rio de Janiero	Brazil	10.3	15
4	Lima	Peru	6.8	28
5	Bogotá	Colombia	6.2	31
6	Santiago	Chile	5.0	38
7	Belo Horizonte	Brazil	3.9	55
8	Porto Alegre	Brazil	3.4	69
9	Medellín	Colombia	3.4	70
10	Recife	Brazil	3.1	79
11	Caracas	Venezuela	3.0	87
12	Salvador	Brazil	2.9	93
13	Fortaleza	Brazil	2.7	102
14	Curitiba	Brazil	2.3	119
15	Cali	Colombia	1.9	150
16	Guayaquil	Ecuador	1.9	155
17	Brasília	Brazil	1.8	162
18	Campinas	Brazil	1.7	181
19	Maracaibo	Venezuela	1.7	183
20	Valencia	Venezuela	1.5	197

Source: United Nations, Department of Economic and Social Affairs.

governance system that was implanted during the Spanish and Portuguese colonial period. The region's growing social divide can be read on its urban landscape. It is estimated that as many as four out of every ten urban dwellers in South America live in conditions of absolute poverty. Regular employment remains elusive for a large proportion of urban dwellers. Many are forced to cobble together meager livelihoods in the urban informal sector, laboring in such low-paying and insecure occupations as street-trading, in-home manufacturing, domestic service, spot construction, and itinerant transportation. Similarly, although elite and professional districts are luxurious, a large proportion of the urban population is housed in inadequate conditions and seeks shelter in dangerous structures with poor sanitation and limited, if any, rights to the land on which their homes are built.

Urban Management, Declining Infrastructures, and Environmental Degradation

According to the terms of contemporary economic reform, municipal governments have been forced to curtail expenditures, payrolls, and services. Such conditions of extreme fiscal constraint make urban management more difficult. The gradual breakdown of urban infrastructure and service systems places enormous stress on an already strained metropolitan system. The lack of appropriate infrastructure contributes to water and air pollution, as household and industrial waste and traffic congestion degrade the urban environment. As basic services

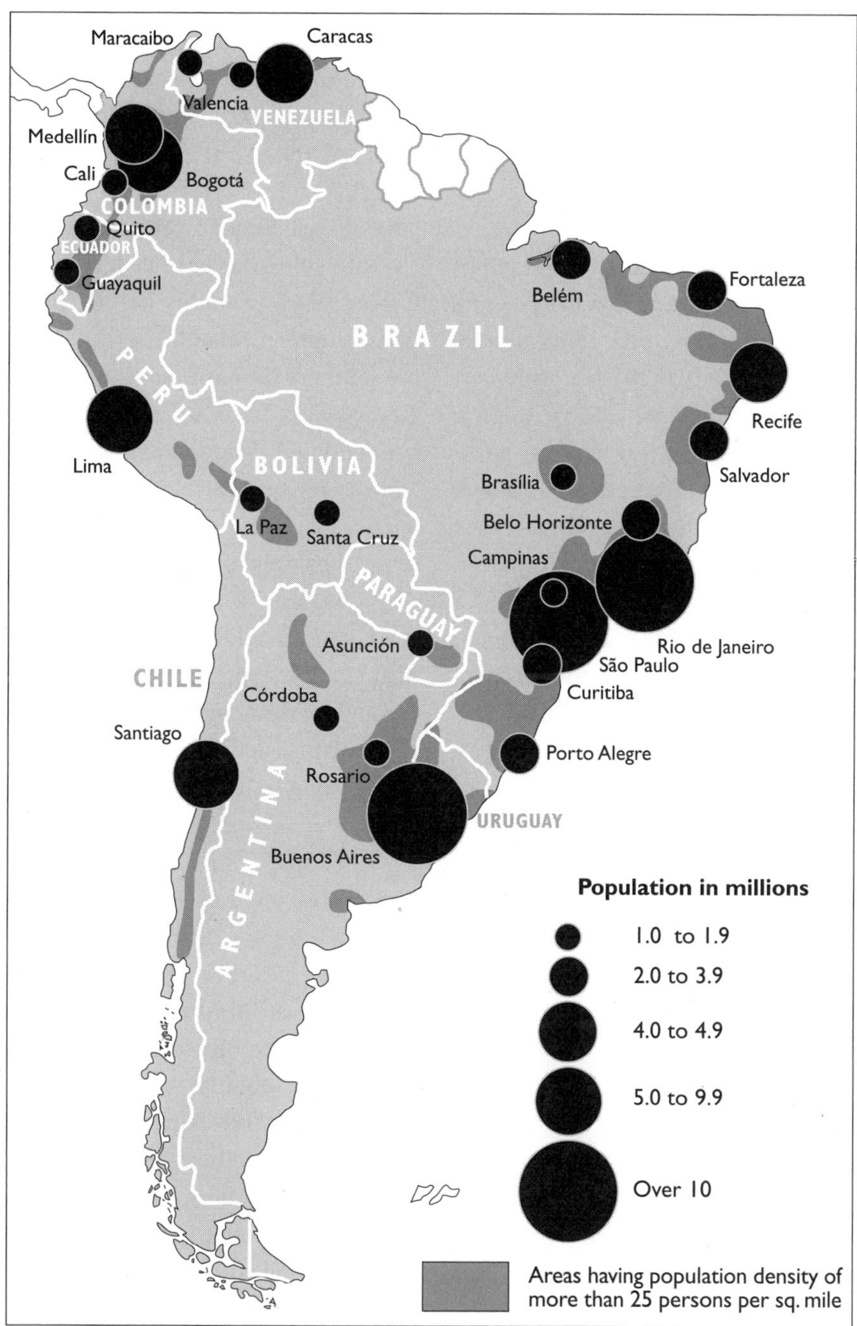

Figure 4.2 Largest Metropolitan Areas of South America. *Source*: Data from United Nations, *World Urbanization Prospects: 2001 Revision* (New York: United Nations Population Division, 2002), www.unpopulation.org.

become increasingly inaccessible, the quality of urban life steadily erodes. Indeed, mortality rates in South America's largest cities are approaching those of smaller cities and rural areas.

Social Movements

While many scholars interpret the contemporary problems of South America's large cities as yet another expression of the intense social and economic divisions that have characterized the region since Spanish and Portuguese colonization, some planners and policy makers hold out hope for a reversal of current trends. Meanwhile, many urban dwellers are taking matters into their own hands by participating in self-help social movements for housing, health care, and service provision as well as wage employment, economic relief, human rights, and environmental justice. Self-help movements have proliferated in the past three decades; so, too, has urban protest, social tension, and political violence. In short, South America's largest cities reveal significant economic polarization and social injustice. They contain a disproportionate concentration of regional wealth and corporate power, as well as a disproportionate concentration of marginalized peoples.

HISTORICAL GEOGRAPHY OF SOUTH AMERICAN CITIES

Pre-Columbian Urbanism

Urban settlements have long played an important role in South American societies. The spectacular settings and monumental beauty of the Inca cities of Cuzco and Machu Picchu spring readily to mind. The Inca, however, were only the final stage in a 4,000-year history of urban development in pre-Columbian Andean America. Even though the urban heritage of Andean America has garnered most of the attention, significant evidence indicates that large sedentary communities existed across a range of ecological settings in the Amazon region as well. Similarly, permanent settlements are known to have existed in the Southern Cone region, primarily in the Andes Mountains of present-day Chile and Argentina, at the southern limits of Inca imperial expansion. Nevertheless, the historical-geographical continuity of urban settlement is strongest in the Andean region, where the conquering Spanish later rebuilt important indigenous centers to serve as colonial cities in their New World empire. One notable feature unites settlements in these distinct cultural-ecological regions: their near total destruction by invading Europeans through violence or disease and, in some cases, their reconstruction to reflect a new and unfamiliar value system.

Early Andean Urbanism

Urban settlement of Andean America evolved over 4,000 years from isolated monumental centers on the arid coast into an elaborate network of cities linked by the extensive road system of the Inca Empire. As settlements spread through the mountains, plateaus, canyons, and deserts of the Andean region, they and the various societies that built them adapted to the exigencies of the harsh Andean environment. Andean settlements reflected their builders' preoccupation with water, fertility, and the supernatural powers believed to control them. Andean societies turned natural features into symbolic landmarks, as the siting, architecture, infrastructure, and layout of settlements followed the dictates of a sacred geography. Buildings faced sacred mountains, canals carried water from sacred springs, and city plans were oriented according to observations of the sacred skies. With time, the diversity and distinctiveness of the Andean landscape created a distinctly Andean urbanism. Serving overarching religious and administrative purposes, cities did not function as market centers in the traditional sense. Rather, they functioned as pilgrimage sites, residences for the political and religious elite, and instruments to manage society. Indeed, Andean cities were vibrant ceremonial centers designed to mediate society's relationship with nature, as expressed in the animal murals, mineral ornamentation, and textiles that adorned them.

The austere and forbidding landscape of Andean America encompasses desert, steep mountains, and tropical rain forest. Survival necessitated access to distant resources. Hence cities looked beyond their immediate regions to dispersed zones of production and exchange. They were commonly built at politically and economically strategic sites with access to agricultural and natural resources from diverse ecological zones. This was the situation of Batín Grande, on the northern coast of present-day Peru. Its metalworkers were supplied with copper from nearby mines and gold from the highlands, while its smelters were fired by wood from surrounding forests. Similarly, cities such as Chavín de Huantar, the highland city that served as a gateway community between the desert coast and the interior rain forest, were often located along natural trade corridors. As Andean societies evolved, cities became linked into local and eventually highly coordinated and centrally planned networks of urban centers. The cities of the Chimú were walled compounds; tightly clustered, cell-like buildings characterized those of the Wari; and those of the Inca were designed around great open plazas. Andean cities coordinated far-flung resources; one, Cuzco in the high Andes of Peru, was able to command an empire that stretched 2,500 mi, from Ecuador and nearby Colombia to northern Chile and Argentina. This was the Inca Empire, which rivaled the empire of Rome in size, but was built without the assistance of iron tools, wheels, coinage, or writing. To this day, the stone masonry of Cuzco's and Machu Picchu's pre-Hispanic urban landscapes is one of the civil engineering marvels of the world.

Early Amazonian Urbanism

Until very recently, pre-European indigenous settlements in Amazonia have generally been portrayed as small, isolated, and transitory clearings in an expansive forest landscape. It was widely assumed that the rain forest and drier upland ecologies were incapable of supporting large populations. The few permanent settlements that had been uncovered were assumed to be incursions from other regions, such as the Andes, where a sedentary lifestyle was entrenched. However, exciting new research is revealing far more numerous, complex, and diverse societies than previously considered. Indeed, evidence indicates that large and fully sedentary communities as well as dense regional population aggregates existed across a range of ecological settings long before the arrival of Europeans. Clearly, the aggregation of populations into permanent settlements was not the result of population movements due to European conquest, as widely proposed, but rather a response to local and regional pressures.

Most physical evidence of early Amazonian urbanism derives from individual case studies, such as the Marajoara mound builders of Marajó Island in the Amazonian floodplain or the ring villages of what is today central Brazil. However, consistently recurring themes suggest that case studies such as these are neither anomalous nor unique, but rather part of a more general settlement pattern of indigenous adaptation to the challenges and opportunities of a diverse habitat. Evidence suggests that, between 400 and 1300 A.D., the Marajoara built hundreds of monumental earthen mounds that served as platforms for settlements of multifamily houses surrounding open spaces. Similarly, ring villages—settlements of residential units arranged in one or more circular, elliptical, or semicircular rings enclosing a central plaza—extended throughout the middle Amazon as well as the drier upland habitat of central Brazil. Evidently, these patterns were a widespread Amazonian phenomenon, as similar societies flourished throughout Amazonia, including the present-day Guianas, Venezuela, and Bolivia.

Evidence reveals that substantial variability existed in settlement patterns across a diverse range of ecological settings and that the carrying capacity of diverse Amazonian settings may have been substantially higher than commonly accepted. Indeed, indigenous populations of this region were highly selective in their use of the natural landscape and, over time, choice settlement locations were not degraded but grew more desirable as human occupation modified them. As settled populations increased, it is probable that both social and spatial organization became more elaborate and enduring and that communities became more committed to village spaces—plazas, monuments, houses, gardens, walkways—and their maintenance. Pre-Columbian Amazonian society was far more complex than the oversimplified images of homogeneity perpetuated by conventional models. Moreover, the Amazon offers proof that urbanism can emerge in ways that differ from the more standard models.

Colonial Cities: Spanish vs. Portuguese America

After their initial voyages of discovery and conquest in the early 16th century, both the Spanish and the Portuguese established settlements to exploit and administer their new territories in South America. Through the Treaty of Tordesillas in 1494, the pope attempted to regulate competition between the two Iberian powers by dividing the world at a line of longitude that crossed Brazil near the mouth of the Amazon River. The line of demarcation was modified by subsequent colonial rivalries, particularly by Portuguese incursions into the Amazon Basin and the Río de la Plata areas. In their urban expressions, the Spanish and Portuguese colonies differed in terms of site selection, general morphological characteristics, and geopolitical strategies. In both cases, however, the enduring importance of the early colonial cities has been perpetuated in the continuing patterns of urban primacy that persist to this day. The enduring importance of the Spanish and the Portuguese is also reflected in the religious and linguistic landscapes of South America's cities. Roman Catholic cathedrals and parish churches dominate central cities and residential neighborhoods, but the continent is split by language into a Spanish-speaking region and Brazil, where the population speaks Portuguese.

The main center of Spanish colonial power in South America lay in the Viceroyalty of Peru, centered on the extensive domain of the former Inca Empire in the Andean highlands. The dramatic fall of the Inca Empire, after Francisco Pizarro captured and executed the unarmed Inca leader Atahualpa and thousands of nobles and warriors in 1532–1533, provided a rich source of labor, silver, and gold. Spain proceeded to extend this initial conquest with expeditions into other areas of the continent. Spain founded towns both on the coast and in highland areas. Port cities such as Callao, Buenos Aires, and Cartagena linked the new colonies to the Spanish homeland. In highland areas, the Spanish subjugated dense indigenous populations, along with their minerals, complex agricultural systems, and other natural resources. They forcibly concentrated the indigenous populations into arbitrarily created villages known as *reducciones,* razed and rebuilt the Inca capital of Cuzco (although Inca construction was so solid, many walls could not be razed), and established such enduring Andean centers as Bogotá, Medellín, Quito, La Paz, and Potosí. Town founding served as a central instrument of colonization, dominating the countryside and imposing a profoundly urban civilization.

Spain did not centrally plan its earliest colonial settlements, but new towns generally adhered to a set of standards established during the late medieval Reconquista of southern Iberia and codified in the Discovery and Settlement Ordinances of 1573. The so-called Laws of the Indies decreed the distinctive physical form and location of Spanish settlements in the New World. The Spanish-American city adopted the distinctive feature of a right-angled gridiron of streets oriented around a central plaza. The imposed urban form of the Laws of the Indies towns essentially served as an effective instrument of social control: urban morphology and social geography were intertwined. Important institutions such as the Roman Catholic cathedral, the town hall *(cabildo),* the governor's palace, and the commercial arcade bordered the central plaza. Spanish residents clustered around the urban core, often in houses built with the defensive architecture of an external wall and an enclosed inner courtyard. Indians and undesirable land uses were banished to the urban periphery, a pattern replicated in contemporary cities. These features continue to distinguish the Spanish-American city from cities founded by the Portuguese in Brazil and by the French and British in the Caribbean.

In Portuguese America, the eastern coast of the continent initially proved less alluring than Spain's Andean empire, with its rich silver and gold mines. Consequently, the early Luso-Brazilian settlements were somewhat smaller and less carefully planned. Early settlements in Brazil generally were located close to the coast, at convenient points of interchange between the rural areas of production and metropolitan Portugal. Except for São Paulo, all the towns established before 1600 were located directly on the coast and functioned essentially as administrative centers and military strongholds, ports and commercial entrepôts, residential and religious centers. To reinforce strategic footholds, the Portuguese crown began to designate captaincies, or land grants, in 1532. The captaincy system divided Brazil's coastal strip and, in theory, extended inland to the Line of Tordesillas. It allowed Portugal to combine elements of feudalism and capitalism and to employ relatively few of the crown's funds. Yet Brazil was constantly under attack from other European powers, so Portugal created a more centralized Spanish-style system in 1549, with Salvador da Bahia as capital (fig. 4.3). From about 1530 to 1650, sugarcane cultivation on coastal plantations became enormously profitable, powered by imported African slaves. With a population of 100,000 by 1700, Salvador grew to become the most important early Portuguese settlement and the second largest city in the entire Portuguese realm, after Lisbon itself.

The coastal location of most early settle-

Figure 4.3 The old city of Salvador (da Bahia) in northeastern Brazil was the original capital of Brazil and still strongly reflects its colonial heritage. (Photo by Jack Williams)

ments underscored the importance of a good port and a defensible site, so settlers often favored hilly and topographically irregular terrain in the extensive Serra do Mar, the rugged mountains that stretch along much of the central Brazilian seacoast. These towns took on polynuclear and linear forms. Irregular mazes of streets focused on a series of squares along the waterfront, as opposed to the more regular grid plans of the Spanish cities. Despite their apparently picturesque confusion of city streets adapted to the topography, Portuguese settlements adhered to coherent but flexible principles of spatial order. The colonial towns were set on defensible hilltop sites, where they prominently featured fortifications, important public buildings, churches and convents, and residential areas, all connected by a maze of winding streets and punctuated by ornate public squares. Class-segregated neighborhoods emerged, as elite mansions for rural aristocracy and urban merchant classes were set apart from slave districts.

Neocolonial Urbanization: Political Independence, Economic Dependence

Between 1811 and 1830, independence came to each of the countries of South America (except for "the Guianas"). However, throughout South America, characteristically colonial urban forms persisted, even after political independence was achieved. Until the mid-19th century, when elites embarked on campaigns of economic expansion, cities remained relatively small. Thereafter, South America became increasingly integrated into the global economy through the export of primary commodities—beef, minerals, coffee, rubber—and the import of manufactured goods. Focused on trade with North America and Europe, economic expansion fostered population growth, social change, and urban morphological adaptation. Urban growth proceeded with the creation of new transportation links, rural-urban migration, urban infrastructures, and general commercial development. First affected were mercantile cities, such as Rio de Janeiro, Montevideo, Buenos Aires, and Santiago. These leading cities in turn diffused technological innovations and capital investments to the inland centers of primary-commodity production, that is, their interior hinterlands. New urban services gave the privileged cities images of modernity and attracted migrants from the interior.

Mounting internal migration and foreign immigration contributed to South America's increasing rates of urbanization. By 1900, Buenos Aires had reached a population of 806,000 and Rio de Janeiro had reached 692,000. Eight other South American cities—Santiago, Montevideo, São Paulo, Valparaíso, Lima, Recife, Rosario, and Bogotá—had between 100,000 and half a million inhabitants. Correspondingly, the percentage of the national population living in the largest city rose in the late 19th and early 20th centuries. Commercial expansion and demographic growth led to widespread deficiencies in urban housing, transportation, sanitation, and health problems, often the subjects of reform movements. The modern city emerged as entrepreneurs invested in new building projects and planners mounted ambitious public works projects to rationalize urban form. Architects, engineers, and planners looked to London, Paris, and Vienna as the main sources of urban inspiration. For example, as the late-19th-century center of Paris was gentrified into an elegant residence for elites, Latin American architects and engineers, often schooled at the École des Beaux Arts in Paris, were inspired to apply similar styles of urban planning in their own cities. The two leading centers, Buenos Aires and Rio de Janeiro, subsequently underwent significant urban renewal programs as they competed for continental leadership. This Eurocentric focus to South American city planning paralleled the continent's political-economic and cultural dependence on neocolonial powers abroad.

SOUTH AMERICAN CITIES TODAY

An Urbanizing Century

As South America moved into the 20th century, the pace of urbanization accelerated. Today, the urban metropolis, not the rural countryside, defines the landscape of the region. The neocolonial trade status that marked South America's place in the world economy in the 19th century determined the course of early industrialization, and consequently urbanization, well into the 20th century. The region's cities were promoted as poles of "modernization," defined in terms of an urban-industrial infrastructure and an expanding industrial labor force. In reality, cities became enclaves of modernization whose existence was premised on facilitating the extraction and basic processing of primary products, principally agricultural and mineral, for an export market. Their fate was dependent upon the transfer of technology and expertise from more technologically advanced trading partners. The benefits of this were confined to the metropolitan region and had little effect on the wider regional economies.

With the worldwide depression of the 1930s, demand for the region's primary products plummeted, unemployment soared, and poverty spread. Discontent coalesced into a movement that challenged the wisdom of prevailing laissez-faire economics, which was blamed for the region's state of underdevelopment and enduring poverty. By the early 1950s, a spirit of economic nationalism gripped most South American governments, as they intervened directly in the workings of their economies. The goal was to alter the pattern of producing primary products for export in favor of producing manufactured goods for domestic, and ultimately foreign, consumption. The development of domestic industry focused on major urban centers, because they offered broad access to the national market, a concentrated pool of labor, political power, and the infrastructure of transport and communication facilities. Investment in the urban-industrial sector was generally favored over the rural-agricultural sector and life became increasingly untenable for small-scale agricultural producers. Thousands of rural dwellers were drawn to cities in the hope of finding jobs, housing, education, health care, and cultural opportunities for themselves and their families. Cities grew at an unprecedented rate, due to both in-migration and relatively high fertility rates.

Initially, most cities were able to accommodate their expanding populations. Rapid industrialization created manufacturing jobs as well as demand for commercial, financial, and public services. New building technologies, coupled with new forms of transportation, ensured that living conditions were at least adequate. Medical technology made cities relatively healthy places in which to live. However, the short-term increase in industrial output experienced by most South American economies came with long-term consequences. Smaller cities languished, as conditions of urban primacy intensified throughout the region. Rapidly growing primate cities were as dependent as ever on imported technology, in the form of modern machinery and replacement parts, fostering external indebtedness and balance-of-payment deficits.

To address these shortcomings, national development shifted from an exclusive focus on nurturing domestic industries to a focus on establishing development growth poles. Growth-pole development precipitated elaborate national development plans with a range of outcomes. In the Southern Cone, it was embraced by Chile, where it served to reinforce preexisting patterns of industrialization and urban primacy. In Brazil, it was invoked in an effort to allay the extreme differences in living standards between the more prosperous and industrializing coastal south and the largely agrarian and impoverished north and northeast. Although growth-pole development can be credited with the expansion of industry in the northeast and large-scale mining and highway projects in Amazonia, it can also be blamed for environmental degradation in Amazonia and the enduring socioeconomic disparity in the northeast. The most successful example of growth-pole development exists in Andean America, where the new town of Ciudad Guayana was founded in 1961 along Venezuela's Orinoco River, in a region without cities. Ciudad Guayana, the beneficiary of hydroelectric power and nearby mineral resources, has arguably become the leading steel and heavy manufacturing center of South America.

By the mid-1970s, many growth poles were perceived to be mere enclaves of foreign capital, since investment favored export industries, which were more closely linked to northern firms than to regional or national economies. Hence, most surplus capital left the region, precluding any significant spin-off of related firms and services. Development failed to trickle down the urban hierarchy and, instead, elicited massive cityward migration and further growth of already dominant cities. Because profits were not invested locally, municipal authorities were hard-pressed to provide the urban infrastructure (e.g., housing, water, sanitation, transportation, and utilities)

Figure 4.4 Carpenters in a Lima shantytown *(pueblo joven)* are typical of the informal economy that is so widespread in Lima and other South American cities. (Photo by Rob Crandall)

required by the growing population. Few well-paying manufacturing jobs were available to the largely underskilled rural migrants who swarmed to the cities. Most were left to seek employment at low pay and low levels of productivity, further polarizing rich and poor throughout the region (fig. 4.4)

Despite this, national governments throughout South America continued to finance costly development—especially industrialization and infrastructure—through borrowing on foreign capital markets. Northern commercial banks aggressively courted both private and state interests in South America, as nearly every country in the region accumulated significant debt. Yet each moved steadily along the economic and social development trajectory. Primate cities were as important as they were in the preceding phases of industrial development. They served as national headquarters for local ruling groups and multinational enterprises and as centers for the accumulation of capital and diffusion of a globalizing consumer-based lifestyle. Moreover, they provided living space for increasing numbers of working-class and marginalized peoples.

By the early 1980s, however, the global economy had experienced a series of unanticipated shocks that would devastate urban life within the heavily indebted countries of South America. Substantial debt had accrued during times of global economic expansion and the International Monetary Fund forced countries to exercise extreme fiscal restraint at every level of national life, in order to build up state revenue for debt service and eventual repayment. The debt crisis and related reforms precipitated a sustained period of deep recession and development reversal. Well into the 1990s, extreme economic conditions debilitated the region and its cities and, early in the 21st century, Buenos Aires ground to a financial halt because of "debt fatigue." Nevertheless, urbanization has continued, although at a slower rate. This has given rise to the phenomenon of urban growth without economic growth and to unprecedented urban poverty. In fact, well over half of South America's poor currently reside in urban centers.

The period between 1950 and 1980 saw consistent improvement in urban living standards. Most urban centers were characterized by an expanding middle class and active government promotion of home ownership. Mortgage systems became more accessible and urban infrastructure and services improved. Water, sanitation, education, medical care, and cultural opportunities were readily accessible. Although updated motorways and increased automobile ownership facilitated the growth of elite suburban communities, cars and mortgages were largely inaccessible to lower-income city-dwellers. Consequently, cities underwent explosive growth in self-help housing—primarily squatter settlements—and related programs to service them.

Since the onset of the debt crisis in the early 1980s, the advantages of urban living have declined dramatically. Factories have closed, public-sector employees have been laid off, and social programs critical to the poor have been slashed. Those fortunate enough to maintain jobs have suffered substantial wage cuts. Underemployment (the underutilization of one's skills or the inability to secure full-time employment) envelops half or more of the economically active population in many cities. The deterioration in physical and social infrastructure is evident in declining educational, health, sanitation, and housing conditions. Throughout the region, access to adequate shelter and public services has worsened. In several urban centers, birth weights have dropped, the incidence of hunger has risen, and diseases related to poverty have become rampant. Similarly, child abandonment, youth delinquency, domestic violence, and petty crime have escalated. Life chances in major cities have deteriorated.

Internal Structure of the Contemporary City: Urban Spatial Models

The spatial structure of South American cities has been an important topic for comparative urban research. The literature on Latin American city structure emphasizes the distinctive qualities of Latin American urbanization, but it downplays internal diversity within the vast region. The best-known model of urban spatial structure is that proposed by Ernst Griffin and Larry Ford in 1980 (see chapter 3). As originally formulated, the model notes the original dominance of a traditional colonial core in Latin American cities, which was transformed by the influx of modern high-rises and commercial activities in the 20th century.

Such generalized models of Latin American urban structure obscure the degree of local variation within the region. For example, one of the most sweeping, and questionable, assumptions is that Brazilian cities followed general Spanish-American patterns of historical development. Although they included no Brazilian case studies, Griffin and Ford argued that Portuguese settlements followed regular Spanish practices of the "Laws of the Indies." However, Luso-Brazilian settlements were notable for their informal, spontaneous, and essentially medieval patterns of organic (as opposed to planned) urbanization. Clearly, the early Portuguese colonial outposts in Brazil were somewhat less regular in form than the Spanish-American settlements, since they lacked the comprehensive Laws of the Indies orthogonal gridiron plan, though they contained coherent elements of spatial order. In addition, recent years have witnessed more complex and decentralized forms of urbanization than predicted by the Griffin-Ford model. As Latin American cities have grown, they have experienced greater sociospatial differentiation: new areas have emerged through processes of inner-city gentrification, affluent suburbanization, and peripheral commercial development of "edge cities." In the larger metropolises, urban realms of varying socioeconomic levels have attained an unanticipated degree of autonomy and local variation.

In response to these and other shortcomings, Crowley recently proposed a highly differentiated model (fig. 3.14) and Ford has offered a "new and improved" model that includes greater peripheral development of mall and "edge city" sectors, separate industrial parks, and selective areas of historic preservation in the core (fig. 4.5). Today, a North American–style metropolis of decentralized urban realms, composed of a series of autonomous activity areas functionally divorced from the older CBD (i.e., the multiple nuclei model; see chapter 1), shows signs of emerging in the larger and more affluent metropolises, such as São Paulo. In the end, no abstract spatial model can fully describe the diversity and complexity of cities in South America, much less in all of Latin America. A better approach may be to start inductively with the historical and geographical record of various cities and then to deduce the general regional processes that stand out.

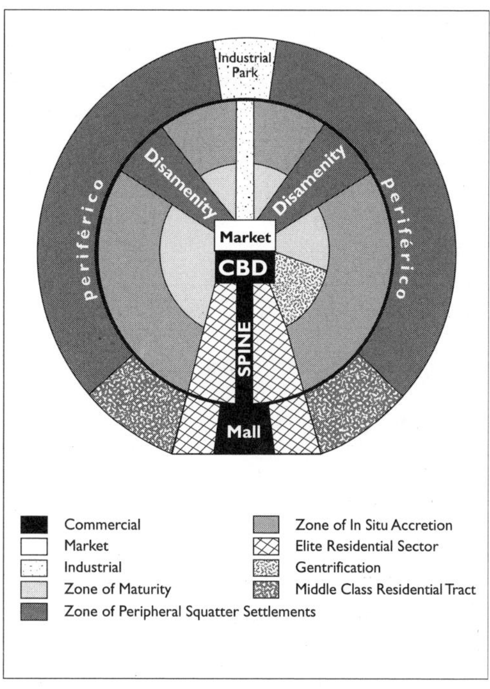

Figure 4.5 Revised Ford Model of Latin American City Structure. *Source*: Larry Ford, "A New and Improved Model of Latin American City Structure," *Geographical Review* 86, no. 3 (1996): 438. Reprinted with permission.

REPRESENTATIVE CITIES

Although contemporary cities of South America look and feel modern and international, they are beset by problems unparalleled in the north. It is tempting to speak of these urban landscapes as "dual cities" in which a modern, affluent, and progressive element has little to do with a poor, obsolete, and unseemly element. In reality, however, the modern, globally linked city and the impoverished, pollution-plagued city are intertwined aspects of the same metropolitan landscape. This landscape of extreme wealth and poverty epitomizes the region's enduring legacy of underdevelopment, economic polarization, and social injustice. Yet each of South America's cities is unique. Rio de Janeiro and São Paulo, anchors of Brazil's megalopolis, epitomize Luso-American urbanization, while Lima does the same for Hispanic-America and Buenos Aires for the Southern Cone. The case of Brasília deserves study because it was the most famous new capital city of the 20th century and a bold experiment in city planning.

Table 4.3 Populations of Rio de Janeiro and São Paulo, 1872–1996

	Rio de Janeiro			*São Paulo*		
Year	*City*	*Metropolitan Region**	*Percent Peripheral*	*City*	*Metropolitan Region*	*Percent Peripheral*
1872	274,972	—	—	31,385	—	—
1900	811,443	—	—	239,820	—	—
1920	1,157,873	—	—	579,033	—	—
1940	1,764,141	—	—	1,326,261	—	—
1960	3,281,908	4,874,619	32.5%	3,781,446	4,796,245	21.6%
1980	5,090,700	9,025,274	43.5%	8,493,226	12,588,725	32.5%
1996	5,551,538	10,192,097	45.5%	9,839,436	16,583,234	40.7%

Sources: Instituto Brasileiro de Geografia e Estatístico (IBGE), *Contagem da Populacão 1996,* Vol. 1. (Rio de Janeiro: IBGE, 1997), 25–26; IBGE, *Anuário Estatístico do Brasil: 1984.* (Rio de Janeiro: IBGE, 1985), 8182.
*Populations of metropolitan regions, available starting in 1960, include both the central city and the adjacent urbanized municipalities.

Rio de Janeiro and São Paulo: Anchors of South America's Megalopolis

Brazil's two leading metropolises, Rio de Janeiro and São Paulo, constitute the central cities of an increasingly integrated urban region. The 266-mi (426-km) expressway trip, the interurban air shuttle, and modern telecommunications link the cities as never before. With a regional population of at least 30 million inhabitants, this sprawling Brazilian megalopolis concentrates much of the country's economic, political, and cultural life. As the country has become overwhelmingly urban, the demographic evolution of the two largest cities reflects Brazil's modern urban-industrial transition (tab. 4.3).

Despite their increasing integration, São Paulo and Rio de Janeiro retain their own distinct identities. Residents of Rio are known as *Cariocas,* those of São Paulo as *Paulistas* or *Paulistanos.* The two groups are famous for their dueling dispositions. The hackneyed image of the fun-loving, easy-going Carioca and the intense, hard-working Paulista is exaggerated, but like many stereotypes they reflect particular social histories. Rio de Janeiro—famous for its spectacular seaside views and a unique popular culture of the samba, bossa nova, and carnival celebrations—has long been an international jet-set playground (fig. 4.6). By the time that Rio lost its title of national capital to Brasília in 1960, rival São Paulo had taken the economic and demographic lead in this rapidly urbanizing country. Now considered the business capital of Mercosur—the emerging common market centered on Brazil and Argentina—São Paulo has become the preferred location for the headquarters of multinational corporations. Far from a laid-back tropical seaside resort, São Paulo is known as a fast-paced, resourceful, temperate metropolis with distinctly urban charms and challenges. Such striking differences between Brazil's two largest cities suggest a significant variation in city structure and underscores the limitations of regional or continental models of urbanization.

Rio de Janeiro was founded as São Sebastião do Rio de Janeiro in 1565 at the entrance of Guanabara Bay, one of the world's great natu-

Figure 4.6 Copacabana Beach in Rio de Janeiro is one of the landmark sites of Brazil and symbolic of Rio's reputation as a tropical playground. (Photo by Jack Williams)

ral harbors. With prosperous local sugar plantations and steady trade, the settlement maintained a population of several thousand, composed largely of African slaves, until the discovery of gold and diamonds in the state of Minas Gerais led to a regional growth spurt in the 18th century. As a result, the colonial capital was transferred from Salvador da Bahia to Rio de Janeiro in 1763. After the Napoleonic invasion of Portugal, the royal family fled to Rio and the city served as capital of the Kingdoms of Portugal and Brazil from 1808 to 1815. Royal sponsorship after the arrival of the Portuguese court stimulated building, and new institutions were founded. Extending along Guanabara Bay and scaling the surrounding hills, the city acquired a linear, polynuclear spatial form.

Rio de Janeiro's status as the main port and capital (1822–1960) of independent Brazil secured its primacy in the national city-system for more than a century. Political patronage and commercial interests encouraged Rio's growth, its infrastructural development, and the continual modification of the settlement's physical site. As Rio was both the capital and the principal national metropolis, its port boomed, industry and commerce prospered, and cultural affairs flourished. By 1872, Rio de Janeiro had a population of 275,000, compared with a mere 31,000 in São Paulo.

Determined to compete with Buenos Aires as South America's most cosmopolitan city, Rio's civic leaders tried to transform Rio de Janeiro into a "tropical Paris." Using yellow fever as a rallying point, municipal authorities mounted an extensive sanitation campaign and demolished thousands of buildings to make way for new boulevards and high-rise structures. The port was transferred from the downtown core to modernized facilities on Guanabara Bay. The new transportation arteries encouraged real estate development in socially segregated neighborhoods during the

Figs. 4.7, 4.8 Rio de Janeiro (and Brazil in general) is notorious for its severe socioeconomic inequalities. This pair of photos dramatically illustrates this. On one side of a valley is a typical squatter settlement, or *favela;* on the opposite side is a posh district of upscale homes and the International School of Rio. (Photos by Jack Williams)

early 20th century. Gradually, the northern zone became predominantly industrial and working class in character, while affluent populations gravitated to such fashionable districts as the world famous Ipanema and, more recently, Barra da Tijuca. Even as Rio de Janeiro has become spatially decentralized, social-class barriers have remained in place. The poor are primarily nonwhite and the middle and upper classes remain overwhelmingly white, a racial disparity that largely coincides with patterns of residential segregation.

The main exception to the sharp north-south split in social geography stems from the highly visible presence of hillside shantytowns, or *favelas,* above the scenic beauty of the fashionable southern districts. By the late 1940s, as a result of the rapid rural-urban migration, the *favelas* overtook the run-down tenements of the central slums as the main form of housing for the urban poor (figs.4.7 and 4.8). Today, nearly one-fifth of the city population is housed in some 600 *favelas.* Providing rent-free housing on government or disputed terrain close to employment, the *favelas* have become a permanent feature on the landscape, despite recurrent efforts by authorities to remove them. Recent programs to ameliorate conditions in the *favelas* focus on infrastructure improvements and better social services, including street paving, building of hillside stairways, water provision, and creation of recreational facilities.

As Rio has grown, environmental problems have mounted. Torrential summer storms often devastate hillside *favelas.* Fifty years ago, the thick vegetation covering the hills of Rio de Janeiro absorbed most of the rainfall, but due

to recent urbanization, most of the rainfall now runs off, dislodging unstable structures and temporarily blocking major transportation arteries in the city. Water pollution is another major problem. State and city agencies have made notable progress in curbing pollution of Guanabara Bay and the popular Atlantic beaches, but much remains to be done to conserve Rio's spectacular natural site.

São Paulo's distinctive colonial origins are traced to its inland site. Jesuits founded São Paulo de Piratininga in 1554 on the gently rolling hills of the inland plateau. The area was strategically located at a critical intermediary point in the transportation routes between the coast and Brazil's plains. São Paulo's locational advantage became apparent only during the 19th century, however, when its fertile soils and mild subtropical climate encouraged the development of a prosperous coffee-growing region. The new British-financed rail system made São Paulo the chief point of transshipment for the lucrative new cash crop. By the late 19th century, the transportation network of the Brazilian southeast centered more on the emerging commercial center of São Paulo than on Rio de Janeiro. As a result, São Paulo grew rapidly, especially through European immigration, largely from Italy, after the abolition of slavery in 1888.

Profits from the coffee trade were often invested in urban commerce, industry, and real estate development. Enterprising immigrant families made fortunes in food processing, textiles, and other early industries. By the 1920s, São Paulo overtook Rio as the principal industrial center of Brazil, though it still lagged behind its Carioca rival in size and political influence. Programs of import-substitution industrialization, initiated in the 1930s, cemented São Paulo's national industrial dominance. Brazil's 1956 Development Plan designated greater São Paulo as the site of the country's first automobile assembly plant, built by Volkswagen. Subsequent factory investments made the city Brazil's largest industrial center.

Modern São Paulo began to take shape in

Figure 4.9 The skyline of downtown São Paulo is evidence of the economic might of Brazil's key commercial/industrial city. (Photo by Brian Godfrey)

the early 20th century, with demolition of inner-city tenements to widen streets. In 1929, the new Boulevard Plan provided a blueprint for opening major avenues in central areas. Large-scale demolition, redevelopment, and new transportation lines led to a burgeoning office and commercial district downtown (fig. 4.9). In outlying areas, served by trains and streetcars, real estate speculation encouraged housing development in socially segregated districts. Working-class districts first emerged in São Paulo's run-down central slums and near industry in the low-lying river basins and railroad corridors. Generally, the wealthy sought higher terrain in the city's southwestern districts. Along the Avenida Paulista, the townhouses of coffee barons and business leaders created a fashionable residential district in the 1920s, but after World War II the mansions here gave way to the headquarters of banks and corporations.

Greater São Paulo has assumed a complex morphology as a result of contemporary economic restructuring, deindustrialization, and decentralization, driven by widespread adoption of the automobile since 1950. With the transition from an industrial emphasis to a commercial and administrative service emphasis in the urban core, the once-compact downtown has been split into two nodes: the traditional business center near the Praça da República and the financial district of the Avenida Paulista (fig. 4.10). Shopping malls now draw customers to the outlying areas. The suburban industrial "ABC region"—Santo André, São Bernardo do Campo, and São Caetano do Sul—with its automobile sector and strong labor unions, faces cutbacks and job loss as industries move away to neighboring states offering attractive tax breaks to lure automobile assembly plants. Meanwhile, outlying satellites are known for their universities and high-technology sectors. São Paulo now constitutes a vast and decentralized metropolis on the scale of New York, Los Angeles, or Tokyo.

Figure 4.10 The juxtaposition of a modern high-rise apartment tower and an older single-family detached home in central São Paulo illustrates the dramatic verticalization that has dominated the city in recent decades. (Photo by Brian Godfrey)

São Paulo also now faces the problems of environmental degradation and related health concerns accumulated during years of explosive growth. Given its inland location, its concentration of heavy industry, its automobiles and buses, and its uncontrolled peripheral growth, Greater São Paulo endures heavy air and water pollution. Air pollution worsens particularly in the winter, when temperature inversions trap pollutants and prevent contaminants from blowing away. State agencies do monitor pollution and use fines with some success to force industries to install filters and to cut contamination. It has proved harder to regulate the more than four million cars and buses, now the main polluters, since automobile emissions are considered a concern of federal regulation. Despite governmental efforts, the construction of sewage and waste treatment systems remains inadequate; continuing migration to the urban periphery results in the digging of new latrines, which often pollute nearby wells. Fiscal problems have hindered ambitious clean-up programs in the befouled Tietê River, which snakes through the metropolitan area.

After decades of rapid growth, Brazil's two leading metropolitan areas thus now face the disadvantages of their massive scale, while industries have shown an increasing tendency to relocate out of the two largest metropolitan areas to small cities in the interior. The fastest-growing Brazilian cities are now the intermediate centers scattered throughout the country's interior, as illustrated by Amazon frontier urbanization. Even as Rio de Janeiro and São Paulo face the challenges of metropolitan decentralization and economic restructuring, the two cities are not likely to lose either their prominence as national centers or their key distinguishing characteristics. As the nerve centers of a vast country, these two cities have sprawled to form the joint nuclei of an integrated megalopolis with the population of a medium-sized European country in southeastern Brazil.

Brasília: Continental Geopolitics and Planned Cities

Urbanization has now spread to South America's remote interior (box 4.1). The founding of new inland cities has presented a prime opportunity for modern urban planning and industrial development, as in Ciudad Guayana of Venezuela and, in Brazil, Goiânia, Belo Horizonte, and most famous of all, Brasília. The transfer of the federal capital from Rio de Janeiro to Brasília in 1960 affirmed Brazil's determination to redistribute the population from the megalopolitan coast to the empty interior. Brasília's spectacular modern design and rigorous land-use controls were intended to contrast with more spontaneous earlier cities, seen to be plagued by chaotic urban growth and generally backward social geographies.

Construction of Brasília began in 1956 on a barren site in the central plateau about 600 mi (970 km) inland from the coast, according to a plan developed by Brazilian landscape architect Lúcio Costa. A Brazilian architect, Oscar Niemeyer, designed the city's most impressive modern buildings. The highly symbolic "Pilot Plan" of Brasília features two great intersecting axes, one governmental and the other residential, together forming the rough outline of an airplane (fig. 4.12). Federal government buildings cluster at the eastern end of Brasília, appropriately located at the "cockpit" of the plane. Called the Plaza of the Three Powers, this area includes the spectacular modern buildings housing Brazil's executive offices, Congress, and Supreme Court. To the east of the plaza lies a large artificial lake, while to the west runs a wide boulevard lined with massive government ministries. Near the central intersection of important boulevards lie the bus terminal, stores, and hotels, which in turn are surrounded by cultural institutions and recreational districts. Farther west, on the plane's central body or "fuselage," are complexes of hotels, a sports arena, and recreational facilities. The residential areas, which extend north and south along the "wings" of the plane, comprise groups of six-story apartment buildings to house government functionaries and their families. Each "superblock" of four buildings contains a school, playground, shops, theaters, and so on. Early residents and architectural critics found Brasília sterile, monotonous, and overly controlled—indeed, a model of authoritarian urban planning—and many government officials maintained homes in the former capital, Rio de Janeiro. In time, however, Brasília filled in with businesses and services and, with the new amenities, the capital developed a certain character. In fact, the United Nations recently designated Brasília a world heritage site, calling it "a landmark in the history of town planning."

Away from the central Pilot Plan of the new capital, spontaneous shantytowns and informal construction quickly proliferated in the federal district's nine satellite cities. Family housing was not provided for the capital's construction crews and other workers, so unplanned communities quickly arose some distance from the attractive residential superblocks of the city center. Several of the older settlements, like Taguatinga, are now affluent centers with good public services, while other, newer areas are still in rudimentary conditions. The bulk of the federal district's population of two million now resides in the satellite cities surrounding the central city.

Despite the widespread criticism of Brasília, the federal district's steady growth suggests a successful pole of in-migration. Yet the inability to plan effectively the entire federal district, symbol of a modernizing regime, underscores

Box 4.1 Frontier Urbanization in Amazonia

In the Amazon Basin, massive and highly contested interregional migrations have peopled one of the last great settlement frontiers on Earth. The Amazon River and its tributaries drain a watershed of approximately 2.7 million sq mi (7 million sq km), or roughly 40% of the South American land surface. Although the Amazon Basin occupies large parts of Bolivia, Peru, Ecuador, Colombia, and Venezuela, about two-thirds of the region lies in Brazil. In all six countries of the basin, contemporary colonization and settlement campaigns attempt to establish national sovereignty and economically develop scantily populated peripheral regions (fig. 4.11).

Figure 4.11 The fledgling boomtown of Xinguara is typical of the Amazon settlement frontier in recent decades. (Photo by Brian Godfrey)

These contemporary projects have resulted in one of the continent's most rapid and disorderly processes of frontier urbanization. Urbanization has been most dramatic in Brazilian Amazonia, which became predominantly urbanized during the late 1970s; by 1991, the population of the North Region of Brazil was about 58% urban. The growth of the number of urban centers has been phenomenal; only 22 centers had more than 5,000 inhabitants in 1960, as opposed to 133 by 1991.

Previous historical boom-bust cycles in natural resources—such as rubber, gold, and diamonds—resulted in two large metropolises in Brazilian Amazonia: Belém and Manaus. Founded during colonial times as defensive and commercial nuclei, these and other regional cities burgeoned during the height of the trade in natural rubber (ca. 1870–1910). Yet both northern cities remained insular and inaccessible by land transportation until the construction of the national highways in the 1960s and 1970s. Subsequently, the cities burgeoned as Amazonian development poles and industrial centers. New housing in these circumscribed riverine cities has come partly from residential towers in central areas, but mainly from self-constructed housing in peripheral, low-lying zones subject to flooding by tides and rains. A large proportion of the metropolitan populations now resides in such precarious peripheral shantytowns.

Even as Belém and Manaus grow to unprecedented sizes, the most significant regional transformation now proceeds in the small towns and medium-sized cities of the interior, which generally experience the highest rates of urban growth. For example, the cattle and timber boomtown of Paragominas (named for its many migrants from the states of Para, Goias, and Minas Gerais) grew by the astronomical rate of 17% over the 21-year period to approach a population of 50,000 by the early 1990s. As in innumerable other regional frontier cities, the transformation of this small town into a booming city has raised considerable problems relating to urban infrastructure, housing, and social services.

Although Brazil's Amazon expansionism attracts significant attention, the Andean countries also have vast, scantily populated, and historically remote eastern regions. In the 1960s, Peru envisioned a Marginal Jungle Highway, which would encircle the upper Amazon Basin from Venezuela to Bolivia. The pan-Andean road network would have linked the various countries and provided a unifying basis for planned urbanization of the upper Amazon settlement frontier. Although territorial suspicions among the Andean countries prevented the full implementation of the ambitious highway network and settlement program envisioned in the original plan, the various governments subsequently all built new roads and launched colonization schemes in their own territories. Most schemes were intended to spur inland migration and thus alleviate crowding in coastal cities. The discovery of oil, gold, diamonds, copper, and other minerals also has fueled inland migrations. The Amazon region will continue to figure prominently in South America's urban development in this century.

the persistence of familiar social problems, such as poverty, self-constructed housing, and the informal sector. The experience of Brasília speaks to the difficulty of implementing centralized planning in a developing country beset by high levels of income concentration and a dearth of basic public services.

Lima: Hyperurbanization at the Global Margin

Historical and modern, cosmopolitan and deprived, luxurious and squalid, problem-plagued and splendid—this is Lima. Although the Lima of today bears slight resemblance to

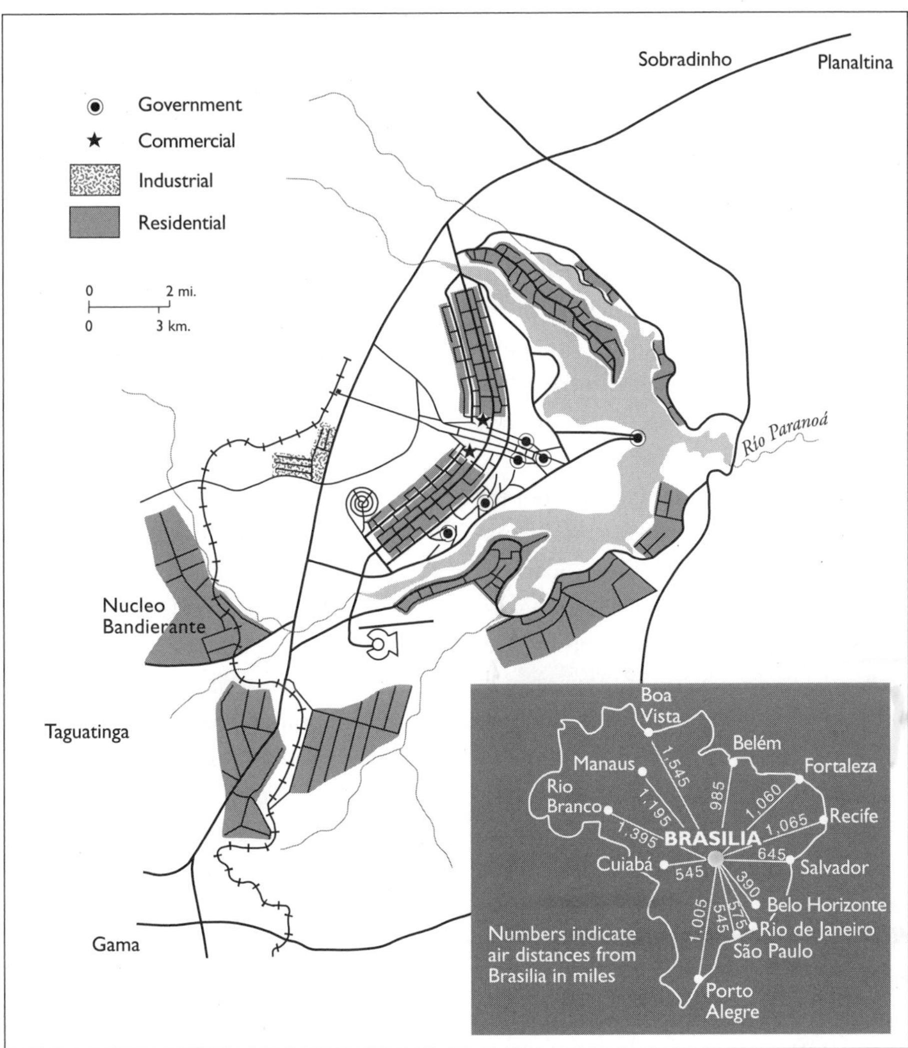

Figure 4.12 Brasília. *Source*: Compiled by the authors.

the settlement established nearly five centuries ago, its most intractable problems date to the historical processes of development and underdevelopment that have shaped the world economy since that time.

Since its founding by the Spanish in 1535, Lima's fate has been interwoven with that of the world capitalist system. Initially, the city served as a point of contact between Spain and its colonial empire in South America, the vast Viceroyalty of Peru, which encompassed most of Andean America and the Southern Cone. Lima quickly evolved into a transshipment point for the mineral, agricultural, and textile wealth extracted from the Andean interior and ultimately it was a market for finished goods produced in more prosperous regions of the world. Lima, capital of Peru since independence, is centrally located on South America's Pacific coast. Along with its port, Callao,

Lima is squeezed into a narrow coastal desert between the Pacific and the Andes. The cold, northward-flowing Humboldt Current creates the heavy, chilling mist that blankets Lima from May through December. The humid and cold ocean air interacts with the dry stable air over the adjacent land to create the unusual combination of heavy cloud cover, high humidity, and little rainfall. Nevertheless, the region can spring into fluorescence with water from the many short rivers that tumble out of the Andean highlands. In fact, some of the most fertile agricultural land in Peru is found along the coast, where a plantation economy took hold during the colonial era and the majority of export crops are cultivated today.

The original site of Lima was located several kilometers inland, along the southern bank of the Río Rímac, from which the city takes its name. Bays on either side of the mouth of the Rímac formed a natural harbor. The natural advantages of the site supported complex civilizations for at least 4,000 years prior to the arrival of the Spanish conquistadors. The site, however, also had its perils: the region is prone to frequent earthquakes, flooding, drought, and other disturbances.

Although Lima was founded before the Laws of the Indies, its founding anticipated them. Hence, the city was laid out in a grid pattern, with streets radiating from a central plaza in a regular east-west and north-south pattern (fig. 4.13). Official buildings and residences of the principal conquistadors were erected around the central plaza. Lima's development was further influenced by its proximity to the Rímac River, which served as a resource for irrigation and waste disposal. Although architecture was Spanish in style and inspiration, the environmental features of coastal Peru influenced it. The dry, temperate climate allowed the use of flat roofs and light materials. The scarcity of local stone necessitated the use of wood and adobe. Frequent tremors limited buildings to two stories. Long vistas of bare adobe walls, interrupted by elegantly carved wooden doors, were the architectural norm of early Lima. In the late 17th century, a surge in the construction of monumental buildings added grandiose Baroque designs. Diagonals—some following pre-Columbian indigenous roads—eased the rigid grid of streets, while numerous small plazas enhanced public space.

Lima quickly emerged as the center of wealth, power, and royal justice for the entire Viceroyalty of Peru. In 1551, the first university in the Western Hemisphere, La Universidad de San Marcos, was founded there. By the close of the 17th century, Lima contained over 30,000 people and displayed all the essentials of a cosmopolitan center and primate city. Its intensely artistic lifestyle confirmed it as the unrivaled capital of Spanish-American high culture. Beyond the ostentation of colonial elites, however, there existed another Lima. Most Limeños subsisted in conditions of poverty and privation. The city was extremely unsanitary and epidemics were common.

Independence in 1821 did little to change the social system or regional hegemony of Lima. However, the demolition of the city's walls in the latter half of the century set in motion a process of significant alteration. A beltway was constructed along the path of the demolished walls, more bridges were built over the Rímac, and broad avenues and rail lines were built to the coast, where upper-class suburbs took hold. By the end of the 19th century, Lima could be considered a fully modern city. Installation of a new sanitation system greatly diminished the incidence of water-borne disease. Electricity throughout the city brought light to homes and power to industry. Trolleys,

Figure 4.13 Plaza Bolívar in downtown Lima is a world heritage site. (Photo by Rob Crandall)

bicycles, and automobiles facilitated movement throughout the city. Medical facilities were improved, fire companies were established, and police protection was extended. For the first time, the death rate in Lima dropped below the birth rate. Meanwhile, population growth, agricultural stagnation, and economic injustice were making life in rural Peru increasingly untenable and set off an early process of rural-to-urban migration.

Demographic growth quickly pushed Lima beyond its old colonial perimeter. Urban development took hold along a set of axes, each of which had a distinctive character. The area westward to the port of Callao became the city's industrial corridor; the seacoast to the south developed into an elite residential zone; and small industry intermingled with working-class housing to the east. Small middle-class and upper-class communities sprang up in the open country between Lima and the coast. By 1960, the areas radiating from the old Lima center to the Pacific coast were fully urbanized. Shantytowns were commonplace in the desert regions to the north and south of the city (fig. 4.14).

Migration to Lima has occurred in a series of waves, each generating distinct changes within the city. Until World War II, mostly rural elites and people from nearby provinces migrated to Lima. Many had family contacts or skills to secure employment. In the two to three decades following the war, migration became a more generalized phenomenon, as people from all regions, lured by new industry, found their way to the city. Finally, the political and economic crisis of the 1980s and 1990s brought an influx of poorly prepared and highly traumatized displaced persons, primarily from the southern highlands, seeking safety and refuge. In relatively short order, provincial migrants and their offspring transformed Lima from a bastion of elitist *creole* culture (European culture within America) into a microcosm of contemporary

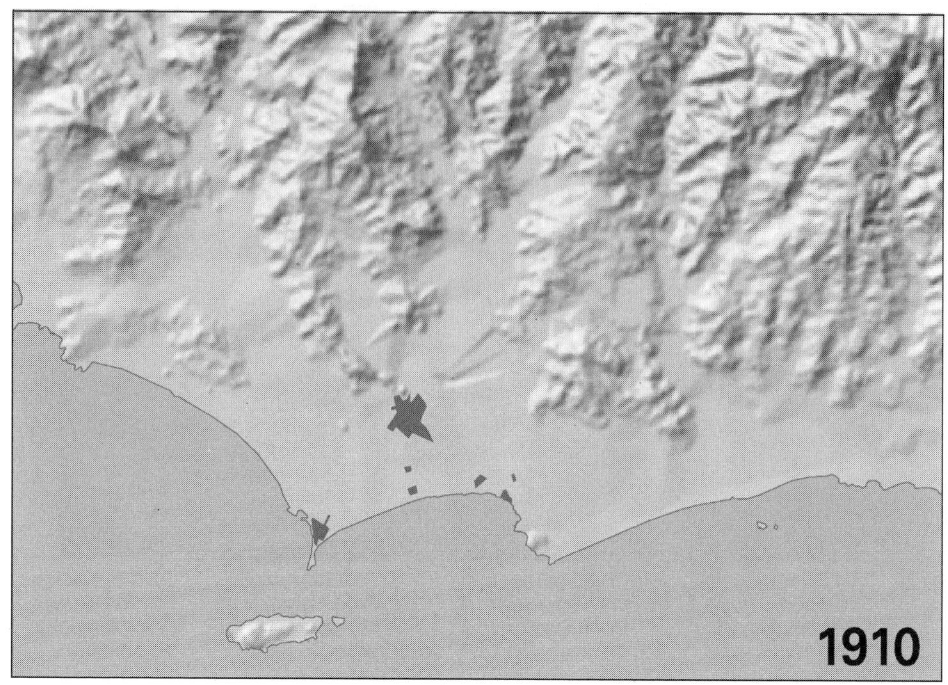

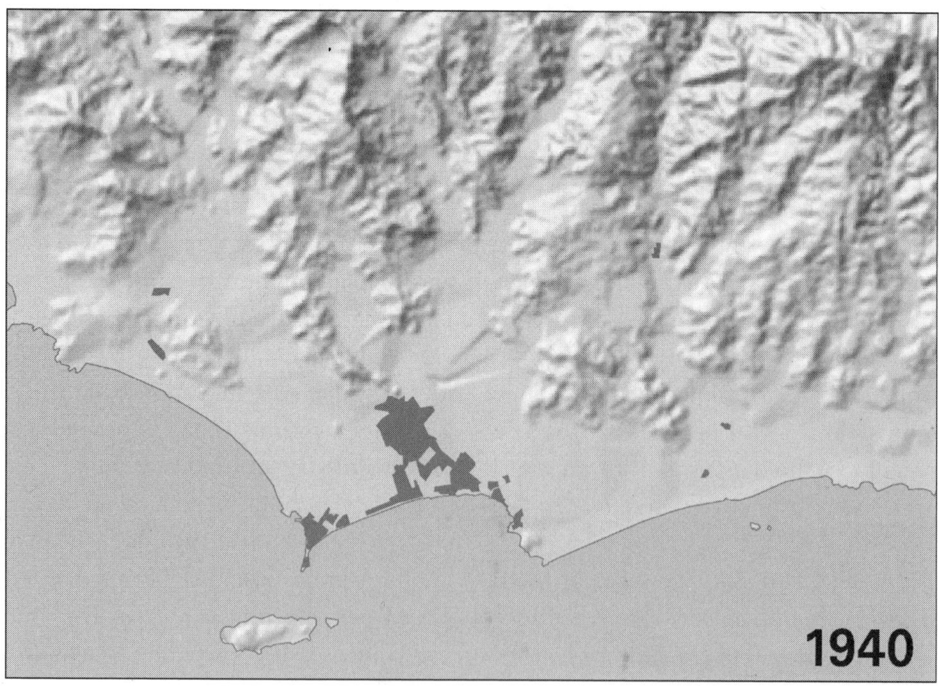

Figure 4.14 Growth of Lima, 1910–2000. *Source*: Centro de Promocion de la Cartographia en el Peru, Avda. Arequipa 2625, Lima 14, Peru

1970

2000

Peru. Today, food, music, dance, crafts, accents, and dress from every region of Peru are found in Lima. Migrant families maintain close ties with their provincial communities. Indeed, many informal housing communities are named for particular provincial communities, while provincial clubs can be found in nearly all urban neighborhoods.

Demographic growth has reinforced the city's primacy. Lima dominates all aspects of national life. Peru's most recent census (1990) indicates that more than 70% of the national population currently resides in cities, with 40% of that population living in greater Lima. Today, upwards of 7 million people live in the metropolitan region, which is more than ten times larger than the next city, Arequipa. Ironically, Lima's primate status is the cause and effect of growth. Due to its location, Lima has long served as the gateway between the outside world and the rest of the country. The concentration of political influence, capital, industry, communications, labor force, and consumers induces further concentration of all these activities. A recent study indicates that Lima accounts for approximately 70% of industrial output, 90% of federal taxes, half of public employees, 75% of the country's phones, 80% of all bank loans and consumer purchases, and 98% of all private investment (excluding mining). Moreover, Lima houses the country's most prestigious institutions of research, learning, and culture.

Today in downtown Lima, ornate colonial architecture contrasts sharply with the modern high-rise buildings that accommodate banks, law firms, businesses, and government services. Most of the remaining colonial mansions have been subdivided into slum housing that accommodates as many as 50 families per building. The enclosed wooden balconies that typified the colonial city have become a point of interest for preservation. In 1991, much of old Lima was designated a UNESCO (UN Educational, Scientific, and Cultural Organization) world heritage site. There is little evidence of gentrification in Lima. Instead, many government agencies and private businesses have moved their offices to the less congested and more secure suburbs. Indeed, the most defining feature of Lima is its expansive *barriadas*, which have been euphemistically renamed *pueblos jovenes* (young towns) and most recently *asentimientos humanos* (human settlements). Hundreds of thousands of shanties have been constructed on the barren, unoccupied slopes that rise above the red-tiled roofs of the inner suburbs and on the flat desert benches that encircle Lima (fig. 4.15). In four short decades, shantytown housing has become the norm in Lima; approximately half of the city's population is estimated to reside in *asentimientos humanos*. Many of these settlements have evolved into permanent communities, having been awarded titles to land and provided basic services. Still others languish in poverty and neglect. Indeed, the only serious outbreak of cholera to occur in the hemisphere in the 20th century began in a shantytown outside Lima in 1991.

The social fabric of present-day Lima is more complex than ever. Race, ethnicity, and class defy easy classification. The enduring difference is that between the rich and influential on the one hand and the poor and powerless on the other. This is visible on the urban landscape. Wealthy Limeños continue the process begun centuries ago of distancing themselves from the poor. Now they are moving not simply to the traditionally more elite western districts of the city, but also beyond to quasirural settings to the east as well as the more distant seaside communities to the north and south. Private security, gated communities, and chauffeurs are markers of their

Figure 4.15 A shantytown *(pueblo joven)* outside of Lima. (Photo by Rob Crandall)

attempt to withdraw. Notwithstanding, luxury and squalor exist side by side. As family stores give way to chic boutiques and hygienic supermarkets in upscale neighborhoods, they in turn are encircled by *ambulantes* (street vendors) selling every conceivable item (box 4.2). Despite the municipality's determination to reclaim the city center for pedestrians and sightseers, bedraggled children join the infirm and elderly in begging.

The economic context of Lima's rapid growth has been one of increasing constraint. Since World War II, national economic policies and international market forces have made life increasingly difficult within Lima. Early attempts to develop domestic industry were financed by hefty borrowing of foreign capital and focused primarily on Lima. New manufacturing jobs were created in industries as diverse as shipbuilding, oil refining, food processing, and the manufacture of automobiles, cement, chemicals, pharmaceuticals, plastics, textiles, and furniture. However, because most of the modern industry was capital-intensive, it provided employment for only modest numbers of skilled and semiskilled workers. Thus this development was inappropriate for the majority of rural migrants who flocked to the capital in the hope of finding jobs and better lives. Ironically, at a time when migration to Lima was increasing, the urban labor market was actually shrinking.

Lima enters the 21st century in dire economic straits and overwhelmed by problems of unprecedented proportion and complexity. Due to its status as national capital and primate city, Lima has turned to the national government of Peru as well as international development agencies for assistance, arguing that Lima's problems are national problems. In many ways, neither the role of Lima in the global economic system nor the conditions of life within the city have changed little through nearly five centuries.

Box 4.2 Women of the Streets

"Cómprame . . . Cómprame casera . . . Cómprame." "Buy me, buy me," they call to the potential customers who pass in the streets. These women are not selling themselves, but rather a vast array of foods and manufactured goods. They are the street vendors, or *ambulantes,* who fill the streets of South America's cities. Street vending, along with prostitution, is one of the few occupations by which women can earn a living on city streets. Whether or not it is considered "proper" is something few women street vendors can afford to consider. They are compelled to earn their livings on the streets by the endemic poverty and limited occupations open to poor women in most South American countries.

Throughout South America, the ranks of street vendors—as all components of the urban informal economy—have swelled as the region's economic crisis has intensified (fig. 4.16). Interviews with women *ambulantes* in cities throughout Peru indicate that, although most are from humble backgrounds, an increasing proportion are relatively well-educated women who cannot find employment in their professions. Those women who depend entirely on their income from street vending tend to be heads of households; they are elderly, widowed, abandoned, single mothers, or wives of imprisoned or "disappeared" men. These women encounter the most restricted range of employment opportunities. Within their set of options, street vending is the most viable. Increasingly, otherwise unemployed men are turning to street vending, heightening competition.

Figure 4.16 A peddler *(ambulante)* selling fresh vegetables in Huancayo, Peru. (Photo by Rob Crandall)

In Huancayo, a bustling commercial center in the Peruvian central highlands, 40% of *ambulantes* are women. As to be expected, they are rational decision makers. More than half deal in volumes of products sufficiently large to gain access to wholesale prices. Those who do not deal in sufficient volume often band together to create the requisite demand. In keeping with the traditional image of women as providers of food and domestic service, they tend to specialize in sales of fresh produce, hot meals, clothing, and household items—the most poorly capitalized product lines, with the lowest profit margins. It is likely that those who sell household items and prepared foods, rather than filling a niche, are creating their own demand. In contrast, nearly the entire supply of fresh produce is commercialized by *ambulantes*. Although the majority of fresh produce vendors are women, they tend to deal in smaller volumes than their male counterparts, thus reaping less than men from this potentially lucrative market.

To assert their interests, many have turned to political activism. Street vendors are organized into trade unions, called *sindicatos,* for the purpose of protecting and furthering the interests of all *ambulantes*. In Huancayo, more than 20% of the leaders of these organizations are women. Women have proven effective in organizing their syndications as well as guiding meetings away from rhetorical exhortations and toward important business matters. Despite this, they tend to be relegated to subservient roles within the organizations—an exercise that only adds to their already heavy workload.

As women everywhere, women *ambulantes* hold worries and concerns as well as hopes and aspirations. Many, especially those who sell prohibited goods, such as raw meat, or who choose to operate without the requisite licenses, worry about harassment by the municipal police. They run the risk of losing their inventory and hence their investment. Many are bound to disadvantageous credit schemes—a cycle that ensures a lifetime of street vending. Bringing their young children to work, seen by some as an advantage offered by street vending, can be a worrisome burden for many women. Children distract their mothers, who must be alert in this competitive occupation. Children are exposed to the elements and many young ones contract respiratory illnesses and die. Once they become toddlers, they play in the streets, where they often sustain injuries. Those who are school age soon become street vendors themselves. Moreover, the streets of their cities are not particularly safe. Petty thieves work them at all hours. Not even the *huachimanes* (night watchmen hired by individual syndicators) can be trusted. They routinely pilfer the stands that *ambulantes* meticulously wrap and leave behind.

Buenos Aires: World City of the Southern Cone

Buenos Aires has long been widely regarded as one of the world's great cities. The historical geography of this national capital, port, and primate city tells the story of Argentina. As the national capital and undisputed economic pivot of one of the continent's leading countries, Buenos Aires stands as the visible symbol of Argentina's historic rise and evolution as an agricultural and industrial power beginning in the late 19th century. The city became a European outpost of immigration, urban design, and popular fashion. Once a minor colonial outpost of Spain, Buenos Aires experienced a "Golden Age" from 1880 to 1940, during which it was known as the "Paris of South America": a sophisticated city of broad boulevards, graceful public squares, neoclassical monuments, and impressive public buildings, all of which carry the impressive symbols of Argentine nationhood. Subsequently, the capital became the stage for the rise of such political movements as Peronism, as dramatized by the famous scenes of Juan Perón and his wife, Eva, addressing the multitudes from the balcony of the Casa Rosada, the presidential palace.

The city's trend-setting residents, known as *porteños* (port dwellers), are largely of European and Mediterranean descent. Metropolitan Buenos Aires has encompassed more than a third of Argentina's total population since 1960, while also representing a disproportionate share of the leading economic, cultural, and administrative sectors of national life. In fact, vast developmental disparities between the cosmopolitan capital and the often backward interior have long troubled Argentina, leading national poet Ezequiel Martínez to call Buenos Aires "The Head of Goliath"—an apt metaphor for a big-headed giant with a weak body.

The founding of Buenos Aires reflected the strategic ambitions of an expansive 16th-century Spanish Empire. After the conquests of Mexico and Peru, Spain turned its attention to securing its vast southern flank in the New World. In 1536, Pedro de Mendoza founded Puerto de Santa María del Buenos Aires (Port of St. Mary of the Fair Winds) at the entrance to a small river on the Rio de la Plata Bay. Subsequently known as La Boca, or "the mouth," this original port of Buenos Aires provided the best maritime landing available at the northeastern rim of the grassy plains called the Pampas, where expeditions could depart for the interior plains.

Lacking the local resources and cooperative native labor needed to sustain the population, and in fact subject to continual attacks by hostile indigenous groups, the original settlement at Buenos Aires was abandoned in a few years. The strategic location of Buenos Aires remained important, however, and Spanish forces refounded Buenos Aires in 1580 as a planned Spanish-American city. The plaza (later renamed the Plaza de Mayo) served as the core of the colonial settlement, surrounded by the important governmental, religious, and commercial structures. The town council building, or *cabildo,* sat on one side of the plaza, across from the cathedral (fig. 4.17). A commercial arcade lined much of the plaza. A gridiron pattern of streets radiated outward, with large plots claimed by leading families.

Despite the strategic location of Buenos Aires, the city and its port suffered from regional isolation and official neglect until late in the colonial period. Cities of the Argentine interior, such as Tucumán, were better connected to overland Andean trade routes than to the Plata estuary. The population of Buenos Aires grew slowly, to about 12,000 by 1750, largely due to the city's role as a center of contraband trade. After 1776, the city became the capital of the newly created Viceroyalty of La Plata. As official trade restrictions were relaxed, the city flourished as a port, and the population grew to about 50,000 by 1800. Soon thereafter, the city became a center of continent-wide agitation for independence. Buenos Aires set up its own government after the revolution of May 25, 1810, and all of Argentina became officially independent in 1816.

Figure 4.17 The colonial *cabildo,* or town hall, now preserved in the historic core of Buenos Aires. (Photo by Brian Godfrey)

If colonial Buenos Aires typified the Spanish-American "Laws of the Indies" town, the city's modern growth and urban planning reflect Argentina's Eurocentric modernization since independence. After decades of political conflicts between those who favored a centralization of power and those preferring a loose confederation of autonomous provinces, the national government federalized the city of Buenos Aires and declared it the national capital in 1880. This Federal District developed rapidly during the late 19th century. British-financed railway lines fanned out from the port city to encompass the Pampas, opening up a vast agricultural breadbasket to world trade. The development of refrigeration allowed transport of Argentine beef to European markets. Buenos Aires' preferred moniker may have been "the Paris of South America," but its new role in the national and international economy made "the Chicago of South America" more appropriate. Like Chicago, it was surrounded by temperate grasslands producing meat and grains and was the hub of the national web of railway connections. In addition, both cities had their urban slaughterhouses and expansive working-class neighborhoods.

As Argentina became an outpost of order and prosperity, the country became a magnet for massive immigration from Europe. More than 6.4 million Europeans officially immigrated to Argentina between 1821 and 1932, a figure surpassed worldwide only by the United States. By 1914, 30% of the Argentine population was foreign born, more than twice the proportion in the United States. Nearly half of Argentina's immigrants were from Italy, about a third came from Spain, and the remainder were Germans, French, English, Syrians, and Lebanese, with a strong Jewish component from Russia. The indigenous population of the Argentine interior, which had resisted assimilation during the colonial period, was soon overwhelmed by the government's military campaigns and European settlement. Since large estates already occupied the best lands, however, most immigrants remained in urban centers, especially in the port of entry,

Figure 4.18 The Diagonal Norte (Northern Diagonal) Boulevard, officially the Avenida Presidente Roque Sáenz Pena, highlights the imposing Obelisk monument in downtown Buenos Aires. (Photo by Brian Godfrey)

Buenos Aires. As a result, urban primacy became a permanent and pernicious component of the Argentine urban system. Although the city's share of the national population has declined due to suburbanization since 1920, that of Greater Buenos Aires has grown steadily. There was such dissatisfaction with the level of urban primacy in Argentina, in fact, that a new capital city in Viedma, on Argentina's Patagonian frontier, almost became a reality.

Rapid urbanization created serious problems of congestion, transportation, sanitation, housing provision, and infrastructure development. The old Spanish gridiron pattern of narrow streets was overwhelmed by burgeoning traffic. In addition, drainage, sewerage, and water provision had always been problems of the city's low-lying, marshy site. Naturally, the emergent country needed a world-class capital city, graced by monuments and public buildings and worthy of Argentina's new wealth and aspirations. Not surprisingly, the urban landscape of modern Buenos Aires came to look like Europe. The 19th-century remodeling of Paris particularly impressed Argentine elites, with the result that the remodeling of Buenos Aires emphasized new boulevards, grand public buildings, and fashionable commercial arteries. In the early 20th century, for instance, several additional boulevards opened in central Buenos Aires, culminating in 1936 with the Avenida 9 de Julio, one of the world's widest boulevards, centered on an obelisk visible from various vantage points downtown (fig. 4.18). The urbane air and elegant public spaces of this Argentine metropolis became apparent with late-19th-century beautification campaigns, which inspired similar urban renewal campaigns in other South American cities bent on remodeling themselves to appear modern and sophisticated.

The social geography of urbanizing Buenos Aires emphasized the importance of socially differentiated residential districts called *barrios*. Unimpeded by physical barriers, Buenos Aires expanded with the addition of new barrios and largely avoided densely inhabited tenement districts. New immigrants originally settled in central-southern barrios, such as San Telmo and La Boca: the Italian-Spanish dialect of Buenos Aires, known as Lunfardo, emerged here, along with the Argentine national dance, the tango. Older industrial and working-class districts are found to the south of the Federal District, upper-class areas are on the northwestern side near the Río de la Plata, and elite suburbs are strung out to the northwest.

The 20th-century growth of Buenos Aires has been powered by industrial and service-sector development. Import-substitution industries, begun during the depression of the 1930s and continued after World War II, offered urban employment just as Argentina's rural economy and provincial centers entered into economic decline. In addition to such common "push-pull" factors, the populist politics of Juan Perón encouraged rural-urban migration as a way to win political power for the masses. This proletarianization process has continued in recent years with the influx of impoverished migrants from the Argentine interior, Bolivia, and Paraguay. Such poverty-stricken migrants have created vast shantytowns on the metropolitan outskirts, providing some aspects of a third world city previously uncommon in Buenos Aires.

Contemporary Buenos Aires has suffered a relative decline in some ways, due to recurrent Argentine problems of political instability and economic stagnation. But with a vibrant city center and a metropolitan population of approximately 12 million in 2000, Buenos Aires remains the primate city of Argentina and one of the trend-setting metropolitan cores of South America. Despite the emergence of suburban shopping centers, office parks, and residential enclaves, contemporary urban redevelopment projects suggest a continuing Parisian-style concern with the status of the central city. For example, the renovation of the long-abandoned downtown piers at Puerto Madero during the 1990s created a new waterfront district of offices, restaurants, convention facilities, and apartments adjacent to the traditional downtown. With such projects, Buenos Aires retains a cosmopolitan air and, given the high degree of Argentine urban primacy, it probably always will. Nevertheless, by 2000 only about a quarter of the metropolitan inhabitants resided in the Federal District, while three-quarters of the population of Greater Buenos Aires resided in suburbs.

FUTURE TRENDS AND PROSPECTS

Ongoing economic crisis has amplified long-standing conditions of economic polarization, poverty, and social injustice in South America's cities. Income constraints have been particularly acute among the poor. In the decade of the 1990s, more than 25% of the urban population lived in poverty, ranging from a low of 10% in Uruguay to a high of 40% in Ecuador and Colombia. Indicators of human development—including health, nutrition, education, housing, purchasing power, and social security—have declined in most countries. Issues of employment, housing, and environmental degradation affect the poor more severely than they do other sectors of urban society. They are creating an increasingly differentiated urban landscape.

The Urban Economy and Employment

Austerity measures accompanying economic adjustment programs have precipitated conditions of economic crisis and social turmoil in cities throughout the region. The crisis has been especially debilitating for low-income and middle-income families. It is not uncommon for many urban residents to spend more

Figure 4.19 This home-based workshop in a Lima shantytown is typical of the informal economy. (Photo by Rob Crandall)

than half their cash income on food—only to barely meet nutritional needs. In the absence of unemployment insurance or an adequate social security system, most South Americans cannot afford to be unemployed. The majority of urban dwellers are forced to turn to their own resourcefulness. Research on urban labor markets in South America indicates that, although participation within the paid workforce has intensified, participation in the informal economic sector has increased far more rapidly. This is especially true among lower-income groups and the more vulnerable (e.g., poor women and children).

Despite indicators of stabilization at the macrolevel (e.g., growth in gross national product), employment problems persist in South American cities. The 1990s saw a continued slowdown in the rate of job creation and the continued expansion of informal-sector employment—now encompassing nearly half of the urban population throughout the region (fig. 4.19). Increases in real wages have favored skilled workers only. According to several recent surveys, unemployment and low salaries are considered the most pressing problems of the region. When underemployment is concentrated among certain social groups or regions, it can generate conditions of social alienation that challenge the cohesion of a society and the stability of a political regime.

Urban Housing

Massive cityward migration, badly distributed income structures, strict limits to wage-labor participation, and constricted private-sector and state-supported construction converge to severely constrain housing options for the middle- and low-income sectors of urban society. Today, one- to two-thirds of the population of any given city resides in informal-sector housing. Similar to its employment counterpart, the informal housing sector exists outside the bounds of "officialdom" in that it ignores building codes, zoning restrictions, property rights, and infrastructure standards. In South America, informal-sector housing is commonly known as "self-help" housing, a term that carries a double meaning. Most commonly, *self-help* refers to the characteristics of the homes and the process through which they are built. Self-help housing tends to be built by the inhabitants themselves, using simple—often hazardous—materials that the owner-builder-occupier has accumulated over time. Additionally, the term conjures up images of impoverished, yet well-intentioned urban dwellers "helping themselves" to unoccupied land—in the absence of a more viable option. Self-help housing communities are commonly considered shantytowns. Many settlements lack basic services, such as running water, sewerage, electricity, and garbage removal. They are constructed of scrap materials that often do not provide adequate protection from inclement weather, have limited access to services, are overcrowded, and lack the security of tenure (i.e., title to the land). Shantytowns—or self-help communities—are marginal in terms of both their location on the urban periphery and the quality of the land occupied, which tends to be undesirable and often unhealthy and dangerous. They may be constructed on the toxic "brownfield" sites, alongside noxious landfills, on steep hillsides, or in gulleys. Their overcrowded conditions are ideal for the transmission of disease. Shanties are the first structures to fall in mudslides and the first to be carried away in floods, and they easily go up in flames.

It is widely assumed that self-help communities strengthen and improve over time. Numerous social scientists have documented the life cycle of squatter settlements. They have illustrated how, after the initial land invasion, settlements evolve into consolidated and well-organized communities. Structures are steadily improved and basic services are addressed in one way or another. With time, municipal governments officially recognize the communities and extend urban infrastructure, supplying water and electricity, paving roads, extending public transportation lines, providing garbage removal, building schools, and staffing clinics. In reality, living conditions have steadily deteriorated within the self-help housing sector since the onset of economic crisis in the 1980s. The decline in real income, experienced by most South Americans, has slowed the self-help consolidation process. Shantytown dwellers have less income to spend on construction materials and, because they are working longer hours to offset their loss of income, they have less time to spend on home improvements. Self-help communities are also receiving fewer services, as utility companies have been forced to either raise rates or curtail delivery of services.

The self-help housing sector is visible testimony to the failure to plan responsibly for the more vulnerable populations in times of crisis. Despite the celebration of the self-help movement in many circles, it is nevertheless a substitute for regulated housing and urban services. Although many international donors are favorably disposed toward the self-help movement—and they display this by providing financial aid, technical advice, and construction materials—the vast majority of self-help housing in South American cities is spontaneously built without assistance of any sort.

Segregation, Land Use, and the Urban Environment

Although South American cities have long been highly segregated, the pattern of segregation is more complex today. Population expansion and variegated topography are bringing distinct social groups into closer contact within many South American cities. As intervening land is occupied, self-help communities and elite developments often exist side-by-side. However, there is little indication that residential segregation is abating. Indeed, South American cities are characterized by greater polarization in lifestyle. The fear of crime has forced the urban elite to retreat into protected areas in luxury apartment buildings or into gated suburban communities where their security is enforced by walls and armed guards and where their children are chauffeured to private schools. Likewise, glass-fronted skyscrapers and shopping malls characterize downtown areas and elite neighborhoods, while peripheral shantytowns are built of scrap materials and lack basic services.

Metropolitan expansion and decentralization have eroded the relative dominance of the traditional city center. Employment in the center is decreasing as industrial activity shifts to peripheral or nearby rural locations, and government and professional offices move to affluent suburbs that are less plagued by traffic congestion and crime. Indeed, Bogotá, Santiago, and Lima proper have experienced net population declines. There is little evidence of sustained gentrification or commercialization in most declining central cities, while empty lots close to the central districts remain undeveloped. Notwithstanding, some major cities are exceptions to this trend. For example, the Brazilian and Southern Cone cities of Rio de Janeiro, São Paulo, Buenos Aires, and Santiago have experienced less central-city decline than have their Andean counterparts, and all now have witnessed the rehabilitation of selected central neighborhoods into vibrant commercial and residential districts. To stave off further decline, Lima has converted its historic district into a world heritage site.

A differentiated urban landscape is further noted in environmental terms. As elsewhere, urban elites are more likely to enjoy the advantages and to escape the disadvantages of urban living. Affluent business and residential districts tend to be better serviced with running water, sewerage, electricity, garbage service, public transportation, paved streets, sidewalks, and public parks. In contrast, low-income districts are characterized by inadequate urban services and infrastructure. Air pollution in some cities, such as Santiago, São Paulo, Caracas, and Lima, commonly surpasses safe levels as established by the World Health Organization. The deregulation of transportation has led to the proliferation of diesel-burning buses and lead-emitting automobiles, compounding air pollution and traffic congestion. The wealthy can more readily escape these negative externalities as they listen to car stereos while waiting out traffic in air-conditioned cars. Meanwhile, the less affluent are crowded onto hot, noisy buses. The discharge of untreated urban sewage into rivers and streams occurs more regularly in low-income districts. Indeed, children who live in shantytowns are especially vulnerable to gastrointestinal and respiratory illnesses, due to the poor water, inadequate sanitation, contaminants, open garbage, and burning refuse that characterize their living space. In contrast, the better-off reside in less polluted areas, are more able to control some aspects of their living environment, and are more able to escape to country clubs and vacation homes. Indeed, it has been suggested that vulnerability to environmental hazards parallels poverty in South American cities, where this vulnerability is further stratified by race, ethnicity, age, gender, and income (box 4.3).

An Uncertain Future

The cities of South America have long played a crucial role in a global urban network and capitalist economy. Economic, political, social, and cultural currents from around the world have flowed through the region's cities

Box 4.3 "A Place for Living"

The following excerpt is about Curitiba, capital of Paraná State in Brazil and a unique city that is a marked contrast with most urban places in South America. Curitiba's remarkable story still intrigues planners and writers, who are trying to figure out how it came about (fig. 4.20).

The first time I went there, I had never heard of Curitiba. I had no idea that its bus system was the best on Earth, that it had largely solved the problem of street children that plagues the rest of South America, or that a municipal shepherd and his flock of 30 sheep trimmed the grass in its vast parks. It was just a midsize Brazilian city where an airline schedule forced me to spend the night midway through a long South American reporting trip. I reached my hotel, took a nap, and then went out in the early evening for a walk—warily, because I had just come from crime-soaked Rio. But the street in front of the hotel was cobbled, closed to cars, and strung with lights. It opened onto another such street, which in turn opened into a broad leafy plaza, with more shop-lined streets stretching off in all directions. Though the night was frosty—Brazil stretches well south of the tropics, and Curitiba is in the mountains—people strolled and shopped, butcher to baker to bookstore. There were almost no cars, but at one of the squares a steady line of buses rolled off, full, every few seconds. I walked for an hour, and then another; I felt my shoulders, hunched from the tension of Rio (and probably New York as well), straightening. Though I flew out the next day as scheduled, I never forgot the city.

Figure 4.20 Curitiba is one of Brazil's larger cities and is famous for its unusual approaches to solving urban problems. (Photo courtesy of Curitiba government)

From time to time over the next few years, I would see Curitiba mentioned in planning magazines or come across a short newspaper account of it winning various awards from the United Nations. Its success seemed demographically unlikely. For one thing, it's relatively poor—average per capita income is about twenty-five hundred dollars. Worse, a flood of displaced peasants has tripled its population to a million and a half in the last 25 years. It should resemble a small-scale version of urban nightmares like São Paulo or Mexico City. But I knew, from my evening's stroll, it wasn't like that, and I wondered why.

Source: Bill McKibben, "A Place for Living," excerpted from Annette Haddad and Scott Doggett, eds., *Travelers' Tales Guides: Brazil* (Redwood City, Calif.: Travelers' Tales, 1997), 131–32.

since the arrival of Iberian conquistadors. Today, as in the past, these global forces and the region's cities continue to shape and influence one another. Indeed, the escalating pace and reach of globalization is adding new urban dimensions to long-standing regional problems of underdevelopment, environmental degradation, and social injustice. The region's intensifying social divide can be read on its urban landscape, which is at once magnificent and tragic. South America's cities contain a disproportionate concentration of regional wealth and power, as well as a disproportionate concentration of marginalized people who are invoking unconventional means of laying claim to their cities. As the world enters the 21st century, unique circumstances and resources abound. It remains to be seen whether these will be deployed to address the historically embedded and seemingly intractable problems that have plagued the region's cities since colonial times. Meanwhile, conflicting and compelling extremes will continue to define the urban scene of South America.

SUGGESTED READINGS

Browder. J., and B. Godfrey. *Rainforest Cities: Urbanization, Development, and Globalization of the Brazilian Amazon.* New York: Columbia University Press, 1997.

Caldeira, T. *City of Walls: Crime, Segregation, and Citizenship in São Paulo.* Berkeley: University of California Press, 2001.

Crowley, W. "Modeling the Latin American City." *Geographical Review* 88, no. 1 (1998): 127–30.

Ford, L. "A New and Improved Model of Latin American City Structure." *Geographical Review* 86, no. 3 (1996): 437–40.

Gilbert, A. *The Latin American City.* London: Latin American Bureau, 1998.

Godfrey, B. "Revisiting Rio de Janeiro and São Paulo." *Geographical Review* 89, no.1 (1999): 94–121.

Griffin, E., and L. Ford. "A Model of Latin American City Structure." *Geographical Review* 70, no. 4 (1980): 397–422.

Hardoy, J. E. *Urbanization in Latin America: Approaches and Issues.* Garden City, New York: Anchor, 1975.

Hays-Mitchell, M. "Globalization at the Urban Margin: Gender and Resistance in the Informal Sector of Peru." In *Globalization at the*

Margins, ed. J. Short and R. Grant, 93–110. New York: Palgrave Macmillan, 2002.

Santos, M. *The Shared Space: The Two Circuits of the Urban Economy in Underdeveloped Countries.* London: Methuen, 1979.

Scarpaci, J. *Plazas and Skyscrapers: The Transformation of the Latin American Historic District.* Tucson: University of Arizona Press, 2002.

Von Hagen, A., and C. Morris. *The Cities of the Ancient Andes.* London: Thames and Hudson, 1998.

Figure 5.1 Major Cities of Europe. *Source*: Data from United Nations, *World Urbanization Prospects: 2001 Revision* (New York: United Nations Population Division, 2002), www.unpopulation.org.

5

Cities of Europe

LINDA McCARTHY AND DARRICK DANTA

KEY URBAN FACTS

Total Population	522 million
Percent Urban Population	74%
Total Urban Population	388 million
Most Urbanized Country*	Belgium (97%)
Least Urbanized Country	Moldova (41%)
Annual Urban Growth Rate	0.11%
Number of Megacities	2
Number of Cities of More than 1 Million	52
Three Largest Cities	London, Paris, Milan
World Cities	London, Paris
Global Cities	London

* Excluding the microstates, such as Monaco.

KEY CHAPTER THEMES

1. Europe contains neither the largest nor the most technologically advanced cities in the world, yet the cities have worldwide appeal for their urban lifestyle and charm.
2. Europe is crucial to the study of urban development because of the long history and extraordinary impact of European urban forms throughout the world.
3. Europe's urban system is dominated by the two megacities and world cities of London and Paris, the consequence of those cities' dominance of two great European empires of the past.
4. Europe has a multitude of cities larger than 1 million, but cities in general are growing slowly compared to other world regions.
5. While there is great variation of urbanization levels, most European countries are now highly urbanized.
6. European cities exhibit great diversity in style and form, the result of the region's complex mix of cultures and nations and its long history.

7. Europe has been a testing ground for all kinds of urban planning theories and schemes over the centuries, many of which have disseminated to other parts of the world.
8. Since the collapse of the Soviet empire at the end of the 1980s, cities in Eastern Europe have been struggling to redirect their development along new paths.
9. Complex land-use patterns within the region's cities are similar in some ways to those of U.S. cities, but are different in other, important ways.
10. Europe's cities today reflect the increasing universality of major urban problems and issues facing other regions of the world, especially more developed countries.

While Europe contains neither the largest nor the most technologically advanced cities in the world, the region is a vital focus in the study of urban geography for a number of reasons (fig. 5.1). First, European cities are quite old, some dating back 3,000 years. Perhaps nowhere else is the urban heritage of feudalism, socialism, and capitalism so well represented. Second, European urban design has spread across the world, so knowledge of these cities is essential to understanding the processes of urbanization elsewhere. Some of the most basic elements of urban planning, such as the grid pattern, derive from Europe. Third, cities here are interesting in their own right; indeed, the great ones, such as London, Paris, and Rome, generally come to mind when we think about Europe or plan a European trip. Finally, a study of European urbanization is made all the more exciting by the tumultuous changes that have gone on within these cities over the past few decades, especially in Eastern Europe.

An important theme in this chapter is the legacy of the history that has so strongly conditioned the character of European cities. An especially significant topic concerns, first, the way in which the development of the cities in Eastern Europe diverged from their Western counterparts during the time of imposed Soviet-style totalitarian governments following World War II and, second, the reconvergence of these socialist cities into the "new" Europe in the transition to capitalism since 1989. While the cities across Europe share many common characteristics, including bustling downtowns, a high population density, and compact form, fundamental differences remain evident, especially between Eastern and Western European cities, in terms of land-use patterns, quality of urban infrastructure, municipal governance, level of retail facilities, and city planning and architectural design.

While there is no standard European-wide definition for exactly what qualifies as a city, Europe contains at least fifty cities with a population of more than a million inhabitants. The majority of people live and work in urban areas. Europe's urban population of 390 million represents 12% of the world's urban population or 38% of the urban population of the developed countries. While Europe as a whole is about 74% urban, wide variation is found from country to country, ranging from lows near 40% in such countries as Moldava and Albania, to virtually 100% in the microstates, such as Monaco. These figures reflect the close correspondence between the urbanization of a country and its economic, political, and even physical geography.

HISTORICAL DEVELOPMENT OF URBAN SETTLEMENT

The Classical Period (800 B.C. to 450 A.D.)

In early Greek culture, the independent city-states were located mainly near coastlines, reflecting the sea-faring nature of these trading peoples, and on easily defensible hill sites, reflecting the need for security. As cities grew in size and population, bands of colonists left to establish cities along the Aegean, Black, and Adriatic Seas and as far west in the Mediterranean as present-day Spain.

Greek towns shared a number of common traits. At the center was the *acropolis,* or high city, which contained various temples, municipal buildings, and storehouses. Below the high city were the *agora,* or open marketplace, more government buildings and temples, military quarters, and residential neighborhoods. Urban facilities generally were available to all citizens equally.

Cities in ancient Greece were laid out on a grid pattern oriented north-south and were surrounded by defensive walls. Cities, though, remained quite small by today's standard. Although Athens probably reached a population of around 150,000 (box 5.1), most large places ranged from 10,000 to 15,000 inhabitants.

Greek civilization was displaced during the second and first centuries B.C. by the expanding Roman Empire. Although the structure of Roman cities was similar in some respects to their Greek predecessors—they were based on the grid system, contained a central plaza or *forum,* were encircled by walls, and were deliberately established in new territories—they had some important differences. For example, Roman cities functioned within a well-organized empire and were designed along hierarchical lines, reflecting the rigid class system of the Romans. Also, Roman cities were established mainly inland and functioned as command-and-control centers.

By the second century A.D., the Roman Empire extended over the southern half of Europe (fig. 5.2). Roman cities, though, remained fairly small. Although Rome probably reached the million population mark by 100 A.D, large Roman towns contained only around 15,000 to 30,000 inhabitants, while most places had no more than 2,000 to 5,000 people. By the close of the classical period, cities had been established across the territory, from Britain to the Balkans, and were connected within a well-integrated urban system.

The Medieval Period (450–1300)

The vacuum created by the collapse of the Roman Empire was filled by various tribes who greatly disrupted urban patterns during the medieval period. Most urban centers became depopulated and their buildings crumbled. At the same time, the constant threat of attack spurred the building of castles and other fortifications in cities in general, including some parts of Eastern Europe that had previously been underrepresented by urban development. Feudalism curtailed the development of European cities during the early medieval period because feudalism's highly structured and self-contained nature favored the self-sufficient country manor as the basic settlement type. The only urban places to thrive or even survive were religious, trade, or defensive centers (fig. 5.3). With the resumption of long distance trade after the so-called Dark Ages, many medieval towns grew along the commercial routes that crisscrossed Europe (fig. 5.4).

Box 5.1 Athens and the Acropolis

If you ask anyone who has visited Athens to describe his most magical memory of the city, you can be virtually certain that the Acropolis, directly or by association, will figure in the reply. The answer may be a recollection of dining out at a roof-garden restaurant with a view of the 2,400-year-old Parthenon (often called "the world's most perfect building") soaring triumphantly against the night sky; or watching a Greek tragedy unfold at the Odeon of Herodes Atticus, an 1,800-year-old white marble theatre nestling against the southern flank of the Acropolis. Alternatively, the visitor may cite the spectacular *Son et Lumiere* on the Pnyx Hill where, each night in summer, the city's marble crown is flooded with the beams of 1,500 spotlights; remember an adventure in Plaka, the ancient *taverna*-packed quarter that tumbles down the northeast slope of the Acropolis in such a tangle of narrow streets and alleys that even Athenians lose their way; or perhaps recall taking a night-cap on the lofty parapet of Mount Lycabettus, a little over a mile from the Acropolis and some 300 ft higher, and seeing one of the most stunning sights on earth: the Aegean sunset turning the white marble of the Parthenon to brilliant gold.

Source: William Wyatt Davenport. *The Great Cities: Athens* (Amsterdam: Time-Life Books, 1978), 6–7.

Medieval cities typically comprised a number of common characteristics. At the center was an open square for holding markets, surrounded in the larger cities by the main cathedral or church, the town hall, the guildhalls, palaces, and the houses of prominent citizens. Close to the center were streets or districts that specialized in particular functions, such as banking or the production and sale of items like furniture or metal wares. The streets and alleys were narrow and unplanned. The enclosing walls could be simple circles or take more complex forms, such as a star shape, to allow greater firepower on advancing armies. The walls, punctuated by gates that were sometimes very elaborate (fig. 5.5), often had water-filled moats or open areas outside to enhance their defensive capacity. Finally, towns of the Middle Ages were decidedly unhygienic. Given their cramped quarters, lack of air circulation, poor sanitation, and absence of waste removal or treatment, it is little wonder that the Black Death (1347–1351) progressed so easily through the towns of Europe, killing one-third of the population.

The lion's share of development during the medieval period occurred in the western and southern portions of Europe that had a Roman heritage of city building. Urban development was impeded in the areas of Southeastern Europe that were under the control of the Byzantine Empire, whereas much of Central, Eastern, and Northern Europe remained largely in a preurban state. Conversely, the Moors, who spread into Iberia beginning in the early 8th century, founded or restored many cities and generally elevated urban culture in what would become Spain.

At the close of the medieval period, Europe had around 3,000 cities containing some 4.2 million people, or 15–20% of the total population. Nearly all of these urban areas had

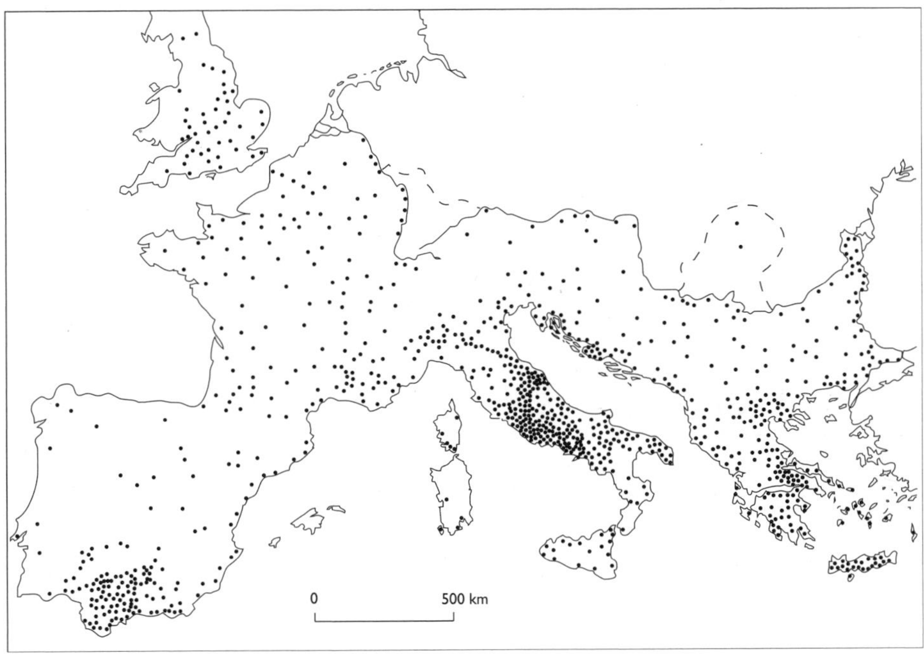

Figure 5.2 Roman Cities in Europe, 2d Century A.D. *Source*: Adapted from N. J. G. Pounds, *An Historical Geography of Europe* (Cambridge: Cambridge University Press, 1990), 56. Reprinted with permission.

fewer than 2,000 people and only Milan, Venice, Genoa, Florence, Paris, Córdoba, and Constantinople had more than 50,000.

The Renaissance and Baroque Periods (1300–1760)

The Renaissance period (1300–1550) was marked by significant changes: in the economic system, which evolved from feudalism to merchant capitalism; in political systems, with the rise of the nation-state; and in art and philosophy. Beginning in Florence in the 14th century, the changes associated with the Renaissance generally spread through Western and Central Europe, but feudalism was still going strong in East-Central and Eastern Europe. Southeastern Europe fell under the grip of the Ottoman Empire, while much of Northern Europe remained outside the progressive influences of the Renaissance.

Spurred by heightened demand for such luxury goods as spices, silks, and cloth introduced into Europe during the time of the Crusades (1095–1291), merchants greatly expanded the trade, wholesaling, and distribution functions of Mediterranean cities; later, the economic center of gravity shifted to the port cities along the North and Baltic Seas (box 5.2).

Changes in the political system, in particular the growth of countries with national capitals within integrated urban networks, had an impact on European urbanization. Best exemplified by Paris and Madrid, the central location of these capitals aided in the process of political consolidation; both of these cities, in turn, were given a further impetus for

Figure 5.3 During medieval times, all buildings, especially royal castles, had to be built lower than the cathedral bell tower, as seen in this view of Old Prague looking across the Vltava River. (Photo by Darrick Danta)

growth by their acquisition of administrative functions, coupled with their enhanced status at the vortex of social, economic, and political change. In like manner, regional centers and seats of county governments emerged to fill out the expanding national urban networks. The overall appearance and structure of cities changed because of the introduction of new forms of art, architecture, and urban planning. Especially in Europe's capital cities, this brought about the greater use of sculpture in public areas, other forms of urban beautification such as fountains, and embellishment on monumental buildings, all of which reached a peak during the baroque period (1550–1760).

The greatest change, though, in the realm of

Figure 5.4 Carcassonne in southern France is one of the best-preserved medieval towns in Europe. (Photo by Darrick Danta)

Figure 5.5 This elaborate church tower preserves the medieval flavor of central Prague. (Photo by Darrick Danta)

urban planning and design, was brought about by several factors. First, after the introduction of gunpowder, the massive walls of medieval times became obsolete. In many cities, the walls were later removed to make space for the wide boulevards that were becoming fashionable. Second, the Renaissance was a period of great accumulation of wealth for the nobility. This burgeoning spending power led to the building of opulent palaces in many cities, notably in Vienna and Paris (fig. 5.7), and to the replanning of cities. Beginning in Paris, many districts containing narrow medieval streets were torn down to make way for wide boulevards that radiated outward from and connected the various palaces and formal gardens laid out for the nobility (fig. 5.8) The emphasis on the control of visual perspective and on the rediscovery of classical models of design marked a significant departure from medieval times.

The European urban network remained largely unchanged during the Renaissance period; however, individual cities got bigger (fig. 5.9). By around 1500, more than a dozen cities in northern Italy, West-Central Europe, and Iberia had grown to more than 50,000 inhabitants. Cities such as Cracow, Prague, and Thessoloniki had grown to more than 25,000 people.

The Industrial Period (1760–1945)

The large-scale manufacturing of the Industrial Revolution began in the English Midlands in the mid-18th century; spread to Belgium, France, and Germany; and reached Hungary by the 1870s. The new mines, factories, foundries, and mills not only changed the structure of cities, but also led to massive in-migration of rural workers.

Box 5.2 The Hanseatic League

A precursor to today's European Union, the Hanseatic League marks the first organization that united a region of Europe in an economic association. Dating back to the 12th century, the League was an association of cities in and around the North and Baltic Seas that entered into agreements for mutual protection and to help develop trade. Over time, more and more cities joined the League in pursuit of the increased opportunities that membership provided; conversely, embargoes were instituted against ports that were hostile to the organization.

By the 14th century, membership in the League numbered some 200 towns spread along the coasts of the Baltic Sea (Riga, Königsberg, Rostock, and Stockholm) and the North Sea (Bergen, Hamburg, and several towns in what is now the Netherlands), along with important inland ports along rivers (Berlin, Magdeburg, Cologne, and Cracow, to name but a few). Later on, several English, Belgian, and even Russian cities joined the League.

By the early 16th century, however, the Hanseatic League began to unravel, a casualty of the turmoil brought on by the Reformation coupled with the desire of towns to exercise greater individual control. By 1648, the Hanseatic League was all but dead. However, a strong architectural legacy is still present in the old Hansa towns, in the design and color of buildings, as illustrated by Rostock (fig. 5.6).

Figure 5.6 "The heart of the Hansa city," this new development in Rostock keeps alive the sense of the Hanseatic League with its use of ornate, colorful buildings. (Photo by Darrick Danta)

Figure 5.7 Schonbrunn Palace, Vienna, gives a glimpse of the prestige and opulence of renaissance European nobility. (Photo by Darrick Danta)

In many cities, whole districts of factory buildings emerged, easily identified by their belching smokestacks, deafening machinery, and the general hustle-bustle of industrial activity. Industrial inputs and products were transported mainly by trains, so new tracks, stations, and rail traffic began to play a significant role in these cities. Public transportation in the form of trolleys and subway systems later modified the look and functioning of cities. Large tracts of worker housing were constructed. This housing, typical of British cities (fig. 5.10), generally was cramped and poorly constructed. The industrial period also heralded the development of the CBD, with its office buildings and corporate headquarters.

The growth of cities closely mirrored the diffusion of industrialization. By the early 19th century, industrial towns in the English Midlands and Scotland had grown to more than 100,000 inhabitants and the proportion of the population living in cities greater than 10,000 had risen to 30%. The growth of industrial cities in France, Belgium, Germany, and countries further east reflected the same pattern. In contrast, expansion of the industrial sectors in Romania, Bulgaria, Albania, and Greece did not occur until the early or middle part of the 20th century.

THE CONTEMPORARY EUROPEAN URBAN SYSTEM

A glance at the map of Europe shows the relationship in *central place theory* between the size and spacing of places that constitute the contemporary urban system in a number of countries: in France, for example, the seven largest metropolitan areas, Paris, Marseilles, Lyon, Lille, Nice, Toulouse, and Bordeaux, are distributed throughout the country; in Hungary, centrally located Budapest is ringed by the regional centers of Debrecen, Miskolc,

Figure 5.8 Paris, looking from the Arc de Triomphe along the Champs-Élysées toward the Place de la Concorde and the Louvre, part of the "Royal Axis" entry to the city. Haussmann replaced the narrow and winding medieval street system with wide boulevards and impressive buildings and monuments. (Photo by Linda McCarthy)

Szeged, and Pécs. Of course over time, political, economic, cultural, environmental, technological, and other changes can alter the role and rank of a place within an urban system hierarchy. The empirical observation of *rank-size distribution* holds for Belgium, Germany, Italy, Norway, and Switzerland. In other national urban systems, a deviation occurs at the upper end of the hierarchy to create *primacy.* Primate cities, which are often national capitals, include Paris, Budapest, Vienna, Reykjavik, Dublin, Athens, and Sofia.

As each country developed its own national capital and urban system, however, few capital cities grew to the size and status of world cities on a par with New York and Tokyo. Of course, London's 15 million people make it one of the world's largest metropolitan regions; Paris is next in the region, with over 9.5 million. While London and Paris reached the one million mark by 1800 and 1850, respectively, quite a few European cities have grown to a million or more inhabitants since 1900. Historically, population movement into cities has been the most important component of urban growth, especially during the industrial period. This form of internal migration within Europe, though, has largely ceased. As the birth rates in most countries have also fallen considerably in recent decades, European cities are now among the slowest growing in the world, averaging just 0.11% growth a year.

However, the cities of Europe have begun

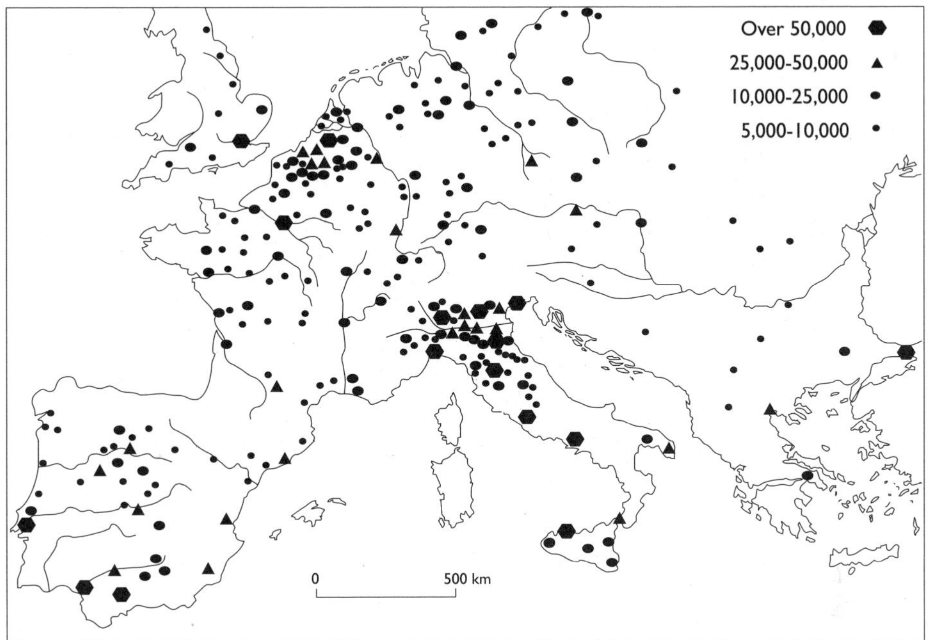

Figure 5.9 Distribution of European Cities around 1500. *Source*: Adapted from N. J. G. Pounds, *An Historical Geography of Europe* (Cambridge: Cambridge University Press, 1990), 222. Reprinted with permission.

to expand outward as a result of transportation and communications improvements. In some instances, the burgeoning neighboring towns and cities have coalesced into massive conurbations. Europe contains about 50 conurbations with more than a million inhabitants.

The Rhine-Ruhr conurbation in Germany has a diameter of about 70 mi and runs from Düsseldorf and Duisburg in the west, through Essen, Wuppertal, and Bochum, and then to Dortmund in the east (fig. 5.11). Of similar diameter is the Randstad, a densely populated horseshoe-shaped region in the western Netherlands. This "ring city" runs from Utrecht, Amsterdam, and Haarlem in the north, through the Hague, Delft, and Rotterdam in the west, to Dordrecht in the southeast (fig. 5.12). Only 60 mi apart, these two conurbations may eventually coalesce along the E36 motorway to become a dominant European metropolitan core. The London, Birmingham, Liverpool, Manchester, Leeds, and Newcastle metropolitan regions form an area of extensive urbanization in England on a par with the Boston-Washington axis in the United States and the Tokyo-Osaka axis in Japan.

The contemporary European urban system displays quite remarkable resilience and continuity—it has survived and adapted to the impacts of tremendous economic, political, social, technological, and other changes since the early days of the Greek city-states. More recently, the wars of the 20th century, especially World War II, unleashed appalling damage, with few cities coming through the conflict unscathed.

Figure 5.10 This view of London working-class row houses is typical of residential districts that sprang up during the industrial period. (Photo by Darrick Danta)

Western Europe

Urban Development after World War II

Separate urban systems developed on either side of the Iron Curtain after World War II. The cities in Western Europe cultivated connections with the capitalist world, and especially with the United States, whose Marshall Plan funded rebuilding in cities that had suffered massive wartime destruction. The reconstruction effort was seen as an opportunity to replan the bombed-out urban areas. Some of the most heavily damaged cities, like Rotterdam, Dortmund, and Le Havre, completely redesigned their street systems for new commercial and industrial buildings. Most cities, including Cologne and Stuttgart, incorporated the surviving historic structures and medieval street patterns into their reconstructed downtowns. Cities like Rouen and Nuremberg went so far as to re-create some of their destroyed historic buildings.

Large-Scale Industrialization and Migrant Labor

The postwar revival of large-scale industrialization generated a strong demand for labor in the cities of Western Europe's more prosperous countries. In the 1950s and 1960s, rural-urban migration fueled rapid urban growth, especially in the largest cities and their central areas. Foreign-born guest workers were brought in to fill low-wage assembly-line and service-sector jobs. The guest workers came from the countries of Mediterranean Europe, including Italy, Greece, Portugal, and Spain, and from former European colonies. West Germany attracted immigrants from Turkey and Yugoslavia, France brought in workers from North and West Africa, while Britain drew on Commonwealth citizens from the Caribbean, India, and Pakistan.

The volume of incoming migrants paralleled the business cycle, with peaks in the mid-

Figure 5.11 The Rhine-Ruhr Agglomeration in Germany. *Source*: Compiled from various sources.

1960s and the early 1970s. By the mid-1970s, there were nearly 4 million foreign immigrants in West Germany, 3.5 million in France, 1.5 million in the United Kingdom, nearly 1 million in Switzerland, and about half a million each in Belgium, the Netherlands, and Sweden.

Beginning in the early 1970s, economic recessions and rising unemployment wiped out demand for new migrant workers. Most governments imposed immigration restrictions. Some countries offered financial incentives to encourage return migration. Inducements were effective only in regions of severe unemployment, such as the Ruhr. Otherwise, the incentives were not enough to motivate migrants to return home to countries where employment opportunities were bleaker than in Europe.

An estimated 15 million foreign workers live in Western European cities today. More than one-third of the migrants in France are concentrated in the Paris region, where they represent more than 15% of the population. Foreign-born residents make up 15–25% of the population in German cities like Frankfurt, Stuttgart, and Munich. More than half the population of Amsterdam is non-Dutch, being composed primarily of individuals from the former colonies of Indonesia and Suriname. The migrants have had a very localized impact within these cities. They took over the

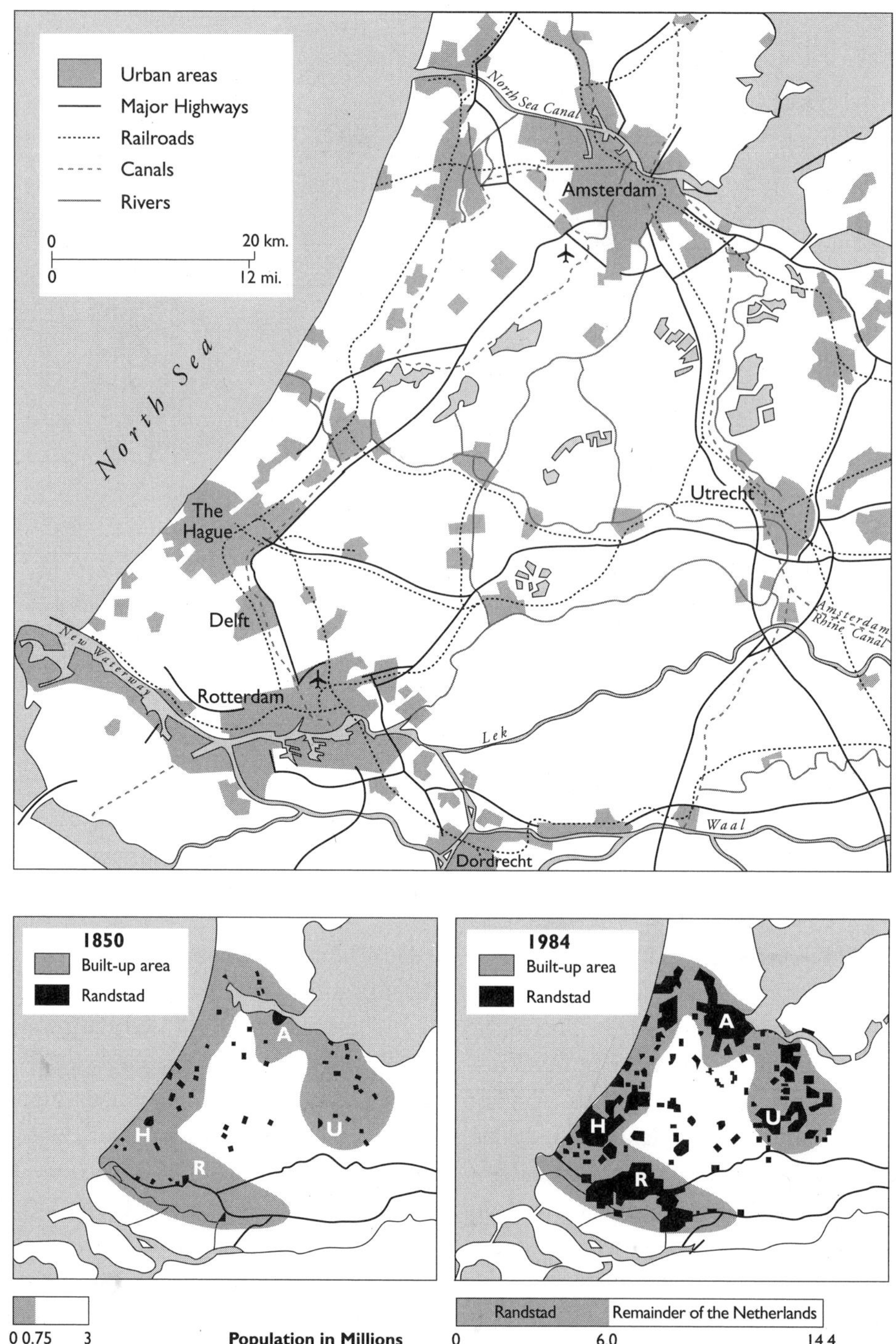

Figure 5.12 The Randstad Agglomeration of the Netherlands. *Source*: Compiled from various sources.

inner-city areas and jobs left vacant because of the suburbanization of the upwardly mobile, native-born population. In continental Europe, a particular ethnic group dominates each inner-city migrant enclave. For example, the ethnic enclaves in Frankfurt, Cologne, and Vienna contain mostly Yugoslavs or Turks, while in Paris and Marseilles these enclaves house Italians, Algerians, or Tunisians. In large British cities, in contrast, there is significant mixing of the different ethnic groups. Although there are large numbers of Asians, West Indians, and Irish, the foreign-born population represents only 15–20% of the population within most neighborhoods. As a general rule, within European cities ethnic groups are highly segregated from each other.

The operation of the labor and housing markets is believed to be more important than outright discrimination in producing inner-city enclaves. Low wages force migrants to rent lodgings in deteriorating inner-city locations. The internal cohesiveness of ethnic groups also contributes to residential segregation. Residents are more likely to share information about vacancies in their neighborhood with members of their own ethnic group.

Metropolitan Decentralization

The process of *counterurbanization,* or metropolitan decentralization, began in the late 1960s. This involved rapid development in suburban areas and nearby small and medium-sized towns while growth slowed in the inner cities. Peripheral areas attracted residents and businesses looking for more space and less pollution and crime. Hardest hit were the national capitals and largest metropolitan regions in the most urbanized countries (fig. 5.13). Counterurbanization affected cities from the traditional manufacturing and port regions of northern Britain, northeastern France, and the Ruhr to the larger, old industrial cities in southern Europe, like Milan, Genoa, and Turin.

Deindustrialization, involving a relative decline in industrial employment and a shift to services, contributes to metropolitan decentralization. In an effort to enhance profitability in traditional manufacturing activities like steel, chemicals, and shipbuilding, corporations restructure their operations by relocating labor-intensive production to lower-cost areas. This leads to massive job losses and urban decline in traditional centers of industry. The jobs created by the relocation of labor-intensive manufacturing have benefited some urban areas in Ireland, Spain, Portugal, and Greece. Branch plant operations like these, however, suffer from vulnerability to decisions made outside the area and from company relocations when government tax incentives expire.

Some CBDs have benefited from the shift to services and have seen an increase in shopping and a growth in the number of offices. Most city centers, however, have lost retail and office employment to outlying areas. Medium-sized cities have attracted employment in expanding sectors of the economy such as information services, high-technology industries, and modern distribution activities. These smaller cities at the periphery of major metropolitan centers avoid the high rents and congestion at the core while taking advantage of the nearby transportation routes, airports, skilled workers, and universities. Many of these cities have escaped serious problems of crime, pollution, and social and ethnic conflict because they are far from declining manufacturing centers. These cities are found in axial regions such as the Rhine between Frankfurt and Mulhouse, the Rhône-Saône valleys from Lyon to Geneva, and the Côte d'Azur east of Marseille.

Figure 5.13 Impacted adversely by metropolitan decentralization, this derelict inner-city area in Dublin contains vacant and deteriorating residential and industrial properties. (Photo by Linda McCarthy)

Some cities in the more peripheral parts of southern Europe continue to experience growth. These include Córdoba and Seville in southern Spain and Cagliari and Naples in southern Italy. Falling agricultural employment promotes rural-urban migration, which has exacerbated the existing housing and unemployment problems within these cities.

Core-Periphery Model

Although criticized for being overly simplistic and static, a *core-periphery model* is often used to describe the spatial pattern of urban development in Europe (fig. 5.14). The dominance of the core cities is based on their superior endowment in those factors that determine the location of economic activity, such as accessibility to markets. The largest cities at the core are connected by the most advanced transportation and communications systems. Labor-force quality and government policies make the core the most attractive area for major modern companies, institutions, and industries.

Cities in the core and periphery are linked in a symbiotic if unequal relationship. Core cities prosper and maintain their economic dominance at the expense of the periphery by capturing flows of migrants, taxes, and investments in cutting-edge industries, such as high-technology manufacturing, and in command-and-control functions, such as the headquarters of transnational corporations. Peripheral cities have more limited potential for economic development and attract tourists, innovation, and investment in branch plants from core locations. In between are the semiperipheral cities that have economic links with both the core and the periphery. An early start gives some cities an initial advantage that leads to localization economies involving clusters of particular industries. As the birthplace of the Industrial Revolution, the English Midlands formed the nucleus of an early industrial core

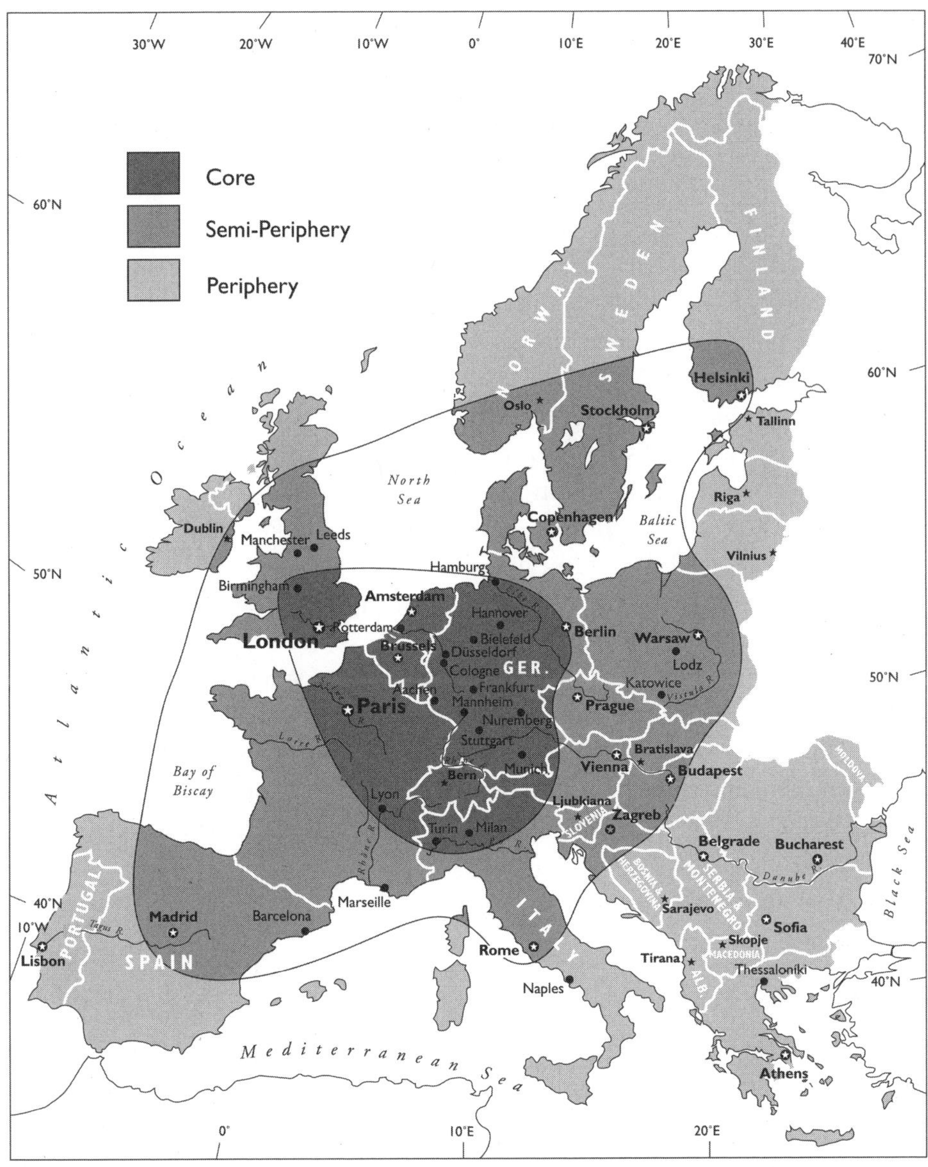

Figure 5.14 Core and Periphery in Europe. *Source*: Linda McCarthy and Darrick Danta

of economic growth. This core extended as far as Paris in the west and the Ruhr cities of Düsseldorf and Dortmund in the east. The periphery included Ireland, western and southern France, Portugal, Spain, Italy, Albania, Greece, Bulgaria, and Romania.

Over time, the core-periphery pattern of development was affected by changes in the locational preferences of companies and industries. From the early 1970s, the old industrial core cities began to experience the severe economic and social impacts of deindustrialization. The shift from labor-intensive freight handling to containerization and bulk transportation methods devastated employment levels in traditional port cities such as Liverpool and Rotterdam. Well-paid heavy-industry jobs were replaced with either low-paying service employment or well-paid high-technology and information services positions. This squeezing out of the traditional middle class has made the urban population more polarized economically and by residential location.

The core has now shifted to the south and east to areas of modern industrial growth. New core cities include Frankfurt, Stuttgart, and Munich in southern Germany, Zürich and Geneva in Switzerland, Milan and Turin in northern Italy, and Lyon in southern France. London and Paris have managed to retain their historic importance because of their size and established positions as major national and international cities in the urban hierarchy. The continued economic strength of the core is reinforced by the considerable political control that accompanies the role of the largest core cities as major centers of international decision making.

European and Global Linkages

European urban areas are part of networks of cities that operate at a number of spatial scales. Since 1989, cities on either side of the former Iron Curtain have become more interconnected in the new European economy. Cities like Berlin, Prague, Vienna, and Ljubljana, formerly at the edge of Western Europe, are well placed to take advantage of increasing trade between east and west and have emerged as vital links at the heart of a reunited Europe. Many of the cities in Western Europe are located within the current fifteen-member-state European Union (EU). The increasing economic and political integration of these countries influences the development of the European urban system. For example, the removal of national trade barriers within the EU in conjunction with the internationalization of the European economy has encouraged population increases along certain border regions. Urban growth zones straddle the boundaries between the Netherlands and Germany, between Italy and Switzerland, and between the southern Rhine regions of France, Germany, and Switzerland. European cities are linked through trade and other mechanisms to major urban areas throughout the global economy. The cities within the EU form part of an international trading bloc containing over 375 million people and with a combined gross national product greater than that of the United States.

A select group of European cities hosts the headquarters of major international agencies, many of which were founded after World War II in an effort to promote economic, political, or military cooperation. Geneva is the main European center for the United Nations. Paris is the headquarters for the Organization for Economic Cooperation and Development (OECD) and the European Space Agency. Vienna is the headquarters for the Organization of Petroleum Exporting Countries (OPEC). The offices of the major decision-making bodies of the EU are located in Brussels, Luxembourg, and Strasbourg. Brussels is also the headquarters of the North Atlantic Treaty Organization (NATO), while Strasbourg serves as the headquarters of the Council of Europe. This organization, with more than 40 countries, including new members from Eastern Europe, promotes European unity, human rights, and social and economic progress.

The major centers of international banking and finance in Europe historically have been London and Paris and now include Frankfurt,

Zürich, and Luxembourg. Frankfurt contains the Bundesbank, Germany's respected and influential central bank. Certainly, this fact played a part in Frankfurt being chosen instead of London in 1998 as the location for the European Central Bank.

London and Paris rank among the small number of world cities that contain the headquarters of some of the most powerful transnational corporations in the world. London contains about 30 of the 500 largest global companies, including Imperial Chemical Industries and General Electric. Paris also has about 30 of these companies, including Aérospatiale and Alcatel. Rome contains the independent state of Vatican City, the seat of the Roman Catholic Church. Milan and Paris are major European centers of culture and design.

Accessibility via the latest transportation and communications technologies allows some cities to strengthen their international positions. The high-speed TGV (Train à Grande Vitesse) reinforces the dominance of cities like London, Paris, Brussels, Amsterdam, Cologne, Madrid, Barcelona, Zürich, and Milan. The busiest airports are in London, Paris, and Frankfurt. Located at the mouth of the Rhine, Rotterdam is the largest port in the world. Rotterdam's annual turnover of about 315 million metric tons of cargo far exceeds that of the world's second-largest port, Singapore. Rotterdam's water and pipeline connections with the Ruhr in Germany make it the main oil distribution and refining center in Europe. Antwerp, Marseille, and Hamburg are also major European ports. Trucking is the most important mode of ground transportation. More than 1,200 billion tons of goods are transported by road each year, compared to only about 230 billion by rail. There are more than 450 automobiles for every one thousand people in Western Europe. At over 500 cars per 1,000 inhabitants, German levels already match those of the United States. A steady increase in automobile ownership has overwhelmed existing and new highway capacity and led to traffic congestion within and between cities.

Eastern Europe

Socialist Urbanization

The cities of Eastern Europe during the post–World War II period developed differently from their Western counterparts, partly because of historical legacy, but also because they were under Communist totalitarian governments until around 1989. One purely political change that affected some cities during the immediate postwar period concerned name changes. Certain place-names were changed to pay tribute to Communist luminaries; an example is Chemnitz, East Germany, which was changed to Karl-Marx-Stadt. Eastern European governments also had to contend with the pressing need to repair and reconstruct the cities that were left in ruins after World War II. The damage sustained by these cities generally was far more severe than that suffered in Western Europe and subsidies were not available through programs like the U.S.-sponsored Marshall Plan.

The urban system in Eastern Europe following World War II thus was underdeveloped compared to that in Western Europe. In 1950, only two cities, Budapest (1.6 million) and East Berlin (1.2 million), contained over a million people; cities like Warsaw, which dropped from a 1940 population of 1.2 million to just 600,000 in 1950, suffered tremendous population losses during the war. Likewise, these countries exhibited relatively low levels of urbanization, ranging from a high of 67% in East Germany to only 21% in

Yugoslavia and Albania. The urban systems that developed in the countries of Eastern Europe under their Communist governments did so more in response to political decision making than as a result of economic forces. Socialist planning concerns greatly affected the growth of particular cities and the overall development of the national urban hierarchies. In the aftermath of World War II, the governments of Eastern Europe engaged in sweeping reform efforts that brought about considerable—though often contradictory—change to their national urban systems.

The earliest stage of postwar economic development involved the rapid expansion of heavy industry that concentrated on the production of iron and steel, chemicals, and machinery. Coupled with increased mechanization in agriculture, this extensive industrial development soon led to a massive rural-urban migration of workers. As a result, the level of urbanization rose quickly, as individual cities—mainly national capitals—experienced rapid growth. The outcome, of course, was rising levels of primacy, increasing congestion, and severe housing shortages. By the late 1960s, for example, Budapest contained 44% of the country's urban population. And this kind of figure masks a reality of an even greater primacy: in a process referred to as *underurbanization,* the number of urban industrial jobs during the early period of extensive socialist industrialization grew at a faster rate than the number of urban housing units; this resulted in workers having to commute to the capital cities over long distances and often for up to a week at a time.

Beginning in the mid-1970s, Eastern Europe entered a phase of intensive industrial and urban development. Governments attempted to place less emphasis on heavy industry, decentralize production from capital cities to smaller ones, develop their settlement networks, and increase the level of infrastructure and housing in cities. Despite these efforts, by 1990, after nearly 45 years of socialism, the urban network in Eastern Europe was still underdeveloped compared to that in the West. Only seven cities, all national capitals, contained more than a million people.

European and Global Linkages

The individual urban systems that evolved or were reinforced in Eastern Europe under socialism were highly centralized. Rail connections were of the "hub-and-spoke" variety, usually with the national capital as the single hub. The border changes associated with the partition of Germany into West and East after World War II severely dislocated the transportation routes and development of the urban systems on either side of the Iron Curtain. First of all, most former rail and road links across the new border were either closed or greatly restricted. More significantly, the government of East Germany had to develop Rostock as a new port to replace Hamburg. An ironic aspect of urban development in Eastern Europe under socialism concerned the lack of international connections. Despite calls for greater cooperation among the socialist countries, close intercity connections did not develop. Indeed, suspicion rather than cooperation generally prevailed; countries tended to site sensitive industries and other vital resources in interior rather than border regions. Likewise, the heightened level of internal security resulted in a decrease in border crossings not only across the Iron Curtain and into the Soviet Union, but even between the countries of Eastern Europe. The dominance of the Soviet Union meant that the headquarters of the international organizations that developed in Eastern Europe, notably the Council for Mutual Economic Assistance

(CMEA, or Comecon) and the Warsaw Pact, were not located in Eastern European cities.

Postsocialist Changes

Since the fall of the Iron Curtain in late 1989, governments have been replaced, Germany has been reunited, and Czechoslovakia and Yugoslavia have devolved into constituent parts. Central economic planning has been abandoned as countries have embarked on the transformation to market economies. The Soviet Union, whose grip had kept Eastern Europe in check during the Cold War, has left the scene, opening the way for Western investment and influences to move in and for people to move out.

These changes impacted the cities and urban systems of Eastern Europe in a number of ways. First, city names that were communist inspired, such as Leninváros (Lenin City) in Hungary, were changed back to their prewar designations. Second, direct foreign investment flooded in, targeted mainly at capital cities, mostly in Hungary, the Czech Republic, Poland, and Slovenia. This investment not only boosted the transformation to capitalism and fueled construction booms, but it also led to the reemergence of a region-wide urban hierarchy. Third, many cities have benefited as trade gateways. Fourth, countless border towns have emerged as important local trade centers. However, the transition has not come without hardship. Indeed, the industrial towns, which were heavily subsidized during the socialist era, have suffered as a result of the closure of outdated plants. Likewise, some cities have lost revenues that previously were generated by the Soviet military presence. Other towns have lost economic status because of the reorientation of trade routes.

Most recently, in the 1990s, there was the widespread destruction associated with the wars in the former Yugoslavia, which technically ceased to exist in 2002. Indeed, a significant portion of the industrial, transportation, communication, and municipal infrastructure, along with housing and religious structures, were destroyed or severely damaged in cities across Bosnia, Serbia, and Kosovo. It will take many years before functioning urban systems can reemerge in this part of Southeastern Europe (figs. 5.15 and 5.16).

THE INTERNAL STRUCTURE OF EUROPEAN CITIES

"Our cities are like historical monuments to which every generation, every century, every civilization has contributed a stone" (Ildefons Cerdà, Spanish civil engineer and town planner, 1867). The surviving historic elements represent an incomplete catalog of urban development and redevelopment. While no two cities are identical, the strong legacy of history is visible as a set of common characteristics that make European cities distinctive.

Major Distinctive Characteristics

Town Squares

The town square, the heart of the Greek, Roman, and medieval towns, has often survived as an important open space. Some medieval town squares in Western Europe boast a continuous tradition of regular open-air markets. The large open square, typical of socialist cities, was used for public gatherings and political rallies and symbolized the open, communal heart of the city (fig. 5.17). Today, many central squares and their historic buildings have been adapted to economic and social change and contain modern commercial functions, such as tourist offices and restaurants.

Major Landmarks

The historic landmarks in Western European city centers traditionally have been symbols of religious, political, military, educational, and cultural interests. Many cathedrals, churches, and statues serve their original purposes. Some town halls, royal palaces, and artisan guildhalls have been converted for use as libraries, art galleries, and museums. Medieval castles and city walls have become tourist attractions. Today, of course, the major landmarks are expressions of economic power—no longer city halls, but the offices of transnational corporations; no longer cathedrals, but sports stadiums.

In Eastern Europe, the hallmarks of socialist cities were the preponderance of massive buildings in "wedding cake" style (fig. 5.18), red stars, and "heroic" statues. Since late 1989, the red stars that had adorned most public buildings have been removed and the many statues of socialist leaders, especially those of Lenin, were destroyed or taken away. Street names, such as "Lenin Boulevard," have been changed from their former designations to completely new names, some to honor individuals or events associated with the "Quiet Revolutions" of 1989.

Complex Street Pattern

The unplanned narrow streets and alleys of the medieval core were developed well before the automobile era (fig. 5.19). Outside the walled town, during the medieval period, suburban areas grew around the long-distance roads that radiated out from the city gates. In the 19th century, cities such as Munich, Marseille, and Madrid made radial or tangential boulevards the axes of their planned suburbs.

Figure 5.15 These high-rise buildings in downtown Sarajevo were badly damaged by the Serbs during Bosnia's struggle for independence. (Photo by Stanley Brunn)

High Density and Compact Form

The constraints of the city walls kept the population density high during medieval times. A number of factors perpetuated the compact, densely built-up form that is now characteristic of large cities in Western Europe. A long tradition of planning that restricts low-density urban sprawl dates back to the application of strict city building regulations in the earliest suburbs. The compact urban form also reflects the relatively late introduction of automobiles in Europe as compared to North America and the high price of gasoline.

Bustling Downtowns

The high density and compact nature of European cities create downtowns that bustle with activity (fig. 5.20). The vitality of the city center is reinforced by the widespread use of public transportation systems (trains, buses, subways) that converge on the core. In larger cities, distinct functions dominate particular districts. Institutional districts house government offices and universities. Finan-

Figure 5.16 Since the end of the Bosnian War, international investment has helped rebuild downtown Sarajevo. (Photo by Stanley Brunn)

cial and office districts contain banks and insurance companies. A pedestrianized retail zone leads to the rail station. Cultural districts offer museums and art galleries. Entertainment areas include theater and red-light districts. Many downtown buildings have multiple uses. Apartments are found above shops, offices, and restaurants. Large department stores, such as Harrods and Printemps of central London and Paris, are prominent features in most European downtowns. Modern downtown malls include Les Halles in Paris and Eldon Square in Newcastle in the northeast of England. Suburban malls are becoming prevalent. Many coastal or riverine cities have also refurbished old port and industrial buildings to house mixed-use waterfront developments such as the one at Liverpool's Albert Dock. Other cities have renovated obsolete historic structures, such as London's Covent Garden, as festival marketplaces with specialized shops, restaurants, and street performers.

In keeping with trends in the West, department, fashion, fast-food, and even video-rental stores began to appear in the downtowns of Eastern European cities during the 1980s. Likewise, the equivalent of shopping malls cropped up, mainly at the intersections of major transportation lines. Pedestrian shopping streets, containing the most exclusive shops, became an important part of the retail structure of Eastern European cities.

Low-Rise Skylines

For North American visitors, the most striking aspect of Western European cities is the general absence of skyscraper offices and high-rise apartments. These city centers were developed long before reinforced steel construction and the elevator made high rises feasible. Master plans and building codes designed to minimize the

Figure 5.17 Skenderbeg Square in Tirana, Albania, shows the premium placed by socialist planners on political showplaces in the heart of the city. (Photo by Darrick Danta)

spread of fire maintained building heights between three and five stories during the industrial period. Paris fixed the building height at 65 ft in 1795, while other large cities introduced height restrictions in the 19th century. Still regulated today, high rises are found only in redevelopment areas or on land at the periphery of the city. Skyscrapers have also been built in the central commercial and financial districts of some of the very largest cities, including London.

In socialist Eastern Europe, there was no private ownership of land and hence no urban land markets. With few transnational corporations doing business in these countries, socialist cities were usually devoid of tall commercial buildings that mark the CBD. The tallest buildings in most Eastern European cities were usually international hotels, massive Houses of the People (also known as Houses of Culture, erected in Soviet socialist style, to serve as cultural, educational, and entertainment centers), or TV towers.

Neighborhood Stability

Western European cities enjoy remarkable neighborhood stability. Europeans move much less frequently than North Americans, while homes maintain the characteristic solidly constructed, concrete block, brick, and stone housing. As a result, older neighborhoods at or near the center of large cities enjoy remarkably long lives, despite suburbanization. The districts of handsome mansions built by speculative developers for wealthy families in the 17th and 18th centuries remain stable, high-income neighborhoods, such as Belgravia, Bloomsbury, and Mayfair in central London. High-income suburban neighborhoods developed typically in the western part of older industrial cities, upwind of industrial smokestacks and residential chimneys. Wealthy residents, in fact, have remained at or near the city center in Western Europe since before the Industrial Revolution. Higher taxes on city land until the late 19th

Figure 5.18 The House of Science in Bucharest is typical of the Soviet-inspired architecture found throughout Eastern European cities. Note the pedestal in front of the building, which formerly supported a large statue of Lenin. (Photo by Darrick Danta)

century kept the poorest residents and immigrants outside the city walls. Beginning with Paris in the second half of the 19th century, this tradition was strengthened by the replacement of areas of slums and former city walls with wide boulevards and imposing apartments.

Since the 18th century in Western Europe, however, urban growth has spread to suburban zones and has even enveloped freestanding villages and towns. Yet these separate urban centers became distinct quarters within the expanding city as they maintained their long-established social and economic characteristics, major landmarks, and shopping streets. During the second half of the 19th century, annexations of groups of these suburban quarters produced distinctive city districts with their own shopping areas and government institutions. In the past few decades, governments in older industrial cities have funded urban renewal projects designed to attract higher-income residents to the revitalized parts of central areas. The success of these large-scale city center redevelopments has given rise to *gentrification* in the surrounding area. Demand for housing that has the potential to be renovated for higher-income occupants, however, has raised property values in certain areas and pushed out lower-income residents.

Housing

Apartment living is common in Europe—residents of all income groups own or rent apartments. Apartments are a good land-use choice in high-density and compact European cities, where space is at a premium and land values are high. Instead of growing outward, cities grew upward, to the limit of the height regulations. The multistory apartment house originated in northern Italy to accommodate the wealthy during the Renaissance period. By the early 18th century, the apartment house had spread to the larger cities in continental Europe and Scotland. Until the invention of the elevator, social stratification within individual

Figure 5.19 Narrow Artillery Lane in London appears frozen in time in a pre-automobile era. (Photo by Linda McCarthy)

buildings was vertical: wealthier families occupied the lower floors, while poorer residents lived in smaller apartments above. Horizontal social stratification also developed within apartment blocks. The large, expensive units were located in the front of buildings, with small low-rent units facing the rear. By the late 18th century, as the Industrial Revolution spurred increasing urbanization, apartment blocks had spread to medium-sized cities. Speculators built large-scale standardized tenements for middle-income occupants and barracks for low-income residents.

The two-story, single-family row house is distinctive to England, Wales, and Ireland. This row house tradition can be traced back to efforts to restrict congestion in London in the late 1500s that made it illegal for more than one family to rent a new building. A variation of the row house, the narrow multistory house with an apartment on each floor, is found across Northern Europe in cities such as Rouen and Lille in northern France and Bremen and Hamburg in northern Germany.

The serious housing shortage that started with the economic recession of the 1930s was exacerbated by the lack of construction and significant destruction during both world wars. The public housing programs that began in Vienna in the early 1920s were stepped up after World War II across Western Europe. Modern architecture and urban design principles were combined with low-cost factory production methods. This resulted in the war-damaged historic houses and dilapidated 19th-century tenements in the central parts of cities being replaced by undistinguished high-rise apartment buildings. In the 1950s and 1960s, most governments adopted a policy of metropolitan decentralization and expansion into inexpensive open land at the edge of cities. Modern high-rise apartment blocks were concentrated in large peripheral estates known by their French name—*grands ensembles.* Developments like Park Hill in Sheffield, Sarcelles in northern Paris, and Chorweiler in Cologne contained 1,000 or more apartments at densities as high as 120 residents per acre.

Traditionally, Western European governments spent more on public housing construction than on rent subsidies. Compared to North America, public housing in Europe is less stigmatized. The very poorest residents are distributed throughout the city in the cheapest private rental units. These poor-quality dwellings are found in damp basements, attic spaces, and run-down rear

Figure 5.20 A busy pedestrianized shopping street in the heart of Dublin. (Photo by Linda McCarthy)

apartments. Where any stigma is associated with public housing, it applies only to specific kinds of government-subsidized developments. These include the housing projects that replaced peripheral shantytowns of poor rural immigrants and postwar refugees in Spain, Italy, France, and Germany.

Historically, the severity of need and the political leanings of governments determined the amount of public housing provided within each city and country. The amount was highest in cities with serious housing shortages and liberal municipal governments, such as Edinburgh and Glasgow in Scotland, where the number of public units grew to well over half the total housing stock. Traditionally, public housing comprised 20–30% of the total in England, France, and Germany and 10% of the total in Italy. Public housing represents only 5% or less of the housing in the more affluent and conservative Swiss cities. Since the 1970s, however, the amount and percentage of public housing have declined due to government cost-cutting privatization programs.

In general, the cities that developed under socialism throughout Eastern Europe were less spatially segregated than those that evolved under capitalism. The prewar residences of the social elite were used for political purposes to house party officials, foreign delegations, or institutes. But housing was viewed as a right, not a commodity; each family was entitled to its own house at reasonable cost. In the face of the tremendous housing shortfalls following the war, the Communist governments during the 1950s to 1970s conducted massive programs for building housing estates: typically, eleven-story, prefabricated, multifamily apartment blocks. These apartments were small (about 460 to 650 sq ft, or 43 to 60 sq m), poorly constructed, and almost universally disliked by residents. Often, housing estates were built in large clusters, sometimes forming massive concrete curtains,

Figure 5.21 An extensive cluster of housing estates located next to a large factory in Bratislava. (Photo by Darrick Danta)

usually on land near the edge of cities (fig. 5.21). Because of this, urban population densities, which are typically higher in Eastern Europe than in North America, were often at their highest near the urban periphery.

Housing estates were often constructed in groups to form a *neighborhood unit* consisting of three to four apartment blocks arranged into a quadrangle surrounding shops, green space, and play areas for children (fig. 5.22). The purpose of these units, in keeping with socialist planning philosophy, was to promote greater social interaction; however, the neighborhood unit concept, along with the construction of housing estates, was abandoned by the mid-1980s, after governments recognized the futility of trying to achieve social engineering through physical planning.

Models of the European City

The concentric zone model is most applicable to British cities. By contrast, Mediterranean cities exhibit an inverse concentric zone pattern. There, the elites concentrate in central areas near major transportation arteries, while the poor live in shantytowns in inadequately serviced parts of the periphery.

A sector model corresponds with the pattern of socioeconomic status in which sectors containing different income groups radiate out from the city center. This social pattern reflects the preferences of the wealthy to locate in pleasant axial areas, such as along monumental boulevards or upwind of pollution sources. Poorer residents are left with unattractive linear sectors of land along railway lines or zones

Figure 5.22 A neighborhood unit in the new industrial town of Dunaujvaros, Hungary, built during the socialist era. (Photo by Darrick Danta)

of heavy industry. The multiple nuclei model fits the pattern of ethnic differentiation—different ethnic groups are concentrated either in nodes within the inner city or in high-rise public housing at the periphery.

While certain common traits characterize the cities of Europe, the richness and variety of their history and geography have produced distinctive regional characteristics. The most visible regional differences are evident by comparing the residential and economic structure of the larger cities in Northwestern, Mediterranean, and Eastern Europe.

A Model of Northwestern European City Structure

In Northwestern Europe, the preindustrial core contains the market square and historic structures such as a medieval cathedral and town hall (fig. 5.23). Apartment buildings contain upper- and middle-income residents above small, street-level shops and offices. The narrow winding streets extend out about a third of a mile. A few wider streets radiate out from the square and form a pedestrianized corridor that runs to the train station and contains national and international department stores, restaurants, and hotels. Skyscrapers are concentrated in the commercial and financial district. There are new downtown shopping malls or festival marketplaces in refurbished historic buildings. Some of the old industrial and port areas contain new retail, commercial, and residential waterfront developments. Wealthy mansions grace the western part of the core. Encircling the core are some zones in transition found in the concentric zone model. The area of the former city wall is a circular zone of 19th-century redevelopment. Some of the deteriorated middle-income housing has been purchased and gentrified by upper-income residents, while other sections provide low-rent accommodations for students and poor immigrants.

Surrounding this area is another zone in transition—an old industrial zone with disused

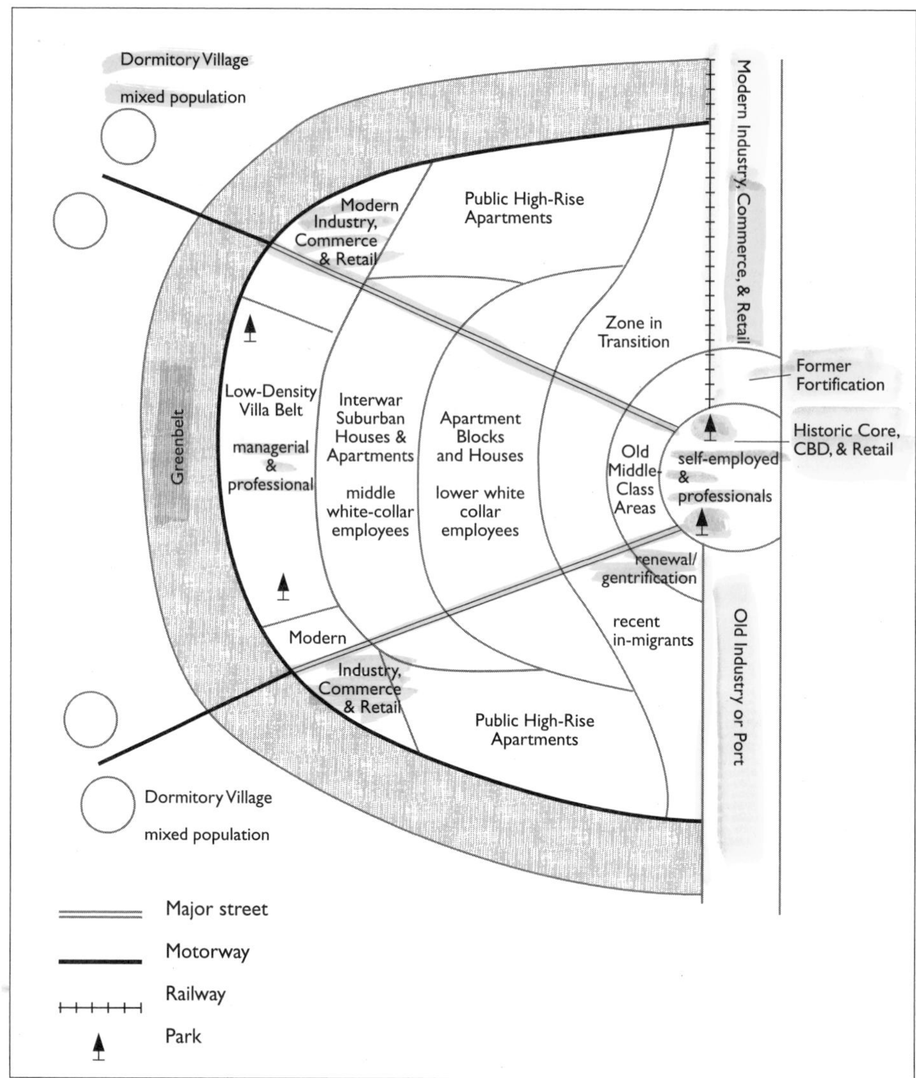

Figure 5.23 Model of Northwestern European City Structure. *Source*: Linda McCarthy

railway lines. In the 1950s and 1960s, new industrial plants, such as for light engineering and food processing, replaced many of the derelict old factories and warehousing. Low-income renters and owners live in the run-down 19th-century housing. Some houses have been refurbished or replaced with new units, while certain neighborhoods are quite distinctive because they house foreign immigrants who live above their exotically painted stores and restaurants.

As in the concentric zone model, beyond this inner area is a zone of "workingmen's homes." This is a stable lower-middle–income zone dating to the first half of the 20th century. These streetcar suburbs contain apartment blocks and houses without garages and are typically anchored by a small shopping area, a community center, a library, and a school. Outside this area are middle-income automobile suburbs containing apartments and single-family houses with garages that correspond with the zone of better residences in the concentric zone model. Further out are nodes containing the most exclusive neighborhoods, as might be expected in the multiple nuclei model.

The multiple nuclei model also explains the estates of public high-rise apartments and new private middle- and lower-middle–income "starter" homes at the urban periphery that lack basic amenities such as shops and banks. The periphery also contains commercial and industrial activities, such as shopping malls, business and science parks, and high-technology manufacturing.

Beginning with Vienna in 1904, many cities delineated a greenbelt at the edge of the built-up area within which development was prohibited. The greenbelt was intended to prevent urban sprawl and provide recreational space. Commuters live outside the greenbelt in dormitory villages and small towns that correspond with the commuter's zone in the concentric zone model. The airport and related facilities, such as hotels and modern factories, are located further out on a major freeway.

A Model of Mediterranean City Structure

The structure of the preindustrial core reflects the distinct history of each European Mediterranean city (fig. 5.24). In Greece and Italy, the historic core can exhibit traces of the grid pattern of streets from the first walled enclosure of Greek or Roman origin, while in Iberia, remnants of the narrow alleys of the Arab quarters date back to the period of Moorish control. The central marketplace is home to markets and festivals; in Spain, it is home to bullfights. The area around the town square contains the cathedral, town hall, and the narrow winding streets of the walled medieval city. Low-income and lower-middle–income residents live at high densities above street-level shops and offices. A retail corridor runs from this old commercial core to the train station. The high-rise offices of the modern CBD are nearby. Labor-intensive traditional manufacturing and port activities survive in some cities. As in the multiple nuclei and sector models, new industries are found in former old industrial sites and in locations well served by the generally more limited transportation infrastructure in Mediterranean cities.

Until the 19th century, urban growth was expressed in increasing densities within the medieval city. Larger cities that removed their medieval walls in the 19th century drew up plans of expansion and laid out new monumental districts in the area within the former city wall. A grand new thoroughfare lined with public works such as statues and fountains extended out from the city. This area attracted commercial development and wealthy residents, as suggested by the sector model. These elite residential areas of parks and tree-lined boulevards were flanked by middle-income and upper-middle–income neighborhoods. In the early 20th century, suburban sprawl became a problem, especially in cities experiencing rapid growth due to industrialization and rural-urban migration. Squatter settlements covered the outskirts of cities. After World War II, these shantytowns were replaced with low-cost, high-rise public housing that today contains low-income and lower-middle–income households. Further out, near a natural resource or industrial operation, are the remote, poorly serviced satellite communities for low-income residents and recent rural immigrants.

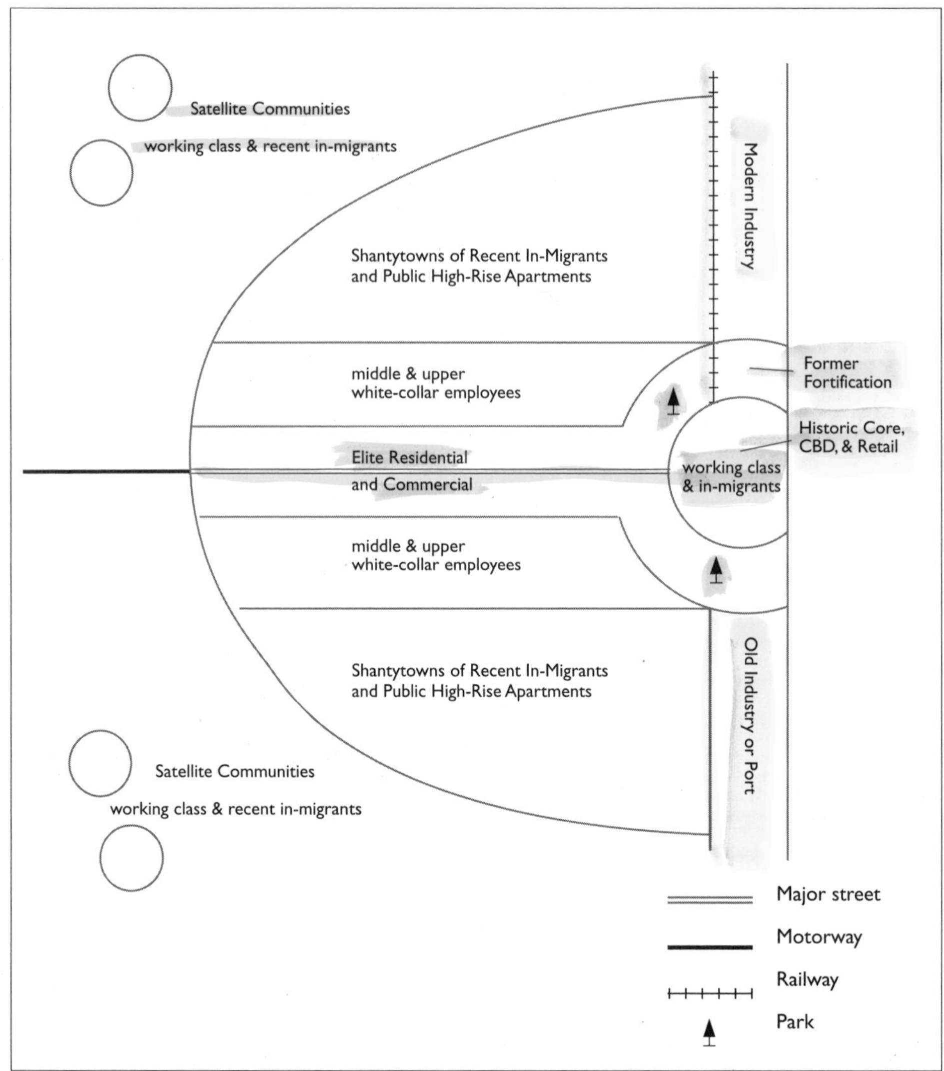

Figure 5.24 Model of Mediterranean City Structure. *Source*: Linda McCarthy

A Model of Eastern European City Structure

Prior to World War II, the internal structures of cities in Eastern Europe were much the same as those in Western Europe. Beginning in the late 1940s, however, the imposition of socialist planning set these cities on a different development trajectory. The principles of socialist economics and planning introduced several common features to the internal structure of the Eastern European city (fig. 5.25).

A typical socialist city contained a central square for political gatherings, often created by razing existing buildings. Former mansions were converted to government use, public buildings came to dominate strategic locations in the city, and statues and other revolutionary symbols dotted the cityscape. Clusters

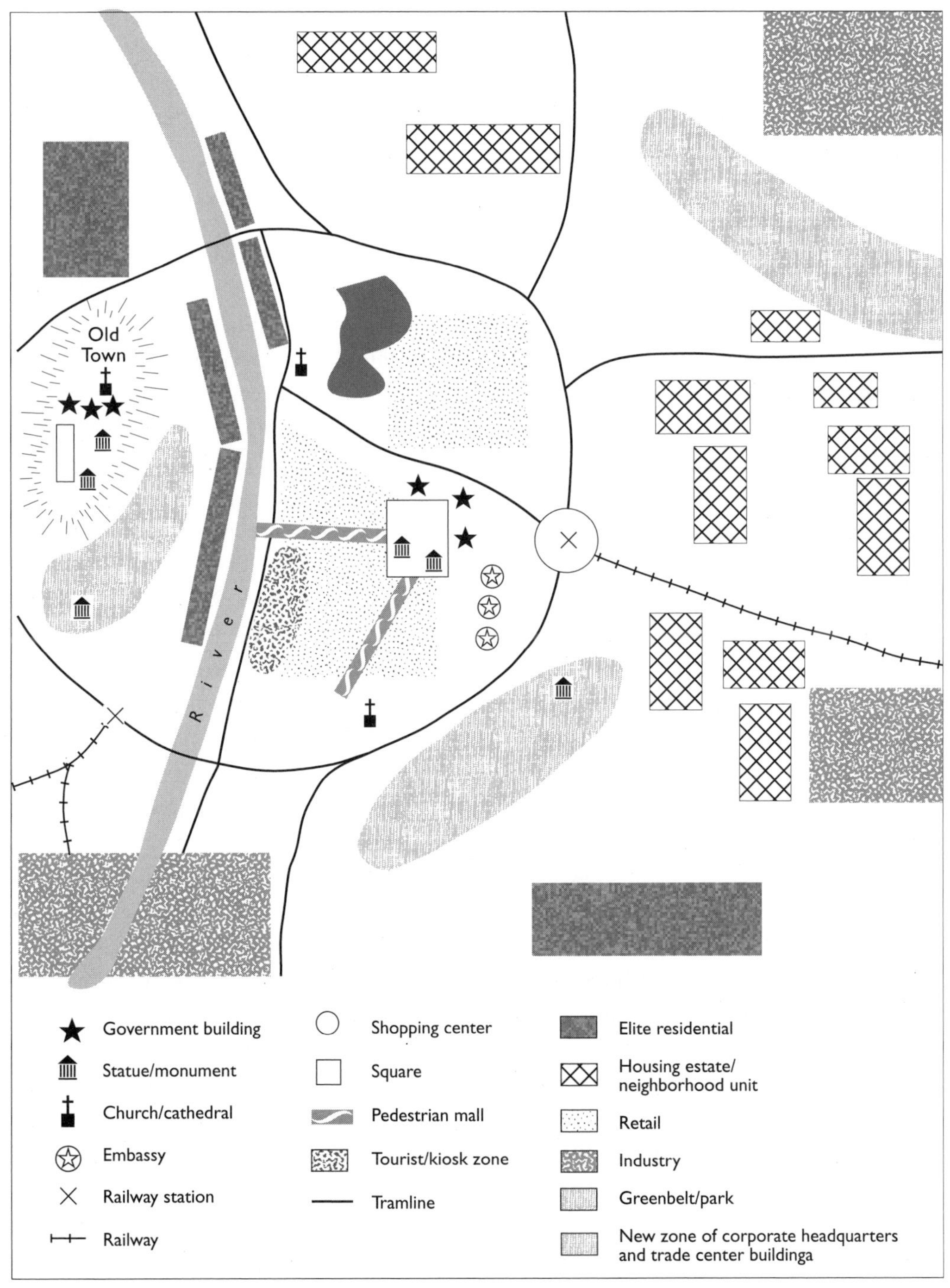

Figure 5.25 Model of Eastern European City Structure. *Source*: Darrick Danta

of housing estates and neighborhood units were interspersed with factories, transport hubs, and retail establishments. Overall, these cities did not conform to Western models of urban structure; rather, since land use was based more on political concerns than economic forces, the cities took on a more haphazard appearance.

Of course, not all places came to exhibit these features to the same degree. Few socialist elements are evident in cities such as Prague that escaped major destruction during the war. The socialist city was most clearly achieved in cities that had been severely damaged during the war, such as Warsaw and Berlin; in the new industrial towns; and in places where socialist ideology was particularly strongly imposed. Socialism was practiced most stridently in Albania, where cities adopted the classic socialist form, religion was officially banned, and private ownership of automobiles was forbidden. Large cities in Bulgaria also developed a rather sterile appearance during the socialist period. In contrast, Polish industrial towns looked much the same as their Western European counterparts.

One of the first changes to occur in the structure of Eastern European cities after 1989 was an increase in tourist facilities—hotels, restaurants, and various forms of entertainment—to cater to foreign visitors. Another change, spurred by economic hardship, was the appearance of informal bazaars lining certain streets where people now sell their own household goods, cheap imported products, and regional craft products, and of *kiosks*, small buildings on the sidewalks of busy streets where printed material, tobacco, and alcoholic products, plus a variety of imported items, are sold. The past few years have also witnessed a building boom. Foreign-owned or foreign-financed office buildings, trade centers, retail outlets, and other establishments are now common features of cities like Berlin, Budapest, Warsaw, and Prague. Very visible signs of change are the proliferating corporate logos and billboards.

REPRESENTATIVE CITIES

A small sample of cities has been chosen as representative of particular aspects of the rich urban history and geography of Europe. London and Paris are centers of national and international significance that have maintained their historic dominance since the Industrial Revolution and are examples of Europe's largest cities. Brussels is representative of cities enjoying growing international importance as a result of the EU. While London, Paris, and Brussels are northwestern capital cities, Barcelona is characteristic of regional ports in the Mediterranean. Oslo is representative of capital cities and major ports in Scandinavia. Berlin provides a fascinating look at the differential operation of two economic/planning realms during the time when it was divided. As a capital city again, Berlin is experiencing the world's most vigorous building boom and is representative of emerging major centers of international investment in the "new" unified Europe. Bucharest is an example of an Eastern European city in transition that is still struggling to address significant challenges in the post-Communist period.

London: The Global City of Europe

London is the preeminent metropolitan area in Europe, based not only on its size but also on its European and indeed global importance. Greater London has a population of more than 7.5 million in more than 700 sq mi

(1820 sq km) of continuously built-up area. Including the metropolitan fringe, London boasts 15 million people. The hub of the British Empire, this city became the center of global economic and political power in the 19th century. Today, London enjoys the kind of *global city* status achieved only by New York and Tokyo. London dominates the UK from its location in Southeast England. It is the seat of national government, the core of the English legal system, the headquarters for major British and foreign companies, and a leading center for banking, insurance, advertising, and publishing. London's newspapers and national television and radio stations reach all parts of the country.

This city has survived major disasters, including a great plague that killed 75,000 of its inhabitants in 1665. The next year, a fire destroyed virtually the entire city. London was rebuilt and many of the historic buildings survived until they were bombed during World War II. London's nickname, "the Smoke," recalls the days when a haze of pollution from industrial and domestic chimneys hung over the city. London has since undergone deindustrialization and a shift to services and modern manufacturing. Despite these changes, London remains firmly rooted in its historic past and cultural traditions.

The historic heart of the city is the most prominent image of London for many people and it is the city's most frequented area. Yet Central London is only a small segment of the city. London's development produced several major concentric zones around this central area, namely, the inner city, the outer suburbs, and the metropolitan fringe. Central London grew around two core areas: a commercial hub with trade and port activities and an institutional center containing religious and government functions. The commercial core developed from a Roman fort on the north bank of the Thames. Between A.D. 43 and 410, Londinium became the fifth-largest city north of the Alps and conducted trade extending as far as the Baltic and Mediterranean.

In the medieval period, London's protected inland site and strategic location for North Sea and Baltic trade allowed port and commercial activities to thrive. The docks spread from the Tower of London into the East End. Specialized market areas developed to the north and east of St. Paul's Cathedral in the original square mile of the Roman city (fig. 5.26). The "City of London" is now the financial precinct. Dominated by the Nat West bank tower, it contains powerful institutions such as the Stock Exchange, the Bank of England, and the Royal Exchange. Pressure from the world's largest banks to locate in this prime financial area pushes up the density and height of office buildings. About two miles upriver, the "City of Westminster" developed around Westminster Abbey as a second core during the medieval period. The present Houses of Parliament were built in the mid-19th century. Queen Victoria made Buckingham Palace the monarch's residence in 1837.

This institutional core grew eastward toward the commercial core along Whitehall, where government offices include 10 Downing Street, the prime minister's residence. The royal hunting grounds in the west became St. James's, Green, Hyde, and Regent's Parks. The area between the parks and The City attracted the mansions of the nobility, centers of culture such as the Royal Academy and the National Gallery, and exclusive shops. In the 17th and 18th centuries, large-scale residential developments of townhouses and squares were speculatively built for the aristocracy. Belgravia, the last of these West End residential developments, has survived as an affluent neighborhood.

Figure 5.26 The commercial core of London. Office towers to the east and north of St. Paul's Cathedral puncture the typical low-rise skyline of European cities. (Photo by Linda McCarthy)

Nineteenth-century growth coalesced the twin cores into an expanding CBD. Major retailing axes developed along east-west Oxford Street and north-south Regent Street. In addition to the West End and The City, the inner city (thirteen of London's 32 boroughs) comprises a ring of 19th- and early-20th-century suburban growth about five miles (eight kilometers) in diameter. From the early 1840s, the railways allowed upper-middle–income families to move further out. The higher density Victorian and Edwardian housing nearer the center included middle-income detached and row houses such as those in Islington and the laborers' cottages in the East End. With increasing industrialization and the incredible growth of new docks and manufacturing facilities, the East End became home to the poorest immigrants (box 5.3). London's population grew from a little more than a million in 1800 to more than 6.5 million by 1900.

Much of the original housing in the East End is gone—destroyed in World War II air raids or replaced by high-rise blocks of already-deteriorating public housing. Any surviving housing is mostly in poor condition. Houses stand in a derelict industrial landscape of old factories, warehouses, docks, railway yards, and gas works. Many of the decaying middle-income residences have been subdivided into low-rent apartments. Except for the West End and The City, the inner city suffers from population loss due to out-migration, high unemployment, vacant and abandoned buildings, pollution, and a lack of amenities. Within the inner city, however, residents are differentiated into neighborhoods, each with its own shopping street, socioeconomic and ethnic mix, and political and sporting allegiances.

Since 1981, an extensive area of London's disused docklands has been rebuilt, refurbished, and gentrified through a combination of public and private incentives. Public

Box 5.3 The Poor in London's East End in 1850

The stranger who has entered London from the West can scarcely believe, after a residence among the princely dwellings and palaces of Belgravia, that there is a quarter in London like that called Spitalfields, and when he sees it for the first time he is astonished above measure. When we first gazed at the destitution and horrible wretchedness of Spitalfields, our blood ran cold at the sight, and whenever we hear the great English metropolis eulogized as the residence of princes in wealth and nobility, we think of some of the sights which our eyes have witnessed, among those parts where the poorer classes herd together, and which we never can efface from our memory.

There is a vast population lying east of Bishopsgate-street, and in wretchedness it may safely challenge a comparison with any people, or class, or nation under the sun. . . . Spitalfields is the residence of the poorest of the poor. In it the buildings are low and black—the interiors small, ill-ventilated, but crowded; and the streets almost too disgusting to describe. In traversing them, one is assailed by the noxious stenches, and the most disagreeable sights. This region is no small part of London, . . . it is the residence of the laboring population of London; there are hundreds of thousands of men, women, and children in it;—some just raised above utter wretchedness; others utterly wretched.

Source: David W. Bartlett, *What I Saw in London; or, Men and Things in the Great Metropolis* (Auburn, N.Y.: Derby & Miller, 1853), 111.

funds were spent on infrastructure and incentives to stimulate private-sector development. The city's tallest building, a fifty-story tower containing offices and specialty stores, was built at Canary Wharf. Dockland revitalization projects now extend as far west as the tiny and largely upscale Saint Katharine Dock, just east of the Tower of London. These dockland developments have attracted higher-income occupants and promoted gentrification of older properties by wealthy residents in adjacent parts of the inner city.

Outer London is a lower-density, seven-mile-wide belt (11 km wide) of interwar housing with some shopping streets and industrial parks. These outer suburbs compose the remaining 19 of London's 32 boroughs. The expansion of the London Underground and the spread of private automobile use promoted suburbanization between 1918 and 1939. A range of middle-income residents lives in well-maintained detached and semidetached houses with gardens. Neighborhood stability is strong, despite a slight decline in the aging population of empty nesters. Second-generation immigrants have moved into pockets of older housing. Private automobile use far in excess of road capacity causes massive traffic congestion.

The outer suburbs end abruptly at a five-to-ten-mile-wide greenbelt ring (8–16 km wide) within which development is restricted, in an effort to prevent urban sprawl and provide recreational space. The villages and small market towns here remain much as they were when the greenbelt was established in 1939. Growth pressures are evident only in the rural dwellings that have been gentrified by new wealthy residents. The prohibition of development within the greenbelt forced growth into either the existing built-up area or the zone outside the greenbelt that begins about 20 mi (32 km) from the city center. Eight new towns were built beyond the greenbelt to house the overspill population from London and the large number of migrants to the Southeast of England from the rest of the UK. This metropolitan fringe now extends up to 50 mi (80 km) from the city center and includes large towns like Guildford, Reading, and Luton. The relatively strong Southeast economy and the growth effects of both the Channel Tunnel link to France and the removal of barriers to trade within the EU have put pressure on housing availability and prices as well as government infrastructure and services. There has been no single government unit responsible for the 32 boroughs and The City since the Greater London Council was abolished in 1986. In 2000, a Greater London Assembly was elected that oversees police, transportation, fire, and emergency services. Despite the advantages of the assembly's coordinated citywide approach, it has limited tax-raising powers to address London's serious inner-city problems.

Paris: France's Primate City Par Excellence

With a population of more than 9.5 million, including the metropolitan fringe, Paris is Europe's second-largest metropolitan area. The more than two million people in central Paris alone make it the largest city by far in France. Paris dominates the national urban system, economy, politics, and culture more than perhaps any other capital city. Paris has adjusted to deindustrialization and become a major international center for modern industry and finance. The outer suburbs contain high-technology plants and research and development companies, as well as vehicle and airplane factories. Inner-city workshops produce exclusive items such as fashion clothing and jewelry.

Paris has survived wars and plagues, including the Black Death, which alone reduced the population by one-third, to 200,000, in 1347. Since World War II, the city has grown almost continuously, due to in-migration from the rest of France and the city's high proportion of young adults of childbearing age. Much of this growth has been concentrated in the outer suburbs. The city center and inner suburbs are losing population to the periphery.

The site of Paris, an island in the Seine, was the first point upriver that could be easily bridged. The Romans seized the town in 52 A.D. from the Parisii, a Gallic tribe, and named it Lutetia Parisiorum ("Midwater Dwelling of the Parisii"). The Romans built a temple and a palace for the city's governor. In addition to royal palaces, the island settlement attracted convents and churches. Begun in the 12th century, the magnificent Gothic cathedral of Notre Dame took more than 170 years to complete.

As a royal center, the grandeur of its architecture and planning made Paris an intensely monumental city. The "Royal Axis" is the imposing entry to the city. It runs from the Louvre (a former royal palace, now the national art gallery) and Tuileries Gardens across the Place de la Concorde, along the Champs-Élysées, to the Arc de Triomphe. The Eiffel

Figure 5.27 The sleek glass pyramid, designed by I. M. Pei, is the new, famous entrance to the Louvre, the national art gallery in a former royal palace, in Paris. (Photo by Linda McCarthy)

Tower was erected for the Paris exposition of 1889. Paris still produces imposing architectural works. Recent, initially controversial structures built in the historic core include the sleek glass pyramid by I. M. Pei in the forecourt of the Louvre (fig. 5.27) and the Pompidou Center, the national museum of modern art, nicknamed the "arty oil refinery" for its multicolored exterior ventilation and service ducts and its steel and glass escalators.

The Paris region, the Île de France, comprises eight administrative units, or *départments,* that date from the French Revolution. Most familiar to tourists, the innermost *départment,* Paris, coincides with la Cité, the historic City of Paris. This high-density area developed within the confines of the medieval walls. Its distinct quarters include the Île de la Cité, the initial tiny island settlement, the seat of administrative and religious authority, despite being only about ten blocks long and five wide. The right bank (facing downstream), the economic heart of the city, contains offices, fashionable shops, hotels, restaurants, and high- and middle-income apartments. The left (southern) bank, the seat of intellectual and cultural life, is dominated by its oldest part, the Latin Quarter, with the Sorbonne University, bookshops, theaters, and middle- and low-income apartments. Unlike in London, there are few large parks. Paris gets its feeling of openness and greenery from the wide boulevards and tree-lined river walkways.

The outer parts of Paris include the little ring *(petite couronne)* of inner suburbs that extend out about 15 mi (24 km) from the center and date from the period between the late 19th century and World War II. Interwar speculative developments of single-family homes were built on the prime sites in this area. Public mid- and high-rise apartments were erected later, on the less marketable land. The big ring *(grande couronne)* of outer suburbs spreads out another 10–15 mi (16–24 km) and contains the postwar public *grands ensembles* of poorly serviced, low-cost, high-rise apartments.

Since the late 1940s and the publication of Jean-François Gravier's book, *Paris and the*

French Desert, national and urban planning has focused on counteracting the extraordinary economic and demographic primacy of Paris. National decentralization policies have attempted to limit growth and congestion problems within the Paris region, while promoting development in the eight *métropoles d'équilibre* (balancing metropolises) of Lille-Roubaix-Tourcoing, Metz-Nancy, Strasbourg, Lyon, Marseille, Toulouse, Bordeaux, and Nantes-St. Nazaire. Five new towns (St. Quentin-en-Yvelines, Evry, Melun-Senart, Cergy-Pontoise, and Marne-la-Vallée) were built along two east-west axes of growth to the north and south of Paris. These new towns grew as extensions to the city, however, and became middle-income dormitory communities for some of the one million daily commuters to central Paris.

Complementing the new towns are four suburban employment centers. The largest and most successful is La Défense (fig. 5.28). It hosts high-rise office buildings containing the headquarters of major financial and other international corporations, shops, public buildings, and housing. The modern Grand Arche in La Défense is visible from the Arc de Triomphe along Avenue Charles-de-Gaulle—the modern extension of the Royal Axis.

Brussels: Centrality and the EU

Brussels is a national capital and an international administrative, financial, commercial, and modern manufacturing center. With a population of more than 1.5 million, Brussels is Belgium's largest metropolitan area. The Franks established a settlement on the Senne River in the 7th century. This site was an island at the furthest point upriver that could be reached by seagoing ships. Brussels grew as a trading center at the crossroads of a major commercial corridor running between England and Germany that included ports on either side of the English Channel as well as cities in Flanders such as Bruges and Antwerp.

During the medieval period, the "Pentagon" was the high-density core inside the five-sided city fortifications. This lower city housed artisans, merchants, and laborers. Its centerpiece, the Grand Place, is a public square containing the Hôtel de Ville, the 14th-century town hall. Many of the ornate 17th-century guildhalls there are now restaurants and shops. In the 18th and 19th centuries, public buildings, royal palaces, and mansions of the nobility were built nearby in the upper, or high, city along wide, tree-lined avenues and spacious squares. A series of boulevards replaced the city walls during the 19th century.

Despite being officially bilingual (French and Dutch), Brussels does not dominate the national political, economic, and cultural scenes in this linguistically divided country. Brussels's location on a linguistic frontier favored its selection as the headquarters for the EU. As a result, English is now also spoken widely. The EU's offices are concentrated in a massive executive district of some 85 city blocks to the east of both the medieval Pentagon and the national government administrative office complex. The demand for office space in the central administrative district has driven significant turnover of land from residential to commercial uses. This trend has reinforced the migration of young professionals to the periphery of the city.

During the interwar years and after World War II, medium- and high-rise apartments were built instead of traditional row houses. Single-family townhouses have also been subdivided into two or more apartments. Despite this increase in the number of dwelling units, the city's population has declined since the 1970s because of suburbanization and the

Figure 5.28 Looking northwest from the Eiffel Tower, Paris. The Palais du Chaillot in the foreground was built for the International Exposition of 1937. In the distance, beyond the Bois de Bologne, is La Défense, a planned suburban employment center. (Photo by Linda McCarthy)

lower fertility of the aging population. Since the 1960s, the number of foreign-born residents has risen to more than 30% of the population. Immigrants from the United States and the richer EU countries such as France and the Netherlands live in the more affluent communes in the east and southeast of the city. Thousands of poorer migrants have come from countries around the Mediterranean and live in the deteriorated old housing in the Pentagon or in the declining traditional manufacturing areas to the north and west of the city. Suburban municipalities now attract the new services and high-technology employment.

Brussels is known for city planning that is laissez-faire at best and dominated by private-sector development interests at worst. Several factors hinder effective urban and metropolitan planning: land-use planning regulations are complicated and fragmented; there is a general aversion to national control of planning in the capital city; and little coordination occurs between the 19 central autonomous communes and the surrounding suburban municipalities.

Barcelona: Capital of Catalonia

With about 1.5 million people, Barcelona is Spain's second-largest city, after the capital, Madrid. Located on the northeastern coast of Spain, Barcelona is the regional capital of Catalonia and the country's largest port and leading industrial, commercial, and cultural center. The Phoenicians founded Barcelona more than 2,000 years ago. The city's street plan reflects its three main phases of growth—its ancient and medieval origins, 19th-century additions, and late-20th-century suburbs. The old town is the symbolic and administrative center of the city. Remnants of the Roman wall and grid pattern of streets are overlain by the high-density, narrow, winding streets of the medieval core. In 1859, Ildefons Cerdà drew up a plan of expansion into the area that had been occupied by the medieval wall. His pioneering urban design was based on a grid pattern with wide, straight boulevards and octangular-sided blocks containing central parks and gardens surrounded by a limited number of apartment houses. Largely ignored during 19th- and early-20th-century speculative growth, Cerdà's plan is reflected in Barcelona's characteristic grid system of streets and was realized only in the Eixample district, a new core precinct that was built just north of the old city. This new development also contains the high-rise offices and apartments of the modern CBD.

After the establishment of the Franco regime in 1939, Barcelona experienced uncontrolled speculative development without adequate public infrastructure and services. Massive rural-urban migration fueled rapid population growth. Tens of thousands of illegal squatters ended up in the shantytowns at the sprawling edge of the city. In the 1960s and 1970s, several hundred thousand poorly designed and serviced, peripheral high-rise public apartments were built to address the acute housing shortage.

Since the mid-1970s and the establishment of a new democratic political system, the increased autonomy of Barcelona's elected local governments has contributed to a rebirth of planning as well as growing prosperity. Barcelona's urban renewal program benefited from funding for infrastructure from the EU. The construction of the 1992 Olympic village helped rejuvenate an area of derelict docks. At the same time, continued in-migration of poor residents has put enormous pressure on housing, infrastructure, and services. These poor migrants become socially, economically, and locationally polarized in the inner-city slums, the peripheral public apartment blocks, or the surviving extensive shantytowns. In contrast, higher-income residents live in nicer central districts or well-serviced, lower-density parts of the suburbs.

Oslo: The Low-Key Capital of Norway

Oslo is the largest urban center in Norway, as measured both by the 500,000 or so people who inhabit the city and by its metropolitan area population of about 750,000. Located on the Oslo Fjorden, this city is Norway's capital, main port, and leading commercial, industrial, communications, and manufacturing center.

The city was founded around 1050, became the national capital in 1299, and joined the Hanseatic League during the 14th century. Given the predominance of wood as a building material, fire was an early problem in Oslo, particularly during the frequent sieges that befell the city. Following a particularly devastating fire that lasted for three days in 1624, King Christian IV designated another site for the town nearer Akershus Castle on the east side of the bay. The new town, renamed Christiana—a name it kept until reverting to Oslo in 1924—was planned with a grid system of spacious streets, a square located between the town and castle, and ramparts protecting the northern flanks. Significantly, buildings in the town were allowed to be constructed only of brick or stone; soon, however, extensive tracts of wooden houses were built on the outskirts of the built-up area. The town, though, grew slowly: it had only around 5,000 residents in 1661 and only 10,000 by 1800.

During the mid-1800s, the administrative function of the city was augmented by industry, based mainly on textiles and wood processing. Important buildings such as the university (1811) and royal palace (1848) also made their appearances. The city expanded in a largely unplanned manner as the population swelled to 28,000 by 1850 and 228,000 by 1900. In the postwar period, Oslo's outward expansion continued, largely as a result of Social Democratic Party policies that heavily subsidized owner-occupied housing.

Despite being Scandinavia's oldest capital, Oslo today is a modern, though low-key, city. As is common throughout Northern Europe, the city extends around the port, is flanked by the centrally located train station, has a royal palace overlooking the historic core, and has a center marked by pedestrian shopping areas.

Berlin: Reinventing Germany's National Capital

Located on a flat, sandy plain on the Spree River, Berlin dates from the 13th century and assumed a prominent role in the Hanseatic League during the 14th century. Berlin owes much of its growth to political factors, in particular after its selection as the seat of power of the electors of Brandenburg (1486) and the kings of Prussia (1701). Berlin continued to grow during the early 19th century as the center of an expanding rail and canal network and as an industrial and commercial center. The city was made capital of Germany in 1871 and soon rose to international prominence. Berlin's population increased from 172,000 in 1800 to 826,000 in 1870 and 4.2 million in 1930.

The city's role as center of the Third Reich (1930s–1940s) made it the focus of Allied efforts to defeat Hitler. Berlin was heavily bombed during the latter part of World War II and received severe damage at the hands of the Russian forces that captured the city. At the end of the war, Germany was divided into East (the German Democratic Republic, GDR) and West (the Federal Republic of Germany, FRG); Berlin, which was located wholly within the GDR, was partitioned into a western zone administered by the United States, Great Britain, and France and an eastern zone administered by the Soviets. In 1949, East Berlin was declared the capital of the GDR, while the functioning capital of the FRG was moved to Bonn.

Tensions soon mounted. Apparently not satisfied with the division of Berlin, the Soviets tried to gain complete control of the city by instituting a blockade on April 1, 1948. The 1.5 million residents of West Berlin suddenly found themselves cut off from all forms of ground transportation and in desperate need of food and other supplies. Rather than allow the residents of West Berlin to submit to this pressure, the United States ordered airlifts of supplies. Within days, American and British pilots began flying fully loaded C-54 and other transport planes into the besieged city. Flights were made 24 hours a day, seven days a week, landing in three different airports approximately every ten minutes, until the blockade was lifted on September 30, 1949. In an effort to stem the tide of people trying to escape from the poverty and harsh political conditions in East Berlin to the relative prosperity and freedom of West Berlin, the Soviets built a wall in 1961 that separated the two zones. The Berlin Wall in general, and "Checkpoint Charlie," the main crossing point between West and East, in particular, soon became poignant symbols of the Cold War. In November 1989, mass demonstrations led to the removal of the wall, the eventual collapse of East Germany, and the reunification of the divided nation in October 1990.

From the 1960s until 1989, the two Berlins developed under very different political and economic conditions. East Berlin became something of a socialist showplace. The city featured a large central square, Alexanderplatz, that was dotted with socialist statues, flanked by a hotel, and punctuated by a highly visible TV tower featuring an observation platform. Leading west from the square, Unter den Linden, historically Berlin's most fashionable boulevard, winds past the Palast der Republic, museum island, and Humboldt University, through much sought-after residential districts, and through the Brandenburg Gate. From 1961 to 1989, the Berlin Wall cut through the city at this point. The wall was heavily patrolled, monitored from strategically placed observation towers, and surrounded by open areas of "no man's land." Today, a section of the wall to the north of the Brandenburg Gate has been preserved, but for the most part little trace remains of this once divisive edifice.

West Berlin was a world away from its Eastern twin. West Berlin's main square, Kurfürstendamm, acted as the center of a typical Western European town, complete with office buildings, department stores and other retail outlets, restaurants, entertainment facilities, and billboards and other symbols of a strong corporate presence. Located here also was one of the few reminders of the war in West Berlin, the remains of a bombed-out church, oddly juxtaposed with a modern church tower. Toward the north and east were the grounds of the zoological gardens and a large park; toward the west and south were the main industrial and residential sections of the city.

The changes in Berlin since 1989 have been dramatic. Five types of building projects have been initiated over the past few decades. First has been the construction of a set of buildings as part of a new government center for Berlin as the capital city. Second has been the massive reconstruction along Friedrichstrasse. This boulevard, which stretches from the former site of Checkpoint Charlie north to Unter den Linden, now contains upscale retail outlets, a mall, and assorted office buildings, making it the "Fifth Avenue of Berlin." Third have been the enormous construction projects at Potsdamerplatz, just south of the Brandenburg Gate. Ironically, this zone of land that ran along the wall—located at the boundaries of East and West Berlin and now at the center of the reunited city—is the most valuable building site in Europe. Following reunification, it was much sought after by corporations eager to take advantage of Berlin as a springboard to Central and Eastern Europe. This multibillion dollar development area, involving such corporate giants as Sony and Daimler-Benz, is significantly changing the look of Berlin (fig. 5.29).

Fourth have been the extensive public trans-

Figure 5.29 The Sony Centre in Berlin is the best example of the postsocialist building boom underway in many cities of Eastern Europe. (Photo by Darrick Danta)

portation improvements. The most pressing need was to reconnect rail and subway lines that had been separated during the Cold War. New subway stations have been constructed, along with improved train stations and an auto tunnel. Fifth, various constructions and memorials concerning the war have been completed. The area containing Hitler's bunker has been preserved, while the "Topography of Terror," an outdoor exhibit illustrating the horrors of SS activity during the war, has been built nearby. Given all these changes, Berlin is already moving forward to take its place among the world's premier urban places.

Bucharest: The Legacy of Soviet Domination

No city in Europe bears the personal imprint of an individual to the extent that Bucharest does of deposed leader Nicolae Ceauçescu. Romania's capital allows fascinating insights into the impact that a megalomaniacal personality can have on a city. Bucharest was founded in the 15th century and became the capital of Wallachia in 1659. During the 19th century, the city became an important transportation hub, acquired a manufacturing base, and became capital of Romania when the country was formed in 1862. The city enjoyed continued growth up to World War II and even came to be known as the "Paris of the East." Population totals for Bucharest rose from about 60,000 in 1830, to 350,000 by 1914, to a little more than one million at the end of World War II.

Following the war, Bucharest was developed according to socialist planning principles: industrial capacity was expanded; new housing was constructed; and former villas were converted into government offices and foreign embassies. Population increased to 1.4 million by 1966, the year Ceauçescu came to power. The new leader's program for urban redevelopment, *systematization*, which was mainly directed at villages in the countryside, led to detached housing in some of Bucharest's suburbs being destroyed and replaced with apartment blocks. Ceauçescu greatly expanded housing estate construction within existing districts and redesigned certain boulevards leading into the city to serve as impressive entryways that would represent the revolutionary ethic being created under socialism.

In the 1980s, the leader turned his attention to central Bucharest. By the time of his overthrow in 1989, approximately 25% of the central area—a zone about 3 mi (4.8 km) long by nearly a mile (1.6 km) wide—had been completely bulldozed to make room for new buildings. At the heart of the scheme was the House of the Republic, a grandiose structure measuring almost 900 by 800 ft (270 by 240 m) on the sides and about 330 ft (99 m) high, making it one of the largest buildings in the world. The structure was to be the new seat of government. This building consumed virtually all the marble in the country during its construction and featured hand-carved wood paneling and crystal chandeliers. The second component of the scheme was the construction of the Victory of Socialism Boulevard. This finely appointed ceremonial route was intended to be longer and grander than the Champs-Élysées in Paris and eventually was adorned by a lavish fountain and lined by Bucharest's finest apartments. Another rather bizarre element of Ceauçescu's modifications involved churches. The leader simply did not like them but rather than being accused of ordering their destruction, he had many of them moved to locations where they were hidden behind other buildings. Although the damage from the December 1989 Romanian Revolution has been largely repaired, the city still suffers from the legacy of Ceauçescu. Today's Bucharest is covered in dust, potholes make driving difficult, apartment blocks are crumbling, construction of the House of the Republic and most of the surrounding apartments is still not complete, and hundreds of homeless children live on the streets.

URBAN TRENDS AND PROBLEMS

Compared to the problems faced by cities elsewhere, and particularly those in less developed countries, European cities are fairly well off. Nevertheless, to varying degrees cities in Europe suffer from problems similar to those experienced in other more developed parts of the world, such as North America.

Western Europe

As the earliest location in the world to experience industrialization, Western Europe was also the first place to be hit by deindustrialization. Rising long-term unemployment among inner-city residents has concentrated poverty and a wide range of social problems in some inner-city neighborhoods of older industrial cities. These neighborhoods also contain the city's oldest and most deteriorated housing and urban infrastructure. Privatization of public housing by governments attempting to cut back on public expenditures has exacerbated the shortage of decent, affordable housing. The enormous cost of upgrading the urban infrastructure in con-

Figure 5.30 Even the main thoroughfares of smaller towns such as Cork in southern Ireland suffer from congestion and pollution problems as they try to accommodate 21st-century automobiles. (Photo by Linda McCarthy)

junction with ongoing budgetary constraints translates into inadequate municipal services in the inner city.

As private automobile ownership has risen, traffic congestion and air pollution, especially in the medieval cores, have reached critical levels (fig. 5.30). Transportation policies in Western Europe have shifted from investment in freeways and central parking facilities to transportation demand management involving ride sharing and public transit. Since the late 1960s, many cities have built or extended subway and light-rail systems. Automobile ownership, however, continues to rise.

The presence of significant numbers of foreign workers and their families has generated a series of problems. Language differences create problems for the educational system in countries with large numbers of children born to foreign workers. These students represent 20–50% or more of the school population in some French, German, and Swiss cities. The general recession and rising unemployment of the early 1990s served to intensify existing prejudices among the indigenous population based on differences in language, culture, or race. Since that time, antiforeigner sentiments have led to vicious attacks on migrants by violent elements within the indigenous population, especially in some German and French cities. At the same time, the general incidence of serious crime—murder, rape, assault—in European cities is much lower than that found in North American cities. Petty crime such as theft or vandalism remains a problem in many cities, though, especially in tourist areas.

Pollution is a problem in nearly every city of the world, though Western European cities rate more favorably than most. Indeed, Swiss, Austrian, and Scandinavian cities are sanitized almost daily and citizens there are conscious not to litter. Many streets and squares in Italy and Spain are routinely scrubbed. Levels of pollution in most of the former heavy industrial regions have fallen. Indeed, air quality in the English Midlands has improved since polluting industries have closed or relocated, while even the Ruhr area boasts clear skies and clean lakes.

Eastern Europe

Beginning in the early 1990s, governments across Eastern Europe faced the daunting problem of transforming their command economies into market-based systems. Virtually all aspects of the economy needed to be privatized. Under socialism, workers were publicly employed and all businesses were owned by the state. Governments have been selling these state-run facilities either to individuals or groups within their countries or to foreign investors. Of course, most economic activities under socialism were run very inefficiently, so privatization has usually resulted in plant closure and unemployment, something unheard of previously. Privatization efforts have had a particularly troubling impact on the housing sector. People in the countries of Eastern Europe were accustomed to paying very little for housing. With privatization and the burgeoning land market, some investors have reaped huge profits; most individuals, though, have suffered economic hardship.

The surviving smoke-belching plants, using outmoded technology, still cause very high levels of pollution. Add to this the lower environmental standards and weaker regulations, use of higher-risk industrial processes, and greater reliance on Soviet-type nuclear reactors, and it soon becomes clear why Eastern Europe is far more polluted than Western Europe.

Another problem concerns the inadequate road system throughout Eastern Europe, particularly in view of the dramatic increase in car ownership rates since 1990, which has placed considerable strain on road systems and parking facilities. Previously, most people could not afford to own a car, waiting periods for car orders were long, and restrictions on ownership applied in some countries. Currently, municipal governments are busily constructing new roads and parking structures.

Finally, the considerable economic and social changes in Eastern Europe have increased the opportunities for criminal activities. In recent years, the incidence of petty crime, such as pickpocketing, has increased. Organized crime has also grown enormously. Besides the more typical drugs, gambling, and prostitution activities, Mafia-type crime organizations have made their appearance in many cities. These groups mainly have sought to control the expanding small-scale retail sector, especially kiosk operators. In scenes reminiscent of 1920s Chicago, small operators are offered "protection" and, if they refuse to pay, their kiosks are vandalized.

URBAN POLICY AND PLANNING

Europe became the birthplace of modern city planning as it reacted to the drawbacks of uncontrolled growth during the industrial period. Policy making and planning to address urban trends and problems now pervade European city life. At different times and places, the goals of planning have been the rational arrangement of different land uses, the efficient functioning of transportation and utility systems, public safety, economic vitality, social equity, environmental quality, aesthetic appearance and architectural design, citizen participation, and the expression of government power.

Modern Urban Planning Traditions

During the past two centuries, European planners have followed six major traditions. Each tradition has attempted to address particular urban trends and problems or to remedy the deficiencies of a previous planning approach.

1. The *authoritarian tradition* laid the foundation for modern planning during the second half of the 19th century. In an extravagant display of institutional power, wide, straight boulevards containing monumental architecture and public works replaced sections of narrow, winding medieval streets. The goals were to beautify cities and remove slums, provide public utilities, create public works employment, and improve traffic circulation and troop movement. Authoritarian planning reappeared during the fascist era in Hitler's Germany, Franco's Spain, and Mussolini's Italy. Out of favor by the early 20th century in Western Europe, it survived after World War II in Eastern Europe.
2. The *utilitarian tradition* was associated with the rise of 19th-century capitalism in Western Europe. City planning in this industrial economy was functional and subservient to the requirements of free enterprise and profit. This kind of urban design produced poor-quality tenement housing for workers that lacked adequate space, ventilation, and light. Negative reactions to the utilitarian tradition in the late 19th century prompted the introduction of legislation governing health, sanitation, and housing conditions.
3. The *romantic tradition* was a reaction to the geometric and monumental authoritarian tradition and the functional and laissez-faire utilitarian tradition. Camillo Sitte, its main proponent, called for enclosed spaces that were designed with imagination and unpredictability, and with aesthetic values that were sensitive to history. Sitte's ideas were reflected in the planning of cities across Europe, including Salzburg and Vienna in the late 19th century and Stockholm, Amsterdam, and Madrid in the early 20th century. His legacy includes city squares offering a focal point, such as a church in Berlin's Zionskirchplatz or a formal garden in the Place de la Nation in Paris.
4. *Utopian planning* was a reaction to the utilitarian tradition and the poor living conditions in early industrial cities. By the early 19th century, Robert Owen in Scotland and Charles Fourier in France had attempted to create model communities. In the second half of the 19th century, industrialists in England built Port Sunlight (William Lever) and Bourneville (George Cadbury). In Germany, Alfred Krupp constructed Margarethenhöhe outside Essen. In the early 20th century, Ebenezer Howard's utopian *Garden City* concept envisioned urban centers of limited size surrounded by greenbelts. Garden Cities include Welwyn Garden City and Letchworth outside London, Hellerau near Dresden, and Tiepolo in Italy. Third Reich planning employed the

Garden City concept to achieve its race hygiene objectives.

5. *Organic planning* built on the achievements of the utopian and romantic traditions. To Scottish biologist Patrick Geddes, cities were living organisms forming natural regions. These regions could be managed scientifically to permit organic metropolitan growth while preventing urban problems from spreading into the countryside. A classic city-region plan in this tradition was Patrick Abercrombie's 1944 Plan for Greater London. This plan involved the shifting of more than a million people to eight new, self-contained towns outside a greenbelt.
6. The *technocratic tradition* was an offshoot of the utopian city plans. This tradition added technical analysis to planning in an effort to design cities that functioned like efficient machines. Architects like Le Corbusier, Mies van der Rohe, and Walter Gropius designed high-rise apartment blocks separated from industrial districts and transportation routes by vast open spaces. These designs formed the basis of the international style of modern architecture that swept Europe after World War II. This style's characteristic, functional concrete, steel, and glass high rises now dominate city center redevelopment schemes, new towns, and peripheral public housing estates. Its capacity to produce nonbourgeois cities made it popular in Eastern Europe.

Contemporary Urban Policy Making and Planning

Postwar planning for redevelopment and growth ended in the early 1970s in Western Europe. Declining population growth rates and widespread economic recession forced governments to reevaluate the efficacy of large-scale, publicly funded projects. There was general dissatisfaction with the technocratic tradition's high-rise buildings and open spaces. Policy shifted to planning for conservation and restructuring, and for combating urban decline.

This reappraisal of policy and planning has two, often conflicting, components. On the one hand, budgetary constraints force governments to actively seek private-sector participation and investment in urban revitalization projects. On the other hand, there is growing concern for issues of social equity, citizen participation, environmental protection, and aesthetic quality. These competing elements are pitted against each other at three main government levels: local, national, and international.

Local Policy Making and Planning

Since the early 1970s, urban revitalization policies in the older industrial cities in Western Europe have promoted economic restructuring away from traditional manufacturing. Cities use local, national, and EU funds to attract private-sector investment in high-technology and service industries. Traditionally in Southern Europe, cities in lower-cost production areas attracted labor-intensive branch-plant industries. More recently, cities such as Montpellier in southern France, Bari in southern Italy, and Valencia in southeastern Spain have focused on providing attractive environments for high-technology industries. Since the early 1990s, cities in Eastern Europe such as Rostock, Budapest, Prague, and Warsaw have actively worked to attract new commercial and industrial investment.

Urban revitalization policies include conservation efforts that reflect the economic importance of tourism in Europe since the days of the European tour. To protect the character of historic districts today, many cities require new construction to be built behind the preserved facade of existing buildings. These policies stem from neighborhood and preservationist activism in the 1960s against proposed city-center clearance and redevelopment schemes. In the 1970s, housing policy in Western Europe shifted away from central slum clearance and peripheral high-rise construction to rehabilitating the existing public housing. In the 1980s, neoliberal privatization policies transferred many public housing units to former tenants. In some Southern and Eastern European cities, rural-urban migration and the poor quality of peripheral public housing remain pressing policy and budgetary issues.

In recent years, most countries in Western Europe have decentralized urban planning, giving over power and responsibility to local governments. In addition, small units of local government have been consolidated into larger regional ones in an attempt to achieve economies of scale. These policy and administrative changes have set the scene for more coordinated regional planning. The "compact city" policy in the Randstad endeavors to curb counterurbanization in this region by concentrating new development within the existing major cities in an effort to maintain their economic competitiveness.

National Policy Making and Planning

In Western Europe, national policies promoted regional decentralization after World War II. Industry, commercial activity, and population were redirected from the large, congested cities to new towns. Many new towns were built as satellite centers or dormitory communities to accommodate spillover population from larger cities across Northern and Western Europe, as in the case of Abercrombie's Plan for Greater London. In the 1970s, declining population growth and widespread economic recessions forced national governments in Western Europe to reassess the need for new-town planning. Since that time, no additional new towns have been budgeted for public funding or even designated in Western Europe.

In the 1980s, a national policy shift reflected the recognition of a number of factors—the difficulty of achieving the decentralization of economic activity, the severity of decline in the central parts of larger cities, and the importance of these larger cities as national engines of growth in a global economy. The UK government established urban development corporations to attract businesses to declining industrial and port areas in cities such as Liverpool and London. In the 1990s, government policy shifted yet again, away from expensive, nationally devised strategies to "community empowerment" initiatives in which local communities carry out revitalization programs and projects that are sensitive to local challenges and opportunities.

In Eastern Europe after World War II, governments were guided by the basic tenets of Marxist-Leninist planning, namely eliminating excessive population concentration in large cities, achieving a balanced urban and infrastructural system, removing the "contradiction" between urban and rural living standards, and creating a classless society. Matching these urban and social planning goals were economic directives that called for the rapid development of heavy industry and the collectivization of agriculture.

In an effort to reduce the size of large cities, governments in most Eastern European countries placed restrictions on the growth of their capitals. In the majority of large cities, however, industrial expansion continued to draw workers from smaller towns or the countryside, thus swelling the large cities' populations. In an attempt to increase overall industrial capacity, balance the urban system, and provide urban functions to underserved areas, governments implemented programs of new-town construction. New towns usually were developed around a large industrial facility, typically an iron and steel mill or chemical processing plant; were consciously sited away from existing towns; and were located either on a vacant piece of land or on the site of an existing village. Whereas residential capacity had been the most important element that influenced the planning and design of the new towns in Western Europe, accommodating industrial capacity and employment was the major issue for the authoritarian planners of the new socialist towns. New towns in Eastern Europe included Eisenhüttenstadt in the GDR, Nova Huta in Poland, and Dimitrovgrad in Bulgaria. These places grew rapidly between 1950 and 1970, eventually becoming important not only for the industrial products that they produced, but also for their roles as urban centers in the hinterlands that they served and in creating a more balanced national urban system for their countries.

By the 1970s and 1980s, planners in Eastern Europe had turned their attention from promoting large-scale industry and new towns to developing light industries and filling out the national urban systems. In many countries, central place theory became either an explicit or implicit guide to development efforts, as planners tried to create multitiered urban hierarchies that provided goods and services to particular regions according to their size and function. This kind of national planning and its outcome, however, varied among the different countries. While most countries built new industrial towns, this form of planning was especially well developed in Hungary, where the National Settlement Development Strategy established the blueprint for the settlement network.

Since the early 1990s, Eastern European cities have been impacted by the national reform strategies that have involved privatizing state-owned housing and industry and promoting new industries and companies. National policy continues to evolve to address urban problems such as the unemployment and homelessness caused by the economic restructuring to capitalism.

International Policy Making and Planning

Western Europe is the scene of significant international urban planning and management initiatives. The Council of Europe promotes historic preservation and urban regeneration through initiatives such as European Architectural Heritage Year. The integration efforts of the EU have led to unprecedented achievements in international policy and planning in Western Europe. Since 1975, for example, EU regional policy has promoted urban development in economically weak peripheral regions or in areas suffering industrial decline. Increasing East-West economic and political integration in Europe as well as the globalization of the economy create opportunities and challenges for the cities of Europe. Certainly, urban policy and planning will continue to attempt to respond to the ongoing changes that impact European cities.

URBAN FUTURES

Since the early 1990s, improved air, rail, and road transportation linkages connecting the major urban centers in both the East and the West have been laying the foundation for the complete integration of the European urban system. The businesses and city governments in the Eastern European countries that are on the waiting list to join the EU have already developed stronger economic and political ties with their counterparts among the existing 15 member states in Western Europe. Membership in the EU will enhance the opportunities of the former socialist cities to address their pressing social and economic problems. Certainly, the future and prosperity of the entire "new" Europe in the global economy depends on creating a more economically and socially equitable situation for all European urban residents. Once EU membership and the use of the common currency, the euro, is extended throughout Eastern Europe, the European urban system will undergo even more profound changes as the governments, businesses, and people in the cities across Europe and elsewhere reorient their activities to take advantage of the new economic and political environment.

At some point in the future, serious consideration will be given to shifting some of the administrative functions of the EU to cities further east. While London, Paris, Frankfurt, Brussels, and Milan will continue to dominate as major financial, political, and cultural centers, Berlin, Vienna, Warsaw, Prague, and Budapest, which have already emerged as important European centers, will surely shift the center of gravity of the core-periphery model further east as the 21st century progresses.

SUGGESTED READINGS

Åman, A. *Architecture and Ideology in Eastern Europe during the Stalin Era: An Aspect of Cold War History*. Cambridge, Mass.: MIT Press, 1992. A fascinating, in-depth, and well-illustrated look at the mindset of planners and architects who produced the buildings and socialist cities of Eastern Europe.

Brunt, B. *Western Europe: A Social and Economic Geography*. 2d ed. Dublin: Gill & Macmillan, 1997. Contains a chapter that provides a thorough and well-illustrated account of "urbanization and urban development" in Western Europe.

Burtenshaw, D., M. Bateman, and G. J. Ashworth. *The City in West Europe*. New York: Wiley, 1981. A wide-ranging book that examines the processes and histories that have shaped Western European urbanization, reviews policies that address various aspects of urban development, and describes urban planning processes.

Enyedi, Gy., ed. *Social Change and Urban Restructuring in Central Europe*. Budapest: Akadémiai Kiadó, 1998. An "insider" look at the recent trends in cities in the postsocialist period.

French, R. A., and F. E. I. Hamilton, eds. *The Socialist City: Spatial Structure and Urban Policy*. New York: Wiley, 1979. The classic on socialist urbanization, includes general chapters plus description of individual cities.

Goodman, David, and Colin Chant, eds. *European Cities and Technology: Industrial to Post-Industrial City*. New York: Routledge, 1999. Considers the impact of new technologies on urban change in Britain, France, Germany, and Russia.

Hall, T. *Planning Europe's Capital Cities: Aspects of Nineteenth-Century Urban Development*. London: E&FN Spon, 1997. Detailed presentations of the historic growth and urban planning of fifteen European capitals.

Hubbard, M., and B. Baer, eds. *Cities of the World*. 4th ed. Vol. 3. Detroit: Gale Research, 1993. A compilation of information on the cultural, geographical, and political conditions in the countries and cities of Europe.

Tilly, Charles, and Wim P. Blockmans, eds. *Cities and the Rise of States in Europe, A.D. 1000 to 1800*. Boulder: Westview, 1994. This book addresses the relationship between cities and political development in selected regions of Europe, from the Middle Ages to the industrial period.

Wagenaar, M., et al., eds. *GeoJournal* 51 (2000). Special issue containing twelve essays on European capital cities, including one by Wagenaar on "Townscapes of Power" (3–13) that examines how central Paris was transformed into an awe-inspiring national capital in the late 19th century.

Figure 6.1 Major Cities of Russia. *Source*: Data from United Nations, *World Urbanization Prospects, 2001 Revision* (New York: United Nations Population Division, 2002), www.unpopulation.org.

6

Cities of Russia

BETH A. MITCHNECK AND ELLEN HAMILTON

KEY URBAN FACTS

Total Population	145 million
Percent Urban Population	73%
Total Urban Population	106 million
Most Urbanized Country	N.A.
Least Urbanized Country	N.A.
Annual Urban Growth Rate	–0.36%
Number of Megacities	0
Number of Cities of More Than 1 Million	12
Three Largest Cities	Moscow, St. Petersburg, Nizhni Novgorod
World Cities	None

KEY CHAPTER THEMES

1. Russia is one of the most urbanized countries in the world.
2. Russia has long been dominated by the primate city of Moscow, in spite of a two-century rivalry with St. Petersburg, the old capital.
3. Russia's urban development reflects the impact of three distinct eras in the country's history: czarist, Soviet, and post-Soviet.
4. Russia's vast size and harsh climate have greatly affected the urban system.
5. The main pattern of the urban system, with its strong reflections of European urban characteristics, was established in the czarist era.
6. The Soviet era (1917–1991) produced the most profound changes in all aspects of urban development and urban life, because of central planning and autocratic rule by the Communist Party.
7. The post-Soviet era has seen the need for complete overhauling and redesign of urban places in a now free-market economy and democratic society.
8. Severe economic recession in the 1990s at least temporarily caused a deurbanization or ruralization of the country.

9. Cities that are prospering are those with superior locations and attractive environments for foreign investment and economic growth.
10. The socialist support system of the Soviet era is gone, crime and corruption are rampant, and a host of problems beset the country as it struggles to reinvent itself.

On December 25, 1991, the eighth—and last—Soviet leader, Mikhail Gorbachev, resigned. Quietly, with no announcement, the Soviet hammer and sickle flag was lowered and the red, white, and blue of the Russian flag was raised, thus signaling the end of one of the most audacious experiments in nation-state development of the 20th century. Today, the Russian Federation (fig 6.1), the country with the largest territory in the world, is in the midst of a triple transition—economic, political, and social. Since the breakup of the Union of Soviet Socialist Republics, these various transitions have both precipitated crises and encouraged their resolution, resulting in trends that seem illogical to those unfamiliar with the country. For example, at the beginning of the post-Soviet period, economic collapse meant factory workers, teachers, and other urban workers moved from cities back to rural areas to practice subsistence farming, a process known as *ruralization.* Not surprisingly in a country nearly twice the size of the United States, the recent emergence of capitalism as a social and economic system, and the visual imprint of capitalism on the landscape, are unevenly distributed across Russian cities. The harsh climate, poorly developed (and frequently impassable) network of roads, and immense distances all exacerbate the fragmentation of the Russian urban system.

The built environment of Russian cities has changed so dramatically since December 1991 that many cities are nearly unrecognizable to those accustomed to the quiet, somber landscapes of the Soviet period. Moscow's Red Square is no longer a nearly deserted public space awaiting military parades. Instead, it is a bustling retail space. The sparsely distributed Communist Party billboards in every city and town have been replaced by brilliant neon and banner-type advertisements along all the major urban thoroughfares. Cities constructed for pedestrians and mass transit are now choked with all manner of vehicles. The typical Soviet rings of large apartment complexes are mixed with Western-style suburban developments of "cottages" and even gated communities.

Post-Soviet Russia is also grappling with changes in the location of urban development and the legacy of the Soviet spatial structure of the urban system. No longer do central planners choose a site for a new factory and then build a city around it, as was the case in the Soviet Union. The Soviet system of planning resulted in construction of cities in unexpected, and ultimately unsustainable, places such as the remote reaches of Siberia and the Arctic. Cities were often sited near natural resources, regardless of the location of those resources. To give but one example, Norilsk, a nickel-smelting city with more than a quarter million inhabitants, was built far above the Arctic Circle. The Soviet system resulted in an urban spatial pattern of economic flows between quite distant cities because the locations of suppliers, intermediate producers, and markets were of little concern in a system where transportation and energy costs were state determined and therefore perceived to be free.

Figure 6.2 In the post-Soviet era, a great variety of street peddlers can be seen on the streets of cities in both Russia and its former republics that have become independent nations, as in this scene from Odessa, Ukraine. (Photo by Jack Williams)

Also gone now is the Soviet emphasis on the military-industrial complex (MIC) in determining the location of investment and urban growth. Many cities became *closed cities* (cities requiring permission to visit) because of their role in the MIC. Cities in the Urals, such as Perm and Magnitogorsk, grew in economic importance and population precisely because they were integral parts of the MIC. Decades of defense-related investments in these cities' industrial bases, housing stock, roads, schools, and other infrastructure influenced the population, economic, and urban geographies in ways that would not have been possible in capitalist economies where economic efficiency is the most important criterion for attracting new factories and urban development.

The demise of the Soviet Union effectively ended central planning, as Russian cities embarked on a new and equally radical experiment, the transition from socialism to capitalism. The 1990s saw the beginning of rapid and widespread change in the location of urban development in response to economic collapse and restructuring, increasing poverty (and especially urban poverty), and large inflows of refugees from other, more troubled parts of the former Soviet Union (fig. 6.2). This change will continue well into the 21st century.

Russia began the 20th century with less than one-fifth of its population living in urban places and ended it with almost three-quarters. Since the middle of the 20th century, the majority of the Russian population has lived in cities, many of which are large urban centers (tab. 6.1). The percentage steadily increased throughout the Soviet period; by 1989, 74% of the population of Russia lived in urban places. After that, the percentage of the population living in urban places declined slightly and then, by the late 1990s, leveled off at about 73%.

Table 6.1 Percentage of the Population Living in Urban Places, by Russian Economic Region, 1959–1996

Economic Region	*1959*	*1970*	*1979*	*1989*	*1996*
Northern	56	64	73	77	76
Northwestern	72	80	85	87	87
Central	59	71	78	83	83
Volgo-Vyatsk	39	53	62	69	70
Central Chernozem	27	40	52	60	62
Volga	48	59	68	73	73
North Caucasus	43	50	55	57	55
Urals	58	65	71	75	74
West Siberian	51	61	68	73	71
East Siberian	53	62	69	72	71
Far Eastern	68	72	75	76	74

Source: State Statistical Committee.

Data on the regional distribution of the urban population (tab. 6.1, fig. 6.1) highlight two important characteristics of urban development in Russia during the 20th century: rapid urbanization due to industrialization and the growth of cities in harsh and inhospitable regions such as Siberia, the Far East, and the Far North. Russia rapidly urbanized during the first half of the 20th century; however, significant levels of urbanization continued to occur in every region of Russia throughout the Soviet period. Even agricultural regions such as the Central Chernozem and North Caucasus regions had more than half of their populations living in urban places by 1979. There were also high rates of urbanization in the Arctic and Siberian regions as early as 1959. Because of the remoteness of these regions, the difficult climate, and the patterns of settlement, most people lived in urban places, but smaller ones than in the rest of Russia. In the late 1990s, the population of the Far North (the Arctic region) was nearly 80% urban, well above the Russian average of 73%.

For both ideological and security reasons, Soviet central planners promoted both rapid urbanization and urban settlement of Siberia, the Far East, and the Far North. On the one hand, Soviet doctrine saw urban life as bringing people closer to Communist ideals. On the other hand, planners used mathematical algorithms to choose the optimum location for investment in economic activities leading to the construction of new cities in previously underdeveloped regions like Siberia. Planners often determined optimum locations close to natural resources. Planners also considered the impact of defense when locating economic activity. They often chose sites that dispersed production to make the national economy less vulnerable to crippling losses if attacked militarily. For example, at the beginning of World War II, Soviet central planners oversaw the dismantling of factories in the western portion of the country, only to reassemble them in the Urals and Siberia.

Finally, these data also illustrate the 1990s phenomenon of ruralization. Small declines in the percentage of population living in urban places in the northern and eastern regions of Russia are due to large numbers of people moving out of these regions, with proportionally more people moving from cities than from rural areas. The small decline in the urbanization rate in the North Caucasus, which is an agricultural area along the southern border, is most likely due to an influx of a large number of in-migrants and refugees from the former Soviet republics who were assigned housing in rural areas.

EVOLUTION OF THE URBAN SYSTEM

During the 20th century, Russia underwent one of the most dramatic urbanization processes anywhere in the world, only to lose urban population and experience a significant urban crisis in the final years of the century. Russia began the 21st century well into a new phase characterized by an equally dramatic reversal of the long-established urban settlement pattern. For centuries, the population had moved from the European core of Russia primarily to cities in the south (often capital cities in Soviet Central Asia) and to Siberian and Arctic cities. In the post-Soviet period, a significant movement out of the Siberian and Arctic cities (as well as from cities in the newly independent countries in Central Asia and the Caucasus), back to European Russia began as a direct result of the change from Soviet central planning to market-driven locational choices. Without central planners, cities in harsh and inaccessible places, such as Norilsk and Surgut, lost population quickly as the introduction of market forces resulted in rapid increases in once heavily subsidized energy and transportation costs. As subsidies dwindled, food, housing, and industrial production costs soared. Faced with ever-increasing costs and the need to ship frequently poor quality goods thousands of miles to distant markets, many factories shut down and unemployment surged. Those who could simply pulled up stakes and moved. Irrespective of the period, however, Russia has experienced a significant mismatch between the location of labor resources, markets, and urban-industrial power in the western portion of the country and the location of natural resources, including energy, in the eastern portion of the country.

The Pre-Soviet Period

The first Slavic cities in the Russian Plain appeared only at the end of the 9th century. Crossed by many important rivers, this plain served as a vital trading route between Scandinavia and the eastern Mediterranean, which was commanded by the Byzantine Empire. The Vikings established a set of city-principalities, at once both military outposts and long-distance trading centers, where they collected tolls from merchants who traveled through the region. Kiev, Novgorod, and Smolensk were among the earliest urban settlements of this type. With time, the Vikings united the Slavic tribes who lived along this trading route, training them in the martial arts, and themselves becoming Slavic-language speakers.

The region gradually began to function independently and one city, Kiev (now the capital of independent Ukraine), became the focal point because of its favorable location where the forests of the North Russian Plain gave way to the grassland steppes. The location of Kiev was attractive to both forest trappers and steppe nomads. The Dnieper River provided access to the Black Sea and Constantinople. By the end of the 12th century, there were more than 300 cities in Kievan Rus, which extended eastward to the Upper Volga River and south to the Black Sea. Kievan Rus was characterized by a set of urban centers with their own feudal organization, and often the cities were in conflict with one another. Most of the cities in Kievan Rus were located along the vast network of rivers in Russia and were originally established as forts, known as *kremlins*. Many of these cities have survived today with their kremlins still intact. The famous Golden Ring of cities outside of Moscow (e.g., Yaroslavl, Suzdal, Vladimir) date back to Kievan Rus and continue to thrive as historic centers of Russian culture.

Despite the prevalence of fort towns intended to protect residents from invasion, from 1237 to 1240 nearly all cities in Kievan Rus were destroyed or plundered by invading Mongol Tatars. This phase of urban decline continued for another two centuries after the formal downfall of the Tatars in 1480. Indeed, as late as 1700, the number of urban centers was still approximately 300.

By the end of the 14th century, the urban system that was to become the core of Muscovy Rus took shape in the more protected, forest-covered part of the Russian plain. Moscow dominated this new region of settlement from its location at the center of a river system, which permitted movement by water in several directions. Access to the Volga and Oka rivers gave a route to the east, although in early days this was blocked by the Tatar khanate of Kazan, which controlled the central and lower Volga. The Western Dvina led to the Baltic and the Don and Dnieper rivers led to the Black Sea. Moscow's favorable location with respect to the major river routes was a key factor in its growth in an era when rivers were important for both trade and communications. Moscow's location also provided security from attack.

Unlike in Kievan Rus, the princes in Moscow sought to eliminate the feudal organization of urban development in order to be able to defeat the Tatars should they attack again, and to consolidate political and economic power in one location. In doing so, the leaders of Moscow could only be described as strongly autocratic, the first in a long line of Russian and Soviet despotic rulers. The Muscovite rulers also sought to isolate the region from external influences and to extend their empire as far as possible. Centuries later, the Soviet leaders continued this tradition.

The importance of hills for defense and rivers as communication main lines during this period explains common features of most old Russian city centers. The surviving fortified core with a stone fortress, or kremlin, was always located on a high riverbank. The layout of streets was usually radial, reflecting the original concern about rapid dispatching of troops from the kremlin. Since medieval cores lay on riverbanks, cities subsequently developed mostly in imperfect circles away from the river, and in many instances new "beyond the river" districts came to be developed with the belated construction of bridges only in the 1960s and 1970s.

Czar Ivan the Terrible defeated the Tatars at Kazan in the middle of the 16th century and Russian settlements expanded eastward across the Ural Mountains into Siberia, encountering little resistance. New settlements such as Tobolsk (1587) and Yakutsk (1632) began as military outposts. Trappers plundered Siberia for furs, but little else of value came from this vast wilderness until 1647, when Russia settled Okhotsk on the Pacific Ocean. As the 17th century drew to a close, Russia remained essentially landlocked, controlling a vast territory with about 300 cities, the same number as had existed three centuries earlier.

Czar Peter the Great founded St. Petersburg in 1703, touching off a spectacular transformation of urban Russia as he sought to catch up to Europe. St. Petersburg was built to be a showcase port city and the country's "window on the West"; the city quickly supplanted Moscow as the new capital. The reforms Peter the Great undertook revitalized both local and long-distance trade. New market centers developed; old urban centers changed and grew. Imperial support meant thousands of serfs were resettled to provide free labor to the trading companies. The creation of this new, Western-oriented city fed into the social tension between those who believed in Westernizing the country and those who preferred to emphasize Russia's Slavic origins. The development of St. Petersburg was also a great precursor of the Soviet belief that humans can conquer nature in the name of economic development. St. Petersburg was originally an inhospitable swamp and thousands of Russians lost their lives while building the city.

The empire continued to expand and by the end of the 18th century there were approximately 400 cities accounting for about 4% of the total population; a century later found 700 cities holding about 16% of the total population. The beginning of industrialization fueled the growth.

Two main regions of industry emerged by the end of the 19th century. In Moscow and its surrounding centers (Tver, Vladimir, Ivanovo, Kostroma), textile manufacturing predominated. The availability of foreign cotton and textile machines meant large brick factories employing thousands of weavers had replaced the original small cottage industries by the 1880s. Beyond Moscow, most new centers of manufacturing were located outside Russia proper. The second area of industrialization and urbanization was the Donbass, in the steppe region of Ukraine, where there were local supplies of coal. The cities in Donbass focused on metallurgy in a maze of coal mines and blast furnaces. Other new centers of manufacturing developed in the non-Russian parts of the empire, including the thriving textile belt of Russian Poland, the engineering center of Riga (Latvia), and Baku (Azerbaijan), a boom city built on oilfields. In fact, most new centers of manufacturing were located outside Russia proper.

The Soviet Period

The Russian Revolution (1917) and ensuing civil war ended with the establishment of a political-economic system unlike any other in the world. The Communist Party took control and used its clout to establish an economic system guided by Communist principles instead of market forces. This new economic system was called the *command economy* because a group of central planners located in Moscow determined not only what was produced, but where, who could acquire products, and at what price. Central planners allocated all investment resources, made location decisions, and set national standards for urban development that had the force of law. Central planning meant national needs superceded local ones, including those related to urban development. Central planning forced a realignment of the urban system to reflect new political and economic priorities. In other words, city governments and city residents had little or no influence over local economic development, urban growth, and the internal structure of cities.

After acquiring a measure of political control over the country, the Communist Party took steps to consolidate its political power and reshape the economy to be consistent with Communist ideology. In 1918, the leadership moved the capital from St. Petersburg (subsequently renamed Leningrad) back to Moscow. The move was both symbolic and strategic: the

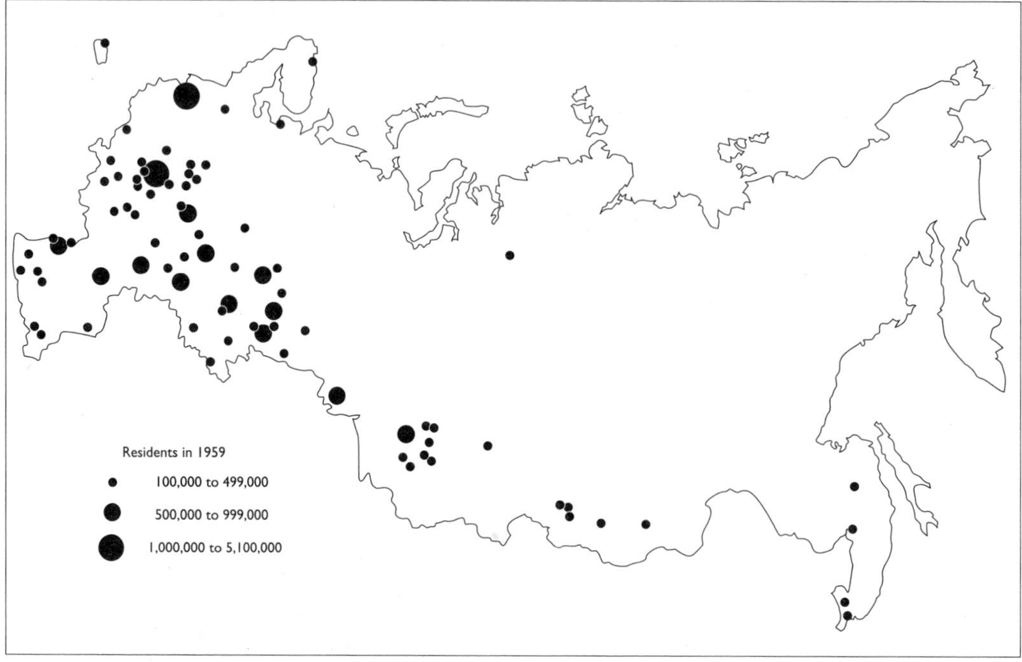

Figure 6.3 Cities in Russia with More Than 100,000 Population in 1959. *Source*: Beth Mitchneck and Ellen Hamilton

relatively recent capital built by the czars as a window on the West was replaced with a far older capital in the country's heartland, which would be easier to defend. The Communist leadership also established a hierarchical urban administrative system to assist in carrying out its political and economic agendas, as well as to reflect the new ideology. By setting up a system of administrative centers in the *oblasts* (political units comparable to states or provinces), central planners were better able to control resource allocation and use in each region. Not surprisingly, these administrative centers benefited disproportionately from central investment decisions and became industrial as well as population centers. By the late 1990s, there were 89 oblasts. In two-thirds of them, the administrative centers accounted for a quarter of the oblast's population.

The new territorial administrative system enabled central planners to realize new economic priorities, especially rapid industrialization, and oblast centers became the locations for massive industrial investment and grew rapidly. Soon, historic industrial centers such as Moscow, Yaroslavl, and Kazan were joined by administrative/industrial centers in Siberia and the Far East (e.g., Omsk, Novosibirsk, Krasnoyarsk, Irkutsk, and Vladivostok). Planners also used investments to develop a system of secondary industrial cities focused on heavy industry (e.g., the automotive industry in Togliatti and aluminum and related industrial production in Bratsk) or natural resource exploitation (e.g., nickel in Norilsk and oil near Surgut).

In time, the concentration of industrial investments in selected regional centers meant

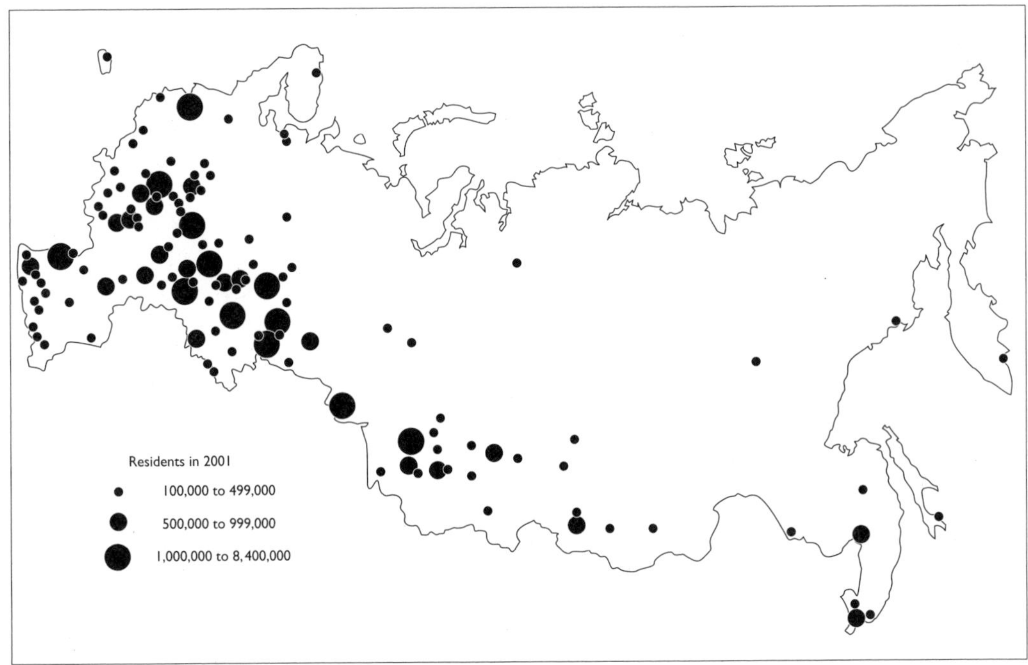

Figure 6.4 Cities in Russia with More Than 100,000 Population in 2001. *Source*: Beth Mitchneck and Ellen Hamilton

that a new system of large cities (i.e., cities of more than 500,000 people) developed in Russia. In a country where big was seen as better, planners and politicians spoke glowingly of cities with more than one million inhabitants. But this enthusiasm was tempered with an understanding that promoting the growth, and consequently the spatial dispersion, of all cities would mean limiting the growth of the largest cities.

As figure 6.3 shows, in 1959 the largest cities, with populations of 100,000 and higher, were located primarily in the western portion of the country. Figure 6.4 illustrates the results of policies to concentrate investments in oblast centers, which resulted in a noticeable shift in the number of largest cities found in the eastern parts of Russia by 2001.

Much of the urban growth took place along the Trans-Siberian Railroad (completed in 1904) or its spurs (fig. 6.5). In the 1970s, Soviet planners began construction on a second Siberian rail route, the Baykal-Amur Mainline (BAM), as a means to further facilitate new natural resource exploitation and the transportation of goods across the vast Russian expanse. These railroads provided a lifeline to cities located thousands of miles from central Russia. In the Far North, cities primarily depended on boats using the Northern Sea Route along the Arctic coastline or Siberian rivers. Not even nuclear-powered icebreakers could ensure access to cities in the Far North year round, while the southerly location of the main railroad lines precluded year-round rail links. Winter roads along frozen rivers often provided the only links for much of the year, until the ice broke up in May or June.

Figure 6.5 Begun as a railway town in the late 1890s, Novosibirsk ("New Siberia") became the administrative center for all of Siberia in 1925. Now, in the post-Soviet era, the skyline is taking on the high-rise profile of cities in the West. (Photo by Donald Zeigler)

While planners directed investment resources to specific cities, they simultaneously pursued a contradictory policy, namely, limiting population growth in many of the same cities. Planners used formal control mechanisms like the *propiska,* a legal permission to live in a city, that were ineffective at limiting urban growth. Many individuals found legal ways around the system, such as marrying someone who had a *propiska* to live in the city or finding employment and having the employer secure a *propiska.* Ultimately, pressures for ever-greater production frequently translated into investments in established sites, instead of new sites, because this made economic sense. But additional investments created additional demand for labor. Attempts by central planners to reap the benefits of economies of scale reduced the effectiveness of city size limitations.

Urban and Regional Planning

In addition to directing investment resources to particular cities, central planners determined the internal spatial structure of Soviet cities. In an effort to create a new kind of city that would be consistent with the ideals of socialism, planners adopted the following guiding principles for urban planning: restricting urban growth in order not to exceed the optimal city size; distributing consumer and cultural goods equitably to the population; minimizing the journey to work and relying on public transportation for spatial mobility; and segregating urban land uses.

The basic building block of Soviet cities was the *microrayon,* which housed 8,000–12,000 people who lived in an area designed as an integrated unit of apartment buildings, stores, and schools intended to provide the consumer

Figure 6.6 This Moscow microrayon shows new construction alongside older apartments from the Soviet era. (Photo by Beth Mitchneck)

with cultural and educational services required by Soviet norms. Microrayons were located near industry and other places of work so as to minimize the journey to work. Built using standardized plans, microrayons were numbingly similar whether in Novosibirsk, Vorkuta, or Moscow (fig. 6.6). Large tracts of identical or similar multistory apartment buildings ring Russian cities, a visible reminder of decades of Soviet construction.

The location of microrayons was determined by the so-called general plans, which determined the precise land use of every plot in the city—what would be built there, what it would look like, and how it would be used. General plans were so detailed that a milk store could not legally be built on a site designated for a bread store. General plans were intended to complement the shorter-term, five-year economic plans, which determined what would be made, how it would be made, who would make it, who would receive the final product, and at what price.

Internal Structure of Cities

The long history of planning in Soviet cities has left an indelible mark on the built environment, precisely because structures were located without reference to market forces. In the United States, demand determines what kind of real estate projects are likely to be profitable and, thus, built. In Soviet cities, by contrast, land was not bought and sold, but allocated for different purposes roughly in accordance with the socialist ideology and planning principles outlined above. Figure 6.7 compares population density in Paris and Moscow according to distance from the city center. In Paris, market forces mean that valuable land near the center of the city is more densely populated than less valuable land on the outskirts of the city. In Moscow, just the opposite is true. The most densely populated parts of the city were on less valuable land far from the city center. Instead of building skyscrapers on valuable land in the

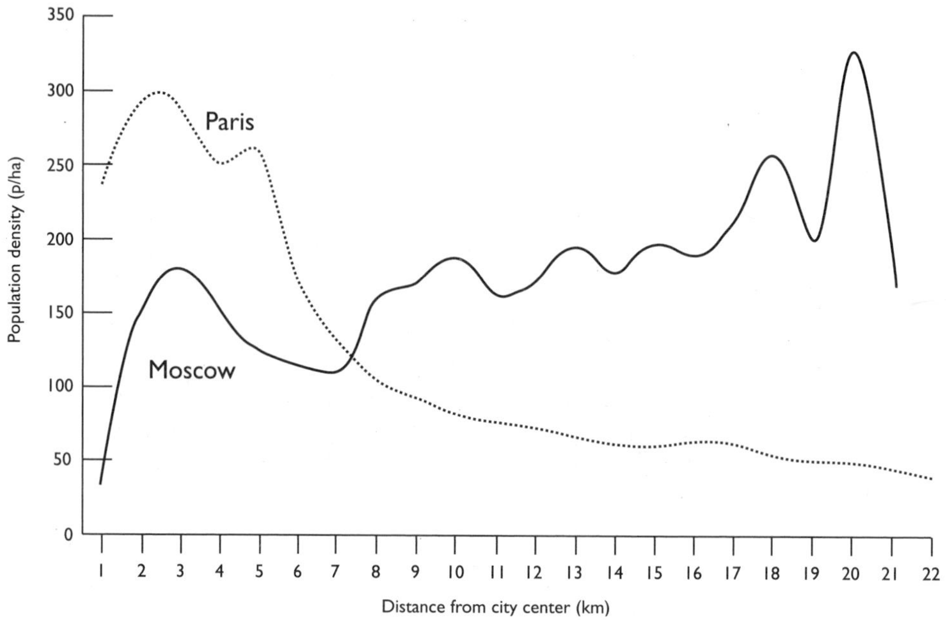

Figure 6.7 Comparative Density Profile in the Built-Up Areas of Moscow and Paris. *Source*: Beth Mitchneck and Ellen Hamilton

city center, central planners built skyscrapers in the suburbs.

Soviet cities were also unique because the absence of a free market meant land was not recycled for other purposes, as would have been the case in cities in market economies. As a result, the rings of development in Soviet cities remain clearly visible today and partially explain why population density increased along with distance from the center. Beginning in the 1930s, huge factories were erected outside prerevolutionary city cores as part of the industrialization drive. In subsequent years, especially after the late 1950s, a near catastrophic housing shortage and renewed determination to improve people's living conditions began decades of housing construction. New apartment buildings were built in successive rings on undeveloped land outside the city core, the existing housing stock, and the existing factories. As the decades went by, prefabricated apartment buildings used nationwide grew taller, and buildings constructed according to these designs were located farther from the city cores.

POST-SOVIET RUSSIA: ECONOMIC COLLAPSE AND THE URBAN SYSTEM

What have economic collapse and the introduction of market forces meant for cities and the urban system? The answer—a great deal. The overnight elimination of central planning has profoundly affected the internal structure of cities, as well as the urban system nationally.

Figure 6.8 New construction has extended well beyond the traditional suburban boundaries of Moscow in the past ten years. Mitino, a new suburb, has upscale apartments, townhouses, and retail and relies heavily upon private transportation links to central Moscow. (Photo by Beth Mitchneck)

Changing Urban Form

Perhaps no event has so profoundly affected the structure of Russian cities as the end of Soviet central planning and the reintroduction of market forces. Single-family houses have appeared seemingly overnight in what has become a new ring of housing development, namely suburbs surrounding the multifamily high rises remaining from the Soviet years (fig. 6.8).

Suburbanization is but one of many visible changes resulting from the development of land and real estate markets in cities where they had been prohibited for most of the 20th century. As land has become a commodity, the old adage of value being determined by "location, location, location" has never been more apparent. Old factories on land surrounding the historic city cores are increasingly being torn down and the land is being reused for other purposes, such as apartment buildings or stores. Existing buildings in poor condition, but in good locations, are purchased, upgraded, and reused for new purposes, such as office space or upscale apartments (fig. 6.9). In contrast, run-down high-rise apartment buildings far from the city center on nearly worthless land are deteriorating rapidly as the better-off tenants move to superior locations, leaving only the poorer people behind in what will likely become vertical slums.

Market forces have also visibly changed the location of economic activity within cities and thus the geography of Russian cities. Previously, retail trade occurred mostly in state-owned stores or in a limited number of farmers' markets. Now, the spatial structure

Figure 6.9 A mixed-use building (residential and commercial) in central Moscow shows the prevalence of new technology (satellite dishes on balconies) in the post-Soviet period. (Photo by Beth Mitchneck)

of urban retail systems has altered dramatically. Each subway station or transportation hub has become a center of retail trade where peddlers vend their wares and where urban retail centers such as malls have been built. Prerevolutionary shopping centers have regained their functions in this new retail environment. For example, GUM department store was remodeled to be a first-class, high-end shopping mall (fig. 6.10). Cities like Moscow have also seen their urban periphery turned into a new retail environment. Enormous retail stores, such as IKEA, are opening up outside of the traditional retail centers, which has the result of spatially extending the retail spaces of Russian cities.

Demographic Change and the Urban System

Societal change has other demographic consequences that are reflected in a restructuring of the urban system. Starting in the 1980s, a pattern of *disappearing cities* signaled changes to the Russian urban system (tab. 6.2). The disappearing or declining towns are spatially distributed throughout Russia, with more than half of them in the industrial core regions around Moscow and St. Petersburg and in the Urals. By the mid-1990s, however, Siberian cities were accounting for a larger proportion of these declining towns. The agricultural regions accounted for the fewest declining towns, suggesting that the phenomenon is firmly rooted in the urban-industrial complex.

Analysis of the functions of the declining towns provides an interesting lens into the impact of restructuring on the urban system. Because of the boom-bust economies surrounding mineral and other resource exploitation, as one would expect, mining towns account for a large proportion of declining towns, roughly a quarter in both time periods. The big story is the large increase in the share of cities from the MIC proportionate to other kinds of declining cities. The MIC cities previously received special attention from the central government, which meant better-than-average access to goods and services, as well as higher salaries for employees in these places. Given the economic changes after the dissolution of the Soviet Union in late 1991, it makes sense that increasing numbers of these formerly privileged places are declining. Nonetheless, this represents a significant change in urban geography. Table 6.2 also suggests another recent phenomenon, namely the loss of population in medium-sized cities, or those with populations over 100,000. This is most likely connected to the decline in MIC cities as well.

An interesting counterpoint to the disappearance of many towns in the post-Soviet period is the appearance of previously unacknowledged cities known as *secret cities* or, in Soviet parlance, "closed administrative-territorial formations." Although some information is now available about these cities, it is still difficult to assess how many there actually were. Some estimates place the number around 40. These were cities where employment was focused on highly classified military production, including nuclear research and missile production. The cities were located in many different regions of Russia, although clusters were found in Murmansk Oblast (related to naval operations), the Far East (also related to naval operations), the Urals, and Moscow Oblast.

Figure 6.10 The famous GUM department store on Red Square in Moscow was originally built to showcase the new retail sector during the late czarist period, but fell into disrepair in the Soviet era. Now renovated, it houses upscale foreign and domestic stores. (Photo by Beth Mitchneck)

Economic Change and the Urban System

The end of central planning profoundly affected the urban system, which had been strongly influenced by decades of an investment policy designed to promote industrialization across the country. Heavy industry was especially hard hit by market forces and the reorientation of the economy away from defense. As the borders opened, Russia was flooded with cheaper and better consumer goods, as demand for everything from locally produced steel to planes dried up. At the same time, regions began to scramble for new investments to replace investments made by the Soviet central government. The introduction of market forces resulted in clear patterns of winners and losers and large differences among places. Some cities benefited; most did not.

Figure 6.11 shows where industrial output per capita in 1998 was highest in comparison with average industrial output per capita for Russia. High rates of industrial output are found in just a few natural resource rich re-

Table 6.2 Function and Size of Declining Towns in Russia

	1979–1980		1989–1994	
	Number of Towns	*Share of total (%)*	*Number of Towns*	*Share of total (%)*
Economic Function of Declining Towns				
Mining	238	24.4	309	24.9
Railroad Service Centers	56	5.7	69	5.6
Forest Products	209	21.4	185	14.9
Textiles	51	5.2	77	6.2
Military Industrial Complex	11	1.3	101	8.1
Recreational	16	1.6	42	3.4
Administrative	0	0.0	29	2.3
Other	396	41.0	430	35.0
Population Size of Declining Towns				
100,000 or more	3	0.3	63	2.1
Less than 3,000	307	31.4	267	21.5

Source: Richard H. Rowland, "Russia's Disappearing Towns: New Evidence of Urban Decline, 1979–1994," *Post-Soviet Geography and Economics* 37, no. 2 (1996).

gions in Siberia and the Far East. In these regions, at least two-thirds of total industrial output results from mining oil, gas, diamonds, and platinum. As this map illustrates, once powerful and economically significant manufacturing regions are no longer as important as they were in the past. The restructuring of the economy away from manufacturing to natural resources has meant that cities dependent on manufacturing are struggling to cope with high rates of unemployment and few opportunities for new development. It is precisely these cities that have been losing population in recent years.

Foreign direct investment provides another example of how economic changes are reshaping the urban system. As figure 6.12 shows, regions that have attracted many foreign investors on a per capita basis have done so either because they are rich in natural resources (oil, diamonds, gold, etc.) or because they are well located and attractive in terms of access to markets (as in the cases of Moscow, St. Petersburg, and Novgorod). Both kinds of regions benefit from per capita foreign investment rates that are more than double the average rate for Russia. The pattern of foreign direct investment is indicative of where international businesspeople believe the economic opportunities lie. These regions are likely to become attractive destinations for migrants from more depressed areas of the country, which will contribute to reshaping the urban system in favor of the former and at the expense of the latter.

Political Change and the Urban System

The introduction of democratization and political decentralization rivals marketization and capitalization as important influences over post-Soviet urban geography. The first democratic elections took place in cities throughout Russia shortly before the end of

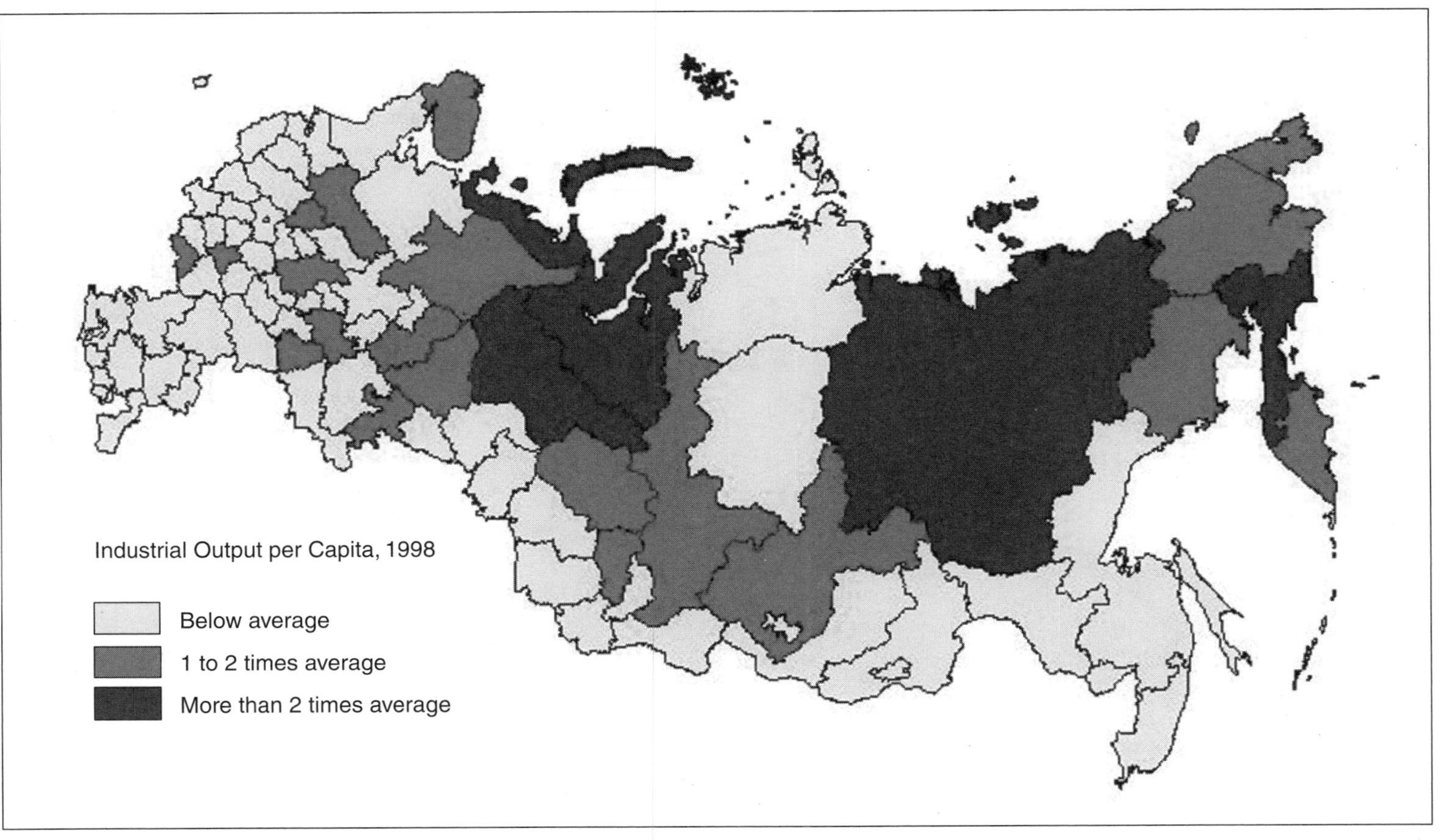

Figure 6.11 Industrial Output per Capita in 1998. *Source*: Beth Mitchneck and Ellen Hamilton

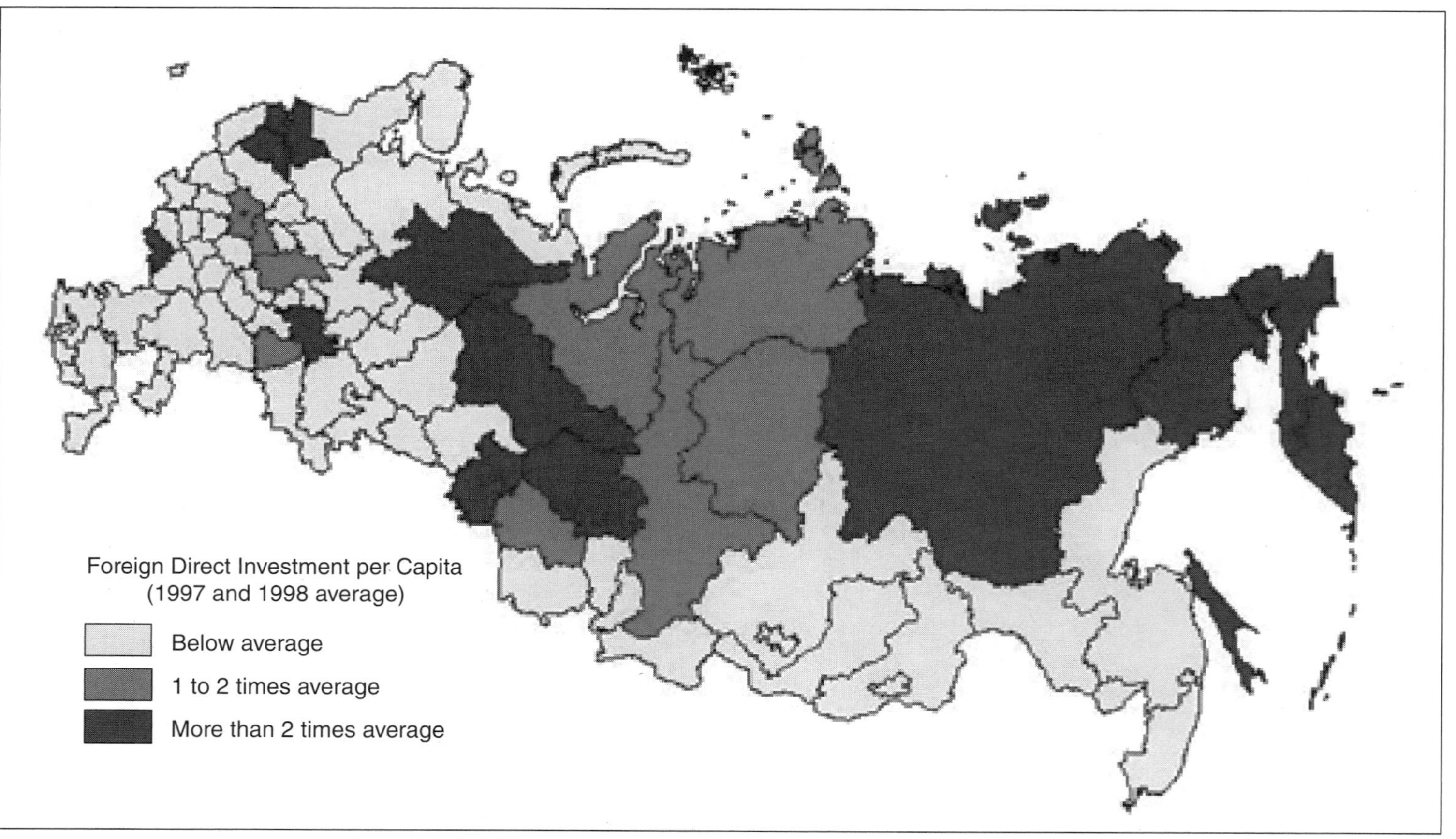

Figure 6.12 Foreign Direct Investment per Capita, 1997–1998. *Source*: Beth Mitchneck and Ellen Hamilton

the Soviet Union. For the first time, local politicians, at least in theory, were accountable to the local population, instead of to higher-level government officials. This accountability has had important implications for the spatial structure of cities, as urban geographies have begun to reflect the needs of the local economy, instead of those of the national one. Democratic local elections are one of the most visible elements of a broader process of political decentralization, which has both empowered local officials and made them more accountable. Local officials now have far more ability to directly and indirectly influence the internal geography of cities than they did a few years earlier.

One immediate result of this newfound local autonomy can be seen in the popularity of renaming cities and streets, in which names associated with prominent Soviet leaders are replaced with historic names dating back to the czarist past. For example, Leningrad reverted to St. Petersburg and Sverdlovsk (named after a local Communist leader) reverted to Ekaterinburg (literally, "Catherine's city," after Catherine the Great). Similarly, streets were renamed; for example, Moscow's Gorky Street, named after the Soviet writer, was renamed Tverskaya Street. The historic names were usually already well known; however, the changes contributed to a feeling among Russians of reclaiming their cities and neighborhoods.

Urban governments also reclaimed their economies. In capitalist economies, urban budgets generally reflect political priorities. In healthy urban economies, budgets grow. Russian cities were protected from the vagaries of fiscal self-management prevalent in capitalist economies because they did not manage their own budget or accumulate budgetary resources until the final days of the Soviet Union. Urban budgets and the revenues that fed those budgets were simply handed down to Russian cities. This meant that urban politicians neither set priorities nor directly influenced the health of the urban economy. Russian city governments managed some of the housing and most of the social services located in their cities, but did not provide funding for these activities. Nor did Russian city governments concern themselves with employment. Under the Soviet system of central planning, employment patterns were largely determined centrally, outside of the direct influence of city managers.

In post-Soviet Russia, everything has changed dramatically and rapidly, as can be seen from survey information. By 1997, nearly 60% of urban politicians surveyed viewed the industrial and economic decline (including the general economy and macroeconomic problems) as one of the three most important problems facing their cities. Transportation and communication were seen to be the second most important problem. City budgets and the housing situation ranked third. The next most often cited short-term priority was protection from crime or "social protection." Virtually overnight, budgets and taxes as well as managing economic change became priorities of urban politicians and important indicators of the rapidity of the introduction of capitalism to Russian cities.

REPRESENTATIVE CITIES

Russia's sheer size and long urban tradition mean it has a large number of cities of varying size and significance. Hence, it is best to focus here on cities that represent as much as possible the most significant changes to Russian cities in the post-Soviet period. Moscow, St. Petersburg, and Novosibirsk illustrate the distinctiveness of capital cities. Moscow and St.

Figure 6.13 St. Basil's Cathedral on Red Square, just outside the Kremlin, is one of the most colorful and oldest Russian Orthodox churches in Russia, and in many ways a symbol of Moscow. (Photo by Donald Zeigler)

Petersburg are the largest cities in Russia and both have served as national capitals, embodying czarist and Soviet eras of Russian history. Novosibirsk is still considered the Siberian capital and it also is an example of an industrial frontier city. Also highlighted in this section are Kazan, an ancient city illustrative of the ethnic diversity of Russia; Krasnodar, a city struggling with refugees in the aftermath of the breakup of the Soviet Union; Obninsk, a former secret city once dominated by the MIC; and Tyumen, a city prominent in the oil industry. These cities and towns reveal how Russian urban landscapes, irrespective of size or national significance, are layered with evidence from czarist, Soviet, and modern Russian histories, each of which left its own distinctive imprint on the cities.

Moscow: Russia's Past Meets Russia's Future

Perhaps no city captures Russia's long history as vividly as Moscow. Modern Moscow is a chaotic blend of brash and unfettered capitalism seen in casino lights and chic boutiques, broad avenues and vast monotonous housing estates built by communism, and the red brick walls and onion-domed churches of the Kremlin, remnants of the czarist past (fig. 6.13). In Moscow, Russia's past lives cheek by jowl with Russia's future.

Founded more than 850 years ago in the declining years of Kievan Rus, the city grew rapidly in importance. Starting in 1485, Ivan the Great and his successors ruled Russia from within the thick red brick walls of the Kremlin for over two centuries, until Peter the Great moved the capital to St. Petersburg. The 1917 Russian Revolution returned the seat of Soviet power to Moscow, and the footfalls of Lenin, Stalin, and other Soviet leaders were heard in the halls of the Kremlin palaces.

In the aftermath of the collapse of the Soviet Union, capitalism exploded through Moscow, which has attracted more foreign investment than any other Russian city. New foreign and Russian capital built business centers, set up real estate companies, and established a new retail sector. Once empty avenues filled with cars seemingly overnight. TVs, VCRs, designer clothes, furniture—Muscovites bought voraciously and then bought some more. In the early 1990s, kiosks appeared everywhere, stocked with an improbable mix of everything from candy bars to vodka, socks, and toys. Five

Figure 6.14 Retailing in Moscow has moved from peddlers clustering near transportation hubs to semipermanent structures, including large commercial malls. This scene is of central Moscow retail development just outside the inner ring road. (Photo by Beth Mitchneck)

years later, stores selling liquor, food, clothing, and toys, as well as every other possible consumer good, largely replaced the kiosks. Now, malls are beginning to replace hastily built and remodeled stores (fig. 6.14).

Historically the political, economic, media, educational, and cultural center of the country, Moscow added to the existing functions as its economy restructured and the city became the banking capital and the consumer capital as well. Moscow is in many ways the primate city of Russia, as was true in past centuries (box 6.1).

Moscow is vastly richer than most other parts of Russia, a result in part of inheriting immensely valuable real estate from the Soviet government and Communist Party. The city used its ownership and control over most real estate in its borders to leverage behind-the-scenes business deals with private-sector investors. Acquiring office space often means establishing a business partnership directly or indirectly with the city. Profits due to the city from these business deals are not paid into the city's budget, but mount up in an unknown number of bank accounts to be used for unclear purposes. Corruption is rampant. Accountability is nearly nonexistent. Not surprisingly, the business climate of the city is highly criminalized. The city's policymaking is often driven by the agenda of organized crime, more than the needs and desires of the city's citizens.

St. Petersburg: Window on the West—Again?

St. Petersburg remains a city of ornate palaces and water-filled canals. Shots fired from the battleship *Aurora,* docked across from the Winter Palace, signaled the start of the Russian Rev-

Box 6.1 Business Services in Moscow and the New Russian Yuppies

Olga Gritsai

In the 1990s Moscow, as the hearth of reforms in Russia, experienced dynamic structural transformations in both the economic and social spheres. One of the new and rapidly expanding sectors was business services; the share of employment in the city for this sector grew from practically zero in 1990 to 8.5–10% in 2000 (still much smaller than in the largest Western cities, but amazingly high after only ten years). Such activities as banking, insurance, advertising, accountancy, corporate legal services, and management consultancies, along with a thriving real estate sector, became well established in the city economy. Big international companies operating in these sectors were among the first to register their offices in Moscow, followed by numerous Russian-owned companies, some of them quickly turning into successful competitors to the international giants.

Companies of this type created a specific job market, recruiting mostly young people with university degrees, good knowledge of foreign languages, and sufficient computer skills. Given the relatively late start of language and computer training in Russia, it is clear why the age limit for the employees in new business services is very low: even those in command of such companies are in most cases not older than 35, and are at maximum 40, while the general cohort of the employees is about 22–26 years old. Many of them start without any relevant education or professional experience, coming with a wide variety of degrees, from geology to journalism, and have to learn the new profession on the job. The same is happening in the service departments of the producing companies; their staff is on average much younger than the personnel in the rest of these companies. The possibility of making a quick career with a high salary (comparable to Western salaries) disinclines these young professionals to leave Russia and look for alternative jobs abroad.

These young, professional, educated, culturally attuned, well-off people have formed their own social group, akin to the Western *yuppie* (young urban, upwardly mobile professional) but combining pragmatism with the extravagancy and nonconformism of the *BoBo* (Bohemian bourgeoisie). They know the price of a good education. Their monthly income is $1,000–$3,000, while for more than 70% of Muscovites it is still below $400. They like comfort, are members of fitness clubs, prefer healthy food, have good cars and mobile telephones, and at the same time are well-informed about cultural events. They attend fashionable films and performances designed for intellectual audiences and are among the

olution in 1917 and hastened the end of St. Petersburg's nearly two-century-long reign as czarist Russia's glittering capital. As the victorious Soviet leaders concentrated economic and political resources to build a vast, highly centralized, and closed society in the new capital of Moscow, St. Petersburg, renamed Leningrad, faded quietly into its new role as the second city in Russia.

Leningrad continued to grow, but not as

most frequent Internet users, considering Internet to be the main source of information and means of communication.

The quick growth of business services and their yuppie-like employees was followed by a boom in a new cultural industry that included elite coffeehouses; small, trendy restaurants that function as leisure clubs; and bowling clubs. Even in such a big city as Moscow the world of yuppies seems to be rather small; very often visitors to these clubs already know each other from university or from other clubs. The norm in these places is "healthy" behavior: freshly pressed juices, alcohol-free cocktails. Exotic types of tea and coffee are more popular here than alcoholic beverages. Many of these cafes and clubs have strong security control at their entrances to protect their images. Material welfare, career, and the freedom of self-realization are the main values for the new young Russians who frequent the clubs, making them a distinct group within the heterogeneous post-Soviet society.

So far, the Russian yuppies seem to be especially a Moscow phenomenon, although they are present in many other Russian cities. Moscow still concentrates 25–30% of national employment in business services, hosts by far the largest cluster of corporate headquarters, and is the major national provider and consumer of Internet services (until 1996, Moscow and St. Petersburg accounted for more than 90% of Russian Internet users). The contrast in prosperity between this group of young Muscovites and people of the same age category in the provinces gives rise to debates about the pathological inequality of opportunity and growing social polarization. But polarization exists also among young Muscovites themselves: those who do not have enough education, intellect, and character to become yuppies may end up as *yuffies* (young urban failures), get involved with drugs or other illegal activities, and slowly become marginalized. The problem is that there is very little middle ground between these two categories of young people.

The easy career making in private business also creates serious generational conflicts. It is indeed very difficult for many people whose professional lives passed mostly in Soviet times to accept that their children, with no experience and hardly any skills, and just after graduating from the university, can get salaries several times greater than those of their parents, not to mention the contrast with their grandparents' tiny pensions. Different values and priorities, rationalism versus the traditionally praised Russian spirituality; preference for the new, technologically more advanced sources of information; and being at ease with the new market reality—all these make the well-known generation gap much wider than it otherwise would be under an economically stable development path.

quickly as Moscow, and the population doubled after 1917 to reach a high of about 5 million in 1989. It is now the second-largest city in Russia. In the post-Soviet period, as with other industrial cities, its official population declined, dropping to about 4.7 million in 2001. Leningrad was the home to a number of prestigious universities and research institutions and its economy depended on educational and research activities, defense-related

Figure 6.15 In the post-Soviet economy, these street musicians perform for money on the streets of St. Petersburg, in the shadow of grand buildings from the czarist and Soviet eras. (Photo by Stanley Brunn)

industries, and the city's unique cultural legacy, including the world-renowned Hermitage Museum, which continues to attract visitors. Leningrad's dependence on the military-industrial complex necessitated some significant movement toward restructuring in the post-Soviet period.

After 1991, the city moved to recapture and build on its distant past. The city's original name was restored. Despite a deteriorating economic and financial situation caused by the near collapse of government support for defense, education, and culture, the newly elected city leadership began to think strategically about the city's future and, in the mid-1990s, the city embarked on a strategic planning process, making it the first city in Russia to do so. After extensive discussions with private businesses in St. Petersburg, as well as residents and local organizations, participants concluded that the city's strengths lay in the highly educated population, a port with the largest capacity in Russia, and a favorable location not far from Finland and Europe with excellent access to major railroads and highways. To improve long-term development prospects, St. Petersburg will work to improve economic growth by making the business climate more favorable and by better integrating the city's economy into the world economy (fig. 6.15). In addition, the European Union is helping to fund the construction of a new highway to provide more efficient linkages between St. Petersburg and Finland. To improve the quality of life for city residents, the city will seek to make budgetary expenditures more effective by using them to improve the city environment and establish a more favorable social environment. For example, road congestion and air pollution have increased dramatically because per capita car ownership has more than doubled in recent years. It remains to be seen whether or not the government of St. Petersburg can improve living standards and promote restructuring, but strategic planning has at least begun the process.

Kazan: Volga Port in Tatarstan

Perhaps no city in Russia better symbolizes the diversity inherent in a country that extends across Europe and Asia than does Kazan. Nearly 1,000 years old, the city is the capital of the Republic of Tatarstan and home to 1.2 million inhabitants. The ninth-largest city in the Russian Federation, Kazan is truly multiethnic. Tatars are the largest ethnic group in the republic; only 43% of the population is Russian. Tatarstan is one of the few "non-Russian" places to have a plurality (48%) of the group for which it is named (Russians are the largest group even in most of the ethnic republics).

Czar Ivan the Terrible succeeded in conquering the independent Khanate of Kazan centuries ago and memorialized his 1552 victory with the construction of the colorful St. Basil's Cathedral on Moscow's Red Square. But despite more than four centuries of Russian (and subsequently Soviet) rule, Kazan remained a Tatar city. The dissolution of the Soviet Union provided an opportunity to reclaim the city's unique past, as well as to renegotiate the terms of Tatarstan's relationship with Russia. Tatarstan is a key leader in seeking more rights and more local government control, and a place the other non-Russian republics have sought to emulate.

In recent years, a new school to educate Russians about Islam has opened in Kazan. The city government helped to construct a new mosque on the grounds of the historic Kremlin. The city's cultural independence from Russia is seen in the historic forms of architecture that make up the built environment of the city. Buildings in the city combine many architectural styles, ranging from baroque to Moorish. Bas-reliefs created by traditional Tatar stone workers also embellish buildings in the city. Minarets dot the skyline, visible evidence of the nearly 1,000 mosques that have opened across Tatarstan in recent years.

Both Kazan and Tatarstan are of major economic significance to the Russian economy, which has provided additional leverage to local leaders to negotiate a unique relationship with Moscow. The city is a major port on the Volga River, the main water route through European Russia, and has served as a transportation gateway for centuries. The European Union is currently investing in modernization of the city's port facilities. Kazan's economy is closely linked to production of transportation equipment, including military helicopters and the gigantic trucks made by KamAz. In addition to being an historic seat of the petroleum industry, the city is home to related petrochemical industries.

Novosibirsk: Siberia's Center

Home to nearly 1.5 million people, Novosibirsk is the center for Novosibirsk Oblast as well as the fourth-largest city in Russia, despite being located 2,000 mi (3,200 km) east of Moscow. Founded in 1893 as a stop along the Trans-Siberian Railroad, Novosibirsk is located on the mighty Ob River, making the city a convenient gateway to other Siberian cities. Novosibirsk continued to flourish as the Soviets pushed east, investing heavily in natural resource extraction and related industrial development, including the decision to move entire factories east in the wake of the German onslaught during World War II. The city remains an important center of the military-industrial complex, despite the need for significant economic restructuring.

Novosibirsk is also the intellectual capital of Siberia, housing numerous educational, scientific, and research organizations. The long distance from Moscow meant that Soviet leaders were less able to keep track of what scholars were thinking and discussing and that ideas circulated more freely here than in Moscow. This alone made the city an attractive destination for intellectuals, despite its long, cold winters and general inaccessibility. A small city on the outskirts, Akedemgorodok, houses the many research institutes of the Academy of Sciences of Russia, as well as Novosibirsk State University. It has long attracted some of the most talented and innovative scientists in Russia. At its height, Akedemgorodok had 65,000 scientists and one could always count upon exceptionally well-stocked stores when others in the metropolitan region were empty. Now, with the collapse of central government funding for research and higher education, many of the scientists have left in search of regularly paying employment.

Despite being located in the harsh Siberian environment, Novosibirsk is like many other Russian cities. With its gray architecture, Soviet-style apartment buildings, and broad streets, it looks like many other Soviet-period cities. Like other cities in the post-Soviet period, it has developed a burgeoning retail sector that gives the look and feel of a city in, perhaps, Asia or Africa, where the informal street economy thrives, although in Novosibirsk these activities are often conducted in underground shopping arcades to escape the Siberian winter. There is brisk trading throughout the city, including bustling open-air markets with vendors selling goods from the United States, Europe, and Asia out of kiosks or behind cardboard cartons. Its location between European Russia and the Far East as well as its role as a transportation hub makes the city an ideal place for wholesale, retail, and informal trade. Vendors in Novosibirsk work in temperatures as low as –40 degrees Celsius (–40F) and are vulnerable to frostbite. While the look and some aspects of the feel may be like other post-Soviet cities, the physical conditions create a very different experience for those living and working in Novosibirsk.

Krasnodar: Russia's Gateway to the Caucasus

At first glance, Krasnodar, just northwest of the now independent Caucasus nation of Georgia, appears to be just another sleepy city grown to substantial size as a result of its role as a river port and railroad center for farming, food processing, and other agriculture-related activities. Krasnodar was founded in 1793 as a military camp. The region's relatively moderate climate has proved beneficial not only to farmers but also to vacationers attracted to coastal resorts along the Black Sea. But Krasnodar's location, so favorable in many ways, has been less fortunate in the aftermath of the collapse of the Soviet Union. As waves of ethnic violence have washed across the Caucasus, hundreds of thousands of people have fled and many have ended up in Krasnodar.

The torrent of so-called forced migrants lies behind Krasnodar's rapid population growth. The population increased from 619,000 in 1989 to an officially estimated 766,000 in 1997 (which is likely much too low)—and this at a time when many Russian cities were losing population. Chechnya is but the best known of the many conflicts in the region, as conflicts in Ingushetia, Ossetia, Georgia, Armenia, and Azerbaijan have all contributed to the stream of refugees and migrants. Although the majority of the new arrivals are Slavs, the influx of non-Slavic Caucasians is the most visible. It is precisely these migrants who have borne the brunt of popular resentment and outright harassment. Krasnodar has continued to use the registration permit, or *propiska* (despite court rulings that the *propiska* is illegal), and harassment of people who do not look Slavic is endemic in the city.

The city has been particularly hard hit by the influx of migrants, because the central government, which has been struggling with its own financial problems, has provided little or no assistance to Krasnodar. At the same time, the end of central planning and the introduction of market forces has left the region struggling to modernize agriculture and food processing with few resources of its own to address these tremendous human problems.

Obninsk: "Atomic City" of the Cold War Era

Just a few years ago, the existence of Obninsk was a state secret. This medium-sized city of a bit more than 100,000 people, located 60 mi (96 km) south of Moscow, appeared on no maps. Obninsk was an "atomic" city where twelve state enterprises and associations were engaged in classified research on nuclear power and the actual production of nuclear energy. Obsessed with secrecy, the Soviet leadership designated Obninsk and approximately forty other cities engaged in similar activities as *closed cities.* Not even the country's own citizens were allowed to visit most of these cities without special permission.

Obninsk and the other secret cities benefited from the best of what the Soviet state had to offer: stores were better stocked, residents were better housed and paid. But the end of the Soviet Union meant that developing new nuclear weapons was a much lower priority and that funding was slashed. Overnight, the city went from being unacknowledged, yet wholly subsidized, to being acknowledged, yet impoverished. Only half of the nuclear scientists continue to be employed in the state enterprises and those who do earn only about $60 per month, which is barely enough to cover basic necessities such as food and utilities.

Despite the economic difficulties, the city has embraced openness and has even set up a website as a conduit to the rest of the world. The city government is now actively engaged in attempting to restructure the city's economy and become financially stable. The government does have a highly educated and skilled workforce to attract international investment. The city has attempted to make connections with its sister city, Oak Ridge, Tennessee, which is home to the Oak Ridge Laboratories, also well known for nuclear research. Obninsk is also trying to develop new economic activity by retooling its factories to produce mineral food supplements.

Tyumen: The Power of Oil

Tyumen is an oil boomtown. In the past ten years, the population has grown by more than 15%, from 476,000 to more than 550,000, in response to dollars pouring into the region to develop the massive oil and gas resources. Located in Western Siberia, in a climate where winter temperatures of –40 degrees Celsius (–40F) are not uncommon, Tyumen is an odd mix of modest Russian wooden houses and new glass office buildings.

As is the case with so many other Russian cities, Tyumen owes its importance largely to its role as a transportation hub. The city has a port along the Tura River and is located at a railroad junction on the Trans-Siberian. But even rail and river connections do not translate into accessibility to most of Russia. The nearest major city, Ekaterinburg, is four to five hours' travel by car or train. The rivers are navigable only during the brief summer season, which limits connections between the city and its surrounding area.

Tyumen is the regional center for Tyumen Oblast, which has been one of the country's largest producers of oil and natural gas since the Soviets began a massive program to develop these reserves throughout Western Siberia in the 1960s. Large investments in physical infrastructure (wells, pipelines, etc.) meant thousands of new jobs and the city grew rapidly. Although the oil and natural gas production occurs mainly in the non-Russian autonomous *okrugs* (political units below the oblast level) of Khanty-Mansi and Yamal-Nenets, Tyumen City is primarily Russian and was originally settled by Russians in the 16th century.

Tyumen has become a destination for migrants simply because of its importance to the oil and gas industry. While most other Russian cities scramble to attract investors and to cope with significant unemployment and social welfare problems, people in this city enjoy a relatively high living standard. Consumer purchasing power is estimated to be up to five times higher than in other Russian cities. Also, even after the financial crisis of 1998, the region and the city itself are home to several major banks, an indicator of the importance of the regional economy to the nation as a whole.

PROSPECTS

Cities in Russia today are the products of czarist, Soviet, and post-Soviet Russian societies, as well as of the many different ethnic groups and cultures that inhabited the region for at least a thousand years. The blending of such a diverse set of cultures and histories results in cities with varied built landscapes. The natural environment, however, has always wielded an important influence over the location of urban settlements, irrespective of the time period or dominant ethnic group. The harshness of the Siberian landscape originally posed a barrier to the expansion of Russian settlement. Like the construction of St. Petersburg, heralded as a triumph although situated in a location where many during the czarist period thought it could not be built, the widespread urban settlement of Siberia became a great accomplishment of the Soviet central planners. This was in spite of the environmental degradation wrought by this settlement, the stranding of people in isolated and inhospitable places, and the immense social and cultural costs, not to mention the immeasurable financial implications.

Cities in the post-Soviet period thus must continue to struggle with the consequences of the Soviet harnessing of nature and the legacy of that era's internal spatial structure of cities. Urban governments as well as the national government are attempting to find ways to integrate, economically and politically, cities as disparate and distant as Krasnodar and Vladivostok. They need to consider the implications of that integration for the internal transportation and communications systems. Alongside internal integration, the integration of former Soviet cities into a larger geopolitical and economic framework stands out as a critical issue for the 21st century (box 6.2). For example, should cities far closer to Tokyo or Beijing than Moscow rely primarily upon trade within Russia for economic direction? What will happen to Soviet cities that were built under one system but must now function under another? How will long-lived structures such as factories, housing, roads, schools, and other buildings be adapted for new uses? How sustainable are cities in extreme environments, such as the Arc-

Box 6.2 Ukraine and Belarus: The "Orphan" States

With the breakup of the Soviet Union, most of the Republics became newly independent states. The question for geographers has been: Which region should they be assigned to when dividing up the world in macro culture realms? Ukraine and Belarus have been dubbed the "orphan" states, in the sense that they no longer fit neatly into any one region. For this text, the decision was to leave Ukraine and Belarus in the Russia chapter, since these two former republics still maintain closer linkages with Russia than with an expanded Europe.

Regardless, from an urban perspective, Ukraine and Belarus present some interesting similarities and contrasts. Ukraine is by far the more important of the two, with a population of 49 million, of whom 68% are urbanized. Moreover, Ukraine has seven cities of 750,000 people or more, dominated by the historic city of Kiev, with 2.5 million, followed by Kharkov, Dnepropetrovsk, and Donetsk in the million-plus category. Ukraine was the number one industrial region of the former Soviet Union. Belarus has only 10 million people and is about 70% urbanized, with it urbanization focused around the old city of Minsk, with 1.7 million. Minsk (and Belarus) have changed hands numerous times in their long history, as the boundaries of Eastern Europe have moved back and forth. Belarus has a much weaker resource base than Ukraine and is heavily dependent on its customs union with Russia to survive economically.

Ukraine and Belarus have been described as a "pair of sluggish Slav countries." When they were part of the Soviet Union, their cities were subsidized to a large extent due to their focus on heavy industry, as detailed in the cases of other Soviet cities in this chapter. With the breakup of the Soviet Union in 1991, the cities, especially in Ukraine, created a tremendous drain on the national budgets. Deindustrialization (i.e., modernization) lagged behind that of Russia, in spite of the fact that Ukraine is often ranked as the one former Soviet republic with the greatest development potential. The result is that the cities of Ukraine and Belarus remain worse off than the Russian cities. The situation has been made worse by difficulties in establishing true democratic systems. Moreover, Ukraine and Belarus have acquired bad reputations as conduits for the smuggling of drugs, migrants, and even weaponry. The two countries definitely have seen better times.

Within the cities, one can especially see the toll of ten years struggling to create viable nation-states and livable cities. Odessa, in southern Ukraine, with a population stagnating at just under a million, is a good example. Beautiful, ornate structures of the czarist era, in varying states of disrepair, share space with the ugly utilitarian structures of the Soviet era. In the 1990s, retail shops appeared sparsely stocked, motor vehicles were not common, and the people seemed to walk through the streets with dignified resignation to their plight. Tickets to concerts or ballets at the Opera House, one of the best places to see the vanished glory of Odessa, could be obtained for a pittance by foreign visitors. Peddlers hawked their wares relentlessly on the steps leading down to the historic waterfront that played a key role in the Russian Revolution so long ago (fig. 6.16). Recent data on quality-of-life measures reveal high rates of alcoholism, lower nutrition standards, and high rates of suicide. It is no surprise, then, that both countries are courting closer ties with the European Union as a possible solution to their complex problems.

Figure 6.16 The Port of Odessa, Ukraine. The city was founded by Catherine the Great in the late 18th century as Russia's principal southern outlet to Europe, through the Black Sea and the Bosporus, past Istanbul. (Photo by Jack Williams)

tic and Siberia? How can cities quite distant from one another remain connected both economically and politically? Perhaps most importantly, what will happen to the people who live and work in Russian cities? What level and nature of integration into the European Union should the Russian government promote? How far down the path of destroying the Soviet housing system should Russian cities go? How best should Russian cities influence land-use change? Answers to these and many other questions confront the people of Russia today, as it continues the process of reinventing its cities.

SUGGESTED READINGS

Andrusz, G., M. Harloe, and I. Szelenyi, eds. *Cities after Socialism: Urban and Regional Change and Conflict in Post-Socialist Societies.* Oxford: Blackwell, 1996. An exploration of how socialist cities are being reshaped as a consequence of the profound economic and political changes resulting from the transition from state socialism to capitalism.

Argenbright, R. "Remaking Moscow: New Places, New Selves." *Geographical Review* 89, no. 1 (1999): 1–22. An interesting view of contemporary Moscow, such that the reader feels what it is like to walk around the city soon after the breakup of the former Soviet Union.

Bater, James H. *Russia and the Post-Soviet Scene.* New York: Wiley, 1996. A study frequently used as a textbook that provides easily understood insights into the post-Soviet world and includes a good chapter on urban development issues.

Bradshaw, Michael J. *Geography and Transition in the Post-Soviet Republics.* New York: Wiley, 1997. A collection of essays examining current human geography in Russia within the context of theoretical developments in contemporary human geography.

French, R. A., and F. E. I. Hamilton, eds. *The Socialist City.* New York: Wiley, 1979. A classic introduction to cities under socialism in the old era.

Hamm, Michael F., ed. *The City in Russian History.* Lexington: University of Kentucky, 1976. The role of cities in prerevolutionary Russia.

Hanson, Philip, and Michael J. Bradshaw, eds. *Regional Economic Change in Russia.* Northampton, Mass.: Elgar, 2000. An examination of regional patterns of economic change in Russia during the transition period.

Harris, Chauncy D. *Cities of the Soviet Union: Studies in Their Functions, Size, Density, and Growth.* Monograph Series of the Association of American Geographers. Chicago: Rand McNally, 1970. An excellent descriptive overview of cities and urban change in the former Soviet Union.

Morton, H. W., and R. C. Stuart, eds. *The Contemporary Soviet City.* New York: Sharpe, 1984. A collection of papers on different aspects of the spatial organization of Soviet cities.

"Moscow as an Emerging World City," *Eurasian Geography and Economics* 33, no. 3 (April–May 2002): 161–270. Five articles devoted to post-Soviet developments and challenges, international links and business developments, environmental problems, social polarization and ethnic segregation, and local activism and civil society.

Orttung, Robert. *From Leningrad to St. Petersburg: Democratization in a Russian City.* New York: St. Martin's, 1995. Political change in St. Petersburg in the aftermath of the collapse of the Soviet Union.

Ruble, Blair. *Money Sings: The Changing Politics of Urban Space in Post-Soviet Yaroslavl.* Washington, D.C.: Woodrow Wilson Center Press, 1995. An investigation of the politics surrounding the use of urban space, especially the politics of property, in the early transition years in the city of Yaroslavl.

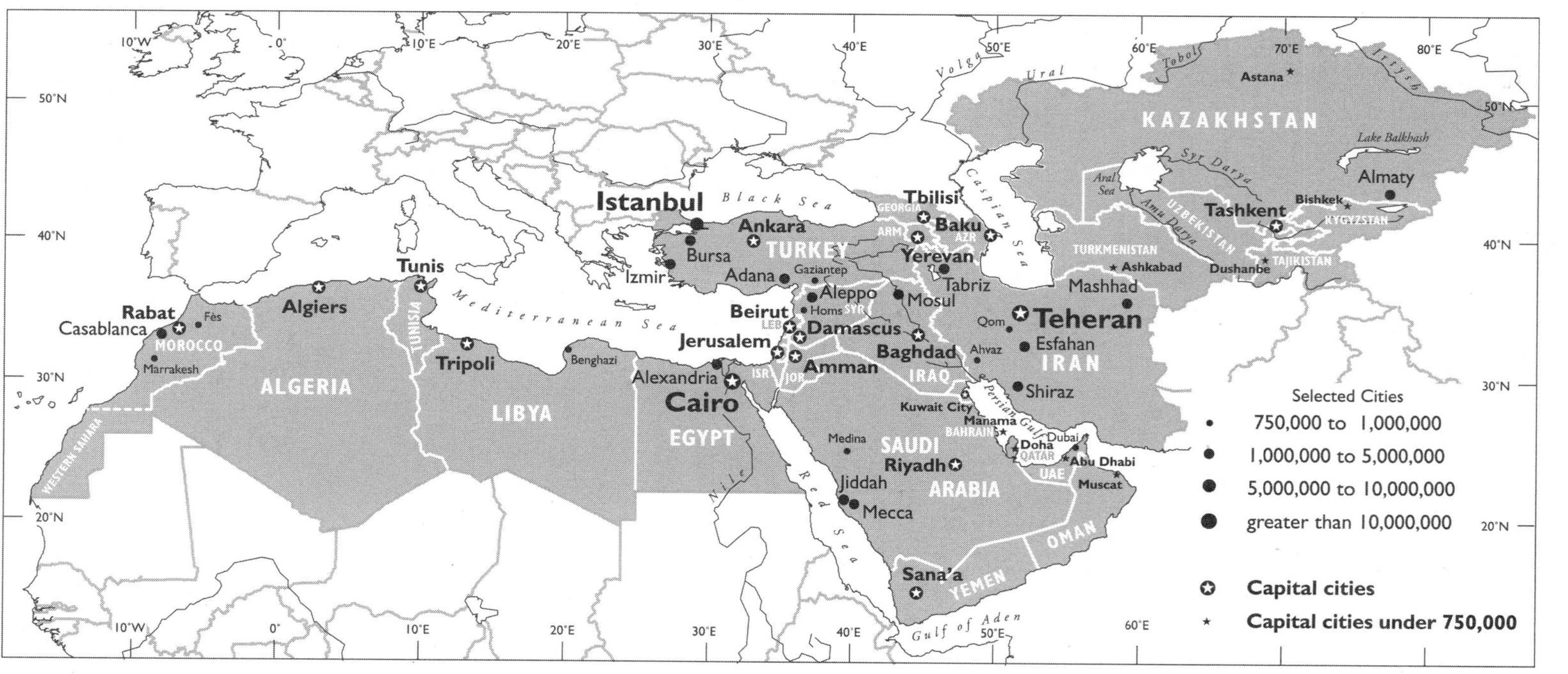

Figure 7.1 Major Cities of the Greater Middle East. *Source*: Data from United Nations, *World Urbanization Prospects, 2001 Revision* (New York: United Nations Population Division, 2002), www.unpopulation.org.

New York: Manhattan, the nerve center of America's global city, lies just north of the harbor (above it in the photo), and is identifiable by rectangular Central Park. New Jersey's busy industrial waterfront is visible on the opposite shore of the Hudson River (left); the other boroughs of New York spread to the right on the other side of the East River.

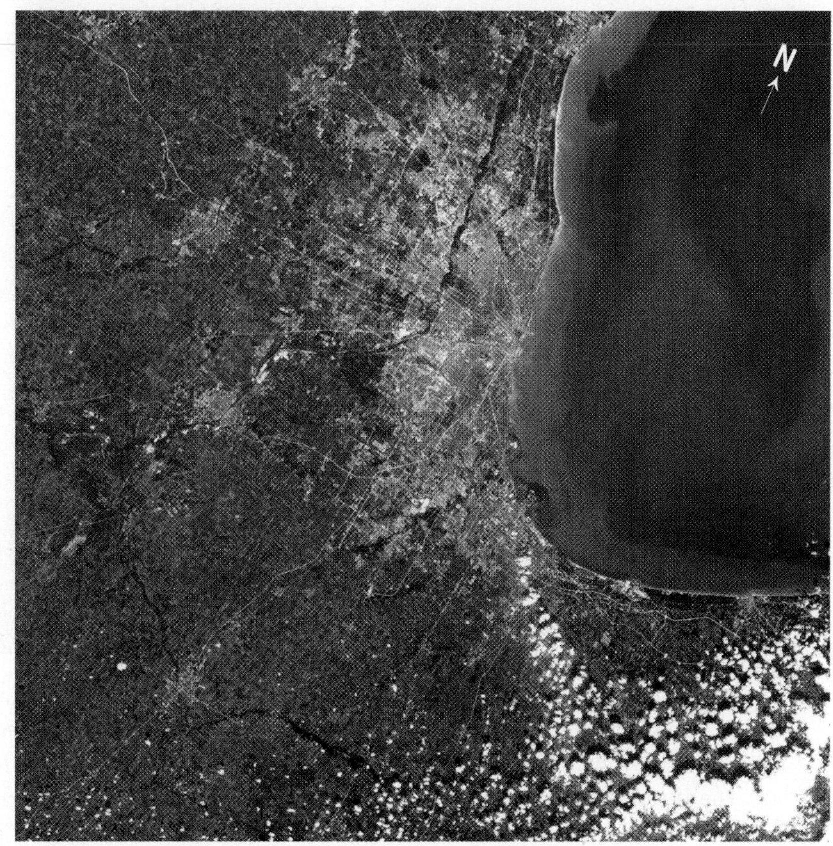

Chicago: The Midwest's premier city radiates outward in a great semicircle from the city's CBD on the southwest shore of Lake Michigan. The grid pattern and growth along transport arteries, especially freeways, so characteristic of American cities, are readily visible.

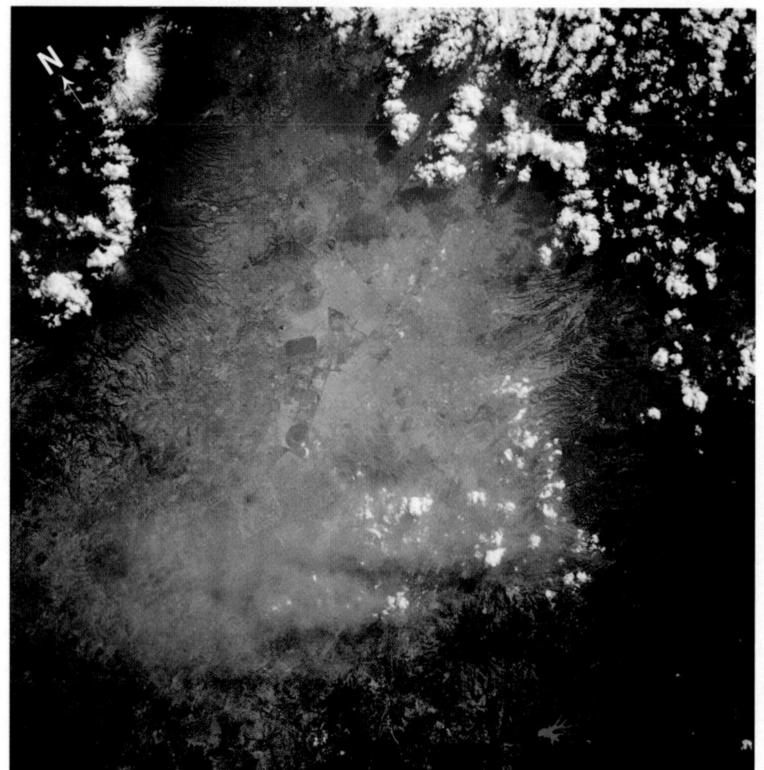

Mexico City: Mexico City, Latin America's largest city, completely fills a mile-high basin surrounded by mountains (with white clouds). The terrain traps smog and reminds residents of the dangers of volcanic eruptions and earthquakes in one of the world's most hazardous urban sites.

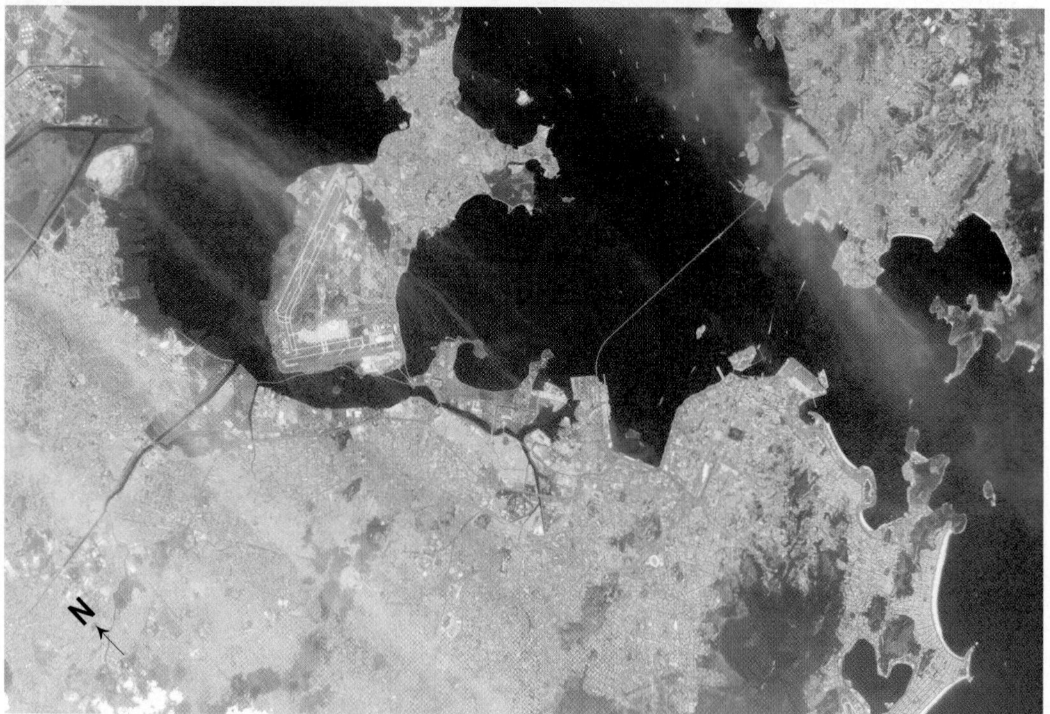

Rio de Janeiro: Brazil's playground city and cultural capital sprawls around the west side of Guanabara Bay. Rugged hills and shortage of level land provide a site renowned for its spectacular beauty but severe limitations for urban growth. A causeway connects Rio with Niterói on the east side. The famous statue of Christ is on top of Corcovado, the dark vegetation-covered mountain in the lower right, with Copacabana Beach immediately to the right, and part of Ipanema Beach below.

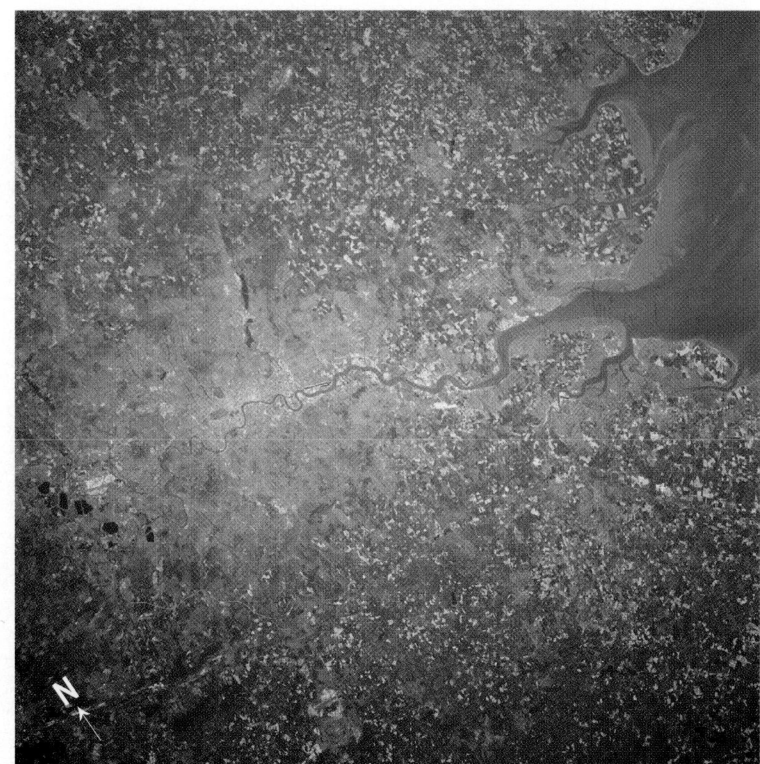

London: Where the Thames River narrows was the Roman settlement of Londinium; out of that emerged over two millennia one of the world's leading cities, now covering the large gray oval area in left center. The green belt, designed to prevent sprawl, is faintly visible around the built-up area.

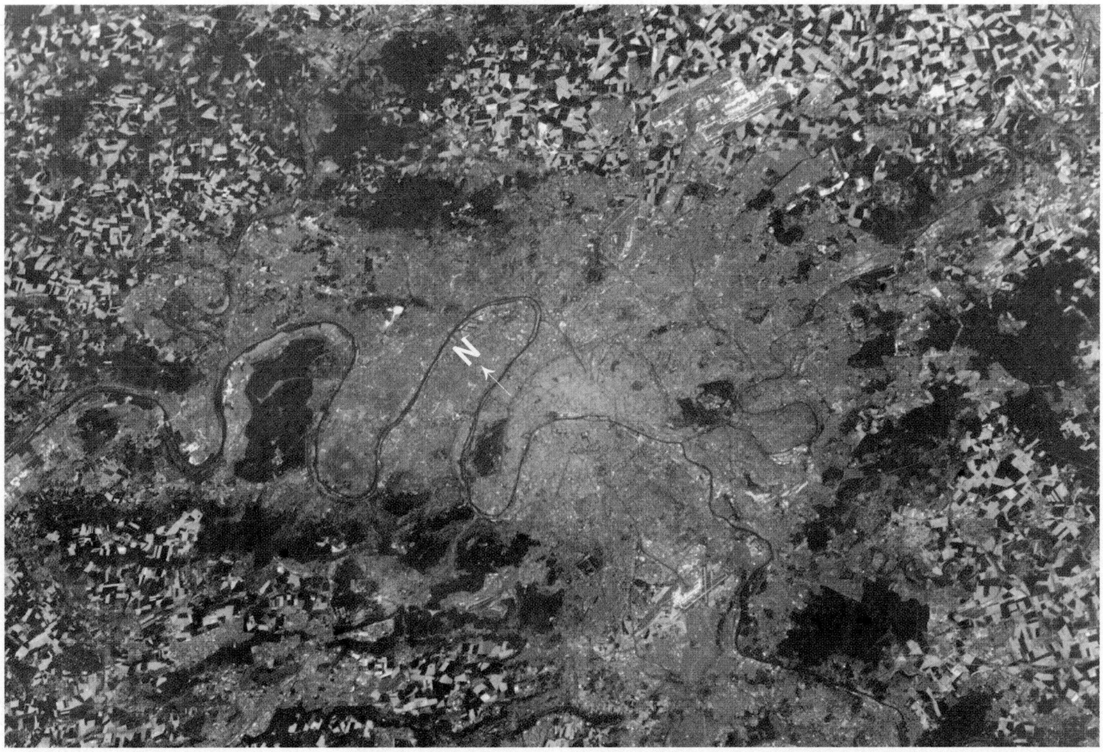

Paris: The modern city of Paris fills much of the large gray area in the middle of this image, through which winds the Seine River. The heart of the city is right in the center, in the slightly lighter area on both banks of the Seine. The dark areas are forests and parks. Small farms/fields show up in the speckled pattern around the perimeter of the image.

Moscow: Moscow, Russia's largest city and capital, sprawls outward on both sides of the Moscow River from the Kremlin, the heart of old Moscow, located on the uppermost bend of the river in left-center. The Ring Road is clearly visible, built on the site of a former city wall.

Istanbul: Europe and Asia meet in Turkey's key city of Istanbul, which sprawls along the Sea of Marmara (lower left) and up both sides of the Bosporus waterway toward the Black Sea (upper right). The two bridges linking Europe and Asia are faintly visible. The Golden Horn, an inlet off the Bosporus, delineates the old city.

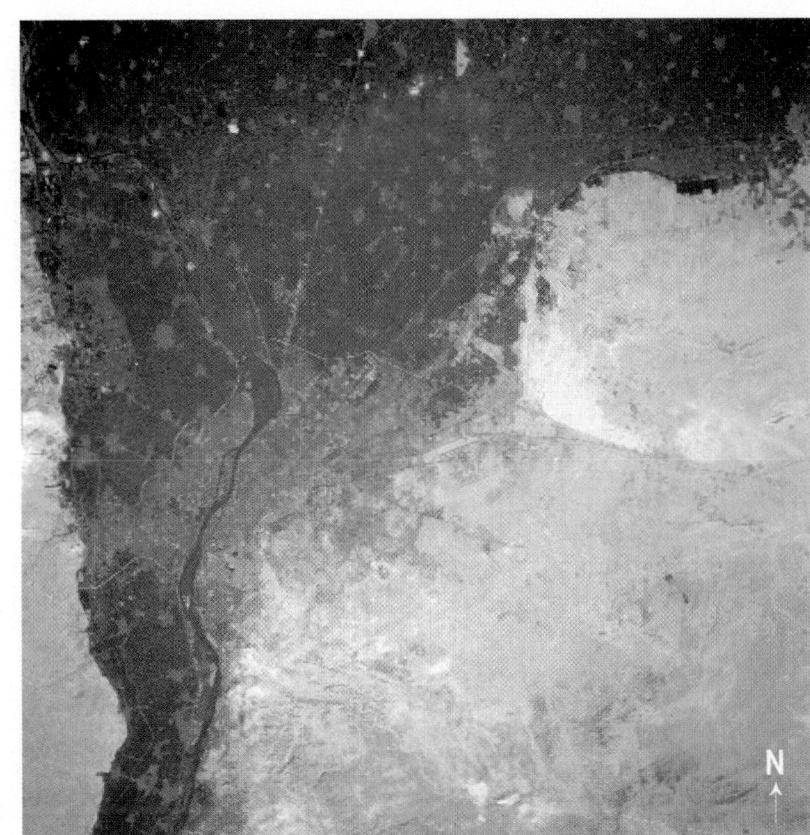

Cairo: As the largest city in the Middle East, Cairo dominates the site where the river Nile meets the delta. Although Cairo is expanding onto the rich delta croplands, attempts are made to direct new developments into the adjacent desert fringes.

Cape Town: South Africa's crown city spreads east of the rugged peninsula whose tip (bottom center) is the Cape of Good Hope, often mistaken as the southernmost point in Africa (the actual site is Cape Agulhas to the southeast, outside this image). Table Mountain, Cape Town's signature landmark, shows up distinctively as a small dark patch near the top of the Cape Peninsula, south of Table Bay, the city's harbor and CBD.

Lagos: Located along the southern and western sides of the Lagos lagoon is Sub-Saharan Africa's largest city. The straightness of Nigeria's coastline is typical of West Africa, the result being that there are few good natural harbors to serve its many states.

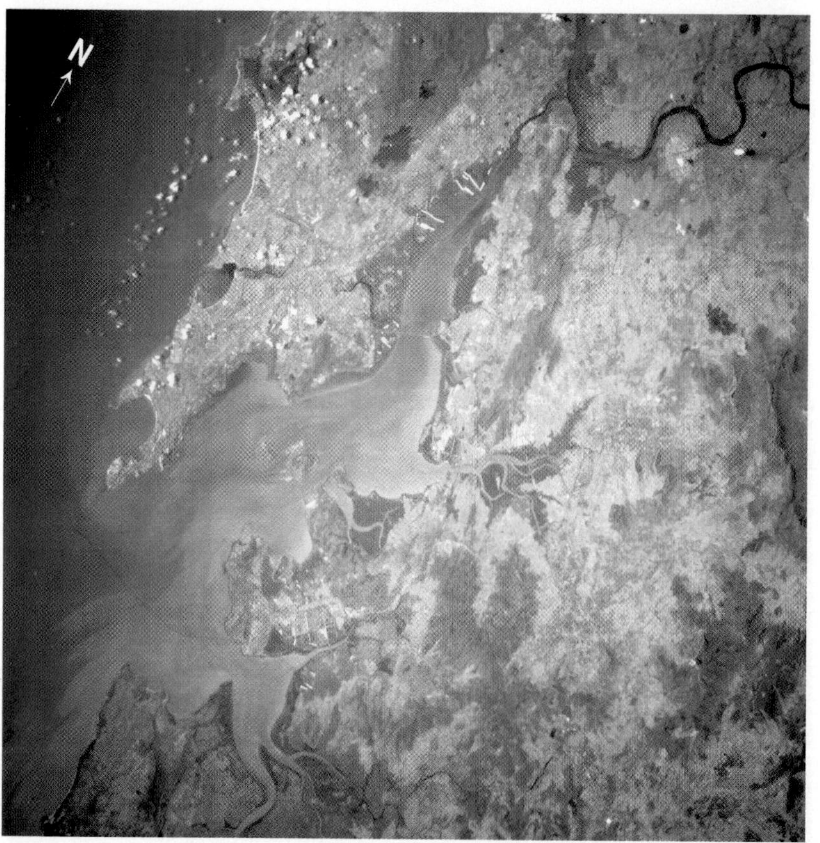

Mumbai: India's largest metropolis and key economic center began on the hook-shaped peninsula jutting into the Arabian Sea in center left, with Nariman Point at the southern tip. Mumbai now sprawls far beyond that original core, around the other side of the estuary.

Singapore: The island city-state lies just off the Malay peninsula, separated by a narrow waterway from the Malaysian city of Johore to the north. This strategic site, at the entrance to the Strait of Malacca to the west (bottom left, with silt showing), combined with a superb natural harbor, have long been Singapore's great geographic advantages.

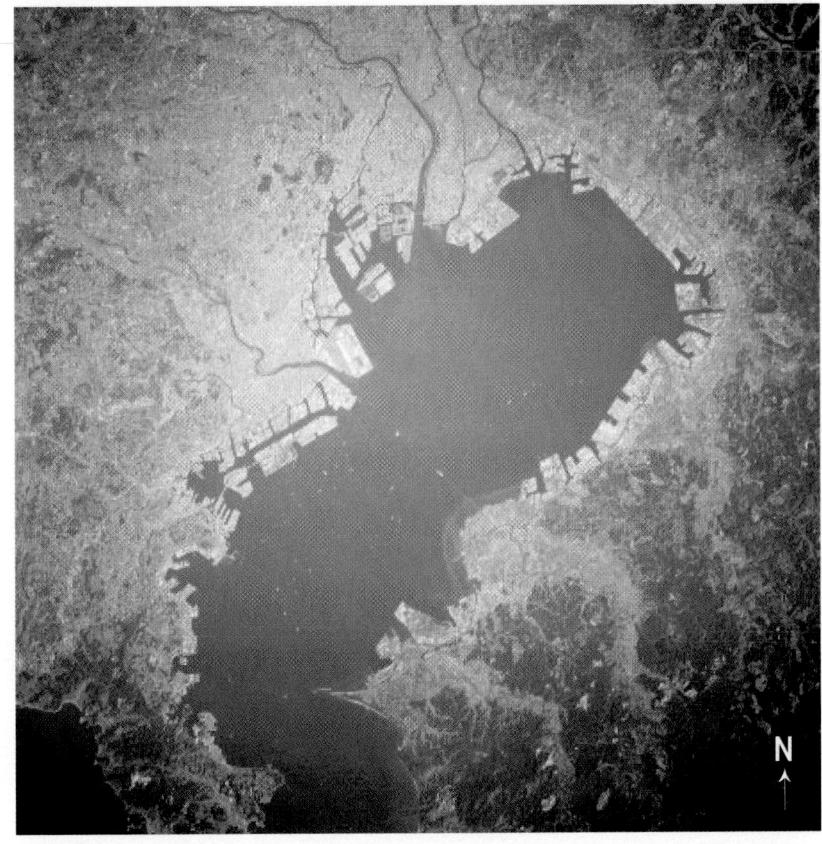

Tokyo: Tokyo Bay is the centerpiece of metropolitan Tokyo. The demand for land has resulted in land being reclaimed all around the perimeter of the bay, evidenced by the sharp angular lines. All the major cities of Japan exhibit such largely human-made coastlines, reflecting the severe shortage of land in Japan for urban expansion.

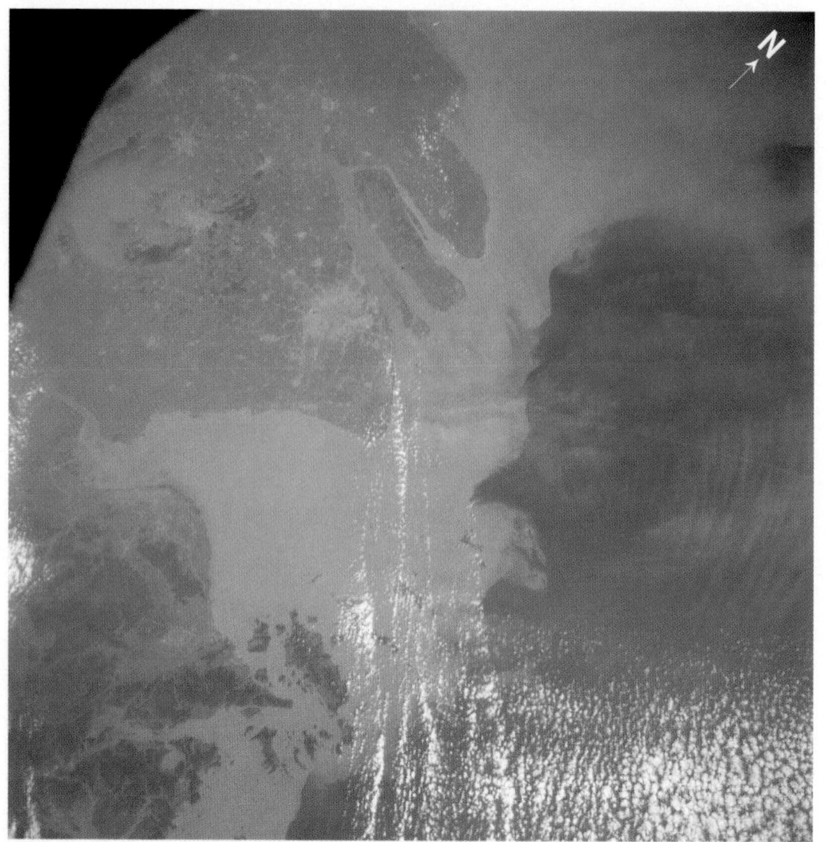

Shanghai: China's largest metropolis lies on the south side of the Chang Jiang (Yangtze R.) delta. The mouth of the river contains a long, large island, part of Shanghai municipality. The main built-up urban area shows as a light grey oval in the upper center. Heavy silt deposits from the Chang Jiang and other rivers color the entire coastal zone many miles out to sea.

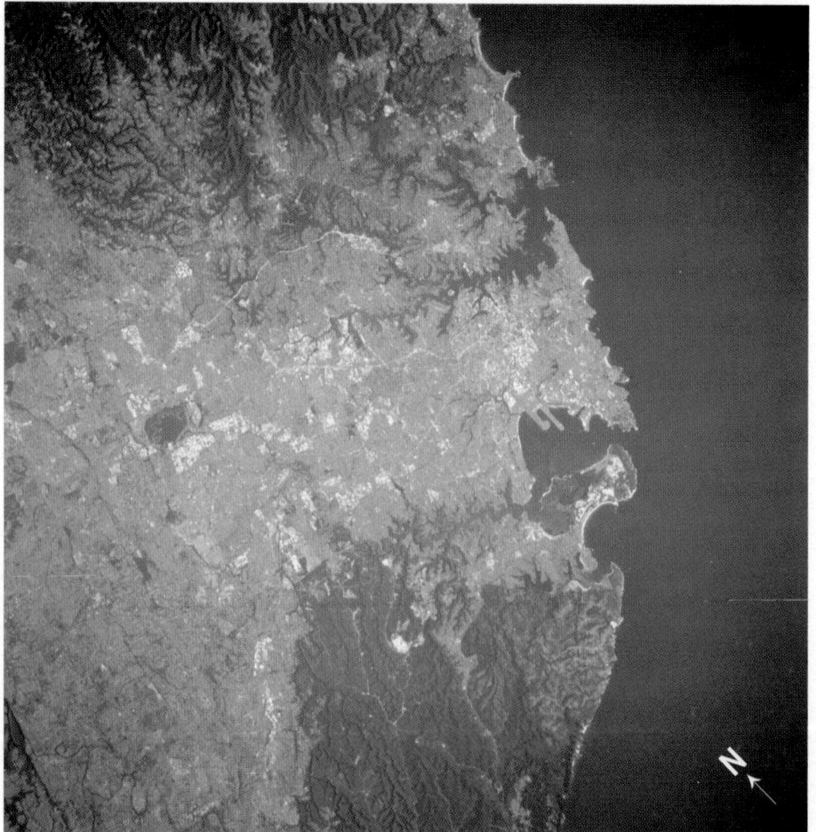

Sydney: Australia's queen city sprawls inland on both sides of the sharply indented Port Jackson (upper center) and many miles further inland, and south to Botany Bay where the city first began. The international airport juts into the bay.

7

Cities of the Greater Middle East

DONALD J. ZEIGLER

KEY URBAN FACTS

Total Population	467 million
Percent Urban Population	58%
Total Urban Population	271 million
Most Urbanized Country	Kuwait (96%)
Least Urbanized Country	Yemen (25%)
Annual Urban Growth Rate	2.3 percent
Number of Megacities	1
Number of Cities of More Than 1 Million	35
Three Largest Cities	Cairo, Istanbul, Teheran
World Cities	None

KEY CHAPTER THEMES

1. Urban landscapes of the Greater Middle East have been shaped by the dry environment and the Islamic religion, as well as by enclaves of Judaism and Christianity.
2. The location of cities has been strongly influenced by the availability of water in the form of rivers, springs, and underground aquifers.
3. The world's first cities grew up in the Fertile Crescent, along the Nile, and on the Anatolian Plateau.
4. Traditional city cores are, or were, walled and dominated by a citadel or *kasbah.*
5. Urban economic geography has traditionally been shaped by the commerce that coursed across the region.
6. Some states have a primate city, some have two or three competing cities, and a few have fully developed urban hierarchies.
7. The "urban triangle" that defines the region's core has a foothold on three continents.
8. During the 20th century, oil and gas revenues have turned some of the least urbanized countries into some of the most urbanized.

9. The urban population geography of the oil-rich states has been transformed by millions of "guest workers," particularly from South and Southeast Asia.
10. Major urban problems range from rapid population growth and unemployment to the preservation of heritage resources.

Urbanism as a way of life seems to have originated in that region we call the Middle East (fig. 7.1). Solidly anchored in this tricontinental junction are the roots of the Western city. Perhaps it is no accident that our word "urban" still carries the name of the world's first truly urban places, Ur and Uruk, in southern Mesopotamia. These early agglomerated settlements, dating from at least the 5th millennium B.C., offered protection, security, and the ability to control resources (such as water) and trade. Ideas about urban development and planning originated here and spread as by-products of commerce and conquest.

Over the course of the 20th century, the "Middle East" as a regional appellation replaced the older "Near East." As a vernacular term, it has also expanded in geographical coverage. For the sake of brevity, the term "Middle East" is used in this chapter to refer to the "Greater Middle East," that crescent of territory stretching from Morocco eastward across North Africa, through the lands of Southwest Asia, to the steppes of Kazakhstan. This great sweep of territory is united by a basic core of shared geographical characteristics (fig. 7.2). First, in its physical attributes, the Middle East is part of the dry world. Second, in its cultural attributes, the Middle East is predominantly Islamic. Third, in its relative location, the Middle East really is in the "middle"—the middle of the Eastern Hemisphere, a frontier between the civilizations of Europe, East Asia, and Africa. In short, cities here have been designed around access to water, God (or gods), and trade.

Dry and seasonally dry, arid and semiarid, desert and steppe—these are descriptors of the Middle East's physical geography. Most of the region suffers a deficit of freshwater. Available water comes from winter showers, orographic precipitation, exotic streams, natural springs, and shallow aquifers. Throughout the dry world, water has historically set the stage for concentrations of population and growth of urban centers. In turn, the dry environment presented a set of natural obstacles that these urban centers had to overcome: scorching sun, high daytime temperatures, desert winds, dusty air, and scarcity of water. The same dry environment—the desert—offered the earliest of cities a set of natural frontiers. An envelope of emptiness protected them.

Contemporary Middle Eastern cities also share a common element of cultural geography, that of religion. This region is the birthplace of three of the world's major religions: Judaism, Christianity, and Islam. All three have left their enduring stamp on the region, but it is Islam that is most widely associated with the Greater Middle East, having begun there in the early 7th century. Within the region, cultures—Arab, Persian, Turkish, Kurdish—vary from place to place, but the cultural matrix is webbed together by the religion of Islam. Christians and Jews (and some smaller groups like the Baha'i, Druze, and Zoroastrians) are found living within the Islamic matrix, but they are the exception, not the rule. Only in a few select areas are urban landscapes punctuated by anything but the minarets of mosques.

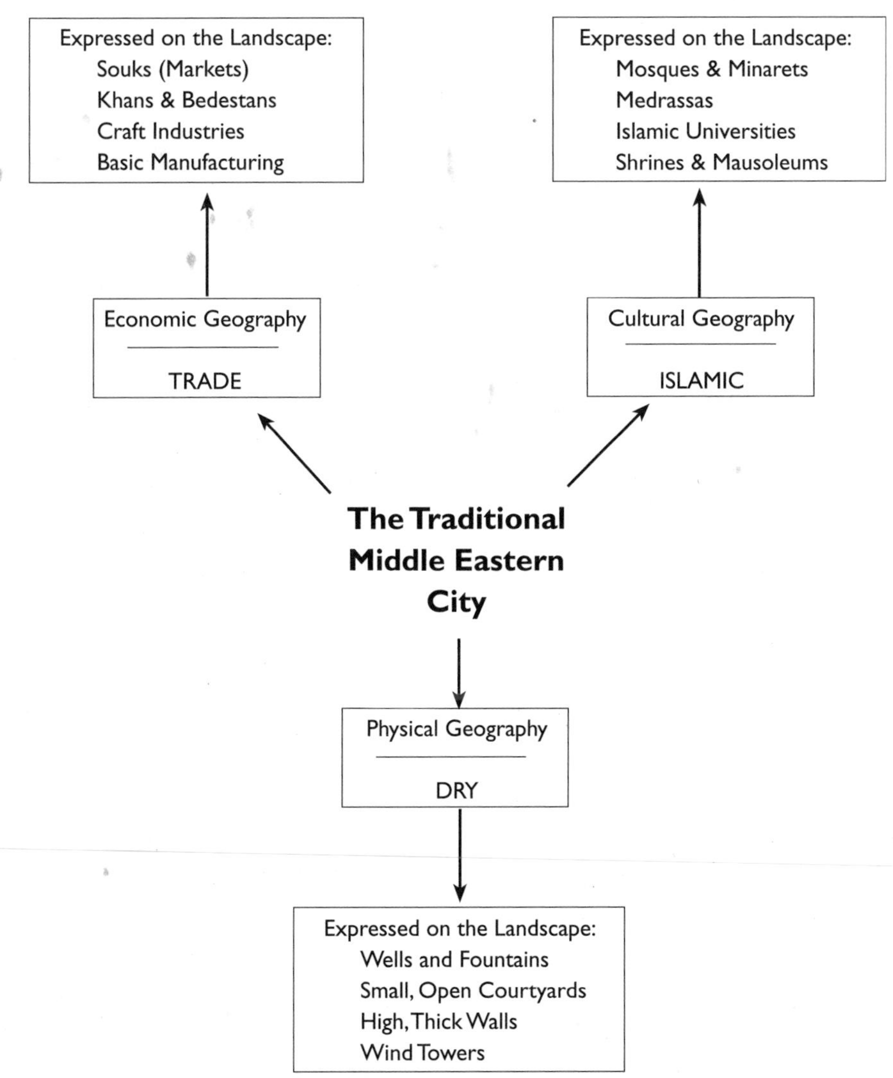

Figure 7.2 The Traditional Middle Eastern City. *Source*: Donald Zeigler

The Middle Eastern city has always been a center of spiritual life and a generator of new ideas about people's relationships with God and each other. Religious ideas run deep here.

The relative location of the Middle East has given its cities a third set of common characteristics: they are centers of trade and commerce. Prior to the 15th-century discovery of water routes around Africa and the world, trade between the great civilizations had to pass through the dry-land crescent separating Europe from East Asia and sub-Saharan Africa. Trade among these three regions—by geographical necessity—passed through the Middle East. In fact, the configuration of land and water—the interpenetration of seas (e.g., the Persian/Arabian Gulf), land bridges (e.g., Anatolia and Persia), and peninsulas (e.g., Arabia), suggested a multitude of routes through this dry-world barrier. Trade in food and fabrics, gold and copper, spices and perfumes, frankincense and myrrh all helped build the cities of the Middle East. In fact, new ideas about how to create and expand wealth, perhaps even capitalism itself, were born in cities here. Their marketplaces—called *bazaars* in the Persian language, *pazars* in Turkish, and *souks* in Arabic—are among the oldest in the world.

In other words, cities in the Middle East have evolved around the well, the house of worship, and the marketplace. Until the late 20th century (and the genesis of oil economies), city size was, in fact, proportional to these factors—larger cities evolved in direct proportion to the availability of freshwater, the abundance of "spiritual capital," and the bounty of trade. Powerful countries were, and are, built around powerful cities. As the concentration of political power in cities increased, it gave rise to a fourth essential element of the urban landscape: the palace. This was the symbol of secular power, the rival of the temple precinct. Today, the palace has evolved into the buildings of governmental administration.

Physical features that commended a site for urban development often took the form of a hill, a natural spring or oasis, a small headland or peninsula, a harbor or river mouth, a confluence of streams, or a point able to command passage through a gap or across a river. It was a peninsula, for instance, that set the stage for the evolution of Istanbul, an oasis that did so for Damascus, a spring for Tehran, a harbor for Beirut, a confluence of streams for Khartoum, and a hilltop for Aleppo.

Site is only half the story, however. Site characteristics may be responsible for the founding of a city, but relative location (with regard to routes of commerce and seats of power) determines whether a city prospers or disappears. Some cities have the potential to be trading hubs or imperial capitals; others do not. Furthermore, what is good in one age may be bad in another. Location matters. Baghdad replaced Damascus as the seat of the Islamic caliphate in 750 A.D. The opening of the Suez Canal drew trade away from the cities of the Fertile Crescent after 1869. Iskenderun (originally Alexandretta) on the Mediterranean was cut off from its natural Syrian hinterland in 1939 when the French transferred the territory to Turkey. All across the Middle East, "dead cities" and archaeological *tells* (hills created as one city was built on top of its predecessors) punctuate the landscape, each an example of how changing relative location influences the geography of growth and decline.

THE ORIGINS OF THE MIDDLE EASTERN CITY

The Middle East was home to the world's first large, agglomerated settlements. These settlements evolved as centers of production, worship, defense, and trade. They distinguished themselves from the countryside by offering the best life had to offer, at least for powerful elites and their clients. The oldest cities in the world, though most often classified as proto-urban, were born during the Neolithic period. They are all associated with the beginnings of agriculture. Their locations form a triangle with one vertex in Iraq, one in Palestine, and one in Turkey. In ancient Mesopotamia (the "land between the rivers") were the cities of Ur, Uruk, Eruidu, Kish, and others. As truly urban places, they emerged in the 4th millennium B.C. They were the largest cities in the world until the rise of Babylon. Only archaeological tells remain, but these forerunners of the modern Middle Eastern city set off a chain reaction in urban innovation that continues to this day. Earlier than this, however, in Palestine, on the other side of the Fertile Crescent, ancient Jericho boasted a wall and watchtower in the 8th millennium B.C. One has only to look at the natural endowments of Jericho's site to understand the impetus for prolific agriculture here. Deep within an arid rift valley, this "city of palms" is located next to a gushing spring and not far from the *wadi* (river bed) that brings runoff from the Judean Hills into the sun-drenched Jordan River valley.

On the Anatolian plateau, just to the north of the Fertile Crescent, stands the most recently discovered prototypical city, Çatal Höyük, which dates to about 6,500 B.C. It was located on a small river in the Konya Plain, today a rather desolate area of Turkey. It had an estimated 50,000 inhabitants and was probably one of the largest and most sophisticated settlements in the world in its day. Why? Because of the successful domestication of wheat and other products. Just as its size proved the viability of largeness, its form proved to be a pacesetter in the development of urban landscapes.

These three centers of incipient urbanism gave us many innovations in city form and function, innovations that remain with us today. Threads of continuity connect the most ancient of cities to the most modern. Indeed, the city idea itself, the idea that urbanism presented a way of life distinct from that of the countryside, was the seed that gave us the world cities of today. Even the earliest of cities illustrated the concept that urbanization meant civilization.

The Plateau of Iran and the Mediterranean basin gave rise to some of the world's earliest, all-encompassing empires. Each conquest opened a new chapter in urban history. Persian culture transformed Babylonian, Median, and Phrygian cities. Under Alexander and his successor generals, Greek culture blended with various "oriental" elements to create a new Hellenistic city. Under the rule of Rome, a new Roman culture transformed Phoenician trading posts and gave rise to a new set of cities in Egypt and Southwest Asia, some built on top of their Hellenistic predecessors. Each of these empires succeeded because they were successfully (if sometimes brutally) administered and promoted trade. As a result, ideas about urban design and city living rolled across their urban landscapes, converging around the institutions of government, commerce, and religion. In the Roman city, wherever it existed, the forum, basilica, coliseum, amphitheater, public baths, and temples provided elements that linger in the landscapes of the Middle East today (fig. 7.3). El Djem, Tunisia, is no longer a major city, but it still has its coliseum, second in size only to Rome's. Istanbul, Turkey, still has its hippodrome, a racetrack for chariots, dating from 330 A.D., when Constantinople was built as a new capital for the aging Roman Empire.

The Roman Empire became officially Christian in the 4th century A.D. Thereafter, the followers of Jesus transformed the cultural landscape and social geography of the empire's cities. Rome's successor, the Byzantine Empire, became the guardian of Christianity in the eastern Mediterranean. Nevertheless, a new religion, Islam, born on the Arabian Peninsula, was to conquer the Byzantine lands of Southwest Asia and North Africa. Between the 7th and 10th centuries, Islam created the unique urban landscapes we know today as "the Islamic city." It was a city of mosques, madrassahs (religious schools), and universities, a city built on free thinking and scientific progress, a city of honest trade, tolerance, and justice. Its daily routines, seasonal rhythms, architectural appearance, and governing sys-

Figure 7.3 Volubilis, in Morocco, was one of the largest cities in the western Roman Empire. Today, it is on the United Nations list of World Heritage Sites. (Photo by Jack Williams)

tem were heavily influenced by Islam. The Islamic city is the city that remains with us today; there is no such thing as a "post-Islamic city." The Islamic city has no counterparts in other parts of the world. Few would refer to a prototypical Christian city, Hindu city, or Buddhist city; but in the Middle East the term "Islamic city" seems to be the most widespread shorthand for distilling the essence of urban geography. That essence is palpable during Ramadan, the month of fasting, when the pulse of urban life is transformed (box 7.1).

Many countries of the Middle East have an urban tradition that transcends not just centuries but millennia: Iraq, greater Syria, Turkey, Egypt, Iran, Uzbekistan. Yet some countries of the region entered the 20th century without an urban tradition at all. The emirates (principalities) of the Persian/Arabian Gulf knew nothing of city life. The Arab side of the gulf was punctuated by small fishing and pearling ports. Saudi Arabia's urban population was almost entirely *hajj*-related (see page 267), with Mecca, Medina, and Jiddah surfacing at the top of the urban pyramid. The ancient cities of the frankincense trade, such as Ubar, had been reclaimed by the desert and the few large seaports, Aden and Musqat, served offshore interests more than their hinterlands. Today, whether a country's cities date back to antiquity or to the recent past, the Middle Eastern population tends to be decidedly urban, a response to the declining viability of nomadism, the rapidly growing numbers of people, the restricted range of arable land, the rise of prosperous fossil-fuel economies, the accessibility to international economic networks, and the political decisions of powerful elites.

Box 7.1 Ramadan in Cairo

Ramadan is a month when Muslims fast from sunup to sundown. Daily rhythms change (stores stay open twenty-four hours), piety prevails (restaurants serve no alcohol), and special foods tickle the tonsils (families enjoy qanafa *and* kataief *after sundown). The following excerpt by Sarah Gauch and Lorraine Chittock captures some of the local color of Ramadan on the streets of Cairo.*

The holy month of fasting is when Egyptians, like all Muslims worldwide, not only abstain from food, drink and sex from sunrise to sunset, but also spend more time in prayer, get out to visit friends and relatives, and give and receive charity. . . . During Ramadan, Cairo is transformed . . . into a kaleidoscope of light and color, with glittery streamers connecting the houses and colored-glass lanterns hanging everywhere. . . .

The frenzied rush to get home for *iftar* (the sundown meal that breaks the daily fast) begins to build around two o'clock as many leave work early. But not everyone goes home: Some break their fast at *iftars* sponsored by companies, clubs, and friends at restaurants and hotels. Others visit "tables of mercy," where wealthy patrons set up seating in the street, or on the sidewalks or even in the grassy medians of thoroughfares to serve free *iftar* meals to the poor. . . .

[I]n the lower-class neighborhood of Bulaq al-Dakrout, people are also out, playing dominoes in small cafes, buying fruit for *suhar,* even getting a haircut at the barbershop. The apartment buildings appear to be almost interwoven with flittering silver-foil streamers and lines of colorful pennants. Shops are covered in flashing colored light bulbs.

. . . "Ramadan is special for everyone."

Source: Sarah Gauch and Lorraine Chittock, *Saudi Aramco World* (January/February 2002), 60–62.

CITIES AND URBAN REGIONS

With 55% of its population living in cities, the Middle East entered the 21st century an urbanized region. In some countries, more than nine out of ten inhabitants now live in cities. Kuwait and Qatar, virtual city-states, fall into this category, as do other Arab states of the Persian/Arabian Gulf and oil-rich, rain-poor countries such as Libya. Likewise, in Israel, more than 90% of the population are urban dwellers. The pattern for Israel applies also to the neighboring states of Jordan and Lebanon, at 78% and 88% urban, respectively. These countries, the most urban, are also the most developed.

The least urban countries are the least developed in the region; in Yemen, Sudan, and Tajikistan fewer than three out of ten inhabitants live in cities. Egypt and Syria, both with enviable agricultural resources, have large rural populations because the ability to make a living off the land holds people in agricultural areas. Egypt's ratio of urban to rural, at 44%

versus 56%, is one of the most stable in the region, with very little change over the past two decades. So is Iraq's, at 68% versus 32%. Likewise, Central Asia has changed little in its urban-rural balance, reflecting the tradition of strong state control over internal migration during Soviet times. In contrast, the proportion of the population living in urban settings has increased dramatically in some countries, typically faster than the rate of natural increase in the population. Oil wealth seems to be the most effective stimulator of urban growth: Oman was 5% urban in 1980 and is 72% urban today; Saudi Arabia was 24% in 1980 and is 83% today; and Kuwait's population increased from 56% to almost 100% urban over the same time period.

Why has urbanization transformed the Middle East during the 20th century? From a demographic perspective, two forces are at work—natural increase and migration. As death rates have declined faster than birth rates since World War II, the population size of every country has soared. In addition, migrants of two types have swollen the urban ranks: migrants from rural areas and, in oil-rich states and Israel, migrants from abroad. For instance, one-quarter of Saudi Arabia's population and 80% of the United Arab Emirates' population is foreign-born. Israel has received a million Russian Jews since the mid-1980s and a tide of Argentine Jews more recently. Rapid city growth in the Middle East is related to developments that have transformed life in urban settings faster than life in the countryside. Technology has created jobs in cites; governments have provided services in cities; and people have greater access to health care in cities. Growth in the urban population may be related to political developments, as well. For instance, Amman, Jordan, a village of 2,000 people in 1950, has grown to a metropolitan area of 1.5 million today. Much of that growth has been the result of refugees moving into Jordan from Palestine in the wake of wars between the Arabs and the Israelis, an economically stimulating peace dividend that followed the treaty between Jordan and Israel, and a stable political climate that has attracted direct foreign investment.

The core of the Middle East is defined by a decagon formed by five seas (Mediterranean Sea, Black Sea, Caspian Sea, Persian/Arabian Gulf, Red Sea) and five land bridges (Anatolia, Caucasus, Iran, Arabia, Sinai). On the perimeter of this core lie three of the world's twenty most populous metropolises. They anchor an intercontinental, international, and intercultural urban triangle (fig. 7.4):

- The African city of Cairo, Egypt, has (with neighboring Giza) almost 10 million people. It is the largest city in the Arab realm.
- The European city of Istanbul, Turkey, has almost 9 million people. It is the largest city in the Turkic realm.
- The Asian city of Tehran, Iran, has more than 7 million people. It is the largest city in the Persian realm.

All three are predominantly Muslim, together accounting for three of the world's five most populous Islamic cities. In 1950, only one city in the entire Middle East, Cairo, had more than a million inhabitants. In 1900, none did. Today, 30 cities have more than one million, including three in Egypt, five in Turkey, and six in Iran. Except for their historical centers, all are products of the late 20th century—they are new cities, not old. Virtually all of their growth postdates World War II. Yet the countries that anchor the Middle East's triangular urban core all have a less developed frontier side, too. Eastern Iran, eastern Turkey, and

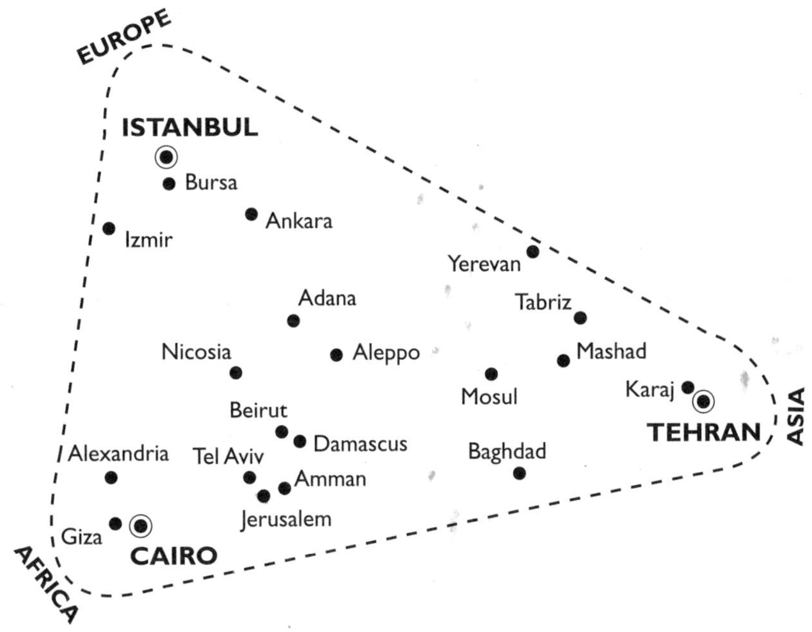

Figure 7.4 The Urban Triangle of the Middle East. *Source*: Donald Zeigler

most of upper Egypt remind us that urbanization has not entirely transformed even the most urbanized countries in the region.

Beyond the Cairo-Istanbul-Tehran triangle and its immediate environs (including Baghdad, with its four million inhabitants), there are important regional metropolises, all of which fall into the one million to two million population range. Only two exceed two million inhabitants: Casablanca, Morocco, and Tashkent, Uzbekistan. One anchors the far west, called Al-Maghreb by Arab geographers. The other anchors the far north, called Central Asia or, in its former incarnation, Turkestan.

Most countries in the Middle East have but a single city with more than one million population. This city, which is usually (but not always) the capital city, anchors the national urban system. The political and economic dominance of the most populous city varies from country to country, however. At one end of the spectrum are the city-states of the region, small cities surrounded by small buffers of sovereign territory. Kuwait, Bahrain, Qatar, and the seven emirates of the United Arab Emirates (UAE) are all microstates governed by emirs from the primate city of each. Other states—Georgia, Armenia, Azerbaijan, and Lebanon, for instance—are slightly larger in territorial extent, but their urban primacy makes them seem like city-states. Sudan's three contiguous cities of Khartoum, North Khartoum, and Omdurman together contain one-sixth of Sudan's population.

At the other end of the spectrum are the countries that have two rival urban cores, a condition that has the potential to set into motion strong centrifugal forces. Perhaps the best example of this is Syria. With about two million inhabitants each, Damascus and Aleppo are quiet rivals. Other countries with dual anchors and intercity rivalries include Yemen (Sana'a and Aden), mostly as a result of its colonial history; Libya (Tripoli and Benghazi), as it was cobbled together by the Italians; Israel (Tel Aviv and Jerusalem), split by its liberal and conservative axes; and Kazakhstan (Almaty and Karaganda), with its Turkic and Slavic flanks. Iraq, by contrast, has a clearly dominant city, Baghdad, but two smaller anchors, Mosul in the north and Basra in the south, have such different cultural geographies that Iraq effectively is a country divided.

In between these two extremes are the states with complex urban hierarchies. Turkey and Iran are both punctuated by booming metropolises, regional centers, small towns, and villages. Morocco, likewise, is a country of cities large and small, many of which have assumed highly specialized roles in the Moroccan urban system. Morocco has a political capital, Rabat, but three other cities—Marrakesh, Fès, and Meknes—have also served in that role. In addition, Morocco has an unofficial economic capital, Casablanca. Its former diplomatic capital (as far as ambassadors were permitted to venture into the country), Tangier, now serves as a bridgehead to Europe. Morocco's traditional religious capital and most important pilgrimage site, Moulay Idriss, marks the final resting place of the founder of dynastic Morocco, Muhammed's grandson, Idriss I. A city in the south, Ourzazate, has even surfaced as one of the movie-making capitals of the world, starring in films such as *Lawrence of Arabia, Star Wars,* and *Gladiator.*

Not only have cities increased in population and territorial extent, they have also begun to coalesce in a fashion reminiscent of Jean Gottmann's Megalopolis. In these urban megaregions, life is at its most intense, a characteristic symbolized by the pace and volume of traffic along connecting thoroughfares. There are perhaps seven megalopolises developing on the 21st-century map of the Middle East. The first four are rather well-defined linear regions. The most populous stretches from Cairo across the Nile to Giza then to Alexandria. Now that the new superhighway has been completed across the desert, development is even more rapidly filling in this 100-mile (161-km) corridor. The second megalopolis is the staple that holds together the continents of Europe and Asia. It is Turkey's Marmara megalopolis, anchored by Istanbul on the European side and Bursa in Asia Minor. It virtually engulfs the entirety of the Sea of Marmara, whose ports attract industry and whose vistas attract residential and recreational developments. Third is coastal Morocco from Casablanca to Rabat and Salé, only about 50 mi (80 km) apart. Fourth is the Israeli megalopolis, which begins in Haifa and Akko, stretches along the coast to Tel Aviv-Jaffa, and then moves up to Jerusalem. Although punctuated by some Arab enclaves, this crescent is essentially a belt of intense Jewish settlement tied together by highways and expanding settlement.

The next three megalopolises are best understood as nests of coalescing cities. The Mid-Mesopotamian megalopolis is anchored by Baghdad, but stretches between the Tigris and the Euphrates Rivers. The Tehran-Karaj megalopolis stretches along the base of the Zagros Mountains. The only international megalopolis is the one that stretches from coastal Saudi Arabia, beginning with the cities of Dhahran and Dammam, and then across the causeway to Bahrain and its capital, Manama.

Capital Cities of the Middle East

In the Middle East today, there are almost 30 countries, each of which has a capital. Indeed the very concept of a capital city originates with the early states and empires that grew up in the river valleys of Egypt and Mesopotamia. Memphis, in Egypt, was one of the world's first real capitals. Its location served as a hinge between Lower Egypt (the delta) and Upper Egypt (the river valley). It was able to command the entire Nile from the Mediterranean to the first cataract. A later Egyptian capital, Thebes (today's small city of Luxor) served pharaonic Egypt, with only brief interruptions, for more than 1,500 years beginning in the 21st century B.C., one of the longest runs in history. Its monumental architecture affirmed one of the rules of capital city development—nothing is too large, too beautiful, or too expensive for the head city of a proud and prosperous state. The power of the sovereign is expressed in powerful landscapes of control, where respect for and obedience to the ruler, or the law, is demanded by the symbolism of the built environment. Thebes is a case study in itself. It is still intimidating and inspiring. The feeling of grandeur, even today, is not unlike that of the 21st century's world capitals—Washington, London, Moscow, and others.

The Middle East may have the largest collection of historical capitals in the entire world. Some are well known—Memphis, Carthage, and Persepolis—while others are now just evocative ruins of the geopolitical past—Sardis, Susa, Ashur, Tuspa. The history of the Middle East is the history of major states and empires, amoeba-like in their evolution and all anchored by capital cities. The 19th and 20th centuries, however, presented a major break with the past. These were centuries of extraterritorial rule, when the capital cities of the Middle East, the decision-making centers of the region, became Paris, London, Moscow, and Rome. Even earlier, Ottoman Istanbul became an extraterritorial ruler of the Arab lands of North Africa and Southwest Asia. With the collapse of the Ottoman Empire, the rule of Europe became even more widespread. Only a few states—Saudi Arabia, Oman, modern Turkey, and, arguably, Iran—avoided colonial domination or protectorate status.

With independence, which came to most states of the region after World War II, a new set of capitals was born. For some states, the choice was simple. Cairo was already serving as the national capital of Egypt. In Syria, Lebanon, and Jordan, the administrative centers that served French and British interests, Damascus, Beirut, and Amman, respectively, became the national capitals. Libya had to decide between two capitals, Tripoli and Benghazi, one in command of Libya's western coast and the other of Libya's east. Only with the creation of a highly centralized, unitary state was Tripoli, the larger of the two, designated as the sole capital. Nevertheless, regional tensions have inspired on-and-off plans to move the capital to a midway point along the coast, the small port city of Sirte, already an administrative center.

Turkey, born out of the Ottoman Empire after World War I, had only one obvious choice of cities for its capital: Istanbul, a city that had served as head of an empire for 1,600 years under Romans, Byzantines, and Ottomans. But instead of Istanbul, in 1923, Kemal Atatürk, as one of his first acts as president, made a not-so-obvious choice: Ankara, a city of the interior. Why make such a dramatic change? To symbolize the death of an old state, the Ottoman Empire, and the birth of a new one, the Republic of Turkey. Turkey was not to be the Ottoman state with a new name, it was to be a new creation rooted in the civilizations of Anatolia, the plateau of Asia Minor. By choosing Ankara, a city of some antiquity, the modern state was able to emphasize its roots in a pre-Ottoman past. Except for the architecture of

Figure 7.5 Inner-city apartments, with balconies, are part of the residential landscape of Almaty, former capital of Kazakhstan. (Photo by Stanley Brunn)

its mosques, Ankara bears almost no trace of the Ottoman period.

Kazakhstan provides the most recent case study of a country that has chosen to relocate its capital. As a modern independent state, it began life in 1991 with Alma Ata, renamed Almaty, as the center of government. Alma Ata, the country's most populous city by far, had served as capital during the period of Soviet rule, when Kazakhstan was a union republic (fig. 7.5). Within a few years, however, the president of Kazakhstan made known his intention to move the seat of government to Akmola, which was eventually renamed Astana, which means "capital" in the Kazakh language. Real and symbolic factors were at work in the decision. Almaty was not centrally located. To boot, it was perilously close to the Chinese border. The choice of Astana solved both of these problems. Moreover, Astana is five meridians closer to Europe, and Kazakhstan takes pride in calling itself a "Euro-Asian" nation, overlapping the continental boundary as it does. Yet, while flirting with the European connection, Kazakhstan draws its national identity from the steppes, the grasslands of Central Asia. Astana, the new capital, presides over those steppes, whereas the previous capital was in the mountainous foothills of Kazakhstan's east.

The urban geographer Jean Gottmann compares a capital city to a hinge; the choice of Astana fits that analogy almost perfectly. First, the new capital serves as a hinge between the pre-Soviet past and the nation-building present. Second, it serves as a hinge (or hopes to) between Asia and Europe. Third, it serves as a hinge between the two sociocultural parts of the nation, the Russified north, inhabited mostly by transmigrant Slavs, and the Turkic south, inhabited by Kazakhs and their Uzbek brethren. By moving the capital city onto the Slavic frontier, Kazakhstan proclaimed its intention to maintain territorial integrity and not to tolerate irredentist claims by Russia (fig. 7.6).

Figure 7.6 One of the few remaining statues of Lenin in the former Soviet Republic of Kyrgyzstan is found in front of the Kyrgyz National Museum (formerly the Lenin National Museum) in Bishkek, the capital. (Photo by Stanley Brunn)

The Middle East also boasts a set of very specialized capitals that no other part of the world can equal: the "head cities" of the three great monotheistic faiths. Mecca, in Saudi Arabia, is the religious capital of the Islamic world, a pilgrimage destination for two million *hajjis* (pilgrims) annually. The flow of *hajjis* also makes Mecca the world's leading tourist city, but a destination reserved strictly for Muslims. Jiddah serves as the gateway to Mecca for those arriving by boat and by air. Those who make the *hajj* visit Islam's second-holiest city as well, Medinat al-Nabi, the "city of the Prophet," commonly called just "Medina." It was to this city that Mohammed fled in 622 A.D., marking the beginning of the Muslim calendar. For a short time under the first caliphs, Medina served as the capital of the expanding Islamic empire. The third-holiest city to Muslims is Al-Quds ("the holy") in Palestine; it is known to the rest of the world as Jerusalem. These three cities are important to the entire Islamic world, but Shia Islam has an additional set of holy cities, Najaf and Karbala in southern Iraq, that are also pilgrimage sites. The "capital" of Islam's predecessors, Judaism and Christianity, is also in the Middle East. The ancient walled city of Jerusalem is the holiest in the world to both Jews and Christians and a focus of world pilgrimage for both. Medieval European maps of the world, in fact, showed Jerusalem to be at the center of the world, exactly where it remains today, if only in a religious sense.

Port Cities of the Middle East

Port cities are gateways to the world. Such is the case with Egypt's major port of Alexandria, founded by Alexander the Great in 331 B.C. Alexandria is on a natural harbor created by an offshore island, while its hinterland comprises the most fertile and productive land in the Mediterranean basin, the delta and valley of the Nile River. Its earliest maritime links connected the port to the entire Hellenistic world, particularly the Greek Aegean. Alexandria hinged together Greek and Egyptian civilizations. The symbol of its commercial prosperity was its lighthouse, the Pharos, one of the seven wonders of the ancient world. The symbol of its intellectual prowess, stimulated by the cultural encounter of these two civilizations, was the library of Alexandria, the greatest of antiquity. Neither the lighthouse nor the library has survived, but the lighthouse remains a symbol of port cities and Egypt recently unveiled its magnificent new library, the Bibliotecha Alexandrina, to commemorate and revive the city's role in the intellectual world.

Just as some of the world's oldest capital cities are located in the Middle East, so are some of the world's oldest port cities—Tyre, Sidon, Acre, Jaffa, Ashquelon, and Gaza—on the eastern Mediterranean coast. Older ports have rarely met the needs of modern countries, however. In fact, if a port is mentioned in the Bible, it is almost surely inadequate for today's commerce. Acre has been superceded by nearby Haifa, Jaffa by neighboring Tel Aviv. Beirut and Alexandria have built new ports beyond their natural harbors. Antioch (modern Antakya), the premier city of the eastern Mediterranean in Roman times, is a port no more. Gaza, which is now challenged to become a modern port for an emergent Palestine, illustrates an important rule of port geography: every country must have a seaport of its own (unless it is landlocked). Where good natural harbors are not available for port development, artificial harbors must be built. The configuration of international boundaries, virtually all products of extraterritorial decision making, heavily influenced the port geography of the Middle East. Syria (historically the entire Western Fertile Crescent), for instance, was cut off from its natural port cities, historic Antioch in Turkey and modern Tripoli and Beirut, by European-drawn boundaries. The result has been a substantial investment in enlarging the small natural harbor at Tartous and building a large new port at Latakia.

Likewise, the impact of international boundaries on port geography is evident at the head of two arms of the sea: on the Persian/Arabian Gulf where Iraq, Iran, and Kuwait converge, and on the Gulf of Aqaba where Jordan, Israel, Egypt, and Saudi Arabia converge. In both places, one port, operating at economies of scale, would make more sense, but political boundaries dictate otherwise. Ditto the UAE, the only federation in the Middle East. Here, there is lively competition among the seven emirates to capture a share of maritime trade and in-transit manufacturing. Consequently, a nation of only two million people has sixteen commercial seaports, the most important of which are in Dubai.

In the Middle East, seaports are not the only port cities. More important historically have been "ports" on the edge of the desert, cities that have dispatched caravans to distant places and opened their gates to merchant traders arriving from afar. The seas traversed by the caravan trade were desert seas—"seas of sand" (even though most are not sandy). Sijilmassa, in southern Morocco, now in ruins and only recently excavated, was one such desert port. It linked the Atlas oases with the Sahel—the southern "shore" of the Sahara—before coastal shipping proved more economical. Sijilmassa served the same function as a seaport, as did its southern counterpart, Timbuktu. Likewise, Damascus grew up around an oasis on the edge of the Syrian Desert. It attracted caravans coming from Mesopotamia. In Uzbekistan in Central Asia, Samarkand, at

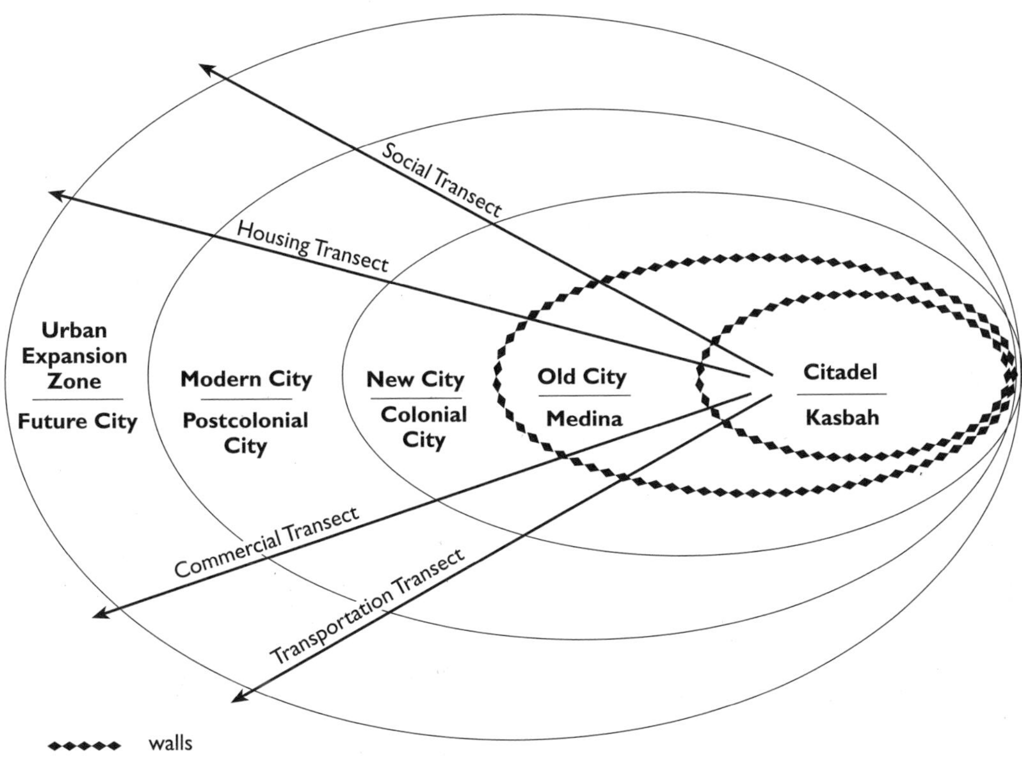

Figure 7.7 Internal Structure of the Middle Eastern Metropolis. *Source*: Donald Zeigler

the foot of the Tien Shan, was also a desert port. Thus on the edges of the Sahara, the Syrian Desert, and the Karakum, ports developed to act as hinges between civilizations.

Models of the Urban Landscape

At the heart of every traditional Middle Eastern city is, or was, a fortress. It may be called the citadel, *al-qalat*, or, in the Maghreb, the *kasbah* (fig. 7.7). It usually covers only a few acres and occupies the most defensible site, often a hilltop. Typically surrounded by a wall, it might also once have been protected by water. Also, it would have served as the administrative heart of the city, the site of the palace. Today, the citadel is most likely to be a preserve of history, valuable as a visual reminder of the past and important in building national identity (fig. 7.8). Its landscape usually exudes a powerful spirit of place. It may or may not continue to be inhabited.

Surrounding the citadel is the old city itself. It, too, was usually walled and its often-ornate gates gave access to the cardinal places in the local universe. In the Maghreb, the old city is called the *medina* (Arabic for "city"). It is the city of antiquity, at least as it has survived conquest, disasters, and well-meaning modernization attempts. Its landscape has imprinted itself on the international consciousness as the typical Middle Eastern city—compact, congested, cellular, and fortified. Its walls, along with their watchtowers, until the 20th century differentiated quite sharply between city and country. Outside the walls were olive groves,

Figure 7.8 In the old part of the Middle Eastern city was the citadel, or old fort, as seen in this remnant in the United Arab Emirates. (Photo by Donald Zeigler)

grazing lands, cemeteries, quarries, and informal markets, not to mention potential enemies (fig. 7.9). At most, the medinas of modern Middle Eastern cities contain 3% of the urban population; residents of modern neighborhoods rarely patronize the old city cores.

Beginning with the colonial era (British, French, or Russian/Soviet), a new city typically developed outside the city walls. In the Maghreb, it was called *la nouvelle ville* ("the new city"). It was a city between two worlds, traditional and modern. The traditional elements of urban form, from mosques to bakeries to public baths, were incorporated into the new city, but they were supplemented by modern amenities and architectural styles, including larger stores and hotels, wider boulevards and traffic circles, Western-style churches, new government buildings, and corporate offices, all plastered with the language of the colonizers.

Gradually, the new city came to be enveloped by the modern, postcolonial city. Courtyard homes all but disappeared from the landscape, their place taken by apartment blocks, with high-income flats and single-family units increasingly common. The postcolonial city became the zone of international hotels, corporate headquarters, and modern universities. It also became the zone of squat-

Figure 7.9 In the classical *medina*, undesirable activities, such as leather tanning, were relegated to the margins of the city, as seen here in Fès, Morocco. (Photo by Donald Zeigler)

ter settlements (which can invade even the inner zones if there is any unoccupied space), where recent in-migrants from the villages find lodging while they work their way up the urban social pyramid. In some countries, such as Morocco, these squatter settlements remain poor, underserved by the urban infrastructure, and socially marginalized. In other countries, such as Turkey, squatter settlements are quickly legitimized by the government, beginning the process of incumbent upgrading.

Beyond the modern city is the urban expansion zone. Here, small villages find themselves undergoing urbanization *in situ.* Here, also, may be new industrial estates, modest new housing tracts, or in the case of Egypt and Saudi Arabia, new cities built from scratch. For the richest countries, those able to afford automobiles and the gasoline to feed them, it can also be a zone of raging urban sprawl. Most often, the international airport is located here as well.

The Middle Eastern city today, therefore, can be seen as an interlocking set of zones patterned in time: citadel, old city, new city, modern city, and urban expansion zone. As one moves from the innermost zone to the outermost, changes in urban form and function are evident. What do transects through these zones reveal?

- *A transect along the social axis:* The old city is becoming increasingly marginalized by society, particularly as the well-to-do move out. The modern city is attracting the lion's share of new neighborhood investment and the best of social services. Even tourists typically stay in the modern city and depend on air-conditioned buses to drop them off at a city gate for brief sojourns into the past.
- *A transect along the housing axis:* The old city (except in Turkey) is a zone of traditional two-story courtyard houses. The modern city is a zone of mid-rise and high-rise apartments. In fact, the multistory apartment block is now the most typical component of the Middle Eastern city's residential landscape (and a reminder of how architecture has pulled away from its indigenous roots).
- *A transect along the commercial axis:* The old city still displays fully functional souks, traditional industries, and small-scale, family-owned artisanal enterprises. The modern city displays its logo-laden landscape of chain stores, international (and national) franchises, and ever more snippets of English (fig. 7.10).
- *A transect along the transportation axis:* The old city reveals narrow streets clogged with pedestrians, donkey carts, and taxis. The new city reveals the proliferation of privately owned automobiles and the amenities, such as gas stations and parking spaces, they require.

These transects of Middle Eastern cities virtually recount the history of cities everywhere. Middle Eastern cities are the places where the 21st century B.C. meets the 21st century A.D.

It is not the periphery that defines the personality of a city, however. It is the center, the old city, the city of history. The preindustrial core also offers a glimpse of the prototypical Islamic city, for Middle Eastern cities seem to be held together by their mosques and minarets. Therefore, in the Islamic city, no one could live or work beyond earshot of a minaret. Without amplification as an aid to the human voice, this meant the network of mosques had to be very dense, indeed. In the traditional Middle Eastern city, the skyline is punctuated by minarets, occasionally joined by church spires in the Christian quarters. The so-called Friday mosques

Figure 7.10 The landscape of Amman, Jordan, shows the signs of global commercialization in the form of this bilingual advertisement for Subway. (Photo by Donald Zeigler)

stand out as the city's architectural masterpieces. The religious landscape of the Middle Eastern city is typically supplemented by Koranic schools, traditional universities, shrines, and mausoleums.

Muhammed, however, was a merchant trader as well as the Prophet, so it is little wonder that *souks* (markets) are another typical part of the traditional Middle Eastern city (fig. 7.11). Often, souks envelop the neighborhood mosques, which the earnings of the souk help to support. The central souks usually evolved around the city's "grand mosque." These souks are specialized affairs: shoes are sold in one area, produce in another, while fast-food (traditional style) is available throughout. Merchants dealing in the same product compete with each other, and the concept of fixed prices does not exist. Shoppers know the techniques of hard bargaining and expect low prices. In the past, the souks were supplied by two institutions: (1) the city's artisans, who made pottery, jewelry, carpets, and everything else, and (2) the city's *khans* (or caravanserais), which served as wholesale centers for goods coming in from distant lands (originally via camel caravans). The khans were essentially inns for merchant traders and their pack animals. In today's traditional city, however, mass-produced goods are as common as locally produced products and khans have been abandoned to other uses or turned into historical landmarks. In other realms of the traditional (but disappearing) city, bread tends to be purchased daily at the bakery itself, public baths *(hammams)* are the social centers of neighborhoods (especially for women), coffeehouses take the place of bars for men (no alcohol is permitted by the Koran), and private life takes place in very private places, like the home.

In fact, the Islamic city is set up to assure privacy, particularly for women and families. Houses are not recognizable as discrete entities; they appear as doors (often brightly decorated) in thick earthen walls (white-washed at most). Along a typically narrow street (often a dead end), doors are staggered and never give casual passers-by a view into the house; windows are well above eye level; and second-story windows are enclosed by a wooden

Figure 7.11 This souk in the old city section of modern Casablanca is a distinctive feature of the medina. (Photo by Jack Williams)

lattice so one can see out but not in. The lattice also wards off the sun and ushers in the breeze. For women, the privacy of the house is carried into the street by the veil or a simple head scarf. The traditional house is built around an open-air courtyard with covered, roomy bays on each side. Rarely does anyone but family make it deeper into the home. Courtyards tend to be small for the same reasons that streets tend to be narrow: to provide shade and to keep distances walkable. The middle of the courtyard is often anchored by a well for water or a fountain to humidify and cool the air. In houses of the Persian/Arabian Gulf and Iran, wind towers were added for the same reason—to channel air downward, creating a breeze. Along the edges of the courtyard, vines and arbors provided shade and produced fruit as a bonus. Mosques, khans, and palaces also included courtyards, making "cellular" one of the words most often used to describe the traditional Middle Eastern city. Supplementing courtyards are flat rooftops (because there is little rain), often enclosed by low walls over which carpets are flung for cleaning. Rising from the rooftops are laundry lines and cisterns, plus antennas, satellite dishes, and solar water heaters. In the summer, roofs may be cluttered with mattress pads at night, not to mention the ubiquitous plastic chairs.

The most coveted space in the preindustrial Islamic city was at the center, close to the seats of economic power and social interaction. Palaces and merchants' houses were central elements of the urban landscape; so were the central souks, the most prestigious of which, such as the book souk, crowded around the city's "great mosque." Noxious enterprises such as tanneries were relegated to the periphery. The residential population of cities, in the traditional city model, tended to be concentrated in "quarters": sections for Jews, Europeans, different Christian sects, different ethnic groups, and people of different village or regional origin. In the past, many of these quarters had gates of their own. Residential space was highly segregated, yet it also mim-

Figure 7.12 Water is precious in the arid environments of most Middle Eastern cities. From these public water urns in Cairo, everyone drinks from the same cups. Note the political ads in the background. (Photo by Donald Zeigler)

icked the security and social cohesiveness of the village by providing a scale of life to which people were accustomed and a set of community institutions that people of like mind could control. Within each quarter lived both rich and poor (fig. 7.12).

As they have survived, the narrow streets of the residential and commercial quarters tend to be penetrable only by foot traffic and donkey carts. Still, this does not stop the occasional taxi or service vehicle. The cramped feeling is heightened by second and third stories jutting out overhead, sometimes joining and creating tunnels. The largest streets lead into the city from gates in the walls, but a large public square dominating the center of town is a rarity (except in Iran). A grid pattern manifests itself (sort of) in towns with a Roman or Byzantine heritage, and it is common for elements of the pre-Islamic landscape, usually unrecognized for their historic value, to become parts of the working city. Roman pavement may lie deep underneath the contemporary street, while what was a wide Byzantine thoroughfare may now be subdivided into three or four narrow, parallel alleys, each serving as a separate souk. Periodically spaced along the most well-traversed routes are richly decorated drinking fountains (or their remnants), often given to the public by wealthy merchants. Otherwise, brightly dressed water vendors wander around high-traffic areas selling drinks to the thirsty.

The preceding generalizations apply to the old cities of the Middle East, those that grew up at oasis sites and prospered because of trade. An entirely new set of cities has grown up on the 20th-century's oil and natural gas fields. They are best exemplified by the cities of Kuwait, Saudi Arabia, Bahrain, Qatar, and the UAE (though oil revenues have transformed cities in Iran, Iraq, Libya, and Algeria, as well). Urban landscapes from Kuwait to Dubai have been built on revenues from the world's largest oil fields. While lacking the historical depth of a city like Aleppo, they do

Figure 7.13 Dubai, with almost a million people, is the most populous city in the UAE and has grown into a major international metropolis over the past three decades as a result of oil revenues. (Photo courtesy UAE)

offer a glimpse of what a modern Middle Eastern city can be. These are cities built on petrodollars, largely since the 1960s. Generally, they consist of two zones patterned in time. First, in the center of each is a tiny core anchored by a fort and perhaps the remnants of a traditional wharf area or well-to-do neighborhood. Although small, these cores are the source of local identity, particularly in layout and architectural styles. Second, around each core is a postindustrial city of high-rise office buildings, shopping malls, gardens, golf courses, apartment complexes, sprawling suburbs, and mosques. With oil wealth, the world's most creative architects are not out of range, and they have built cities in the region that blend modern structures with traditional themes. One of the surprising elements of these new urban landscapes is how green they are. Turning itself into a Garden City, in fact, has been one of Dubai's urban planning objectives (fig. 7.13). Figuratively, oil is turned into water, water into green space. Oil is also turned into new human geographies. Petroeconomies have, by governmental design as well as economic magnetism, virtually eliminated nomadism as a way of life. The rural population has become urbanized. In addition, the faces of the oil-engorged boomtowns have also changed. The economic magnetism of Kuwait, Damman, Abu Dhabi, and others draws unskilled workers from as far away as India, Pakistan, Sri Lanka, and the Philippines and skilled workers from Europe and the United States, as well as other parts of the Arab world.

Figure 7.14 The Jebel Ali Export Processing Zone illustrates the effort to develop a more diverse economic base in the United Arab Emirates. (Photo courtesy UAE)

What is missing from the landscapes of Arab cities on the gulf is the industrial era. Manufacturing is limited to local craft industries and manufacturing-in-transit at the free ports of the region, most notably those in the Emirate of Dubai (fig. 7.14). As banking and trading centers of the Middle East, however, some of these cities—Manama, Dubai, Abu Dhabi—have been thriving as increasingly important transactional nodes in the economic systems reshaping the region. The center of Arab World banking has shifted (in part) from Beirut to Manama, Bahrain, as a result of Lebanon's civil war. Doha, Qatar, is now the headquarters of Al-Jazeerah, the most popular satellite television network in the Middle East. Since the 1990s, the port cities of the Persian/Arabian Gulf have been the entrepôts supplying Central Asia with cars, electronics, and other high-end goods. While built on oil, the cities of the gulf are likely to continue thriving only if they diversify and lay the groundwork for postpetroleum economies.

With the growth of the Internet, all cities in the Middle East are developing into *cyber cities* (see chapter 13). The region's universities, manufacturing establishments, and traders are increasingly tied to constant flows of information that arrive by waves, wires, and photo-optic cables. Every computer terminal becomes its own harbor in the postindustrial landscape. The public is demanding frontage on these harbors. Hence, Internet cafes have appeared in cities all across the Middle East, with few exceptions. The Internet cafe, born in 1984, numbered fewer than 100 worldwide by the early 1990s. Today, there are thousands throughout the Middle East alone. Turkey, Israel, and the emirates of the Persian/Arabian Gulf lead the region, but Iran and Egypt are catching up. The UAE and its primary city, Dubai, have the highest Internet bandwidth of any country in the region (followed by Egypt and Morocco). Kuwait is also developing into a major cybercity, even as it lags in the development of a petrochemical industry.

REPRESENTATIVE CITIES

Cairo: Al-Qahirah, *"The Victorious"*

Al-Qahirah means "the victorious," and Cairo has emerged victorious, as the most populous city in the Arab World, in the Middle East, and on the continent of Africa. The Arabic-language cinema and popular Arab music have made Cairo—along with Beirut, Lebanon—one of the cultural epicenters of the Arab universe. *Al-Ahram*, a Cairo daily newspaper, has the largest patronage in the Arab world, and its English edition circulates globally. As the headquarters of the League of Arab States, Cairo is also the head city of pan-Arab politics, a role facilitated not only by the city's size, but also by its relative location. Cairo is positioned between the western Arab world of North Africa and the eastern Arab world of Asia.

As capital of Egypt, Cairo takes advantage of its position between the country's two rival regions: Upper Egypt (the valley) and Lower Egypt (the delta). The same sedimentation processes that have built the delta have built Cairo's midriver islands. Now free from the annual flood, these islands have become ever more valuable as sites for upscale neighborhoods, high-density apartment communities, posh sports complexes, and the landmark Cairo Tower. The urbanized area's shape also reflects the transition from an elongated valley to a fan-shaped delta—southern Cairo is confined by flanking escarpments to an area along the river, while northern Cairo opens up onto flatter alluvial terrain. The natural direction of spread for the city, in fact, has been northward, but that has brought urban development into conflict with agriculture on some of the most fertile land in the world. In an effort to stem the tide of urban expansion onto valuable farmland, the government began to redirect growth into the desert. The result was, first, a series of new suburbs built on Cairo's arid flanks and, more recently, entirely new satellite cities deep in the desert. The 10th of Ramadan City, for instance, located between Cairo and the Suez Canal, was built to have an industrial base of its own, with several thousand factories. Since the 1970s, it has offered jobs, housing, and a full range of urban services to an ever-expanding population, helping to relieve pressure on Cairo itself.

Greater Cairo is really a product of the 20th century, but as it has grown it has engulfed dozens of predecessor settlements and unique historical landscapes (fig. 7.15). These visual reminders of the past, numbering in the hundreds, make Cairo's landscape a vast open-air museum. Their distribution most closely resembles the multiple nuclei model, as large tracts of 20th-century blandness separate such historical nucleations as the following:

- The great pyramids (and sphinx) of Giza, on the west bank of the Nile, date back to the Old Kingdom, but have been encroached upon by an expanding city, deflating some of the excitement for first-time visitors.
- Heliopolis (on the way to the airport) was one of the ancient world's cult centers, but only a single obelisk—now in the middle of an urban park—remains.
- Babylon-in-Egypt, now known as Coptic Cairo (because of its Coptic Christian inhabitants), has a history associated with the world's most famous refugee family—Mary, Joseph, and Jesus.
- Al-Qahirah, a walled settlement that emerged as the core of Islamic Cairo ("Old Cairo"), was planted by conquering caliphs from Tunisia.
- The elevated Citadel was built by Saladin in the 12th century and later transformed by the Ottomans.

Figure 7.15 The vast metropolis of Cairo sprawls to the horizon from the base of the old Citadel. (Photo by Jack Williams)

When the Ottoman Empire seized Egypt after 1568 and made it into a tributary state of Istanbul, Cairo's role in world affairs shrank. It was only in the 19th century that Cairo began to reemerge as the premier metropolis of the Arab world, and not until 1927 did Cairo's population first reach one million. Today, the metropolitan area has 16 million. One element of its polynucleated landscape is unique in the world; this is "the city of the dead," which comprises the cemeteries colonized by more than 250,000 squatters taking advantage of some "empty" and highly accessible space complete with shelters (tombs) and shops.

Whether counted in people or cars, the growth of Cairo has been meteoric. Today, the city's traffic snarls are of world renown. Not until the late 1980s was Cairo's long-anticipated metro rail system opened to help move the city's millions. It has since expanded to include a subway line tunneling under the Nile to the west bank. The new metro stations are conveniently sited, brilliantly lighted, and immaculate. The metro lines link some outer suburbs (but not yet the satellite cities) with the center of the metropolis and include at least one car on every train that is reserved for women. Trips that at one time took three hours by car now can take as little as half an hour. As the city's circulation system continues to become more efficient, so will its economy.

Damascus and Aleppo: Fraternal Twins

The Arabs call them Sham and Halab. Outsiders know them as Damascus and Aleppo.

With two million people each, they are the most populous cities in Syria. Each makes for itself the same superlative claim, as "the oldest continuously inhabited city on earth." It was Damascus that Mohammed deliberately decided never to visit because he wanted to enter Paradise only once. But it was Aleppo where Abraham (the father of monotheism) stopped to milk his cow on the journey south from Haran. Such stories tell more about the pride each city takes in its heritage than the cold facts of history. Like fraternal twins, their looks and personalities differ, but you can tell they are from the same family.

The location of each city is impressive enough to give credence to their storied histories. To appreciate the site of Damascus, one need look no further than the mosaics of the Umayyad Mosque, built at a time when the city was the capital of the first Muslim empire, the only time in history when the entire Islamic world was politically united. In green and gold tiles, the mosaics portray a lush oasis where life was at its best. Thanks to the Barada River, Damascus is, in fact, one of the world's premier oases. The Barada comes tumbling down the slopes of Mount Hermon and, as the river's velocity diminishes, the channel splits into a handful of distributaries and water sinks into the ground, forming an oasis. Ancient Damascus, as if to avoid occupying precious agricultural land, lies to one side, where growth has pushed it up the side of the last fold in the mountains of Lebanon. These mountains and the Syrian desert protected Damascus.

Damascus's site is more dramatic from the air, where one can see the whole oasis clawing its way into the desert. Aleppo's site is more dramatic from the ground. Rising from the surrounding plain is the citadel, a fortified hilltop that identifies the original city. The north Syrian plain is a steppe (grassland) that stretches southward from the Anatolian plateau until it grades off into the Syrian Desert. In northern Syria, nature has set the stage for dry farming and the Syrians have made the land even more productive with irrigation. The region is a center of wheat, olive, almond, and pistachio production. Aleppo's potential as a breadbasket holds even more promise for the future, a promise noted by the United Nations when it located the International Center for Agricultural Research in Dry Areas there.

No matter how productive the oasis nor how impregnable the hill, neither Damascus nor Aleppo would have occupied a pivotal role in Middle Eastern history had they not been situated at the crossroads of trade. The oldest trade routes followed the parabolic shape of the Fertile Crescent: from the Tigris and Euphrates Valleys, along the spring line at the base of the Anatolian Plateau, and south along the mountainous littoral of the eastern Mediterranean, thence on to Egypt and beyond. Between the two arms of the Fertile Crescent is the Syrian Desert. The desert provided a series of east-west shortcuts. The northernmost shortcut focused on Aleppo, halfway between the Euphrates and the coast. The shortcut that passed through Palmyra (today's Tadmour) focused on Damascus. Both Aleppo and Damascus were also on the north-south axis of trade and thus became urban growth poles early in their history.

Damascus and Aleppo are modern cities today, but not as modern as they might be were it not for the protectionist, almost isolationist, stance of the Syrian government. Only in the early 1990s were strict rules of socialist planning and government ownership eased. The result was a minirenaissance in economic activity in both cities, but too many restrictions remained in place, so the renaissance soon reached a plateau. One positive result is that authentic Arab traditions, not the artificial niceties contrived for tourists, remain triumphant in both cities. The global economy has yet to overtake either one. Each city has a character of its own. One feels a greater reverence for the party line (the autocratic Baath Party) in Damascus. Aleppo, farther from the corridors of power, has a more freewheeling, freethinking air about it, yet more of its women are still fully veiled and the largest stores are no bigger than an American 7-Eleven. Damascus is the almost-monopolistic gateway to the entire country, while Aleppo, despite its comparable size, seems to yearn for some recognition of its own in the modern world.

Jerusalem: Clash of Religion and Politics

Jerusalem occupies neither an attractive site nor a strategic location. It is not central in a geographical sense and lies astride no major trade routes. It is a city that should have been bypassed by time. Instead, Jerusalem has become an epicenter of religious veneration and conflict. It is regarded as a holy city by three religions: Judaism, Christianity, and Islam. Muslims rank it behind only Mecca and Medina in importance. For them, it is the place from which Mohammed made his "night journey" to heaven to talk personally with God. To mark the place of his ascension, Muslims built the Dome of the Rock in 691 A.D. It is one of the oldest Islamic structures in the world. To Jews, Jerusalem is the city of David's kingship and Solomon's temple. Only the wall, which buttressed the platform on which the temple was built, remains, however. It is called the Western Wall and is the focal point of Jewish prayers. The area in front of the wall serves today as an outdoor synagogue. According to Jewish tradition, the Dome of the Rock is built on the site of Solomon's temple, on top of Mount Moriah. To Christians, Jerusalem is the city where Jesus of Nazareth proved himself to be the Messiah. Since Byzantine times, the Church of the Holy Sepulchre has sheltered the place of the crucifixion, entombment, and resurrection of Jesus; it is shared today by six Christian sects.

One always speaks of "going up" to Jerusalem. It began as a hill town at the very southern tip of the western Fertile Crescent, but its hilltop location did not give it a commanding position. The land enclosed by the "old city" walls is lower in elevation than the land to either north or east. The only feature of the physical environment that commended the site at all was a spring, now known as the Gihon. The Jebusite village at the site of the spring was destined for prominence, because its relative location made a difference 3,000 years ago. The village was conquered by the Hebrew king David, who needed a centrally located capital city between the northern and southern tribes of the Hebrew people. Jerusalem fit the bill. With the decision to move the Arc of the Covenant there, the city began to acquire the religious capital needed to sustain its spiritual centrality for three millennia. When the first temple was completed, Jerusalem became the place where the God of Moses and Abraham permanently resided. In fact, the very first Muslims prayed facing Jerusalem, not Mecca. Religion endowed Jerusalem with elements of centrality that geography could not (fig. 7.16).

The current walls of the old city of Jerusalem date to the Ottoman period. Within the walls, Jerusalem is divided into four quarters: Muslim, Jewish, Christian, and Armenian. The men-

Figure 7.16 In present-day Jerusalem, one can visit a large three-dimensional open-air model of old Jerusalem in the time of King Herod. (Photo by Jack Williams)

tal map conjured up by such a description, however, belies the reality of the city's cultural geography. In fact, almost the entire old city, save for the Jewish Quarter, has an Arab feel about it. Furthermore, the boundaries of the so-called quarters do not now (and probably never did) define the cultural divisions of the city. Instead, the old city's cultures overlap, merge, and separate. Movement into and out of the four quarters further challenges the idea that they are homogenous neighborhood groupings of like-minded souls (fig. 7.17). Muslims and Jews are the primary actors, Christians are diminishing in numbers, and Armenians are doing what they have done best for over 1,500 years, surviving as a culturally distinct Christian minority. Muslim Arabs are expanding into the Christian quarter, the traditional niche of Christian Arabs. Jews are solidly in control of the Jewish quarter, but they are also acquiring and conspicuously marking property in the other three quarters with signs, synagogues, and Israeli flags (fig. 7.18). Jews moving into the old city are more likely to be extremely religious, while those leaving are more likely to be secular. Armenians, especially seminarians, flow through the Armenian quarter from all over the world, their identity bolstered since 1991, when Armenia reappeared on the map of sovereign states.

The "old city" is only one of two Jerusalems. The other is the sprawling modern metropolis. While the walled city is no larger than a college campus, metropolitan Jerusalem has over 1.5 million people. Despite being governed as a single municipality, the metropolitan area is bisected by a cultural fault line. West Jerusalem is thoroughly Jewish and provides the site for Israel's parliament, the Knesset. East Jerusalem is primarily Arab (including both Muslim and Christian Arabs), a collection of Arab villages, one of which may someday become the capital

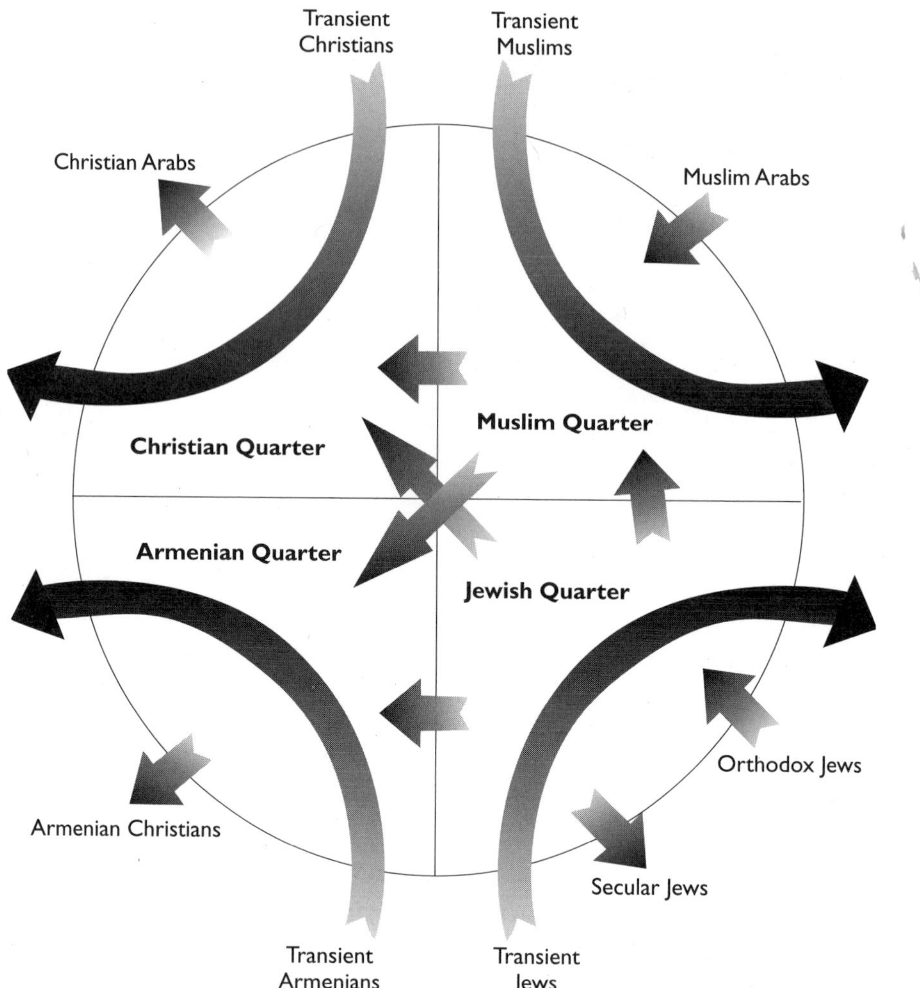

Figure 7.17 Jerusalem: Population Dynamics of the Old City. *Source*: Donald Zeigler

of a Palestinian state. "Occupied" East Jerusalem, however, is not as homogeneous as West Jerusalem. In the east, Jewish settlements occupy a dozen hilltop sites, all of them new (post-1967), wealthy, and strategically positioned to maintain control of greater Jerusalem for the Israelis. To the north, south, and east of Jerusalem, where border crossings are patrolled by Israeli soldiers, the Palestinian Autonomy begins. The city's relative location between Israel proper and the West Bank gives it a frontier feel, a feeling of being along a tension-ridden international boundary with a developed country on one side and a less developed country on the other.

The future of Jerusalem will be determined by the ability of the Israelis and the Palestinians to negotiate a peaceful resolution to their conflicting ambitions. In the meantime, repeated conflict between the Israelis and the Arabs has destroyed the infrastructure of many West Bank cities, such as Ramallah and Jenin.

Figure 7.18 The Dome of the Rock and the Western Wall are symbols of a religiously divided Jerusalem. (Photo by Donald Zeigler)

Istanbul: Bicontinental Hinge

It has existed for almost 27 centuries (since 657 B.C.), for 16 of them as an imperial capital. Its original name was Byzantium, but it was rechristened the New Rome in 330 A.D. Almost immediately, the people began calling it Constantinopolis, Emperor Constantine's city. Today, it appears on the map as Istanbul. It has been "The City" ("-bul" is from the Greek *polis,* meaning city) of the eastern Mediterranean realm for more than a millennium, having surpassed a million inhabitants by 1000 A.D. Something about this location just begs for an urban place.

Istanbul's location makes it a hinge between continents. From its situation on the European side of the Bosporus, it is positioned to control overland trade between Europe and Asia and the shipping lanes between the Mediterranean and Black Seas. The huge empires that Istanbul commanded—Roman, Byzantine, Ottoman—also gave it the ability to control overland access to Arabia, the Indian Ocean, and East Asia. Until the round-Africa route was fully opened in the 16th century, Istanbul was able to call the shots in trade between north and south, east and west. As imperial capital of the Ottoman realm since 1453, it reached its peak in the 16th century, when the Emperor Suleyman commanded so much wealth that he was known to the world as "The Magnificent." His city was at that time larger in population than London, Paris, Vienna, or Cairo. During that century, however, the power of Constantinople began to wane. No longer did Ottoman subjects hold a monopoly on the ancient silk routes across Asia or on the fertile crescent caravan trade from the eastern Mediterranean to the Persian/Arabian Gulf. As technology enabled mastery of the sea, caravels replaced camels as the most reliable and economical modes of transport. Well before the end of the 19th century, the Ottoman Empire was the "sick man of Europe" and Istanbul was a city in decline.

The core of Istanbul, the historical city, occupies a peninsular site with deep water on three sides. Crowning the peninsula, and visually dominant from the sea, are seven hills, just like in Rome, the city it replaced as capital of the Roman Empire. The peninsula is bordered on the south by the Sea of Marmara, on the east by the Bosporus, and on the north by the Golden Horn, the large, sheltered harbor that enabled the city to dominate the shipping trade. The Bosporus and its companion strait, the Dardanelles, enabled oceangoing vessels to penetrate central Eurasia. On the Black Sea's northern shore, the ancient Greeks implanted colonies engaged in trade. The fertile hinterlands of these colonies became a breadbasket, producing wheat for the Aegean core of the Hellenic world, wheat that went to market via the Bosporus. The first "world-class" city to dominate these straits existed in the Bronze Age. Its name was Troy and it was located at the southern end of the Dardanelles. Troy was the Istanbul of its day.

In the 20th century, the Bosporus provided one of the Soviet Union's few outlets to the world ocean and was consequently a point of strategic significance during the Cold War. By controlling Istanbul's strait, the North Atlantic Treaty Organization could deprive Moscow of dominating one of the world's most strategic locations. Even now, the Bosporus continues to be important to the Soviet successor states, especially the Russian Federation. The strait has also taken on a new strategic significance in the flow of crude oil from the landlocked Caspian Basin fields, much of which may be routed by pipelines to Black Sea ports, loaded into tankers, and transited through the Bosporus. Already, the Bosporus is one of the world's busiest straits. At Istanbul, it is at its narrowest, assuring full and busy roadsteads and shipping lanes, the ingredients of potential collisions, particularly given the swift currents that flow out of the Black Sea.

Oil is not the only commodity that is likely to stimulate the growth of Istanbul in the 21st century, for the city is newly repositioned to capitalize on its hinge function. During most of the 20th century, Istanbul was all but severed from its European hinterland by the Iron Curtain and the animosity of neighboring Greece. Now, however, Eastern European nations have opened their borders. The routes of commerce between Europe and Asia are once again funneling traffic across the Bosporus, and Greece has muted its objections to considering Turkey for European Union membership. Trade is flowing again. It is nowhere more powerfully symbolized than in the growing volume of truck traffic navigating the transcontinental Bosporus bridges, completed in 1974 and 1988 (fig. 7.19). Istanbul is taking on new significance in "the new Europe" and Turkey is increasingly calling itself a European nation. At the same time, it is emerging as a gateway to Central Asia, where the Turkish people originated and where most of the languages spoken are Turkic. As if to affirm its global centrality, Istanbul opened one of the world's newest airports in 1999.

Fès and Marrakesh: Imperial Rivals

In Morocco, it was Fès and Marrakesh that gave rise to the country's urban system and

Figure 7.19 The second bridge across the Bosporus, linking Asiatic and European Istanbul, was opened in 1988. (Photo by Jack Williams)

served as the solidification points of Moroccan culture. Neither city functions as the capital today, but both have in the past. Nor is either located in the Rabat-Casablanca megalopolis, or even along the coast. Instead, Fès faces east toward Morocco's Arab Islamic heritage, while Marrakesh faces south toward the desert oases of Africa.

The seeds of Fès, and with it the seeds of the Moroccan state, were planted shortly after "the Arab conquest," about 790 A.D. The Arabs arrived via the Taza Gap, the only natural corridor between the Maghreb and the rest of North Africa. An Arab village joined a Berber village on a tributary of the largest river in Morocco. This city, Fès al Bali, commanded passage through the Taza Gap to the east. It was also located near well-watered and forested mountains to the north and south and had a rich agricultural hinterland to the west. As trade developed, the souks of Fès became the best in the Maghreb.

Marrakesh was born in the 11th century, when the indigenous peoples of the Sahara established a trading post just north of the snow-capped High Atlas mountains. Their rulers were so successful in consolidating power and trade routes that the city soon became their capital. As their territory expanded, the city became synonymous with the country itself. As a result, Marrakesh and Fès both claim to be the historical core of the Moroccan state, Fès contributing its Arab and Andalusian culture (Arab culture transplanted from Spain) and Marrakesh contributing the culture of the Sahara.

A comparative analysis of the cultural landscapes of Fès and Marrakesh illustrates their roles in building the national urban system. As with cities everywhere, the personality of each of these cities is expressed most clearly in its center, within the walls of the old city, the *medina.* All Moroccan cities have their medinas, but the finest in the entire Maghreb, and arguably the best-preserved preindustrial city in the world, is Morocco's first imperial capital, Fès. The second-finest medina may be in Marrakesh, the imperial capital of Morocco's

Box 7.2 World Heritage Sites

The United Nations Educational, Scientific, and Cultural Organization maintains a prestigious list of "world heritage sites." See the World Heritage List at http://www.unesco.org/whc/heritage.htm. Here is what UNESCO has to say about Fès (Fez) and Marrakesh.

MEDINA OF FEZ:

Founded in the 9th century, Fez reached its height in the 14th century under the Marinides and again in the 17th century. In 1912, when France established Rabat as the new capital, its political importance declined, but its religious and cultural role continues today, centered as it is around the two famous mosques of Al-Qarawiyin and Al-Andalus in the heart of the medina.

MEDINA OF MARRAKESH:

Marrakesh, founded in 1071–72, was the capital of the Almoravids and later the Almohades. The lively medina contains an impressive number of architectural masterpieces, including the walls and the monumental gates, the Kutubiya Mosque with its 77-metre-high minaret, the Saadian tombs and characteristic old houses.

Source: "The World Heritage List," http://www.unesco.org/whc/heritage.htm.

south. So authentic are the landscapes of intramural Fès and Marrakesh that they were among the first to be placed on the United Nations' World Heritage List (box 7.2). Fès and Marrakesh have shaped the culture that is uniquely Moroccan, and their medinas present the symbols of Moroccan nationhood and the images for which Morocco is known around the world. One image common to both Fès and Marrakesh is the souks. They are the rabbit warrens of shops and craft merchants competing to provide not only the necessities but also the finer goods and higher-level services that marked the differences between urban and rural life.

Both Fès and Marrakesh served as focal points of commerce, political power, religious life, and public celebrations. But why have these ancient walled cores been able to stall the passage of time so well? Their survival is related to the survival of Morocco itself. More than most other places in the Middle East, Morocco held conquest at bay, turning back both the expanding European kingdoms to the north and the Ottoman Empire to the east. Few Westerners even laid eyes on the interior of Morocco until the French established a protectorate there in 1912. For an "infidel," penetrating Morocco was the equivalent of penetrating Tibet—one did it only under cover. Many of Morocco's medinas, therefore, survived intact. Fortunately, when the colonizing French did arrive, they chose not to modernize them, but to build new cities outside the old walls, thus saving medieval urban landscapes from disfiguring modernization.

The best-known symbols of Fès are the Kiraouan and Andalusian mosques. The first is among the most revered in the entire Muslim world. In this distinction, it stands not alone, but with its university, among the oldest in the world, and the tomb of the founder of Fès. The spiritual and intellectual life of Fès set the tone for the evolution of Moroccan culture. Like Fès, the most recognizable site in the Marrakesh medina is a mosque, the Koutoubia mosque, built by a Berber dynasty that recentralized power in the south. The Koutoubia's minaret, its most conspicuous feature, arose as a statement of political power, as a mirror image of the mosque built in Córdoba (Spain), where Andalusian culture thrived. In Marrakesh, commercial power blended with political power, whereas in Fès commercial and political power blended with the power of Islam. It was probably that religious anchor that kept the capital city function returning to Fès.

The physical settings of Fès and Marrakesh have influenced each city's urban landscape. The Fès medina, wedged into a narrow, V-shaped valley, epitomizes preindustrial urban crowding. Every square inch of space is accounted for. As a result of a more northerly location and a higher altitude, Fès's climate is cooler and rainier. The Marrakesh medina, by contrast, seems to epitomize the desert, which begins south of the High Atlas. The spaciousness of the desert is reflected in the public square in the center of the old city. Such an expanse of open space in a Middle Eastern city is a rarity.

Tashkent: Anchor of Central Asia

With 2.5 million people, Tashkent is Central Asia's largest city. Since independence from the Soviet Union in 1991, it has come to see itself as the region's anchor and gateway, and as a transcontinental bridge linking east and west. It is also the capital city of Uzbekistan, the most central state of Central Asia. Uzbekistan borders every other country in the region (but not Russia), giving it a pivotal geopolitical role to play in the 21st century's "great game" for influence over people, trade corridors, and resources (natural gas, gold, uranium, cotton). Many of the decisions that will mold Eurasia's new political geography will be made in Tashkent's corridors of power.

Almost every city of Central Asia originated as a trading post on the "silk roads." Tashkent is no exception. It was a port on the edge of the desert, a "stone town" on the northern route from Kashgar (now in China) to the Caspian Sea and thence on to Europe. Its founding goes back at least 2,000 years to the place where the Syr Darya's tributaries back up to the water-laden Tien Shan mountains. With such enviable access to the region's most precious resource, water, Tashkent offered opportunities for modern growth. The city is also situated near the entrance of the Fergana Valley, one of the choice spots for fruit and vegetable production in the region, and in a commanding position relative to the cotton fields snaking across the irrigated desert to the Aral Sea. These economic attractions, combined with the region's gold resources, resulted in the Russian conquest. Tashkent was in the first khanate to be absorbed by Russia, in 1865, during a time when Europe had been cut off from American supplies of cotton by the Civil War.

During the Soviet period, Tashkent was selected to be the capital of the Uzbek Soviet Socialist Republic, replacing Samarkand in 1930. Before World War II, its population was only half a million, but during the war the Soviets mounted a massive industrial effort and protectively located many strategic industrial operations beyond the Urals, thus swelling the city's population. In fact, Tashkent's most renowned product is still airplanes; Seattle, Washington, home of Boeing Aircraft, is one of Tashkent's "sister cities." When the Soviet Union collapsed, the city was the country's fourth largest. It was also the most Soviet city in Central Asia, thanks to two factors—Communism's emphasis on state planning and the forces of nature. Tashkent was almost completely destroyed by an earthquake in 1966. The Soviets seized upon the opportunity to refashion the landscape in a socialist mode: as "a new Soviet city" for "a new Soviet man."

Tashkent's ancient core survives only in the four historic M's: market, mosque, madrassah, and mausoleum. Since independence, a fifth M has been added, a new museum—dedicated to the life of Tamerlane. Although Tashkent was not Tamerlane's capital, the city has seized upon Amir Tamur as the quintessential symbol of its independence and quest for respect. Like many states that cast off Communist regimes, Uzbekistan has mined the archives for inspiration drawn from its pre-Soviet and pre-Russian past. The opening of the Tamerlane Museum symbolizes transition. Tashkent was a regional city beholden to Moscow. Today it is the capital city of an independent state seeking to play the same role in the modern world that Tamerlane's empire did when it stretched from the borders of Europe to the borders of China.

It is iconography rooted in Turkic culture that is now remaking the landscape of Tashkent (even though Tamerlane was probably Mongol and his capital was Samarkand). Lenin and Marx are gone; heroes on horseback and other images of the steppes have taken their place. Government buildings fly flags that are Turkic blue, not Soviet red. New structures are conglomerates of steppe-colored brick, not piles of cinder blocks. One out of every five cars is a Daewoo, from Korea. Traditional domes and arches (bedecked with blue tiles) are replacing socialist perpendiculars. Mosques are being built again, after decades of antireligious propaganda. Uzbek, a Turkic tongue, replaced Russian as the official state language (in 1989) and it is being written in the Roman alphabet, not Cyrillic, a fact of life easily read in the city's linguistic landscape.

Meanwhile, Tashkent still has a predominantly Soviet feel and appearance. About a third of the population is Slavic in origin and speaks Russian. Nine-story apartment blocks dominate residential neighborhoods. European-style parks and open space, a positive contribution of socialist planning, were incorporated into the landscape after the earthquake. Opera, ballet, and the puppet theater still dominate the performing arts. The only subway system in Central Asia offers Tashkent the same efficient service and rich artistry as Moscow's metro. Flights to Moscow still far outnumber flights to any other destination, 30 each week (as compared to six for Istanbul). The Lada (Soviet-era automobile) is still a common sight on city streets.

Tashkent's urban landscape represents layers of history. Its position on the silk road (now navigated by trucks, not camels) is commemorated by the traditional marketplace; the Islamic conquest is commemorated by the nearby mosque, madrassah, and mausoleum; the peak of its stature as a global power by the Tamerlane Museum; the Soviet period by the socialist planning model that shaped its spatial structure and architecture; the period of independence by a return to Turkic traditions. Finally, a layer of transnational landscape elements has appeared: Western products in the stores, logos of multinational corporations downtown, American fast-food chains, copious commercial advertising, and the international tourist trade, which has come to exploit the lure of Asia's "old silk road."

KEY PROBLEMS

Middle Eastern cities do many things well. First, they reflect the hospitality of their inhabitants, people who easily talk to visitors, are eager to communicate despite linguistic barriers, and have time to spend in casual conversation on the street (fig. 7.20). Arabs, Turks, and Iranians are among the friendliest people in the world and their cities make you feel at home. Second, Middle Eastern cities, with few exceptions, are safe day and night. There are "eyes upon the street" all the time, whether you can see them or not, and family networks, undergirded by strict codes of conduct, hold family members accountable. Plus, alcohol consumption among Muslims is prohibited, so drunkenness is uncommon. Third, the generations mix freely. Neither the old nor young are warehoused; parents are seen with children; teenagers use the same streets as the elderly; and young apprentices are common in the city's businesses. Households are often multigenerational. Fourth, homelessness, although it does exist, is less common than in Western cities. It is taken for granted that some people will not be able to live self-sufficient lives, so families compensate for personal inadequacies and many social needs are taken care of by the Islamic emphasis on required almsgiving and charity. Fifth, almost every city takes pride in its food, whether served in sit-down restaurants or on the street. Middle Eastern cuisine helps to define both national cultures and urban life. Furthermore, it is healthy food, not overprocessed, and rarely fried. Sixth, cities are well served by a variety of transportation. Cars are not required; in the old cities they may be a hindrance (box 7.3). City buses, taxis, service taxis (often 12-passenger vans), and fixed-rail lines (in a few cities) always make it possible to get around at very low cost. Besides, cities are compact, so walking is always a possibility.

Figure 7.20 The coffee urn is a symbol of hospitality throughout the Arab world, as seen here in Jordan's capital, Amman. (Photo by Donald Zeigler)

Urban life in the Middle East is not utopian, however. Cities have their problems, some seemingly intractable, just as in other world regions. These troubles include overly rapid population growth, unemployment and underemployment, transportation chaos (much of it caused by the automobile), and shantytowns or squatter settlements. In the case of the latter, unique names have been developed to describe them: *gecekondu* ("built overnight") in Turkey and *bidonvilles* (after the tin containers for kerosene, *bidon a pet-*

Box 7.3 Car Meters

It seems we are going European. Around 1300 car meters are going to be installed around Amman. This is a first ever in Jordan and we should say Hurrah to the Amman Municipality. Whoever came up with such a brilliant idea should be given a medal. Seriously though, the reasoning behind the parking meters is to organize the state of parking and reduce random parking in Jordan, and the idea that any vehicle owner can park anywhere he pleases. The Amman Municipality will be making an extra JD 219,000 for such a move.

Source: Star (Amman, Jordan), March 1, 2001, 3.

role, used to build them) in the Maghreb and other former French colonies.

Other problems acutely felt in the Greater Middle East are those of freshwater, cultural homogenization, and preservation of the region's heritage.

Freshwater

There is a shortage of water in the Middle East. As cities expand, they can accommodate growth only by developing water resources for new homes, businesses, and industries. Surface and groundwater resources are being utilized to the maximum throughout most of the region. Even the "fossil waters" of the Sahara are being used by the Libyans to supply their urban populations in the north, while the Arab states of the Persian/Arabian Gulf have all gone heavily into desalination. Nevertheless, most cities do not use their water resources efficiently. What water they do have could go farther if leaky pipes were repaired, if water-conserving technologies were used, and if irrigation systems could make do with less. Plus, the water problem is not simply a problem of quantity; it is also a problem of quality. Virtually every city must concentrate on upgrading its water treatment operations so that tap water is safe to drink.

Cultural Homogenization

The trend throughout the region is toward more culturally homogenous populations, a concomitant of European-style nation building. Istanbul is more ethnically Turkish and more thoroughly Muslim than ever before in history; Alexandria and Cairo are more Arab. Slavs have left Tashkent by the thousands since independence from the Soviet Union. Many Israelis see Jerusalem as becoming ever more thoroughly Jewish. Religious minorities have been squeezed out of virtually all cities in Iraq and Iran. Europeans, seen as "the colonizers," have abandoned the cities of the Maghreb. The Jewish population of every Middle Eastern city outside of Israel has decreased substantially or disappeared since 1948. Some see this tendency toward "ethnic purity" as a problem.

Heritage

In all cities of the Middle East, modernization threatens heritage resources. New roads cut through walled cites, suburban expansion buries Roman villages, and property owners upgrade without considering historic preservation. In the architectural realm, urban expansion zones are looking more and more alike throughout the world. Meanwhile, the integrity of old urban landscapes is scarred by deterioration or unregulated incumbent upgrading. The landscape of central Beirut, for instance, has been rebuilt after Lebanon's civil war in an "international style," quite in contrast to Sana'a, the capital of Yemen, which has used UN aid to maintain the architectural unity of its historic core, despite rapid population growth.

These problems, along with others too numerous to mention, are not unique to Middle Eastern cities. They are worldwide. As a majority of the world's population has become urban, the problems of cities are increasingly the problems of all humanity. Having invented the city in the 4th millennium B.C., the people of the Middle East are now challenged to see if they can perfect it in the 21st century A.D.

SUGGESTED READINGS

Abu Lughod, Janet L. *Cairo: 1001 Years of the City Victorious.* Princeton, N.J., Princeton University Press, 1971. A chronicle of Cairo from 969 to 1970 and a glimpse of how to make sense of any urban landscape.

Benvenisti, Meron. *City of Stone: The Hidden History of Jerusalem.* Berkeley: University of California Press, 1996. Offers a balanced view of Jerusalem's urban landscapes, boundaries, and demographics.

Blake, G. H., and R. I. Lawless, eds. *The Changing Middle Eastern City.* London: Croom Helm, 1980. Articles on cities from Morocco to Turkey and Iran, including their social, economic, ethnic, and environmental patterns and problems.

Bonine, Michael, ed. *Population, Poverty, and Politics in Middle East Cities.* Gainesville: University Press of Florida, 1997. Profiles of various cities and articles on political, historical, and gender-related themes.

Hitti, Philip K. *Capital Cities of Arab Islam.* Minneapolis: University of Minnesota Press, 1973. Thoughtful profiles of historical capitals: Mecca, Medina, Damascus, Baghdad, Cairo, and Cordova.

Hourani, A. H., and S. M. Stern. *The Islamic City.* Philadelphia: University of Pennsylvania Press, 1970. Delves into the question of whether there is an "Islamic" city, with specific reference to Damascus, Samarra, and Baghdad.

Kheirabadi, Masoud. *Iranian Cities: Form and Development.* Syracuse, N.Y.: Syracuse University Press, 2001. A thorough treatment of the spatial structure and physical form of Iranian cities.

Lapidus, Ira M. *Middle Eastern Cities.* Berkeley: University of California Press, 1969. Papers on ancient, Islamic, and contemporary Middle Eastern urbanism as tied to the cultural and physical environment.

Serageldim, Ismail, and Samir El-Sadek, eds. *The Arab City: Its Character and Islamic Cultural Heritage.* Riyadh, Saudi Arabia: Arab Urban Development Institute, 1982. Photographs, drawings, and readable text on city form and urban planning.

Wheatley, Paul. *The Places Where Men Pray Together.* Chicago: University of Chicago Press, 2001. Analyses of cities and urban systems in Islamic lands between the 7th and 10th centuries.

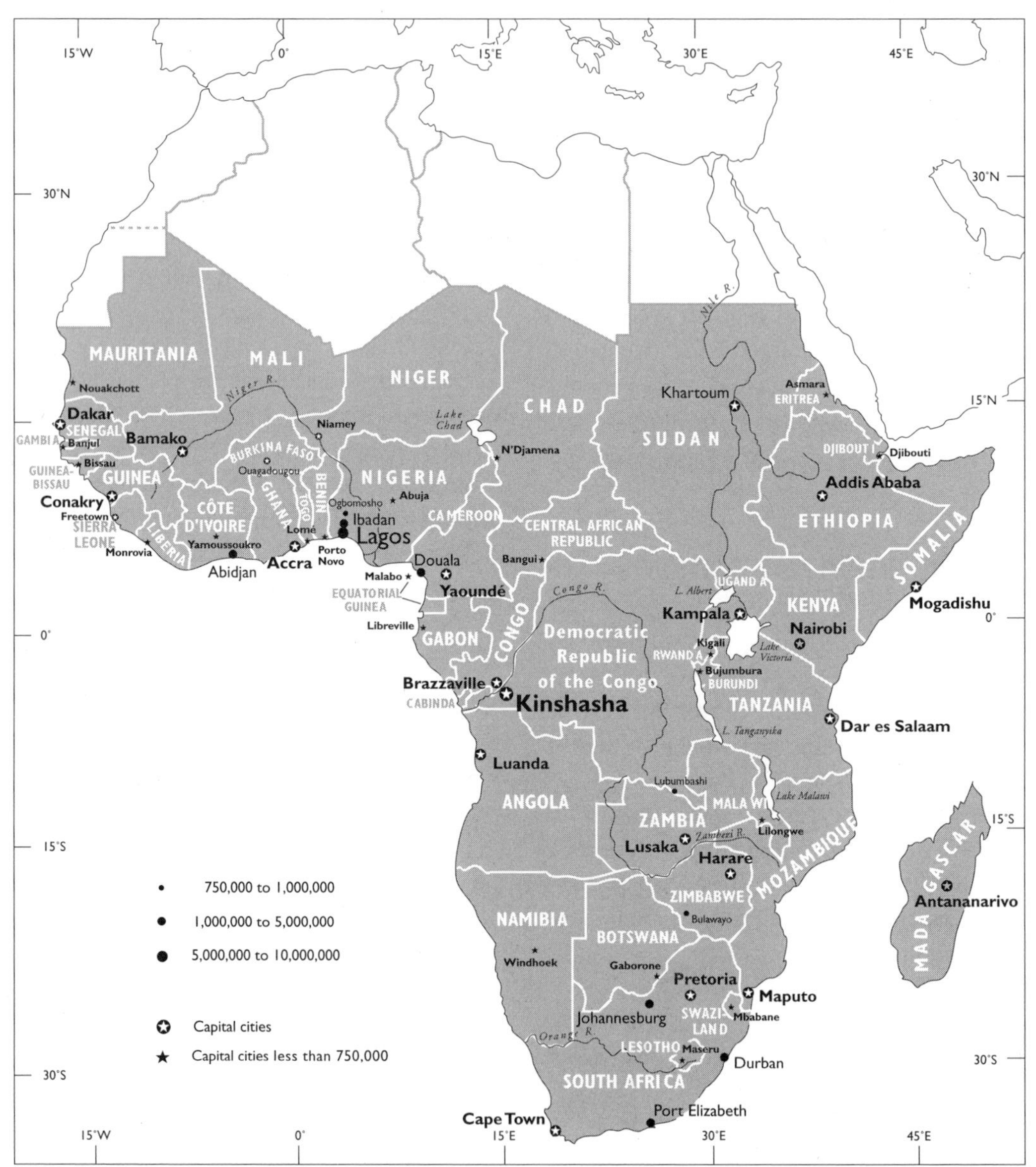

Figure 8.1 Major Cities of Sub-Saharan Africa. *Source*: Data from United Nations, *World Urbanization Prospects, 2001 Revision* (New York: United Nations Population Division, 2002), www.unpopulation.org.

8

Cities of Sub-Saharan Africa

ASSEFA MEHRETU AND CHRIS MUTAMBIRWA

KEY URBAN FACTS

Total Population	635 million
Percent Urban Population	35%
Total Urban Population	231 million
Most Urbanized Country	Gabon (82%)
Least Urbanized Country	Rwanda (6%)
Annual Urban Growth Rate	4.2%
Number of Megacities	1
Number of Cities of More Than 1 Million	25
Three Largest Cities	Lagos, Kinshasa, Abidjan
World Cities	None

KEY CHAPTER THEMES

1. Sub-Saharan Africa remains one of the least urbanized regions of the world.
2. Cities are growing at extremely high rates, primarily because of rural-to-urban migration.
3. Only one megacity exists and there are relatively few large cities for a region of this size.
4. A rich urban tradition preceded the arrival of colonialism in some parts of Sub-Saharan Africa.
5. Colonialism had a profound impact on urban development, especially in the creation of what were to become coastal primate cities.
6. The region today is overwhelmingly focused around primate cities, with the exception of South Africa.
7. Most of the region's cities reflect varied forms of internal land use (structure) that bear little resemblance to Western models.
8. Many of the cities have very limited hinterlands and hence small markets, which makes them economically unviable.
9. Most countries consist of a dominating primate city core and an impoverished and neglected periphery (hinterland).

10. Of all the world's culture realms, this region is perhaps the least engaged with the world global economy.

From an urban and regional development perspective, to many outsiders Sub-Saharan Africa (SSA) seems to be a realm, almost without exception, of dysfunctional cities and dysfunctional countries (fig. 8.1). As with all stereotypes, the reality is much more complex. Nonetheless, dysfunctionality does exist and is reflected in the economic, cultural, political, and environmental realities of the continent. First, the rate of SSA's level of urbanization changed from about 15% of the population in the 1960s to more than 35% by the turn of the millennium. This is phenomenal growth compared with the inability of the region's cities to absorb so many migrants so fast. Economic growth in SSA hardly kept pace with population growth, much less with urbanization. Per capita income growth was a fraction of the growth in urbanization. Second, the social and physical characteristics normally associated with urbanism and the growth of cities failed to materialize in SSA, because of the weakness of the macroeconomic system in responding to contemporary challenges of urban-based modernization. This has made most African cities architectural kaleidoscopes of structures with disparities in housing quality, urban amenities, and social capital. Shanty and slum dwellings without rudimentary urban services such as potable water and sewerage are juxtaposed with expensive homes and gleaming modern buildings with creature comforts that match those in Europe and the United States. Qualities of public education and health services have become so strained by the weight of the urban poor that there has emerged an exclusive dual system of service provisioning, with a high-quality and high-cost private sector for those who can afford it and a rapidly deteriorating, low-quality public system that is on the verge of breakdown. Third, the process of urbanization in SSA has caught many African city-dwellers between order and chaos as they try to survive within a political and cultural framework that is foreign and hostile to their rural moorings. Whatever political clout and social standing rural-urban migrants may have enjoyed in their rural lives become irrelevant in the city, where compensating democratic rights are rarely realized. Most SSA governments demand acquiescence to an order whose benefits rarely trickle down to the common folk. This has created a unique dimension in SSA primate cities that function as indispensable political centers and whose control is essential to govern the state.

Being a large and very diverse region ecologically, culturally, and historically, SSA exhibits a variety of patterns of urbanization. Of the 48 countries in SSA, only seven—Djibouti, Equatorial Guinea, Gabon, Namibia, Réunion, South Africa, and Zambia—show higher than 50% levels of urbanization. These countries are either minuscule territories with large port settlements, as in Djibouti, or are settler economies with a large mining sector, as in Namibia, Dem. Rep. Congo, Zambia, and South Africa. Fifteen countries have urbanization levels equal to or higher than 40%. They are midsize to smaller countries such as Cameroon, Congo, and Liberia. Five countries—Burkina Faso, Burundi, Lesotho, Rwanda, and Uganda—have less than 10% urbanization levels. Large countries such as Nigeria, Sudan, Tanzania, and Ethiopia have levels of less than 25%. There are few clusters of major urban agglomerations in SSA. The most clustered agglomeration is found in West Africa, between Abidjan and Lagos. Smaller clusters are found in South Africa, around Johannesburg, and in Zambia, along the rail line between Lusaka and Ndola. Other principal towns in Africa are scattered and isolated from one another. This has been one of the obstacles to regional development, as many national markets anchored in the capital cities are balkanized or isolated in their own watertight compartments, with little to no cross-border traffic of people or commodities between them.

Contemporary SSA urban development produces several discernible patterns. First, one of the more significant effects of the colonial period was the development of coastal settlements to the detriment of historical centers of trade and civilization in the continent's interior. Second, because of the selective development of urban centers following colonialism, the distribution of major cities became uneven over the region. This is evident from the size and importance of port capitals as compared to inland towns. Third, African cities are characterized by varied forms of internal morphology as a function of their site, ethnic composition, function, and historical background. Conventional Western typologies would be inappropriate to describe them. More often, the towns are a reflection of colonial zoning influences that continue to be followed after independence or are a result of postindependence rezoning and city planning efforts that once again failed to take into account the indigenous requirements. Fourth, SSA primate cities and major urban agglomerations constitute socioeconomic cores or central regions that depend for their existence on unequal relationships between them and the hinterlands.

EVOLUTION OF CITIES

It is estimated that only 20% of Africa's major cities are attributable to colonialism. A great many of the present urban centers claim their origins from indigenous civilizations. A good number also emerged, particularly in the coastal regions of Africa, during the precolonial period of African exploration and trade between Asiatic states and Europe. A few have also been established since the 1960s. It is not easy to separate those cities that were indigenously initiated from those that were founded due to precolonial and colonial European intervention, partly because at various times the colonial powers took over some indigenous centers and altered them to the point where the original characteristics disappeared. Thus, for example, Kinshasa of the Democratic Republic of the Congo is said to have originated as one of the largest centers of the Kongo kingdom after being founded before 1530, while it is also described as a colonial city established in 1881 as Leopoldville.

Early Traditional Urban Centers

A great number of SSA's historic cities are either gone or no longer very important, partly because of the advent of colonialism and partly because of the continuous internal shifts of centers of influence. Nonetheless, the imprint of great civilizations around Meroë, Axum, and Adulis in East Africa, which flourished for centuries before Christ, is a vivid reminder of ancient glory (fig. 8.2). Lying westward along the Savanna belt were kingdoms whose urban centers, such as Timbuktu, were the termini of a network of caravan routes that crisscrossed the Sahara, supplying goods to Tripoli and oases in the Maghreb. West African commodities reached Western Europe via ports on the Mediterranean.

Figure 8.2 Historical Centers of Urbanization in Africa. *Source*: Assefa Mehretu

Some of the Sub-Saharan centers had achieved such repute in the medieval world that they became nodes of empires that claimed prominence and considerable influence from the 13th to the 17th century. Although major cities did not materialize in this region before the colonial period, the prosperity of the area supported centralized kingdoms and extensive interregional trade.

In Southern Africa lay two important centers. The ruins of the Great Zimbabwe, the capital of the Rozvi Mutapa Empire, which flourished between the 4th and 19th centuries, demonstrated one of the most remarkable organizational and architectural features of African civilizations. Although Zimbabwe itself may not have reached great urban status in number of urban inhabitants, it served as the

Figure 8.3 An upscale home in Zanzibar is illustrative of socioeconomic inequality in Sub-Saharan Africa. (Photo by Assefa Mehretu)

most influential locus of political control for numerous towns that developed around the gold-rich—and ivory-rich—hinterlands between the Zambesi and Limpopo rivers. West of Great Zimbabwe, Bulawayo sprang up as the capital of an Ndebele empire and continued to dominate the area until the colonial scramble. The Zulu kingdoms to the south also developed influential centers around which emerged some of the most powerful political organizations and military might on the continent.

Many of the ancient African cities have lost their influence to newer indigenous towns or colonial capitals, but it must be remembered that many of those ancient cities have now transformed themselves into some of the major metropolises in the continent. Omdurman (Sudan), Addis Ababa (Ethiopia), Kumasi (Ghana), Kano and Ibadan (Nigeria), Kinshasa (D. R. Congo), and Bulawayo (Zimbabwe) are only a few of the existing urban centers that predate foreign intervention.

Medieval Trade Centers of East Africa

Of particular significance to the development of urbanization in East Africa are the ancient coastal trade centers on the Red Sea and Indian Ocean, around which flourished an extensive trade with the Arab and Persian peoples of Asia. Some of these centers acted as coastal city-states; beginning in the 9th century, they became important beachheads for Arab maritime traffic, which included the export of gold, ivory, and slaves from Africa in exchange for textiles and jewelry. These East African coastal centers also derived their growth, character, and political organization from the increasing number of Asiatic settlers who used the trade contacts to make permanent homes in Africa. Major urban centers grew out of this, such as Mogadishu, Malindi, Mombasa, and Zanzibar (fig. 8.3). The urban structures of these cities, some of which are still important, combined African, Arabic, and Persian building styles. A number of centers in the interior were also affected, particularly with the expansion of Islam south from the Maghreb and west from the Red Sea and the Gulf of Aden.

Precolonial Urban Development

Europe's impact on SSA began with intermittent coastal contact in the era of exploration,

Figure 8.4 In Cape Town, South Africa's crown jewel city, the harbor area has been redeveloped into this handsome tourist mecca. (Photo by Jack Williams)

starting with the Portuguese in the first half of the 15th century. For about two and a half centuries, most contact between European traders and Africans occurred in coastal installations whose size and infrastructure grew as European traders gradually developed the trade network for tropical commodities, such as rubber, ivory, gold, hardwoods, and hides and skins. The slave trade of course contributed to the development of coastal trade centers where warehouses and permanent installations were needed to accommodate commodities and people drawn from the interior. The Portuguese made their first contact in West Africa by establishing the town of St. Louis in 1445 at the mouth of the Senegal River. Dominating the 16th-century scene in trade and urban development, the Portuguese were responsible for founding a number of centers, among which were Bissau in Guinea; Luanda, Benguela, and São Salvador do Congo in Angola; and Lourenço Marques (now Maputo), Sena, and Mozambique in Mozambique. As the Dutch, British, and French strengthened their hold on African coastal commerce in both West and Southern Africa and as the Arabs retrieved their supremacy in the east, the Portuguese role in Africa declined markedly.

Knowledge about Africa from the era of exploration resulted in growing European interest in African lands and resources. This brought the Dutch, French, and British into action. The Dutch founded Cape Town in 1652 (fig. 8.4) and the French and British established forts along the West African coast. The competition led to clashes among the Europeans. From this period emerged towns such as Conakry in Guinea; Accra in Ghana; and Calabar in Nigeria. Most of these towns were merely forts, such as that of Accra, which was originally the site of Fort Usher, established in 1650 by the Dutch, and Fort James, founded in 1673 by the British. The 18th century contributed little to new urban growth. A few towns did emerge, such as Port Louis in Mauritius and Freetown in Sierra Leone in 1736 and 1787, respectively, but their populations were very small.

During the first half of the 19th century, urban growth in Africa was very pronounced. The Yoruba towns in Nigeria, such as Oshogbo and Ibadan, witnessed considerable growth. Elsewhere in West Africa, Monrovia in Liberia, Banjul in Gambia, and Libreville in Gabon were founded in the same period, as were Khartoum in the Sudan in East Africa and a number of South Africa's major cities, including Port Elizabeth, Durban, Pietermaritzburg, Bloemfontein, East London, and Pretoria, in Southern Africa.

During the period of European contact before the colonial partition, SSA's urban pattern began to take form, but under the following constraints. First, most of the European contribution in settlement development was coastal and no significant penetration of the continent occurred during this period. Second, many of the coastal settlements were intended as transshipment points for trade and they lacked the regular urban facilities, except those structures that served as European housing or as port and defense establishments. Third, there was a lack of diffusion of European technology and culture to the interior, indigenous urban centers. The interior towns, while serving as important nodes of precolonial trade, obtained very little in terms of European technology.

African Urbanization during Colonial Times

By the beginning of the 20th century, the European scramble for African land had been completed. The principal spheres of urban influence were the British, French, Portuguese, Belgian, and Dutch. These five countries had divided almost all of Africa among them. Social and physical aspects of urban development followed the social and political objectives of these European powers. With the abolition of slavery, the supply of raw materials to Europe from Africa had to be ensured and the colonial powers saw that they had to make an aggressive thrust into the interior and support the flow of the commodities. The required infrastructure and colonial settlements to ensure this flow were built. By the beginning of the century, the railway pattern in Africa resembled that of a system of coastal rivers draining the continent to the sea. Virtually all of the coastal termini from Dakar to Luanda became the capitals and/or primate cities in their respective countries, with external trade as their major function. In East Africa, where the resource hinterlands are far in the interior, towns such as Khartoum, Addis Ababa, Kampala, Nairobi, and Salisbury were linked by railways to ports in each country, such as Port Sudan in Sudan, Djibouti in Ethiopia, Mombasa in Kenya (fig. 8.5), and Beira serving Rhodesia (now Zimbabwe). Other East African centers, such as Dar es Salaam (fig. 8.6) and Maputo, became important ports.

In South Africa, the pattern was somewhat different. Major European penetration predated colonial partition, with the massive Dutch immigrations into the interior plateau region of Southern Africa starting in 1836, from their earlier coastal holdings that dated from the mid-17th century. Because of the long-standing white settlements, urban development, commodity flows, and infrastructure here are different from elsewhere in Africa. In South Africa, as a result, there are at present numerous urban centers in the in-

Figure 8.5 The old CBD of Mombasa still evokes the ambiance of the colonial era in this tropical city near the equator. (Photo by Jack Williams)

terior that are served by a number of ports all around the southern tip of the continent. The railway pattern is much more intensive, with a high degree of connectivity between urban centers in the plateau hinterland as well as between the interior settlements and the port cities.

Although the growth in Africa's principal urban centers did not start until after World War II, most, if not all, of the primate cities had been established before that, in the majority of cases by the colonial powers. Since colonial policy did not encourage real industrialization, except what was needed to facilitate efficient transfer of minerals and commodities to the metropolitan centers, fixed capital in secondary activities was not a major factor in urban development. However, primary commodity processing for export was responsible for growth of urban population in mineral-rich regions. Good examples are the mining towns of the Zambian copper belt and Shaba province of Congo, in which, for example, Ndola and Mufulira in Zambia and Lubumbashi and Kilwezi in Congo have become major urban centers.

The colonial period also introduced other factors that have played important roles in urban growth. To support the scale of trade that flowed between Africa and Europe, a commensurately large administrative operation had to be established. Modern social infrastructure and amenities required by the bureaucratic and business elite led to the introduction of European urban characteristics that were later to be inherited as the most important problem as well as an opportunity facing primate cities in Africa.

REPRESENTATIVE CITIES

Addis Ababa: The Indigenous City

With only 15% of its population living in towns, Ethiopia is one of the least-urbanized countries in Africa. Addis Ababa, the capital and primate

Figure 8.6 Along this commercial street in present-day Dar es Salaam, one can buy a hot dog, a pool table, a school uniform, jewelry, chocolate, and seeds, according to shop signs. (Photo by Assefa Mehretu)

city with 2.6 million inhabitants, accounts for a large portion of the urban population. Perched on the ridge above the Great Rift Valley at about 8,000 ft (2,400 m) above sea level, Addis Ababa (which means "new flower") is one of the highest capital cities in the world. By virtue of its site, Addis has one of the most pleasant climates in Africa, similar to those of Nairobi and Harare. The physical beauty, climate, location, and abundance of wood for fuel and water, including hot springs, convinced King Menelik II of Ethiopia to establish Ethiopia's new capital in the foothills of the imposing Entoto Mountains in 1886. Menelik's decision to make Addis a permanent capital represented an end to the practice of "roving capitals," which Ethiopian emperors used for various reasons. Addis Ababa became the last of these rotating capital cities, which began with pre-Christian Axum, all in northern Ethiopia. Addis is the southernmost in Ethiopia's succession of capitals and by far the most remote from the core of the feudal power of historic Ethiopia. The geographic situation of Addis, also characterized by its location almost the dead center in the nation and at the meeting line of the old north and new south, gave Menelik II immense powers not only to consolidate the nation, but also to frustrate colonial intrusions.

The development of Addis as a primate city overshadowing older centers in the north was based on four factors. The first was Menelik's victory over Italy at Adwa in 1896. Menelik (as did King Haile Selassie I following World War II) used Italian prisoners of war to help build roads, churches, office buildings, and other types of public works for which the country lacked the skilled manpower. The second factor in the growth of Addis was the completion of the Djibouti-Addis Ababa railway in 1917, which connected the Ethiopian hinterland to international markets. The third was finding a lasting solution to the domestic fuel wood shortage brought about by the rapid depletion of the original forest around Addis. Menelik had a Swiss national bring eucalyptus trees from Australia and had them planted around the capital. This saved Addis from becoming abandoned as had happened to former capitals when fuel wood became depleted. Finally, in the late 19th century Menelik began initiating a number of innovations in tertiary functions, such as the establishment of radio and telephone communication, a common currency, postal services, modern schools, printing presses, and banks, which were all centered in Addis. He even had the first automobile brought in and shocked his followers by not only learning how to drive but also showing a preference to riding in the four-wheeled device rather than on his usual horse or mule. In the early part of the 20th century, Addis Ababa became a distinctly modernizing city.

The Italian occupation of Addis Ababa (1935–1941) and its planned use as the hub of Italy's short-lived colonial empire brought about several social as well as physical changes to Addis. First, the experimentation that Menelik began in 1886, extended by Haile Selassie until 1935, of judiciously grafting modern technology onto strongly traditional Ethiopia, came to an end with the drastic methods of the Italian occupying forces, who altered the technological environment to serve solely their own purposes and the small but powerful Italian settler community that followed. Second, the Italians attempted an "apartheid"-type solution for urban residential and commercial land use and divided the town into separate sectors, one for Ethiopians and another for Italians. The Ethiopian residents were to be relocated to a newly developed zone in the west of the town, now called Addis Ketema (New Town), that adjoins the Merkato d' Indigino (the natives' market), which itself had been relocated from its old location to free up the area for the piazza in the Italian zone of the city. Third, the Italians undertook major construction efforts in public building programs for housing and government functions and in roads both within Addis and radiating from the city to provincial capitals throughout the country. This is considered one of the most important contributions of the Italian occupation to the modernization of Addis Ababa. As many of the Italians opted to stay in Ethiopia following liberation in 1945, they continued to have a varied social impact through their language, food, and music. Addis once featured some of the best Italian restaurants and cafes in all of Africa.

Addis Ababa is composed of six principal quarters. The first is the central district, in which are located St. George Cathedral; the ultramodern City Hall; the piazza, which contains fashionable downtown shopping, and entertainment sector; and Churchill Avenue, the principal north-south axis connecting older and newer quarters of the central business district (fig. 8.7). Second, to the north, northwest, and west of the central district, are the residential quarters, which include Addis Ketema, with its Roman-style grid pattern designed by Italians, and the adjoining Merkato, the central market. Third, to the northeast, are the extensive embassy grounds that Menelik II granted to the major European powers of Britain, France, the Soviet Union, Italy, and Belgium, to which were later added embassies of the United States and Kenya. Fourth, to the southeast, are more residential quarters, which include a fashionable and upscale residential area that adjoins the Bole International Airport. Fifth, to the south of the central district, is the famous Ethiopian Railway Station, built by the French. South of the railway station are more low-income residen-

Figure 8.7 Modern high-rise architecture is beginning to appear in Africa's cities, including this scene of a building under construction on the fashionable Bole Road in downtown Addis Ababa. (Photo by Assefa Mehretu)

tial quarters. Sixth, to the southwest, are two residential quarters that contain some high-density pockets of very low-income residents. Farther out toward the southwestern suburbs is the prestigious quarter of the Old Airport area, in which are found upscale residential quarters and embassies (fig. 8.8).

Addis Ababa, unlike many Sub-Saharan primate cities, does not exhibit distinct separation of colonial and indigenous quarters. As the Italian plan to divide the city along those lines was aborted by the defeat of the occupying forces, the city grew in haphazard fashion and its rapid growth overtook the many attempts to guide its internal structure. Addis, like Lagos and Ibadan in Nigeria, has perhaps one of the most indigenous flavors of any SSA metropolis. The visitor to the city can marvel at tradition and modernity woven together both socially and physically. One can find some of the most modern of structures alongside extensions of rural living where residents keep cows, sheep, and chickens in fenced-in compounds.

Addis grew from about a quarter million inhabitants in 1950 to about 1.9 million in 1990 and it now has 2.6 million inhabitants. It is projected to have 5.1 million by 2015. Recently, the city has been growing by about 5% annually. In the 1960s, the growth of Addis was aided by its choice as the location of the secretariats of the African Union (formerly the Organization of African Unity) and the United Nations Economic Commission for Africa, both of which brought fame and recognition to Addis as one of the most pleasant and charming cities in SSA. The city also gained from the increasing number of international civil servants who lived in Addis and the numerous international conferences and seminars for which Addis became known, partly because of the excellent network of its national airline and hotel accommodations.

As in many African primate cities, Addis has faced the problem of having too many residents for the jobs and amenities available. The housing and sanitation problems in some sec-

Figure 8.8 This upscale neighborhood of Ethiopia's capital city of Addis Ababa illustrates the country's international linkages. (Photo by Assefa Mehretu)

tors of Addis are far beyond what the city government can cope with. The nationalization of urban land and rental property by the marxist government (1974–1990) exacerbated the situation. The city went into disrepair with state ownership of all rental property. New housing construction almost ceased until late in the life of the regime, when massive, low-cost housing construction began in the eastern suburbs of the city. The current government, preoccupied by security concerns brought on by its own ill-advised policy of ethnic federalism, has not had the time or resources to address the massive urban problems left by the marxist regime. To make matters worse, the current government has maintained the marxist regime's nationalization of land and put in place a strange regulatory system of urban land use that has highly inflated urban land access fees and priced most of the city's inhabitants out of decent housing opportunities. In most sectors of the city, the policy has depleted incentives to repair and maintain the housing stock, leaving most of the city in total disrepair (fig. 8.9).

The future challenges for Addis Ababa are based on five factors. First, because of push factors of political instability, ethnic division, resource constraints, and food insecurity, rural-urban migration has accelerated. The city has no capacity to provide a decent urban life for so many people. Second, the standard of living for most has declined over the years because of the long-neglected national economy. Third, there exists an astronomic disparity between those who are well off and those who struggle to make a living. Some of this is due to the corruptive environment the government has incubated, which has allowed some of the political and business elite to take advantage of their positions of influence to make themselves obscenely rich. A recent crackdown has landed many such in-

Figure 8.9 This scene of lower-quality housing, from Dar es Salaam in Tanzania, could be replicated in most cities of Sub-Saharan Africa, including Addis Ababa. (Photo by Assefa Mehretu)

dividuals in prison, facing charges of corruption. Fourth, the nationalization of land and the ludicrously expensive lease arrangements that the government has devised will not serve the majority of the city-dwellers. The policy has become a recipe for denial of decent housing for many, including people who should be enjoying middle-class status. Finally, the city's reputation as the center for innovation and locus of industrial development that would beneficially engage the hinterland has been damaged. The city suffers from the perception of it as the center of an oppressive government that has little to no interest in the welfare of rural folk. For a large nation like Ethiopia that has resource constraints in many of its highly populated regions, the government's policy of development should be partly anchored in urbanization; Addis should be developed to play a lead position in a more balanced national urban hierarchy.

Harare: The Colonial Legacy

In Zimbabwe, 32% of the population lives in urban settlements, about the average for Africa. Harare is not only the capital city of Zimbabwe, but also increasingly its primate metropolis. Until independence in 1980, cities like Harare (formerly Salisbury) were planned and developed by British settlers who colonized Zimbabwe (then Southern Rhodesia) beginning in 1890. Reflecting its colonial background, Harare contains certain discriminatory spatial and socioeconomic structures common to Southern African towns. Some of these are unlikely to be completely eradicated in spite of the postcolonial removal of segregation laws that created the high-density

African townships at the geographic margins of the urban core. At the outset, the overall colonial urban development policy in relation to the indigenous African population was to restrict them from permanent urban residence and to provide low-cost housing only for the gainfully employed male population in the townships. The expectation was that the unemployed would always return to their tribal trust lands (renamed communal lands) set aside for them in the rural areas through a series of land tenure acts. The intended effect was to ensure racial segregation in all the towns and thereby discourage rural-urban migration and urbanization of the indigenous population. However, African rural-urban migration increased over time and households with children became more and more noticeable in the city. Since colonial urban planning was based on the principle of segregation, town planners of the time located the African townships far away from the "European city" to and from which they shuttled at dawn and dusk for work. The situation marginalized and disrupted the Africans who spent too much time commuting back and forth to a city whose functions they could not benefit from except by earning wages.

Like other urban places in Zimbabwe, Harare today is experiencing several postcolonial growth problems as it tries to readjust its structure and function to serve as the administrative and economic capital of a "desegregated" country. Its first growing pains came from an increased influx of the African population, which was no longer subject to colonial control. This meant that many migrants headed for the city and began stretching the limits of the "African townships." Since the African townships were not designed to absorb large numbers of urban residents, they began to experience serious problems from unemployment, urban poverty, and overcrowding. This produced slum and shanty dwellings in the built-up areas and squatter developments in vacant lots within the municipal boundaries. Today, Harare's principal zones of urban development remain essentially the same as when they were put in place in the colonial era—the African Townships, downtown CBD, industrial area, low-cost residential zone, mid-cost residential quarters, and high-income residential suburbs.

The development of the African townships has an interesting history. In the early stages in the history of the colonial town of Salisbury, the first African residential area, or "native location," was sited at the southern outskirts of the city. It consisted of huts built by the occupants that were later replaced with municipal-built flats to accommodate the workingmen needed in the adjoining industrial zone and for domestic work in the city. This represented the first major African urban presence near the town's commercial and industrial center. In 1907, this area became known as the Harare African Township (now Mbare). After the establishment of Mbare Township, more African townships were located and developed in the south and west, close to the industrial areas where black laborers were required the most. As the population of the city increased over the years, more African townships were established using various low-cost housing schemes, but they were progressively farther away from the city center and European residential areas.

Recent changes to urban life and residential development did not alter the colonial spatial structure of urban marginality. With the dismantling of racial legislation that had prohibited freedom of movement and permanent African urban settlement, Harare experienced rapid population growth. According to the censuses of 1982 and 1992, the population increased during that time from 656,000 to 1.2 million and accounted for 33% of the total urban population of the country in 1982 and 36% in 1992. Consequences of rapid population growth in Harare, such as chronic unemployment, acute housing shortages, and an inadequate municipal services infrastructure, have continuously burdened the city and intensified the poverty experienced by most of its high-density township residents.

The majority of African residents in Harare continue to live in varied conditions that reflect the colonial legacy. The structure of the city and its urban governance persist in the form of "economic apartheid." The economic hardships of the urban poor and those living in crowded suburbs make it impossible for them to make significant changes to their lifestyles. The distances from the core of the city vary from 5 to 30 km, and in some cases are even greater, and the cost to low-income residents in time and money is considerable. Also, crowding in residential areas means great pressures on public transport and on the shopping, recreational, and educational facilities within the townships. Likewise, demands on household and public toilets are excessive and the dangers of disease and illness often overload public health facilities and strain household budgets. However, this is not the impression that one gets from visiting downtown Harare, which is one of the most attractive and modern cities in Africa.

The duality of Harare is clearly manifested in the contrasting characteristics of, on the one hand, the city's rich sectors downtown and in the residential suburbs to the north and, on the other, the African township of Mbare in the south. Mbare is the major entry point for Africans into the capital city. It serves as the city's major hub for long-distance bus transport and the retail market center. It is a residential area of first choice for most low-income families. From the early 1980s on, it gradually absorbed large numbers of rural-urban migrants. In the early 1990s, in-migration was increased by the drought, which pushed rural people to seek refuge and shelter in the immediate hinterland of the bus terminus. Consequently, Mbare degenerated into a slum of backyard shelter developments characterized by overcrowding, extreme poverty, and widespread pollution. Unlike with the equally illegal open space habitats of squatter settlements elsewhere in the city, which are often raided, demolished, and cleared of their residents, city authorities have conveniently overlooked the Mbare problem of squatter settlements in the face of an extreme shortage of low-cost housing. The socioeconomic and environmental conditions associated with squatter settlements in Mbare reveal some very disturbing patterns of coping in the residential margins. Regular amenities are in short supply, affecting hygienic conditions. Economic hardships are significant, with unemployment rates reaching almost 70% and only 10% having reliable incomes above the national poverty line of US$30 per month.

The transition from colonial to independent administration of Zimbabwe accelerated rural-urban migration and increased the many urbanization problems that cities like Harare face. Zimbabwe's urban problems are directly associated with rural poverty caused by limited access to arable farmland, a by-product of the colonial land apportionment laws. The lack of economic opportunities in rural areas has made moving to urban locales the only option available. The government has made many attempts to reduce socioeconomic disparities between and within rural and urban areas. The state made it a priority to develop rural areas

Figure 8.10 In this outdoor market in Dar es Salaam, modern plastic ware seems to be overtaking traditional basketry. Markets such as this are common in the cities of Sub-Saharan Africa, including Harare in Zimbabwe. (Photo by Assefa Mehretu)

by infusing resources into rural infrastructure such as roads, schools, health facilities, clean water supplies, telephone communications, and electricity. With international support in loans and grants, the development plans made significant progress, until they were negatively impacted by adverse macroeconomic conditions in Zimbabwe and by the failure of the state to bring about meaningful land reform and redress the spatial mismatch between population density and land potential in the countryside.

The recent political turmoil that has arisen from long-neglected issues of land distribution following more than 20 years of independence is taking shape in a strong opposition to the status quo. Old wounds from colonial days and the independence movement are being revisited, with the parties in contention for power taking shots at each other for their own ends. Whatever the outcome in this power struggle in an increasingly polarized Zimbabwe, the situation in the cities will continue to be unstable until the lopsided land distribution inherited from colonial Rhodesia finds a resolution in an orderly, fair, and equitable manner without jeopardizing the productive sectors of the country's economy (fig. 8.10).

Lagos: Megacity of SSA

Nigeria's population is more than 36% urbanized. Lagos, with 13.4 million inhabitants in 2000 and 23.2 million projected for 2015, qualifies as SSA's most populous city and one of the world's megacities. The development of the petroleum industry in Nigeria has given a boost to urban development, including that of Lagos. It is often said that Lagos owes its growth and dynamism to European influence. Yet it is also true that, with the exception of inland centers such as Ibadan and Ouagadougou, Lagos, in its development dynamic, owes more to early African urban development than does any other city in West Africa. Lagos was established in the 17th century, when a group of Awari decided to cross over the lagoons and settle in a more secure setting on the island of Iddo. They later crossed over to Lagos Island in search of more farmland. In this manner, the three important parts of the city of Lagos were founded as fishing and farming villages by the indigenous population, well before major external influence in the 18th century.

Another important historical factor in the development of Lagos is its significance in the slave trade between 1786 and 1851, in which Africans, especially the Yoruba, were willing participants. Lagos was not a slave market until 1760, but it soon became one of the most important West African ports in the slave trade. Lagos Island became an important center where slaves were barricaded as they awaited their export along with primary commodities, particularly foodstuffs and Yoruba cloth, which reached markets as distant as Brazil. Although in 1807 the British passed an act to abolish the slave trade, Lagos, because of its locational advantage, continued the trade until it was halted by the British invasion of the city in 1851. British bombardment of the city also caused a temporary decline in the city's population. With the cession of Lagos to Britain as a colony in 1861, the colonial era for Lagos had begun. Thereafter, Lagos's population and urban activities began to grow even faster.

People continued to move into the "free colony," leaving behind slavery, war, and instability in the interior. Freed slaves also returned from Brazil as well as Sierra Leone and made their homes in Lagos. Toward the end of the 19th century, Britain intervened to stop internal hostilities and established a protectorate over the whole of Nigeria. A railway from Lagos, begun in 1895, reached Kano in 1912. Its effective hinterland now expanded to the interior of Nigeria, Lagos became even more important as a trade and administrative center. By 1901, the city had a population of more than 40,000 and, by this time, the future prominence of the "modern metropolis" was pretty much established.

Lagos is a city with many problems rooted in its rapid growth. It has been called the "biggest disaster area that ever passed for a city." That may be overstating it, but Lagos has acute, sometimes incomprehensible, problems of congested traffic; inadequate sanitation, housing, and social services; and urban decay. With the expansion of oil wealth now tapering off, the problems of the city have been aggravated on all fronts.

Lagos is a primate city. The disparity in socioeconomic status between the elite and the mass of urbanites is very wide. That also means the city reflects two contradictory modes of living: one that is an extension of European style brought about by those who can afford the luxuries of a high level of technology and another that is an extension of the traditional mode of living, which has been distorted to fit an urban milieu. This curious amalgam, as it reflects itself in an African urban setting, loses the beauty, charm, and convenience of either of its parts and becomes a nuisance, as exemplified by the traffic congestion and slum dwellings of Lagos.

As a primate city, Lagos has the typical problems of rapid population growth and insufficient employment opportunities. The net effect of these problems is enormous. It depresses urban wages to almost marginal subsistence levels and adds to the pressure on urban amenities and housing, as well as to numerous other social problems, especially in the slums of Lagos and peripheral residential communities. Lagos is a good example of an African primate city whose growth rates and attendant problems in distorted consumption patterns have created a stultifying effect that a weak and often disorganized city government is incapable of handling.

There are, however, some positive developments underway. Abuja, in the vicinity of the confluence between the Niger and Benue rivers, has been designated as the new capital city of the country and all government functions are being moved to that more central location. This will mean a major step toward decentralization and reduce the concentration of functions in Lagos. There is no doubt that Lagos is a long way from ever receiving the praises given Dakar and Abidjan, but then Lagos, as with Ibadan and Addis Ababa, is a truer expression of the African response to an inappropriate and misplaced urban design. It should be remembered that Lagos, even in the colonial period, had less than 5,000 expatriates. Hence, compared with Dakar, Abidjan, Nairobi, and Kinshasa, the character of the city and its spatial organization were considerably less a function of the impact of the Europeans. The process that Lagos is undergoing, if there is any recognizable process at all, may throw light on the problems of indigenization of African primate cities that have been, and in most cases still are, enclaves of European economic systems and often as alien to their people as cities in Europe. Lagos is a bona fide African city and, as disorganized as it is, it may be one of the few cities in Africa to offer a lesson on the transition from a colonial to an indigenous urban environment.

Nairobi: The Inertia of History

Only 20% of Kenya's population lives in cities. It shares with Zimbabwe some characteristics of a settler colony, including low rates of urbanization among the African population. Nairobi, as the capital and primate city of Kenya, currently has 2.3 million inhabitants. Among African cities, Nairobi has perhaps one of the most unusual histories. The site was known as Enkare Nairobi, or "cold water," by the pastoral Maasai, who also regarded this area, uninhabited and fully covered by virgin forest and swamp, as a natural buffer between them and their traditional enemies, the Kikuyu to the north. The Nairobi River, however, was a strategic resting spot for the traveler from the coast. In 1896, the first rail was laid to link Mombasa on the coast with the most important part of its hinterland at the time, Uganda. The railway reached the site of Nairobi three years later, in 1899. Because of the natural advantages of the site, Nairobi was chosen as the headquarters of the railway, taking that function from Mombasa. In addition, the administrative center of the province to which Nairobi belonged, which was located at Machakos, about 40 mi (65 km) to the southeast, was moved to Nairobi in 1899. Although drainage and health problems plagued the early settlement, in 1906 the colonial government endorsed the location, fixing Nairobi where it was for good.

By 1906, the new city contained more than 13,000 people. Nairobi soon became the most important colonial capital in East Africa. This role was greatly strengthened during the two world wars, when the city was an important base of operations for British military forces in Africa. By 1948, the city's population exceeded 100,000. After that, Nairobi shared with other African primate cities the postwar boom in growth that continued until the independence movement of the 1950s.

The factors that stimulated the establishment and growth of Nairobi were to produce some of the important problems the city faces as a burgeoning African metropolis. First, the city's site, which was considered ideal for railway sidings at the outset, proved disastrous when it came to problems of sanitation, which is still an important constraint on the city's development.

Second, Nairobi has never been considered by the Africans as a suitable place to live. Because of the absence of any indigenous rationale for its creation, and because of an initial monopoly of the site by foreigners of European or Indian origin, Africans were not attracted to the city. This was of course exacerbated by colonial marginalization of the local population. There have always been high numbers of men in the city and relatively few women and children. Although Nairobi is a city in Kenya, it has very few characteristics that qualify it as representative of Kenyan indigenous life.

Third, Nairobi's three major ethnic groups, Africans, Asians, and Europeans, were stratified by occupation and separated residentially. The Europeans had been responsible for all administration, resource ownership, and financial institutions. The Asians, who were initially introduced into the area to work on railway construction, worked as artisans, merchants, and shopkeepers. From the outset, the Africans were relegated to whatever menial jobs the city was able to create for them. Residentially, the three peoples were largely separated into three zones within the city.

Fourth, responses to growth, especially among the African population, are similar to those of the colonial days. Unlike the European and Asian property owners who lived in their carefully demarcated zones, most Africans lived in rented housing built by the city or their employers. The African residential zone of Eastlands was also characterized by instability, not only in the frequent turnover of inhabitants, but also in the continuous rebuilding and construction throughout the colonial period. Another major development has been the growth of squatter settlements in Nairobi, which has come about as a result of population pressure in the city proper and of the growing labor force, which generally finds marginal or no employment in the formal sector.

Nairobi has now achieved the status of a major African metropolis with diverse local as well as international functions. As a primate city with exclusive advantages in attracting important secondary, tertiary, and quaternary functions, it plays a dominant role in a core-periphery relation in a highly dualistic economy. As the major core in Kenya, Nairobi displays an internal morphology in which a modern enclave continues to operate in almost the same mode as it did in colonial days, abated only by the emerging indigenous elite, which has started to make inroads in the traditionally European and Asian niches and enclaves. Figure 8.11, a model derived from empirical analysis of a number of Sub-Saharan African cities, including Nairobi, reveals the generalized placement of the major land-use categories in such cities today.

Nairobi continues to suffer from the inertia of history. Its most important problem emerges from the fact that the city is regarded as an alien introduction. As far as the general population is considered, Nairobi's primary purpose has been to offer nonagricultural employment just as an industrial enclave would in a rural environment. European residents, who still consider Europe as their home, use Nairobi as a means of economic enterprise. The Asians maintain their primary connections with India and Pakistan. Many Kenyans have not been fully integrated in the "core" functions of the city nor are attracted to it as a permanent residence. The average Kenyan

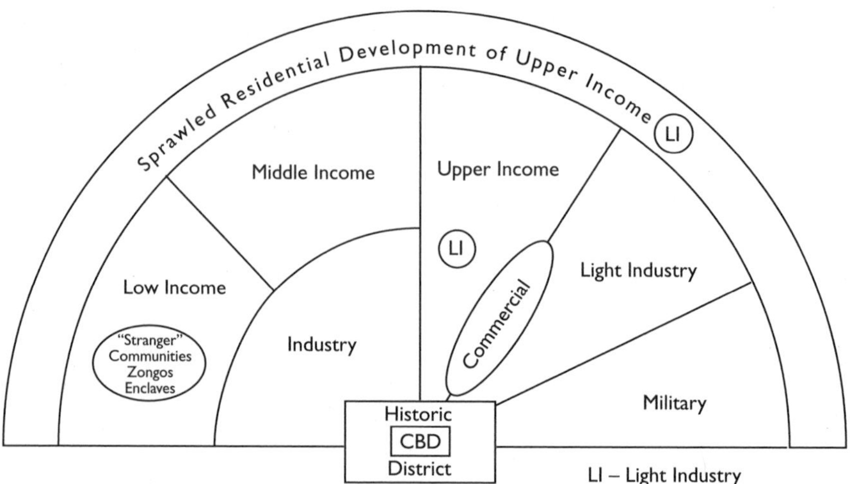

Figure 8.11 A Model of the Sub-Saharan African City. *Source*: Samuel Aryeetey-Attoh, "Urban Geography of Sub-Saharan Africa," in *Geography of Sub-Saharan Africa*, edited by Samuel Aryeety-Attoh (Upper Saddle River, N.J.: Prentice-Hall, 1997), 193. Reprinted with permission.

maintains a special attachment to his or her rural homestead. Although such primordial linkages are not as important as they were before, Kenyans regard their rural moorings with fondness and it is to them that many Kenyans retreat for rest and recreation, and eventually retirement.

Contemporary development of an urban elite of indigenous origin has, of course, initiated a change in the ethnic character of employment strata, residential separation, and residential stability in the city. Many Africans have moved into occupations that have been traditionally European and Asian. Among the elite, there are many who were born, raised, and educated in the city and consider it home. Some of these who are prosperous enough to afford the price have moved into traditionally European and Asian neighborhoods. However, such trends, although significant, only affect a minority in the higher economic and political echelons. Upper Nairobi and the "Hill" residential areas continue to be dominated by European single-unit and fashionable homes complete with servants' quarters. In Parklands-Eastleigh live most of the Asians of the city. Here, they have tried to maintain their cultural uniqueness through architectural style and through community and religious functions. The quality of the dwellings here, however, is not uniform. The well-to-do Asians inhabit Parklands, adjacent to the European sector. The poorer Asians live in Eastleigh. Some of the Asian population has moved to a second Asian quarter in Nairobi South.

The majority of Africans live in Eastlands, which borders Eastleigh. This sector contains the working-class estates often built by the city or employers. The western section of Eastlands contains older units. More recently, newer and better-quality units have been built to the east. But overall, the quality of residence here cannot be compared with that of the two

Figure 8.12 Regarded by many Africans as an artificial city, Nairobi nonetheless has risen in the century of its existence to be the key city of not only Kenya but East Africa as well. (Photo by Assefa Mehretu)

areas discussed previously. The Eastlands residential area is flat, monotonous, short on amenities, and has a residentially unstable population. Also, the three major ethnic residential areas are still distinct. The few Africans who inhabit other sectors are either servants or members of the African elite who have the means to acquire property in these areas.

Nairobi's land use includes three other functions, which are found in the central and southern areas of the city. The industrial zone has been laid out to the east of the railway station, complete with railway sidings and access roads in the southern sector of the city. To the north of this is the central business district, which is located in the heart of the city, marked off by natural as well as artificial boundaries. This central area of Nairobi represents one of the busiest spots in the continent (fig. 8.12). The CBD's most prominent functions are commerce, retailing, tourism, banking, government, international institutions, and education. It is also very modern, with multistory buildings, double-lane streets with streetlights, buses, congestion, gigantic billboards and neon lights, and automobiles from all over the world. This is the heartbeat of Kenya, where where almost every major national decision is made and where all new major urban functions gravitate. The ultramodern city that Nairobi has become is a mosaic of the three subcultures it represents. The ordinary Africans set out from their Eastlands homes to work in the CBD's menial and often informal-sector jobs and in the industrial estates. There is very little in Nairobi for them in terms of recreation, except perhaps the bars in the residential zone. The average European, African elite, or Asian drives a car from a comfortable home in Upper Nairobi or Parklands and works in the CBD or some other similar enclave, often in extremely modern, clean, and comfortable surroundings, with occasional interruptions to visit the plush hotels, bars, and supermodern shops in the CBD. Before dusk, those people probably go for a game of golf or tennis at the Golf Club or the railway sports grounds, located conveniently between the CBD and "the Hill," a fashionable bedroom district of the economic and political elite.

Dakar: Senegal's City of Contradictions

Senegal is about 42% urbanized, one of the higher figures for SSA. With 2.1 million inhabitants, Dakar is one of the principal primate cities in West Africa. The city is known for its beauty, modernity, charm, and style. Because of its agreeable climate, excellent location, and urban morphology, it is often described as the Marseille or Nice of West Africa. But, of course, this image applies to only part of Dakar. As with Nairobi and Harare, Dakar is a city of phenomenal contradictions.

The city was founded in 1444, when Portuguese sailors made a small settlement on the tiny island of Gorée, located just off the Dakar Peninsula. In 1588, the Dutch also made the island of Gorée a resting point. Although the French came to the site in 1675, they did not move into the mainland until 1857 and used Dakar as a refueling and coal bunkering point. A number of developments expanded Dakar's functions, leading it to be, in a relatively short time, the most important colonial point on the west coast of Africa. In 1885, Dakar was linked to St. Louis, the old Portuguese port, by rail and this gave it an added importance as a trading center. Because of its situation and site advantages, added to its moderate climate, Dakar soon became a focus for a number of colonial functions that France wanted to introduce in the region. In 1898, Dakar became a naval base and in 1904 it became the capital of the Federation of French West Africa. Dakar is situated in the westernmost part of the continent. This made it the most strategic point for ships moving between Europe and Southern Africa and from Africa to the New World. As capital of French West Africa until 1956, it served a hinterland stretching from Senegal in the west to the easternmost part of Francophone West Africa, which included Mali, Burkina Faso, and Niger.

After the French moved from the island of Gorée to the peninsula in 1857, there was some uneasiness about living in quarters surrounded by African villages. Although a policy of racial segregation was not officially pursued, the French settlers had always wanted to keep the two communities separate. However, only because of a natural calamity that befell the Africans could the French finally accelerate the establishment of their exclusive holdings. Progressive displacement of African dwellings was underway before the outbreak of a yellow fever epidemic in 1900, but the Europeans, invoking sanitation requirements, displaced the Africans at a greater rate afterwards, pushing them northward. Between 1900 and 1902, numerous African homesteads were burned down as a "sanitary measure" and the occupants were relocated after receiving compensation for their holdings. Another epidemic in 1914 again brought destruction of African homesteads in the south and more relocation of Africans to the north. On the eve of World War II, the French succeeded in almost completely dominating downtown Dakar, often called Le Plateau or Dakar Ville, concentrating the Africans in what became known as the African Medina, in the north-central part of the peninsula. The problem of "cohabitation," as the French called it, was at the root of the whole displacement campaign. Although the colonial authorities would never admit a policy of official segregation, many recommendations were made to openly enforce a system based on race. A commission charged with the study of Dakar in 1889 put forth a recommendation for separate

Figure 8.13 New housing developments such as this in Dar es Salaam are increasingly common in the region's cities. (Photo by Assefa Mehretu)

residential quarters for European and African populations. In 1901, another report proposed relocating the Africans outside the confines of the city. A new plan, implemented in 1950–1951, gave further excuse to the colonial administrators to displace more Africans, particularly those who had formed squatter dwellings in open spaces, especially in the north of Le Plateau.

The present internal morphology of Dakar reflects this historical background. Although rigid, exclusive ethnic domains are no longer in evidence, Le Plateau still contains one of the most Westernized sectors in Africa. It compares easily with any European city. The African Medina, by contrast, reflects its background as a concentration of Africans into high-density housing projects and bidonvilles (squatter settlements). Modern Dakar has four main divisions. Le Plateau, the most modern sector of the city, contains upper-class residential quarters, commercial and retail functions, and government offices and institutions (fig. 8.13). To the east is the port of Dakar, where port administration and numerous port functions are handled. This part of the city has an atmosphere reminiscent of its European background, with high-rise buildings, expensive shops, exclusive restaurants, business offices, and many Europeans. The Grande Medina, which is located to the north of Le Plateau, contains the old African Medina; this is the African Dakar. Its functions are primarily residential, but it also contains shops, markets, and cultural features. The Medina contains the industrial laborers and those employed in the informal sector, both outside and inside the Medina. The population of the Medina and the adjacent bidonvilles of Ouakem and Grand Yof is uniformly poor, living in high-density and sometimes inadequately serviced quarters of the city.

East and northeast of the Grande Medina is the industrial sector of Dakar, conveniently located with its southern flank resting on the port section of Dakar. This sector contains the bulk of the industrial activity of Dakar. North of the Medina, recent expansions of the city have resulted in the development of a sector called Grand Dakar, which contains a mixture of modern residential quarters, industries, and bidonvilles. Southwest of Grand Dakar is also found the section of the city called Farm, with its plush residential quarters and the University of Dakar.

As with many African primate cities, Dakar faces the problem of rapid population growth. In 1914, the city had a total population of 18,000; by 1945 it had 132,000; and by 2000 it had more than 2 million. Clearly most of the growth is attributable to rural-urban migration, which is characteristic of all Sub-Saharan primate cities. The rate of natural increase of the city's population has also been much higher than the national average on account of better sanitation and medical services.

Rapid population growth is an important problem for planning in Dakar. Since 1956, at which time the city ceased to be the capital of the Federation of French West Africa, it has lost a considerable amount of its function in both governmental administration and commercial and industrial activity, both of which relied on a hinterland many times larger than Senegal. The French had an elaborate colonial administrative system in Dakar. Supported by a budgetary allocation from France, Dakar had the largest contingent of French expatriates in government administration and economic and social functions, including education, commerce, and industry. The question after 1956 was whether Dakar could survive as a Senegalese capital after having lost a good part of its functional hinterland.

Yet, there is no doubt that Dakar is still an important center whose functions reach far beyond its national boundaries. Its ideal location still makes it a center of maritime as well as airline traffic. Many international organizations are located in Dakar on account of its situation and agreeable urban environment. Many international conferences and meetings are held there. Above all, it is one of the most favored vacation spots in West Africa for European tourists, especially those from the Mediterranean, who find a familiar climatic comfort in exotic surroundings.

The future of Dakar, nevertheless, depends largely on confronting two challenges. One is to stem the tide of rural-urban migration by a sound policy of regional and rural development, including development of satellite cities and subsequent decentralization. The other, as in other African primate cities, is to bridge the gap between the city's ultramodern sectors and the bidonvilles and make Dakar a true African city.

Johannesburg: Industrial and Mining Center

With more than 2.5 million inhabitants, Johannesburg, once a mining camp, is the largest city in South Africa. The city is also the largest mining and industrial center on the African continent. Johannesburg owes its establishment and phenomenal growth to the discovery of gold in 1886. The rush of settler communities from the south to share in the riches of the land caused the town's population to increase to 10,000 within a year of its birth. Things changed fast for the mining town. It had not only the country's first electric light, but also horse trams for public transportation. By 1895, hardly ten years after its establishment, the city had about 100,000 people, half of whom were European. Johannesburg was the creation of the mining companies, which until this day have perhaps more to do in determining the spatial organization of the city, particularly as it relates to the Africans, than do the civil authorities in the city.

The city had unfortunate beginnings, from a social perspective. It became a microcosm of a notorious experiment in social engineering of separate development—eventually to be known as *apartheid*—for settlers and the aboriginal African population. Apartheid started with the assertion in 1886 that no native tribes could live within 70 mi (112 km) of the site of the new town. According to the Europeans, the Africans were attracted to the site of their own free will in search of employment, to earn cash, with the objective of returning to their Kraal, where they would invest in cattle. When the "native" problem first arose in 1903 and when it surfaced again in 1932, with the creation of the Native Economic Commission, the European settlers argued that Johannesburg had been built by the Europeans, for the Europeans, and belonged to them alone. They maintained that the "natives" were needed for unskilled labor and came to the city to work but not to live in it, mainly because of their inability to handle European civilization. In this manner, the largest of the "European" cities in Southern Africa came into being. Consistent with the ideological position that Africans cannot be detribalized and will always continue to have their links with their tribal villages, Africans were denied permanence of dwelling while they worked for the city and were absolutely barred from living in the city, restricted to guarded compounds during the tenure of their urban employment. The "pass law" (requiring all Africans to carry passes, or internal passports) inaugurated in 1890 and the "compounding system" (restricting Africans to certain residential areas) contributed to the severe urban structural problems with which Johannesburg still has to cope in multiethnic, independent South Africa.

Johannesburg became Africa's largest manufacturing center and this "City of Gold" was also a principal center of culture and education. The prosperity of the city, which was derived from the labors of all the races, was appropriated by the European minority, who enjoyed perhaps one of the highest living standards in the world. Today, the city is clean, with well-planned streets, skyscrapers, and extremely plush residential quarters. The downtown area is similar to that of any industrial city in Europe and North America, with high-rise development to house the offices of the numerous companies, trading firms, and government institutions. In the suburbs of Johannesburg, such as Houghton and Hyde Park, are residential homes for the well-to-do Europeans, whose architecture and amenities more than match those of their European and North American counterparts.

The policy of separate development under apartheid became a formal national policy by the late 1940s, building on decades of gradual evolution, and it was enforced by the minority European government (box 8.1). Apartheid was a socially engineered, hegemonic tool to maintain a privileged status for the European settler population so that its small number could appropriate the vast amount of wealth that was being generated in the country. The impact of this policy was perhaps felt more in places like Johannesburg than anywhere else in the country. Apartheid's application was severely tested in the dynamic environment of Johannesburg, which was attracting a great number of Africans to supply the labor requirements of a rapidly growing industrial conurbation. The authors of apartheid followed a myopic vision by engineering an unsustainable institution of separate development for Africans in their native homelands, as they were later forced to tolerate ghettoes such as Soweto, the infamous African township, growing by

Box 8.1 Apartheid and Urban Development in South Africa

Apartheid has been gone from South Africa since 1993, but the legacy of that dreadful system lingers on in many facets of South African life today and probably always will to some extent. Anyone trying to understand this complex and most important of all nations in Sub-Saharan Africa, and comprehend how difficult it has been for it to throw off the shackles of its past, needs to understand the basic philosophy and practices of apartheid.

Racial segregation had long existed in South Africa. But it was the rapid urban/industrial growth from World Wars I and II, resulting from rich mineral wealth (especially gold and diamonds), that prompted the creation of apartheid. Industrial growth in the cities, plus associated growth in mining and agriculture, all controlled by whites, brought millions of blacks into the cities. By 1946, the blacks were on the verge of becoming predominantly urbanized. Whites saw this as a threat to their continued absolute control of the country's political and economic systems.

Thus, petty apartheid, or the segregation of the races in the use of public and private facilities (similar to the segregation found in the U.S. South before the civil rights movement of the 1960s) evolved into the dreaded Homelands Policy. This involved the forced deportation of blacks from urban areas into reserves known as *bantustans,* or homelands. As Boyd summarized it:

> The ultimate aim was that the black labor force on which the white areas and cities depended would be permitted in those areas only as "foreign" migrant labor, without any right of residence or claim to citizenship in South Africa; their only political rights would relate to "homelands," which many of them would never see unless they were expelled to them. Thus, by a skillful juggling of the "homeland" fragments on its map, South Africa would cease to have a black majority; it would be mainly a white nation that provided employment, on its own terms, for millions of black "foreigners" whose own "homelands"—lacking mines, cities, industries, or even good farmland—could not support them. (Andrew Boyd, *An Atlas of World Affairs* [New York: Methuen, 1983], 88)

In theory, the homelands were supposed to be the rural areas from which the blacks and their ancestors originally migrated. Each homeland would be a self-governing state in which the citizens would be allowed to develop in their own way, independent of white society. The South African government was to provide technical and financial assistance and encourage white businesses to set up plants on the margins of the homelands. In each homeland, towns and cities were supposed to be established, to provide the urban structure necessary to create viable "nation-states" within the Republic of South Africa. There were to be nine homelands in all, for the nine main African tribal groups, as the government defined them (see fig. 8.14). In effect, the South African government was trying to create a series of uninational states rather than a multinational state.

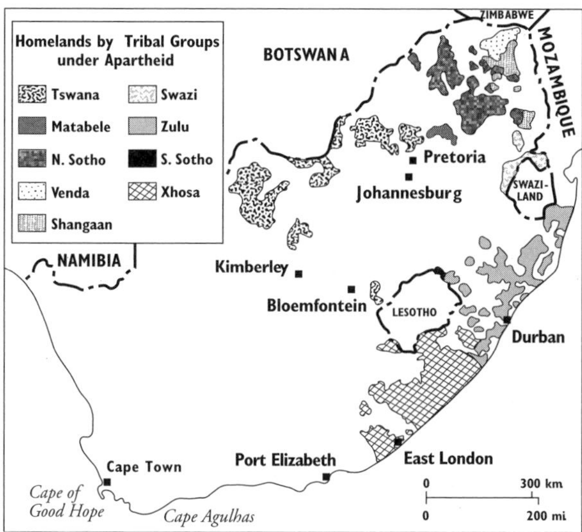

Figure 8.14 South African Homelands during Apartheid.
Source: Compiled from various sources.

The reality of the homelands is that they were located on the most marginal lands that could be found, in a roughly horseshoe-shaped area surrounding the white-controlled urban/industrial core region of the Witwatersrand, centered on Johannesburg. It would have been impossible for the homelands to develop economic independence, and fragmenting the black population in this way served to create cheap labor pools and to reduce political threats to the whites. Much of the urban and economic development promised by the government failed to materialize and the homelands that did come into existence remained largely isolated holding pens for dependents of blacks working in the urban areas who returned to their homelands only for holidays.

Since the early 1990s and the coming to power of a black-dominated government, the homelands have all been abolished and new administrative divisions have been laid out within the country in an attempt to erase the physical remnants of apartheid. But social/cultural evidence of apartheid is much harder to eradicate, not to mention the vast economic gulf that separates most whites from blacks. In spite of the magnanimous efforts of Nelson Mandela, the country's first black president, to promote a climate of reconciliation, the political, social, and economic reality in South Africa remains stained by apartheid's legacy. Thus, the central cities remain dominated by white elites, as in the beautiful central city of Cape Town spreading out at the foot of Table Mountain, while vast numbers of blacks, including recent migrants from neighboring countries, fill squatter settlements that seem to stretch for miles around the central cities. In terms of urban models, it is a classic inverse concentric zone pattern—rich center, poor periphery. Closing the gap between blacks and whites remains the paramount hurdle for this richly endowed country.

leaps and bounds in the shadows of Johannesburg. Apartheid was doomed to succumb to the social disorder its authors never anticipated. The 1976 race riot in Soweto was a watershed in the development of nonracist South Africa. The impatience of the world community with the brutal regime brought moral outrage from outside and increased violence from within. Under the weight of these two dynamics, and aided by a visionary and forgiving leader, Nelson Mandela, South Africa finally emerged from its nightmare by 1993, when apartheid came to a formal end, a year before Mandela was elected president of the nation.

The future of Johannesburg (not to mention other South African cities) now lies in how the root causes of urban instability created by apartheid are dismantled while maintaining the city's ability to continue as South Africa's most important industrial and business center. The challenges that Johannesburg faces are evident from what has been happening in attempts to resolve the severe socioeconomic disparities. With the enforcement mechanisms of the apartheid influx control laws gone, an orderly transition from a divided city into an integrated city will be a daunting task for policy makers and city planners. Johannesburg residents now suffer from incidents of crime such as carjackings and armed robbery, consequences of the collapse of the unsustainable social walls that apartheid created. Johannesburg is in the process of becoming a megalopolis, as a series of mining towns and industrial areas merge together. The previously marginalized townships, such as Soweto and Alexandra, scattered around the city and containing more than a million inhabitants, have to be integrated into the metropolitan life in a more orderly fashion. With a nonracial central government at the helm and with ample human and physical resources for economic progress, all signs point to a more progressive trajectory for cities like Johannesburg. Success depends on whether people of all ethnic groups living in the city deal responsibly with the history of their relations and choose to build a diverse society in which everyone has a stake in the new South Africa's development.

PROBLEMS OF URBAN DEVELOPMENT

Primate Cities

Urban primacy continues to dominate the African scene (fig. 8.15). In fact, the study of urbanization in Africa has often been the study of the primate cities whose backgrounds, characters, and dynamics are usually quite different from indigenous urban centers. One of the more significant factors in urban transformation in Africa in the post-World War II and postindependence period has been the dramatic growth of the primate cities. The degree of primacy in Africa is high. Primate cities contain more than 25% of the total urban population. In places such as Lesotho, the Seychelles, and Djibouti, primate cities contain 100% of the urban population. Generally, in those countries where urbanization has had a relatively long history, the ratios are lower. But the degree of primacy will continue to be a significant pattern in Africa's urban development for quite a long time.

In the 1960s, most primate cities in Africa accounted for about 10% of the urban population. By the year 2000, many cities, such as Lagos, Kinshasa, Lusaka, Accra, Nairobi, Addis Ababa, Luanda, Dakar, and Harare, increased their share of their respective nation's urban population to over 20%. However, since the second half of the 1980s, some encouraging

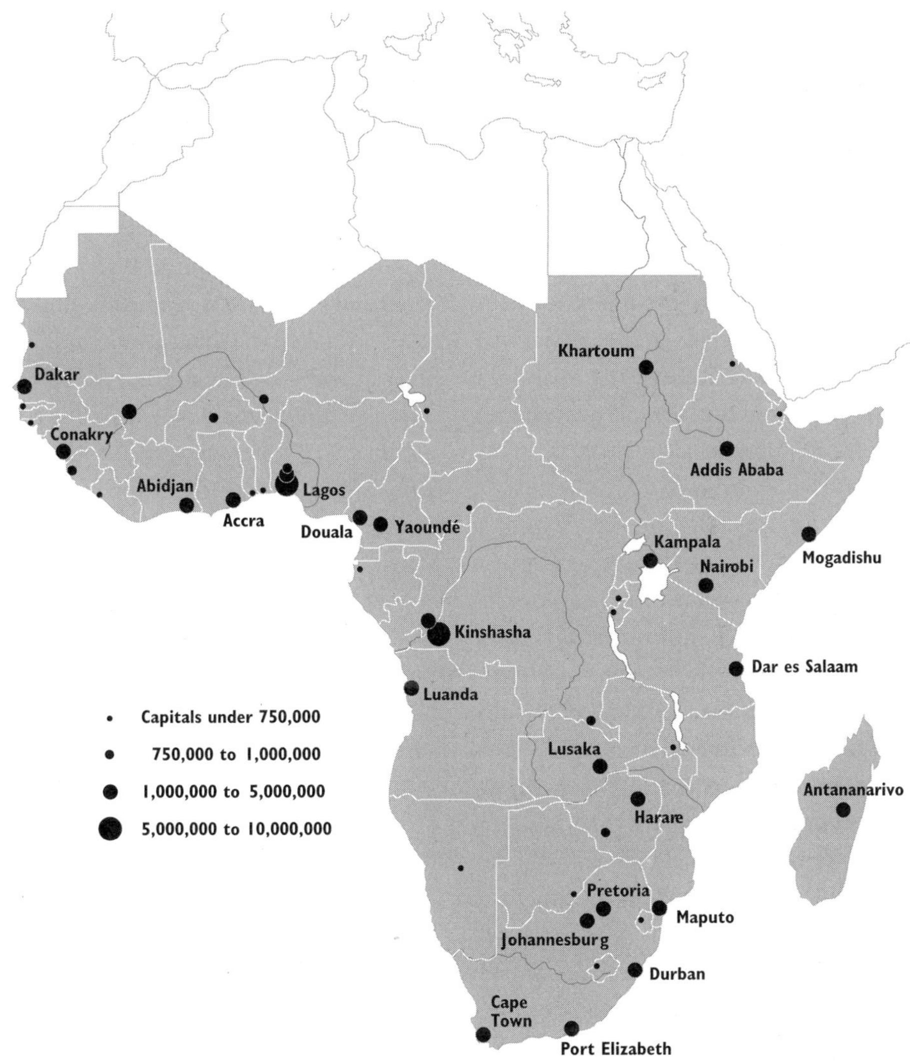

Figure 8.15 Principal Urban Centers of Sub-Saharan Africa. *Source*: Data from United Nations, *World Urbanization Prospects, 2001 Revision* (New York: United Nations Population Division, 2002), www.unpopulation.org.

signs of deconcentration around primate cities have been observed. The ratios of urban populations that reside in primate cities seem to be stabilizing.

Primate cities in SSA have a more disproportionate influence than is warranted by the magnitude of the populations living in them. They dominate the political, economic, infrastructural, and cultural scene of their countries. The strong influence they exercise also enables them to preempt a good portion of the national social and industrial investments. Concentration of power in these cities has produced large disparities in standards of living between those who live in them and the rest of the country. As these disparities are the result of nonmarket forces that help the primate cities to prosper at the expense of the countryside, strong resentment prevails, often inviting sudden changes of government by nondemocratic means. Unfortunately, the frequent overthrowing of governments has only worsened the role of primate cities, most of which have become nodes of heavy-handed governments that have resisted the introduction of pluralistic and democratic systems and free-enterprise economies.

Site and Situation

As with many other aspects of African development, the growth of most African cities has not resulted from careful planning. With perhaps a few exceptions, neither has growth reflected genuine indigenous requirements of spatial organization. Situation has been by far more important than site in the founding of cities. Furthermore, many cities were founded by the colonial powers to function as transshipment centers for efficient handling of raw-material exports. It was not in the interest of colonial administrators to build functional towns to serve indigenous interests, hence site and situation of towns in terms of internal space organization requirements were unimportant considerations, so long as the outward flow of commodities was ensured. Consequently, the sites of some of the largest cities in Africa suffer from limited areas for expansion and development. Some of the cities, such as Lagos, Dakar, Conakry, Monrovia, and Durban, are restricted to island or peninsular sites. Cape Town, Freetown, Addis Ababa, and Nairobi are among towns that are handicapped by mountain barriers, hilly sites, or historical background. Others, such as Khartoum and Banjul, which are sited on flat areas and flood plains, have drainage problems. Most large cities, particularly those in the Guinea coastal region, continue to reflect a maritime orientation located at the margins of the hinterland of their respective nations. With the increasing importance of cities in the interior—such as Bouaké in Ivory Coast (Côte d'Ivoire on map, p. 292), Kumasi in Ghana, Kano and Abuja in Nigeria, and Yaoundé in Cameroon—the situation of the present maritime bias may be rectified. In West Africa, two countries have moved their capitals from the coast to more central locations. Nigeria's capital is now Abuja, while the official capital of Ivory Coast is now Yamoussoukro. Generally, the maritime orientation of urban development, transport and communication infrastructure, industrial development, and market function continue to dominate.

Rural-to-Urban Migration

Between 50% and 60% of the urban growth in SSA comes from rural-to-urban migration. This migration is one of the most crucial problems facing African governments at present. A massive flow of people into the few urban centers that became the locus of power and investment, particularly in the period following decolonization of the continent, has strained the carrying capacity of most urban centers. Concern about the rate of SSA urbanization would hardly seem justifiable, considering the very high magnitude of its rural population. However, the urban growth pattern, often dominated by the primate city and the high rate of growth of such centers, is far beyond the capabilities of the urban socioeconomic system to generate the needed employment opportunities, housing, and social services (fig. 8.16). As a consequence, the primate city has become, in most instances, a liability to the overall development process.

The paradoxical fact that rural-urban migration continues to grow in spite of rising unemployment in urban centers of LDCs has given rise to a migration theory based on rural-urban income differentials. This theory assumes that migration is "primarily an economic phenomenon" and that the potential migrant makes a calculated move in order to realize much higher "expected" earnings with varying probabilities. Whether in fact the current massive rural-urban migration is caused primarily by economic phenomena related to rural-urban income differences might be open to debate. However, the fact remains that the SSA primate city is a major factor in the contradictions between urban and rural life. Because of its monopoly of economic opportunities and political power, the city has created a perception on the part of rural-urban migrants of certain and immediate opportunities for socioeconomic improvement, a perception that is rarely realized. The growth of shantytowns and squatter settlements and the proliferation of informal employment in the city are the result of this miscalculation (box 8.2).

Figure 8.16 In Mombasa, Kenya's port city, hundreds of workers in this government-supported enterprise carve wooden handicrafts for tourist markets. These kinds of enterprises help to create badly needed jobs in today's African metropolises. (Photo by Jack Williams)

Functional Concentration

Ethnic background, culture, occupational characteristics, residential stability, and overall standards of living differentiate the inhabitants of most African cities. There is some resemblance between African cities and those of the industrialized countries, but the resemblance is limited to the physical structure of the domain of the African and expatriate elite who have surrounded themselves with the trappings of a modern environment. The difference lies in the existence, within the same municipal boundary, of a highly marginalized population that is poor and finds itself in a condition of subservience to the more privileged social classes in the modern system. As a result of this condition, the African city exhibits in microcosm the disparity that exists between the city (core) and the countryside (periphery) as a whole. The system portrays two enclaves operating within the African city, one composed of the urban elite and having strong functional linkages with the international system, with the other composed of poorer masses who maintain stronger economic, political, and social affinity with the rural population of the country or with the vast

Box 8.2 HIV/AIDS and Urban Development

In the past 20 years, a new scourge has appeared in Sub-Saharan Africa that is creating havoc among already weak and struggling nations. HIV/AIDS is a worldwide threat, but is particularly concentrated in SSA. Moreover, it is in the growing cities of this realm that one finds the greatest impact of this disease, which threatens to make even worse the many problems plaguing these countries and their cities, as detailed in this chapter. Cities, by their very nature of concentrating large numbers of people in small areas, increase the speed of transmission of HIV.

By the end of the 1990s, SSA accounted for 70%, or 24 million, of HIV infections in the world and more than 80%, or 13 million, of AIDS deaths. The hardest hit countries in 2000, in terms of percent infection among ages 15–49, were (in descending order): Botswana (36%), Swaziland (25%), Zimbabwe (25%), Lesotho (24%), South Africa (20%), Zambia (20%), Namibia (20%), Malawi (16%), and Kenya (14%). These numbers are concentrated in the southern part of the continent, but most countries in SSA are affected to some degree. In many of these countries, the rate of infection among pregnant women is even higher, with ranges of 25–50%.

Why such a disproportionate share in this already beleaguered part of the world? The reasons are many:

- Governments in SSA have been in denial, refusing to recognize the existence or severity of the threat.
- The health-care system, including availability of effective drugs and blood-screening procedures, is woefully inadequate to the challenge.
- Widespread poverty and ignorance make it extremely difficult to educate people about the dangers and how to prevent infection.
- There are large numbers of people in high-risk groups (sexually active workers, sex-industry workers, migrants, military personnel, truck drivers, drug users who share needles).
- Male-dominated societies put women at particularly high risk.

and complicated informal sector that has evolved within the city (fig. 8.17). From the viewpoint of the urban masses, the crucial problem that militates against an integrated development is the fact that the African formal sector has been unable to disengage its political, economic, and cultural links with the outside world and turn its face toward its own people and make modern urbanization work for them. There is little chance for those people in the informal sector to make the transition to the modern and more prosperous sector. Modern technology, which is relatively accessible for those in the formal sector, is virtually unreachable to the inhabitants of the informal sector.

POLICY IMPLICATIONS

Solutions to the current urban problems imply policies whose impacts should go beyond the confines of the SSA city. One of the chief factors

The disease mostly affects adults in their early productive years, thus directly impacting development of social capital and creating large numbers of orphans. This witches' brew obviously makes it even harder for SSA nations to attract foreign investment and turn the tide economically. Some nations that have among the highest incidence thus are caught in a downward spiral that eventually could result in depopulation, economic decline, and political collapse.

There are glimmers of hope, nonetheless, in various parts of SSA, where initiatives of a wide variety are making some progress, often in localized areas. In Uganda, for example, the government supports awareness programs through the media and schools. South Africa was in complete denial for a number of years, but has finally faced the facts and begun public education programs, too. A good example there of a local group that seeks to educate the public is a group in Cape Town called Wola Nani (wolanani@Africa.com). This group airs radio announcements in the various languages of South Africa and provides counseling, home care, workshops, training for those living with someone infected with HIV, community AIDS education, and other activities. Certainly just creating public awareness of the threat and then educating people how to avoid infection are critical first steps. But these are just beginning in SSA—some of the countries have not even started—and time is running out. Most of the millions already infected are probably doomed to an early death, since there is little likelihood the health-care system can ever properly take care of more than a fraction of them.

From an urban development standpoint, this may well mean that some cities in SSA will stop growing, and even decline, in population in coming years. Declining economies and political/social instability in the cities might well discourage people from migrating to the cities, thus slowing or even reversing the current trend of increased urbanization. SSA thus might be the one region of the world in the 21st century to deviate significantly from the trends observable in cities of most other developing realms.

inhibiting economic growth and developmental urbanization is the balkanization of the continent into economically feeble markets that, under existing conditions, can hardly hope to evolve into viable economies in the foreseeable future. To make matters worse, most African nations also operate under conditions in which political boundaries act as socioeconomic sheds across which virtually no trade, migration, or diffusion of ideas take place. This stands in the way of economies of scale, which would be essential for common-market-based industrial development. Instead, most significant flows in this insular spatial economy gravitate toward the primate city. To solve this dysfunctional situation, a system of subregional interaction and common-market arrangements should be seriously considered in the long run. Although most African nations seem rigid about yielding any part of their sovereignty, a lasting solution to the problems of economic insularity can be effectively achieved only by encouraging direct links between the economic core areas of the African nations, at least on a subregional basis.

Figure 8.17 In this open-air market in downtown Cape Town, merchants sell every conceivable commodity to locals and tourists, evidence of post-apartheid South Africa's more open economy and society. (Photo by Jack Williams)

This not only would bring about all of the advantages of coalesced markets, but also would help to restructure the spatial orientation of the economy by integrating "peripheral" areas into the economy. The current deliberation among African leaders once again to revive notions of African integration and common markets is progressive.

The problem of primate-city dominance can also be abated by sound internal regional development policies that would introduce measures for improving the flow of development investment and infrastructural development. Development poles, satellite towns, and rural service centers can be identified from the existing system of central places and made to receive higher shares of the development investment than has been the case up to now. The new system of investment and settlement planning should aim at making the primate city yield those services and activities that can be effectively handled by smaller and more accessible centers. The development of appropriate surface transport networks would make this transition possible. Improving road connectivity between selected lower-order central places and supplying the rural population with alternative accessible centers for urban functions would have a significant impact in reducing the excessive gravitation toward the primate city.

A focus on rural development has taken hold in many African countries. Although results are not dramatic, experience indicates that increased commitment in this area could have a significant impact on the transformation of urban-rural relations. If planned and executed in a more integrated fashion, rural development based on the productive potentials of agriculture and natural resources can help redress existing rural-urban disparities and also alter the present trade and resource transfer relations whose terms of exchange favor the primate cities and other major urban centers in each country. A rural development strategy not only could bring about improvement in rural productivity and hence opportunities for better levels of living, but also enable a more equitable distribution of development benefits.

The solution to the current state does not lie in the frequent self-righteous pronouncements that come from the leadership in Africa for selflessness and sacrifice on the part of a segment of the educated population. To use coercion by dispatching people to serve in outlying areas or to try to stem the tide of rural-urban migration by any other forceful means is counterproductive. The only viable option is to make outlying areas more attractive to live and work in. Smaller towns and rural centers must be made to acquire competitive conditions of income and amenities so that they can attract people on their own merit. The willingness to work outside the primate city must be dealt with in a spatial fashion by effecting adjustments in income and provision of social services. Few SSA countries can afford a large-scale decentralization policy involving many towns. However, a concerted effort to restructure the spatial organization of the socioeconomic system, which is now dominated by the primate city, should be a major goal for development planning for many years to come.

SUGGESTED READINGS

Bernstein, Ann. *Cities and the Global Economy: New Challenges for South Africa.* Johannesburg: Centre for Development and Enterprise, 1996. A brief study of South Africa's attempts to transform its previously segregated and unequal cities in the light of a changing world economy and South Africa's role in a global marketplace.

Bond, Patrick. *Cities of Gold, Townships of Coal: Essays on South Africa's New Urban Crisis.* Trenton, N.J.: Africa World Press, 1999. A collection of political economy articles from the 1990s about the uneven development of South Africa's cities and black townships and the struggle to correct these imbalances in the post-apartheid era.

Hance, William A. *Population, Migration, and Urbanization in Africa.* New York: Columbia University Press, 1970. Perhaps one of the best readings available on the general character of African urban systems, their problems, and possible solutions. It also has a section giving profiles of some African cities.

Herskovits, Melville J. *The Human Factor in Changing Africa.* New York: Knopf, 1962. A seminal work on the history of African cultures that provides excellent background on development in SSA. The chapter on culture regions focuses on regional differences in urban structure.

Hull, Richard W. *African Cities and Towns before the European Conquest.* New York: Norton, 1976. An excellent summary of the background of major urban regions that had been investigated to this date.

Miner, Horace, ed. *The City in Modern Africa.* New York: Praeger, 1967. Various authors discuss a number of problems of African urbanization. The chapters on processes of modernization and size classification are particularly interesting.

Pedersen, Poul O. *Small African Towns: Between Rural Networks and Urban Hierarchies.* Brookfield, Ill.: Avebury, 1997.

Simon, David D. *Cities, Capital and Development: African Cities in the World Economy.* New York: Halstead, 1992. An analysis of the essence of African cities, especially primate cities, from a political economy viewpoint.

Tarver, James D., ed. *Urbanization in Africa: A Handbook.* Westport, Conn.: Greenwood,

1994. An examination of Africa's urban experience, with some chapters on the history of urbanization, fourteen chapters on selected African countries, and several chapters on special topics such as HIV/AIDS and urbanization.

Tomlinson, Richard. *Urban Development Planning: Lessons for the Economic Restructuring of South Africa's Cities.* Johannesburg: Witwatersrand University Press, 1994. One of the first urban planning perspectives on how to rebuild South Africa's cities and economies in the post-apartheid era.

Tostensen, Arne, Inge Tvedten, and Mariken Vaa, eds. *Associational Life in African Cities: Popular Responses to the Urban Crisis.* Uppsala, Sweden: Nordiska Afrikaininstitutet, 2001. A collection of seventeen case studies of various parts of Africa on aspects of urban life, including informal networks, religion and identity, land and housing, infrastructure and services, and community initiatives.

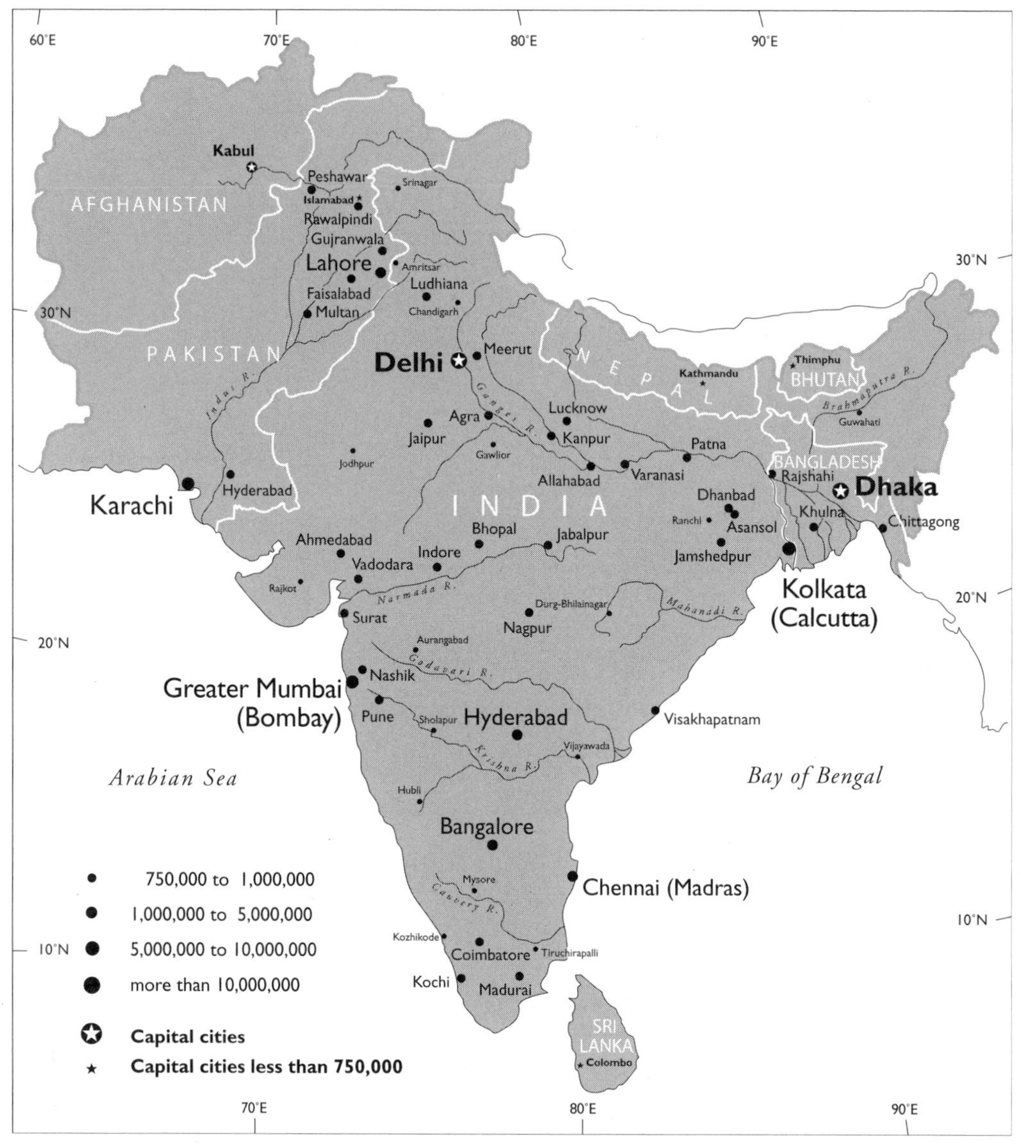

Figure 9.1 Major Cities of South Asia. *Source*: Data from United Nations, *World Urbanization Prospects, 2001 Revision* (New York: United Nations Population Division, 2002), www.unpopulation.org.

9

Cities of South Asia

ASHOK K. DUTT AND GEORGE M. POMEROY

KEY URBAN FACTS

Total Population	1.378 billion
Percent Urban Population	28%
Total Urban Population	382 million
Most Urbanized Country	Pakistan (33%)
Least Urbanized Country	Bhutan (7%)
Annual Urban Growth Rate	4.1%
Number of Megacities	5
Number of Cities of More Than 1 Million	45
Three Largest Cities	Mumbai, Kolkata, Dhaka
World Cities	None

KEY CHAPTER THEMES

1. True primate systems characterize all countries in South Asia, except India.
2. There are three basic types of cities: traditional, colonial, and planned.
3. There have been five major influences on the development of cities: the Indus Valley civilization, the Aryan Hindus, the Dravidians, the Muslims, and the Europeans.
4. The current urban system most distinctly reflects the presidency towns of the colonial era.
5. The urban form of the cities is reflected in two basic models: the colonial-based city model and the bazaar-based city model, with permutations of both.
6. India's urban system is relatively well balanced in terms of rank-size profile and urban primacy, compared with the other countries of the region.
7. Massive rural-to-urban migration in recent decades has led to exploding urban populations and overwhelmed urban systems.
8. Civil wars and political instability have been major contributing factors to the destabilization of urban areas over the decades, most recently in Sri Lanka and Afghanistan.
9. Planned cities and new towns have played an important but subsidiary role in the region for a long time, with Islamabad (Pakistan) and Chandigarh (India) as notable recent examples.

10. The cities' huge problems today reflect the region's limited integration into the modern global economy.

South Asian cities are often portrayed as overcrowded, overgrown, and underfunded, with seemingly insurmountable problems of inadequate shelter, lack of clean water, overwhelmed infrastructure, filthy air, and unemployment and underemployment. Indeed, these cities do exhibit among the worst urban conditions and problems to be found anywhere in the world. Such conditions, combined with inadequate resources, contribute to a feeling of despair and hopelessness for those confronting urban issues. Kolkata (formerly Calcutta), India, more than any other city, is often regarded as the epitome of such despair and hopelessness.

Yet, it is within these same cities that one finds hope and opportunity—more hope in fact than the small flicker that is reflected in the French author Dominique LaPierre's Kolkata-based novel *City of Joy.* While the stereotypes described above contain degrees of truth, the cities of South Asia are beacons of hope that attract hundreds of millions of people from across the subcontinent and serve as powerful engines of social and economic change. Furthermore, South Asia's vibrant mosaic of diversity is well reflected in its urban centers. The megacities of South Asia, the most cosmopolitan of which is Mumbai (formerly Bombay), draw migrants from throughout their hinterlands, transforming these cities into exciting kaleidoscopes of language, faith, and ethnicity (fig. 9.1).

South Asia may be among the world's most populous regions, but with only 28% of its population living in cities, it is not among the most urbanized. Because of its gargantuan size relative to the other countries in the region, India in large part determines this average; in fact, its proportion urban is nearly the same as the regional percentage. While the levels of urbanization are changing only incrementally, the absolute numbers certainly are not. Above an urban base for South Asia of 72 million in 1950, an additional 310 million people live in urban areas today, equaling approximately the entire population of the United States and Canada combined. What surprises many is that these numbers pale in comparison to the projected number of urban dwellers in 2030—913 million—which is an increase of more than a half billion over the present figure. The largest numbers belong to India, where in the past fifty years, 225 million have been added to the 62 million previously residing in the cities. The figure is expected to rise by 348 million in the next three decades. Next largest in absolute numbers of urbanites are Pakistan, with 58 million of its 156 million residing in urban areas, and Bangladesh, with 27 million in its cities.

A large number of major cities, and a good share of the world's megacities, also characterize the region. Although cities at all levels of the urban hierarchy are growing, there are now forty-five urban agglomerations that have passed the million mark and more than 370 other agglomerations of greater than 100,000 population. Karachi, Delhi, and Dhaka are the 13th, 14th, and 15th largest, respectively, in the world. Kolkata is the 9th largest urban agglomeration and Mumbai is the 3d largest, trailing only Tokyo and Mexico City. Mumbai is expected to overtake the latter in the next ten years to become the planet's second-largest urban center, with a projected population of 26 million in 2015—comparable to the New York and Chicago metropolitan areas combined. It is projected that Dhaka and Karachi will also climb in the rankings to 5th and 6th places, respectively. Two other cities, Hyderabad (India) and Lahore (Pakistan), will join the megacity club by 2015. Several individual cities have seen remarkable growth. In India, cities within urban corridors, such as Thane (in the Mumbai metropolitan region), experienced annual growth rates of 6% through most of the 1990s. As with many other world regions, rural-urban migration continues to form a large component of urban population growth in South Asia.

Except in India, urban primacy characterizes the urban systems of all countries in South Asia. For India, three cities each in the north and south of the country stand out. In the north, Mumbai, Delhi, and Kolkata anchor the points of a rough geographical triangle. A similar hierarchy exists in the south, with Hyderabad, Bangalore, and Chennai (formerly Madras) forming the points on the triangle. These six cities together make up a very large chunk (21%) of India's urban population. For Pakistan, one in five urban dwellers lives in Karachi, which is nearly double the size of the largest secondary city, Lahore. For each of the remaining four countries, the largest city also serves as the national capital. Dhaka, with 40% of all urban dwellers in Bangladesh, is quadruple the size of Chittagong, the second-largest city. For both of the next two largest countries, Afghanistan and Sri Lanka, the largest cities, Kabul and Colombo, respectively, serve as administrative centers for national governments that have difficulty maintaining full control over their nation's territories. Kabul once had slightly less than half of Afghanistan's urban population, but Taliban rule in the 1990s and the subsequent U.S.-led antiterrorism war, beginning in 2001, left the urban situation in that country very unstable. Colombo has nearly one quarter of Sri Lanka's urban population, but the ongoing civil war there contributes to an unstable urban situation in that country also. Kathmandu's share of Nepal's urban population has recently declined to 23%, while tiny Thimphu's 22,000 residents are 19% of Bhutan's urban population.

South Asian cities may be divided into three basic types: traditional cities, colonial cities, and planned cities. Traditional cities are those that were part of a thriving urban system prior to Western colonialism, whether as centers of trade and commerce, centers of administration, or religious pilgrimage destinations. Cities have been a part of the cultural landscape of South Asia for about 5,000 years, with the Indus Valley system serving as one of several urban hearths. Many traditional cities, including Delhi, flourished with colonization, as Western mercantile capitalist activities became commonplace and in some cases eventually overwhelmed, or at least came to dominate, traditional activities. Others stagnated as the colonial mercantile trade activities and networks bypassed them. Traditional cities were often distinguished as trade centers, such as Surat on India's west coast, or as centers of religious pilgrimage, such as Varanasi, which is on the banks of the revered Ganges River.

Several of the region's largest cities, most notably Mumbai, Kolkata, and Chennai, were products of British colonialism, thus making them of the second type of South Asian city. In the postindependence period, the various traditional and colonial cities have evolved further into commercial/industrial cities, to serve the expanding economies and national development plans of the region.

The third basic urban type is the planned new city, which consists of two kinds: one group designated as political and administrative centers, such as Islamabad in Pakistan and Chandigarh in India, the other intended as industrial centers for steel and related heavy industrial activities. The latter cities include Durgapur in West Bengal and Jamshedpur in Bihar, both in India.

EVOLUTION OF CITIES

The cultural, linguistic, and religious diversity, and in turn the urban fabric, of South Asia are derived from five distinct influences. Chronologically these are (1) the Indus Valley civilization, 3000 to 1500 B.C.; (2) the Aryan Hindus, since 1500 B.C.; (3) the Dravidians, since about 200 B.C.; (4) the Muslims, since the 8th century; and (5) the Europeans, since the 15th century.

The Indus Valley Era

The Indus Valley is among the world's oldest urban hearths. The preeminent cities of the Indus Valley civilization, Mohenjo Daro and Harappa in what is now Pakistan, were established as planned communities as early as 3000 B.C. They flourished for about 1,500 years and were the largest urban centers of an extensive settlement system that included at least three other urban centers and perhaps more than 900 smaller centers. First excavated in 1921, the ruins of Mohenjo Daro reveal a carefully constructed city reflective of a highly organized and complex society. No other city outside the Indus civilization possessed such an elaborate system of drainage and sanitation, which signified a generally high standard of civilization. This urban civilization came to an end around 1500 B.C., when the newly arrived Aryans—less civilized but more adept in warfare than the Indus people—overpowered the Indus civilization and turned the northern part of the South Asian realm into a mixture of pastoralism and sedentary agriculture. With the collapse of Mohenjo Daro, the realm entered a dark age lasting approximately a thousand years.

The Aryan Hindu Impact

Eventually the demands of trade, commerce, administration, and fortification gave rise to the establishment of sizable urban centers, particularly in the middle Ganges Plains. Originating from a modest 5th-century fort, Pataliputra developed into the capital of a notable Indian empire, the Maurya (321–181 B.C.). Its location coincides with that of modern Patna. Pataliputra possessed the urban forms of a capital city of the Aryans. The city was organized to conform to the functional requirements of the capital of a Hindu kingdom: residential patterns based on the function-based, four-caste social system, along with the requisite royal administrative features.

While caste is not as important in determining contemporary residential patterns in cities as it was in Pataliputra, it is still socially significant today. Caste, the designation of social status by birth, places a person into one of four broad-groups—*Brahmins, Kshatriyas, Vaisyas,* and *Sudras.* The Untouchables, lowest among the Sudras, are deemed so because the touch or even the shadow cast by one could pollute someone of higher caste. Traditionally, each caste and its subcastes has certain designated occupations. Brahmins (the priest caste) are at the top, followed by Kshatriyas (the warrior caste), Vaisyas (the commercial and agricultural caste), and Sudras (the manual labor caste). Caste still plays a major role in society. Marriages are generally within caste and broad connections can be made between caste status and income, quality of life, and social connections. This is true even after years of legal reforms such as a reservation system (similar to affirmative action in the United States) and broader social campaigns led by leaders such as Gandhi. The caste system also is still reflected in urban land-use patterns and socioeconomic structures.

In Pataliputra, one could clearly see the spatial distribution of castes. Near the center and a little toward the east were the temple and residences of high-ranking Brahmins and ministers of the royal cabinet. Farther toward the east were the Kshatriyas and the rich merchants and expert artisans of the Vaisya. To the south were other Vaisyas, including government superintendents, prostitutes, musicians. To the west were the Sudras, including Untouchables, along with ordinary artisans and low-grade Vaisyas. Finally, to the north were artisans, Brahmins, and temples maintained for the titular deity of the city. A well-organized city government, hierarchical street system, and elaborate drainage system accompanied this functional distribution of population in Pataliputra. With the eclipse of the Maurya Empire in the 2d century B.C., the Gupta Empire (320–467) made Pataliputra its capital, but the city lost its importance thereafter and was eventually buried under the sediments of the Ganges and Son rivers. Only small parts of the old city have recently been excavated. Other Hindu capitals that developed in both North and South India changed and modified the many urban forms used in Pataliputra.

Dravidian Temple Cities

In contrast to the North, Hindu kingdoms in South India had relative control for most of the historical period; distinctly Hindu forms of city development evolved uninterruptedly, minimizing Muslim influences. The rulers of South India constructed temples and water tanks as nuclei of habitation. Around the temples grew commercial bazaars and settlements of Brahmin priests and scholars. The ruler often built a palace near the temple, turning the temple city into the capital of his kingdom; examples are Madurai and Kancheepuram, both of which remain important pilgrimage centers today (fig. 9.2). The loftiness and the grandeur of the temples imparted to the subjects a sense of protection by the Almighty. Thus, the kingdom was endowed with celestial favor, the king wielded power derived from Him, and a god-king concept was woven into the city design. Such city forms were exported to Southeast Asia, where they were further elaborated and modified; Angkor Wat (A.D. 802–1432) in Cambodia is one example.

Mentioned by Ptolemy, Madurai, the second capital of the South Indian Hindu kingdom of Pandyas, dates back to about the beginning of the Christian era. The geographical advantage of the city was its situation by the side of the river Vaigai, which provided a natural defense. The major evolution of Madurai's cultural landscape dates to the 16th century, when it became the capital of a Hindu Nayak dynasty. Though Madurai is now several times the size of the old walled city, with imprints from a brief Islamic period and a longer British dominance, its religious importance is nearly comparable to that of the North Indian city of Varanasi, which is the foremost pilgrimage center, followed by Tirupati (box 9.1)

The Muslim Impact: Shahjahanabad (Delhi)

The first permanent Muslim occupation that significantly influenced the realm began in the

Figure 9.2 A Hindu temple in the major pilgrimage city of Madurai in South India. (Photo by Paul Karan)

11th century A.D. and resulted in the adding of many Middle Eastern and Central Asian Islamic qualities to the urban landscape of South Asia. Shahjahanabad is a particularly good example of Muslim impact. The Moghul emperor Shah Jahan, who planned the Taj Mahal in Agra as a tomb for his wife, moved his capital from Agra to Delhi and started the construction of a new city, Shahjahanabad, on the right bank of the Yamuna River. The city was built near the sites of several previous capital cities and took nearly a decade to complete (1638 to 1648). Its architecture was a fusion of Islamic and Hindu influences. Though the royal palace and mosques, with their arched vaults and domes, adhered to Muslim styles, Hindu styles were found in combination. The Muslim rulers were most concerned with the magnificence of their royal residences and courts, massiveness of their fortresses, and typical Islamic loftiness in the design of their mosques. These features were represented most vividly in Shahjahanabad. Surrounded by brick walls and without a moat, the city was completely fortified. Moreover, many settlements, including the extensive remains of the earlier city, were sprawled out in four different suburbs, all outside the walls.

Box 9.1 A Visit to the Pilgrimage City of Tirupati

George Pomeroy

As our vehicle wended its way through a number of hairpin turns to the top of the escarpment, I could sense immediately that we would be arriving in a different type of city. The road traffic was less varied, consisting mostly of buses, and the road was lined with occasional flowers, as well as warning signs about oncoming traffic and sharp turns. As we made our way to the 3,500-foot elevation, the temperature cooled and one could view the surrounding green slopes of the Eastern Ghats ranges, as well as occasionally glimpse the town from which we had embarked. As we neared the end of the road, the path took on a different character. Long stretches of it were sheltered and sometimes the road was lined with fencing. This was the "queue" that I had heard of. During peak season, people will line up for twelve hours or more to enter the pilgrimage city of Tirupati.

Located in the state of Andhra Pradesh, Tirupati is the home of the 1,200-year-old Sri Venkateshwara Temple and is second in India only to Varanasi in the number of pilgrims who travel there, which sometimes exceeds 100,000 persons daily. The astounding number of pilgrims has generated the development of a city unto itself, complete with numerous guest houses, restaurants, vendors, and of course, the temple, subtemples, and accessory features. There is even a building, several stories in height, specially built to hold the "queue" during the peak pilgrimage periods. The temple is one of only a few in India that allows non-Hindus to enter its inner chambers. Those who pay a special *darshan* (a premium offering or donation) can be expedited to the front of the line, instead of waiting many hours to enter the temple. A nearby building is made conspicuous by the shaven heads of men, women, and children emerging from it. Having one's head shaved, a practice called *tonsuring,* is considered auspicious by those visiting Tirupati.

The guesthouses are scattered throughout the carefully planned and highly organized city complex. Some cater to the wealthy, others to those with more modest incomes. There is even a special guesthouse that dignitaries, such as the president of India, visit on occasion. The entire area is beautifully landscaped. With our visit occurring in the quietest part of the pilgrim calendar, the entire city seemed peaceful and bucolic, which is in stark contrast to most South Asian cities and seemed especially so given that we had been in the bustling city of Chennai earlier that day.

There are numerous pilgrimage cities throughout India. Some, especially Varanasi, are better known in the West. Most venerate either Shiva or Vishnu. Tirupati is devoted to the latter. The city's municipal governance is unique in being managed by a special board of trustees as a religious community, as opposed to a secular one. What makes Tirupati most remarkable, however, is that it is the richest temple city in all of India, generating billions of rupees in donations, all of which is reinvested back into the *choultries,* or pilgrim's accommodations, or nobly used to fund orphanages, homes for the poor, and craft-training and education programs.

Figure 9.3 The Red Fort is a central feature and popular tourist site in Old Delhi. (Photo by Jack Williams)

Planned as a parallelogram with massive red sandstone walls and ditches on all sides except the side by the river, the fortress (Red Fort) had an almost foolproof defense. It was situated at the eastern end of the walled city. Inside the fortress were a magnificent court, king's private palace, gardens, and music pavilion, all built of either red sandstone or white marble in the exquisite designs of Moghul architecture. The Red Fort remains a central feature of Delhi today, as it often serves as platform or backdrop for political proclamations and is a well-known tourist destination (fig. 9.3).

The two main thoroughfares, which connected the city with the fortress and the outside world, were lined with merchant shops. One of these thoroughfares, Chandni Chowk ("silver market"), ran straight westward from the Red Fort toward the Lahore Gate of the city. The Chandni Chowk was one of the great bazaars of the Orient. The other thoroughfare, Khas Road, a shopping area of lesser importance, was built a little to the east of the Great Jama Mosque, largest and most famous of all the mosques in South Asia.

Shahjahanabad ceased to be the capital of India, more precisely North India, when British rule started in the 18th century, but it continued to be a functional city. Today, the area is known as Old Delhi and it is part of the Delhi metropolis. Most of the city walls are gone, though all the basic structures of the Red Fort and Jama Mosque remain intact. Chandni Chowk continues to be a traditional, busy bazaar where motorized vehicles are prohibited. It is very densely populated with a mixture of Hindus and Muslims. Large parts of Old Delhi are gradually being transformed into commercial and small workshop uses.

The Colonial Period

After Vasco de Gama discovered the oceanic route to the east via the Cape of Good Hope and landed on the southwestern coast of India in 1498, the Western colonial powers of Portugal, Holland, Britain, and France became greatly interested in developing a firm trade connection with South Asia. Though initially all four powers obtained some kind of footing in India, the sagacious diplomacy and "divide-and-rule" policy of the British succeeded in ousting the other Europeans from most Indian soil. Eventually, the British established three significant centers of operation—Bombay, Madras, and Calcutta. In the 1990s, each was renamed to reflect indigenous cultures and further downplay India's colonial heritage.

The British needed a firm footing in seaports for the convenience of trading and for receiving military reinforcements from the parent country. Kolkata, Mumbai, and Chennai were the seaports. Hence, these three cities were designed as the headquarters for the three different presidencies into which the British divided South Asia for administrative purposes. Consequently, the cities are referred to as the "presidency towns."

The Presidency Towns

When Mumbai, Chennai, and Kolkata were established as presidency towns, their nuclei were forts. Outside these forts were the cities. Inside the cities, two different standards of living were set for two different groups of residents, the Europeans and the "natives," each of whom occupied their own part of the city (see "The Colonial-Based City Model," next page). The rich comprised the absentee landowners from rural areas, moneylenders, businesspeople, and the newly English-educated Indian elite and clerks. The poor comprised servants, manual laborers, street cleaners, and porters. The rich needed the service of the poor and, therefore, the houses of the native rich in many instances stood by the houses of their poor servicing people.

As local industries grew in the 19th century, a new working class developed. In Kolkata, the industrial workers worked mainly in jute mills and local engineering factories; in Mumbai, they worked in the expanding cotton and textile-related industries; and in Chennai, they worked in tanning and cotton textiles. As these trades grew, the presidency towns turned from water to rail and roads for inland transportation. Train services were started in South Asia in 1852. The presidency towns also developed huge hinterlands that catered to the needs of the colonial economy. The hinterlands supplied the raw materials to the three seaports for export to the United Kingdom; in return, the British sent consumer-type manufactured goods through the same ports. Thus, the presidency towns became the main foci of the colonial mercantile system.

Accompanying the new technology, such as railways, were new forms of architecture, particularly the expanding use of the Western Gothic and Victorian styles, often combined with South Asian motifs (fig. 9.4). The public buildings of the presidency towns, such as railroad terminals, post offices, the governor's house, high courts, the central and provincial secretariats, the museums and educational institutions, were built in these designs. One of the best examples of the use of these architectural styles in combination with some Indian forms is the Victoria Memorial Building (built 1906–1921) in Kolkata. The building was done in white marble with European designs and the architects originally intended it to surpass the Taj Mahal in massive grandeur.

Figure 9.4 The "Gateway of India" was built in 1911 on Mumbai's harbor shore to commemorate the landing of King George V. The arch remains a distinctive symbol of India's largest city. (Photo by Ashok Dutt)

MODELS OF SOUTH ASIAN CITY STRUCTURE

The search for models to explain South Asian cities has prompted some theorists to apply mechanically the Western concentric zone theory of Burgess and to prepare all-purpose models, irrespective of their applicability. No comprehensive model explaining the growth pattern of the indigenous city structure has yet been suggested. But it is important to note that two principal forces, colonial and traditional, have acted in creating the existing forms of South Asian cities.

The Colonial-Based City Model

The colonial city patterns in South Asia parallel those found in other world regions, but the Indian subcontinent presents a specific and hybrid model, being neither Western nor Indian nor the same as in other world regions. The need to perform colonial functions demanded a particular form of city growth relevant to the subcontinent (fig. 9.5) that produced the regional characteristics:

1. The need for trade and military reinforcements required a waterfront location accessible to oceangoing ships because the colonial power operated from Europe. A minimal port facility was a prerequisite and was the starting point of the city. Thus, coastal locations became the main attractions for the colonial city site.
2. A walled fort was constructed adjacent to the port with fortifications, white soldiers' and officers' barracks, a small church, and educational institutions. Sometimes located inside the fort, factories processed agricultural raw materials to be shipped to the mother country.

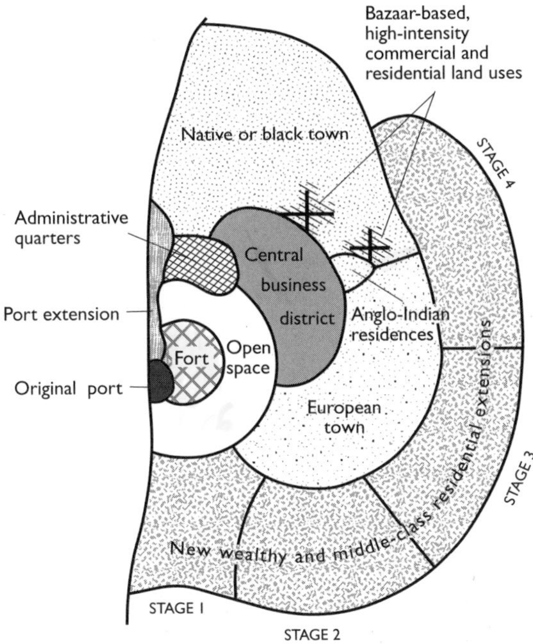

Figure 9.5 A Model for the Internal Structure of a Colonial-Based City in South Asia. *Source*: Ashok Dutt

Thus, the fort became not only a military outpost but also the nucleus of the colonial exchange.

3. Beyond the fort and the open area, a "native town" (a town for the native peoples) eventually developed, characterized by overcrowding, unsanitary conditions, and unplanned settlements; it serviced the fort and the colonial administration, as the CBD and further administrative activities developed near the fort and the native town.
4. A western-style CBD grew adjacent to the fort and native town, with a high concentration of mercantile office functions, retail trade, and a low density of residential houses; the administrative quarters consisted of the governor's (or viceroy's) house, the main government office, the high court, and the general post office. In the CBD, there also were Western-style hotels, churches, banks, and museums as well as occasional statues of British sovereigns, viceroys, and other dignitaries, reminiscent of royal eternity, at important road intersections (fig. 9.6).
5. The European town grew in a different area or direction from the native town. It had spacious bungalows, elegant apartment houses, planned streets with trees on both sides, and a generally European look; clubs for afternoon and evening get-togethers and with European indoor and outdoor recreation facilities; churches of different denominations; and garden-like graveyards.

6. Between the fort and the European town, or at some appropriate nearby location, an extensive open space *(maidan)* was reserved for military parades and facilities for Western recreation, such as races, golf, soccer, and cricket. The racecourse opened on Saturday afternoons, when the whites and a few moneyed native people frequented the track to gamble.
7. When a domestic water supply, electric connections, and sewage links were available or technically possible, the European town residents utilized them fully, whereas their use was quite limited in the native town.
8. At an intermediate location between "black towns" (or native sections) and "white towns" (European areas) developed the colonies of the Anglo-Indians, who were the offspring of mixed marriages (European and Indian) and were Christians; they were never fully accepted by either the natives or the European community.
9. Starting in the late 19th century, the colonial city became so large that new living space was necessary, especially for the native elite. Extensions to the city were made by reclaiming the lowland or developing the existing nonurban area in a semiplanned manner and in stages.
10. From the very inception of such colonial cities, the population density was very low at the center, which housed the Europeans, while a much larger group of "natives" lived outside the colonial center. When the European center was gradually replaced by a Western-style CBD during the second half of the 19th century, there was a further decline in the population of the center, giving rise to a density gradient with a "crater effect" at the center. Though the crater effect is typically a Western large-city feature, it existed in colonial-based cities of the developing countries right from their inception.

As the colonial system became deeply entrenched in the Indian subcontinent and an extensive railway network was made operational, the waterfront locations accessible to oceangoing ships were no longer a prerequisite for a colonial headquarters. Kolkata, Mumbai, Chennai, and Colombo were not the only suitable locations on the subcontinent for high levels of administration. Hence, in 1911, the capital of British India was moved to the inland city of Delhi, which was not a seaport. Thus, a new inland colonial city was implanted by the side of Old Delhi. It was designated New Delhi.

Three other lesser (but widespread) colonial urban forms (cantonment, railway colony, and hill station), were also introduced to the subcontinent to serve very specific purposes.

Cantonments

These were military encampments, numbering some 114 in all by the mid-19th century and housing a quarter of a million soldiers, both European and native. Strict segregation by class and ethnicity was practiced in these encampments.

Railway Colonies

These surrounded a railroad station of a regional headquarters for railway operation and administration and also imposed strict segregation in their design. Often situated near urban centers, railroad colonies eventu-

Figure 9.6 One of the first buildings constructed (1889) in Allahabad University is typical of British colonial structures, with a melding of Gothic and Indian architectural styles. (Photo by Ashok Dutt)

ally formed part of the greater urban area. These colonies were innumerable; wherever the railroad went, they followed.

Hill Stations

These stations, at altitudes between 3,500 and 8,000 ft (1,067 to 2,440 m) served as resort towns for Europeans seeking to escape hot summers on the plains and spend time in the midst of a more exclusive European community. There were 80 such stations, such as Simla and Darjeeling, by the time of independence (fig. 9.7). The Europeans transplanted all the class distinctions and characteristics of the lowland cities to these smaller centers in the hills and mountains.

The Bazaar-Based City Model

The traditional bazaar city is widespread in South Asia and has certain features that date back to precolonial times. Ordinarily, the city has grown around a trade function originating from agricultural exchange, temple location, the city's existence as a transport node, or various administrative activities (fig. 9.8). Usually, at the main crossroads a business concentration occurs where commodity sales dominate. In North India, such an intersection is known as *chowk,* around which develops the houses of the rich. Most merchants live either on the upper floor or in back of their shops. Often, the same house is used as a warehouse.

The bazaar, or the city center, consists of an amalgam of land uses that cater to the central-place functions of the city. The commercial land use, dominating the center, consists of both retail and wholesale activities. As the greater portion of family income is spent for the basic necessities of life—food, clothing, and shelter—most streets are related to the retail sale of foodstuffs and clothes. Perishable

Figure 9.7 Simla, a hill station and former summer capital of colonial India, lies at about 7,500 ft (2300 m) elevation in the Himalayas, thus providing cooling relief for British colonials during India's torrid season. The town remains a popular tourist destination for all today. (Photo by Ashok Dutt)

goods, such as vegetables, meat, and fish—which consumers buy fresh daily because of lack of refrigeration facilities in most homes—are sold in specific areas of the bazaar, which often lack enclosed walls but have a common roof. In the process of bazaar evolution, functional separation of retail business occurs: textile shops stay together, attracting tailors; grain shops cluster together near the perishable goods market; and pawnshops are adjacent to jewelry shops. Sidewalk vendors are present almost everywhere in the bazaar.

Wholesale business establishments also form part of the bazaar landscape. Situated near an accessible location, they tend to separate according to the commodities they deal in, such as vegetables, grains, and cloth, depending on the size of the city the bazaar serves. Traditionally, the public or nonprofit inns provide modest overnight accommodation in the bazaar for a nominal fee. However, as a result of Western impact, some kinds of hotel accommodation are now available in the medium-sized and large cities. Prostitutes and dancing girls, once a source of evening entertainment in the bazaar, have been supplanted by cinemas, which in turn have declined due to the prevalence of television and VCRs. Traditionally, the shops selling country-made liquor were never located in the bazaars, probably because drinking liquor in public places was considered ill mannered by both Hindu and Muslim societies. Only in recent years have Western bars and liquor stores started to appear in the center. Whereas at one time the only doctors were practitioners of indigenous medicines, now practitioners of modern Western medicine join them near the main streets of the bazaar. Bar-

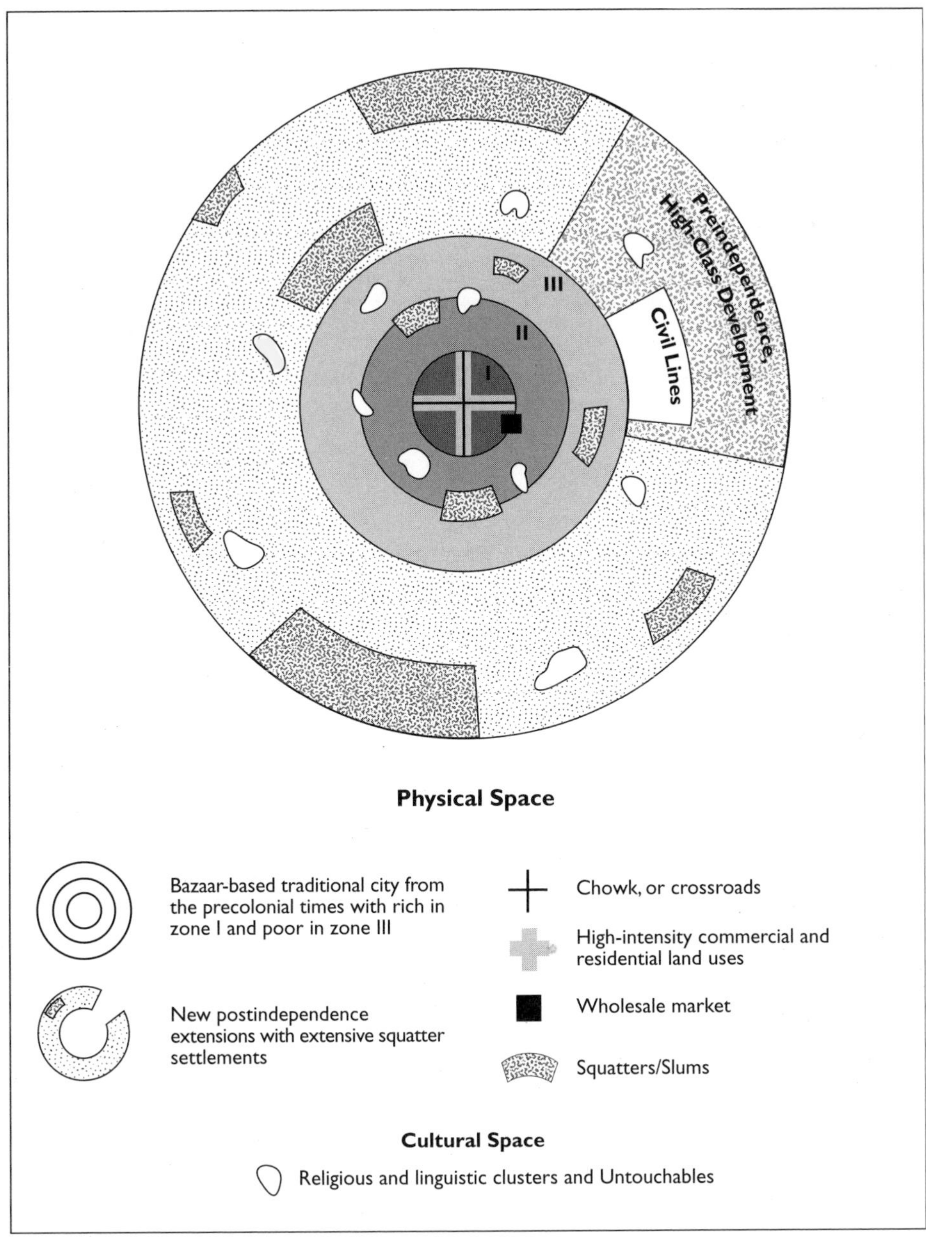

Figure 9.8 A Model for the Internal Structure of a Bazaar-Based City in South Asia. *Source*: Ashok Dutt

bers, who used to serve only outdoors, have regular shops like those of Western countries, although many still operate on the sidewalks. Barbers' establishments, unlike those of other trades, are scattered all over the bazaar. Long-distance private telephone centers along with Internet access enterprises have become commonplace in city centers.

Thus, the inner core of the city develops an increased concentration of trade, commerce,

Figure 9.9 The old and the new mix in this scene from Patna, India, which could be duplicated many places throughout South Asia. Bicycles, carts, cars, and cows all mingle in front of modern high-rises. (Photo by Paul Karan)

and wealthy people. Beyond this inner core, in a second zone, the rich people live in conjunction with the poorer servants, but not in the same structure. The rich need the service of the poor as domestic servants, cleaners, shop assistants, and porters. The residences of the poor surround this second zone in a third area, where the demand for land is less and its price low. Beyond the third zone, "civil lines" (which housed various civil functions) were established during the colonial rule, with the native rich and middle class settling in these neighborhoods, particularly after independence, and squatter settlements developing alongside. One sees here, thus, elements of the inverse concentric zone model (fig. 9.9).

As the city grows, ethnic, religious, linguistic, and caste neighborhoods are formed in specific areas. Their location varies in accordance with the time of their settlement and the availability of developable land. The Untouchables always occupy the periphery of the city, although sometimes other housing develops later, beyond their neighborhoods. In Hindu-dominated areas of India, the Muslims always form separate neighborhoods. Similarly, Hindu minorities in Srinagar and Dhaka live in enclaves of the old city. Often, people who have migrated from other linguistic areas form specific neighborhoods of their own.

Planned Cities

Though there were several ancient planned cities in the subcontinent, such as Mohenjo Daro and Pataliputra, they did not survive. There were others, however, that were planned during the precolonial, colonial, and independence periods that not only survived but also formed nuclei for major urban developments. Jaipur is an example of a precolonial planned city and Jamshedpur is an example from the British colonial period. Jaipur, India's twelfth-largest city, with an estimated

Figure 9.10 The old fort towers over Jaipur, in the arid country of western India. Originally a planned city, Jaipur is a favored tourist destination today for those wanting to ride elephants and glimpse some of the grandeur of India's golden age. (Photo by Jack Williams)

2.1 million people, was founded as a planned city in 1727 by the Maharajah of Jaipur (fig. 9.10). A hierarchy of streets divided Jaipur into sectors and neighborhoods. Though the planned city covered only 3 sq mi and is now surrounded by a built-up area of about 22 sq mi (57 sq km), the original identity of the 18th-century planning has been retained.

Similar is the case of Jamshedpur, planned as a company town for the first steel mill in the subcontinent by the Mumbai-based industrial family of the Tatas. Jamshedpur is about 150 mi southeast of Kolkata; the raw materials for the steel making—iron ore, coal, and limestone—are found nearby. The city underwent four different plans during colonial times and one during the independence period. The Koenigsberger plan (after a German Jew who took Indian citizenship) in 1943 remodeled Jamshedpur on the basis of the neighborhood unit concept, a novel idea that made the plan probably the first of its kind on the subcontinent. Fortunately, not only did Koenigsberger's innovative experiment prove successful for one city, but also almost all the new industrial and administrative cities of the subcontinent now incorporate this idea in their plans.

In 2000, the city of Jamshedpur itself had about 900,000 residents, while the wider metropolitan population was well over 1 million. Metropolitan growth has spread much beyond the city's original planned area, which still dominates the city landscape. Thus, true to the characteristics of the planned city model, Jaipur, Jamshedpur, and other such cities have a planned central core that has undergone modifications over time and is surrounded by unplanned traditional developments and semiplanned postindependence extensions.

Mixtures of Colonial and Bazaar Models

The functional demands created by activities in the colonial, the bazaar-type, and the planned city generated interaction among these models. The British administrative requirements in the traditional cities resulted in the establishment of *civil lines*, generally on the periphery of the city. The civil lines were composed of a courthouse, treasury, jail, hospital, public library, police facilities, clubhouses, and residential quarters for the high administrative and judicial officials. The streets for the civil lines were well planned, were paved, and had trees planted on both sides. In the provincial capitals, a governor's house, secretariat, and extensive residences for different levels of government employees were also constructed. In the native states of the subcontinent, where an indirect colonial rule was operational, a British regent with his staff resided at the state capital within a civil station, which looked like a colonial appendage attached to the bazaar or planned city.

During the 20th century, both before and after independence, when the local rich needed to build houses of their own, several governmental, semigovernmental, cooperative, and private agencies planned developments surrounding the traditional city. Consequently, many traditional cities developed new extensions on their peripheries. For the most part, however, colonial cities never grew as conceived by their colonial masters. Traditional factors played an unavoidable role in altering the colonial forms. The traditional bazaar thrived side by side with the CBD. As a result, to correctly model classical colonial cities, such as Kolkata, Mumbai, Chennai, and Colombo, it is essential to consider the impact on them by the traditional bazaars. All colonial cities bear imprints from bazaar forms, just as the bazaar cities were impacted by colonial functional demands.

Planned cities, when expanded, added colonial and bazaar city forms, and sometimes the two latter types expanded by creating new planned entities. The basic characteristics of the three types of cities (bazaar, colonial, and planned) are summarized in table 9.1.

REPRESENTATIVE CITIES

With so many large and distinctive cities in South Asia, selecting which ones to highlight as representative is a difficult task. Clearly, the three great presidency towns of Kolkata, Mumbai, and Chennai must be included. Each represents a quite different geographical setting and regional hinterland, but they all share the commonality of creation by the British. Delhi, a combination of colonialism and tradition, represents the political center of India today. Karachi for Pakistan and Dhaka for Bangladesh illustrate the nature of primate cities in the region. Lastly, the three smaller capital cities of Colombo (Sri Lanka), Kabul (Afghanistan), and Kathmandu (Nepal) not only are the key cities of those three countries but also are examples of smaller regional capitals. All three share very troubled political and economic environments.

Kolkata: Premier Presidency Town

The image of Kolkata among foreign commentators through time has evoked a number of nicknames, including Rhoads Murphey's "City in a Swamp," Dominique LaPierre's "City of Joy," and Rudyard Kipling's "Cholera Capital of

Table 9.1 Typological Characteristics of South Asian Cities

	Land Value	*Population Density Gradient*	*Physical Aspect*	*Land Use Composition of the City Center*	*Historical Roots*	*Mixture of Three Forms*
Bazaar City	Highest at the center; declines as one moves to the periphery	Highest at the center and declining inversely as one moves to the periphery	Narrow streets, commercial establishments at the center occupying the road; front, back, and second-/third-floor residential; generally congested and dirty	Retail and wholesale business mainly, with limited recreation and combined with high-density residential	May have origins from ancient, medieval, or recent times and accordingly may have imprints from Dravidian, Hindu, Muslim, or Western forms at the periphery	When a bazaar city was implanted with colonial aspects, garden-like, semiplanned "civil lines" were added; similar addition of planned neighborhoods also made at the periphery after independence
Colonial City	Highest at the center; generally declines as one moves to the periphery, but relatively higher in the European town compared to the "native" town	Center with minimum density, with highest densities around the CBD, creating a "crater effect" at the center; thereafter declines as one moves to the periphery	Wide streets at the center and the European town, with garden-like, affluent appearance; the "native" town characterized by narrow, sinuous streets and generally shabby condition	Offices, banks, main post office, transport headquarters, government buildings with large open space, hotels, retail and recreational activities, and residential use	Origins no earlier than 16th century; Victorian, neo-Gothic, and other Western forms widely prevalent; native forms also implanted	Parts of colonial city—particularly adjacent to the CBD and some specific locations in the "native" town—evolving characteristics of the bazaar center; planned neighborhoods added, particularly adjacent to the periphery of the Europen town after independence
Planned City	May vary according to predetermined values for different locations	May vary at different locations of the city, but the initial plan is for low density	Organized and generally pleasing appearance	Combination of retail, office, and recreation in a systematic fashion	May have origins in any historical period, but over time bazaar aspects will begin to dominate the center if restrictions are not strictly adhered to	Planned towns with addition of "civil lines" at the periphery and bazaar central forms evolving at one or many locations

Source: A. K. Dutt and R. Amin. "Towards a Typology of South Asian Cities," *National Geographical Journal of India* 32 (1995): 30–39.

the World" and "City of Pavement Dwellers." As administrative capital for much of the colonial period and as an important commercial center since before then, Kolkata set the tone for urban imagery in South Asia.

"City in a Swamp" appropriately describes the city even today. Sited on the levees sloping east and west from the riverbank, the forty-mile-long metropolitan district is for the most part at or below 22 ft above sea level. The site's proneness to flooding, already high at this low elevation, is aggravated by the monsoon, which brings most of the city's annual rainfall of 64 in (1,600 mm) from June to September, when runoff from upstream already causes the river to swell. Waterlogged soils and extensive flooding substantially impact three out of every five slum dwellers. Despite these physical disadvantages, the city's location on the Hugli (a distributary of the Ganges) provided the advantages that were critical to its growth. Its location 60 mi (96 km) upriver from the Bay of Bengal allowed access to 19th-century ocean vessels, provided a populous hinterland with rich mineral and agricultural resources, and allowed access to the Gangetic Plain via waterborne transport on perennial river systems. These advantages, coupled with the later development of extensive rail and road connections, spurred growth and development. Finally, the establishment of the trading post and military garrison by the British in 1756 provided the mechanisms through which trade was conducted.

Spatial growth of the city and the business district in particular centered on the original fort and continued from that point, even after its relocation several years later. A European component grew from the south end and a native town grew in the north. The native town included a wealthier and middle-class component that resided at the northern edge of the CBD. This area, the Barabazar, is reminiscent of the traditional bazaars. It remains the most desirable residential area today, especially for wealthy Marwari and Gujarati merchants who migrated from western India and are now a bulwark of the business community. With such commercial activities (particularly commodity sales), high residential and commercial densities, and an incumbent population of wealthier residents, Barabazar presents many characteristics of a traditional bazaar center. Immediately to the south of the area is the Western-style CBD, mainly an office, administrative, and commercial district with a low density of residential population (fig. 9.11).

As the city grew, its northern part reflected more traditional characteristics, while the southern section presented more of a European look. In between lay the CBD, including the Chauringee, the main activity center of the metropolis. With the formation of the Kolkata Improvement Trust in 1911, new areas were reclaimed in the southern and eastern portions of the city, to be inhabited mostly by wealthy Bengalis, the native inhabitants of the state.

Kolkata is a leading port in India and the capital of the state of West Bengal. The Kolkata (Calcutta) Metropolitan District (CMD), of which the city of Kolkata is part, has an area of 500 sq mi (1,300 sq km) and a population of 12.9 million. The colonial characteristics of Kolkata city, however, were restricted to its own municipal jurisdiction. The CMD expanded along both banks of the Hugli River in a linear and continuous pattern for about 50 mi (80 km). The CMD consists of about 500 local governing bodies in which the City of Kolkata is the largest, with its 40 sq mi (104 sq km) and 4 million inhabitants. Away from Kolkata, the local centers of the CMD, including Kolkata's twin city, Howrah, typically present the traditional bazaar kind of land uses

Figure 9.11 Kolkata's Grand Hotel is part of the old colonial CBD that still dominates in India's second-largest, and much maligned, city. (Photo by Ashok Dutt)

and are devoid of any imprint of a Western-style CBD.

The situation of the city was advantageous in forming an industrial nucleus. In the 19th century, its seaport facilitated the import of wholesale machinery for the jute industry, the most significant industrial activity of the metropolis. Raw jute was produced in the nearby fields of the Ganges delta. From then until today, the jute industry has grown, as a chain of mills has stretched along the banks of the Hugli River, forming the largest concentration of jute mills in the world.

Because of its role as British colonial capital (1757–1911) and through the introduction of Western education in the early part of the 19th century, Kolkata was regarded as a pacesetter in terms of education and politics. As a pioneer center of education, it was often viewed as possessing an elitist heritage. The large number of Kolkata University graduates migrating to different parts of India, and their roles in patriotic political activities, helped generate the common saying that "What Bengal [meaning Kolkata] thinks today, India thinks tomorrow." After independence, with the strong attraction of Delhi, the national capital of independent India, this leadership role for Kolkata has significantly diminished.

Today, the CMD is highly industrialized. Postindependence industrial activity was initially hurt by partition, which severed the jute mills of the city from their supply areas in East Pakistan (now Bangladesh), contributing to the city's relative industrial decline. Today, it is the engineering industry, concentrated on the right bank of the Hugli in Howrah, that is the important component of the local economy. Other important industries are paper, pharmaceuticals, and synthetic fabrics. Information-technology firms and related employment are growing, but Bangalore and the Mumbai-Pune corridor remain ahead of Kolkata in this area. Commercially, the city now ranks second to

Figure 9.12 A sidewalk vendor in Kolkata's CBD sells a peanut mix. Such humble retail trade suffices to sustain vast numbers of urban poor in South Asian cities. (Photo by Ashok Dutt)

Mumbai. It hosts headquarters of native business firms, banks, and international corporations.

In spite of recent stagnation in Kolkata's economy, the city attracts migrants from many different parts of northeastern India. Many Hindu refugees arrived from East Pakistan when partition occurred. Their arrival boosted the proportion of those speaking Bengali, who now account for two-thirds of the city's population (fig. 9.12).

Mumbai: India's Economic Capital

Mumbai, for centuries known as Bombay, has surpassed Kolkata as India's largest urban agglomeration and most cosmopolitan city. Two dimensions have been critical to its rise to preeminence, one financial and one cultural. First, the skyscrapers in the Nariman Point area are the heart of the city's, and the nation's, financial sector and signify the city's role as the single most important command-and-control point in the national economy. The three stock exchanges of Mumbai, fully computerized, handle 70% of the country's stock transactions. Second, in one aspect the city has emerged as the nation's cultural capital through its prolific film industry, which is among the world's largest; "Bollywood" films are eagerly consumed not only by the viewing public in India, but also by audiences in Bangladesh, the Middle East, and Africa (box 9.2).

In 1672, Mumbai became the capital of all British possessions on the west coast of India. The 17th-century British possession of the seven islands, which now form the oldest part of this city, initiated the construction of the fort. Beyond the fort grew a filthy "native town," where sanitary conditions were miserably poor. Drainage was the main problem. The "European town" grew on higher ground around the fortress and protective walls were erected around it. The native or "black" town was separated from the European town by an esplanade, which was kept free of permanent houses. The main impetus to Mumbai's development occurred when Britain's supply of raw cotton temporarily diminished in the 1860s during the U.S. civil war and Mumbai became an important supplier. This resulted in an amassing of huge capital by Mumbai-based businessmen, as

Box 9.2 Cinema and the City: Mumbai's Film Industry

What city produces more motion pictures than any other? While Hollywood may come to mind first, it is "Bollywood" that provides the correct answer. Each year, the Mumbai movie industry churns out over 700 films, surpassing the number produced in any other country. "Bollywood," with its stars, studios, and magnetism, is in part synonymous with the city itself.

Most of the films are in Hindi, though anyone viewing a typical Bollywood film for the first time will likely figure out the plot. Characterized by generous quantities of glitz and glamour, at least a half dozen songs, and nearly as many dance sequences, the stories are usually quite simple and crammed with clichés. Many are love stories—handsome young man meets sweet, beautiful woman and falls in love, they are separated, and then, later, they are haphazardly brought together again and live happily ever after. Though much is implied that is not shown on the screen, the movies are actually rather clean, with kissing as risqué as it gets. Also, good wins out over evil almost without exception. A closer analysis reveals that most of the films are based on a distinctive style with a mix of nine critical elements—love, hate, sorrow, disgust, joy, compassion, pity, pride, and courage—as dictated in the ancient *Naya Shastra* (Science of theater).

The movie production process can be chaotic. Scripts are sketchy, if prepared at all. Actors may be working on various films at a single time. Directors make abrupt last-minute changes during filming. After production and domestic viewing, the films are exported to other parts of Asia and to Africa, where they are also popular. Bollywood and the rest of India also produce many critically acclaimed movies, including art films. However, like cinema worldwide, the market has an appetite for glamour and action, so many audiences are getting what they want—simple, escapist fun.

Such a thriving film industry implies profitability, but surprisingly only one in five movies turns a profit. Audiences are often poor and pay as little as twelve rupees (twenty-five cents) for admission and, therefore, many viewers are needed for a film to be profitable. The entire industry generates only US$1.3 billion in revenue each year. Production costs are kept low and stars live modest lifestyles that rarely resemble their onscreen glamour. Financing is difficult to secure, in part because of government restrictions, so it is often secured at outrageous interest rates as high as 24%–36%. Mafia-type organizations have stepped forward to fill this financial void. These organizations extort protection money from movie stars, directors, and producers alike. So the film industry, like the property markets and construction industry in Mumbai, has been plagued by organized crime.

Mumbai, with its thriving film industry and its financial markets, in a sense serves as both the Los Angeles and New York of India, adding to the magnetism of the city and bolstering its ranking among the great urban centers of the world.

Figure 9.13 The Mumbai Municipal Corporation Office in front of the Victoria Terminus in the old colonial center of town mixes Western design and European Gothic design to create one of the landmark buildings still serving Mumbai. (Photo by Ashok Dutt)

the city became the main cotton textile center of the realm. In 1853, the opening of railways eventually connected Mumbai with a hinterland covering almost all of west India. Mumbai further prospered with the opening of the Suez Canal in 1869, which enhanced the city's trade advantage by cutting the distance to Europe. This closer proximity helped earn the city the nickname "Gateway to India."

When the fort area developed into a Western-style CBD, the British, followed by rich Indians, moved to Malabar Hill, Cumballah Hill, and Mahalakshmi, on the southwestern portion of the island. In the 1940s, the rich settled in another attractive area of the island, Marine Drive (now renamed), which lay along the Back Bay. Because of the ever-increasing demand for commercial and residential land in the fort area and the lack of land on the narrow peninsula and the island city, dozens of skyscrapers have been erected since the 1970s at Nariman Point, generating a skyline resembling a miniature Manhattan. The most recent phenomenon of Mumbai's commercial land-use change is the partial shifting of office- and financial-related activities to the newly built high-rise buildings of Nariman Point, though the old fort area is still considered the main core of the CBD. Mumbai is the world's ninth most expensive city in terms of office occupancy costs. The poor, the middle class, and a few native businessmen settled mostly at the center and the north of the island. Presently, the more Western colonial influence created by European settlements can be observed in the southern part of the city proper (fig. 9.13). The more traditional influences have remained observable in the north. Most recently, the northern part of Greater Mumbai, which lies north of Mahim Creek and the city proper, has undergone the development of semiplanned residential suburbs and industrial parks. Unsanitary slums, built of flimsy materials, mushroom all over the city.

As a state capital and largest metropolis in South Asia, Mumbai has also become the largest port on the entire subcontinent. It handles about 25% of India's foreign trade. Though cotton textiles employ about half of the city's workers, general engineering, silk, chemicals, dyeing, and bleaching are also important employment sources. The Mumbai Metropolitan Region accounts for about 11% of India's industrial employment and fixed capital, while the Mumbai-Pune corridor is India's second most important center of employment for information technology.

The city attracts an enormous number of migrants from the western and central parts of India, thus giving it a religious and linguistic diversity that surpasses all others in South Asia. Mumbai does exhibit certain religious characteristics common to some other South Asian cities as well. For example, the decline in the Muslim population between 1941 and 1951 resulted from the partitioning of British India into India and Pakistan in 1947, prompting the mass exodus of Hindus and Sikhs from West Pakistan and Muslims from India, as well as causing the departure of many Hindus from East Pakistan (now Bangladesh) to India. Hindus are thus the dominant group today, accounting for 69% of Mumbai's population, followed by Muslims, Sikhs, and a mix of Christians, Jains, and Buddhists. Two other minority religious groups play a socioeconomic role far beyond their numbers. First, the Zoroastrians, or Parsis as they are called in Mumbai, are a small but significant minority group. Even though their numbers in Mumbai are small, more Parsis live here than anywhere else across the globe. Also significant are the Jains, mainly migrant businessmen from Gujarat State who were drawn by Mumbai's increasing commercial importance. The number of Buddhists has increased as a result of the mass conversion of local Untouchables during the Neo-Buddhist movement, launched in Maharastra in the 1950s. In terms of linguistic characteristics, Mumbai is unique among metropolises of the subcontinent. The regional language, Marathi, is spoken by less than half the population. Mumbai is a microcosm of India itself.

Chennai: Regional Center of Tamil Nadu

Long considered among the most provincial of the country's largest urban centers, India's fourth-largest city is increasingly cosmopolitan. Along with Bangalore, it has even become the preferred location for many of the nation's software companies.

Situated by the side of the Bay of Bengal, Fort St. George was the focal point of Chennai's settlement at the inception of the colonial era. The "black town" situated north of the fort walls was known as Georgetown. Georgetown's southeast corner, called Parry's Corner, forms the focal point of the present CBD. The whites' bungalows spread out toward the west and southwest from the fort and were separated by a large open space, Island Grounds, and public buildings such as hospitals. South of the "white town" was Mount Road (now Anna Salai), which eventually attracted large-scale commercial activities. In the extreme south and southwest of the city, areas were developed by government and semigovernmental agencies for planned residential expansions after independence.

Chennai, a seaport and capital of Tamil Nadu State, had an estimated population of 6.6 million in 2000 and is a typical regional center. Three-fourths of the residents speak the language of the state, Tamil; Telegu and Malayalam are also important. True to the city's regional characteristics, 84% of the population is Hindu, while the remainder are Muslim and Christian. The high general population density is due to the density of older areas of the city, particularly around the center. In general, Chennai's urban characteristics reflect a combination of colonial and traditional effects. Like Kolkata and Mumbai, the CBD has a low population density and is surrounded by a high-density "crater rim," while the density declines as one moves to the periphery. The areas north of the CBD show a more traditional influence, with large tracts of low-lying areas inhabited by poor slum dwellers (fig. 9.14). In the south and southwest, the colonial Western impact is more perceptible, though slums are spread in a linear fashion along both banks of the Buckingham Canal.

Figure 9.14 Piped water is a luxury in most South Asian cities. Most people make do with public water outlets like this one near the beach in Chennai (Madras) for bathing and washing clothes. (Photo by Jack Williams)

Delhi: Who Controls Delhi Controls India

Delhi, the capital of India, combines a deep-rooted historical heritage with colonial and modern forms. Historical records confirm that 18 different capital sites in the Delhi area have been chosen in the past 3,000 years; 17 sites have actually been identified through physical evidence. Fifteen different names have been given to the various capital sites, but in spite of the many efforts by the rulers to change the city name, the name "Delhi," derived from Dilli, one of the earliest capital sites, has remained.

The attraction for Delhi as a capital site is rooted in South Asia's physiography, locations of advanced civilization centers, and migration/invasion routes. Delhi occupies a relatively flat drainage divide between the two most productive agricultural areas of the realm, the Indus and Ganges plains, where the most notable centers of civilization and power developed in the past. North of these plains and Delhi lie the barrier of the Himalayas; in the southwest lies the inhospitable Thar (Rajasthan) Desert. Following the strategic Khyber Pass and entering the vast Indus plains of Punjab, the continental migrants and invaders from the northwest frontiers of South Asia were impelled to control Delhi to insure a firm hold over the North Indian Plains. The control of Delhi was so vital to the rule of North India that a popular saying arose: "He who controls Delhi controls India." Moreover, Delhi's location gave it access to the year-round waterborne traffic of the northern part of South Asia.

Most of the historical sites of Delhi were located between the Delhi ridge (on which the 19th-century British cantonment was located) and the Yamuna River, but the extensive developments that occurred after India's independence caused expansion of the city across the ridge and on the east of the river (fig. 9.15). Old Delhi (the former Shahjahanabad), the

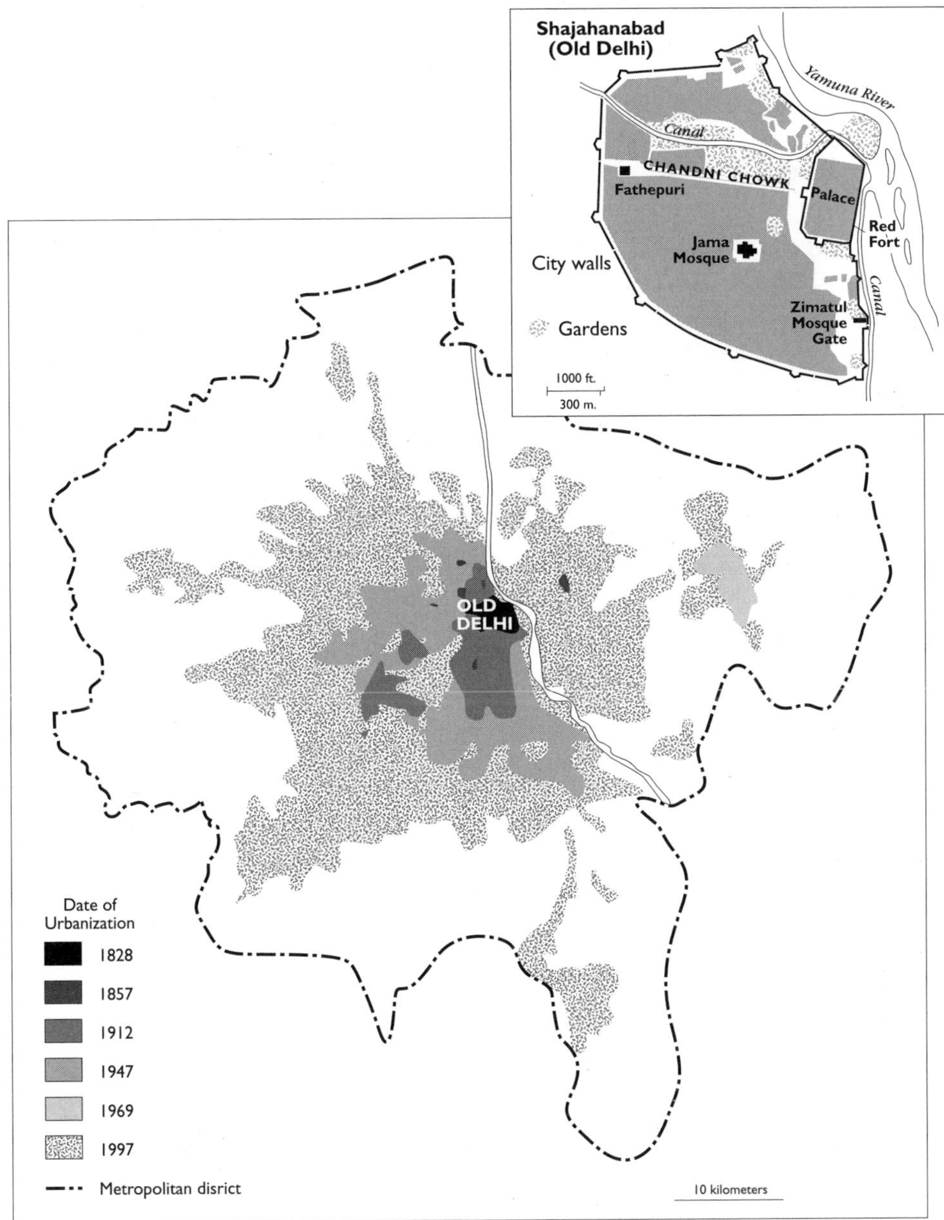

Figure 9.15 Delhi and Shahjahanabad (Old Delhi). *Source:* Ashok Dutt and George Pomeroy

only living urban relic of Delhi's past, is a traditional bazaar-type Indian city with the Chandni Chowk as the main commercial center. Here, sanitation used to be one of the main problems, but since independence the area has been fully provided with underground sewers and piped water. Rich merchants and ordinary working people live here, close to one another. West of the Yamuna, connected by bridges with the main city, is a postindependence, semiplanned area as well as squatter developments, where one-third of Delhi's population

Figure 9.16 The circular Parliament House, constructed in the 1920s in the new colonial capital of New Delhi, is the seat of India's government today, in which both houses of Parliament have their chambers. (Photo by Ashok Dutt)

lives, some in unhealthy slums with very little or no basic facilities of water, sewer, electricity, or paved roads.

New Delhi, situated south of Old Delhi, is a majestic colonial creation that emerged as a new city after the capital of British India was moved from Kolkata. The capital was temporarily moved to Delhi's civil lines and cantonment in 1911, before being installed in New Delhi in 1931 (fig. 9.16). New Delhi was planned by a British architect, Edwin Lutyens, in a geometric form that combined hexagons, circles, triangles, rectangles, and straight lines. Spacious roads, a magnificent viceroy's residence (now the President's Palace), a circular council chamber (which is now Parliament House), imposing secretariat buildings, a Western-style shopping center (Connaught Place) with a large open space in the middle, officers' residences in huge compounds, and a garden-like atmosphere formed the main elements of New Delhi. The new capital was separated from the congested, unsanitary, and generally poor conditions of Old Delhi by an open space. The congestion was so pathetic to British eyes that in 1937 a Delhi Improvement Trust was formed to tackle Old Delhi's problems.

The main economic base of New Delhi is government service. After India's independence, an increasing demand for housing was created by new government employees, which led to large-scale public housing developments around earlier settlements of New Delhi. The most noticeable feature of such developments was the segregation of larger neighborhoods according to the rank of the government employees and foreign residents. Class rather than caste determined the new neighborhood composition. Delhi has expanded in a planned manner, as the Delhi Development Authority has worked to coordinate the land development process with an innovative revolving funding scheme. The dark side of this strategy is that the lower and middle classes are left without affordable housing options. That a third of Delhi residents live in slums negates any gains registered.

Air pollution caused by motor vehicles and industrial activities is so intense that Delhi is considered among the worst five in the world in air pollution. India's Supreme Court had to intervene in the 1990s, forcing pollution controls. Since 2001, diesel-run commercial vehicles have been banned. Motor vehicles are forced to use unleaded gasoline, while commercial vehicles are required to use compressed natural gas, thus reducing transportation-related emissions.

Karachi: Pakistan's Port and Primate City

Situated at the western edge of the Indus River delta, Karachi is highly industrialized and has a busy port. Not only is Karachi Pakistan's largest city and chief port, but it also anchors the country's industrial core—with cotton textiles, steel, and engineering—and the most important educational/medical facility center. After independence, it became the federal capital of Pakistan for a short period.

In 1941, Karachi had a population of 435,000. At that time, the city's industries consisted of a few servicing workshops and small handicraft establishments located in and around the traditional bazaar-type center. Subsequent large-scale industrialization, including the establishment of industrial estates at the city's edge as early as the 1960s, stimulated an acceleration in the already rapid pace of growth. As a result, Karachi's population is now approximately 11.7 million, making the urban area one of South Asia's megacities. This rapid industrial growth provided an urban "pull" not only for Pakistanis, but also for large numbers of Muslim refugees leaving India, especially in the period immediately following partition. Thus, the city has a relatively small percentage of natives.

While the city has become more homogenous in terms of religion as a result of the inmigration and the effects of partition, it has also become more linguistically diverse and politically unstable. The partition led to the departure of all but a few thousand Sindhi Hindus, while Urdu-speaking Muslim immigrants came in large numbers from the north and central parts of India. After the 1947 partition, Urdu became Pakistan's national language, providing an additional impetus for its becoming the majority language of Karachi's citizens. Before partition, however, there was a base of Gujarati Muslim refugees from India. Thus, apart from English (a lingua franca of the elite), three languages are prevalent in the city: Urdu, Sindhi, and Gujarati. A considerable influx of Pushtu-speaking Pathans (Pashtuns) from the Northwest Frontier Province and Afghanistan in the 1980s often clashed with the Urdu-speaking migrants from India. Only a few Afghan refugees returned to Afghanistan after the Soviet pullback in the late 1980s. With the increased violence, a number of warring groups have materialized. The combination of linguistic and ethnic differences, exacerbated by ineffective and corrupt law enforcement, a bureaucratic judicial system, and the availability of arms supplied by the United States during the Afghan War in the 1980s, has contributed to an alarming level of violence.

This violence has escalated since and continues today. This crime, along with declining employment opportunities and crumbling infrastructure, has led to urban discontent and near anarchy.

The center of Karachi represents a true bazaar model: high population density, high intensity of commercial and small-scale industrial activity, and relatively higher concentration of rich people. Toward the east from the center of the city were the planned cantonment quarters that originated during the British occupation dating back to 1839. During much of colonial times, after Karachi became the capital of the new province of Sind, the city remained confined by a land-use pattern that placed the docks in the southwest, the bazaar in the center, and the civil lines and military establishments in the east and toward the north. After independence, new suburban residential developments surrounded the eastern two-thirds of the colonial city, while planned industrial estates were built mainly toward the northern and western fringes. Thus the trends of colonial expansion continued, with the native rich settling toward the east, adjacent to the former civil lines and cantonment.

Dhaka: Capital, Port, and Primate City of Bangladesh

Modern Dhaka, Bangladesh's capital and largest urban center, is a city of mosquitoes and cycle rickshaws. Its streets are jammed with vehicles, each of which is attempting to overtake the others. The contrast between rich and poor is glaring. Dhaka's noise pollution is deafening and generated from horns, sirens, and the loudspeakers of restaurants and mosques, the latter of which broadcast prayers five times a day, along with the festivities of an occasional wedding party. The city's large number of cinemas show "Bollywood" films, generally filled with overtones of sex and violence. The observance of *purdah* (seclusion of women) has declined among both urban women (since the 1950s) and rural women (at present), but women still keep a low public profile.

Situated in the center of the country, Dhaka is sited on the left bank of a tributary of the Meghna-Ganges system (fig. 9.17). Founded in the 7th century A.D., the city was subsequently governed by Hindu Sena kings (beginning in the 9th century) and Muslim rulers (1203 to 1764), for whom it served as an intermittent regional capital, while attaining great commercial importance. Toward the end of the 17th century, the city had more than 1 million inhabitants and stretched for 12 mi (19 km) in length and 8 mi (13 km) in breadth. The European traders, largely Portuguese, Dutch, English, and French, started coming to Dhaka after 1616. The loss of regional capital status in 1706, however, precipitated a decline that continued well into the colonial period. Kolkata, with its status as a colonial capital and trade center, eclipsed Dhaka and its sphere of economic and political influence.

The early 20th century and the city's status as a temporary regional capital brought about important changes, resulting in a resurgence of growth that took the population from 104,000 in 1901 to 239,000 in 1941. Partition in 1947 prompted large-scale immigration of Muslims from India and also stimulated industrial growth from an almost nonexistent base. Spearheading the industrial growth was jute processing, now taking place in Bangladesh as a result of the new international boundary, which provided an effective barrier to the jute mills of Kolkata. Subsequently, Dhaka's Urdu speakers swelled in numbers. At least as significant in spurring growth and development af-

Figure 9.17 Lying in a floodplain, Dhaka, the capital of Bangladesh, is periodically ravaged by floods that wreak havoc and bring huge loss of life to this desperately poor city and country. (Photo courtesy of UNICEF-Davies)

ter partition was Dhaka's reclaimed role as regional capital (this time for East Pakistan) and, after establishment of an independent Bangladesh in 1971, its newfound role as national capital. The resultant multifarious administrative-commercial activities provided the necessary pull factors to trigger the most rapid growth in Dhaka's history. Today, the metropolitan population of approximately 11 million makes it the fifth most populous city in South Asia.

The long history of Dhaka has left its obvious imprints on the city's landscape and internal structure. The legacies of successive Hindu, Muslim, and British rules are present in various buildings and place-names. With a Muslin population of more than 90% of the city's total, mosques are so numerous in Dhaka that it is often called the "City of Mosques." Hindus are the most important minority group, followed by Christians and Buddhists. Linguistically, Dhaka is very homogenous, as more than 95% of the population speaks Bengali, the native language. During the Pakistan period (1947–1971), a substantial number of Urdu-speaking Muslims who came from either North India or West Pakistan were in the city, but since the creation of Bangladesh, the majority of them have been forced to depart. It was during the 190 years of British rule that a more active Muslim culture was superimposed over the city's indigenous Hindu base. The conspicuous products of Muslim construction, combined with Western styles and urban expansion, led to diversity in the Dhaka landscape.

Colombo, Kabul, and Kathmandu: Peripheral Capitals and Regional Centers

Colombo, Kabul, and Kathmandu are the premier cities and have served as the national capitals of Sri Lanka, Afghanistan, and Nepal, respectively. Recently, the capital of Sri Lanka has officially moved to Jayawadenepura, not too far from Colombo, the earlier capital. The city of Colombo, nonetheless, continues to be the de facto capital. The three cities are greatly different in size: Kabul has 2.7 million people, Colombo 684,000, and Kathmandu 756,000.

All three are historic cities. Kabul, the oldest, was referred to in the *Rig Veda,* a 3,500-year-old Hindu scripture, and by Ptolemy in the 2d century A.D. Kabul's strategic position by the side of the Kabul River and at the western entrance of the famous Khyber Pass, through which came the Hindu Aryan and other migrants and invaders to India, gave the city great political and trading significance. Sited at an elevation of 5,900 ft (1,800 m), Kabul has served as a regional or national capital for numerous regimes over the centuries, most notably, the Moghul Empire (1504–1526) and, after 1776, an independent Afghanistan. Later attempts by both the Russians and the British to subjugate the country and its capital failed. After 1880, modern buildings and gardens were constructed, but these have not diminished the identity of the old bazaar city.

The city has suffered greatly since the 1970s, as a result of internal and international conflict. The overthrow of the king in 1974 initiated a series of events that included the establishment of a Soviet-backed marxist government (1978), the establishment of a weak puppet state (1989), a period of warlord-dominated chaos (1992), the establishment of the Taliban regime (1996), and the creation of an interim civilian government (2002). Under the socially repressive Taliban, Afghanistan served as a haven for those responsible for the World Trade Center attacks of September 11, 2001. Retaliation by the United States led to intense and destructive bombing of Kabul, as well as Kandahar and other cities. As of 2002, the new, post-Taliban regime seemed determined to establish stability and democracy. In the wake of almost continuous strife, however, it remains to be seen if the government will be able to rebuild the country and its cities and provide a stable socioeconomic setting.

Kathmandu, in the Kathmandu Valley, lies in the midmountain region of the Himalayas, at an elevation of about 4,400 ft (1,350 m). Because of its physically sheltered valley location, it remained free from invasion from the plains of India. Kathmandu occupies a central position for most of Nepal and is the most important commercial, business, and administrative center in the country. The Gurkha ethnic group, after conquering Nepal, made Kathmandu its capital in 1768. Reconstruction efforts after the devastating 1934 earthquake plus post–World War I developments added more buildings, but the older section of the city has retained the bazaar characteristics. Though the overwhelming majority of Kathmandu residents are Hindus, there are also some Buddhists. Parliament is seated here. However, the city's significance as the seat of government for the only Hindu kingdom of the world is now in jeopardy, due to a murder and suicide rampage by the crown prince, which left most members of the royal family dead in the summer of 2001. Sporadic violence by maoist guerillas has contributed to further instability. Nonetheless, the city remains a major center of South Asian tourism and is a launching ground for mountain treks.

Situated on the west coast of the tear-shaped island of Sri Lanka (known for cen-

Figure 9.18 This sleek, modern hotel in Colombo, capital of Sri Lanka, represents the efforts of the government to develop Colombo (and Sri Lanka) as a tourist destination and international business center, a worthy goal made very difficult by the country's two-decades-long civil war. (Photo by Jack Williams)

turies as Ceylon), Colombo has functioned as an important port city since at least the 5th century. Nonetheless, it was Western contact, beginning with the Portuguese settlement in 1517, that really started the growth of Colombo as the key port for Sri Lanka. The Dutch occupied the port in 1656, but the British replaced them in 1796 and turned the city into their main administrative, military, and trading place in Sri Lanka. After independence in 1948, Colombo became the national capital. It continues to be Sri Lanka's most important city in terms of business, administration, education, and culture. It is a colonial-based city. The CBD-like center, with its high-level government offices situated within the former colonial fort area, lies next to the old section of the city, Pettah (Tamil for "the town outside the fort"). Pettah represents the characteristics of the bazaar city enclave. Cinnamon Gardens, the former cinnamon-growing area of the Dutch period, has been turned into a high-class, low-density residential quarter. The city has expanded significantly since independence; its industries are mainly those that process the raw materials that are exported through the port of Colombo. To diversify the national economy through industrialization, an export-oriented free trade zone has been established near the port (fig. 9.18).

The impacts of the prolonged Tamil insurgency have detrimentally affected the development and growth of Colombo, as well as of most other urban centers throughout Sri Lanka. With the conflict having dragged on for two decades now, industrial activities and critical infrastructure investments are becoming even more spatially uneven. Transportation across the island has been split in two, as the northern and eastern portions of the island have become war zones. Finally, the costs of rehabilitation and reconstruction are substantial.

URBAN PROBLEMS AND SOLUTIONS

Several important problems inherent in the urbanization process of the developing countries are prevalent in South Asian cities, among them the post–World War II urban population explosion, housing shortages, insufficient development of utilities (water supply, drainage, sewerage, and electric supply), increasing water and air pollution, and financial incapability.

Rural-urban migration and high rates of natural increase have led to rapid increases in city populations. This has happened without a reciprocal increase in the manufacturing-sector employment, resulting in large-scale unemployment. Moreover, most rural migrants, being unskilled, are incapable of employment in modern industries. They are forced to swell the ranks of the informal sector, working as porters, rickshaw pullers, domestic servants, construction workers, or other low-paid manual laborers. Even a large number of educated youth find it difficult to obtain suitable employment.

Housing shortages emanating from large-scale in-migration and a relatively lower rate of new house building plague all the cities of South Asia. The demand for housing leads people to live in small units and unsanitary environments. As many as 67% of the households in Kolkata and 83% in Greater Mumbai have only one room; in Delhi and Chennai the figure is more than 60%. Moreover, the average number of persons per room in households is increasing. To compound difficulties, existing houses lack utilities; in Dhaka, for example, 16% of the population lives without electricity, 46% without piped water, and 50% without sewers or septic tanks.

A large number of people who cannot afford to rent a house often become pavement dwellers. In 2000, there were an estimated 250,000 pavement dwellers in Mumbai alone and more than 50,000 in Kolkata. In Kolkata, they are concentrated in the central areas of the city, where there is the greatest need for instantly accessible, low-skill, low-paid transport laborers. They are predominantly males aged 18–57, though nearly a third are children, most of whom add to the family income by begging and scavenging (fig. 9.19).

Slums, or *bustees,* have developed in almost all the major cities of South Asia. The term *bustee* is used in Kolkata and Dhaka, the term is *jhunggi* in Delhi, *chawl* in Mumbai, and *katchi abadi* in Karachi. The *bustee* has been defined by the Indian government's Slum Areas Improvement and Clearance Act of 1954 as a predominantly residential area where dwellings (by reason of dilapidation, overcrowding, faulty arrangement, or lack of ventilation, light, or sanitary facilities—or any combination of these factors) are detrimental to safety, health, and morals. Moreover, the slums mainly consist of temporary or semipermanent huts with minimal sanitary and water supply facilities and are usually located in unhealthy, waterlogged areas (fig. 9.20). They develop ubiquitously in the metropolises, though there is always a greater concentration of large slum areas away from the central business area. They begin with temporary settlements, sometimes started by landlords, but oftentimes by illegal squatting on public lands, by the sides of railroad lines or canals, on unclaimed swampy lands, in public parks, or on any other vacant land. In Chennai, though the slums consist of just 6% of the area, they accommodate 32% of the city's population. In the city of Kolkata alone, 39% of the population lives in *bustees* where 50% has no access to sewerage facilities. The unsanitary conditions of such slums made

Figure 9.19 A picture of hope, in this street scene from Lahore, Pakistan, in which a teacher uses the side of a boulevard as a makeshift, outdoor classroom for his young charges, part of a broader UNICEF program to help Pakistan's urban poor. (Photo courtesy of UNICEF-John Issac)

Kolkata an endemic center of cholera up until the 1960s. Kipling once described Kolkata as the "cholera capital of the world." Most lowlands in Mumbai flood during the monsoon season and are inhabited by slum dwellers, giving rise to highly unsanitary living conditions. Compared to cities in the Deccan plateau, in the cities in North India and the east coast plains a greater proportion of the population lives in slums.

In India, slum upgrading policy for the nation as a whole has seen several policy shifts during the past 50 years. Through the 1950s, slum upgrading policy consisted of slum clearance—that is, the bulldozing of slums, a policy wholly unrealistic in solving housing supply problems. This was followed by a period in which policy emphasized improving housing structures and the sanitary environment in the 1960s and 1970s. Since then, the slum policy has been focused on general improvement of housing and sanitation, under the slogan "shelter for all." These policies are reflected in the metropolitan plans of the Indian cities and in India's five-year national development plans. In spite of various policy approaches, slums remain places of little hope, low incomes, and a generally poor quality of life.

The increasing population causes increased densities. The greater the number of people the more demand on the water supply, school space, recreation grounds, and transportation

Figure 9.20 In Mumbai and many South Asian cities, drainage is often poor. Here a semistagnant creek by the side of slums and middle-class apartments is also a garbage and sewage dump. (Photo by Ashok Dutt)

facilities, all of which are inadequate in the cities. Mumbai has only 0.25 acre (0.10 ha) of open space per 1,000 population, though 4 acres (1.6 ha) was the suggested standard by the Master Plan of Greater Mumbai. The city of Chennai has one park for every 30,000 people and one playground for every 17,000.

Both fast-moving vehicles and slow, human-pulled or animal-driven vehicles frequent the CBD of Kolkata. The mixture of vehicles causes uncontrollable chaos on the streets. Free movement of animals, particularly "sacred cows" in the medium-sized and small cities, adds to the traffic problems. Almost four-fifths of the vehicles entering the CBD of Kolkata are motorized, with most of these private automobiles, taxis, buses, and trolley cars. Up until the early 1990s, the Howrah Bridge was the only connection between Kolkata and Howrah. The number of vehicles and pedesetrial commuters traversing this bridge is greater than the number at any other location in Kolkata. A second (toll) bridge, much less used, was built in the early 1990s.

The increasing number of automobiles causes extensive pollution. In Mumbai, where vehicular density has been estimated to be about 800 per sq mi (309 per sq km), 15 tons of carbon monoxide are thrown into the air daily. In Chennai, automobile pollution is greatest in the areas where vehicular traffic is slowest. Coal-burning industrial furnaces and domestic ovens, commonly used for cooking, are responsible for about 250 tons of particulate matter and 75 tons of sulfur thrown into the air daily in Kolkata.

South Asia's urban problems are enormous. The facilities cannot keep pace with the ever-increasing population. Because South Asian nations are poor, their limited financial resources constrict the developmental programs; even some of the rudimentary urban facilities cannot be provided.

Planning

Modern town planning began in South Asia in 1864, when the British appointed sanitary commissions for the three presidencies of Madras, Bengal, and Bombay. Rudimentary water-supply and sewage systems were introduced first. In following years, electric street lights, public parks and playgrounds, and even trolley systems or suburban electric railways, especially in the largest cities, were provided. Improvement trusts were established, such as the one in Mumbai in 1898. These worked to further drain swampy areas, reclaim and develop land, and provide elements of infrastructure, including sewage systems, water lines, and roads. Poorer people living in older areas rarely received the benefit of such planning, especially in the central parts of bazaar cities.

Perhaps the most influential early planner was Patrick Geddes, who emphasized the "folk" aspect of city planning and other ideas considered novel at the time. Instead of focusing on infrastructure or architectural layouts like many other planners of the period, Geddes appreciated the importance of grassroots activity, the maintenance of historical character, and the creation of a Garden City atmosphere, of course with improved hygiene. The results of his efforts are most prominent in Indore, Lucknow, and Lahore.

With independence in 1947, the new national government of India provided impetus to urban planning activities. Dilapidated areas of cities, especially slums, were given greater attention. Planning activities from this period were systematic, modeled after those in Britain and the United States. Over the next several decades, metropolitan planning organizations and their master plans, along with slum clearance programs, were developed, presented, and implemented for the metropolitan areas of Delhi, Mumbai, Kolkata, Chennai, Karachi, and Dhaka.

Comprehensive rational planning approaches, which rely upon top-down technical expertise and the exclusion of public participation, were characteristic of the period. Notable departures from this were the Chennai Structure Plan of 1980 and, much later, the Dhaka Metropolitan Development Plan of 1995, which were both based on strategic planning. No planning body has yet adopted the recently conceived planning approach of "consensus building" or "collaborative planning," wherein the planner involves the public in a format that encourages participation by a wide variety of interests.

In each setting, particular projects addressed problems that were common to all. In Delhi's earliest metropolitan plan, efforts to combat congestion visualized two complete ring roads complemented by a national highway along the Yamuna River. A greenbelt around the metropolis was also proposed, with several towns outside this greenbelt designated as secondary growth centers to assist in the decongestion of the core. Despite the plan, commercial centers seemed only lightly impacted and many of the problems remained. Later Delhi area plans gave given greater attention to the regional urban hierarchy, ecological considerations, and conservation of urban heritage.

Mumbai's planning activities envision a polynucleated region with new growth centers in New Mumbai and other complexes, new housing and the provision of acceptable services in slums, and an improved transportation infrastructure. New Mumbai is a new town developed to draw development pressure away from Mumbai itself, but it has been only marginally successful in that respect.

Kolkata's earliest metropolitan planning activities (in 1962) were assisted by the Ford

Foundation and the government of India and were seen as a model of comprehensive planning activity. However, there has since been a succession of plans that have never been fully implemented. With time, Kolkata's planning efforts have become more gimmicky and piecemeal. Much more pragmatic are Kolkata's slum improvement efforts. The slums, or *bustees,* are in the process of being cleaned up by the Kolkata Development Authority under a special legislative provision. Slums are being provided with underground sewerage, individual sanitary toilets in households, tap water connections inside homes, paved lanes and streets, and electrification of homes and streets. The government has introduced all these improvements from tax resources. By the same legislation, the landlords of the *bustees* are forbidden to increase rent or evict tenants unnecessarily. Thus, the public money spent for *bustee* improvement is not used for the profit of *bustee* landlords, but for the improvement of the hut dwellers' sanitary conditions, without making any basic change in the structure of the buildings.

Dhaka's planning endeavors, most recently based on a strategic planning approach for the years 1995–2015, have served to shape all new areas of the city, addressing residential provisions for middle- and upper-income groups, industrial and commercial development, and intracity transportation. More recently, special attention has been given to flood abatement, agricultural farmland preservation, and infrastructure. Flood abatement efforts have notably incorporated retention ponds in the east and west.

New Towns

New towns have been built as separate entities to serve as industrial, transport, university, or capital cities. Western planning imprints are evident in all the towns, because the towns have been planned by either Western planners or native planners trained in Western systems. Broad streets separated by neighborhoods, a garden-like atmosphere, clean housing with adequate utilities, and separation of nuisance-causing land uses, such as heavy industry and transportation terminals, from residences are generally common to all contemporary new-town planning. The best-known new towns of South Asia are Islamabad, planned by Constantinos Doxiades, and Chandigarh, planned by Le Corbusier.

Islamabad

Islamabad, capital of Pakistan and situated at the foothills of the Himalayas at an elevation of 1,800 ft (540 m), is at an undulating site of exquisite natural beauty. City building started in 1961 and people started to settle there in 1963. The city plan combines an extensive Islamabad Park toward the northeast, adjacent to which administrative and university centers have been established. Linear blocks of built-up land separated from each other by broad boulevards and a central open space have been designed in such a way that each one of the uses can be extended southwestward toward Rawalpindi, because it is in that direction that Islamabad is likely to grow. Only small-scale industries such as bakeries, printers, and other services for meeting the daily needs of the citizens have been allowed in the inner city. As these industries have no nuisance value, they have been located next to residential strips. A separate space has been reserved for the larger and nuisance-causing industries on the south-central periphery of the city. The administrative center, the seat of the central government, has been located in the north so that it can be extended along the foothills in the future. The residential areas comprise small townships or neighborhoods linked by a central commercial district and several trading units. Thus, such daily requirements as shopping, schooling, and recreation can be found in neighborhoods themselves. Pedestrian and vehicular traffic have been separated. The CBD and special institutions have been designed to contain multistoried buildings. The Islamabad capital site has an area of 350 sq mi (910 sq km), half of which consists of Islamabad Park. Islamabad had a population of more than a million in 2000.

Chandigarh

Like Islamabad, Chandigarh is located in the gently sloping terrain of the Himalayan foothills. Originally, the site was chosen for the capital of East Punjab; now it functions as the joint capital of two states of India—Punjab and Haryana—and as capital of the Union Territory of Chandigarh. The city was designed by Le Corbusier and built during the 1950s and early 1960s on a neighborhood plan containing fifty-three sectors, each self-contained with shopping areas, schools, hospitals, and parks. Le Corbusier also divided the traffic and roads into seven hierarchical levels, from regional roads down to small roads and pathways leading to houses. A western-style CBD is located at the center. The street system is based on a grid pattern. The capital complex is situated at the northern end of the city. Immediately to the south are the rich neighborhoods, with the middle class and then the poor living further out. Though the greenbelt was created around the Union Territory in order to check unplanned developments, it became less effective after Punjab was divided in 1966, giving rise to another state, Haryana. Eastern Chandigarh bordered Haryana, while to the west was Punjab. In 1968 the Punjab government took the first step to create an extension of Chandigarh outside the plan. It created SAS Nagar in the same grid pattern, extending the city toward Punjab in two further rows of sectors. Haryana developed a new town of Panchakula adjacent to Chandigarh, from which it was separated by a thin greenbelt. Thus, both Panchakula and SAS Nagar are satellite towns of Chandigarh, uncoordinated by Chandigarh city planning.

Although the Le Corbusier plan was designed to accommodate half a million people, Chandigarh has surpassed that number, with 642,000 according to the 2001 census. Chandigarh planners are in the process of relaxing the regulations on vertical development of the residential quarters in order to accommodate a higher density of population. Though the road system mostly follows the rectangular grid, the continuous open space along the median between the main roads and several east-west strips provides an uninterrupted vista of openness.

Chandigarh today has a rather disheveled, shabby appearance, the consequence of India's poverty, overpopulation, and insufficient financial resources to adequately maintain the city; also, the 1960s modernism of Le Corbusier's design now looks quaint and very out of place in the Indian cultural setting. With the look of a concrete jungle and without the use of readily available and locally produced bricks and stones, Chandigarh suggests the impropriety of hiring Western designers to plan cities for non-Western cultures. Indian building designs are absent. The buildings have been planned for withstanding summer heat without taking into consideration the harsh winters. Though the city has not aged well, it still is cleaner, more organized, and more livable than most other cities of India.

Box 9.3 Bangalore and Hyderabad: Silicon Valley and Globalization Come to South Asia

Former and current executives of software companies such as Microsoft are falling over themselves to invest in India's software industry. Near Hyderabad, one of India's largest cities and the capital of Andhra Pradesh state, a former Microsoft executive has spent millions of dollars of his company's money building a business park for software engineering, complete with the latest technologies and amenities—fiber optic cables, recreation centers, and even an ice rink!

Meanwhile, one state away, in Karnataka, IBM and other high-tech companies have already made substantial investments in such facilities. Millions have been spent on high-tech "campuses" where back-office functions for firms such as Infosys Technologies take place. As a result of such globalization, customer assistance centers for General Electric and British Airways take calls from all over the world. Rarely do the callers, in, say, the United States, even realize they are speaking to someone in India! While the annual salaries are not high by Western standards, they certainly are attractive in India. India's software industry is growing by leaps and bounds, already generating several billion dollars in revenue per year. This total is projected to increase exponentially in the next several years. Some project the technology sector in India at large to be a $90 billion industry by the year 2010.

Why has India emerged as an alternative location for software development and, of all places, why Bangalore and Hyderabad? After all, India is a country with a per capita GDP of $485, a telephone network that used to be considered inefficient, and an overburdened power-generating infrastructure. First, India is a country with highly developed universities and technical schools in relation to its level of development and overall literacy. This is in part because of postindependence development priorities, indigenous attitudes, and possibly, the colonial legacy. The emphasis on higher education and advanced technical skills has provided a large cohort of capable, yet underemployed workers in search of opportunity. Second, these locations offer a special combination of factors critical to a high-tech growth pole. Bangalore provides an entrepreneurial spirit, government flexibility, and the labor force to complement the venture capital. Similarly, in Hyderabad, the state's chief minister has pulled out all the stops in providing investment incentives and infrastructure to high-technology-related development. Third, the forces of globalization have allowed transnational corporations to take advantage of lower costs in other parts of the world. Technology has made distance less of a cost barrier and allowed what was unthinkable a generation ago, and first contemplated only several years ago, to become a reality today.

Both Chandigarh and Islamabad have been built at enormous cost. It is unlikely that construction of other new towns can even begin to solve the stupendous urban problems of South Asia. New towns will serve only the particular functions for which they are built. The future health of South Asian cities depends on new planning ideas melded into the South Asian setting. Several cities have already established a basic organizational infrastructure for such planning, which must be linked with larger regional plans. The success of city planning will depend on how financial investments are made for the improvement of the city, how city planning is integrated with each country's development, and how ingenious are the plans formulated to solve the unique problems of the region.

Ultimately, a country's ability or inability to solve its national development problems will be directly reflected in the cities. South Asia is a region still only marginally connected to the global economy and, as such, has not yet significantly benefited from the infusions of capital and the development prospects that have so greatly helped other world regions, such as East Asia. The cities are barometers of this reality (box 9.3).

SUGGESTED READINGS

Chapman, Graham P., Ashok K. Dutt, and Robert W. Bradnock. *Urban Growth and Development in Asia, Vol. II: Living in the Cities.* SOAS Studies in Development Geography. Aldershot, England: Ashgate, 1999. See, especially, Ashok K. Dutt and Anindita Parai, "Defining Urban Corridors: Case Studies of Four Mega Cities of India," 93–107; George Pomeroy, Ashok K. Dutt,and Vandana Wadhwa, "Spatial Patterns of Crime in Indian Cities," 292–99; and Wilke Ruiter, "Equity and Slum Redevelopment in Mumbai," 205–221.

Dupont, Veronique, Emma Tarlo, and Vidal Denis, eds. *Delhi: Urban Space and Human Densities.* New Delhi: Manohar, 2000.

Dutt, Ashok K., Animesh Halder, and Chandreyee Mitra. "Shifts in Slum Upgrading Policy in India, with Special Reference to Calcutta." In *Regional Development and Planning for the 21st Century: New Priorities, New Philosophies,* edited by Allen G. Noble et al., 125–50. Aldershot, England: Ashgate, 1998.

Evenson, Norman. *Chandigarh.* Berkeley: University of California Press, 1966. A comprehensive anatomy of planning in Chandigarh.

King, Anthony D. *Colonial Urban Development: Culture, Social Power, and Environment.* London: Routledge and Kegan Paul, 1976. A comprehensive sociological analysis of colonial urban forms of New Delhi, the hill station of Simla, and cantonment towns.

LaPierre, Dominique. *City of Joy.* New York: Warner Books, 1986. A novel set in Kolkata that became a Hollywood movie.

Misra, R. P., and Kamlesh Misra. *Million Cities of India, Vol. 1.* New Delhi: Sustainable Development Foundation, 1998.

Moorehouse, Geoffrey. *Calcutta.* New York: Holt, Rinehart and Winston, 1983. A popular classic that examines the city with passion and intensity; a riveting story.

Neville, S. Arachchige Don. *Patterns of Community Structure in Colombo, Sri Lanka: An Investigation of Contemporary Urban Life in South Asia.* Lanham, Md.: University Press of America, 1994.

Noble, Allen G., and Ashok K. Dutt, eds. *Indian Urbanization and Planning: Vehicles of Modernization.* New Delhi: Tata McGraw-Hill, 1977. More than 20 chapters on a variety of cities and issues in India's urban history.

Patel, Sujata, and Alice Thorner, eds. *Bombay: Mosaic of Modern Culture.* New York: Oxford University Press, 1995.

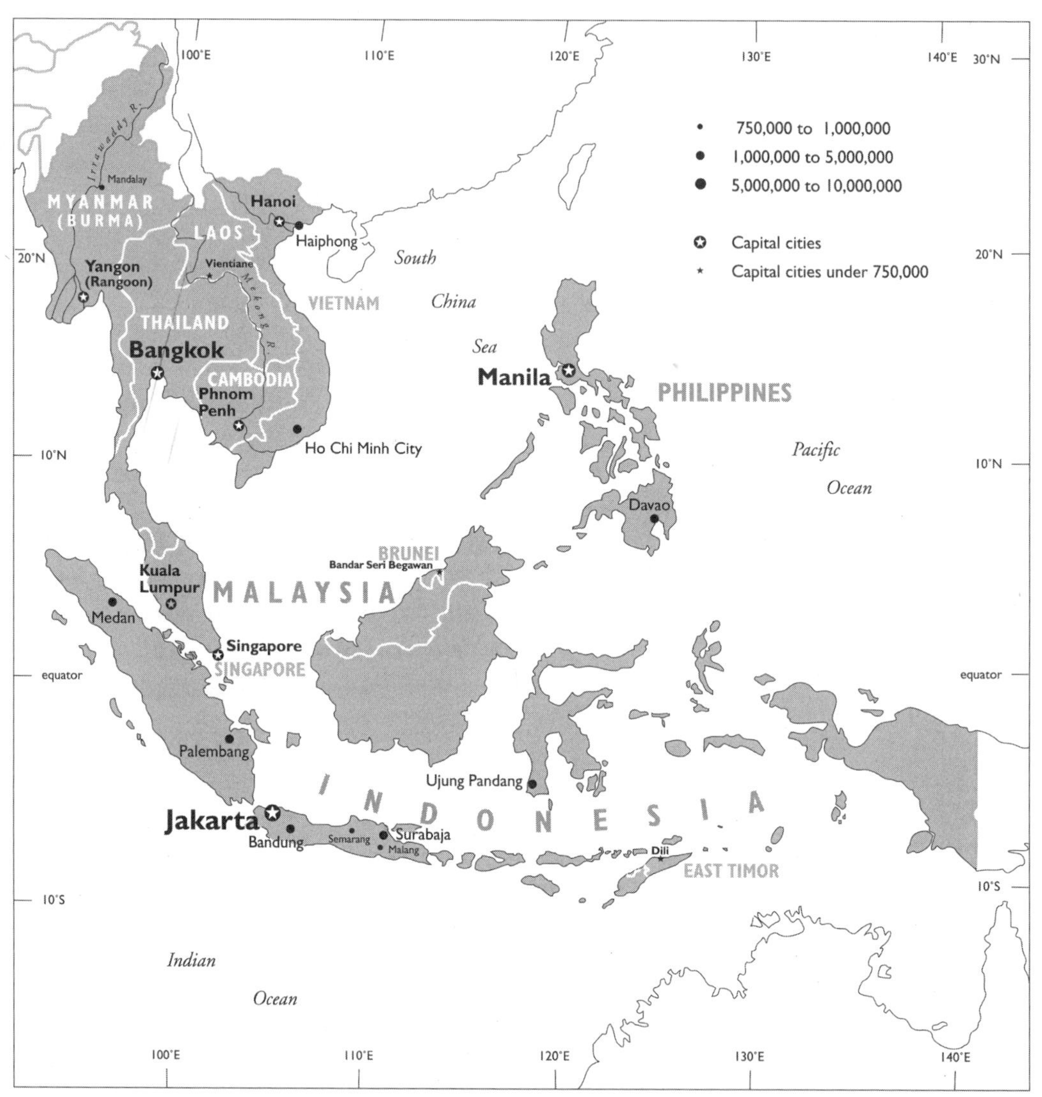

Figure 10.1 Major Cities of Southeast Asia. *Source*: Data from United Nations, *World Urbanization Prospects, 2001 Revision* (New York: United Nations Population Division, 2002), www.unpopulation.org.

10

Cities of Southeast Asia

JAMES TYNER

KEY URBAN FACTS

Total Population	530 million
Percent Urban Population	38%
Total Urban Population	203 million
Most Urbanized Country*	Philippines (59%)
Least Urbanized Country**	Cambodia (18%)
Annual Urban Growth Rate	3.7%
Number of Megacities	3
Number of Cities of More Than 1 Million	18
Three Largest Cities	Jakarta, Manila, Bangkok
World Cities	Singapore

* Excluding Singapore (100%) and Brunei (78%)
** Excluding East Timor (7.5%)

KEY CHAPTER THEMES

1. Urban landscapes of Southeast Asia have been shaped by Chinese, Indian, Malay, and international influences, especially colonialism.
2. All of the world's major religions are represented in the landscapes of the cities.
3. All of the major cities of the region have experienced rapid population growth since independence.
4. Primate cities (notably, Jakarta, Manila, and Bangkok) dominate the region, but the key urban center of Southeast Asia is Singapore.
5. Foreign influences, especially through foreign direct investment, play a critical role today.
6. Land reclamation is increasingly used in port areas to provide land for urban expansion.
7. Land-use patterns in the cities are very similar throughout the region.
8. Many cities are restructuring their economies to become "information technology" cities.
9. Some of the world's largest cargo ports—notably Singapore—are located here.
10. Transnational cities, which reach across national boundaries in their influence, are becoming more important.

Towering glass-encased skyscrapers, flashing Coca-Cola signs, McDonald's restaurants—the increasingly universal symbols of central cities around the world are very evident in the cities of Southeast Asia, especially the larger ones, giving the cities a deceiving sense of familiarity (fig. 10.1). Closer examination, however, reveals many subtle, and sometimes not-so-subtle, differences. Southeast Asia as a whole is a cacophony of cultures, with hundreds of different languages and many distinct religions. Nestled between two dominant culture hearths, China and India, Southeast Asia is a blend of indigenous and foreign elements. This diversity, not surprisingly, has been and continues to be inscribed upon the urban landscapes of the region, from the lotus-blossom-shaped stupas of Buddhist temples in Bangkok to the brightly colored Hindu temples in Singapore, from the golden-domed Muslim mosques of Kuala Lumpur to the Roman Catholic cathedrals in Manila.

Yet most people do not think of Southeast Asia as urbanized. The typical image of the region is agrarian—huts surrounded by brilliantly green rice paddies, with perhaps a water buffalo grazing disinterestedly nearby. While it is true that Southeast Asia is one of the least-urbanized regions of the world, it would be misleading to discount the long and varied urbanization process in Southeast Asia. Indeed, prior to the era of European colonialism (from the early 16th to the mid-20th century) Southeast Asia was one of the world's most urbanized regions. As late as the 15th century, for example, the population of Angkor (in present-day Cambodia) had a population in excess of 180,000; Paris, in contrast, had a population of only 125,000.

Five hundred years of colonialism and post-colonialism, dramatically altered the course of urbanization in Southeast Asia. Many countries, as well as cities, suffered tremendous population declines. Malacca (Melaka), for example, was once the premier entrepôt on the strait that shares it name. After capture by the Portuguese in the 16th century, however, it declined from over 100,000 to about 30,000 inhabitants. The history of Malacca and many other cities reveals a dynamic process of ebb and flow in the urbanization process.

Only four countries—Singapore, Brunei, Malaysia, and the Philippines—are more than 50% urbanized. Other states are more rural in character: Cambodia, Laos, Myanmar, and Vietnam, for example, are all less than 30% urbanized. Yet, with the exception of Thailand, all of the countries of Southeast Asia throughout recent years have exhibited urban population growth rates in excess of 3% per year, with some countries (Cambodia and Laos) at more than 6%. In short, the cities of Southeast Asia, following a period of stagnation or decline, are now experiencing rapid growth (table 10.1). In 1940, for example, no city in Southeast Asia registered a population of more than a million; by 1950, just two cities had surpassed this mark. In 2000, however, 13 cities exceeded the one million threshold. Three megacities—Jakarta (13.7 million), Manila (11.8 million), and Bangkok (10.3 million)—have also emerged. These massive urban agglomerations contain a disproportionate share of the region's urban population. Bangkok, for example, contains more than 54% of Thailand's urban population, while Manila accounts for nearly a third of the Philippines' urban population.

EVOLUTION OF CITIES

Precolonial Patterns of Urbanization

Southeast Asia is characterized by more coastline than perhaps any other major world region, and

Table 10.1 Southeast Asian Urbanization Trends and Projections

	Percent Urban				
Country/Region	*1970*	*1980*	*1990*	*2000*	*2010*
Southeast Asia	20.4	24.3	30.2	37.3	44.8
Indonesia	17.1	22.2	30.6	40.3	49.7
Thailand	20.8	24.5	32.0	40.0	n.a.
Philippines	33.0	37.5	48.8	59.0	66.6
Malaysia	33.5	42.0	49.8	57.5	64.4
Myanmar	22.8	24.0	24.8	28.4	35.4
Cambodia	11.7	12.4	17.6	24.1	31.6
Vietnam	18.3	19.2	19.9	22.3	27.4
Laos	9.6	13.4	18.6	25.1	32.6
	Urban Population Growth Rates (Average Annual Percentage)				
Country/Region	*1970–75*	*1980–85*	*1990–95*	*2000–05*	*2010–15*
Southeast Asia	4.2	4.3	4.0	3.4	2.8
Indonesia	4.9	5.3	4.5	3.6	2.6
Thailand	5.5	2.7	2.5	3.0	3.2
Philippines	4.2	5.2	4.2	3.1	2.2
Malaysia	4.8	4.4	3.9	3.0	2.2
Myanmar	3.3	2.1	3.3	3.9	3.7
Cambodia	–2.1	6.6	6.2	5.1	4.5
Vietnam	2.9	2.5	3.1	3.7	4.0
Laos	5.5	5.6	6.1	5.3	4.6

Source: Gavin W. Jones, "The Thoroughgoing Urbanization of East and Southeast Asia," *Asia Pacific Viewpoint* 38, no. 3 (1997): 237–44, table 1.

much of this coast is accessible to sea traffic. Indeed, Neptune's vast domain in Southeast Asia is approximately four times the combined land area of the 11 countries that make up the region. It is not surprising, therefore, that maritime influences have contributed significantly to the Southeast Asian urbanization process. The region also contains many fertile river valleys drained by the Mekong, Chao Praya, Irrawaddy, and Red rivers and their tributaries. Consequently, densely populated, agrarian societies also emerged throughout, especially on the mainland.

Although it is commonplace to speak of the global economy as beginning in the 16th century, it is important to recognize that international trade existed long before European states like England and Spain began colonizing the Americas, Africa, and Asia. Indeed, long-distance trade existed between China and India, and linked these areas with places as far afield as Africa, as far back as the early centuries of the first millennium A.D. The importance of long-distance trade in the eastern Indian Ocean and South China Sea regions, in fact, led to the appearance of a series of cities and towns along the coast of the Malay Peninsula and on the islands of Sumatra and Java.

Southeast Asia's geographical location made it a natural crossroads and meeting point for world trade, migration, and cultural exchange. A century before the Christian era began, seafarers, merchants, and priests entered the region, contributing to the urbanization process. Most Southeast Asian societies were influenced primarily by India, and this is most pronounced in religious and administrative systems. The process of "Indianization," however, was not marked by a mass influx of population, such as the movement of Europeans into North America. Neither was this process a replacement of indigenous Southeast Asian culture with Indian elements. Rather, the influence of India on Southeast Asia represented a more gradual and uneven process of exposure. China provided the other major cultural impetus, although this impact was greatest in Vietnam and through tributary arrangements with various maritime Southeast Asian kingdoms bordering the South China Sea.

Two principal urban forms emerged in precolonial Southeast Asia: the *sacred city* and the *market city*. Although both types of cities performed religious as well as economic functions, the two exhibited many differences. First, sacred cities were often more populous; wealth was gained from appropriating agricultural surpluses and labor from the rural hinterland. Market cities, in contrast, were supported through the conduct of long-distance maritime trade. Through the market cities passed the riches of Asia, including sandalwood, pearls, silks, tin, porcelain, and spices. Second, sacred cities were sprawling administrative, military, and cultural centers, whereas market cities were mostly centers of economic activity. In physical layout, sacred cities were planned and developed to mirror heaven and earth; that is, the cities served as symbolic links between human societies on earth and the forces of heaven. Monumental stone or brick temples commonly occupied the city center. Market cities, in contrast, tended to occupy more restricted coastal locations and thus had more limited hinterlands. These cities were more compact in their spatial layout. Lastly, compared with sacred cities, market cities were ethnically more diverse, populated by traders, merchants, and other travelers from all parts of the globe.

The earliest city to emerge in Southeast Asia was associated with the empire of Funan. Located along the lower reaches of the Mekong River, it flourished between the 1st and 5th centuries A.D. and was an important center for the exchange of cargo, ideas, and innovations. Indian influences were seen in the judicial and political systems of Funan, as well as in its language and writing systems. Funan became an important port for both Chinese and Indian traders, as well as other seafarers from as far away as Africa and the Middle East. The growth of Funan was related to its location at a place where the landscape enabled overland portage between the Bay of Bengal and the South China Sea. The decline of Funan began when, by the 5th century, advances in navigational technology opened up more efficient sea routes through the Strait of Malacca and the Sunda Strait.

Srivijaya was another important maritime empire, flourishing between the 7th and 14th centuries. It depended on international maritime trade and China's sponsorship through a tributary system, which meant paying tribute (goods and money) to the Chinese emperor in exchange for independence. Located on the Malacca Strait on the island of Sumatra, Srivijaya controlled many important sea-lanes, including the Sunda Strait. Evidence suggests that the Srivijayan Kingdom had numerous capitals, one of which was Palembang, located on the southeastern tip of Sumatra. Palembang provided an excellent, sheltered harbor and served as an important Buddhist pilgrimage site. To this day, Palembang remains an important port city and marketplace in Indonesia.

Another example of a market city is Malacca (fig. 10.2). Founded around 1400 on the west-

Figure 10.2 Malacca is one of the oldest towns in Southeast Asia and has changed hands many times, as successive rulers and colonial powers came and went. Today, it is an important commercial and tourist city in modern Malaysia. (Photo courtesy Malacca government)

ern side of the Malay Peninsula, Malacca was a counterpart to Palembang and emerged as an important entrepôt and key node in the global spice trade. Although Malacca never had a permanent population of more than a few thousand people, it was an extremely vibrant city, inhabited by many foreigners as well as indigenous Malays. Other important market cities located throughout Southeast Asia included Ternate, Makasar, Bantam, and Aceh.

Sacred cities often occupied more inland locations. One of the first of these was that of Chenla, an early successor state to Funan. Developed during the 6th century A.D., Chenla succumbed to the Java-based Sailendras. From their agricultural surplus wealth, the Sailendras were able to construct the world's largest Buddhist temple, Borobudur, on the island of Java. Built between A.D. 778 and 856, the ten-level Borobudur corresponds to the divisions within the Mahayana Buddhist universe and is one of the great cultural treasures of Southeast Asia. A UN-sponsored program rebuilt the complex several decades ago to preserve it for posterity.

The reunification of the two Chenlas led to the development of perhaps the best known of all inland sacred cities, Angkor (fig. 10.3). Located at the northern end of the Tonle Sap basin, the Angkorian Empire, at its peak, included present-day Cambodia and parts of Laos, Thailand, and Vietnam. The Angkor Kingdom was founded in 802 A.D. and by the 12th century contained a population of several hundred thousand. Similar to Borobudur and other sacred cities, Angkorian cities were designed to mirror the complex Hindu and Buddhist cosmologies. Angkor itself is composed of numerous temple complexes, such as Angkor Thom and

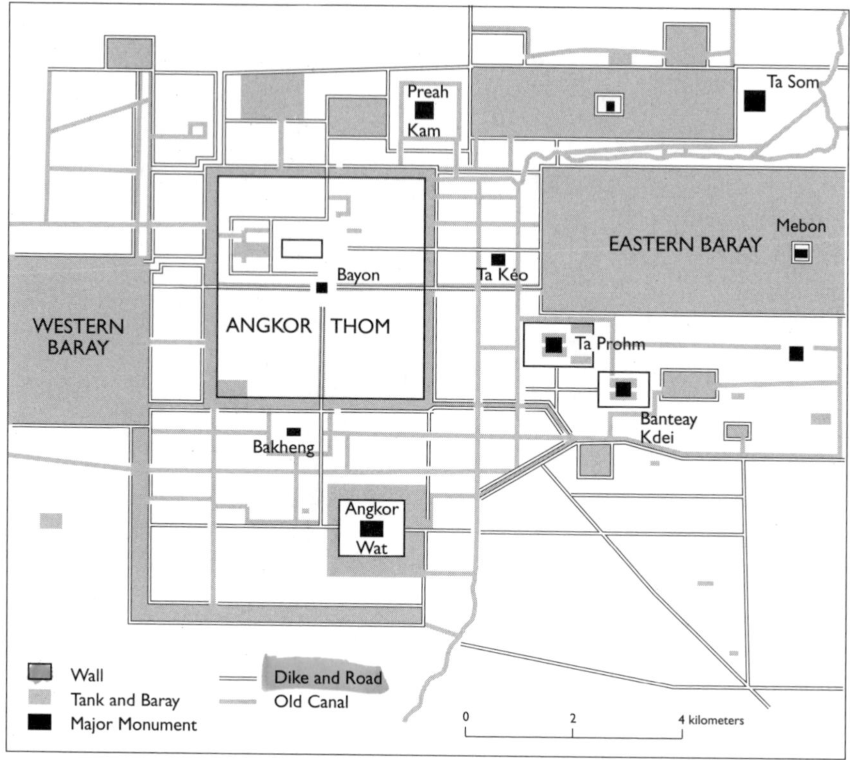

Figure 10.3 Plan of the Angkor Complex, ca. A.D. 1200. *Source*: T. G. McGee, *The Southeast Asian City* (New York: Praeger, 1967), 38.

Angkor Wat. In total, the temples of Angkor cover more than 200 sq mi (520 sq km).

By the 16th century, many of the once-prosperous inland sacred cities had declined. Numerous coastal market cities, such as Palembang and Malacca, continued to thrive on maritime trade. Through these cities diffused many of the world's major religions, including Hinduism, Buddhism, Islam, and Christianity, all of which have left their imprint on the urban landscapes of Southeast Asia.

Urbanization in Colonial Southeast Asia

Southeast Asia, compared to other world regions, was relatively urbanized at the time of European colonialism. By the 16th century, there were at least six trade-dependent cities that had populations of more than 100,000—Malacca, Thang-long (Vietnam), Ayutthaya (Siam, present-day Thailand), Aceh (Sumatra), and Bantam and Mataram (both on Java). Another half-dozen cities had at least 50,000 inhabitants. Spatially, the urban system of Southeast Asia was characterized by a predominance of strategic coastal locations that served an extensive international maritime trading system. Only the Philippines, because of its more peripheral location relative to the major sea-lanes, lacked an urban tradition. But even there, by the early 16th century, the seeds of urbanization had been planted. The sultanate of Brunei had extended its authority into the Philippine ar-

Box 10.1 Brunei Darussalam

Golden-domed mosques, soaring minarets, and offshore oil rigs. These are the symbols of Brunei. Situated on the northern coast of Borneo, Brunei Darussalam (meaning "abode of peace"), as the country is officially recognized, is an oil-rich Islamic sultanate. At 2,226 sq mi (5,788 sq km)—roughly the size of Delaware—Brunei is, with the exception of Singapore, the smallest state in Southeast Asia. Brunei is also exceptionally prosperous, with considerable income derived from its petroleum industries. Citizens of Brunei thus enjoy a high standard of living based largely on a massive state welfare system under the paternalistic leadership of the sultan, one of the richest men in the world. Health care and education are provided free and inexpensive loans are made available to citizens. Brunei thus resembles some of the oil-rich sheikdoms of the Persian Gulf.

Brunei is a highly urbanized state, with approximately 60% of the country's 336,000 residents living in cities. Bandar Seri Begawan, formerly Brunei Town, is the national capital and primate city of Brunei. Home to 50,000 people, Bandar Seri Begawan is the country's major commercial and business center and the home of the Royal Palace. More than half of the city's population lives in Kampong Ayer, the world's largest stilt village. Kampong Ayer is historically significant in that villagers have lived in these stilt houses perched over the Brunei River for more than 400 years. Seven miles to the northeast of Bandar Seri Begawan, situated on Brunei Bay, is Muara, the country's national port. Other important cities include Seria and Kuala Belait, both located on the northwest coast. These two cities function as important centers for the oil and gas industries, as well as for port operations. Seria has been the center of Brunei's petroleum industry since oil was first discovered there in 1929.

chipelago and with this came the spread of Islam (box 10.1).

In 1511, however, a Portuguese fleet captured the port city of Malacca, thus ushering in nearly 500 years of European colonialism. The Portuguese came primarily to gain access to and control of the lucrative spice trade and they were subsequently followed by the Spanish (1521), the British (1579), the Dutch (1595), and the French (mid-17th century). Other colonial activities, such as religious conversion, were less important at this time.

The early years of European colonialism in Southeast Asia were similar to colonialism in Africa and the Americas. Europeans captured or built garrisons in coastal cities, established treaties with local rulers, and thus brought about a transformation of the urban process in Southeast Asia.

During the first three centuries of colonialism, European influence was most pronounced in two regions: in Manila (the Philippines) under the Spanish and in Jakarta (Indonesia) under the Dutch. The first permanent Spanish settlement, Santisimo Nombre de Jesus (Holy Name of Jesus), was not established, however, until 1565 on the island of Cebu; in 1570, the Spanish occupied a site on the northern island of Luzon, situated on the Pasig River and proximate to Manila Bay. Two existing fishing villages known as Maynilad (from which the city takes its name) and Tondo were occupied and expanded. Apart from accessibility, defense was often an important consideration in early city planning. Dutch and Portuguese forces, as well as Chinese pirates, threatened the early settlement of Manila. Consequently, after 1576, construction began on a fortified structure known as the *Intramuros* (walled city). In time, Manila would become the commercial hub of the Philippines and a key node in the Spanish galleon trade that stretched from India to the New World.

The early European presence was also pronounced in Java. The Dutch East India Company during the 17th century established a few permanent settlements, one of which, Batavia, was to become the largest city in the region. The city is now known as Jakarta. Batavia had numerous locational advantages. Geographically, it was situated near both the Sunda Strait and the Malacca Strait, thus allowing easy access to maritime trade. The first Dutch building, a combination warehouse and residence, was built in 1611. In 1619, a plan was laid out for the city and Batavia replaced Bantam as the preeminent city of Java. Much of early Batavia was modeled after the cities of Holland; canals were dug and the narrow, multistoried Dutch residences were also copied. However, the architecture found in Europe was not functional in hot, humid locations such as Java, so building styles were altered to better fit the tropical environment.

Many of the great cities of Southeast Asia today trace their roots to European colonialism (fig. 10.4). Singapore (from the Malay words *singa*, lion, and *pura*, city), for example, began as a small trading post located at the southern tip of the Malay Peninsula, at the entrance to the Strait of Malacca, the premier passage through the island-studded seas of Southeast Asia. The town was known as Temasek (Sea Town) before 1819, when Sir Stamford Raffles of the British East India Company signed an agreement with the Sultan of Johor allowing the British to establish a trading post at the site. Benefiting from its strategic location and deep natural harbor, the incipient Singapore began to attract a large number of immigrants, merchants, and traders. As a British colony, Singapore emerged as one of the paramount trading cities in the region.

Saigon (now Ho Chi Minh City), which became the capital of French Indochina, likewise began as a small settlement, one that included a citadel and fortress surrounded by a Vietnamese village. Saigon's location in the Mekong delta region—one of the world's great rice granaries—provided the city an important function as agricultural collection, processing, and distribution center.

Bangkok, the capital of Thailand, was never colonized by the European powers, yet it still reflects considerable Western influence. Bangkok proper is a relatively new city; it was not founded until 1782. Prior to this date, the capital of Siam, as Thailand was then known, was located at Thon Buri along the Chao Praya River. Beginning in 1782, however, construction began on an easily defensible but swampy site located opposite Thon Buri, on the east bank of the Chao Praya. Later, during the reigns of King Mongkut (r. 1851–1868) and his son, King Chulalongkorn (r. 1868–1910), major public works were initiated. This is particularly evident in the expansion of rail and road networks, port facilities, and telegraph services.

The most significant impact of colonialism was the establishment of urban nodes, such as Bangkok, Manila, Batavia, Saigon, and Rangoon (now Yangon), that would grow into primate cities. Geographically, these cities were located at sites that provided access to seas or

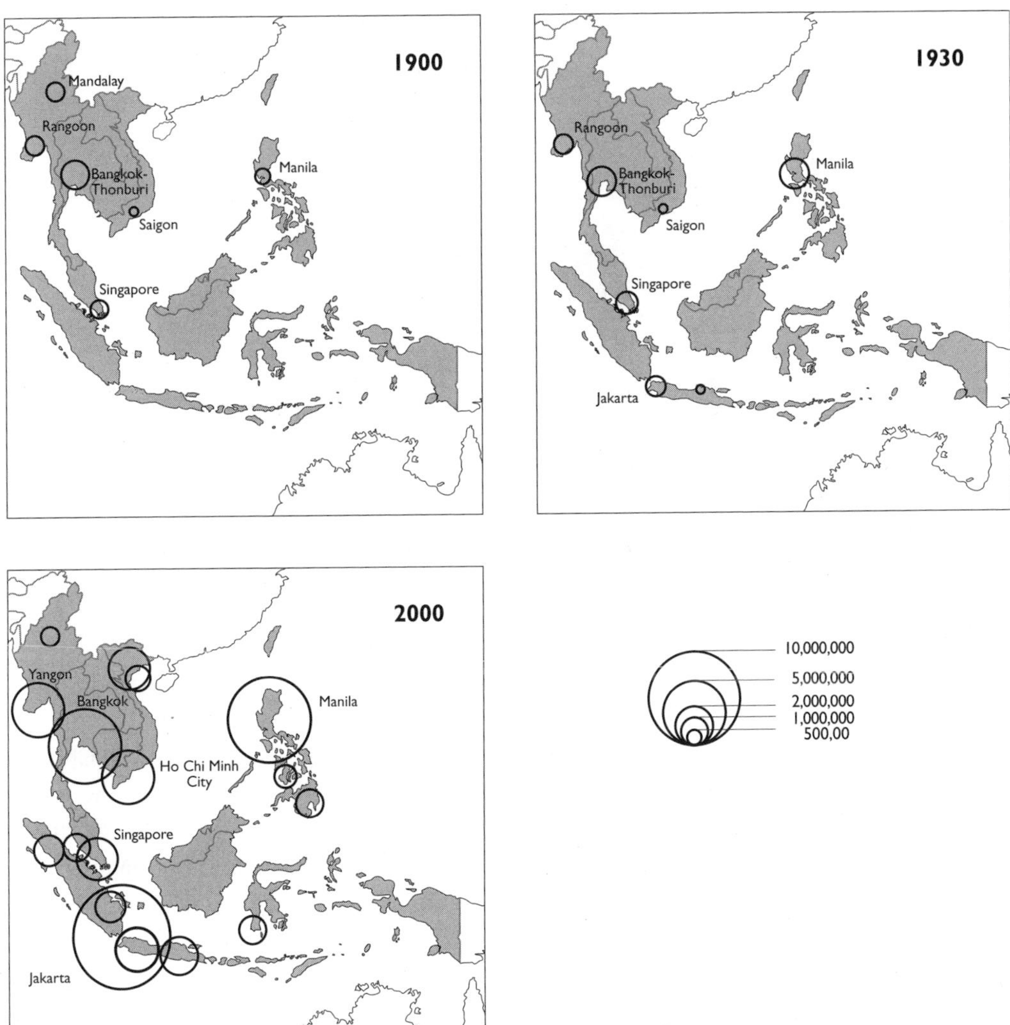

Figure 10.4 Urban Growth in Southeast Asia, 1900–2000. *Source*: Compiled by the author from various sources.

rivers. These locations afforded the European colonizers easy access, so that their ships could export primary products from the region and import secondary products from Europe and elsewhere. Such a dependence upon maritime trade, and the subsequent concentration of political and economic functions in these selected cities, contributed to the decline of other, more inland cities. In this manner, the urban system of Southeast Asia was turned inside out, as development was encouraged on the coast and suppressed inland.

The primate cities also provided multiple functions. Thus political, commercial, financial, and even religious activities were concentrated in these urban areas. Saigon, for

Fig 10.5 The Overseas Chinese are a pervasive presence in Southeast Asia, especially in the cities. This Chinese temple is in Georgetown, Penang, one of the original Straits Settlements that began British colonial rule in Malaya, and which brought the Chinese here. (Photo by Jack Williams)

example, was an administrative and manufacturing center, as well as the dominant trading port of Indochina. The primate cities also became exceptionally large. Stemming from the increased concentration of economic and political functions, these cities became magnets for both internal and international migration. Moreover, their populations were characteristically diverse. In many of these regions, the colonizers encouraged contract labor. The British, for example, actively encouraged the importation of labor from China and the Indian subcontinent, with the effect that, by the 19th century, immigration facilitated the establishment of Chinese communities in cities such as Singapore and Manila and of an Indian community in Singapore. Thus, segregated foreign quarters and Chinatowns emerged, for example, Cholon in Saigon (fig. 10.5). It was not uncommon for these segregated areas to arise through European force and prejudice. In Manila, for example, the Spanish government issued a series of decrees that required, with few exceptions, all Chinese, Japanese, and Filipinos to leave the Intramuros section of Manila before the closing of the city gates at nightfall. Additionally, Spanish authorities enacted regulations enforcing ethnic segregation and commercial activity.

Apart from the establishment of primate cities, a second impact European colonialism had on Southeast Asian cities was the establishment or transformation of smaller cities throughout the region. This included the establishment of mining towns, such as Ipoh in Malaysia, or regional administrative centers such as Medan on the island of Sumatra and Georgetown on the Malay Peninsula. Also notable was the emergence of upland resort centers or hill stations. To escape the oppressive heat and humidity, colonial powers would establish cities high in the mountainous regions. Bandung, for example, a small city located in a deep mountain valley on the island of Java, was established by the Dutch. The cool climate of Bandung served as a welcome relief from the tropical climate and also facilitated the cultivation of coffee (still known as "Java" worldwide), cinchona (for quinine), and tea. Other examples of hill stations included Dalat, a French-built city located 4,800 ft above sea level in the Central Highlands of Vietnam; Baguio City, a mountain resort developed by the Americans in the early 20th century, nestled atop a 4,900 ft (1,470 m) plateau in the Philippines; and the Cameron Highlands of peninsular Malaysia.

Lastly, European colonialism significantly affected the development of regional transportation and urban systems within Southeast Asia. Along the Malay Peninsula, for example, the British-built railways ran from the Perak tin-mining areas to the coast and were later expanded along a north-south axis to provide access to the ports and tin-smelting facilities in Penang and Singapore. Consequently, the major urban areas along the western coast of the Malay Peninsula—Kuala Lumpur, Ipoh, Seremban, and Singapore—formed an interconnected urban system that remains evident today. Similar patterns are also visible in Indonesia, wherein road and rail networks reflect access between sites of resource extraction (plantations and mines) and ports, and to a lesser extent can be seen in the Philippines and the former French Indochina. Colonial powers also exploited river systems (such as the Irrawaddy in Burma) for internal transportation systems, to exert political and economic control, to link their administrative functions throughout their colonies, and to provide access to sites of resource extraction (such as tin mines in Malaya).

REPRESENTATIVE CITIES

Decolonization and independence in Southeast Asia began at the turn of the 20th century, but did not formally end until the pullout of the Portuguese from East Timor in 1975. The forces of war, nationalism, and independence all changed the face of urbanization in Southeast Asia. Independence was the stepchild of carnage in Vietnam, Laos, and Cambodia, and their cities showed the scars. Hue, for example, which had served as Vietnam's capital until 1945, was practically destroyed in the Vietnam War. Phnom Penh suffered the same fate. Even in cities that were not scarred by war, the urban landscape changed. In Manila, for example, Dewey Boulevard, named after Admiral George Dewey, who defeated the Spanish at Manila Bay in 1898, was renamed Roxas Boulevard, after Manuel Roxas, the first president of the independent Philippines. In Jakarta, President Sukarno ushered in a period of massive monument building to provide Jakarta with new, highly visible symbols that would reflect new ideologies. One such is the National Monument, or *Monas,* a towering 429 ft (132 m) marble obelisk with a bronze and gold top designed to look like an eternal flame.

The list of key urban themes at the start of the chapter summarizes the more significant developments and characteristics of cities in the region since independence. Following are vignettes of key representative cities of the region: Singapore, Kuala Lumpur, Jakarta, Manila, Bangkok, and the evolving socialist cities of Phnom Penh in Cambodia and Ho Chi Minh City and Hanoi in Vietnam.

Singapore: World City of Southeast Asia

There truly is no other city in the world quite like Singapore (fig. 10.6). Its striking modernity, Disneyland-like cleanliness, and orderliness seem unreal, especially if one has just arrived from the sprawling, chaotic cities of

Figure 10.6 Singapore's ultramodern skyline towers over remnants of the British colonial era, a vivid reminder of how far this unique city-state has come. (Photo by Jack Williams)

Bangkok, Jakarta, or Manila. To some, Singapore is a model of efficiency, a mosaic of well-manicured lawns, efficient transportation, and planned development. To others, however, Singapore represents a draconian police state masquerading as utopia. The reality, of course, lies somewhere in between, depending on one's personal tastes and values.

Singapore remained a colonial possession of the United Kingdom until 1963. At that time, the city became part of the newly independent state of Malaysia. This arrangement lasted only two years, however, as in 1965 Malaysia set Singapore adrift. Singapore is unique within Southeast Asia, and in the world, in that it is both a city as well as a sovereign state.

Despite its small size—at just 246 sq mi (640 sq km), it is one-fifth the area of Rhode Island—Singapore is second only to Japan in per capita income in Asia. Historically, it has benefited from its strategic geographic location, superb natural harbor, and small size, which helps protect against uncontrolled rural-urban migration. Effective government policies and dynamic leadership have propelled Singapore into its role as Southeast Asia's leading port and industrial center, as well as a leading banking/commercial center. Indeed, Singapore ranks along with Tokyo and Hong Kong as one of the three key urban centers in Asia in today's global economic system.

Singapore's economy is based on a strong manufacturing sector (initially processing raw materials such as rubber, but more recently electronics and electrical products), oil refining, financial and business services, and tourism. The economic success of Singapore has translated into a very favorable quality of life. Singapore registers the region's lowest infant mortality rate and the lowest rate of population increase, in addition to the highest per capita income. This quality of life is facilitated through subsidized medical care and compulsory retirement programs.

Singapore has evolved into a truly cosmopolitan and world city. The affluence of Singapore is dramatically seen along the city-state's major shopping and tourist corridor, Orchard Road. In the 1830s, this area was home to fruit orchards, nutmeg plantations, and pepper farms. Today, Orchard Road stretches for approximately 1.5 mi (2.4 km) and is lined with major shopping centers, luxury hotels, and entertainment centers such as the Raffles Village (built around the lovingly restored classic Raffles Hotel, one of the great hotels of the past).

Singapore continues to reflect its rich ethnic heritage. Currently, approximately 75% of Singapore's population is ethnic Chinese; Malays and Indians constitute 15% and 7% of the population, respectively (fig. 10.7). To serve this diversity, Singapore has four official languages—English, Mandarin Chinese, Malay, and Tamil, a language of southern India. The immigrant history of Singapore is vividly preserved in the architecture. The Chinatown area of Singapore, for example, located at the mouth of the Singapore River, began in 1821, when the first junk load of Chinese immigrants arrived from Xiamen, in Fujian Province. It was there that Chinese immigrants in 1842 completed the Thian Hock Keng Temple, dedicated to Ma-Chu-Po (Matsu), the goddess of the sea. Nearby is Nagore Durgha Shrine, built by Muslims from South India, and further down the road is the Al-Abrar Mosque, also known as Indian Mosque, which was built between 1850 and 1855 (fig. 10.8). Because of land reclamation projects, the ultramodern skyscrapers of Singapore's financial district now eclipse Chinatown's oceanfront view.

Given the large number of historical temples and monuments, urban preservation is important in Singapore, although this has not always been the case. During the 1960s and 1970s, for example, many older buildings were demolished to make room for a more modern infrastructure. However, a movement to preserve Singapore's urban history was initiated; today, many areas, such as the waterfronts along Collyer Quay and Boat Quay, have been renovated (fig. 10.9).

Singapore is also instructive for its public housing programs. Beginning in the 1960s, the Singaporean government—primarily through the efforts of the Housing Development Board (HDB)—moved to ensure adequate housing

Figure 10.7 Arab Street in Singapore is a quaint reminder of the multicultural environment that lies beneath the city-state's Chinese majority population. (Photo by Richard Ulack)

Figure 10.8 The gaudy Indian Temple in Singapore is one of the best-known cultural landmarks of the city and a center of the Hindu minority population. (Photo by James Tyner)

for its population. The result was the establishment of numerous new towns and housing estates. The Queenstown housing estate, for example, located in the central region of Singapore, was one of the earliest estates developed by the HDB. Tao Payoh New Town and Ang Mo Kio New Town, both located within the Northeastern Region, were begun in 1965 and 1973, respectively. A more recent development is Woodlands New Town, located on the northern coast of Singapore. New towns are designed to be self-sufficient communities of many thousands of residents. Ang Mo Kio, for example, registered a 1990 population of 223,000 occupying more than 54,000 housing units. As such, new towns also exhibit a mixed land use. In Ang Mo Kio, for instance, one-third of the land is devoted to residential use; one-third is either undeveloped, water, or open space; one-sixth is commercial/industrial/institutional; and the remaining sixth is mostly road and infrastructure. By 2000, nearly 90% of Singaporeans lived in one of the high-density housing estates built by the HDB. Moreover, in recognition of Singapore's ethnic diversity, the government has mandated ethnic-based occupancy rates to offset the emergence of hyper-segregated enclaves.

New towns perform functions beyond housing. In particular, these areas are thought to contribute to an overall employment/housing balance in Singapore, enhance environmental conservation, and contribute to economic growth. The Woodlands Planning Area, for example, is envisioned to serve as a regional hub and gateway between Singapore and Malaysia.

Despite these successes, urbanization in Singapore remains, and will continue to remain, hindered by two physical obstacles. First, Singapore cannot readily expand its area, because it occupies only a small island. In response, the Singaporean government has utilized land reclamation schemes and has also been working to expand its growth beyond its own political boundaries into neighboring Malaysia and Indonesia (see the discussion on growth triangles in "Models of the Southeast Asian City"). In this manner, the government hopes to exploit the comparative advantages of Singapore and neighboring countries. A second, and perhaps more immediate, obstacle confronting Singapore is that of water (box 10.2). Despite these physical limitations, though, Singapore must be considered one of the more remarkable cities in all of Southeast Asia.

Figure 10.9 Sir Stamford Raffles, founder of Singapore, stands along Collyer Quay with restored shop houses on the opposite bank as reminders of Singapore's colorful past and tourism present. (Photo by Jack Williams)

Kuala Lumpur: *Twin Towers and Cyberspace*

The skyline of Kuala Lumpur is becoming as recognizable as that of Paris or San Francisco because of what looks like a giant double-barreled beehive, the massive 88-story Petronas Twin Towers, that dominates the capital city of Malaysia (fig. 10.10). As of the turn of the 21st century, the Petronas Towers (the tallest buildings in the world at the time of their construction) had become a symbol not only of Kuala Lumpur but also of the lofty goals set by the Malaysian government.

Like Bangkok, Kuala Lumpur is relatively young. The city was founded in 1857 by Chinese tin miners at the swampy confluence of the Klang and Gombak rivers (the name "Kuala Lumpur" translates as "muddy confluence"). The settlement grew rapidly and, by 1880, had become the capital of the state of Selangor on the Malay Peninsula. A railroad connected it with the coast in 1895 (fig. 10.11) and in 1896 Kuala Lumpur became the capital of the Federated Malay States.

Despite its growing political importance, Kuala Lumpur throughout much of the early 20th century was still overshadowed in population by other cities, known as the Straits Settlements, along the Malay Peninsula, including Georgetown and Singapore. And although designated capital of the Federated States of Malaysia in 1963, Kuala Lumpur still trailed both Singapore and Georgetown as preeminent commercial centers on the Malay Peninsula. In 1972, however, Kuala Lumpur gained city status and was declared a Federal Territory (similar to Washington's District of Columbia).

Kuala Lumpur experienced tremendous population growth throughout the late 20th century. Currently, the population is close to two million. However, unlike in the cities of

Box 10.2 A Thirsty Singapore

Water is arguably the single most critical site need for a city to survive and prosper. The case of Singapore provides a perfect example of this issue, which all the cities of the world must face. In Asia, Singapore and Hong Kong especially share this problem. Given that Singapore is an island located in the tropics and receives an average of 95 in of rainfall per year, it is ironic that water constitutes one of the greatest obstacles to the city-state's future. Residential and industrial water consumption amount to approximately 1.3 million cubic meters of water per day. Over the past decade, annual consumption has increased by nearly 5%.

Yet, water is a serious problem because the island contains no significant rivers or lakes to collect freshwater and so must rely on reservoirs and storm-water collection ponds to provide freshwater for its 3.5 million residents. Most water, however, is supplied by Malaysia. Two bilateral agreements (set to expire in 2011 and 2061) guarantee Singapore access to water; currently, approximately 52% of its water is provided by its northern neighbor. However, this dependency remains a source of concern, especially as 2011 approaches, because as Malaysia industrializes and its population continues to increase, it may have less water to export. Consequently, Singapore has been impelled to obtain alternative sources of water, both within the country and from without.

Singapore has initiated a series of conservation measures. These include public education and publicity programs advocating rational use of water. The installation of water-saving devices, such as flow regulators and low capacity flushing systems, is mandatory. This latter measure is especially significant since household water use—and particularly the flushing of toilets—accounts for more than 50% of water consumption. Within the industrial sector, the recycling of water and the substitution of nonpotable water (e.g., sea water, rain water) for potable water, has also been encouraged. Other measures, including water consumption taxes, have been implemented.

Aside from the conservation of water, Singapore has pursued means of obtaining more water. The installation of desalinization plants is a possibility. However, energy requirements are enormous for these plants; indeed, desalinated water is approximately eight times as expensive as natural freshwater. Moreover, the operation of desalination plants is affected by oil prices; during the 1970s oil crises, for example, many desalination plants around the world were forced to shut down in response to rising energy costs. Nevertheless, three new desalination plants are or will be under construction. Additional reservoirs may also help ease Singapore's thirst, although the development of these projects is hindered by land shortages. Lastly, Singapore has looked beyond its geographic boundaries to obtain sources of water. In 1991, for example, Singapore signed a memorandum of understanding with Indonesia to draw water from Bintan Island in the Riau Archipelago and from the Kampar River in Sumatra. This solution, though, simply replaces Singapore's dependency on Malaysia with one on Indonesia.

One thing is certain: a glass of drinkable water in Singapore will cost more in the future than it does today.

Figure 10.10 Kuala Lumpur, Malaysia's capital, competes with other Asian cities in the contest to have the tallest building in the world, with the beehive Petronas Towers already toppled from their title. (Photo by Richard Ulack)

Bangkok and Manila, there has been a more concerted effort to manage the urban growth of Kuala Lumpur. The planned development of satellite cities, for example, was designed to relieve the urban congestion of the primate city. In the 1950s, the satellite city of Petaling Jaya was established, and it is now home to more than 500,000 residents and is a major industrial center. Nearby, the satellite town of Shah Alam, initially planned to be half residential and half industrial, was built in the 1970s. Although shantytowns are visible in parts of Kuala Lumpur, as a whole the city exhibits a sedate orderliness more reminiscent of Singapore than of other major cities of Southeast Asia.

The economy of Kuala Lumpur, once dominated by tin mining, is now an exceptionally diverse mix of manufacturing and service activities. Many of these industries are clustered within the Klang Valley conurbation, an urbanized corridor stretching from Kuala Lumpur

Figure 10.11 The Moorish-style Railroad Station in Kuala Lumpur is one of the most distinctive buildings left from the British era and is now a treasure of the city. (Photo by James Tyner)

westward through Petaling Jaya and Shah Alam to the port-city of Klang. Also, indicative of the information economies emerging in Southeast Asia, Kuala Lumpur is pegged to become an anchor in an emergent "Multimedia Super Corridor" (MSC) in what is envisaged to be a setting for multimedia and information-technology companies. Designed to catapult Malaysia's economy into the global information age, the MSC will consist of more than 240 sq mi (624 sq km) of research, development, manufacturing, marketing, and distribution services. Two new cities are being constructed to the south of Kuala Lumpur: Putrajaya, which will become the administrative capital of Malaysia, and Cyberjaya, billed as an "intelligent city," complete with a state-of-the-art, integrated infrastructure that will attract multimedia and information-technology companies.

Jakarta: Megacity of Indonesia

Most visitors to Indonesia arrive first in Jakarta, a sprawling metropolis situated on the north coast of Java. At two and a half times the size of Singapore, Jakarta is the largest city in population and land area in Southeast Asia. From its origins as a small port town called Sunda Kelapa, the Special Capital Region of Jakarta (Daerah Khusus Ibukota, or DKI Jakarta) has experienced phenomenal growth over the past five decades. From fewer than 2 million in 1950, Jakarta's population had swollen to more than 9 million by 1990 and had reached more than 13 million by 2000. As with many primate cities in Southeast Asia, urban growth has sprawled into the hinterland. In recognition of this sprawl, in the mid-1970s officials began to refer to the entire region as Jabotabek, an acronym

Figure 10.12 The sprawl of massive Jakarta is visible in this bird's-eye view that simultaneously shows the old (the central Mosque, the largest in Southeast Asia) and the new (a line of the rapid-transit system designed to ultimately help bring order to Jakarta's traffic chaos). (Photo by Jack Williams)

derived from the combination of *Ja*karta and the adjacent districts of *Bo*gor, *Ta*ngerang, and *Bek*asi. When the entire Jabotabek region is considered, the population of the Jakarta metropolitan area swells to more than 17 million and will contain an estimated 24 million people by 2005 (fig. 10.12). Similar to other major cities in the region, Jakarta's population is also impacted by seasonal and daily commuting. Hundreds of thousands of workers, the majority of whom live in the Jabotabek region, commute daily to Jakarta.

Jakarta remains Indonesia's largest and most important metropolitan area. It is the national capital and the principal administrative and commercial center of the archipelago. The city also plays a vital role in Indonesia's international and domestic trade and receives a disproportionate share of foreign direct investment. This investment, focused primarily on manufacturing but also on construction and service sectors, operates as a multiplier effect for Jakarta's economy. In some respects, though, Jakarta has undergone a period of deindustrialization similar to that of other cities in the world, such as London. Thus, although the city remains an important manufacturing center, economic growth has been accounted for largely by increases in both tertiary and quaternary sectors (especially financial services, communications, and transportation).

Economic changes have contributed to changing land-use patterns. The central core of Jakarta has experienced significant changes over the past decades, such as a conversion

Figure 10.13 Only a minority of Jakarta's residents have access to piped water, so water vendors such as this wend their way through the streets selling this precious commodity. (Photo by Jack Williams)

from residential to higher-intensity commercial and office land use, as well as the emergence of luxury high-rise apartments. In the Jabotabek region, the development of new towns (e.g., Lippo City, Cikarang New Town, and Pondok Gede New Town) and corresponding large-scale residential subdivisions has also transformed previously agricultural land into urban spaces. Indeed, upwards of eighty thousand new housing units are added each year to the Jabotabek region. Other changes include the emergence of larger industrial estates as well as leisure-related land uses (e.g., golf courses).

Jakarta reflects the urban woes characteristic of primate cities, including a lack of adequate public housing, traffic congestion, air and water pollution, sewage disposal, and the provision of health services, education, and utilities (fig. 10.13). Because of the megacity's sheer size, not to mention the heightened political, social, and economic instability of Indonesia since the overthrow of President Suharto in 1998, Jakarta's problems are magnified to dangerous levels.

Manila: Primate City of the Philippines

Unlike walking the regimented, disciplined streets of Singapore and Kuala Lumpur, travel within Manila is an experience unto itself. Indeed, with the possible exception of Bangkok, no other city in Southeast Asia is as famous—or infamous—as Manila for its traffic. Throughout the day, and frequently at night, traffic grinds slowly through the maze of highways and alleys that constitute Manila's road network. Diesel-spewing *jeepneys,* rickety old buses, and luxury sport-utility vehicles all compete in bumper-car–like fashion (fig. 10.14). Turn lanes and even stoplights are largely ignored. Yet, beyond the chaos and congestion that puts the freeways of Los Angeles to shame, Manila exhibits its own charm and appeal.

Politically, socially, economically, and in

Figure 10.14 Unique to Manila, the *jeepney* is a form of urban transport that got started after World War II using old U.S. jeeps. Decked out with frills and gaudy decoration, the jeepneys play an important role and have become a symbol of Manila. (Photo by Jack Williams)

terms of total population, Manila far surpasses all other cities in the Philippines. Indeed, with the exception of Thailand, no other major country in the region has a higher primacy rate than does the Philippines. Currently, Manila is approximately nine times as large as the Philippines' second-largest metropolitan area, Cebu. Similar to Jakarta's Jabotabek, the Manila Metropolitan Area (MMA) is composed of many different political units. In 1975, the MMA was formed through the integration of the four preexisting, politically separate cities of Manila, Quezon City, Caloocan, and Pasay, plus thirteen municipalities.

The Metro Manila region, reminiscent of the multiple nuclei model, is a polynucleated area with many distinct personalities. Binondo, for example, located next to the Pasig River, was originally a Christian Chinese commercial district during the Spanish colonial period and to this day remains Manila's Chinatown. Nearby is Tondo, today an impoverished, densely populated district of rental blocks; prior to the arrival of the Spanish, it was a collection of Muslim villages. To the south, abutting Manila Bay, is Ermita. Once a small fishing village, the area developed into a prime tourist destination, packed with bars, nightclubs, strip shows, and massage parlors. In recent years, however, these establishments were closed down in Ermita and have since relocated to other areas of Manila. As a final example, Makati, originally a small market village, is now Manila's major financial center, occupied by banks and multinational and national corporations. Makati also contains some of Manila's most expensive housing subdivisions, sprawling shopping centers, and five-star hotels.

Named after Manuel Quezon, who served as president of the Commonwealth of the Philippines (1934–1946), Quezon City served as national capital from 1948 to 1976. Now it is home to many important government buildings, medical centers, and universities,

Figure 10.15 The informal economy thrives in the cities of Southeast Asia, as with this vendor selling corn on the cob in the streets of Manila. (Photo by Richard Ulack)

including the main campuses of the University of the Philippines and Ateneo de Manila University. Quezon City also consists of upscale gated residential communities patrolled by armed guards. These estates are equipped with luxurious air-conditioned homes, tennis and basketball courts, golf courses, and swimming pools. However, reflective of Manila's complex land usage, as well as the highly polarized nature of Philippine society, just outside of these gated communities are numerous squatter settlements.

Characteristic of large cities in Southeast Asia, Manila exhibits increasing consumer spaces. In recent years, large shopping malls have been built. For many visitors, these malls are remarkably similar to those found in the United States and Europe. Major department stores anchor the malls, while in-between are dozens of specialty stores, food courts, and entertainment venues (fig. 10.15). The SM Megamall, for example, in addition to its numerous stores and restaurants, contains an ice-skating rink, bowling lanes, a twelve-screen cinema, and an arcade room.

Similar to both Jakarta and Bangkok, the increased concentration of foreign direct investment into the Philippines has translated into rapid changes in the economy of Manila as well as in land use. During the 1990s, the greater Metro Manila region and surrounding provinces experienced phenomenal industrial and manufacturing growth. This expansion, however, occurred at the expense of Manila's rural hinterland. Metro Manila is, in fact, located at the center of the Philippines' major rice-producing area, and continued urban sprawl is rapidly encroaching on these agricultural areas.

Urban poverty and landlessness continue to be major problems in Manila; the extent of these problems, however, remains a contested issue. Estimates of the number of poor vary widely, ranging from 1.6 million to more than 4.5 million. What is certain, however, is that landownership in Manila is decidedly uneven, with the majority of its population landless. High urban land values mean that the majority of residents are unable to obtain legal housing, a situation exacerbated by continued high rates of in-migration. Their recourse is to resort to illegal housing and to settle in urban fringe areas, such as along railroad tracks and in vacant lots. Residents of squatter settlements are subject to deplorable health conditions and pollution problems. Historically, squatter settlements have been demolished and their residents evicted (box 10.3). Aside from poverty, Manila faces other serious problems. Accessibility to water, for example, looms large. Manila is also confronted with serious air and water pollution problems, as well as an inadequate sewerage system. Indeed, during the rainy season many streets throughout Manila, such as those in the port district and Tondo, become impassable due to flooding.

Bangkok: Los Angeles in the Tropics

Bangkok, at 34 times the size of Thailand's second-largest city, Nakhon Ratchasima, is the textbook example of urban primacy. While only one-fifth of the country is urbanized, fully two-thirds of this urban population is concentrated in the Bangkok Metropolitan Region (BMR). Currently, the core of Bangkok has a population of about 6 million; when the entire BMR is considered, the region's population is more than 10 million. The population of Bangkok does fluctuate, both daily and seasonally. An estimated one million people commute daily into Bangkok. Additionally, Bangkok experiences a distinct pattern of seasonal migration wherein in February—a slack agricultural period—many workers move to the city in search of temporary jobs in the informal sector.

The official name of Bangkok is Krung Thep, which translates as "The City of Angels" (the same meaning as Los Angeles). In many respects, Bangkok might be considered the Los Angeles of Southeast Asia. At the dawn of the 21st century, Bangkok was poised to become an international communications and financial center, as well as a major transportation hub in Asia. Initially, much of Bangkok's growth was tied to massive amounts of investment brought about by the United States' involvement in the Vietnam War. During the 1960s, in particular, Bangkok served as a major military supply base. In subsequent decades, it has continued to attract large sums of foreign investment. Between 1979 and 1990, nearly 70% of all foreign investment projects in Thailand were concentrated in the BMR. Economically, Bangkok has capitalized on its reserves of cheap labor, favorable tax incentives, and political stability.

Similar to Jakarta and Manila, Bangkok is a multinucleated city. And while the "old city" remains the principal administrative and religious core of Bangkok, considerable expansion has occurred into the surrounding districts of Pratunam, Raja Prasong, Siam Square, Silom, and Suriwong. Bangkok has also experienced a rapid conversion of land use, with many residential areas in the city being converted to commercial use and former small shop houses being transformed into high-rise office buildings and large shopping complexes.

Radiating outward in a concentric pattern, urban growth surrounding Bangkok has largely been haphazard and unplanned. Indeed, until 1992 Bangkok did not have an official city plan. And even now, former prime rice-producing and fish-farming areas are being converted to industrial uses and capital-intensive enterprises.

The overurbanization of Bangkok has resulted in serious environmental problems. Air and water quality have deteriorated in recent years, while the disposal of solid waste is a perennial problem. Also, Bangkok is sinking. Due to the overdrawing of well water, the city suffers from land subsidence, as its elevation drops at a rate of about 10 cm per year. Indeed, some areas have subsided by more than three feet since the 1950s.

Bangkok is also plagued by severe transportation problems. The number of motor vehicles (excluding motorcycles) increased from 243,000 in 1972 to more than a million in 1990;

Box 10.3 Smokey Mountain

Trash, or garbage, bedevils cities around the world, as population and consumption both rise. What to do with trash is a chronic problem everywhere. Smokey Mountain, a 70 acre (29 ha), smoldering garbage dump north of Manila, was home to more than 13,000 people. Throughout its five decades of existence, it came to symbolize the extreme poverty and squalid conditions of many third world cities. However, Smokey Mountain also provides a case study in collective action and self-reliance.

Located next to Manila Bay, the area known as Smokey Mountain was originally the site of numerous small fishing villages. Beginning in the 1950s, as Manila experienced rapid growth, garbage began to be dumped in the area. Initially, much of the refuse washed out to sea, but as the pace of urbanization increased, the natural mechanisms for removing the garbage were overwhelmed. With rapid rural-urban migration and a lack of adequate housing, people began living in the area. By the late 1980s, there were approximately 3,500 families (more than 13,000 individuals) living in the squatter settlement. The majority of the residents worked as scavengers on Smokey Mountain. Others engaged in street scavenging throughout Manila.

Historically, government policy was to demolish squatter settlements and to relocate the residents. In 1978, however, missionaries of the Society of the Divine Word (SDW) began to build *Basic Christian Communities* on Smokey Mountain. The concept of the Basic Christian Communities was to help the residents of Smokey Mountain to help themselves. This began through the organizing of the communities. The communities were structured around three dimensions: spiritual, economic, and historical. Spiritually, the communities served to uplift the residents through the provision of Christian guidance. Accordingly, self-reliance, personal empowerment, and communal responsibility were stressed. Economically, the communities facilitated the formation of locally based cooperatives. A long-range goal was to have no one on Smokey Mountain earn a living via scavenging. Through the assistance of local and international, private and government organizations, the residents learned management and leadership skills, obtained occupational training, and learned to write grant proposals. Numerous cooperatives were formed, such as for health, education, and day care. Networks and alliances were formed with other local groups throughout Manila and the rest of the Philippines.

Smokey Mountain, however, no longer exists. Since 1992, when President Fidel Ramos closed the dump site, the area has witnessed a massive face-lift. Through private development, the shoreline property is steadily being converted into a major commercial and industrial park. Additionally, more than 30 permanent, medium-rise condominiums are being or will be built to provide housing. Most of the former residents live in a Smokey Mountain Development and Reclamation Project housing compound, waiting to move into the condominiums. Most of the former residents have been able to obtain nonscavenging jobs.

Poverty, for many people living in Southeast Asia, is a fact of life. But the lessons of Smokey Mountain speak of hope and inspiration rather than passivity or victimization.

Figure 10.16 All cities have traffic problems, but the primate city of Bangkok, one of Southeast Asia's largest, chokes on its traffic congestion. (Photo courtesy Bangkok government)

concurrently, only about 50 mi of primary roads were added. As a result, the average speed on most roads in Bangkok is less than six miles per hour (fig. 10.16). Numerous proposals and strategies have been advanced to rectify traffic congestion, including increased road capacity, improvements in public mass-transit systems, improvements in the traffic control system, and strategies to control the volume of traffic (e.g., staggered office hours to reduce peak commuting traffic). The government is also encouraging the growth of satellite cities as a means of promoting regional economic growth and relieving the congestion of Bangkok.

Phnom Penh, Ho Chi Minh City, Hanoi: Socialist Cities in Transition

In early morning, the dusty streets of Phnom Penh are alive with swarms of noisy motorbikes that surge like schools of fish. Luxury cars compete for space with the motorbikes. Plodding along the roadsides are converted tractors with wooden trailers that ferry scores of young women—all dressed in identical green-and-white uniforms—to the foreign-owned factories that ring the periphery of the city. Such is Phnom Penh in the 21st century: a frantic, disorderly city that is rebuilding after decades of tumultuous revolutions and genocide. The experiences of Phnom Penh, Ho Chi Minh City, and Hanoi provide vivid proof that urbanization is intimately associated with broader social movements, including revolutions.

Socialist cities in Southeast Asia have experienced, and reflect, a different pattern of urbanization than is the case with capitalist-based cities. The urbanization process in Southeast Asia's socialist countries has been analyzed in a three-stage model. The first stage consists of a process of deurbanization whereby major cities were depopulated. As the Khmer Rouge assumed control of Cambodia in 1975, the socialist government undertook a forced evacuation of the capital city, Phnom Penh. Prior to this date, the population of Phnom Penh had swollen in size from around 700,000 in 1970 to approximately 2.5 million by 1975. This population increase resulted mostly from an inflow of refugees from the countryside escaping the guerrilla fighting. By the end of April 1975, however, the city's population was only about 2,000 and consisted mainly of soldiers and a few workers attached to the Khmer Rouge government, along with their families. The cause of this massive deurbanization process was ideological in nature. In effect, the socialist revolution in Cambodia constitutes a classic example of social engineering. Upon their ascension to power, the Khmer Rouge attempted to transform Cambodia into an agrarian, preindustrial society. The purported goal was to recapture Cambodia's golden age of Angkor. Since Angkor was a predominantly agrarian, rice-based society, the Khmer Rouge leaders believed that cities constituted the evils of capitalism and Western influence. The evacuation of Phnom Penh, however, was genocidal in nature. An estimated 1 to 3 million people were killed during the Khmer Rouge's attempt to transform the country. People were either executed outright or worked to death on communal farms.

Today, the city of Phnom Penh still bears the scars of its genocidal past. With the exception of its major thoroughfares, many of the streets in Phnom Penh are unpaved and pockmarked with potholes. Numerous partially destroyed buildings remain as silent reminders to the brutality of recent history. Yet, Phnom Penh is rebuilding, reflecting a new orientation toward the global economy. For example, along the major road linking Phnom Penh and Cambodia's International Airport, multinational corporations have established a visible presence, while in the capital many side streets are lined with English-language schools.

In Vietnam, a similar, though less brutal, process of deurbanization occurred. The population of Saigon, like that of Phnom Penh, had also increased dramatically through inmigration and refugee flows. By 1975, Saigon had an estimated 4.5 million people. Following the communist victory of the Democratic Republic of Vietnam, the new government planned to move as many as 1.5 million people out of Saigon; ultimately, however, only about one million people were relocated. The process of deurbanization in these socialist countries was often accompanied by a refashioning of the cities. Initially, Western-style establishments and customs were replaced with a spartan milieu. Cities were drab and monotonous, composed of row upon row of uniform, box-like buildings. Conforming to socialist ideology, the new governments attempted to eliminate the private sector; shops, restaurants, hotels, and services were generally run by either government enterprises or cooperatives. Consequently, cities were typically devoid of the mass advertising that is commonplace in capitalist cities. The new governments fostered symbolic changes as well. The renaming of Saigon to honor Ho Chi Minh, who led the fight against the French and established communism in Vietnam, provides the clearest illustration. Another visible difference was the traffic. In Hanoi, the streets were practically empty of motor vehicles, save for an occasional Soviet-era limousine and a few battered and decrepit buses. Instead, bicycles thronged the streets, especially during peak hours, when residents cycled to and from work and school. In short, the newly formed socialist governments attempted to wipe clean, so to speak, the slate of capitalist-based urbanization.

Following this initial stage, socialist gov-

Figure 10.17 The former French governor-general's mansion in Hanoi, beautifully restored and used as a government building today, is an elegant reminder of the French colonial history in Vietnam. (Photo by Jack Williams)

ernments entered into a second, bureaucratic stage wherein longer-term strategies of socialist urbanization were implemented. The socialist government in Vietnam, especially, developed spatial strategies to ameliorate the problems of large cities, including the provision of adequate food, employment, and housing. Policies were enacted to restrict population mobility, thereby affording relief to the infrastructure of large urban areas, such as Ho Chi Minh City and Da Nang.

Socialist reform constitutes the third stage of the model. Although economic reforms were first introduced in Vietnam in 1979, it was not until 1986, with the introduction of *doi moi* (renovation), the slogan for the government's new development strategy, that substantial improvement occurred. *Doi moi* entails the gradual introduction of capitalist elements, including private ownership, foreign investment, and market competition. In short, Vietnam remains politically committed to socialism but economically is exhibiting a shift toward capitalism and a greater level of integration into the global economy.

Spatially, economic reforms have focused predominantly on the southern region of Vietnam, and especially Ho Chi Minh City, because of that city's much longer tradition with free-market economics and linkages with the outside world. By analogy, Hanoi is Vietnam's Beijing (fig. 10.17) and Ho Chi Minh City is the country's Shanghai. Approximately 80% of all foreign investment into Vietnam is directed toward the south. Investments in tourism, assembly, and manufacturing are concentrated in the larger urban areas. Not surprisingly, therefore, regional disparities of foreign investment and economic reforms have transformed urban areas. Indeed, the cities of Hanoi and Ho Chi

Figure 10.18 In the reform era of *doi moi* in Vietnam, private enterprise is now actively encouraged, as evidenced by these shops and street-side vendors in Ho Chi Minh City. (Photo by Jack Williams)

Minh provide stark contrasts in the evolution of cities in socialist Southeast Asia. Although both retain remnants of their colonial histories, Hanoi—the political capital of Vietnam—remains the more sedate, regimented, and subdued of the two, while Ho Chi Minh City is a bustling metropolis (fig. 10.18), an urban forest of hotels, restaurants, bars, nightclubs, and discotheques. It has returned to its prewar capitalist character, with luxury hotels—such as those of Hyatt, Ramada, and Hilton—competing side by side with government-run hotels. Hanoi, conversely, contains many symbols of Vietnamese nationalism, such as the Ho Chi Minh Mausoleum and the Ho Chi Minh Museum. By the end of the 1990s, however, Hanoi was beginning to show the effects of the increased globalization of Vietnam and beginning to take on some of the color and dynamism of its rival in the south.

COMPONENTS OF URBANIZATION IN SOUTHEAST ASIA

Urban growth in Southeast Asia is the result of five different processes.

First, areas formerly classified as rural may be reclassified as urban. Indeed, urban populations may change simply through administrative acts, as in the case of Malaysia, where the number of people needed for an area to be classified as urban changed from 1,000 to 10,000 in 1970.

Second, urban areas may grow in population through natural increase, that is, the excess of births over deaths. If urban-based women exhibit higher fertility levels than their rural-based counterparts, the urban population will increase more rapidly vis-à-vis rural areas. Although rural areas in general exhibit higher fertility than urban areas in Southeast

Asia, this relationship may be reversed if the urban area receives a large number of migrants who are in their reproductive years. In general, natural increase accounts for about one-half of the urban population growth in Southeast Asian countries. It is important to remember, however, that while overall natural increase may contribute to *urban growth,* it may not contribute significantly to *urbanization,* that is, the increasing proportion of people living in urban areas relative to rural areas.

Third, urban areas may increase more rapidly than rural areas, thus contributing to urbanization, if the mortality of urban-based people is lower than that of their rural-based counterparts.

Fourth, a net redistribution of people from rural to urban areas through migration will contribute to urban growth. Studies reflect that, overall, rural-urban migration has played a major role in both the rapid urbanization and urban growth in Asian countries over the past two decades. Internal migration is extremely important to the urban growth of Thailand, for example. In 1990, the Thai census recorded more than 1.5 million rural-urban migrants—although there were more than twice as many rural-rural migrants—and currently, approximately one out of every seven urban residents in Thailand is classified as a recent migrant.

Fifth, international migration may contribute to urban growth, as overseas migrants tend to move to urban areas as opposed to rural areas. Singapore and, to a lesser extent, Kuala Lumpur, are two of the major immigrant receivers in Southeast Asia. That said, many governments—including Singapore's—often try to prevent immigrants from settling permanently. Thus, urban growth via international migration—for Southeast Asia—remains a relatively insignificant component.

The components of urban growth by country for the periods 1980–1985 and 1990–1995, and those projected for 2000–2005, are presented in table 10.2. It is immediately obvious that, within Southeast Asia, over the past two decades the combined components of migration and reclassification account for the largest portion of urban growth. There was also considerable variation among countries. Urban growth in Myanmar, the Philippines, and Vietnam, for example, has occurred primarily through natural increase, whereas natural increase has assumed a lesser role in Cambodia, Thailand, Malaysia, and Indonesia. The importance of internal migration to the urbanization process of Cambodia, of course, is a consequence of the forced displacement of urban-based people during the murderous Khmer Rouge regime (1975–1979). The urban growth of Singapore, not surprisingly, consists only of natural increase.

Aggregate numbers such as these mask significant social and economic changes that are occurring. Internal migration in Southeast Asia, for example, is increasingly dominated by female migrants. In Thailand, the share of female migrants increased from 53% of all Bangkok-bound migrants in the 1970s to more than 62% in the 1980s. The increased feminization of internal migration in Thailand is related to structural changes occurring in both the rural and urban areas. The majority of these women—most of whom are in their early twenties—originate from northeastern Thailand, one of the most impoverished regions in the country. Faced with minimal prospects in the rural areas, these women are increasingly moving to Bangkok to obtain employment in unskilled factory work, the service sector, or the informal sector. Also,

Table 10.2 Components of Urban Growth in Southeast Asia (percentage of urban growth)

	1980–1985		*1990–1995*		*2000–2005*	
	Natural Increase	*Migration and Reclassification*	*Natural Increase*	*Migration and Reclassification*	*Natural Increase*	*Migration and Reclassification*
Southeast Asia	49.1	50.9	44.9	55.1	41.7	58.3
Cambodia	70.9	29.1	49.5	50.5	30.6	69.4
Indonesia	35.2	64.8	37.0	63.0	36.7	63.3
Laos	43.8	56.2	44.7	55.3	43.8	56.2
Malaysia	22.0	78.0	38.0	62.0	40.0	60.0
Myanmar	110.0	–10.0	63.2	36.8	44.5	55.5
Philippines	66.0	34.0	62.4	37.6	57.0	43.0
Singapore	100.1	–0.1	100.1	–0.1	98.9	1.1
Thailand	39.6	60.4	31.4	68.6	31.2	68.8
Vietnam	71.7	28.3	50.5	49.5	38.1	61.9

Source: Graeme Hugo, "Demographic and Social Patterns," in *Southeast Asia: Diversity and Development,* edited by Thomas R. Leinbach and Richard Ulack, 74–109 (Upper Saddle River, N.J.: Prentice Hall, 2000), table 4.17.

a certain number of these migrants find employment in the sex business and end up working in brothels, massage parlors, or strip shows. Likewise internal migration to Jakarta has become more feminized in response to the city's structural transformation to a more service-based economy.

Not all internal migration is permanent. Indeed, many cities in Southeast Asia are impacted by daily or seasonal circular migration. Three factors are readily identifiable. First, circulation is highly compatible with work participation in the urban informal sector. Migrant laborers are able to circulate between rural villages and urban sites depending on the season. Circulation thus offers a flexible solution to the seasonality of labor demands; laborers are able to work on the nearby farms during the peak agricultural period, while during downtimes these same workers are able to participate in the informal economy in the city. Second, circular migration diversifies families' income-generating activities. Depending on the relative economic strength of urban and rural areas, workers may alternate their activities accordingly. Third, circular migration has, with advances in transportation systems, become a more viable option. Improvements in transportation systems, such as paved roads and mass-transit bus lines, have permitted people to move with greater ease, thus contributing to the growth of residential suburbs.

Malaysia provides a good case study to examine more closely the varied components of urban growth. Table 10.3 indicates the components of population growth of major urban areas in Malaysia for two time periods, 1970–1980 and 1980–1991. During the first period, the cities of Kuala Lumpur, Kuala Terengganu, and Kota Bharu increased partly due to reclassification, as all of these cities experienced substantial boundary changes. Indeed, reclassification accounted for nearly 42% of Kuala Lumpur's population increase. Other cities in Malaysia, such as Georgetown, declined in urban population, mostly because

Table 10.3 Components of Population Growth in Peninsular Malaysia, 1970–1980 and 1980–1991 (thousands)

		Population Change Due to		
Urban Areas	*Change in Population*	*Natural Increase*	*Reclassification*	*Net Migration*
1970–1980				
Kuala Lumpur	467.6	167.6	196.3	103.7
Ipoh	45.9	51.3	0.1	–5.5
Johor Bahru	110.2	50.2	16.8	43.3
Klang	78.4	48.6	12.5	17.4
Petaling Jaya	115.1	28.3	20.4	66.4
Kota Bharu	112.8	40.8	67.1	4.9
Kuala Terengganu	127.0	33.2	78.2	15.5
Georgetown	–21.3	42.6	—	–64.0
Kuantan	88.1	23.9	30.7	33.5
Seremban	51.8	25.7	19.4	6.7
1980–1991				
Kuala Lumpur	225.7	267.4	—	–41.7
Ipoh	175.0	90.3	96.3	–11.6
Johor Bahru	195.3	95.0	7.1	93.3
Klang	176.3	113.2	56.5	6.7
Petaling Jaya	143.2	85.7	43.4	14.1
Kota Bharu	66.7	67.0	6.9	–7.2
Kuala Terengganu	47.8	70.1	—	–22.2
Georgetown	–28.6	41.9	—	–70.5
Kuantan	70.9	37.1	1.5	32.3
Seremban	60.3	40.2	3.1	17.0

Source: Department of Statistics, Malaysia, *Urbanisation and Urban Growth in Malaysia,* Population Census Monograph Series, no. 1 (Kuala Lumpur: Department of Statistics, 1996), table 6.4.

of out-migration. The satellite city of Petaling Jaya, conversely, increased appreciably in size because of net in-migration. The second time period reveals some important changes. Although Kuala Lumpur registered an increase of nearly 270,000 people through natural increase, the city also lost more than 41,000 people through out-migration. Many of these migrants relocated to the newer residential areas surrounding Kuala Lumpur, principally Petaling Jaya and the port city of Klang. These latter two cities, along with Ipoh, also increased in size due to reclassification.

MODELS OF THE SOUTHEAST ASIAN CITY

For more than three decades, much thinking about Southeast Asian urbanization has developed out of T. G. McGee's model of city structure (fig. 10.19). Building on a long tradition of urban modeling in North American cities, McGee's model presumed, first, that no clear zoning characterizes land use of the large cities of Southeast Asia. Instead, McGee proposed that only two zones of land use remained relatively constant, these being the

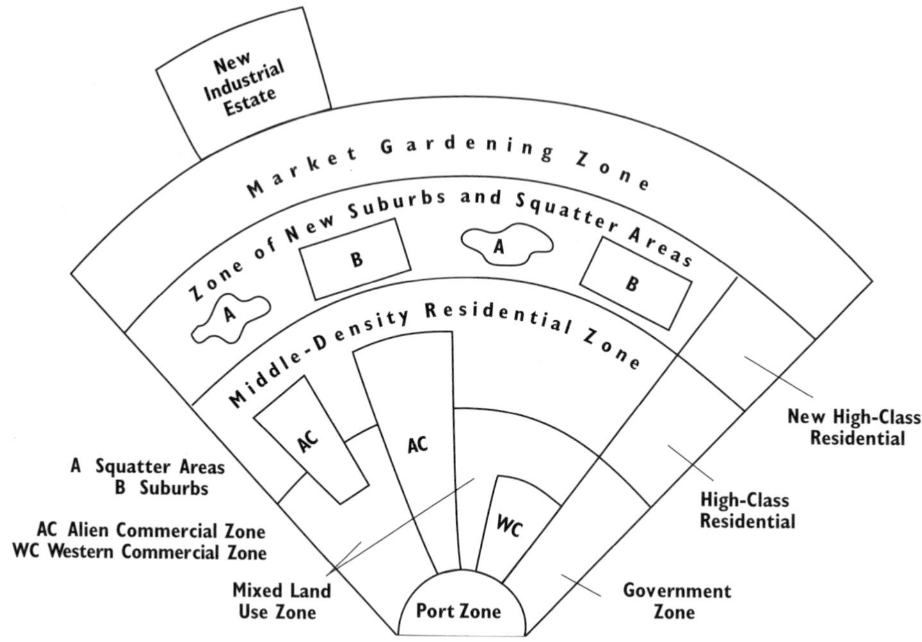

Figure 10.19 A Generalized Model of Major Land Use in the Large Southeast Asian City. *Source*: T. G. McGee, *The Southeast Asian City* (New York: Praeger, 1967), 128.

port district and, on the periphery of the city, a zone of intensive market gardening. In between were areas of mixed economic activity and land use with other areas of dominant land use, such as spines of high-class residential areas and clusters of squatter settlements.

As cities in Southeast Asia have experienced rapid urban growth, as well as important economic transformations, our understanding of these places has changed considerably. While remnants of McGee's initial model are still visible, e.g., a central port zone and mixed land-use patterns, other aspects of Southeast Asian cities have been radically transformed. Urban scholars now speak of *extended metropolitan regions* (EMRs). This distinctive form of Asian urbanization has its origins in the way in which Asian cities have been incorporated into the global economy. The colonial-induced primate cities are increasingly penetrating their surrounding hinterlands, urbanizing the countryside, and drawing rural populations deeper and deeper into the urban economy. In certain respects, EMRs are similar to metropolitan regions in the United States. However, EMRs in Southeast Asia differ from their North American counterparts in that the former exhibit a greater population density in both the urban cores and surrounding rural periphery.

EMRs may be differentiated into three basic forms. The first is the *expanding city-state.* Singapore provides the only example. In recent decades, Singapore has extended its political and economic influence into the territory of its neighbors, Indonesia and Malaysia. This process is elaborated later. A second type is the *low-density* EMR, exemplified by Kuala Lumpur. These EMRs have been able to maintain relatively low population densities through the successful development of satellite cities that fringe the dominant urban area. In other words, low-density EMRs reflect controlled and managed growth, as opposed to the more rapid and unplanned growth of other cities. The third, and most prevalent, type is the *high-density EMR*. This type of EMR, epitomized by the massive cities of Jakarta, Manila, and Bangkok, exhibits a chaotic spillover of urban economic functions into the rural hinterland, with an accompanying loss of agricultural land to residential and industrial development.

Related to EMRs is a new urban form, identified by McGee as *desakota*. The term itself is derived from the Indonesian words for village *(desa)* and town *(kota)* and is meant to capture the process whereby urbanization overtakes its surrounding hinterland. A number of elements have been associated with *desakota*. First, these cities exhibit considerable diversity in their land use. Characteristically, a *desakota* region encompasses cities with mixed residential and industrial land uses, as well as a densely populated wet-rice agricultural area. Within *desakota*, moreover, there is considerable interaction between village and town. This is made possible by an integrated transportation system that permits high levels of population mobility. Indeed, the increased daily commuting patterns seen in Bangkok testify to this increased circulation within *desakota*. Second, these regions also are strongly integrated into the global economy. Foreign investment is generally important in these areas, as multinational corporations are able to tap into large available labor supplies. The process of formation of the *desakota* is perhaps more important than the resulting pattern itself, because surrounding rural areas become urbanized without the transfer of population that occurs in, say, rural-urban migration.

Whereas proponents of the *desakota* model view the contemporary Southeast Asian urbanization process as unique, some writers contend that the high-density EMR is largely synonymous with the *desakota*, while some are convinced that the *desakota* is not unique at all. Others contend that Southeast Asian cities are not that distinctive, suggesting a series of alternating phases of convergence and divergence from, especially, Western European cities. They contend that from traditional, precolonial forms, during the peak period of colonization from about 1880 to the 1930s, there was considerable convergence between Southeast Asian and Western European cities. This convergence was manifest in the urban landscape, as reflected in architectural styles and land-use patterns. By the late 19th century, for example, most large Southeast Asian cities had distinct central business districts that were dominated by European firms; ethnic residential segregation was also prevalent. Singapore perhaps best exemplified the European colonial city. Other cities, of course, were remade by the European powers. These include Rangoon (occupied by the British in 1834) and Saigon (occupied by the French in 1859). Even Bangkok, which avoided colonization by the European powers, was still influenced by both the British and the French. The years spanning the 1940s through the 1970s constituted a period of divergence. These decades witnessed considerable rural-urban migration, a proliferation of informal-sector employment, and an expansion of squatter settlements. These were the years of decolonization, and cities in Southeast Asia reflected an increased nationalism and symbolic transformation of their urban landscapes. Lastly, the 1980s and 1990s reveal convergence again with Western cities. These transformed cities are increasingly becoming characterized by a rise of private transport, an increased consumption and emergence of consumer landscapes (e.g., shopping malls), a privatization of space (e.g., a proliferation of gated, and often armed, residential communities), and a decline in urban planning. These decades likewise witnessed the emergence of massive plaza malls throughout Manila, Bangkok, Jakarta, and Kuala Lumpur. In part, these urban transformations are associated with the emergence of a large middle class, a group that is increasingly seeking private ownership and more secure and luxurious suburban living spaces.

Apart from urban growth associated with primate cities, Southeast Asia is also experiencing a rise in "transnational cities." Similar to urban changes occurring in East Asia, cities in Southeast Asia are increasingly extending their scope across national boundaries. Variously known as *regional economic zones, borderless cities, ecumenopolises, growth triangles,* and *urban corridors,* these urban forms consist of social, political, and economic linkages between two or more states. These are usually government-created economic regions that represent a new organization of space across national boundaries. Within Southeast Asia, the three countries of Singapore, Indonesia, and Malaysia best illustrate the concept of transnational cities. In 1989, Singapore announced the formation of a growth triangle linking Singapore, Indonesia's adjacent Riau Archipelago, and the Malaysian state of Johor. Known by the acronym of *Sijori* (from the combination of *Si*ngapore, *Jo*hor, and *Ri*au), the arrangement combines Singapore's capital, technology, and managerial talents with land and labor provided by Johor and the Riaus. Linkages have been expanding within the Sijori growth triangle, including sizable flows of goods, capital, information, and people. Examples include the development of Batam Island's international phone system, which is routed through Singapore, as well as a possible extension of the Singapore subway system into Johor.

In 1993, an agreement was reached between Indonesia, Malaysia, and Thailand for a Medan-Penang-Songkhla growth triangle. This would incorporate the four northern states of Malaysia, two provinces in northern Sumatra, and five provinces in southern Thailand. Elsewhere, a potential growth triangle may also link southern Mindanao (the Philippines), northern Sulawesi (Indonesia), and Sabah (Malaysia). Many of these zones are informal arrangements and they are often defined in name only. In other words, few of these megaurban corridors have any official recognition by the countries involved.

PROBLEMS OF URBAN AREAS

Cities in Southeast Asia, as the preceding sections have indicated, are not immune to serious problems. Clearly, the inability of urban residents to obtain adequate employment and housing loom among the largest. Many inhabitants of these cities remain mired in poverty. As of the early 1990s, for example, more than 30% of Metro Manila's population lived below poverty, as did nearly 30% of Indonesia's urban population. The figure for Indonesia escalated sharply in 2000–2001, as the country struggled with instability of all kinds.

In part, these conditions exist and persist because the urban economies are unable to satisfy the labor demands brought about through natural increase and rural-urban migration. As a case in point, during the 1980s Jakarta's population grew at an annual rate of 3.8%, while urban employment grew at only

2.8%. One obvious solution is the promotion of labor-intensive businesses. In Malaysia, for example, small-scale business operations have been encouraged. Moreover, these have been assisted through credit management schemes and other forms of assistance. Thailand, likewise, has pursued income-generating projects and the decentralization of industries and employment based on urban centers in outlying regions. The Thai government has proposed to expand highway and communication links between urban areas in the BMR and emphasize different roles for urban centers throughout the country. The government also plans to broaden urban planning practices to include region-serving development functions, such as agroprocessing services, regional marketing, and communications functions, and formulate a regional network or cluster strategy of urban and regional development. Not all regional growth programs, of course, are successful. The Philippines, for example, initiated a regional policy initiative in 1973 to help lessen the overurbanization of Manila. Included in this policy was a proposed ban on locating new manufacturing plants within 31 mi (50 km) of Manila. This policy, however, resulted in an intensification of urban growth around the fringes of Manila, thereby adding to the congestion of the city.

Even without the problem of continued population growth, the generation of employment is not an easy task. Many of the labor-intensive industries initiated in Southeast Asia have been extremely exploitative. Seen especially in the export-processing zones controlled by multinational corporations, these jobs are low paid, often of a temporary nature, and lacking in health and safety benefits. Employment opportunities are also gender selective, as factory managers prefer to hire—and exploit—female workers.

Another option is for governments to obtain overseas employment for their citizens. Since the 1970s many governments in Southeast Asia, specifically the Philippines, Thailand, and Indonesia, have initiated overseas employment programs. Evidence is mixed as to the effectiveness of these programs. For example, the Philippines is currently the world's largest exporter of government-sponsored temporary international labor migration; annually, more than 700,000 Filipinos are deployed to more than 160 countries and territories. However, this number is offset by the estimated 700,000 new entrants to the Philippines' labor market each year. Thus, unless other alternatives are pursued, overseas employment will remain a stopgap program.

Conditions of unemployment and underemployment are reflected in inadequate housing. For example, in the 1990s in Manila, approximately 40% of the urban population was estimated to be living in squatter settlements, with another 45% of the population living in slum conditions. In Bangkok, 23% of the population was estimated to be living in slum and squatter settlements; in both Kuala Lumpur and Jakarta, squatters constituted approximately 25% of the population.

The rise of squatter settlements and slum areas is explained by other factors besides population increase. Escalating land prices, compounded by real estate speculation, for example, exacerbate the problem of housing. So, too, does the creation of artificial land scarcity. In Metro Manila, for example, large tracts of land, even within the central business district of Makati, remain vacant.

Sadly, many governments continue to view eviction and demolition as the most effective means of confronting squatter settlements. In the Philippines, for example, more than 100,000 people were evicted from Manila each year between 1986 and 1992. Not surprisingly, a policy of relocating squatters to sites 20–50 mi (32–80 km) outside the city and placing them in high-density residential apartments proved ineffective. Only Singapore has achieved substantial results in the provision of public housing. Other cities, especially Manila and Bangkok, trail woefully behind. While many of these governments have agencies charged with developing public housing, most lack the required economic resources and political resolve to be effective.

Many Southeast Asian governments also are unable to provide adequate services, such as clean water, sewerage, and other utilities. Only about 7% of Burma's urban population, for example, have access to piped water. In Jakarta, only a quarter of the population has solid waste collection; in the remainder of the city, it is collected via scavengers. One effective strategy has been Indonesia's Kampung Improvement Program (KIP). This program is a far-reaching initiative that concentrates primarily on the improvement of infrastructure and public facilities. Specific projects include footpaths, secondary roads, drainage ditches, schools, communal bathing and shower facilities, and health clinics. Since its inception, the KIP has been expanded to more than two hundred cities throughout Indonesia and has benefited more than 3.5 million people.

Air pollution poses serious health hazards to residents and visitors alike in Southeast Asian cities. Jakarta, for example, exceeds the health standards for ambient levels of airborne particulate matter on more than 170 days of the year. Moreover, topographical features may augment pollution problems. The surrounding hills of the Klang Valley around Kuala Lumpur, for example, confine pollutants in the region and thus exacerbate air quality problems.

Water pollution, likewise, remains a major obstacle to the quality of life in Southeast Asian cities. Many rivers, including the Pasig in Manila, the Chao Phraya in Bangkok, and the Ciliwung in Jakarta, are considered biological hazards. The canals and waterways in Bangkok, especially, are highly polluted from a combination of industrial and household discharge. Only 2% of the city's population is connected to Bangkok's limited sewerage system, most solid waste is discharged into waterways, and more than 15% of the garbage disposed of daily is left uncollected.

An additional problem is traffic congestion. The traffic problems in Bangkok and Manila were discussed previously. In Jakarta, as in these cities, private car ownership has outpaced road construction. Some governments, including those of Malaysia and Indonesia, have utilized toll roads to reduce traffic congestion. Other efforts concentrate on the development of mass-transit systems, such as the construction of light-rail transit systems in both Manila and Kuala Lumpur. These projects are extremely expensive, however, and following the financial crises of 1997, many have been temporarily halted. To this day, half-completed overpasses and bridges and incomplete rail systems stand as silent reminders of continued underdevelopment.

DECENTRALIZATION POLICIES AND URBAN PLANNING

Recognizing the strong concentration of economic activity in the largest cities, as well as a lack of alternative employment opportunities, some governments have initiated strategies designed to decentralize industry, reduce regional disparities, and develop peripheral locations. As we have already seen, both Singapore and Malaysia have introduced programs designed to lessen the pressure on their core urban areas. Malaysia, especially, has established industrial estates in the vicinity of all medium-sized cities throughout the peninsula; in the process, Kuala Lumpur's proportion of manufacturing has been substantially reduced. Elsewhere in the region, Thailand has attempted to foster growth in its eastern seaboard as well as along the Thai-Laos border. Apart from economic considerations, there are also political motivations behind policies of decentralization. Specifically, these policies are responses to previous regimes of authoritarian rule, irredentist sentiment, and extreme levels of urban primacy.

Decentralization policies, in general, entail a devolution of powers to local governing units or a deconcentration of functions, and the transfer of authority, from national or central government departments to regional offices. Theoretically, a policy of decentralization offers the potential for maximum participation of government levels, hastens decision-making processes, and decongests central government functions. As a case in point, the Philippines has made various efforts since independence toward decentralization. Arguably, the most significant act was the Local Government Code of 1991. This act, among its many features, transferred to local governments both the responsibility for the delivery of basic services and the enforcement of certain regulatory and licensing powers, increased the internal revenue allotment of local governments, expanded the taxing powers of local governments, and broadened the definition of governance to include the participation of nongovernment organizations and people's organizations.

Decentralization strategies should not be viewed, however, as panaceas for the woes of Southeast Asian cities. Potential problems exist in the implementation and effectiveness of these policies, including financial stability, administrative capability, and contests between national and local governments and the private sector. Moreover, those municipalities with an adequate preexisting infrastructure that includes sufficient links to transportation and communication are likely to benefit the most.

AN EYE TO THE FUTURE

Like Gregor Samsa in Franz Kafka's novella *The Metamorphosis,* the cities of Southeast Asia have awoken from unsettled dreams to find themselves changed into something monstrous—agglomerations of skyscrapers and street vendors, palatial residential neighborhoods, and impoverished squatter settlements.

What does the future hold for the cities of Southeast Asia? Three themes come to mind. First, continued population pressures and environmental degradation will most likely accelerate rural-urban migration, thereby exacerbating overurbanization problems. Consequently, the cities of Southeast Asia will likely continue to expand into their hinterlands. How this development occurs, however, and how governments respond to this growth, will greatly affect the livability of these cities. Will growth continue unabated, in an unplanned, haphazard fashion, or will decentralization strategies and growth-diversion measures effect desired changes? In economically poor countries, or those saddled with massive foreign debts, fiscal capacity, management, and political motivation may hinder these attempts.

A second theme is that these cities will continue to be incorporated into the global economy. Thus, manifestations of globalization processes at the local scale will become more apparent. For example, the mushrooming of McDonald's and Kentucky Fried Chicken franchises will continue. But apart from these superficial changes lie deeper, structural transformations resultant from the infusion of foreign capital. Just as political revolutions had impacts on urban areas in the socialist countries, social changes are likely to stem from urban transformations. Conversely, separatist movements in Indonesia and the Philippines, for example, may manifest themselves in the urbanization process.

Part and parcel of an increased globalization is the continued mobility of workers throughout the region. Whether internal movements or international migrations, the resultant population changes may further test the social and political stability of these cities. Likewise, the ethnic diversity of some cities, such as Singapore and Kuala Lumpur, may continue to influence urban planning efforts.

Southeast Asia, because of its strategic location and key cities, with Singapore as the anchor of the region, is destined to grow ever more important in world affairs and in urban development in this century.

SUGGESTED READINGS

Askew, Marc. *Interpreting Bangkok: The Urban Question in Thai Studies.* Bangkok: Chulalongkorn University, 1994. A look at various facets of Thailand's primate capital.

Berner, Erhard. *Defending a Place in the City: Localities and the Struggle for Urban Land in Metro Manila.* Quezon City, Philippines: Ateneo de Manila University Press, 1997. An examination of the complex issue of land rights and squatters in overburdened Manila.

Berry, James, and Stanley McGreal. *Cities of the Pacific Rim: Planning Systems and Property Markets.* London: E & FN Spon, 1999. A study of the interactive relationships between the operation of the planning system and the role and performance of property development and real estate markets in fourteen Pacific Rim cities.

Dale, Ole Johan. *Urban Planning in Singapore: The Transformation of a City.* Oxford: Oxford University Press, 1999. A study of the process of urban planning in Singapore that traces its early growth on the banks of the Singapore River to its present structure.

Ginsburg, Norton, Bruce Koppel, and T. G. McGee, eds. *The Extended Metropolis: Settlement Transition in Asia.* Honolulu: University of Hawaii Press, 1991. A variety of authors look at various aspects of some of the key cities of Asia, including Jakarta and others.

Leinbach, Thomas R., and Richard Ulack. *Southeast Asia: Diversity and Development.* Upper Saddle River, N.J.: Prentice Hall, 2000. A comprehensive geography of Southeast Asia, including a chapter on urbanization.

Logan, William S. *Hanoi: Biography of a City.* Seattle: University of Washington Press, 2000. An exploration of the many layers of Hanoi's built environment and how the shape of the city reflects changing political, cultural, and economic conditions over a thousand-year period.

McGee, T. G. *The Southeast Asian City: A Social Geography of the Primate Cities of Southeast Asia.* New York: Praeger, 1967. Still a classic work on the subject.

McGee, T. G., and Ira M. Robinson, eds. *The Mega-Urban Regions of Southeast Asia.* Vancouver: University of British Columbia Press, 1995. A multiauthored study of the megacities of Southeast Asia, building on earlier work by McGee and others.

Ness, Gayl D., and Michael M. Low. *Five Cities: Modelling Asian Urban Population-Environment Dynamics.* Oxford: Oxford University Press, 2000. New research on the dynamic interactions between population and the urban environment in Faisalabad, Pakistan; Khon Kaen, Thailand; Cebu, Philippines; Pusan, South Korea; and Kobe, Japan.

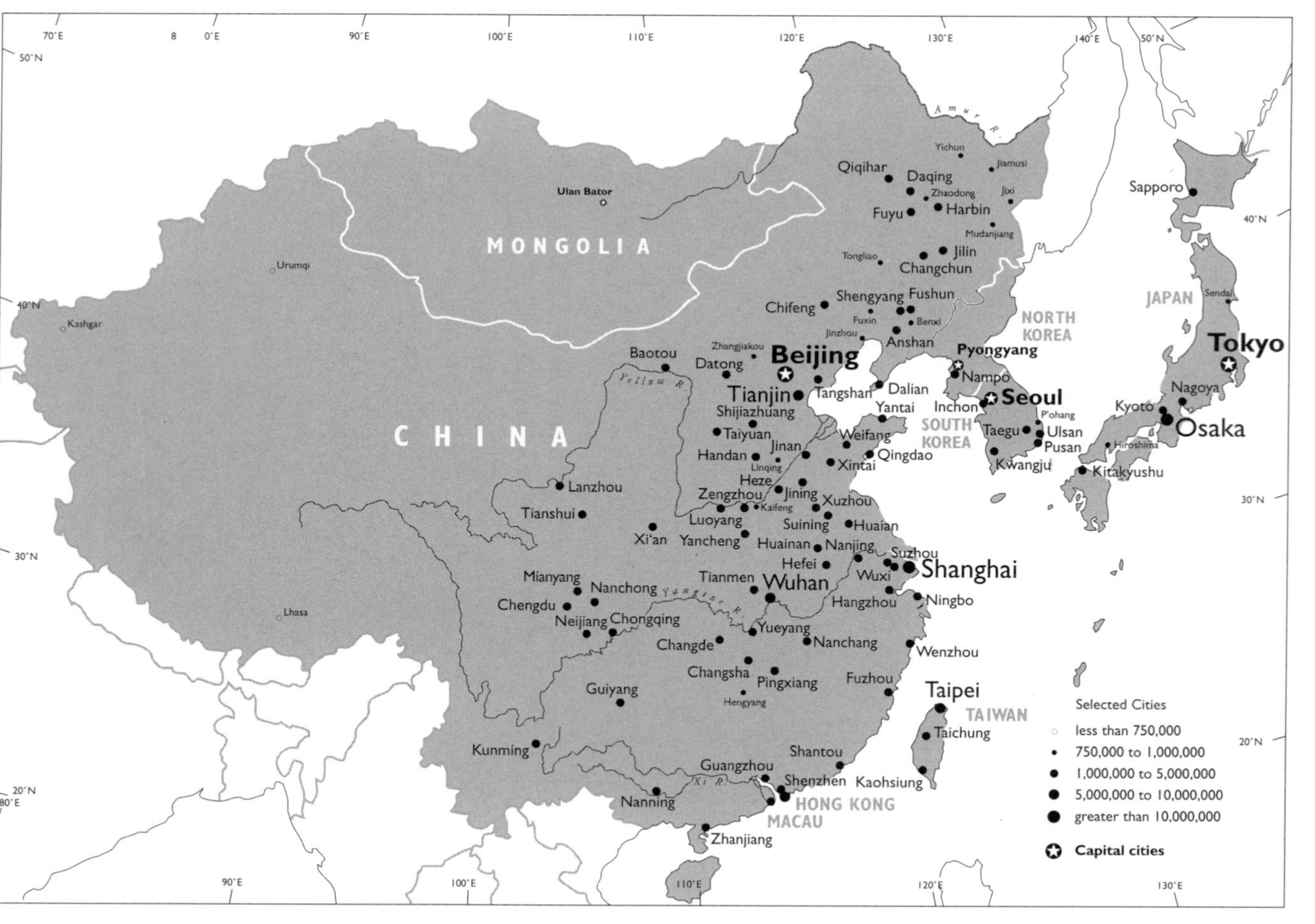

Figure 11.1 Major Cities of East Asia. *Source*: Data from United Nations, *World Urbanization Prospects, 2001 Revision* (New York: United Nations Population Division, 2002), www.unpopulation.org.

11

Cities of East Asia

JACK F. WILLIAMS AND KAM WING CHAN

KEY URBAN FACTS

Total Population	1.51 billion
Percent Urban Population	
China	37%
Remainder	71%
Total Urban Population	
China	479 million
Remainder	172 million
Most Urbanized Country	South Korea (83%)
Least Urbanized Country	China (37%)
Annual Urban Growth Rate	
China	3.5%
Remainder	1.2%
Number of Megacities	4
Number of Cities of More Than 1 Million	
China*	90 (incl. Hong Kong)
Remainder	23
Three Largest Cities	Tokyo, Shanghai, Osaka
World Cities	Tokyo, Hong Kong
Global Cities	Tokyo

*China has a remarkably large number of cities of more than one million because villages (mostly farm population) are included in city districts in the suburban areas. Thus, the population sizes of many cities based on city districts are likely to be larger than their true "urban" populations.

KEY CHAPTER THEMES

1. East Asia consists of two distinct parts—China and the remainder—in terms of urban development history.
2. China is one of the original centers of urban development in history and has some of the oldest continuously occupied cities in the world.

3. China influenced early urban development in the other states in the region, but urban centers developed outside of China primarily under different circumstances and in different forms.
4. Colonialism had a less important role in urban development in East Asia compared with other parts of Asia and the colonial realms; nonetheless, many large Chinese cities were treaty ports under colonialism, while Hong Kong and Macau were entirely creations of colonialism.
5. Japan, South Korea, Hong Kong, and Taiwan are already highly industrialized and urbanized and deeply involved in the global economy.
6. China has been following in the footsteps of the rest of the region since the late 1970s and now is one of the most rapidly urbanizing countries in the world.
7. China is unique in being still primarily rural in its population distribution, yet having the largest urban population and the greatest number of million-plus cities of any country in the world.
8. East Asia has a large number of the first- and second-order world cities, led by Tokyo, which ranks with London and New York as the only three truly "global" cities, evidence of this region's economic power.
9. North Korea is the lone holdout in East Asia in clinging to a rigid, Stalinist socialist system in its cities and economic development, in contrast with China and Mongolia.
10. Although the cities of East Asia have experienced the usual panoply of urban problems, a number of the region's cities, especially outside of China, are regularly ranked as among the most livable in Asia.

East Asia exudes power and success. Nowhere is this more evident than in its great cities, such as Tokyo, Beijing, Shanghai, Seoul, Hong Kong, and Taipei (fig. 11.1). Emerging in the past half century to rival the old power centers of the world—North America and Europe—East Asia's cities have been the command centers for the prodigious economic advances of much of this region. These are also among the largest cities in the world. Yet, compared with the often-struggling agglomerations found in poorer realms of the world, East Asia's cities have been more successful in coping with rapid growth and large size. The region is sharply split between China, which is rapidly urbanizing but still only about 37% urban, and the rest of the region, which is already 72% urban. This dichotomy is reflected in the character of the cities and the processes, past and present, that have shaped them.

THE EVOLUTION OF CITIES

The Traditional or Preindustrial City

East Asia, especially China, is one of the original centers of urbanism in world history. Many cities here can trace their origins directly back two millennia or more. One can see interesting parallels with the earliest cities in other culture realms, with their focus on ceremonial and administrative centers planned in highly formal style to symbolize the beliefs and traditions of the cultures involved.

Changan

In its idealized form, the traditional city reflected the ancient Chinese conception of the universe and the role of the emperor as intermediary between heaven and earth. This idealized conception was most apparent in the national capitals, but many elements of this conception could be seen in lesser cities at lower administrative levels. The Tang capital of Changan (present-day Xi'an) was one of the best early expressions of the classic Chinese capital city. Founded more than 3,000 years ago, Changan was the capital of a number of dynasties and states around the valley of the Wei River (a branch of the Yellow River). But the city reached its true flowering during the brilliant Tang dynasty (A.D. 618–906).

As typified in Changan, the city was a physical expression of the cosmological beliefs of an agricultural people. Thus, the city was divided in a grid pattern, into four parts representing the four quadrants of the heavens. Each side of the square enclosed by the city wall could be identified with a daily position of the sun or with one of the four seasons. The royal palace represented the polar star, which dominates the universe, so the palace at the center dominated the city (and in a broader context, the nation as a whole) and separated markets from centers of religious observance. The main north-south street through the city represented the celestial meridian. The city wall and gates were oriented to the cardinal directions. South, toward the sun, was the most favorable direction; hence, the palace (or lesser administrative headquarters in lower-order cities) always faced south. Some cities did not even have north gates. In short, the city represented in highly formalized morphology the interrelationship between people and nature. Inevitably, the demands of modern urban development have necessitated, in the eyes of planners at least, the tearing down of most city walls, and thus the removal of a colorful legacy of the past. The sites of the old walls commonly become the routes of new, broad boulevards. One of the few cities whose original wall has been retained almost in its entirety is Xi'an, because of its historic role.

Beijing

Of all the historic, traditional cities, none is more famous than Beijing (Peking), the present national capital. Although a city had existed on the site for centuries, Beijing became significant when it was rebuilt in 1260 by Kublai Khan as his winter capital. It was this Beijing that Marco Polo saw. The city was destroyed with the fall of the Mongols and the establishment of the Ming dynasty in 1368. Nanjing served as national capital briefly after that, but in 1421 the capital was moved back to the rebuilt city (now named Beijing, or "Northern Capital," for the first time), where it has remained with few interruptions until today. The Ming capital was composed of four parts, the Imperial Palace (or Forbidden City), the imperial city, the inner city, and the outer city, like a series of nested boxes. It is the former Forbidden City that can still be partially seen within the walls of what is today called the Palace Museum.

The Chinese City as Model: Japan and Korea

Changan was the national capital at a time when Japan was a newly emerging civilization adopting and adapting many features of China, including city planning. As a result, the Japanese capital cities of the period were modeled after Changan. Indeed, the city as a distinct form first appeared in Japan at this time, beginning with the completion of Keijokyo (now called Nara) in 710. Although Nara today is a rather small prefectural capital, it once represented the grandeur of the Nara period (710–784). Keiankyo (modern-day Kyoto) was to survive as the best example of early Japanese city planning. Serving as national capital from 794 to 1868, when the capital was formally shifted to Edo (now Tokyo), Kyoto still exhibits the original rectangular form, grid pattern, and other features copied from Changan. However, modern urban/industrial growth has greatly increased the size of the city and covered or obscured much of the original form. Moreover, the Chinese city morphology, with its rigid symmetry and formalized symbolism, was essentially alien to the Japanese culture to begin with. Even the shortage of level land in Japan tended to work against the full realization of the Chinese concept of the city.

Korea also experienced the importation of Chinese city-planning concepts. The Chinese city model was most evident in the national capital of Seoul, which became the premier city of Korea in 1394. The city has never really lost its dominance since. Early maps of Seoul reveal the imprint of Chinese city forms. Those forms were not completely achieved, however, in part because of the rugged landscape around Seoul, which was located in a confining basin just north of the lower Han River. Succeeding centuries of development and rebuilding, especially in the 20th century during the Japanese occupation (1910–1945) and after the Korean War (1950–1953), obliterated most of the original form and architecture of the historic city. A modern commercial/industrial city, one of the largest in the world, has arisen on the ashes of the old city (reinforcing the popular, other name for Seoul, the "Phoenix City," after the mythological bird that symbolizes immortality). A few relics of the past, such as some of the palaces and a few of the main gates, stand today as a result of restoration efforts.

Colonial Cities

The colonial impact on East Asia was relatively less intrusive than what occurred in Southeast and South Asia, but was notable nonetheless.

First Footholds: The Portuguese and the Dutch

The Portuguese and the Dutch were the first European colonists to arrive in East Asia. Seeking trade and the opportunity to spread Christianity, the Portuguese made some penetration of southern Japan via the port of Nagasaki in the latter 16th century. Their greatest influence was actually indirect, through the introduction of firearms and military technology into Japan. This led to the development of stronger private armies among the *daimyo* (feudal rulers) of Japan, which in turn led to the building of large castles in the center of each *daimyo*'s domain. These castles, modeled after fortresses in medieval Europe, were commonly located on strategic high points, surrounded by the *daimyo*'s retainers and the commercial town. These centers eventually served as the nuclei for many of the cities of modern Japan.

Macau

The Portuguese also tried to penetrate China. Reaching Guangzhou (Canton) in 1517, they attempted to establish themselves there for trade, but were forced by the Chinese authorities to accept the small peninsula of Macau, near the mouth of the Pearl River, south of Guangzhou. Chinese authorities walled off the peninsula and rent was paid for the territory until the Portuguese declared it independent from China in 1849. With only 10 sq mi (26 sq km) of land (land reclamation in recent years has added a little to the total), Macau remained the only Portuguese toehold in East Asia, especially after the eclipse of their operations in southern Japan in the 17th century. Macau was most important as a trading center and a haven for refugees. The establishment of Hong Kong in the 19th century on the opposite side of the Pearl River estuary signaled the beginning of Macau's slow decline, from

Figure 11.2 Macau's international airport, opened in the late 1990s, stretches on reclaimed land between the two islands of Coloane and Taipa. In the distance, on the peninsula, is the main urban area of Macau. Collectively, these three pieces of land form the Macau Special Administrative Region of China. (Photo courtesy Macau government)

which it has never fully recovered. In the post-1950 period, Macau survived largely on tourism (as a sort of seedy reminder of what Hong Kong looked like before being Manhattanized) and gambling (as a downscale Asian version of Las Vegas, gangsters and all). In the 1990s, Macau attempted some modest industrialization, as it integrated with the Zhuhai Special Economic Zone just across the border and sought to become a regional air hub by constructing an international airport (still greatly underutilized) on reclaimed land (fig. 11.2). Since reversion to the People's Republic of China (PRC) in 1999, Macau has faced a somewhat uncertain economic future within the South China economic zone.

The Dutch impact in East Asia was much less important. Primarily concerned with Southeast Asia and the Dutch East Indies (present-day Indonesia), the Dutch penetrated East Asia primarily for the brief period in which they controlled the island of Formosa (Taiwan), during 1624–1662, which first brought the island to the world's attention. During that time, the Dutch began to develop modern agriculture and established the site of the city of Tainan, the original capital and oldest city on the island.

The Treaty Ports of China

It was the other Western colonial powers, arriving in the 18th and 19th centuries, that had the greatest impact on the growth of cities and urbanization in China. Most important were the British and Americans, but the French, Germans, Belgians, Russians, and others were also involved, as were the Japanese, who joined the action toward the close of the 19th century.

It all began officially with the Treaty of Nanjing in 1842, which ceded to Britain the island of Hong Kong and the right to reside in five ports—Guangzhou, Xiamen (Amoy), Fuzhou, Ningbo, and Shanghai. Further refinements of this treaty in succeeding years gave to the other foreign powers the same rights as the British (the "Open Door" policy). A second set of wars and treaties, in 1856–1860, led to the opening of further ports. By 1911, approximately ninety cities of China—along the entire coast, up the Chang Jiang (Yangtze) valley, in North China, and in Manchuria—with a third of a million foreign residents, were opened as treaty ports or open ports (fig. 11.3).

The treaty ports introduced a dynamic new order into traditional Chinese society. The Westerners established themselves in the ports to make money, but they also had the right of extraterritoriality, which guaranteed them coverage by Western legal procedures. Gradually, taxation, police forces, and other features of municipal government were developed by the Western countries controlling the treaty ports. China's sovereignty thus was largely supplanted in cities in the concession areas, leased in perpetuity by the foreigners for modest rents paid to the Chinese government.

Shanghai

Shanghai (literally, "On the Sea") had existed as a small settlement for two millennia. By the 18th century, the city was a medium-sized county seat with a population of about 200,000 and built in traditional city style, with a wall. Deposition of silt by the Chang Jiang over the centuries, however, had made Shanghai no longer a port directly fronting the sea. The town was now located about 15 mi (24 km) up the Huangpu River, a minor tributary of the Chang Jiang.

Western control of Shanghai began with the British concession in 1846 and expanded over the years to cover most of the city. In 1863, the British and American areas were joined to form the Shanghai International Settlement, which by the heyday of the 1920s contained some 60,000 foreigners, the largest concentration in China. The Shanghai Municipal Council dealt with all the problems of the large city—roads, jetties, drainage, sanitation, police, recreation, and the rest. Hence, Shanghai, as well as the other treaty ports, served as magnets for wealthy Chinese entrepreneurs and for millions of impoverished peasants seeking a haven in a deteriorating China. The wealthy Chinese invested in manufacturing and other aspects of the commercial economy; the peasants provided abundant cheap labor. By the end of its first century under Western control, just before World War II, Shanghai handled half of China's foreign trade and had half the country's mechanized factories. The city's population of four million made it one of the largest cities in the world; it was more than twice the size of its nearest rivals, Beijing and Tianjin. Shanghai even gave its name to a new word in the English language—to be "shanghaied" (i.e., kidnapped to serve on the ships plying the trade routes between the Western world and China).

The Westerners simply profited from a natural locational advantage near the mouth of the Chang Jiang delta for handling the trade of the largest and most populous river basin in China. During the 20th century, Shanghai's manufacturing was able to compete successfully with that of other centers emerging in China, despite the absence of local supplies of raw materials, because of the ease and cheapness of water transport. This was achieved also in spite of a relatively poor site—an area of

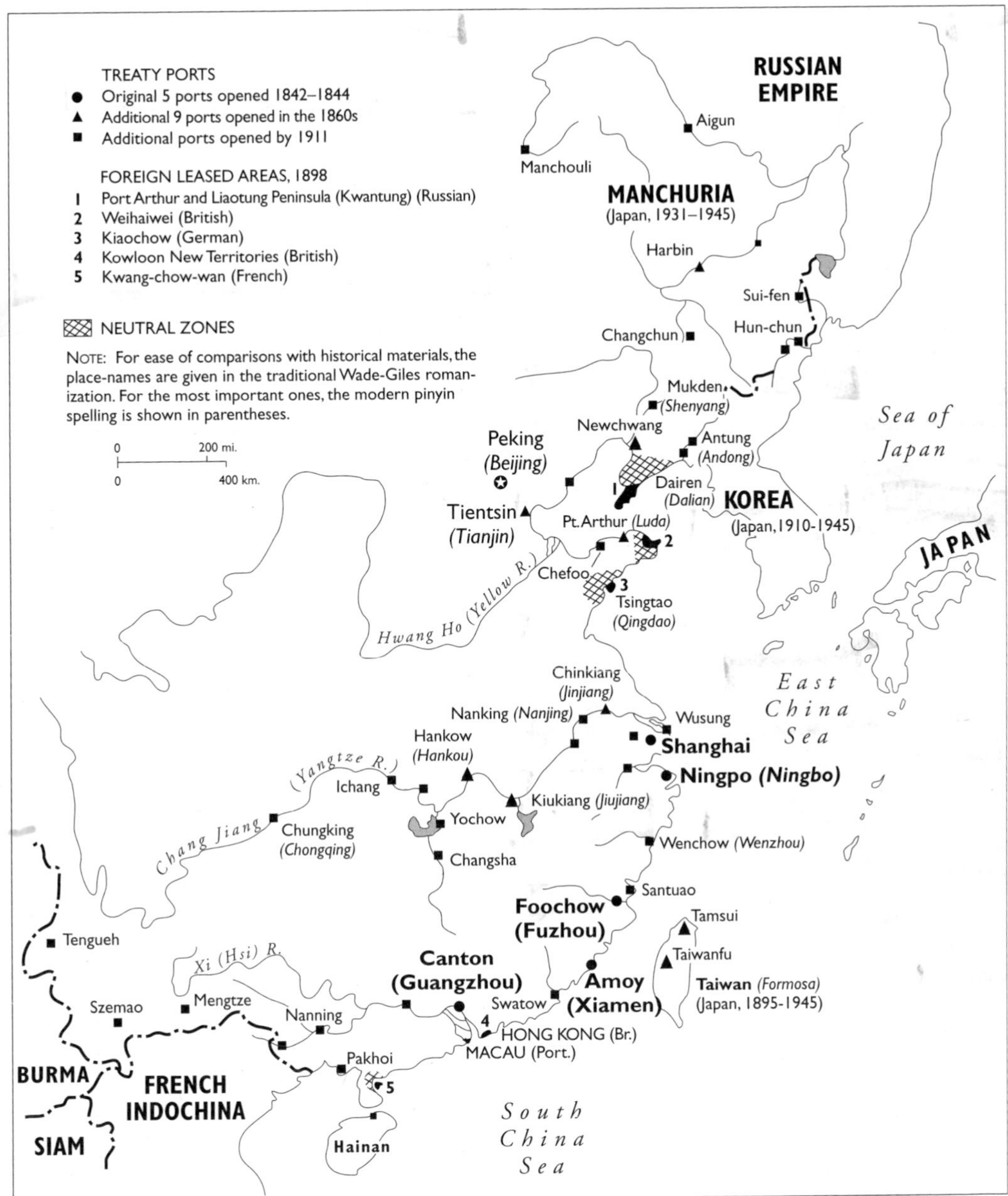

Figure 11.3 Foreign Penetration of China in the 19th and Early 20th Centuries. *Source*: adapted from J. Fairbank et al., *East Asia: Tradition and Transformation* (Boston: Houghton Mifflin, 1973), 577.

deep silt deposits, high water table, poor natural drainage, insufficient water supply, poor foundations for modern buildings of any great height, and a harbor on a narrow river that required regular dredging for oceangoing ships.

The Japanese Impact

There was a colonial impact on other Chinese cities, too, of course. Particularly significant was the Japanese impact. In Manchuria (northeastern China), which the Japanese took over in the

1930s, many of the major cities were modernized and developed along the Western lines that the Japanese had adopted in development of their own cities after 1868. The Japanese also introduced the beginnings of the industrial base that was to make Manchuria the most important industrial region in China. Industry was concentrated in a string of major cities, particularly Harbin, Changchun, and Shenyang, connected by the railway network that the Japanese built. As with Shanghai, in these cities there arose a new Western-type commercial/industrial city alongside the traditional Chinese city, which was eventually engulfed and left behind as a remnant of the past.

The Japanese also greatly influenced the urban landscape of their two other colonies in East Asia. During their rule of Taiwan (1895–1945) and Korea (1910–1945), the Japanese introduced essentially the same Western-style urban planning practices, filtered through Japanese eyes, that they later brought to Manchuria's cities. Taipei was made the colonial capital of Taiwan and transformed from an obscure Chinese provincial capital into a relatively modern city of about 250,000. The city wall was razed, roads and infrastructure were improved, and many colonial government buildings were constructed. The most prominent was the former governor's palace, with its tall, red-brick tower, which still stands in the heart of old Taipei, now used as the presidential office and executive branch headquarters for Taiwan's democratic government. Like Taipei, Seoul was transformed to serve the needs of the Japanese colonial rule of the Korean peninsula. In Seoul's case, however, this meant deliberately tearing down traditional palaces and other structures to be replaced by Japanese colonial buildings as part of a brutal effort to stamp out Korean resistance to Japanese rule.

Hong Kong

Hong Kong (literally, "Fragrant Harbor") differed from other treaty ports in that there was little pretense of Chinese sovereignty here (though the PRC government insisted after 1949 that Hong Kong was part of China). Hong Kong was ceded to Britain at the same time Shanghai was opened up in the 1840s. Hong Kong became second only to Shanghai as the most important entrepôt on the China coast during the following century of colonialism.

The reason for the importance of Hong Kong was not difficult to find. In 1842, the city began with acquisition of Hong Kong Island, a sparsely populated rocky island some 70 mi (113 km) downstream from Guangzhou. The Kowloon (literally, "Nine Dragons") peninsula across the harbor was obtained in a separate treaty in 1858. Then, in 1898, the New Territories—an expanse of islands and land on the large peninsula north of Kowloon—were leased from China for 99 years (hence, reversion to China took place in 1997), creating a total area of about 400 sq mi (1,040 sq km) for the colony. The site factor that so strongly favored its growth was one of the world's great natural harbors, between Hong Kong Island and Kowloon. Indeed, the advantages of the harbor outweighed the site disadvantages—limited level land for urban expansion, inadequate water supply, and insufficient land nearby to feed the population. The city's location at the mouth of southern China's major drainage basin gave Hong Kong a large hinterland, which greatly expanded when the north-south railway from Beijing was pushed through to Guangzhou in the 1920s. Thus, for about a century, Shanghai and Hong Kong largely dominated the foreign trade of China.

Japan: The Asian Exception

Following the classic capitals of Nara and Kyoto around the 8th century, other cities followed in Japan, principally the centers of feudal clans. Most of these were transitory, but a sizeable number survived into the modern era. One of the best-preserved historic towns today is Kanazawa, on the Sea of Japan in the Hokuriku region. The city was left behind by Japan's modernization after 1868 and escaped the devastation of World War II, since it had no industrial or military importance. Historic preservation since the 1960s has kept much of the lovely 19th-century architecture and character of the old city, a rare exception to the urban development patterns found throughout most of Asia.

Japan is referred to as the "Asian exception" because it had only a minor colonial experience. Indeed, Japan was itself a colonial power in Asia. Hence, the urban history of Japan involved an evolution almost directly from the premodern, or traditional, city to the modern commercial/industrial city. Japan did have treaty ports and extraterritoriality imposed on it by the Treaty of 1858 with the United States, which led to foreigners residing in Japan as they did in China. This colonial phase was short-lived, however. Japan was able to change its system and reestablish its territorial integrity by emulating rather than resisting the West. Extraterritoriality came formally to an end in 1899, as Japan emerged an equal partner among the Western imperial powers. The relatively benign impact of the Western colonial presence in Japan can still be seen in a few places, nonetheless, such as the former colonial residential area in Kobe.

Gradual political unification during the Tokugawa period (1603–1868) led to the establishment of a permanent network of cities in Japan. The castle town served as the chief catalyst for urban growth. One of the most important of these new castle towns to emerge at this time was Osaka. In 1583, a grand castle was built that served as the nucleus for the city to come. Various policies stimulated the growth of Osaka and other cities, including prohibitions on foreign trade after the mid-1630s, the destruction of minor feudal castles, and prohibitions on the building of more than one castle to a province. These policies had the effect of consolidating settlements and encouraging civilians to migrate to the more important castle communities.

The new castle towns, such as Osaka, were ideally located (fig. 11.4). Because of their economic and administrative functions, they generally were located on level land near important landscape features that gave the castle towns an advantage for future urban growth. Thus, Osaka emerged as the principal business, financial, and manufacturing center in Tokugawa Japan. The cities of that period were tied together by a network of highways that stimulated trade and city growth. The most famous of these early roads was the Tokaido Highway, running from Osaka eastward through Nagoya (which emerged as another major commercial and textile manufacturing center) to the most important city of this period and after, Edo (Tokyo).

Among the major cities of Asia, Tokyo was a relative latecomer. It was founded in the 15th century, when a minor feudal lord built a rudimentary castle on a bluff near the sea, about where the Imperial Palace stands today. The site was a good one, however, for a major city—it had a natural port, hills that could easily be fortified, and plenty of room on the Kanto Plain behind for expansion. Tokyo really got its start, though, a century later, when Ieyasu, the Tokugawa ruler at that time, decided to make Edo

Figure 11.4 The beautifully restored castle of Hikone, in Shiga Prefecture, central Honshu, is a classic example of an old castle town from Japan's feudal past. (Photo by Jack Williams)

his capital. Much of Tokyo still bears the imprint of the grand design that Ieyasu and his descendants laid out for Edo. They planned the Imperial enclosure, a vast area of palaces, parks, and moats in the very heart of the city. Much of the land on which central Tokyo stands today was reclaimed from the bay, a method of urban expansion that was to typify Japanese city building from then on, reflecting the shortage of level land and the need for good port facilities. By the early 17th century, Edo already had a population of 150,000 surrounding the most magnificent castle in Japan. By the 18th century, the population was well over one million, making Edo one of the largest cities in the world (fig. 11.5).

Edo's growth was based initially on its role as a political center, tied to the other cities by an expanding network of roads. An early dichotomy was established between Osaka, as the business center, and Tokyo, as the cultural and political center, that lingers even today in the rivalry between the two. With the restoration of Emperor Meiji in 1868, Japan's modern era began. The emperor's court was moved from Kyoto to Edo, which was renamed "Tokyo" ("Eastern Capital") to signify its additional role as national political capital. This transfer of political functions, plus the great industrialization and modernization program that was undertaken from the 1870s on, gave Tokyo a boost that started it on its astounding growth during the 20th century.

INTERNAL STRUCTURE OF EAST ASIAN CITIES

It is not easy to generalize about the internal structure of cities in East Asia. This is partly because of the basic division between socialist and nonsocialist urban systems that characterized the region for so long. It also is because

Figure 11.5 Waterfront development in Tokyo's Chuo Ward is an effort to preserve some remnants of premodern Tokyo. (Photo courtesy of Tokyo City Government)

of the imperfect fit of Western urban models to even the nonsocialist cities of the region. The socialist urban model is discussed elsewhere in this book, particularly the chapters on Europe (chapter 5) and Russia (chapter 6). The Chinese variant of the socialist urban model is briefly examined in this chapter.

In the rest of East Asia, and now increasingly also in reformist China, the forces that have produced and shaped cities are much the same as in the Western world, but with modifying local conditions peculiar to each country and society. These forces include: rapid industrialization focused in cities, leading to high rates of rural-urban migration, rates which have now largely tapered off in the more developed economies (Japan, South Korea, Taiwan), but that are escalating in China; private ownership of property and dominance of private investment decisions affecting land use; varying degrees of government involvement in zoning and urban planning, some of it successful but a great deal of it ineffective; high standards of living and consumption, and increasing reliance on the private automobile for transportation, in spite of often very good public transport systems; and a relatively high degree of racial homogeneity but sometimes significant stratification into socioeconomic classes. These and other factors have had varying degrees of impact on the growth of cities, and on how space is used in cities, and hence on the types and severity of problems. Western urban models of the internal structure of cities, discussed elsewhere in this book, do not entirely fit the cities of East Asia. Nonetheless, elements of each model can be found, as noted in various places in this chapter.

REPRESENTATIVE CITIES

With the exception of (British) Hong Kong and (Portuguese) Macau, the colonial era in East Asia ended with the defeat of Japan in 1945. The emergence of communist governments in the late 1940s in China (PRC) and North Korea (Democratic People's Republic of Korea), joining the already communist government of Mongolia (Mongolian People's Republic, established in the 1920s), split the region into two distinctly different paths of urban (and national) development: the path of the socialist cities of China, North Korea, and Mongolia versus that of the nonsocialist (free-market) cities of Japan, South Korea, Taiwan, Hong Kong, and Macau. This became the basic classification of cities of the region until the late 1970s at least. At that time, China entered the post-Mao or reform era, in which free-market forces increasingly began to drive the economy and determine the path of urban development. Only North Korea remained basically wedded to a rigid socialist path.

One can also classify the major cities of the region on the basis of function and size. From this perspective, several cities illustrate the distinctive types: megalopolises or superconurbations (Tokyo), recently decolonized cities (Hong Kong), primate cities (Seoul), regional centers (Taipei), and formerly socialist cities undergoing transformation (Beijing and Shanghai).

Tokyo and the Tokaido Megalopolis: Unipolar Concentration

Japan illustrates especially well the phenomenon of superconurbations or megalopolises. A distinctive feature of Japan's urban pattern is the concentration of its major cities into a relatively small portion of an already small country. In spite of more than a century of industrialization, Japan did not pass the 50% urban figure until after World War II. Between 1950 and 1970, the percentage of people living in cities with a population of 50,000 or more rose from 33% to 64%, while the total urban population reached 72%, a figure comparable to that of the United States in the same year. In other words, it took Japan only 25 years to go through a process that took many decades in the United States. Since 1970, the proportion of urban population has continued to increase, but more slowly, reaching 78% by the late 1990s (and projected to reach 85% by 2025). As the urban population grew dramatically, so did the number and size of cities. Small towns and villages (those with fewer than 10,000 people) declined sharply in numbers and population, while medium and large cities grew rapidly, all the natural outcome of Japan's phenomenal economic growth after the war.

Almost all of the major cities are found in the core region. (The one significant exception is Sapporo, the regional center of the northern island of Hokkaido.) This region consists of a narrow band that begins with the urban node of Fukuoka/Kitakyushu/Shimonoseki at the western end of the Great Inland Sea, which separates the major islands of Japan. The core then stretches eastward along both shores of the Great Inland Sea (of the islands of Honshu and Shikoku) to the Tokyo region. In between, especially along the southern coast of Honshu, are strings of industrial cities, such as Hiroshima, which grew to importance in the last century.

Within this core is an inner core, containing more than 44% of Japan's total population of 126 million, known as the Tokaido Megalopolis (named after the Tokugawa-era road through this area) and consisting of the three urban/industrial nodes of Keihin (Tokyo-

Yokohama), with more than 30 million people; Hanshin (Osaka-Kobe-Kyoto), with more than 16 million; and Chukyo (Nagoya), at nearly 9 million. Within this inner core, Tokyo dominates. There really are two distinct parts to Japan, in a classic core-periphery imbalance—the "developed" capital region centered on Tokyo and the "underdeveloped" regions (in a relative sense) elsewhere in Japan (fig. 11.6). Rapid growth from the late 1950s through the early 1970s saw a shift from rural areas to big cities in general. Since then, the migration and growth have been increasingly toward Tokyo at the expense of the rest of the country, including Tokyo's long-standing rival, Osaka, a phenomenon dubbed *unipolar concentration.* Tokyo continues to expand, draining people and capital investment from the other regions, many of which are stagnating. The Osaka region (also known by the premodern name of Kansai) has not seen growth of new industries to replace the smokestack industries, such as steel and shipbuilding, while Osaka businesses continue to relocate to Tokyo. This combination encourages out-migration and depresses personal consumption. Nagoya has fared somewhat better than Osaka by managing to maintain employment and urban vitality in its central city. For people eager to be in the mainstream of modern Japan, living in or near Tokyo is essential.

Tokyo is truly a primate city; its dominance within Japan is awesome. Tokyo's roughly one-quarter share of Japan's total population is concentrated in barely 4% of the nation's land area. As a result, population density in Tokyo is 16 times that of Japan as a whole. Whatever quantitative measures one wishes to use, Tokyo has a disproportionate share, whether it is of workers, factories, headquarters of major corporations and financial institutions, institutions for higher education, industrial production, exports, or number of college students. As the national capital, Tokyo of course has all the key governmental functions concentrated here. As a result, all 47 prefectural governments have branch offices in Tokyo, in order to maintain effective liaison with the national government. One observer likened the situation to that of the Tokugawa era of the 18th century, when the provincial feudal lords were required to maintain a second household in what was then Edo, as a means of maintaining the power of the Tokugawa Shogunate. The obeisance to Tokyo remains to this day, albeit in a new form.

Tokyo City itself has increased in population only slightly, while the 23 wards of the central city have actually lost some population. By contrast, the three key prefectures surrounding Tokyo (Saitama, Chiba, Kanagawa) gained significantly, evidence of the suburban sprawl of the built-up area into satellite towns and cities. Because land became so scarce and expensive in Tokyo, virtually the entire perimeter of Tokyo Bay now consists of reclaimed land (fig. 11.7).

Western influences played some role in the prewar development of Tokyo. Unfortunately, the devastation of the 1923 earthquake and the urgent need for quick rebuilding precluded widespread adoption of Western urban planning ideas. The devastation from World War II bombing had the same effect. In spite of ambitious plans drawn up immediately after the war, few of those ideas were implemented. The result was a tendency for the city to grow haphazardly in a manner that resulted in congestion and a disorganized city layout. By and large, growth has been concentrated around key subcenters, such as Shinjuku (now the city government headquarters) and Shibuya, and along the key transport arteries (rail and ex-

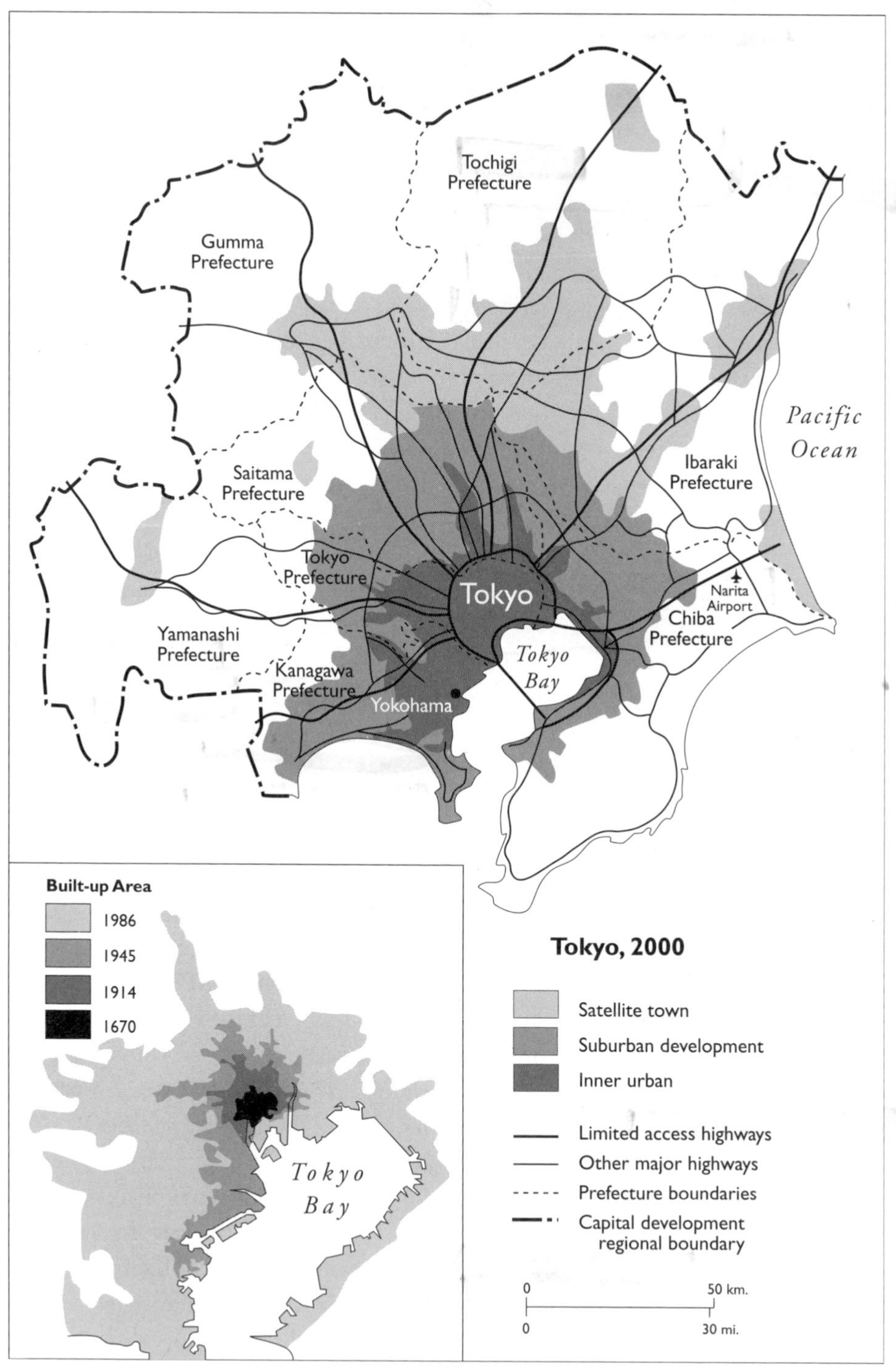

Figure 11.6 Tokyo Capital Development Region. *Source*: Tokyo Metropolitan Government

Figure 11.7 This Landsat image of the Tokyo Bay region dramatically illustrates the vast sprawl of Greater Tokyo, which completely surrounds Tokyo Bay along a largely human-made coastline. The new Tokyo Bay Aqua Line, a combination bridge/tunnel connecting Tokyo City in the northwest with Chiba Prefecture in the southeast, is faintly visible (the white streak in the middle is the entrance to the tunnel).

pressway) radiating outward from the old historic core of the Imperial Palace (Chiyoda District). Hence, the city has a distinct concentric ring pattern intermixed with elements of the multinucleic model. The city also has taken on elements of the American-style "doughnut" model, because of spiraling land costs in the 1980s and desertion by middle-class people seeking affordable housing in outer areas. They commute to the central city to work in the daytime, but return to the suburbs in the evening. Unlike in U.S. cities, however, there are no serious racial/socioeconomic class differences fueling this residential pattern (except relating to the minority *burakumin,* or untouchables, and the Korean minority, who tend to live in their own ghettoes).

Japan's "bubble" economy burst starting in the early 1990s, when both residential and commercial land prices peaked at 200–300% of what they had been in the early 1980s. Land prices have slid precipitously downward since then, returning to early 1980s levels or lower by 2001. The bottom of the real estate bust appeared to have been reached, at least for Tokyo.

Beijing: The Less Forbidden City

Beijing, the great "Northern Capital" for centuries, was a horizontal, compact city of magnificent architecture and artistic treasures of China's past grandeur when the New China began in 1949 (although, to be sure, the city had suffered greatly from general neglect during the hundred years of foreign intrusion, civil war, and internal strife since the 1840s). Centered on the former Forbidden City (Imperial Palace), Beijing was renowned for its sophisticated culture and refined society. The beautiful Beijing dialect became the national spoken language after the collapse of the dynasty in 1911. The city's only real function was as political and cultural center of a vast nation. There was hardly any industry and the population was not large.

The situation changed dramatically after 1949. For starters, for the half century after 1949, the city expanded from just 1.7 million people in 24 sq mi (62 sq km) to a vast metropolis of about 12 million in its 13 city districts (or about 14 million people in more than 6,500 sq mi, or 16,800 sq km, including rural counties under Beijing's administration). The population growth was due to the physical expansion of the urban area, natural population growth, and net migration. Especially since the early 1960s, the population has been strictly regulated. Indeed, because of its prime importance as the restored national capital (Nanjing was the national capital during the Republican era, from the late 1920s until 1949), migration to Beijing, like Moscow under the Soviets, was the most strictly controlled among all China's cities. Functionally, Beijing was also transformed into a *producing* city, as it became one of China's key industrial centers, while retaining its ongoing function as center of government, culture, and education. Other functions such as commerce and services were greatly curtailed. With a command-type economy geared to central planning and five-year plans—much like those of the then Soviet Union—Beijing became even more the power center of China, analogous to Moscow.

The changes inflicted on Beijing's landscape were enormous in the Maoist era (1949–1976), especially during the Cultural Revolution (1966–1976). Although objectives, policies, and urban plans for Beijing fluctuated during the Maoist era, the end result was the transformation of Beijing into a vast, gray city of arrow-straight, wide boulevards and huge government buildings, punctuated by seemingly endless rows of drab apartment blocks in the socialist style. The charming traditional courtyard houses in *hutong,* or narrow alleys, in the old city were gradually subdivided for multiple families, but often without the necessary updates and maintenance (fig. 11.8). A huge area in front of the Tiananmen ("Gate of Heavenly Peace") entrance to the Palace Museum was cleared of structures, greatly expanding the existing square. The largest open square of any city in the world, Tiananmen became the staging ground for vast spectacles, parades, and rallies organized by the government on national days

Figure 11.8 Millions of Chinese urban residents still live in old, dilapidated housing, as in these *hutong,* or alleys, of old Beijing. (Photo by Stanley Brunn)

or during mass political campaigns. Mao and other party leaders stood on top of the gate like a latter-day imperial court (this area is now open to tourists to gawk and take photos). Not surprisingly, after Mao died in 1976 his body was embalmed and put in a crystal display case inside a huge mausoleum on the south end of Tiananmen Square, exactly along the north-south axis running through the Palace Museum. The parallel with the display of Lenin's body in Red Square in Moscow is obvious, as is the attempt to link Mao with the imperial tradition of China and the role of Beijing as an expression of cosmological beliefs. Though the square was designed and used mostly by those in power, for their own purposes, it was also the staging ground of major protests organized by students, intellectuals, and workers, from the famous May Fourth Movement in 1919 to the failed Pro-Democracy Movement in 1989.

The greatest sacrilege, in the eyes of some critics, was the tearing down of Beijing's city walls, sparing only the one around the former Forbidden City. The sites of the walls became ring roads designed ostensibly to ease traffic flow. Only a few crumbling city gates were kept as relics of another era. A subway system lies under the Erhuan Lu, or Second Ring Road. Removal of the walls totally shattered the original form of Beijing and forever altered its architectural character. Critics lamented that Beijing under Mao was a city primarily designed to express the government's power and control of China.

To be fair, the government was faced with enormous problems, especially in providing housing and meeting basic human needs. Historic preservation tends to take a backseat to more urgent human needs in almost every country. Moreover, the government did keep the Forbidden City (plus some other national treasures, such as the magnificent Temple of Heaven and the fascinating Summer Palace in northwestern Beijing) and work toward restoration of its former grandeur, transforming the huge enclosure into the Palace Museum—a collection of former palaces, temples, and other structures, many housing collections of art from the imperial ("feudal") past. The motive was largely political, but the net result was indeed historic preservation. The Palace Museum (Gu Gong) today is one of the top cultural treasures of the world, not just of China.

China's large cities in the Maoist era were both production (manufacturing) centers, as well as administrative nodes of the economic planning system that focused on both national and regional/local self-reliance. The functions of business and commerce were weak. Most cities tried to build relatively comprehensive industrial structures, resulting in much less division of labor and exchanges among manufacturing centers. The periurban (rural) areas controlled by the municipalities served the role of providing food for the cities. Some satellite towns in the outskirts of large cities were developed to accommodate the spillover of industries. Without a land market, many self-contained work-unit neighborhoods dominated the landscape of large cities, resulting in less functionally differentiated urban spatial structures. Large cities expanded in concentric zones, as in the model generalized by Lo (fig. 11.9). Beijing was no exception to this pattern.

The new policies beginning in the late 1970s were meant to cover some of the above weaknesses and transform Chinese cities through a series of marketization reforms. Those reforms have brought rising affluence, especially in the eastern coastal provinces and cities, reflected in the urban consumption boom of the 1980s and 1990s. In Beijing, this has translated into thousands of new stores and restaurants. Through large redevelopment projects, Beijing now has major commercial/financial districts, such as Xidan, a busy shopping area with modern architecture and expensive shops, and Wangfujing, an old retail strip that went through a major facelift in 1999, when the street was fully pedestrianized.

Growing per capita income also fueled a housing boom in the 1990s. With a real estate market beginning to function, a greater demand for floor space has intensified use of urban land. Greater separation of workplace and housing has become increasingly feasible for a portion of the labor force. In the late 1980s, suburbanization on a large scale also began. Foreign investment now focuses not only on export processing but also on retail, insurance, finance, and producer services in the city, and this has increased the functional differentiation of city centers and suburbs, as well as other sites not centrally located but linked by highways.

To attract industry, Beijing's government has established more than a dozen development zones, mostly in the urban fringe. Zhongguancun, set up in the Haidian District close to China's top universities in the northwestern part of the city, is China's "Silicon Valley," where a large number of high-tech domestic and joint ventures are concentrated. On a larger scale, Beijing's growth is increasingly linked to the southeast with Tianjin, an international port city with provincial-level status, and to the east with Tangshan, a major center of heavy industry and coal mining, to form one of China's extended metropolitan areas. This process of outward expansion will intensify as China becomes even more integrated with the world, especially now that China has become a member of the World Trade Organization (WTO). Beijing, already home to many major multinational firms, will continue to be a major player in the globalization of the Chinese economy.

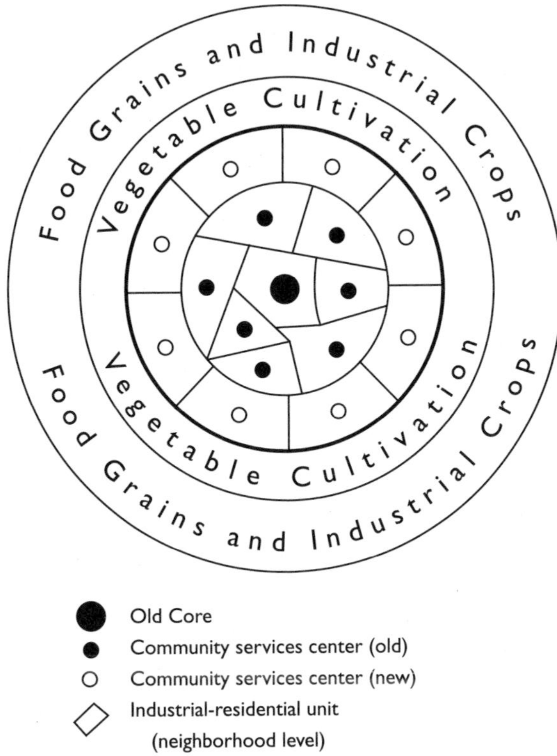

Figure 11.9 A Model of the Socialist City in Maoist China. *Source*: C. P. Lo, "Shaping Socialist Chinese Cities: A Model of Form and Land Use," in *China: Urbanization and National Development,* edited by Chi-keung Leung and Norton Ginsburg, Department of Geography Research Paper, no. 196 (Chicago: University of Chicago, 1980), 154. Reprinted with permission.

The rise in personal income is also paralleled by a noticeable increase in income disparities and social differentiation. In the outskirts at the north of Beijing, expensive, detached, Western-style bungalow houses have begun to appear, catering to expatriates and the new rich. At the same time, with the relaxation in migration controls since the mid-1980s, Beijing now has a large migrant population of about three million. These mostly rural migrants fill many low-level jobs shunned by the locals. Migrants tend to be poor and they often congregate based on their place of origin and provide mutual help to each other. Several migrant communities have sprung up in Beijing's outskirts, such as the "Zhejiang Village" (fig. 11.10) and "Xinjiang Village." Living conditions in these migrant villages provide a stark contrast with those of wealthier neighborhoods. In the inner city, laid-off workers from bankrupt state enterprises are gradually forming Beijing's new urban poor.

In the early 1980s, the government became

Figure 11.10 Lunchtime in the "Zhejiang Village" on the outskirts of Beijing, a community made up largely of recent migrants from Zhejiang Province in south China. (Photo by Kam Wing Chan)

serious about planning for the aesthetics of Beijing's future, bringing air and water pollution under control, and giving the city a more human feel. The Asian Games, held in 1990, provided the stimulus for much beautification effort and for improvements in urban infrastructure, such as several major expressways extending across the city and connecting the central city with the airport. Another round of even larger-scale construction is now under way as Beijing prepares to host the Olympic Summer Games in 2008. Many residents hope this will transform Beijing into a truly world-class city.

Shanghai: *Head of the Dragon?*

Shanghai is considered by many to be China's most interesting and vibrant city. This is because of its unique colonial heritage and because in many ways it is the New York of China—the center of change and new frontiers in social and economic behavior. Shanghai still is the largest and one of the most Westernized cities in China (along with perhaps Guangzhou) and has one of the highest standards of living.

Of all China's cities, Shanghai offers about the best example of the Chinese socialist city, because of its special role within socialist China in both urban planning and the economic development of the nation. Shanghai city itself is part of the Shanghai municipal region, comprising 17 city districts and three rural counties covering a huge area of more than 2,400 sq mi (6,300 sq km) with a combined total population of more than 16.7 million. The city itself, within the 17 city districts, is more than 14.7 million in population (fig. 11.11).

In terms of meeting the criteria of a true "producing" city in the socialist model, Shanghai comes the closest of just about any Chinese

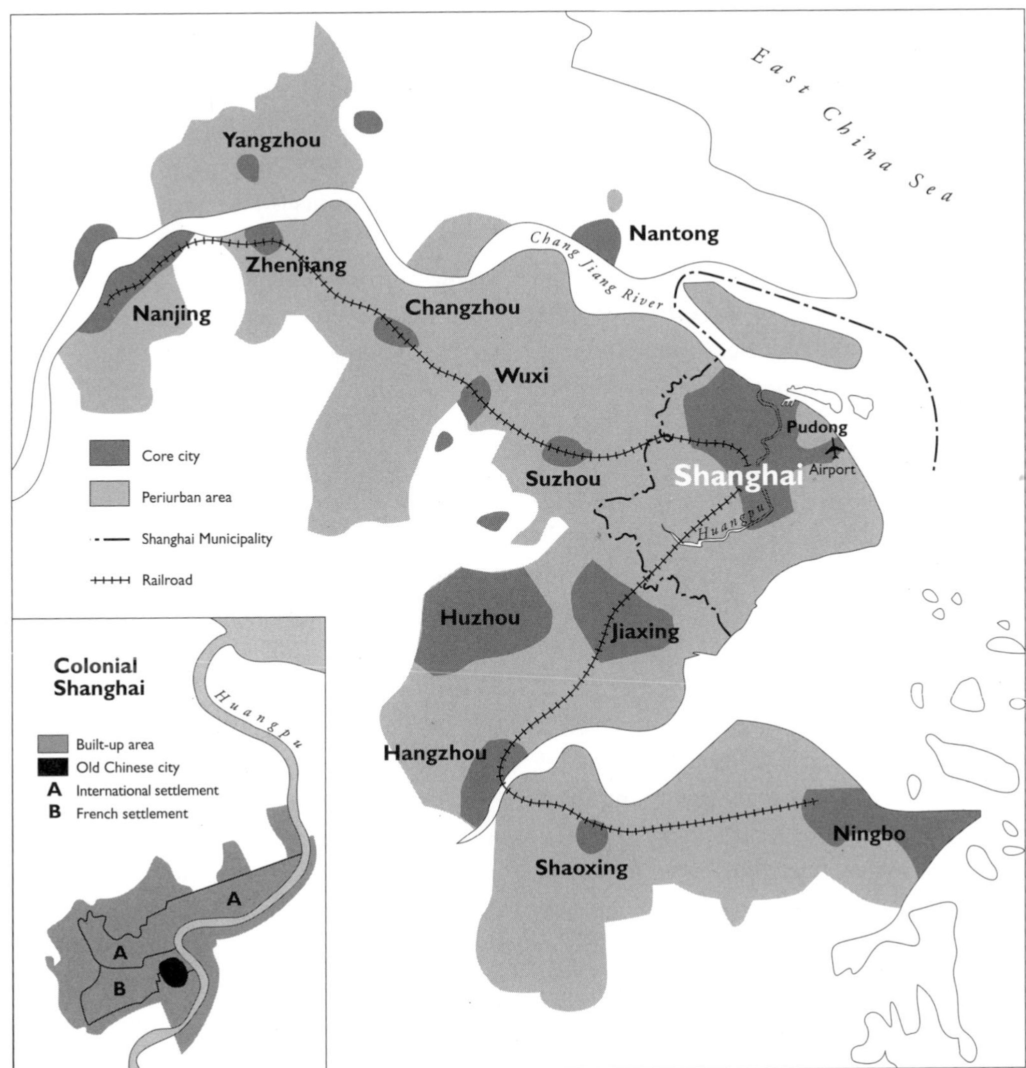

Figure 11.11 The Shanghai Extended Metropolitan Region. *Source*: Adapted from Gu Chaolin, Yu Taofang, and Kam Wing Chan, "Extended Metropolitan Regions: New Feature of Chinese Metropolitan Development in the Age of Globalization," *Planner* 18, no. 2 (2000): 16–20.

city today. Prior to the reform era, revenues for the Chinese government relied heavily on taxes on state-owned enterprises (SOEs); Shanghai, being the prime center of SOEs, bore a heavy burden. It is estimated that Shanghai alone contributed about one-sixth of government revenues between 1949 and 1978. This "extraction" by the central government, however, was partly balanced by the advantages Shanghai enjoyed. Typically, industrial producers such as Shanghai were heavily favored by the central government and protected over agricultural producers. Not only was competition limited for industry, prices of manufactured goods were often set high in Shanghai's favor. In the period between 1953 and 1978, economic growth of Shanghai averaged about 9% per year, clearly higher than the national average. In 1978, the city accounted for 8% of China's GDP, 12% of its industrial output, and 18% of its exports.

As with many cities in the Maoist era (with the exception of Beijing), little was reinvested in Shanghai in terms of new construction and upgrading of facilities. The downtown area, particularly around the Bund, or riverfront, district, where the major Western-controlled activities had been concentrated, had the look of a 1930s Hollywood movie set, with aging, poorly maintained, Western-style buildings that once housed banks and offices, hotels, and other commercial functions. In 1933, the Park Hotel was built on Nanjing Road, a major commercial artery of Shanghai. That hotel remained the tallest building in the city for 49 years, until 1982, when high rises began to be constructed once again. Although fascinating to an outside visitor, the city was falling apart. It was the relative neglect of many cities, including Shanghai, that contributed to the impression that the Maoist government was "antiurban," although the reality was far more complicated.

With the reopening of China in the late 1970s, under the "New Open Door" policy, foreigners again began to return to China, particularly the coastal zone in Guangdong in the south. Although Shanghai was designated as one of the 14 "open cities" (for foreign investment) in 1984, Guangdong was really the initial region chosen to be developed in cooperation with foreign (including Hong Kong) capital. In the 1980s, Shanghai thus lagged behind Guangdong in attracting foreign capital and in its rate of economic growth, averaging about 7% a year, much less than Guangdong's spectacular double-digit growth. Shanghai's share of the nation's exports declined sharply, to only 7% in 1990 (compared to 20% for Guangdong). Shanghai's share of the nation's GDP also slipped, to only 4%. The turning point for the city came in 1990 in the aftermath of the 1989 Tiananmen events, as the government struggled to regain foreign investors' confidence. In an effort to restart the momentum of the economy, China decided in April 1990 to rejuvenate Shanghai and its hinterland by developing Pudong ("East of the Pu," i.e., the Huangpu River, which bisects Shanghai), a zone on the east side of the old city core (fig. 11.12).

The new development plan established a package of preferential policies, very similar to those in China's five export-oriented special economic zones (SEZs), to woo foreign capital. These policies included lower profit taxes, lease rights on land, retention of revenues, and others. The Pudong plan gave emphasis to high-tech industries and financial services rather than simply export processing. Pudong was supposed to be the answer to choking congestion in the old city center and to be the catalyst for the renaissance of Shanghai as a whole. Foreign investors have been encouraged to get in on the ground floor of what is touted as one of China's most ambitious undertakings of the 1990s and the new century. Among the foreign investors, Taiwanese businesses have shown the most intensive interest in Pudong. Shanghai is now home to some 3,000 Taiwanese companies, while an estimated 100,000–200,000 Taiwanese business people regularly stay in the Shanghai region. A "Little Taipei" is developing in the Zhangjiang High-Tech Park in Pudong.

With the full backing of the central government, Shanghai improved its infrastructure and through the 1990s greatly strengthened its role as China's prime economic and financial center (figs. 11.13 and 11.14). The Shanghai

Figure 11.12 In the space of just ten years, Shanghai's new CBD has arisen across the river in Pudong, centered on the futuristic TV observation tower around which modern high-rise buildings have sprung up. Pudong and Shanghai are to be the "Head of the Dragon" in development of the Chang Jiang valley and the rest of China. (Photo by Jack Williams)

Stock Exchange was set up in December 1990. Throughout the decade, Shanghai's annual economic growth rate stayed above 10%. Today, more than half of the world's Fortune 500 corporations have set up offices or plants in Shanghai. One survey in the late 1990s showed that Shanghai had outdistanced Beijing as the most popular city in China in which to make a career.

Today Shanghai's development is part of a larger, dynamic Chang Jiang delta urban region composed of some 13 closely linked cities and surrounding counties. This region, stretching from Hangzhou and Ningbo in the southeast to Suzhou and Nanjing in the northwest, contains about 70 million people. It also includes other major industrial cities, such as Wuxi, Suzhou, and Changzhou, and newer county-level cities, such as Kunshan, Jiangyin, Zhangjiagang, and Xiaoshan (see fig. 11.11). Shanghai has definitely reacquired some of its prerevolutionary glamour. Shops and architecture in some sections of the city have a cosmopolitan feel and there is a sizable expatriate community in the urban area once again.

However, there are some who doubt whether Shanghai will truly become the "head of the dragon"—an economic powerhouse that will somehow stimulate development of the whole Chang Jiang valley (the "body" of the dragon)—as the Chinese government hopes. Critics have pointed to problems, such as inadequate port facilities, unwise location of the new international airport, excess supply of real estate in Pudong, serious traffic congestion, air and water pollution, and the lack of bottom-up development based on rural enterprises in the counties. Perhaps most important of all, Shanghai still lacks the "software" required to make good use of its hardware,

Figs. 11.13, 11.14 (facing page) These two photos dramatically illustrate the transformation of Shanghai since the end of the Maoist era. In the mid-1970s, Nanjing Road, a key commercial artery of old Shanghai's International Settlement, slumbered in socialist stagnation. By the end of the 1990s, much of Nanjing Road had been turned into a glittering, throbbing pedestrian mall devoted to high mass consumption and the free-market economy. (Photos by Jack Williams)

that is, a well-enforced legal system and protection of intellectual property rights. China's dragon has yet to roar.

Hong Kong: Rendezvous with Destiny

At the stroke of midnight on June 30, 1997, Hong Kong was officially handed over to China and became the Hong Kong Special Administrative Region (HKSAR). This was an extraordinary historic event, with Governor Chris Patten, Prince Charles, China's President Jiang Zemin, and other dignitaries presiding, marking the end of the colonial era in Asia and the rise of China's power. Hong Kong was one of the last two colonial enclaves left in all of Asia by the late 20th century. The other colony, Macau, likewise was returned to China by Portugal in December 1999. Hence, as China entered the new century, its intense, humiliating experience with foreign colonialism finally came to a definite end after almost 160 years.

The 1997 event was a result of a joint agreement signed by China and Britain in 1984, which committed China to guarantee Hong Kong 50 years of complete autonomy in its internal affairs and capitalist system. China would have control only over Hong Kong's defense and foreign relations. Since 1997, Hong Kong has been under the model of "one country, two systems." The latter refers to the socialist system in the PRC and the capitalist system in Hong Kong. In the years before the handover, the biggest question that stirred up concern was what would happen to Hong Kong after 1997. In one of the gloomiest predictions,

Fortune magazine in 1996 pronounced the city dead. Indeed, in the decade preceding the transition, these concerns had triggered an exodus of about half a million Hong Kongers, mostly wealthy professionals, most of whom ended up in Canada (especially Vancouver and Toronto), Australia, and the United States. But other observers believed that the inherent assets of Hong Kong, which had fueled its extraordinary rise over the previous 40 years to a position as a powerful mini-industrial state, would see Hong Kong through the stresses of political transfer to the PRC. So far, the optimists seem generally vindicated.

Back in 1949, when Shanghai and the rest of China fell to the communists, few thought that Hong Kong could long survive under British rule. The UN embargo on China during the Korean War effectively cut off most of Hong Kong's trade, which at that time was mainly movement of goods into and out of China. The population soared from half a million in 1946 to more than two million by 1950, as refugees flooded the colony. Huge squatter settlements were everywhere and the economy was in a shambles. The British, in collaboration with Chinese entrepreneurs—including many wealthy industrialists who had fled Shanghai and other parts of China, such as the father of the HKSAR's current chief executive, Tung

Chee Hwa—began to turn Hong Kong's economy around. They did it by recognizing the need to industrialize and develop products, "made in Hong Kong," for export. Hong Kong could no longer survive as just a trade center for China's goods. It was a spectacularly successful transformation. Adopting a laissez-faire (probusiness) policy, including generous tax policies, the authorities in Hong Kong encouraged foreign investment, which poured in from Japan, the United States, Europe, and the overseas Chinese. There was ample cheap, hardworking labor. Site limitations were overcome by massive landfill projects to provide new land for factories and urban expansion, while freshwater and much of the city's food supply were purchased from Guangdong Province across the border.

The strategy worked because China wanted it to work. One of the paradoxes of Hong Kong was that the government of China continued to permit this arch symbol of unrepentant Western capitalism and colonialism to exist and thrive on what was rightly Chinese territory. The Chinese did this partly because Hong Kong made lots of money for them, too—several billion dollars a year in foreign exchange earned from the PRC's exports to Hong Kong and from investments in banking and commerce. Wisely, China did not try to take over Hong Kong, because the PRC saw practical advantage for a struggling socialist China in keeping the door open a crack to the outside world (and also in not being responsible for solving Hong Kong's then staggering problems). During this era, one of the most striking sights could be seen in Statue Square on Queens Road Central in downtown Hong Kong, where lined up side by side were the Bank of China, the Hong Kong & Shanghai Banking Corporation, and the Chartered Bank of Great Britain. The latter two represented the local financial strongholds of Great Britain and private capital, while the Bank of China represented the command center for the PRC's interests in Hong Kong. Banker's Row became even more impressive a sight when, in the 1980s, the Hong Kong & Shanghai Bank opened on the same site a new structure, the most expensive ever built in Hong Kong up to then. The new building was an instant architectural controversy because of its postmodern design, by Norman Foster. This avant-garde building was soon overshadowed, however, by the new Bank of China building, opened in 1991. Designed by I. M. Pei, the renowned Chinese-American architect, the building is regarded as one of the most architecturally outstanding buildings in the world today, and a not very subtle reminder of who after all is the ultimate authority in Hong Kong.

Those two buildings symbolized not only the political duality and economic dynamism that have characterized Hong Kong throughout most of its history, but also the cosmopolitan and sophisticated "world city" that Hong Kong had become by the 1980s. One of the top tourist meccas in the world, Hong Kong is, by any standards, a stunning sight whether one is arriving for the first time or the hundredth (fig. 11.15). The skyline is spectacular, especially at night, with its glittering, ultramodern high-rise buildings packed side by side along the shoreline. There is so much money to be made in Hong Kong that every inch of space is extremely valuable and must be used to maximum advantage. The authorities have used remarkable ingenuity in designing the road system and other urban features, especially on crowded Hong Kong Island, where the strip city snakes along the north shore. Kowloon, on the mainland side, has relatively more land, but even there the intricacy of the urban design is impressive.

Figure 11.15 This view of Hong Kong, taken from Kowloon across the harbor, dramatically conveys the modernity and wealth of modern Hong Kong. The Central Plaza building towers over the wave-like profile of the Convention Center, where the handover to China took place in 1997. (Photo by Kam Wing Chan)

Less eye-catching to the average tourist, but themselves impressive accomplishments, are Hong Kong's public housing and new-town programs. The two were begun simultaneously as measures to cope with the large influx of migrants from China in the early 1950s. The programs gradually expanded into some of the world's largest, quite an anomaly for a laissez-faire economy. Today, about half of Hong Kong's population of seven million lives in public, largely rental, housing. Indeed, public housing, because of much lower rents, has been a major mechanism for decentralizing the population outside of the main urban area (fig. 11.16). Reclamation has been a main strategy for creating new land for the city. Many of the large new towns, such as Shatin (about 600,000) and Tuen Mun (500,000), were built almost totally from scratch. Public housing was crucial in maintaining the social and political stability of the city, especially from the 1950s through the 1970s, when the city faced enormous pressure from the rapidly growing, largely low-income population.

Until the late 1980s, the economy that had fueled the creation of this machine—where making money, as much and as fast as possible, is the raison d'etre for most people—was heavily based on consumer goods manufacturing and exports, especially textiles, electronics, and toys. The top markets remain the United States, Europe, and Japan. With China's opening in the late 1970s, Hong Kong quickly took advantage of the cheap land and labor in the Pearl River Delta and since then has steadily *offshored* (moved its manufacturing capacity) to the delta (while company headquarters remain in Hong Kong). Currently, some 100,000 Hong Kong-invested enterprises operate in the delta region and employ a total of 5–6 million

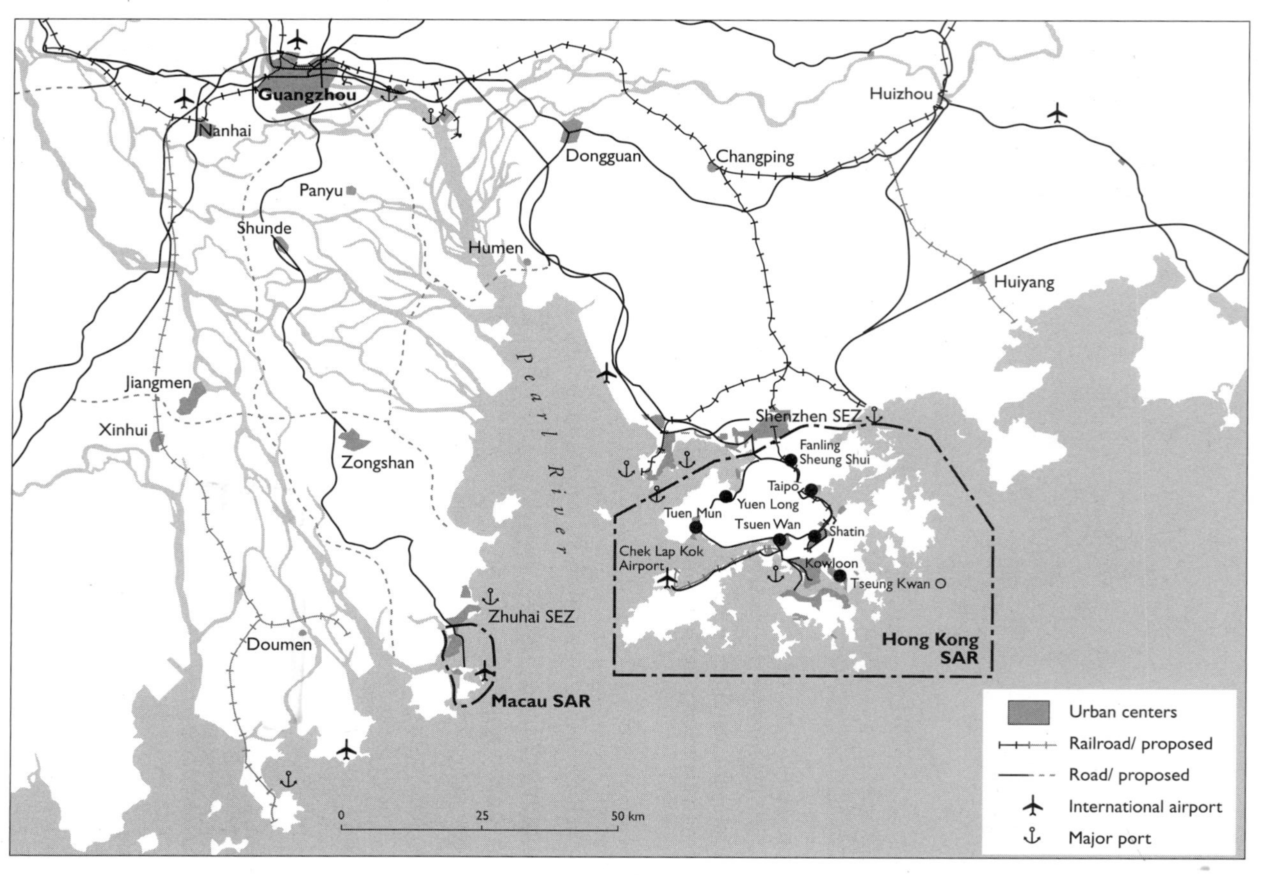

Figure 11.16 The Hong Kong Extended Metropolitan Region. *Source*: Adapted from various sources.

workers. In many ways, the delta and Hong Kong are now a highly integrated region, one that has become one of the major global export centers, with Hong Kong serving as the "shop front" and the delta as the factory (see fig. 11.16).

The rise of this region in world trade has reinvigorated Hong Kong's role as an entrepôt. Hong Kong is the banking and investment center for the China trade, as well as regional headquarters for many international corporations. In the rapid opening of China in the past two decades, Hong Kong has played an extremely crucial role as the intermediary between China and the world, such as in serving as middleman for Taiwan's huge economic dealings with the PRC. Tourism remains vital as well, with people coming for different purposes—Japanese and Taiwanese tourists, to take advantage of what seems like one giant shopping mall dedicated to extravagantly high mass consumption, or the more curious American tourists, to get a taste of the "Orient." Many tourists are now from the PRC, for whom Hong Kong is their first taste of the Western capitalist world.

In a period of less than two generations, Hong Kong has evolved into a global center boasting a per capita income on a par with Europe and the United States. In the past 15 years, Hong Kong has advanced further into the postindustrial phase, into information services, as one of the key world centers of international trade and services, along with Tokyo, Singapore, New York, and a few others. Now, at the beginning of the 21st century, the biggest worry Hong Kongers have does not seem to be the issue of China's political intervention after handover. Instead, a series of mishaps in the city after the handover have cast doubt on the touted managerial capacity of the government. Hong Kong is still in the economic doldrums that started with the Asian financial crisis of 1997–1998 and continued into the aftermath of September 11. Faced with greater economic competition (including from other Chinese cities, especially Shanghai, Guangzhou, and Shenzhen), many people are seriously questioning if the previous formula for success will continue to work for Hong Kong in the new millennium. In the past two decades, Hong Kong has successfully used its special connection with China to its own advantage. Will this continue to work, now that the world economy is more globalized and China has joined the WTO? What is Hong Kong's market niche under these new circumstances? Whatever happens, there is no doubt that Hong Kong's future is closely tied to that of China.

Taipei: A Regional Center in Search of a Region

Although regional centers are found throughout East Asia, a particularly good example is the city of Taipei, which has been emerging from its provincial cocoon in recent years and acquiring some of the aura of a world-class city, following in the footsteps of Hong Kong. There is some ambiguity about how to classify Taipei, because since 1950 it has been the "temporary" capital of the Republic of China (ROC) government-in-exile and, as such, has experienced phenomenal growth beyond what it might have undergone if it had remained solely the provincial capital of an island province of China. For certain, if the communists had succeeded in capturing Taiwan in 1950, as they had hoped to, Taipei would be a vastly different place today, probably something akin to present-day Xiamen (Amoy) across the Taiwan Strait. Instead, Taipei skyrocketed from the modest colonial capital city of a quarter million in 1945 to the present metropolis of more than six million in

Figure 11.17 The Taipei Metropolitan Region completely fills the Taipei Basin and spills out toward the northwest, northeast, and southwest, as shown in this Landsat image.

a metropolitan region that completely fills the Taipei basin and spills northeast to the port of Keelung, northwest to the coastal town of Tanshui (now a high-rise suburb), and southward toward Taoyuan and the CCK International Airport (fig. 11.17). Functionally, the city shifted gears from being a colonial administrative and commercial center to becoming the control center for one of the most dynamic economies in the postwar world.

When the ROC government retreated to Taiwan in 1950, the provincial capital was shifted to a new town built expressly for this purpose in central Taiwan, not far from Taichung. Taipei was theoretically concerned with "national" affairs and hence had all the national government offices re-created there (transplanted with administrators and legislators from Nanjing). The provincial capital dealt with agriculture and similar island (local) affairs. This artificial dichotomy, designed to preserve the fiction that the ROC government was the legal government of all of China, held until the early 1990s, when the government finally publicly admitted it had no jurisdiction over the mainland. The impact on Taipei over the decades was great, however, resulting in a large bureaucracy and the construction of national capital–level buildings in the city. This was possibly because huge tracts of land formerly occupied by the Japanese were taken over by the government after 1945 and the single-party authoritarian political system under the Kuomintang (KMT) allowed the government to develop the city in whatever way it desired, largely free of open public opposition.

This even included renaming many streets in Taipei after well-known mainland cities and places. After President Chiang Kai-shek died in 1975, as another example, a huge piece of military land in central Taipei was transformed into a gigantic memorial to Chiang, one of the largest structures in Taiwan. Two huge concert halls, also built in the classic palace architectural style, were added to the immense grounds of the memorial in the 1980s to signify the coming of age of Taipei as a world-class city and center of sophisticated culture.

Taipei has come to assume many primate-city functions, although statistically only twice the size of Kaohsiung, the main heavy industrial center in the South. Besides being the "national" capital, Taipei is overwhelmingly the center of international trade and investment and includes a large expatriate community. Culture, entertainment, and tourism are all focused on Taipei. Japanese business people and tourists especially like Taipei because of the colonial heritage; Taipei's culture has a distinctly Japanese flavor to it. The Taipei metro region also is one of the key industrial areas of the island; most of the manufacturing is now concentrated in a number of satellite cities, to the west and south, such as Sanchung, Panchiao, and Yungho. The old port of Keelung, once the key link with Japan, serves as the port outlet for the Taipei Northern Industrial Region. As with Seoul, most of the city's huge population increase over five decades was the result of in-migration from the densely populated countryside, a migration that in recent years has been primarily toward the suburban satellite cities. By 1999, the Northern Industrial Region had a total population of 9.5 million (out of Taiwan's nearly 23 million people), of which Taipei Municipality accounted for 2.6 million and the surrounding satellite cities accounted for 3.9 million, or 6.5 million total for the urban agglomeration.

The city has been growing toward the margins. Eastern Taipei ("New Taipei"), focused symbolically around the World Trade Center and along Tunhua Road, has seen especially astounding growth, with hundreds of high-rise luxury apartment buildings and office towers springing up. Large-scale suburbanization has also taken place, as affluent yuppies have moved to the northern suburbs, to high-class residential neighborhoods in Tienmu and Neihu, or southward toward Hsintien. High housing costs and overcrowded central-city conditions have encouraged this out-migration.

In some respects, Taipei looks like Seoul on a smaller scale, with modern buildings, broad, tree-lined boulevards, and a high standard of living. Substantial cleanup and improvements came with the 1990s as the political system was democratized, the environment became an important concern, and urban development became an open topic for public input. An expanding subway system is helping to ease the transportation crush, composed of hordes of motorcycles and increasing numbers of private automobiles. As with cities around the world, parking is a monumental problem for all drivers.

Seoul: The "Phoenix" of Primate Cities

Seoul exhibits urban primacy in an especially acute form. It is home to 10 million people, more than 25% of South Korea's total population of 27 million, putting it in the ranks of the world's megacities (making it one of four such in East Asia). More than 40% of the country's population lives within the greater Seoul metropolitan region. In 1950, Seoul had barely more than one million people, just slightly more than second-ranked Pusan, the main port on the southeast coast. By

2000, Pusan had just under four million people.

As the national capital, Seoul has a large tertiary sector devoted to the national government and the large military forces that South Korea must maintain. In addition, there is a large expatriate community, composed mostly of U.S. military forces and civilians (mostly business people and diplomatic personnel). Seoul is the political, cultural, educational, and economic heart of modern South Korea, the nerve center for the powerful state that South Korea has become. Although Seoul does not rank with Tokyo or New York as a true world city, it is nonetheless moving in that direction and certainly has become much more cosmopolitan in the past ten years, with the democratization and globalization of South Korea, as with Taipei and Taiwan.

The rise of Seoul to become one of the largest cities in the world is surprising, if only from a locational viewpoint. The city's site, midway along the west coast plain of the Korean peninsula, where most of the people are located, was originally a logical place for the national capital of a unified Korea. However, since the division of the peninsula in the late 1940s and the bitter stalemate between North and South Korea since 1953, Seoul's location just 20 mi (32 km) from the demilitarized zone (DMZ) makes the city highly vulnerable. Suggestions for moving the capital functions to a more southerly and defensible site have regularly met with indifference or outright opposition. This is partly because most Koreans believe that national reunification is inevitable. When that happens, Seoul would then resume its historic role as national capital, revered by all Koreans for what the city symbolizes.

The city was nearly leveled during the savage seesaw fighting in the Korean War, when the North occupied the city twice. Growth since the 1960s has been primarily the result of massive rural-urban migration, encouraged by Korea's transformation into an urban/industrial society. The economic takeoff started in the 1960s, as the South embarked on an export-oriented industrialization strategy, much of it concentrated in the Seoul area. Urbanization thus accelerated and the South passed the 50% urban mark in 1977. Seoul has spilled over into other areas, as well as sprawling south of the Han River and completely filling the basin of the river, covering an area equal to the entire island of Singapore. The southerly expansion was made possible by increasing the number of bridges across the Han from the original two to more than 20 currently. Residential and commercial growth has been rapid.

Seoul has its own grandness and beauty, in certain places, such as in the layout of new districts or restored monuments of the past. But parts of the city are still terribly congested and shabby, especially some residential areas built on steep hillsides as a result of spontaneous rather than planned urbanization. Seoul could be said to have come of age when it hosted the Olympic Summer Games in 1988, which gave authorities the rationale to spend billions of dollars to beautify the city and upgrade its infrastructure. In addition to a huge Olympics complex (used also for the Asia Games and other events since), an extensive subway system was completed (fig. 11.18). The downtown CBD is a typical conglomeration of high-rise luxury hotels and office buildings, interspersed with relics of Korea's past. Newer high-class residential/commercial districts, such as Kangnam south of the Han River, now contribute to a multinuclei pattern of development. Just south of the downtown and the prominent Mt. Namsan (whose observation tower still affords the

Figure 11.18 Seoul constructed an impressive subway system for the Olympic Summer Games in 1988. Each station is different in its architecture and artistic decoration. This is the handsome Kangnam station. (Photo courtesy Seoul city government)

best overall view of Seoul) is Itaewon District, long the center for U.S. military personnel, a honky-tonk reminder of an era of the past and of the uneasy fit of American pop culture with Korean values.

URBAN PROBLEMS AND THEIR SOLUTIONS

The relatively clear-cut dichotomy between the socialist path of China, North Korea, and Mongolia and the nonsocialist path of the rest of East Asia that characterized the region through the 1970s is no longer really valid. China has been largely abandoning socialism in many aspects of its economy since the late 1970s. North Korea occasionally hints that it might be tempted to do so also, but then slips back into its Stalinist suspicion of the outside world (box 11.1). Mongolia, like Russia, abandoned not only a socialist system but also single-party rule forthwith, and is now struggling to join the world, too (box 11.2). The colonial era is now completely over in the region. As a result of all these changes, urban problems and solutions take on new guises and, except for North Korea, are becoming increasingly similar across the region.

The Chinese Way

To appreciate what China has attempted and accomplished in the reform era, one needs to briefly review urban development policies before then.

The Maoist Era (1949–1976): Antiurban?

By nationalizing the economy, taking control of all the means of production, and adopting a planned, or command, type of economy, China's government after 1949 thought it had the solution to the country's immense problems. Events proved them wrong. The overwhelming emphasis on industrial growth; suppression of personal consumption (the

Box 11.1 Pyongyang: Reclusive City of Chosun

The government of North Korea (which likes to use the old name for Korea, "Chosun") rules this austere nation of some 22 million from the capital city of Pyongyang. At 3.5 million, Pyongyang is three times larger, in classic primate fashion, than the next two largest cities, Nampo and Hamhung. This is hardly a surprise, given the rigid, centrally planned, Stalinist system that hangs on, long after the Soviet Union, Maoist China, and communist Mongolia saw the light. Leveled to the ground during the Korean War (1950–1953), Pyongyang was totally rebuilt in the true Stalinist, socialist city model of the past, with broad boulevards (although they are still little utilized) and massive government buildings. Few foreigners get to personally visit this city and nation; few have kind words to say after they leave. There is a small expatriate community, composed of diplomatic personnel and those associated with international food relief efforts. In spite of the widely publicized food shortages (even famine conditions), the declining per capita incomes and life spans, and the escape of thousands of North Koreans into China, visitors remark that the authorities are adept at keeping Pyongyang and other visitor sites clear of tell-tale evidence. Hence, the city is starkly revealed for what it is: a superficially modern showcase for socialist dogma, but not a real city for life, creativity, and resident happiness. Drab apartment blocks have few amenities, the shops are bleak and empty of goods, security forces are visible everywhere.

"nonproductive" side of cities); the guaranteeing of the welfare of urban dwellers through the *iron rice bowl* welfare system, to the relative neglect of rural areas; strict controls over internal migration within the country through the *hukou* (household registration) system (box 11.3); strict monitoring of peoples' lives in the cities through neighborhood committees (box 11.4)—these and other policies produced an artificial, unworkable urban and national system that was clearly failing by the mid-1970s, when Mao died. The system had to change.

The Reform Era (1978–—): Opening China

Starting in the late 1970s, China's leaders began radical reversals of policy across the board, abandoning or severely diluting many of the key policies of the Maoist era, including those in urban development. One major exception was in the Communist Party's retaining a rigid, one-party, authoritarian political system that was increasingly at odds with the many reforms that were instituted.

The major policy change was in the *kaifang* ("opening") policy, or what might be dubbed the "New Open Door" policy (a voluntary opening, in marked contrast to the forced "Open Door" policy of the colonial era in the 19th century). China was thrown open to foreigners for investment, trade, tourism, technical assistance, and other contacts. The policy of self-reliance was set aside. Rapid growth in links with the outside world had a profound impact, but especially on cities and urban development in the coastal zone, which was earmarked for preferential treatment. The establishment of export-processing zones with concessionary tax policies to attract foreign investment included the desig-

Box 11.2 Mongolia

With a huge land area equal to more than 40% of China, but a miniscule population of just 2.6 million, Mongolia ranks simultaneously as one of the largest yet smallest of nations in the world. Easily ignored, in spite of its territorial size, in the early 1990s Mongolia threw off the communist system imposed on it in the 1920s (as the second communist nation in the world, after the USSR) and the subservient status imposed by the Soviets. Today, a democratic Mongolia is struggling to modernize, with a still powerful Communist Party competing. With 57% of Mongolia's population urbanized, the days of nomadic herders are diminishing, as urban life gains popularity. The capital city of Ulan Bator (Ulaanbataar) has only about three quarters of a million people, but that is 30% of the national total and the population of the city is projected to be just less than a million by 2015. Ulan Bator still displays the drab grayness of the socialist era, as new structures start to go up. There is little industry and the economy depends largely on tourism and processing of animal products. The second largest city is Darkhan, with about 70,000. Urban primacy yet again in even more stark an imbalance! It is much easier to visit Mongolia today, and visitors report an open, urbanizing, but poor society eager to modernize and join the world. Still, this nation and its cities are likely to always play a marginal role in the affairs of East Asia and the world.

nation of four special economic zones (SEZs) (Shenzhen, Zhuhai, Xiamen, and Shantou) in Guangdong and Fujian in 1979 and of 14 "coastal open cities" in 1984. At the end of the 1980s, Hainan Island became both a new province and the fifth SEZ, while Shanghai's Pudong district joined the category of "open" zones. By the mid-1990s, practically the entire coastal region was one large open zone. One of the most notable consequences was the creation of the new city of Shenzhen, just across the border from Hong Kong. A small village at the border-crossing point became, within a decade, a city of more than one million, with one of the highest standards of living in China and very much the look of a younger Hong Kong. Coupled with the Shenzhen SEZ, this delta area has become increasingly wealthy, Westernized, and sophisticated.

The negative side of this policy was to increase regional imbalances, so that the increased standard of living in favored coastal areas left more backward parts of interior China further behind (fig. 11.19). This was the result of a deliberate policy by the Chinese government, which abandoned any pretense of "egalitarianism" with Deng Xiaoping's famous dictum, "To get rich is glorious!" In addition, the government has relaxed controls in many areas. With decollectivization and the return to private smallholdings (under the Household Responsibility System), agriculture showed significant increases in labor productivity, with greatly improved living standards in the countryside. At the same time, though, many rural workers became unneeded, putting pressure on the government to relax restrictions on internal migration. Out of this has emerged the "floating population" of migrant workers, at least 100 million strong, who provide plentiful low-cost labor and help make Chinese industry competitive in international markets. The

Box 11.3 Cities with Invisible Walls: The *Hukou* System in China

The development strategy pursued by China during the Maoist era (1949–1976) was based on strictly controlling rural-urban migration. The principal means for doing this was the *hukou* (household registration) system, set up in 1958. Under this system, all citizens were classified as either urban or rural residents. Urban residents had state-guaranteed food grains, jobs, housing, and access to an array of subsidized welfare and social services (known as the *iron rice bowl*). Rural residents had very few of these benefits and had to rely on themselves or their collectives. These obvious disparities generated strong incentives for rural residents to migrate to urban areas. For the great majority of the rural population, however, the option of migrating to the cities was not open to them. The government used strong administrative measures to stem migration to the cities. By law, anyone seeking to move to a place different from where his or her household was registered had to get approval from the *hukou* authorities, typically the public security bureau. But approval was rarely granted. In essence, the *hukou* system functioned as an internal passport system very similar to the *propiska* system used in the former Soviet Union and the *ho khau* system in Vietnam. While old city walls in China had largely been demolished by the late 1960s, the power of this newly erected migration barrier is likened to "invisible" city walls.

The reform era that began in the late 1970s has put much pressure on the *hukou* system. Development of a market-oriented economy and relaxation (but not abandonment) of migratory controls have resulted in at least 100 million people (the so-called *floating population,* or migrant workers) staying outside their place of formal *hukou* registration. These workers, when in the cities, are not considered urban "residents" and are not eligible for many urban social services or education programs. This unequal treatment of the migrant population has drawn much attention and controversy inside and outside China.

Source: Kam Wing Chan, *Cities with Invisible Walls: Reinterpreting Urbanization in Post-1949 China* (Hong Kong: Oxford University Press, 1994).

migrants fill many jobs shunned by urban laborers. But they also create enormous headaches for urban governments, because of their numbers and the lack of governmental control over them. Increased crime rates, increased congestion in already overburdened transportation systems, difficulties in enforcing family planning laws—these are among the problems that have surfaced.

There has also been an exponential growth in the number of people living in towns (distinguished from cities) over the past 20 years because of the government's relaxation of controls over entry into the economy by non–state-owned enterprises. This has led to a burgeoning of rural enterprises (Township-Village Enterprises, or TVEs) and of small-scale entrepreneurs going into business for themselves. These activities have absorbed a huge amount of the surplus labor in the countryside. Rural people can now more easily gain permission to transfer to a town, as long as

Box 11.4 China's Urban Neighborhood Committees

One unique institution in Chinese cities, one that has survived from the Maoist era, albeit with modifications, is the neighborhood residents' committee. First established in 1954, these committees now number some 100,000 and are found in every urban center. The size varies but the average population per committee is 3,000 to 4,000. The duties include publicizing state law and policy; safeguarding residents' interests; urging citizens to honor their obligations; administering a variety of public affairs concerning social welfare; mediating civil disputes; helping maintain social order and security; helping the government do work in the interest of the residents; and reporting to the government the opinions, needs, and recommendations of the citizens. In short, the committees are part social welfare agencies and part neighborhood watch agents and watchdogs for the government. Retired women usually run the committees. During the period when the one-child policy was heavily emphasized (in the first half of the 1980s), committee workers (nicknamed the "granny police") often had to snoop into intimate aspects of individuals' lives. In the 1990s, many of these committees, especially those in the inner cities, served mostly to provide services for laid-off workers and their families and manage migrant residents. Nonetheless, the neighborhood residents' committee remains one of the more durable features of the old socialist city system, adapted to the needs of a rapidly changing China.

they have a job and a place to live, although gaining permanent residency status in cities remains impossible for the average peasant. The government thus continues to try to contain the growth of large cities, but the pressure at the gates is immense.

The new focus on markets and private enterprise in cities, alongside the state-owned economy, has created a demand for advertising and the need to spruce up storefronts and display windows. Urban life appears more and more similar to that of the rest of the region. Urban life has unquestionably improved for most residents, as it now offers a much greater variety and quality of goods and services, as well as an end to the stifling conformity and drabness of the Maoist years. Unfortunately, one of the costs has been that inflation has exceeded increases in incomes, making life more difficult for some, especially those on relatively fixed incomes, such as retirees and state-owned enterprise (SOE) workers. Unemployment is likely to worsen in the face of continued population growth and difficulties in creating jobs fast enough to absorb the surplus population.

Other Paths in East Asia

As with big cities around the world, the industrial cities of East Asia are experiencing profound problems of overcrowding, pollution, traffic congestion, crime, and shortages of affordable housing and other urban services. Yet most people in the cities of East Asia are relatively well off. This has been a region of extraordinary economic growth and advancement in recent decades, so that residents of these cities have standards of living among the highest in the world. They dress smartly, are well fed, and have considerable disposable income. Western-

Figure 11.19 China has embarked on urban development throughout its realm, including here in Lhasa, the capital of Tibet. Center of international controversy, Lhasa is being transformed into a Chinese city. (Photo by Stanley Brunn)

ization (more properly now, globalization) is very evident in its impact in terms of popular culture and lifestyles. Retail stores of all types provide every conceivable consumer good for the affluent residents. At night, the cities glitter with eye-popping displays of neon, nowhere more dazzling than in Japan. Significantly, surveys of the quality of life in Asian cities, such as that done annually by Hong Kong's *Asiaweek* magazine, regularly put Japan's cities and Hong Kong in the top ranks, while others, such as Seoul and Taipei, have steadily moved nearer the top. China's cities, understandably, still rank further down, but are making steady progress.

Expensive land is a major constraint to the development of these cities. Increasingly, thus, the major cities are following in the footsteps of most other large cities with high-rise syndrome. There is even a growing competition among the cities of the region to see which can build the tallest skyscraper, as if having the tallest building somehow conveys status and superiority. Shanghai, Taipei, Seoul, and other cities are involved in this one-upmanship (fig. 11.20). Even Japan's cities, long characterized by relatively low skylines (because of earthquake hazards), have succumbed to the trend toward high-rise construction, such as in the cluster of 50-plus-story buildings centered around the new city government complex in Tokyo's Shinjuku district. Japanese cities (and, increasingly, other cities in the region) also make effective use of underground space, with enormous, complex underground malls interconnected by subway systems.

Movement outward from the central city is the only other alternative to going upward or downward. Skyrocketing land values, suburbanization, and rapid population increases have been experienced around the big cities. New communities have sprung up, including bedroom towns somewhat in the American fashion, where young couples, for less money, can obtain better housing with cleaner air and

Figure 11.20 Seoul competes with other Asian cities to have one of the tallest skyscrapers. (Photo courtesy Seoul city government)

less noise, even though doing so often means long commutes to work. Fortunately, most of the large cities have developed relatively good public-transport systems. Nonetheless, the automobile culture is spreading rapidly, with the private automobile purchased as much for status as for convenience in getting around. The automobile culture first took hold in Japan in the 1960s, but other countries have followed suit and even China is now firmly on the private automobile bandwagon.

Closing the Gap: Decentralization in Japan

The Japanese have been struggling for several decades to decentralize their urban system and reduce the relative dominance of Tokyo, by and large without success. The task really has two dimensions: improving living conditions in Tokyo and physically decentralizing the urban system. Within Tokyo, the solution to overcrowding and the (still) high cost of land lies in finding new land, such as through continued landfill projects to expand the shoreline and make greater use of Tokyo Bay, as well as moving further outward toward less-developed areas in the Tokyo region. Many such projects were planned or underway during the 1990s, but the continuing stagnation in the economy caused cancellation or delays in these, as with the Tokyo Teleport Town and the 1996 World City Expo. One project that was completed in 1997 was the Tokyo Bay Aqua Line, an expressway across the middle of Tokyo Bay connecting Tokyo with Chiba Prefecture and designed to enhance development along the eastern and southern shore. The hope is that Chiba Prefecture, occupying the whole peninsula opposite Tokyo City, will be the new high-growth area for the Tokyo region, anchored around three new core cities—a high-tech Kazusa Akademia Park, Makuhari New City, and Narita Airport (fig. 11.21).

An alternative supported by many is to decentralize. How to decentralize is a tough question over which there is anything but consensus. Over the decades, Japan has had a succession of National Development Plans, all of

Figure 11.21 Chiba Port already handles the largest volume of freight among Japan's port cities and also illustrates the widespread practice of creating artificial land for urban expansion in Japan's post–World War II growth. (Photo courtesy Chiba government)

which have addressed in some way the need for more balanced regional development. Proposals for relocating the national capital out of Tokyo have gone nowhere. Various kinds of subcenter ideas have been tried; however, none have been substantially successful in reducing the drawing power of Tokyo. Neither has the decline of regions such as the Kansai been stopped, in spite of efforts such as the opening of the new Kansai International Airport on an artificial island off the coast of Osaka in 1990, in an effort to give Tokyo's Narita some competition.

Nonetheless, the dream persists. If Japan had not suffered such economic stagnation for the past ten years, the prospects for real change would be better today. Now, fearing that Tokyo might be supplanted as Asia's premier business center by some other city, especially Hong Kong or Singapore, the government has already stepped up its efforts to revitalize the capital under a new program called Urban Renaissance. In sum, the inability of Japan—with its enormous wealth and relatively homogeneous society—to solve this regional imbalance problem does not suggest a high probability of success for solving the same problem in many other countries.

Seoul: The Problems of Primacy

Somewhat like its larger cousin, Tokyo, Seoul suffers from the typical problems of urban primacy. There is crushing traffic congestion, made worse by a growing middle class determined to have the status symbol of private cars in a society where status means everything. There is smothering air pollution caused by too many motor vehicles, by the burning of charcoal and coal (a minority of homes receive piped gas), by the presence of thousands of factories, and by a basin topography that traps pollutants beneath temperature inversions, as occurs in Los Angeles or Mexico City. There is a severe shortage of affordable housing; with land so scarce and expensive, the small Korean homes cluster together like bees on the steep, rocky hillsides. Elsewhere, especially south of the Han, huge apartment complexes march to the horizon in a monotonous precision of layout. Property values soared in the 1980s as redevelopment contributed to large-scale real estate speculation, a problem common in East Asia. The property bubble burst in the early 1990s with a gradual decline in prices, spurred further by the Asian fiscal crisis of 1997–1998. The crisis hit South Korea the hardest and actually contributed to a decrease in Seoul's total population from its peak of 12 million in 1999 to the present 10 million. The economy is slowly recovering, but property prices are still high in Seoul.

Seoul would probably be even larger and more congested than it is today if the government had not adopted a policy of promoting urban/industrial growth elsewhere in the country. In spite of the attraction of Seoul to would-be migrants, considerable urban growth has occurred in secondary and tertiary cities in the urban system, including Pusan, Ulsan, Taejon (Daejon), and Kwangju (Gwangju). The government has also attempted to decentralize the Seoul metropolitan region by constructing new towns, such as Guri, Banweol, and Sungnam. These have had limited impact, however.

Taipei: Toward Balanced Regional Development

Taipei has made dramatic progress in recent years in solving some of its urban problems. Completion of the Mass Rapid Transit system and stepped-up enforcement of traffic rules have brought order to what was once one of the worst cities in Asia for traffic chaos. Pollution has been drastically cut through various programs. While housing is still expensive, it is becoming relatively more affordable. Overall, the city is cleaner and decidedly a better place in which to live or raise a family. Although many people have moved to the suburbs, a large residential population still lives within the central city, so that the "doughnut" phenomenon really does not fit Taipei. The multinucleic model is perhaps more applicable.

In part to solve the problems of overcrowded Taipei, the national government embarked on island-wide regional planning in the early 1970s. The end result was a development plan that divided the island into four planning regions, each focused around a key city. The Northern Region, centered on Taipei, has about 40% of the island's total population. Through a variety of policies, including rural industrialization, massive investment in infrastructure (especially transportation, including Taiwan's own version of the "bullet" train, between Taipei and Kaohsiung), and programs to enhance the quality of life and economic base of other cities and towns, Taiwan has managed to slow the growth of Taipei and diffuse some of the urbanization. The dominance of Taipei is not as severe as that of Tokyo or Seoul. Government policy is aimed at lowering the relative proportion of population and economic activity in the Northern

Region and spreading it more evenly among the other three regions. The Central Region (around Taichung) has seen the most rapid growth in recent years.

PROSPECTS

Urban dwellers in many poorer cities around the world must look at the prosperous cities of East Asia and wonder what the residents are complaining about, given their high standards of living and relative comfort. To citizens of the region, however, and especially to urban planners, the overall problem of most cities of East Asia is how far short the cities still fall in what they could be. Note the following remarks of leading Japanese observers on their country: "Japan's foremost urban centers lack anything resembling the character and depth of their European counterparts. Instead, they seem to be forever under construction." "There is huge potential demand for urban redevelopment." "Japanese city planning shows little vision regarding a living environment." One could probably elicit similar statements from observers in the other countries of the region.

So where do these countries and cities go from here? East Asia is unquestionably going to be a region of continuing high economic growth, with strong continued urbanization, especially in China. There are vast amounts of capital in the region for urban development. Marshalling that capital to maximize the quality of urban life is the challenge facing all of these states. East Asia is in the forefront of the information technology and transportation revolutions, which are rapidly diminishing the importance of distance. Transnational urban linkages within the region and between the region and the rest of the world, especially Southeast Asia and North America, are going to become stronger. The cities of East Asia are destined to play leading roles in world affairs in the 21st century, belonging as they do to one of the three power centers of the global economy.

SUGGESTED READINGS

Chan, Kam Wing. *Cities with Invisible Walls: Reinterpreting Urbanization in Post-1949 China.* Hong Kong: Oxford University Press, 1994. A study of the complex changes in China's urban development experience.

Esherick, Joseph W., ed. *Remaking the Chinese City: Modernity and National Identity, 1900–1950.* Honolulu: University of Hawaii Press, 2000. A collection of papers about various Chinese cities that underwent great change in the half century leading up to the establishment of the PRC.

Gaubatz, Piper Rae. *Beyond the Great Wall: Urban Form and Transformation on the Chinese Frontiers.* Stanford, Calif.: Stanford University Press, 1996. A geographer examines five cities (Kunming, Lanzhou, Xining, Hohhot, and Urumqi) on China's inland frontiers, from ancient times to the present.

Karan, P. P., and Kristin Stapleton, eds. *The Japanese City.* Lexington: University Press of Kentucky, 1997. A collection of ten papers about various aspects of Japanese cities, including a good overview chapter by Paul Karan. Nicely illustrated.

Knapp, Ronald G. *China's Walled Cities.* New Paltz: State University of New York, 2000. The history and importance of walls in such cities as Changan (Xi'an), Beijing, and Nanjing.

Kornhauser, David. *Urban Japan: Its Foundation and Growth.* New York: Longman, 1976. Still one of the best overviews of the geographic and historical aspects of Japan's urban experience, from earliest times to the pre–World War II era.

Seidensticker, Edward. *Low City, High City: Tokyo from Edo to the Earthquake.* New York: Knopf,

1983. A classic account by a leading scholar of Japan about how the Shogun's ancient capital became a great modern city in the period 1867–1923.

Sit, Victor F. S. *Beijing: The Nature and Planning of a Chinese Capital City.* New York: Wiley, 1995. A detailed analysis of China's cultural and political capital.

Speare, Alden, Jr., Paul K. C. Liu, and Ching-Tung Tsay. *Urbanization and Development: The Rural-Urban Transition in Taiwan.* Boulder, Colo.: Westview, 1988. A collection of writings from over the years by three leading authorities on urban development in Taiwan.

Tang, Wenfang, and William L. Parish. *Chinese Urban Life under Reform.* Cambridge: Cambridge University Press, 2000. A sociological look at the profound changes taking place in China's cities and urban society.

Yatsko, Pamela. *New Shanghai: The Rocky Rebirth of China's Legendary City.* New York: Wiley, 2000. A journalist takes a critical look at Shanghai and its potential to be China's "head of the dragon."

Yee, Albert H. *Whither Hong Kong: China's Shadow or Visionary Gleam?* Lanham, Md.: University Press of America, 1999. A group of top-notch China watchers offer their perspectives on various facets of Hong Kong's past, present, and future.

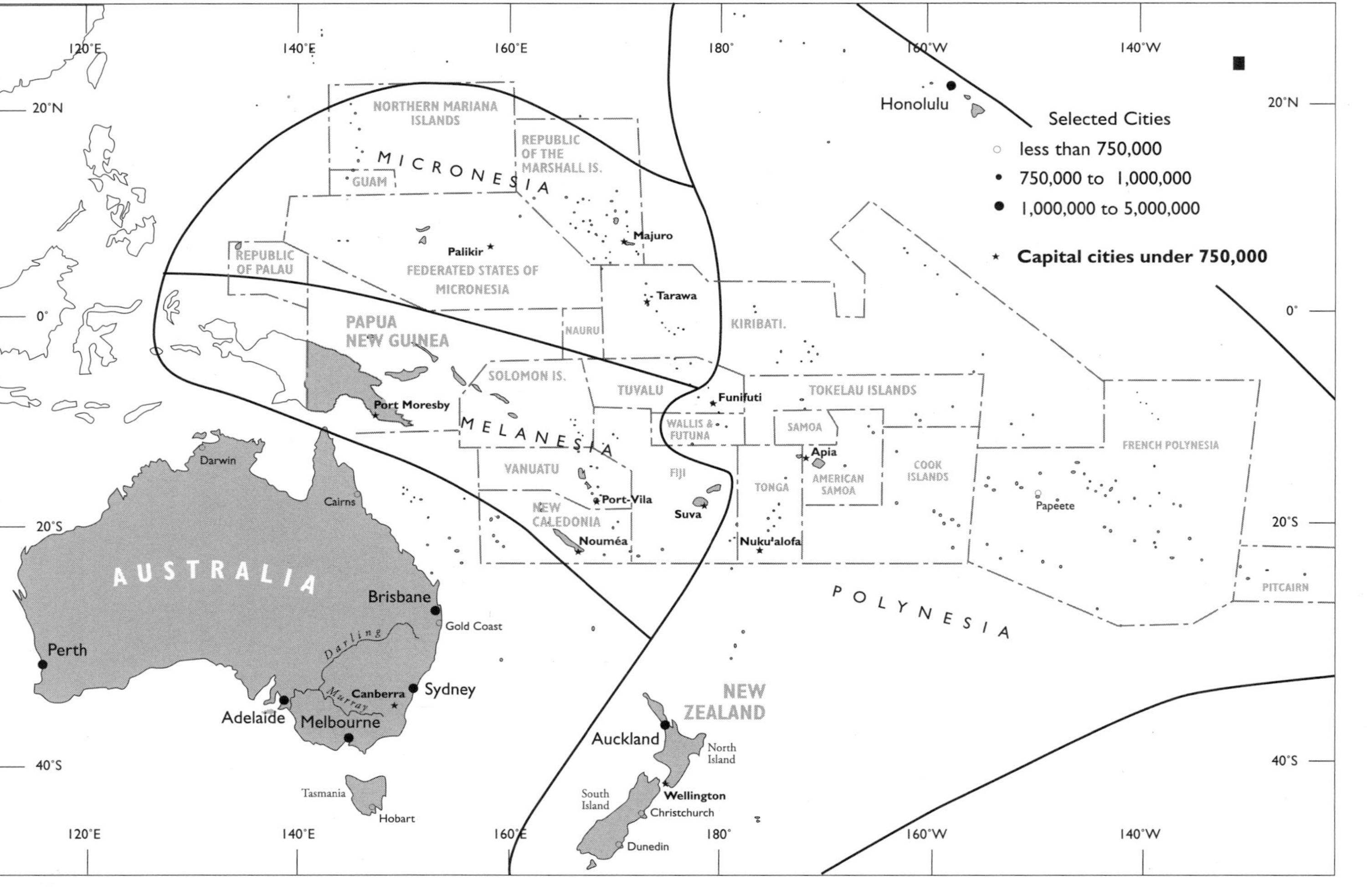

Figure 12.1 Major Cities of Oceania. *Source*: Data from United Nations, *World Urbanization Prospects, 2001 Revision* (New York: United Nations Population Division, 2002), www.unpopulation.org.

12

Cities of Australia and the Pacific Islands

ROBERT J. STIMSON AND SCOTT BAUM

KEY URBAN FACTS*

Total Population	31 million
Percent Urban Population	
Australia/New Zealand	90%
Pacific Islands	27%
Total Urban Population	
Australia/New Zealand	21 million
Pacific Islands	2.1 million
Most Urbanized Country	Australia (91%)
Least Urbanized Country	Papua New Guinea (18%)
Annual Urban Growth Rate	
Australia/New Zealand	1.4%
Pacific Islands	4.1%
Number of Megacities	0
Number of Cities of More Than 1 Million	6
Three Largest Cities	Sydney, Melbourne, Brisbane
World Cities	Sydney

*Excluding Hawaii

KEY CHAPTER THEMES

1. Oceania has two realms—Australia/New Zealand and the Pacific Islands—with distinctly different urban characteristics.
2. Australia is by far the most important country in this region in all respects, including from an urban development perspective.
3. All the nations in this realm, big and small, are dominated by primate cities.
4. The cities of Australia/New Zealand have the reputation of being among the most attractive and livable in the world.

5. Australia/New Zealand exhibits many of the urban characteristics of other developed countries, such as the United States, while the Pacific Islands' urban character is similar to that of less developed countries.
6. Sydney is by far the most globally linked city and the key economic center in this vast realm.
7. In the early 20th century, Australia built a new national capital, Canberra, to tie together its states after federation was achieved.
8. Australia has experienced its own version of "sunbelt" migration and depopulation of certain areas as the result of economic change.
9. Suburbanization, "edge cities," and mega–metropolitan developments are increasing phenomena in Australia.
10. While the cities of Australia/New Zealand still bear a predominantly British heritage, increasingly, nonwhite immigration is changing the ethnic character of cities, especially Sydney and Melbourne.

THE REGIONAL SETTING

Australia and the Pacific Islands (comprising Australia, New Zealand, and the Pacific Islands found in Micronesia, Melanesia, and Polynesia) form a unique region with lots of space and few people, most of whom live in urban places, most of which are in Australia (fig. 12.1). For simplicity's sake, this realm is also sometimes called *Oceania*. Today, no part of the world is so dominated by its major metropolitan concentrations; the term *primate city* might well have been coined to describe the dominance of the capital cities or main cities of the former colonial territories and nations that now make up this region.

Colonization, Development, and Urbanization

Two hundred years ago, cities and towns as we know them did not exist in Oceania. The entire continent of Australia, plus Tasmania and most of the southern half of New Zealand, was devoid of permanent settlements. In Australia, the Aborigines were hunters and gatherers dispersed widely and in small numbers across the vast continent. Across the other 10% of the land area of Oceania, in northern New Zealand, the remainder of Polynesia, and the island clusters of Melanesia and Micronesia, permanent settlements were limited to small villages of horticulturalists. The urban systems that have emerged over the past two centuries are a result of colonization and penetration by the new settlers: the British, Dutch, Germans, French, Americans, and Indians.

During the colonial era, a lot of attention was given to the formal elements of town planning. Officers of the colonial governments introduced British town design across Australia and New Zealand, as well as to the islands of Oceania. Only in the French territories of New Caledonia and Polynesia and in Rabaul (in Papua New Guinea) and Apia (in Samoa), where there was a German presence for a time, were other patterns of town development followed.

The colonial and postcolonial development of the lands and later the nations of Oceania occurred throughout prolonged eras of global commerce, technological change, and industrialization. But because Oceania lacked the levels of urbanization commonly found elsewhere among agrarian civilizations of the preindustrial world, it is logical to describe the present-day urban systems as the creations of the expansive colonial mechanisms of mercantile and industrial Europe of the 19th century. Towns were the gateways for trading agricultural, pastoral, mineral, and other resource products to the motherland. Conducting this trade was extremely difficult, because of the tyranny of distance, that is, the long distances separating the colonial settlements from the homeland. However, as technology advanced over time, especially with the invention of agricultural machinery and improved modes of transportation and communication, there was a diminished need for large numbers of rural workers. Thus, urbanization became the norm throughout Oceania.

Still, the evolution of the urban systems of the lands of Oceania requires an understanding of the geographical character of these territories, as well as the political and economic bases of their territorial organization.

The Archipelagos

Across the archipelagos of Oceania there is a logic to the geography of the numerous nations, most of which comprise many, mostly very small, islands. Before European colonization, political integration within each of the island groups rarely existed, and where it did it was mainly limited to a few villages within a single tribal area restricted mostly to the one island. The colonists imposed a common political rule over whole archipelagos and these new colonial territories became the embryonic urban systems of modern nation-states such as Fiji, the Solomons, Samoa, and Vanuatu. Some isolated islands, like Nauru, became nation-states in themselves. Two of the archipelagos are politically partitioned: in the case of the Samoan Islands, the small Tutuila remains under American control, rather than part of independent Samoa, while Bougainville, the largest island of the Solomon group, is part of Papua New Guinea, not the Solomon Islands nation-state.

New Zealand

New Zealand is by far the largest island state in Oceania. Two large main islands—North Island and South Island—stretch over a distance of about 1,000 mi (1,600 km). From 1840, the British colonists set up a string of town settlements along the coasts. In 1865, the capital was shifted from the relatively peripheral town of Auckland in the far north to Wellington at the southern base of the North Island. Wellington gained political ascendancy over the many coastal settlements, as well as over Dunedin and Christchurch, the two major settlements established on the South Island. However, it was not until 1874 that the conclusive subjugation of the native Maoris was achieved.

For some years, there was both a geographical and statistical balance to the urban hierarchy in New Zealand, but gradually this was to change. Access to the most productive hinterland within a small national economy meant that Auckland progressively emerged as the undisputed primate city. Its position has become even more dominant through waves of immigration from Europe, as well as through the influx of Pacific Islander populations. The North Island has become more dominant, while the South Island is now in a state of depopulation. As a nation, New Zealand loses many people each year who emigrate mainly to settle in Australia.

Papua New Guinea

Papua New Guinea consists of the eastern half of the large island of New Guinea, the Bismarck Archipelago, and Bougainville in the Solomons. It is located immediately north of Australia. Before European settlement, there was a degree of interaction through trade among the various regional clusters of coastal village settlements. But there was no political integration. Imperial Germany established a claim to the northern part of the main island and to Bougainville, while the British claimed the southern part, along with the Solomons to the south of Bougainville. In 1906 Australia took over from Britain the administration of Papua and, in 1919, was also given the mandate to administer German New Guinea.

It was not until after World War II that urban development took off to any degree in Papua New Guinea. At the time of the Japanese bombing in 1942, none of the largest towns had more than 10,000 people. But after World War II, Australia amalgamated the administration of Papua and the Territories of New Guinea into a central government with the capital at Port Moresby, the original capital of Papua. Even though it was not centrally located for the major areas of population and economic production, which were concentrated in the northeast and in the highlands, Port Moresby had the advantage of easy access to Australia, along with a reasonable port and regular air services. As a result, it developed quickly as a primate city. When Australia ceded independence to Papua New Guinea in 1975, Port Moresby had a population of more than 80,000. It was twice the size of Lae, located on the north coast, and three times the size of Rabaul, the capital of the former German territories.

Australia

Australia dominates Oceania in all respects, including urban development.

The Image and the Reality

Often, the popular image of a place and its people portrays something quite different from the reality. There are two common international images of Australia. One is of a land of kangaroos and rugged stockmen doing battle with a sun-burnt land and wild beasts, as portrayed by Paul Hogan in the Crocodile Dundee films. The other is of a land of sun and golden beaches where bronzed young men and women ride the waves. But the reality is that Australia is a highly urbanized, multicultural nation where almost seven in ten people live in just five big cities. It has an economy in which the services sector now accounts for three-quarters of the nation's gross domestic product. In fact, the largest city, Sydney, is among the top eight financial centers in the world.

Australia is a vast and largely arid land, simultaneously the world's largest island and its smallest continent, about the same size as the contiguous 48 United States. To emphasize Australia's remoteness in the world, it takes about eight hours to fly nonstop from Sydney to Singapore, more than 10 hours to fly to Tokyo, and 13 hours to fly to Los Angeles.

History of Settlement

Australia's indigenous peoples—the Aborigines and Torres Strait Islanders—have lived on the continent for more than 40,000 years. The onset of British colonization in the late 18th century began what the indigenous peoples see as the invasion of their land. Although Dutch explorers had reached the northwest coast of Australia much earlier, the "discovery" by Captain Cook did not occur until 1770.

Settlement by the British began with the establishment of a few penal colonies, notably at Sydney in New South Wales and at Port Arthur in Tasmania. Eventually, six separate colonial territories were formed, each focused on a colonial administrative town located on the coast. These were to become the capital cities of the states, which formed separate entities within the British Empire. Three colonial settlements—Sydney in New South Wales, Adelaide in South Australia, and Perth in Western Australia—formed the primary foci of British settlement. The original territory of New South Wales incorporated all the eastern third of the continent, plus the island of Tasmania to the south.

Distance and slow transport combined to stimulate separatist movements in areas distant from Sydney. Over the first few decades of the 19th century, Tasmania, Victoria, and then Queensland were given separate colonial status, with their respective capitals at Hobart, Melbourne, and Brisbane. From the late 1830s, the scene was thus set for a separate settlement pattern to evolve within each of the six colonies, each of which was in fierce economic competition with its neighbors. This was mitigated only by a sense of common origin among two groups of new settlers: the prisoners sent by the British to the penal settlements of the new colonies and the British colonial officials and free settlers. But among both groups there was a common allegiance to the British Crown.

It was from those initial colonial coastal settlements that first exploration and then settlement and transport systems spread into the interior and along the coast. This was to generate a classic core-periphery process of economic development and settlement that was hastened by the advent of the railway era. The inland and coastal areas were exploited for their resources, including the products of pastoralism and farming and of mineral exploration and mining, especially of gold. In the middle to late 19th century, gold rushes occurred in many parts of Australia, attracting large waves of immigrants, including many Chinese.

The railways funneled all this resource production to the coastal towns, and in particular the colonial capitals. They were the focal points for the transport and communications system, as well as the centers of administration, commerce and trade, and manufacturing. Surpluses were exported to imperial Britain and elsewhere in Europe, while the capital needed to build an infrastructure and develop resources and manufacturing came from Britain. This made the colonial capitals all powerful in terms of both commerce and politics, giving them an unstoppable dominance and turning them into the primate cities of their states. The main factors involved during the 19th century in the urbanization of Australia are summarized in figure 12.2. Associated with this colonization were inevitable conflicts between the new settlers and the indigenous peoples, whose numbers were greatly reduced, often through violence on the part of the new settlers.

Federation and a New National Capital

It was not until 1901 that the six colonial states agreed to form the federation known as the Commonwealth of Australia. Trade between the states was open and unencumbered under the new nation's constitution, but the states retained authority and responsibility over many issues, much like in the United States. With na-

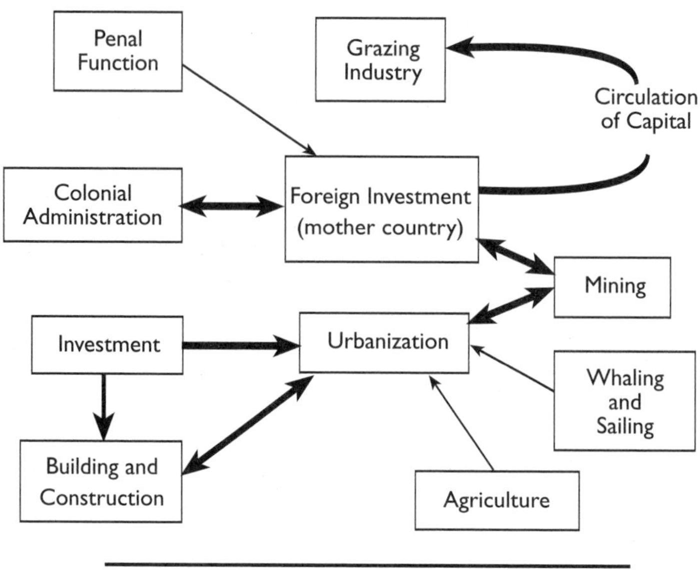

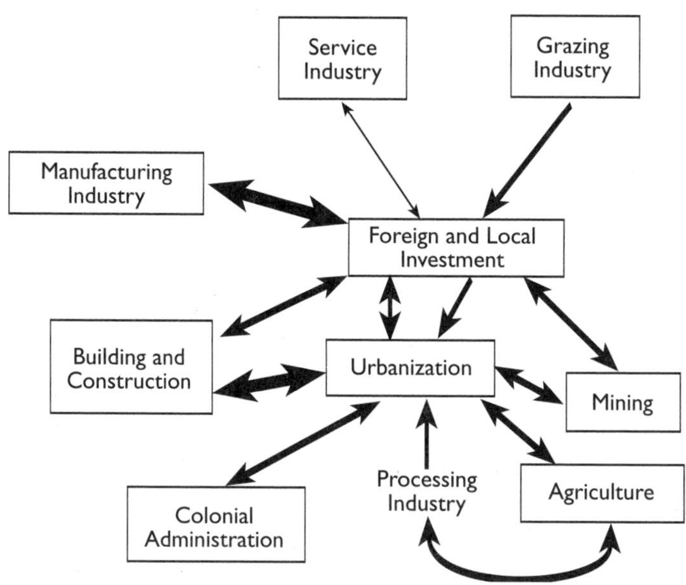

Figure 12.2 Main Factors in 19th-Century Australian Urbanization. *Source*: Burneley (1980)

tionhood came the decision, through agreement between the colonial states, for a new national capital to be developed, to be called Canberra. By the time of federation, Australia's population had grown to almost four million and, by the turn of the 21st century, it had exceeded 19 million. It has become even more urbanized with the progression of time.

POPULATION PATTERNS AND THE SETTLEMENT HIERARCHY

Within Oceania, the huge continent of Australia presents a very different scale of geographic space for the evolution of an urban settlement pattern than do the many small island states of the archipelagos. For example, the Cook Islands, a self-governing dependency of New Zealand, consists of only small, inhabited islands, with a combined population of only about 25,000, scattered across thousands of square miles of ocean. However, even Australia has a small population in world terms; its population of 19 million is just over half that of California.

Primacy and Subservience

Over time, a state of urban primacy has emerged in which the original colonial administrative settlements have grown to dominate the urban hierarchy in each territorial unit of Oceania. This is not surprising. The colonization that occurred from the late 18th century happened in a context in which the intention of the colonial settlers was to maintain continuous contact and interaction with the mother country. It was thought this would best be achieved by bringing an extensive territory under the tight control of a central government. The proper and orderly mode of settlement of the new lands was the town, with trade, agriculture, and commerce flowing from the frontier settlement to the main colonial administrative town, through which the surplus was exported.

Also, by the mid-19th century the Industrial Revolution in Europe and North America had produced rapid technological advances. Thus in Oceania much of the period of colonization coincided with the advent of railways and the application of machinery in agriculture and mines. All this enabled primary production to be achieved by a relatively small workforce so that there was no need for large numbers of rural workers.

In New Zealand, the movement of the Maori population from their small rural holdings to the towns also assisted the rate of urbanization. In the archipelagos and Papua New Guinea, the local population densities of horticulturalists often was quite high in some of the well-cultivated and richer-soil areas. Often, the native systems of communal land tenure hindered the conversion of rural production to a commercial basis. All these factors, combined with the relatively late date of European penetration across the islands and into the inland areas, worked against the development of large rural populations.

Thus across Oceania a high level of urbanization was the norm from the beginning of colonization. Over the past century, this has been further enhanced by (1) the evolution of more highly capitalized and mechanized modes of primary production; (2) the bypassing of small urban settlements in favor of large towns and cities by the farmers seeking urban services; (3) the post–World War II policies of governments to develop metropolitan-based manufacturing and to attract large numbers of immigrants from overseas; and (4) more recently, the shift to services-dominated economies with economic activity and employment growth located primarily in the big cities (box 12.1)

The Urban Hierarchy

Sydney and Melbourne are the only first-tier cities in Australia and indeed all of Oceania, with populations estimated at more than 4 million and 3.4 million, respectively, in 1999. They are big cities in world terms. Only four other cities in Oceania have populations over one million—Brisbane, Auckland, Perth, and Adelaide, which form a second tier of cities. In Australia, no other city has a population above 350,000 and only Canberra, the Gold Coast, Newcastle, and Wollongong have populations above 200,000. In New Zealand, only Wellington, Christchurch, Dunedin, and Hamilton have populations above 100,000.

Contemporary Urban Patterns

The contemporary distribution of Australia's population by scale of settlement is shown in table 12.1, which also indicates the projected change over the first decade of the 21st century. More than 60% of the nation's population is found in just three big cities with populations above one million, and their share is predicted to increase little. Only 11 other places have populations over 80,000, where just under 14% of the nation's people live. The remote settlements, such as the isolated mining towns and the sparsely populated rangelands, account for only about 4% of the nation's 19 million people.

Most of Australia's population is concentrated in a relatively narrow belt along the east, southeast, and southwest coastal areas and extending up to about 125 mi (200 km) inland, beyond which settlement is very sparse, as fertile farmlands and the less-watered rangelands give way to the semidesert and desert areas of the outback. However, significant shifts have been occurring in Australia's settlement pattern, particularly through sunbelt migration to the urban centers of the coastal areas of Queensland, northern New South Wales, Western Australia, and even parts of the Northern Territory. Rural-urban migration continues, as does movement out of the small country towns to the larger regional centers. There is also movement out of some of the big cities, especially from Sydney and Melbourne to their surrounding hinterland areas and the coastal urban areas, as well as to metropolitan Brisbane and Perth. But the largest volume of internal migration shifts occurs within the large metropolitan areas, from inner and middle suburbs to the outer and fringe areas.

Mega–Metropolitan Regions

By far the largest absolute growth in population continues within the major cities and their surrounding regions. This results in a blurring in the distinction between the traditional metropolitan areas and their hinterlands (referred to in Australia as *periurban* areas) and even to a linking up with other nearby cities to form very large multicentered urban structures within almost continuous urbanized regions. These may be referred to as *mega–metropolitan regions* (although they are smaller than true megacities elsewhere in the world). The five mega–metropolitan regions centered on Sydney, Melbourne, Brisbane, Perth, and Adelaide have all grown rapidly outward over the past half-century and, since the 1970s, those regions collectively have maintained a constant 70% share of Australia's population.

From the 1950s into the 1970s, the rapid growth of those cities occurred largely as a result of government policies of import substi-

Box 12.1 Honolulu

Honolulu is a city difficult to pigeonhole. On the one hand, it is the largest city, and capital, of the state of Hawaii in the United States. On the other hand, its cultural roots are very much in the Pacific Region, with its initial settlement by Polynesians, followed centuries later by European and American colonists and waves of immigrants from Asia, especially Japanese, Chinese, and Filipinos. The resulting cultural mix is distinctly polyglot. Economic ties, likewise, run in all directions, with dependency on the U.S. mainland (especially for food and basic consumer goods) as well as Asia (especially for tourists and investment capital). Geographically, Honolulu (and Hawaii) are on the northernmost fringe of Oceania, but very much linked to the region. For example, Honolulu is the key Pacific airline hub for routes to Australia, New Zealand, Fiji, Tahiti, and just about anyplace else in the South Pacific.

One feature that Hawaii shares distinctly with the rest of Oceania is that of primacy. Honolulu is overwhelmingly the primate city of Hawaii, with 870,000 (73%) of Hawaii's 1.2 million population (2000 census). In many respects, Hawaii is Honolulu, in terms of government, education, culture, and the economy. In a manner of speaking, Honolulu is an "artificial" city, in the sense that it would be impossible to sustain a metropolitan center of this size on a small island in the middle of the Pacific Ocean without the many lifelines stretching back to the U.S. mainland and to various parts of Asia, especially Japan. Honolulu thus is the largest, by far, of all cities in the Pacific Islands, excluding Auckland in New Zealand, and the biggest thing happening between Los Angeles and Sydney.

Unfortunately, Hawaii and Honolulu did not share that much in the boom times of the 1990s in the United States and have especially suffered in the downturn of the new century. It's an age-old set of problems in the Pacific—isolation, limited economic opportunities, and the dangers of relying on tourism as the mainstay of an economy. Honolulu's own "Gold Coast" (Waikiki Beach) was begging for visitors as the new century started, and things only got worse after September 11, 2001. There's really not much hope for diversification. Pearl Harbor and the American military presence are not enough to take up the slack. Agriculture is dead. Efforts at high-tech manufacturing, to supplement if not supplant the aloha shirt and tourist-trinket sector, have been all talk, not action. Honolulu (and the whole state of Hawaii) will likely always see its fortunes crest and ebb on the waves of the tourist industry.

tution through subsidizing development of mass manufacturing of automobiles and household consumption goods. That growth was accompanied by large-scale subsidized immigration of mostly unskilled workers from Britain and Europe. Housing was provided in new suburban estates, by both public housing authorities and private developers. The big cities thus grew rapidly outward, as new suburbs to house the increasing urban population and the new factories were developed. Thus began the suburbanization of the population, jobs, and shopping centers.

Since 1980, however, new processes of globalization and economic restructuring have created different outcomes and patterns. This has

Table 12.1 Australia's Population Distribution by Scale of Human Settlement: 2001 and Projections to 2011

	Total Estimated Population 2001	*Share of population 2001(%)*	*Projected Population 2011*[1]	*Share of population 2011(%)*	*Annual Average Rate of Growth 1991–2001(%)*	*Projected Annual Average Rate of Growth 2001–2011(%)*
Big cities[2] (more than 1 million)	11,517,061	60.7	13,001,535	61.6	1.2	1.0
Other cities (80,000 to 1 million)	2,600,720	13.7	2,914,838	13.8	1.5	1.0
Large regional/rural[3] (25,000 to 80,000)	1,281,895	6.8	1,349,681	6.4	1.5	1.0
Small regional/rural[3] (10,000 to 25,000)	1,271,603	6.7	1,337,903	6.3	0.6	0.4
Other regional/rural[3] (fewer than 10,000)	1,825,789	9.6	1,936,494	9.2	0.6	0.4
Remote centers[3] (more than 5,000)	225,004	1.2	251,048	1.2	0.6	0.7
Other remote[3]	328,779	1.7	328,745	1.6	–0.1	–0.1
Australia	18,963,615	100.0	21,119,244	100.0	1.14	0.9

Source: Australian Bureau of Statistics (ABS), *Regional Population Growth,* cat. no. 3218.0 (Canberra: ABS, 2000); ABS, *Census Data 1996* (Canberra: ABS, 1996).

[1] Data for 2011 are based on ABS projections.

[2] Includes Sydney, Melbourne, Brisbane, Perth, and Adelaide.

[3] Following Department of Primary Industry and Energy information. This Rural, Remote, and Metropolitan Areas (RRMA) classification is widely used by AIHW in their Environmental Health Reporting. Metropolitan = big cities plus other cities; rural = large, small, and other regional/rural. Other classifications are emerging but were not available for this report.

meant that many manufacturing jobs in the big cities have been lost, to be replaced by jobs in the producer services industry and other service industries, such as tourism, health, and education. New high-tech manufacturing activities have also emerged. These new jobs often require higher levels of skills and training; they are not all located in the outer suburbs; and many have favored women over men in part-time rather than full-time jobs.

But the big cities continued to grow. The mega–metropolitan regions have attracted about three-quarters of the total value of nonresidential construction in Australia since 1980. By the mid-1990s, these mega–metropolitan regions were the locations for 85% of Australia's economic establishments in the property and business services sector, 79% of finance and insurance services, 78% of wholesaling, and 78% of manufacturing. Thus these regions dominate both the population and the economic geography of the nation.

Nonmetropolitan or Regional Australia

While the big cities dominate Australia's settlement system, a significant number of people do live elsewhere and much economic activity is to be found both in the country cities and towns and in the remote settlements of rural and regional Australia.

The changing pattern of settlement is being strongly influenced by migration to the "sun belt" coastal areas of Queensland (including Brisbane and the Gold Coast) and northern

Figure 12.3 Perth sits in splendid isolation on the southwest coast of Australia, the primate city for a vast, underpopulated region. (Photo courtesy Australian government)

New South Wales, as well as to Perth and parts of the southwest coast of Western Australia (fig. 12.3). While an important component of this internal migration stream is retirees relocating for amenity and lifestyle reasons, rapidly growing urban areas in the sunbelt are actually attracting a wide spectrum of people. However, relatively few immigrants have settled in those places. The rapidly growing urban centers of the sunbelt tend to have relatively high levels of unemployment and high levels of dependency on welfare payments, and many people who have been displaced by manufacturing job losses in the big cities as a result of economic restructuring have relocated to such areas.

The love affair that Australians have with the coast is demonstrated dramatically by the fact that over the five years between 1991 and 1996 there was an increase of more than 266,000 in the number of people who lived within 2 mi (3.2 km) of the seashore, with 98,000 of that growth being in the coastal urban settlements of Queensland and 81,000 in New South Wales.

Away from the coast, the pattern of settlement in inland rural and regional Australia has evolved through periods of both growth and decline, with the impacts being uneven over both time and space. Thus the fortunes of particular towns have waxed and waned as a result of demographic, social, and economic change and also as a result of the impacts of new technologies. Some parts of inland rural and regional Australia have experienced substantial population growth, as in some of the towns of the Northern Territory and the remote mining towns of Western Australia. But the restructuring of mining through fly-in–fly-out operations has spelled the end of the era of development of new mining towns and is now signaling their population decline.

Across Australia's wheat/sheep belt, and in some of the irrigated agricultural regions of the interior, many of the large regional service towns are growing and show a strong economic performance. However, the viability of many of the smaller towns of these inland regions has been threatened for a long time by advances in transport and communications and the restructuring of business operations, which means that rural folk bypass the smaller towns in favor of a few large regional centers. Both private business and government service functions increasingly are concentrated in those larger places.

Thus, many once prosperous smaller towns are experiencing both population and economic decline. This is exacerbated by young people having to move out for senior high school and postschool education and to get jobs in the large regional cities or the metropolis. In addition, there has been population and economic decline in many of Australia's regional cities and towns that once prospered under the era of protected manufacturing development. These include mill towns such as Launceston in Tasmania, the energy-generation towns in Victoria's La Trobe Valley, and iron and steel or metals-production towns such as Whyalla, Port Augusta, and Port Pirie in South Australia's iron triangle. However, a few regional centers have boomed as a result of the development of new manufacturing industries producing mineral products, such as Gladstone on Queensland's central coast, with its alumina smelter and other metal-refining industries.

The Changing Urban Hierarchy

The changes between 1971 and 1996 in the rank order of cities and towns in Australia's national urban hierarchy are shown in figure 12.4. This captures the impact of those processes of urban change and development discussed above. While Sydney and Melbourne continue to be ranked 1 and 2 (fig. 12.5), Adelaide was ranked 3 in 1971, but since the 1980s has been displaced by Brisbane and Perth. The national capital of Canberra has risen from rank 11 to 6, while Hobart has dropped from rank 8 to 11 and Darwin in the Northern Territory has risen from rank 50 to 16. Regional industrial cities like Newcastle and Wollongong have experienced a drop in rank, as have many of the wheat/sheep belt regional cities, despite their continuing growth and strength as regional service centers. It has been the coastal urban centers, fed by retirement migration and others seeking amenities and a better lifestyle, that have increased their rank positions, with the Gold Coast-Tweed Heads rising in rank from 19 to 7 and Maroochydore-Mooloolaba on the Sunshine Coast just north of Brisbane rising from below rank 50 to 27.

Indigenous Settlement

In marked contrast to the overall pattern of population distribution in Australia is the settlement pattern for the indigenous peoples, who numbered fewer than 400,000 by the end of the 1990s. Almost one-third of this group live in small, dispersed remote-area settlements; one-fifth live in small, regional and rural settlements of fewer than 10,000 people; and only a little more than one-quarter live in the mega–metropolitan regions. There are more than 1,300 discrete indigenous

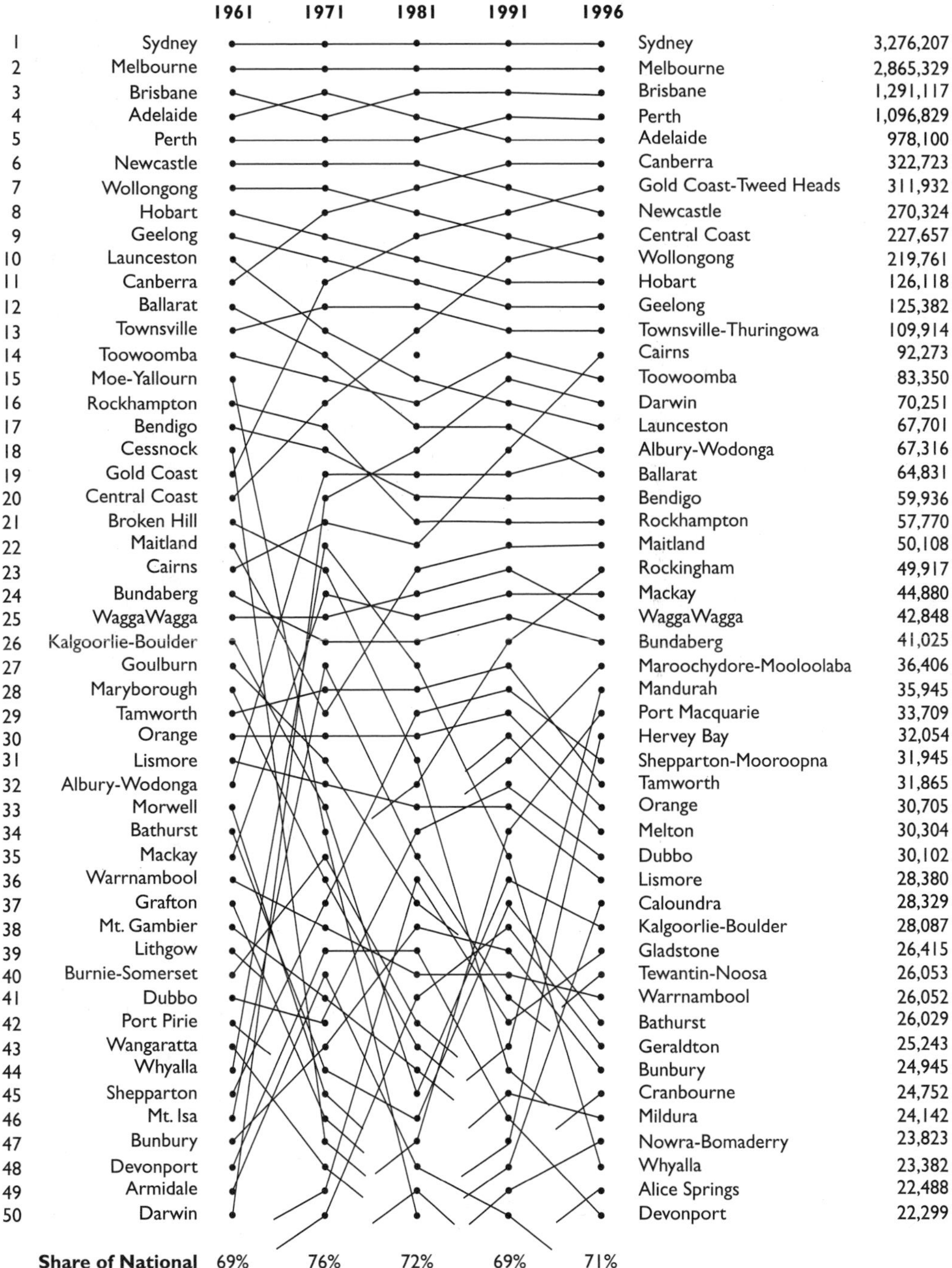

Figure 12.4 Changes in Population and Rank of Australia's Fifty Largest Urban Centers, 1961–1996. *Source*: Australian Bureau of Statistics Census, Urban Centre Populations

Figure 12.5 Australia's second-largest city and a major industrial center, Melbourne prides itself on being more traditional than exuberant Sydney, its long-standing rival to the northeast. (Photo courtesy Australian government)

settlements across Australia with a combined population of about 110,000, but only about 350 of them have more than 50 people.

There is a high level of mobility of people between indigenous settlements, especially in the rural and remote areas. There is a high propensity among indigenous people to locate their housing in close proximity to family and kin, giving rise to a high degree of segregation from the wider population and to the existence of a small number of localities within the big cities where indigenous people tend to congregate. The incidence of transience and of homelessness are high, as are unemployment and levels of morbidity from many aspects of ill health.

REPRESENTATIVE CITIES

Sydney: Australia's World City

Sydney is indisputably Oceania's world city. With a regional population approaching 4.5 million and covering an area of over 7,700 sq mi (12,400 sq km), Sydney is Australia's largest city, and a large city in world terms. It has many of Australia's icons—the Opera House and the Harbor Bridge, not to mention the natural beauty of Sydney Harbor itself (fig. 12.6). Sydney also was the location of Australia's largest international party ever—the 2000 Olympic Games.

The point of first settlement in Australia, at Sydney Cove on Port Jackson, has developed

Figure 12.6 Sydney is widely regarded as one of the most beautiful and distinctive cities anywhere, not least because of its spectacular harbor and signature Opera House, which has become the symbol of the city. (Photo by Jack Williams)

as the functional heart of metropolitan Sydney (fig. 12.7). As the colonial settlement grew, development spread up the shallow valley from Sydney Cove, following the roads that fanned out to the south, southwest, and east. Settlement also spread up the harbor to link with Parramatta, an early settlement established to the west of Sydney. The rail network was growing rapidly by 1850 and it remained the dominant force driving the settlement pattern until the rapid spread of automobiles from the 1930s gave greater freedom and flexibility in travel. This was to spawn the suburban development that has progressed ever since. Sydney's population of 652,000 in 1911 grew to almost 1.5 million by 1947 and the subsequent rapid growth associated with large-scale immigration and suburban development in the post–World War II era saw Sydney's population expand to 4 million by 2000.

Physically, Sydney is effectively confined to a basin, hemmed in by geographical obstacles. The suburbs themselves—especially the great western expanse stretching over 25 mi (40 km)—are largely undistinguished, many of the inhabitants having been forced to live in the city's peripheral new suburbs by continually rising housing costs in the inner city and middle suburbs. Long fingers of both harbor and bushland extend deep into Sydney's metropolitan heart. Consequently, some parts of the city are vulnerable to bushfires, as tragically underlined in the summers of 1994 and 2002, when fires engulfed many suburban homes and even came close to the city center.

As Sydney's population expanded, the physical fabric kept pace and molded its form to meet new needs, new tastes, and new technologies. Before 1880, Sydney was tightly built, with most of its housing in terraces (row houses);

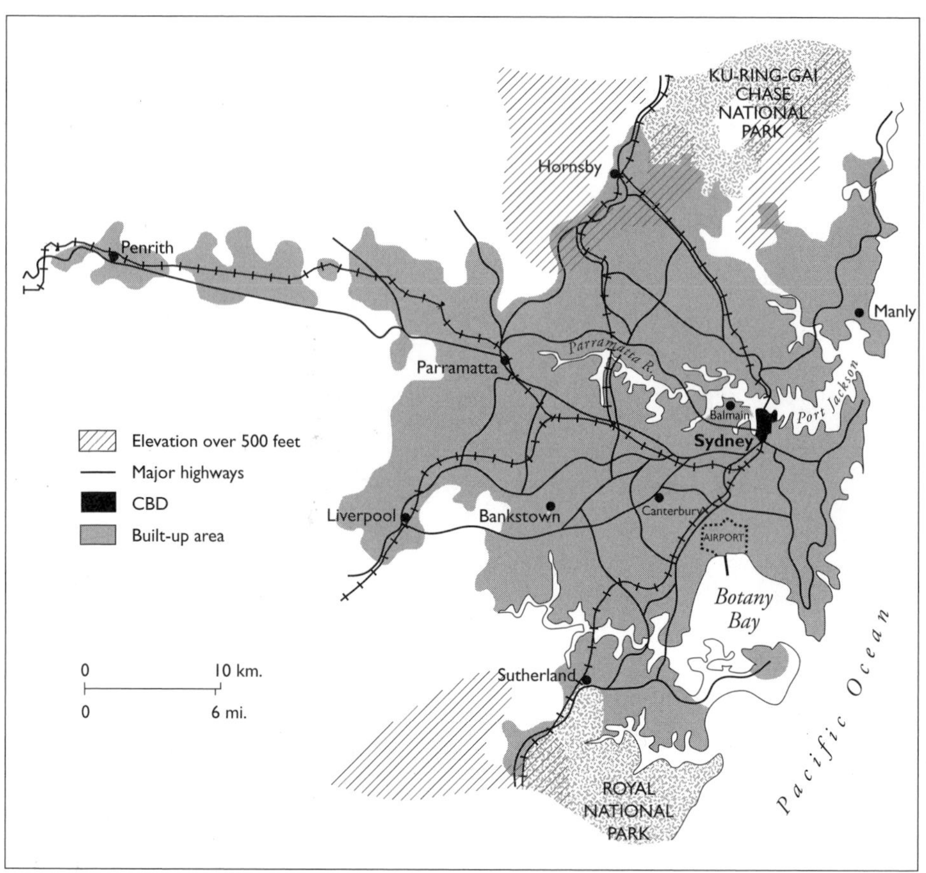

Figure 12.7 The Sydney Metropolitan Region. *Source*: Compiled from various sources.

water supply and sewage disposal were constant problems given the sandstone base rock; and in the summers intestinal diseases were rife and infant mortality levels high. During the city's first century, only the rich could afford separate, more solidly built houses. But the row houses made for lower general densities than existed in many contemporary cities of comparable size. The main roads radiating out from the early imposed grid pattern of the original town were notable for following ridge lines in the direction of open country, rather than adhering to the compass points as in the new American urban foundations.

The rail network that began developing in 1850 soon supplemented the roads as the major determinant of the direction of urban expansion. The trains were challenged as the providers of public transport by the trams (streetcars) and harbor ferries. Most of the development occurred south of the harbor, namely in single cottages on individual plots of land after 1890. The inner area was the focus, providing employment in commerce, transport, manufacturing, and government functions. In 1932, the Sydney Harbor Bridge connected the CBD to the North Shore.

The rapid expansion in car ownership from the 1930s, plus the huge increase in population after 1947, grafted the patterns of the automobile urban forms onto the rail-conditioned fabric of Sydney. Suburbs have sprawled and shopping centers have grown to serve them. Industry has expanded and moved out from congested central locations. The office buildings of the CBD have erupted skyward through numerous commercial building boom times, while high-rise apartments have appeared at choice harborside sites as well as across the inner redevelopment areas of favored points and high transport access. However, unlike American cities, Sydney was slow to develop freeways and it still lacks a fully integrated freeway network. Since the 1960s, though, the city has seen the construction of sections of freeway, including a cross-harbor tunnel with a link to the airport, and sections that eventually will link with the freeways radiating out through the suburbs and on to the urban centers to the north, west, and south.

More so than the other big cities in Australia, Sydney has been transformed by immigration. While it remains true that most "Sydneysiders" are of British and Irish descent, Sydney has become a truly multicultural city. By the mid-1980s, 23% of Australia's Italian-born population, 73% of its Lebanese, and 39% of its Vietnamese lived in Sydney. At the same time, the Aboriginal population of Sydney stood at only 18,600, constituting 0.6% of the city's total population. Today, Sydney is where more than 40% of the new immigrants to Australia choose to live. Sydney's cosmopolitan flavor is enhanced by tens of thousands of Asian students studying at its five universities.

Sydney's economy revolves around commerce, finance, and tourism as well as advanced manufacturing, retailing, and telecommunications. Increasingly, it is the producer services sector that is so important to the economy. Sydney is one of the most significant financial centers in the Asia-Pacific region. Sixty of Australia's largest corporations have established their headquarters there. It is the hub of information technology and telecommunications, commanding more than 40% of Australia's telecommunications market. As Sydney is a major commercial center, public- and private-sector business and administration occupy much of the workforce. However, manufacturing continues to be important: metals, machinery, clothing, processed food, electronic equipment, pharmaceuticals, and petroleum products are some of the wide range of Sydney's manufactured products. Sydney's container ports and airport also handle a significant proportion of Australia's foreign trade. Exported wheat, wool, and meat are some of the items that flow through the city's Port Jackson or through the large port complex on neighboring Botany Bay. The Kingsford Smith International Airport is the busiest in Oceania, with about 55% of inbound international business and tourist passengers to Australia visiting Sydney.

A couple of decades ago, Melbourne had some claim to being Australia's financial center, with companies such as BHP-Billiton headquartered there. But today, Sydney has become the indisputable business champion of Oceania. Much of this globally linked economic activity is located in the high-rise office towers of Sydney's CBD, which has experienced a series of massive office construction booms, especially during the 1980s. That construction has spread to the suburbs as well and, by the 1990s, Sydney's urban form and structure had changed to incorporate the "edge city" phenomenon of suburban business centers with high concentrations of producer service functions. These large suburban concentrations of economic activity have become the focal nodes of metropolitan subregional labor markets (box 12.2).

More than Australia's other big cities, Syd-

Box 12.2 "Welcome to Megacity"

If the forest of cranes on the skyline, the huge earth moving projects that tangle traffic into snarling knots, the breaking every other week of another real estate price barrier, or the nose-to-tail procession of planes entering and leaving the city don't point to Sydney pulling away from the pack, the selection of water at Balmoral's Bathers' Pavilion does. Only a certain kind of city can support a beachside eatery that sources each of the five brands of bottled water and four flavored spring waters on its bar list by country . . . and charges upwards of $7 a bottle.

Welcome to Sydney . . . restyled as Australia's principal center as a Global City. . . . It is pretty much the center of the universe as far as Australia goes.

Beyond the hype, there's a pile of evidence to support the view that it has been lifted into a different league from other Australian cities.

- In Sydney . . . the share of manufacturing in total jobs has been declining more rapidly than the national average.
- People in Sydney earn more on average than elsewhere in New South Wales, and people in New South Wales earn more than people in the rest of Australia.
- Around 60 percent of all business done through the centralized Australian Stock Exchange is done through Sydney screens.
- Of the top 100 companies, more than half are based in Sydney. . . . In the new global order, positioning is everything. And it is difficult to argue against Sydney having maneuvered itself into a highly advantageous position as it approaches 2000.

Source: "Welcome to Megacity," *Bulletin* (Sydney), September 12, 1999, 53–56.

ney is experiencing a boom in inner-city redevelopment (fig. 12.8). The origins of this may be traced back to the 1950s, when gentrification began to occur in some of the old industrial working-class housing areas of the inner suburbs, as white collar professionals began to move in to buy up and renovate the old terrace houses in suburbs like Paddington. Over the decades since, this gentrification process has spread more widely across the near inner-city suburbs and beyond. In the past decade or two, the redevelopment of old inner-city industrial landscapes and waterfront areas has seen the conversion of warehouses into upscale apartments, and the bulldozing of old factories, railway yards, and docklands to make way for the building of flashy new high-rise apartments and townhouses. As a result, housing prices in the inner city have skyrocketed and the attraction of older "empty nester" households and "yuppie" (young professional) singles and couples to this new and renovated housing has resulted in a turnaround from decades of population decline in Sydney's inner suburbs to modest population increases since the late 1980s.

Figure 12.8 "The Rocks" in Sydney is a gentrified part of the old city, developed now into a handsome area for tourism and upscale commercial/residential use. (Photo by Jack Williams)

But most of the actual growth in population, as well as a large proportion of investment in many economic activities in the big cities such as Sydney, continues to be in the outer suburbs, except for sectors like offices and hotels (tab. 12.2). Thus, while the landscapes of Sydney's inner-city areas have been transformed in the past two decades by new up-market housing developments, office towers, high-rise hotels, and tourism facilities focused on redevelopment, outer suburban expansion and growth continues apace, featuring low-density housing developments on greenfield sites, suburban shopping malls, and new factories in industrial zones.

One result of the processes underlying the growth and development of Sydney has been the formation of divides in its socioeconomic structure. Functional patterns and terrain have always divided Sydney. Along the harborside and across Sydney's northern reaches the land tends to be hilly and the scenery pleasant; to the south and west, the surface is relatively monotonous, the scenery is boring, and the summer temperatures are high. The north, free of noxious industry, developed primarily as a residential area, while to the south and west it is heavily industrial, the streets carry the largest volume of heavy transport, and housing tracts never seem to be far away from the generators of noise and atmospheric pollution. These divisions are paralleled in significant measure by many of the patterns of Sydney's social geography. The vast subregional differences in Sydney are seen particularly in housing prices, reflecting spatial variations in incomes.

The gentrified inner-city suburbs are the work environments for the "symbolic analysts" employed as professionals and managers in information economy activities, with their high incomes and "cafe society" lifestyles. In contrast, the lower-income people who compete

Table 12.2 Distribution of Population, Dwelling Approvals, and Investment in Construction Activities within Australia's Metropolitan Areas

	Zones within Metropolitan Areas			
	Core (in and around CBD) %	*Inner Zone Suburbs %*	*Middle Zone Suburbs %*	*Outer Zone Suburbs %*
Population 1998	7.5	11.4	34.1	47.1
Population growth				
1986–1991	–0.5	–1.8	14.6	87.7
1991–1996	7.8	4.0	13.1	75.1
Dwelling approvals	8.3	6.0	24.8	60.9
Value of construction investment, 1988–1998				
Offices	72.2	6.2	14.2	7.3
Factories	7.3	5.9	41.5	45.3
Other business premises	17.3	14.9	38.3	29.5
Shops	19.9	10.0	29.9	40.2
Hotels	72.8	6.4	11.5	9.3
Education facilities	25.2	10.9	27.3	36.6
Health facilities	24.8	11.8	38.8	24.5

Source: Derived from Australian Bureau of Statistics Data
Note: The data in each row are percentage shares of the total for all metropolitan areas. Rounding means that the percentages may not add exactly to 100%.

for the often restricted number of jobs as "routine production workers" in factories, call centers, and data-processing establishments are confined in their housing choices to the less-expensive outer suburbs, where increasingly these types of jobs are located. Many of these latter residents of Sydney do not have the need to go to the CBD and, in fact, never do so.

Thus today Sydney is more and more characterized by the divide between, on the one hand, the "globally linked" industries and high-skill occupations and the places where such people live and, on the other hand, the "domestic-linked" industries and lower-skill occupations and the places where those people live.

Auckland: A Second Tier City and New Zealand's Growth Center

Auckland is the only primate city in Oceania that has grown to primacy in an urban system, despite the fact that it is not the capital city (fig. 12.9). Founded in 1865, it in fact became the second capital of colonial New Zealand, but the capital was later transferred from Auckland to Wellington. Auckland achieved city status in 1871 and in the late 19th century it quickly overtook the older southern settlements of Dunedin and Christchurch to become New Zealand's largest city. It has grown ever since, to now more than one million spread across a metropolitan area of more than 360 sq mi (580 sq km). Along with Brisbane, Perth, and Adelaide, Auckland is one of four second-tier metropolitan cities in Oceania, with populations exceeding one million. Auckland lies across a volcanic isthmus separating two harbors and is recognized as a water lover's paradise, with the largest boat ownership per capita in the world.

The history of the Auckland region is traced back to pre-European times, when it is

Figure 12.9 A city built on an isthmus and connected to a rich hinterland, Auckland, New Zealand, now hosts many activities found in major world cities, including a sky tower casino that dominates the skyline. (Photo by Richard Le Heron)

estimated more than 20,000 Maori lived in the area. A number of the extinct volcanic cones around the harbors were transformed into fortified villages. The rich hinterland ensured that Auckland prospered as a post for exporting agricultural and forestry products and as a service center. In its physical setting and the layout of its street plan, Auckland is reminiscent of Sydney. The similarity is enhanced by the preference for subtropical species in street tree plantings. Auckland lays claim to being the "Queen City," not only of New Zealand but also of all Polynesia. In large measure, this claim is justified in terms of the city's commercial and industrial preeminence at home and its commercial and social integration with the island world of tropical Polynesia.

Auckland's ethnic diversity increased dramatically after World War II, when employment opportunities in a booming postwar economy attracted many new settlers from the Pacific Islands, as well as immigrants from the United Kingdom and Western Europe, especially the Netherlands. It has become a multicultural city, with 74% of its population being of European descent, 10% Pacific Island Polynesian, 8% New Zealand Maori, 4% Asian, and 4% European–Maori or other European–Pacific Island.

Today Auckland is New Zealand's principal seaport, airport, and naval base and the dominant commercial and manufacturing center. Within the greater Auckland area, and surrounding the central city, are three new, large suburban city developments—North Shore City, Waitakere City, and Manukau City. Main manufacturing products from the metropolitan area include iron and steel, processed food, machinery, textiles and clothing, motor vehicles, and fertilizers. But increasingly the Auckland economy and its jobs are focusing on commercial and business activities. As an evolving modern city, Auckland has undergone a renaissance—with an ever-changing skyline, a pulsating redeveloped waterfront, and a new infusion of restaurants and bars. The city has become a mecca for nightlife, buzzing with an atmosphere of fun and excitement, stimulated to a significant extent by the city's successful hosting of the America's Cup yachting event.

Canberra: Developing the Bush Capital

Canberra is one of a handful of cities in the world built specifically to undertake the role of government. Like its counterparts—Washington, Ottawa, Brasília, New Delhi—Canberra was developed to fulfill a symbolic function, to be a "national" city in a federal union by overcoming the rivalries of preexisting states. It was agreed that the new capital should be in the territory of New South Wales, but not too close to Sydney and not on the coast. The site agreed upon was Canberra, located 200 mi (320 km) southwest of Sydney on the way to Australia's second-largest city, Melbourne.

The history of Canberra begins prior to European settlement of the area and is bound up with Aboriginal habitation and white pastoral expansion. Archaeological evidence suggests that Aborigines were living on the limestone plains here for at least 21,000 years before white settlement and possibly even longer. The whites came very late, even in terms of their own history in Australia, as it was not till December 1820 that Europeans first sighted the district. Over the ensuing years, large estates were established, along with village settlements, which were to become some of the suburbs of modern Canberra.

The national capital period of Canberra's history began slowly. World War I meant that little was done immediately about physically establishing the national capital, even though the Australian Capital Territory had been proclaimed and an American town planner, Walter Burley Griffin, was commissioned to design the new capital. The Commonwealth Parliament finally relocated there from Melbourne in 1927. But the depression of the 1930s ensured that progress remained sluggish at best and by 1947, Canberra's population was only 16,000.

Since World War II, however, Canberra has been among Australia's fastest-growing urban areas, as federal government functions progressively were relocated there from Melbourne and Sydney. The subsequent vast expansion of government and bureaucracy brought about a parallel rapid growth in population, but up until the late 1980s the majority of jobs were in the public sector. The building trade, working overwhelmingly on government projects, also has been a large employer, but manufacturing in general is not and Canberra lacks a significant blue-collar sector.

The planning and development of Canberra derived from the original plan by Griffin. That plan incorporated a Parliamentary Triangle, with radiating boulevards and linking circuits. The original residential areas were planned on a crescent street layout. The rapid growth of the national capital since the 1950s was achieved through strict planning under the National Capital Development Commission, with an ordered sequencing of new town construction separated by greenbelts. This has created a sprawling, low-density urban area with a population fast approaching 350,000.

The idea was to decentralize the location of both residential areas and jobs, including public service departments, into new town centers to promote self-containment. But this did not work, as people frequently changed jobs and households and many workers commuted to parts of the city other than where they resided.

As a result, complex cross-metropolitan travel patterns have emerged and Canberra has become very dependent on the automobile. In the 1980s, controls restricting the development of Civic (the original town center) as a CBD were eased and this acted as a catalyst for substantial private-sector investment. But the town centers of the new towns are the locations not only for shopping malls, but also for office developments that predominantly house government functions.

The suburban residential development of Canberra is characterized by a mix of medium-density flats and townhouses around the town centers, but the predominant form of housing is separate dwellings on a large block of land. Each new town comprises a number of discrete suburbs with complex internal street patterns providing a limited number of entry points from ring roads that form the arterial road system. Each suburb has a neighborhood shopping center and services; the size of each suburb was planned to provide a catchment area to support a primary school. Generally, the residential neighborhoods of Canberra provide a high-quality environment incorporating parks, bikeways, and streetscaping. Many outsiders regard Canberra as dull and boring, lacking urban soul, and devoid of vitality and night life. However, the local Canberrians appreciate their highly planned urban landscape, which provides a quality environment highly suitable for bringing up a family. It is an exceedingly civil city built for civil servants.

Unlike its counterparts in other lands, Canberra has hesitated to embrace the monumental and the grandiose. The avenues tend to be avenues and one cannot always see the buildings through the trees. But Canberra does have many cultural, architectural, heritage, and surrounding natural attractions and in recent decades has begun to experience considerable growth in domestic and international tourism in its role as the national capital. Today, Canberra's built form offers many impressive sights among the many symbolic public buildings within the Parliamentary Triangle, including the Houses of Parliament, the High Court, the National Gallery, the National Botanic Gardens, the Australian War Memorial, the National Library of Australia, the National Film and Sound Archive, the Australian Museum, and a number of key government department buildings. Fine parklands fringe the large, artificial Lake Burley Griffin, which cuts through the city.

Of these attractions, the New Parliament House is a highly original creation (fig. 12.10). This "House on the Hill' was opened in May 1988, superseding the original Parliament House (opened in 1927), which was simply too small. The design for the new building, by an American firm, Mitchell Giurgola, in partnership with Australian-born architect Richard Thorp, was selected in 1980 from 329 entrants in a worldwide competition.

Situated on Capital Hill, at the apex of the Parliamentary Triangle, the new building was designed not to be an imposing presence on the landscape, but to merge into the profile of the hill itself. The circular form of Capital Hill is suggested in two planes—along the majestic curved walls and over the gentle rise of the central roof, which is covered in lawn, recalling the original hilltop. The flag mast is the

Figure 12.10 Canberra's distinctive but controversial Parliament House is difficult to appreciate from the outside, because much of the structure is underground. The inside is breathtaking, filled with beautiful art work and materials native to Australia. (Photo by Jack Williams)

pinnacle of the building, standing high above the roof and flying a huge Australian flag.

More than 60 countries have established diplomatic missions in Canberra. Most are within close range of the Parliamentary Triangle, in choice residential areas. Many of these chancelleries and residences are constructed in the architecture of their homeland and together are a distinctive feature of Canberra.

Canberra is a bureaucrat's town. It has been developed for the purpose of government and the function of government has been the major driving force in its economic and social growth. However, following the downsizing of many government functions, during the era of economic rationalism and privatization that lasted through the 1990s, Canberra witnessed a change in its fortunes, with increasing economic problems and, for some time, a stagnant population. In recent years, however, there has been a reversal of those trends with a shift in the economic and demographic characteristics of the city, as private-sector growth has taken over from the public sector as the catalyst for the local economy. Much of that growth, however, has been related to outsourcing of information technology and other functions from government. But Canberra in its own right is also attracting firms as a good location to do business.

Gold Coast: A "New Consumption" Urban Landscape

The best-known new coastal urban center to emerge in Oceania as a result of internal migration to Australia's sun belt and the growth of tourism is Gold Coast City, which covers a large area spanning the New South Wales–Queensland border. Gold Coast City stretches along 36 mi (57 km) of coastline. While it is clearly a city in its own right, the Gold Coast is part of what is now an extended metropolitan region in southeast Queensland that stretches north to

Noosa and Maroochydore on the Sunshine Coast and takes in Brisbane, the capital of Queensland (fig. 12.11). The Gold Coast is a leading example of the "new urban consumption space and place" based on tourism and the lifestyle desires of the in-movers.

From humble beginnings as a timber-filling area in the 1840s, the Gold Coast region developed an agricultural base early on. From the turn of the 20th century up to World War II, the population grew quite rapidly, especially following the building of the rail connection from Brisbane to Southport, the region's main service town, and then further south to Coolangatta. This hastened the development of the region as Brisbane's "south coast," attracting weekend as well as longer-term holiday makers to the pristine beaches of the coastal strip. In the 1970s, agricultural production declined in importance and numerous grand schemes were initiated to develop horticultural production to supply the Brisbane market. From the 1930s to the 1950s, the south coast continued to grow, but development was spread unevenly and Southport remained the main town. The really rapid growth and boom times were to begin in the mid-1950s.

Figure 12.11 Queensland's capital city of Brisbane sparkles in the Gold Coast sun as a model in many ways of effective city and regional planning, and as one of Australia's most handsome cities. (Photo by Jack Williams)

The Brisbane newspapers first used the name "Gold Coast" in the late 1940s when referring to the real estate opportunities available there. In 1958, the South Coast Town Council adopted the name Gold Coast Town Council. Tourism, first domestic and later international, took off. The boom times that have continued ever since have been punctuated by periodic busts in property construction. In particular during the 1970s and 1980s, the Gold Coast became notorious as a haven for property developers seeking the "quick buck," leading one author to write a book about the emergence of this new urban center with the colorful title, *A Sunny Place for Shady People.*

The Gold Coast now has an estimated resident population in excess of 400,000, making it the second-largest local government area in Australia. It will soon be the sixth-largest city in Australia. Throughout the 1990s, the annual growth in population was about 4%, with a very significant proportion of that growth due to internal migration from other parts of Australia, as well as immigration from New Zealand.

The attraction of the Gold Coast is due to several factors. People move there because of its

Figure 12.12 Like some futuristic vision, high rises on the Gold Coast soar above the beaches that draw tourists by the millions to Queensland's coast. (Photo by Jack Williams)

"sun belt" attributes of climate and lifestyle, to be closer to family and friends, and also for perceived employment opportunities. While many people who come to the Gold Coast retire after relocation, retirees now actually account for a declining minority of the in-migrants, with the highest proportion of in-movers now being in the age range of 20–29 years.

The continuing rapid growth that has occurred on the Gold Coast is changing the nature of the residents and their way of life. One side of this change is the increasing multicultural character of the city, as the proportion of people born overseas increased from less than 4% in 1986 to more than 24% in 1996. However, the 9% that were born in other than the main English-speaking countries is substantially lower than the figure of 13% for Australia as a whole, although their actual numbers have increased dramatically since the mid-1980s.

The boom in tourism on the Gold Coast and the gradual diversification of its economic base means that the city is now better able to ride out the inevitable boom-bust character of construction activity (fig. 12.12). But behind the glitzy façade of the tourist strip, the Gold Coast experiences higher levels of socioeconomic disadvantage compared to other parts of Australia. It is characterized by a relatively high incidence of lower-income households, high levels of unemployment, a low proportion of workers with tertiary educational qualifications, and a high proportion of workers in lower-paid jobs associated with tourism. Lower incomes can be partially attributed to the proportion of older people, including retirees, with 23% of the Gold Coast's population aged 55 years and over in 1996, compared to the average of 21% for Australia as a whole.

The importance of tourism to the Gold Coast is beyond dispute, as it provides the greatest number of job opportunities and its revenues are important in supporting other industries, such as residential development and

Box 12.3 Surfers Paradise Hangs in for Next Wave

Twice daily, in Surfers Paradise, a $1 million carillon clock heralds the promised new wave of Gold Coast wealth. It adorns the recently completed Imperial Plaza and its three levels of Asian restaurants in European-style architecture. Incongruous though it may seem it reflects expectations of a new era on the Gold Coast. Owner-developer Jenny Wong sells exclusive European labels in her fashion boutique, there are 300 restaurant seats for Chinese cuisine, 120 for Japanese, and "Viennese style" dining for 100 that offers "Trevel Hendy Weet-Bix" and $10 glasses of champagne for breakfast.

Wong's plan fits snugly with the latest trends in Gold Coast tourism, which is estimated at $2 billion a year. Last year, for the first time, the number of "other Asian" tourists (443,000) exceeded the number of Japanese (410,000). The "other Asian" component is the rapid growth sector, and is made up mainly of people from China and Taiwan, and Chinese citizens of Singapore and Hong Kong. Europeans and North Americans have faded into the background. Of the one million foreign visitors 74 percent are Asian.

A Singaporean investor, Ong Beng Seng, is seeking approvals for a $300 million, 1,200 room hotel of "intergalactic" design. The plan represents the promise of a new wave of investment for the Gold Coast. Civic and business leaders are expecting investment from Singapore, Hong Kong, South Korea and Malaysia to follow the new trends in Asian tourism.

. . . There is enthusiasm for the relatively low price at which a "lifestyle" can be bought, and some Sydney and Melbourne people practically commute from the Gold Coast. About $750,000 will buy an expansive waterfront home with pool, tennis court, private jetty and moorings in a prime location. . . . This appeal is being marketed, and foreigners are buying in.

Source: M. Massey, "Surfers Paradise Hangs in for Next Wave," *Business Review Weekly,* February 27, 1997.

education. Annually, more than 3 million visitors come here (one-third are international), excluding the day-tripper market, estimated at as many as 10 million per annum. A notable aspect of tourism on the Gold Coast is the large concentration of tourists from Asia, particularly Japan.

Associated with that rapid growth in both domestic and international tourism has been a necessary revolution in the nature of the available tourism product. New tourist facilities have been developed since the mid-1980s, much of them financed by foreign direct investment. In the hinterland areas, this includes tourism theme parks—including Movie World, Sea World, and Dream World—as well as scores of golf courses and many integrated tourist resorts to supplement the high-rise hotels and apartments that are concentrated along the coastal strip focusing on Surfers Paradise (box 12.3). The Gold Coast epitomizes a new urban landscape based on pleasure and leisure—sun, surf, and golf. It is Australia's equivalent of Miami in the United States.

Port Moresby: The Trials of an Archipelagic City in a New Nation

Port Moresby is the capital city of Papua New Guinea, located on the south coast of the island of New Guinea. The city is built in an area of plantations with experimental livestock and dairy farms. Its exports are copra, coffee, rubber, plywood, timber, and gold. Saw milling, brewing, tobacco processing, and the manufacture of local crafts and concrete are the principal industries, while fishing is also important. But Port Moresby was created specifically by and for government and achieves its eminence less from its size than from its role in integrating a fragmented land.

Local geography creates a microclimate in Port Moresby. The rain shadow created by the Owen Stanley Range means that the city receives far less than the average rainfall on New Guinea Island. The relatively dry climate thus created leads to occasional drought and shortages of drinking water, but the mountains also shield the city from the heavy rains that regularly sweep across the rest of New Guinea from May to November.

The area has been occupied for thousands of years. Europeans became aware of the area when British explorer John Moresby sailed through the Gulf of Papua in 1873. About 15 years later, Britain established the colony of British New Guinea here and named Port Moresby the capital, after Moresby's father, Admiral Moresby. The British annexed the area in 1883. Port Moresby was an important Allied military base during World War II. After the war and under Australian administration, the city grew and prospered and by 1961, its population had grown to 29,000; it had grown to 76,500 by 1971 and to about 150,000 by the turn of the century.

The original commercial center of Port Moresby is now remote from the geographical center of the urban area. Development has spread east toward the airport and north in the direction of the University of Papua New Guinea. The old town is largely separated from the new areas by steep hills and a sharp embankment. The planned new residential development is strongly reminiscent of the suburbs of Canberra, designed as tidy, intricately plotted suburban tracts separated from each other by empty space. But these new settlements often have been the focal point of simmering resentments among rival tribal groups, exacerbated by increasing ethnic diversity within the city.

There are major difficulties of physical communication between Port Moresby and the rest of Papua New Guinea, as the city has road contact only with its neighboring coastal strip. The city is cut off from land transportation contact with the major population concentrations beyond the mountains, thus the airport is the key point in the slender web of air connections that hold together this troubled nation. Local industrial development has helped spur the growth of Port Moresby in recent years. Today, the population continues expanding at a rapid pace, but the city struggles with urban violence and a high crime rate. The sharp and widening income disparities are such that many live in temporary shanty settlements.

TRENDS, ISSUES, AND CHALLENGES FOR PLANNING

The problems facing the cities of Oceania seem pale reflections of those facing cities elsewhere in the world. No vast reservoirs of rural folk are seeking liberation that an urban location supposedly confers. But relative to the limited populations and available resources there, the integration of further rural people will undoubtedly tax the authorities in cities such as Port Moresby (Papua New Guinea) and Suva (Fiji). In Australia and New Zealand, the growth of some of the big cities continues to be at a relatively rapid rate, but the prime engine of this urban growth is essentially interurban migration and immigration rather than rural-urban movement.

Nonetheless, there are significant issues presenting challenges for planning and servicing urban development in Oceania.

The Organization of Urban Government

The organization of government itself raises questions about collecting and distributing resources and who is responsible for providing services and facilities and doing the planning for urban development. In Australia, the three levels of government (national—or Commonwealth—state, and local) have specific but sometimes conflicting roles in urban development and planning, especially at the state and local levels. The desire for grassroots participation, through local councils, sometimes leads to inefficiencies and conflict.

Urban Environmental and Management Issues

Among the key issues facing urban planners and developers today are stemming rapid growth and sprawl of suburban development, reducing car dependency, improving energy efficiency, reducing demand for water, reducing waste outputs, better managing the impact of development on coastal ecosystems, incorporating sustainable development principles into planning, enhancing local authority capacity, dealing with depopulation of small inland towns, and addressing the issues facing indigenous communities.

Commuting Patterns and Mode of Travel in Cities

Providing transport infrastructure—both public transport services and road networks for passenger and freight movement—is a major planning issue for all the big cities. This is especially the case in Australia, with the strong preference for private automobiles as the mode of travel and with the seemingly never-ending, low-density, outward sprawl of the cities. Strategies to encourage use of public transport run up against mass indifference and stubborn dependency on automobiles.

The City versus the Bush

One of the big talking points of the past decade or so in Australia and New Zealand has been the increasing divide between "the city" and "the bush." The so-called crisis is seen legitimately at times in terms of falling or poor commodity prices, declining rural and regional employment opportunities, and a deterioration of traditional infrastructure. An increasing gap between metropolitan areas and rural and regional areas in access to new telecommunications and information technology is being referred to as the "digital divide."

But in Australia it is simplistic and even wrong to assume that all of the rural and regional areas are in crisis, as many places are doing well. Rural and regional Australia continues to be an important contributor to the nation's export effort, and the same is true in New Zealand. Regional cities like Shepparton in Victoria's "food bowl" and Griffith in the irrigation areas of southern inland New South Wales are booming. Once-remote places like Cairns in far

Figure 12.13 Cairns, in the far north tropics of Queensland, has developed in recent years as a major tourism center and the gateway to the Great Barrier Reef and its attractions. The gambling casino here in Cairns is designed to help tourists part with their money before venturing elsewhere. (Photo by Jack Williams)

northern Queensland have experienced a rapid growth of international tourism through vastly improved air transport linkages (fig. 12.13). The towns of Australia's many wine regions are also experiencing strong economic performance.

It also is simplistic to think that everything is great in the big cities. Within the individual large metropolitan area there are also distinct divisions. The contrasts are stark. There are the gentrifying inner-city suburbs with their increasing numbers of highly skilled and well-paid professional workers in the information industries where the housing markets are booming. Then there are the high concentrations in dormitory suburbs with low-income households, unemployed people, and workers with low skills living in cheap housing that is poorly serviced by transport and located where job opportunities are limited and the incidence of part-time work is high.

The Island Cities

The problems of the major towns in the archipelagos in Oceania do not stem so much from sheer large scale, as places such as Suva (fig. 12.14), Apia, and Nouméa have limitations on their size simply because they are located in some of the world's smallest and least-populous states. Rather, towns have problems such as those that occur when people from villages of the outer islands find themselves needing to pay cash for living costs, when their support is in the home village far away. These are the traditional problems relating to the urbanization of rural people.

Port Moresby, however, is potentially different, as it could grow into a large city and as it has been experiencing rapid growth. While the quasitribal solution to the transition from village to city is operating in Port Moresby, unfortunately, law and order have become major

Figure 12.14 Outdoor markets, such as this one in Suva, the capital of Fiji, are a staple of life in the scattered towns of the Pacific Islands. (Photo by Richard Ulack)

problems. Moreover, as the city grows, heavy capital outlays are needed to provide basic water and energy supplies that are well above the levels of the sustainable environment.

SUGGESTED READINGS

Australia Department of Housing and Regional Development. *Urban Australia: Trends and Prospects*. Special issue of the *Australian Urban and Regional Development Review*. Canberra: Department of Housing and Regional Development, 1995. An overview of population trends, patterns of settlement, employment and investment, infrastructure, social structure, environmental issues, and urban planning and management.

Badcock, Blair, and Andrew Beer. *Home Truths*. Melbourne: University of Melbourne, 2000. An overview of housing in Australia.

Burnley, Ian, Peter Murphy, and Robert Fagan. *Immigration and Australian Cities*. Leichhardt, New South Wales: Federation, 1997. Discusses the impact of immigration on Australia and its cities.

Forster, Clive. *Australian Cities: Continuity and Change*, 2d ed. Melbourne: Oxford University Press, 1999. An overview of the big cities in Australia, their foundations, development, employment, housing, residential mosaic, governance, and future planning issues.

Gibson, Katherine, and Sophie Watson. *Metropolis Now*. Leichhardt, New South Wales: Pluto, 1994. A postmodernist perspective on planning and urban development in contemporary Australia, including edge cities, housing, and cultural planning.

Newton, Peter, and Martin Bell, eds. *Population Shift: Mobility and Change in Australia*. Canberra: Australian Government Publishing Service, 1996. Discusses geographically such topics as international migration, interregional migration, interurban mobility, and social aspects of Australia.

O'Connor, Kevin, Robert Stimson, and Maurice Daly. *Australia's Changing Economic Geography: A Society Dividing.* Melbourne: Oxford University Press, 2001. Provides an overview of the impacts of globalization and of economic and social change on spatial patterns of economic performance in Australia's states, big cities, and nonmetropolitan regions.

Stilwell, Frank. *Understanding Cities and Regions: Spatial Political Economy.* Leichhardt, New South Wales: Pluto, 1992. Topics discussed include urban and regional development, inequalities, and planning.

13

Cities of the Future

STANLEY D. BRUNN AND RINA GHOSE

AN URBAN WORLD WITH TWO FACES

We have approached cities and urbanization from historical and contemporary perspectives in the regional chapters of this book. Now it is time to think about the future (see box 1.1). One prediction we can make with certainty: within a decade, the majority of the world's population will live in urban regions. The United States reached the urban-majority mark in 1920. The world will reach the urban-majority mark well before 2020. What does the future hold for such a world and its people? Will present trends continue or will there be a sea change in the very nature of urban life? Will cities in MDCs continue to stabilize in population and eventually decline, while those in LDCs experience continued high growth rates? What will be the consequences of divergent development paths on urban economies, communication and transportation, and human organizations and interaction? These are among the questions that intrigue urban geographers as we examine the early 21st century.

A global perspective on these global urban changes from 1950–2050 is depicted in figure 13.1. In 1950, urban residents numbered approximately 750 million worldwide. By 2000, the figure was 2.8 billion and by 2050 it is expected to be 6.5 billion. In 1950, Africa and Southwest Asia had 6% of all urban residents, while Europe had 32% and Asia about 30%. Between 1950 and 2000, Africa more than doubled its city residents, while Asia's urban population grew by 40%. In 2000, Europe's share of the world's urban population had declined to about 15%, North America's to only 8.5%. By 2050, more than one in four urban residents will be living in African and Middle Eastern cities and one in two will be living in Asian cities. Europe and Latin America will have almost the same number of city residents, while U.S. and Canadian urbanites will almost equal in number those of West Africa. In aggregate, there are currently more rural than urban residents in LDCs, but this pattern will be reversed by about 2020 (fig. 13.2).

LARGEST AGGLOMERATIONS IN 2015 AND 2050

The largest cities now are in LDCs and they still will be in 2015. Significant questions emerge from this fact, including what implications the changes in numbers, sizes, rankings, and distributions will have on human and natural resource bases and the future of humanity. Tokyo (27 million) is expected to remain the world's largest agglomeration, but it will be followed by cities in the LDCs: Dhaka

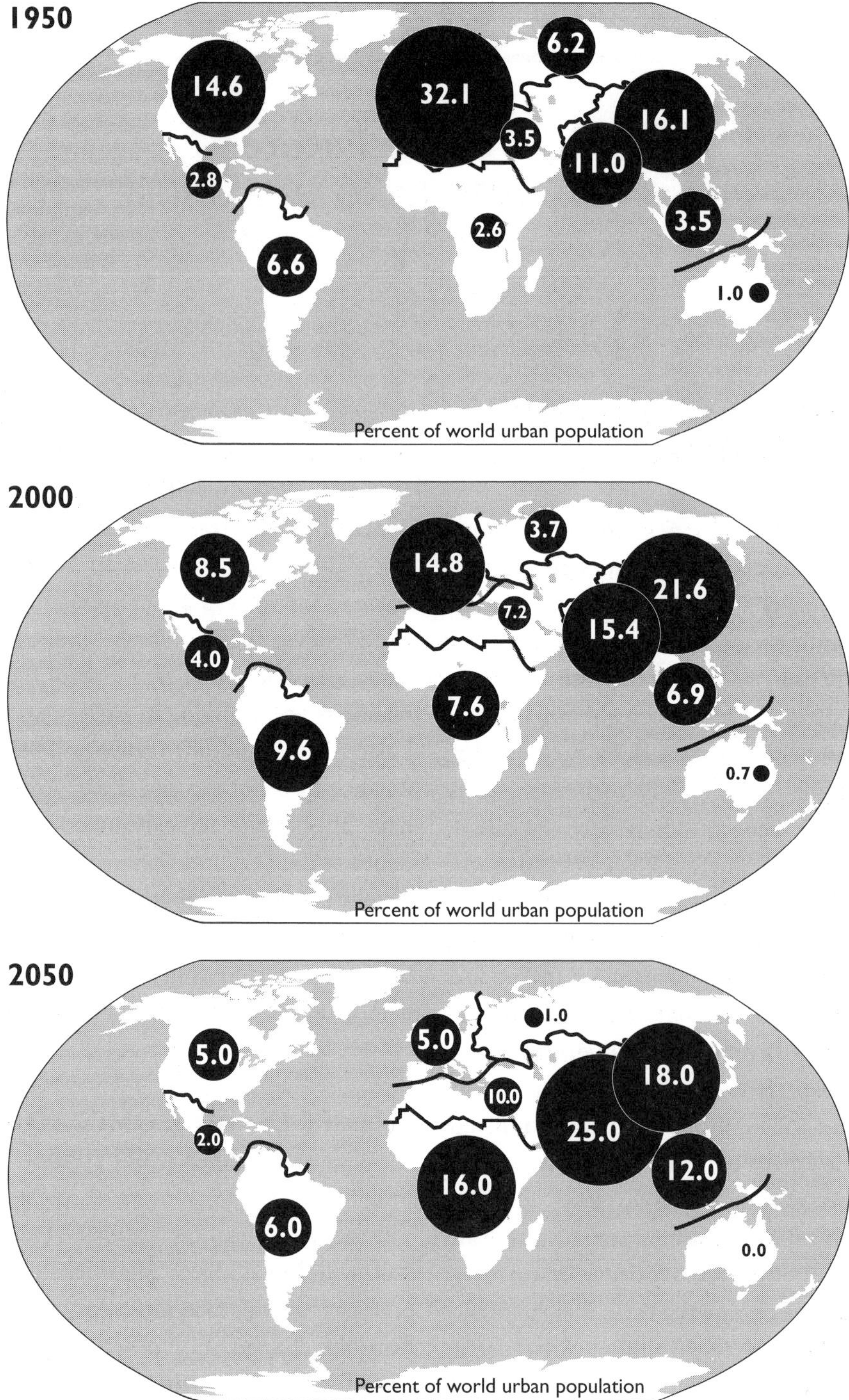

Figure 13.1 Urban Populations: 1950, 2000, 2050. *Source*: Data from United Nations, *World Urbanization Prospects, 2001 Revision* (New York: United Nations Population Division, 2002), www.unpopulation.org. Projections for 2050 by authors.

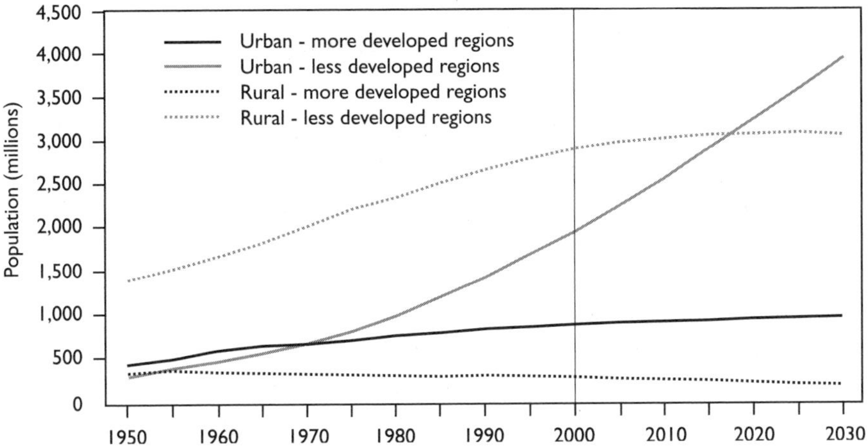

Figure 13.2 Urban and Rural Populations in MDCs and LDCs, 1950–2030. *Source*: United Nations, *World Urbanization Prospects, 2001 Revision* (New York: United Nations Population Division, 2002), www.unpopulation.org.

and Mumbai (each about 23 million), São Paulo (21 million), and Delhi (20 million). Lagos and Istanbul will move up in the rankings, while Mexico City, Los Angeles, New York, Buenos Aires, and Rio de Janeiro will move down. The UN lists 524 urban agglomerations with 750,000 inhabitants or more in 2000 (see the appendix for a complete list). Their combined population was 1.2 billion, or 40% of all urban dwellers. More than 40% of these agglomerations were in China (with 119), India (with 50), and the United States (with 46). Altogether, in 2000 the top nine countries had 303 agglomerations exceeding 750,000 and 57% of the world's urban dwellers.

To gain some perspective on these numbers, we used the populations of the 30 largest cities in 1950, 1975, 2000, and 2015 to calculate what cities the residents would come from, proportionately, if we had a global village of just 100 people (box 13.1). The shifts described above are confirmed—fewer will come from New York, London, and Paris and more each succeeding generation will come from major cities in East, South, and Southeast Asia.

The burgeoning populations of LDC cities can also be illustrated by using the 2010–2015 expected growth rates to project the populations of the largest agglomerations to 2050. At midcentury, 48 agglomerations are likely to have more than 10 million residents each (tab. 13.1). The distribution of these giant cities can be seen in map form in figure 13.3. Dhaka will have nearly 48 million people, followed closely by Delhi at nearly 41 million and Mumbai at 38 million. These are staggering numbers, as never in human history have we had cities this large. Tokyo, expected to rank first in 2015, will slip to sixth place. Seven of the ten largest agglomerations will be in Asia. São Paulo, Mexico City, and Kinshasa are projected to have 25–26 million each. New York and Los Angeles will be the only U.S. agglomerations having more than 10 million. Istanbul will replace Cairo as the largest city in the Greater Middle East. The combined population of these 48 largest agglomerations will be approximately 850 million.

Box 13.1 A Global Village

How has the composition of the world's urban population changed during the past half century? What changes are possible based on future UN projections? One way to answer this large question in a meaningful way is to consider the 30 largest agglomerations in 1950, 1975, 2000, and 2015 and reduce the huge numbers into a "global village" of only 100 people. This approach can give us some idea where residents of the world's largest cities come from, that is, from what cities and what regions.

The largest number of residents in our village in our first year would be from New York (10 residents), but then Tokyo would have more residents in the other years (9, then 8, and then 7). Both cities would be losing citizens in each year, so that by 2015 New York would have only 4 residents and Tokyo only 7.

Not unexpected from what we have seen described elsewhere in this chapter are declines in the numbers from European and U.S. cities and increases from LDC regions. Europe and the United States would account for half of all villagers in 1950, but only 13 combined by 2015. Manchester, Birmingham, Rhine-Ruhr, and Boston would have lost representation. Another 19 villagers would have come from East Asia in 1950, with 30 by 1975, but only 29 by 2015. The largest number of newcomers would come from South and Southeast Asia, growing from 6 in 1950 (all these from South Asia) to 36 from 10 different cities in these regions in 2015. The lion's share of these additions would hail from Dhaka, Mumbai, and Delhi with 5, 5, and 4 residents, respectively, in 2015.

There would be no Russian residents in this village after 1975 (4 would come from Moscow and 2 from St. Petersburg in this year) and there would be none any year from Oceania. Sub-Saharan Africa would have none in 1950, but 6 residents (from Lagos and Kinshasa) in 2015. Cairo would have 1 resident in 1950 and by 1975 it would be joined by Tehran as the only cities with a resident from the Greater Middle East; these two cities would have 6 residents combined in 2015. Mexico City would be the sole representative of Central America; there would be 2 from this agglomeration in 1950 and 5 in each succeeding year. South American cities would always be represented, initially by Buenos Aires and Rio de Janeiro, but later by São Paulo, Lima, and Bogotá. By 2015, there would be 15 residents in our village from these 5 cities, with most from São Paulo.

What is clear from the cities of origin of residents in our "global village" is that the number from MDC regions would decrease and the number from LDC regions would increase. Whereas in 1950 there would be 61 villagers from 18 different cities in North America, Europe, and Russia, by 2015 there would be only 13 citizens from just 4 cities in those regions. By contrast, the numbers and composition from LDC regions would increase, from 12 cities and 39 residents of our village population of 100 in 1950 to 26 cities and 87 residents by 2015.

Note: Japan is included in the East Asia region. If counted with the MDC regions, the numbers would change somewhat.

Table 13.1 Projected Populations of Largest Agglomerations in 2050

Based on population increases from 2010–2015 and projected for 2050

Rank	*City*	*Population (millions)*
1.	Dhaka	48
2.	Delhi	41
3.	Mumbai	38
4.	Karachi	32
5.	Jakarta	32
6.	Tokyo	28
7.	Kolkata	26
8.	Mexico City	26
9.	São Paulo	26
10.	Kinshasa	25
11.	Lagos	21
12.	New York	21
13.	Lahore	18
14.	Shanghai	18
15.	Los Angeles	17
16.	Bangkok	16
17.	Beijing	16
18.	Buenos Aires	16
19.	Istanbul	16
20.	Bangalore	15
21.	Riyadh	15
22.	Tianjin	15
23.	Wuhan	15
24.	Bogotá	14
25.	Chittagong	14
26.	Chongqing	14
27.	Manila	14
27.	Hyderabad	13
29.	Kabul	13
30.	Lima	13
31.	Chennai	13
32.	Rio de Janeiro	13
33.	Surat	13
34.	Addis Ababa	12
35.	Abidjan	12
36.	Ahmedabad	12
37.	Luanda	12
38.	Pune	12
39.	Tehran	12
40.	Baghdad	11
41.	Cairo	11
42.	Guatemala City	11
43.	Ho Chi Minh City	11
44.	Hong Kong	11
45.	Jiddah	11
46.	Osaka	11
47.	Seoul	11
48.	Yangon	11

Source: 2010–2015 data available in United Nations, *World Urbanization Prospects,* 2001 Revision, table A12, www.unorganization.org.

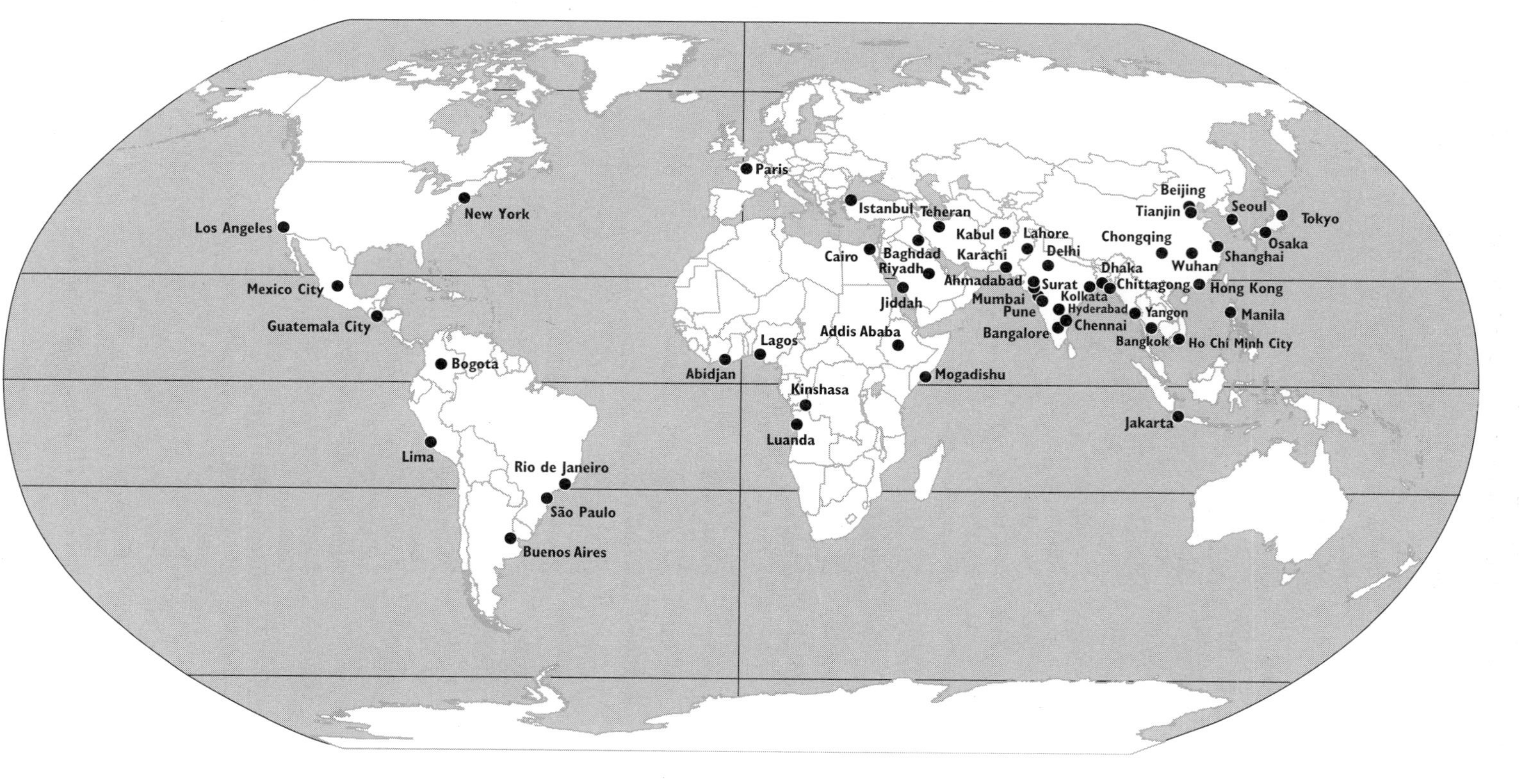

Figure 13.3 The Fifty Largest Cities in the World, 2050. *Source*: Projected from United Nations, *World Urbanization Prospects, 2001 Revision* (New York: United Nations Population Division, 2002), www.unpopulation.org.

TEN HUMAN GEOGRAPHIES OF THE EARLY 21ST CENTURY

Economic, social, and political futures in any region are affected by local cultures and events as well as external regional and global actions and institutions. These futures are likely to surface first in large cities. In some form, the following scenarios are probable (in no particular order of likelihood):

1. *An urbanizing world.* Urbanization will continue to concentrate a growing population on comparably less land. Urban agglomerations will grow bigger and urban institutions will increasingly dominate even rural areas. Interactions, associations, and communications are likely to be increasingly between cities near and far rather than between cities and their rural trade areas.
2. *Urban connectedness, anomie, and placelessness.* Faster transportation and *information and communication technologies* (ICTs) may lead people to lose their sense of place. The result could be anomie—alienation and social instability. Cell phones, fax machines, the Internet, and wireless communications are likely to speed up the interconnected world in which we live and diminish the significance of place.
3. *Meshings of the local and global in daily life.* Scale meshings will be evident in transactions and interactions—where one works, with whom one works, and the destinations of goods and services produced, such as luxury crops, telecommunications equipment, digitized health records, or components in a global product (computer or motor vehicle). While some urban residents will interact at very local scales, others will interact at extraregional and global levels. The size of the ellipses in figure 13.4 are roughly proportional to the geographic and personal scale of interactions for various individuals in different sizes of human settlement.
4. *Asianization of Europeanized worlds.* A significant contemporary global process will be the continued impress of Asian diasporas on traditionally Europeanized worlds. While non-Asian culture groups are also involved in worldwide migration, Asians are having a particularly significant impact, especially on cities. The movement of large numbers of skilled and unskilled, legal and illegal Asian residents into gateway cities throughout most of urban Europe and North America, for example, is already highly visible. These new cultures add new layers of food, music, entertainment, and intellectual diversity to city life. Figure 13.5 is designed merely to suggest the movements and general destinations of Asian migrants.
5. *Increased regional and global awareness.* The diffusion of mass communication technologies and instant global reporting of major events will increasingly transcend traditional cultural, national, and political boundaries and raise the awareness of planetary concerns. International boundaries will further diminish in importance. Examples include the free flow of goods, services, labor, and capital throughout the European Union, the importance of global and regional environmental treaties, and global pressure to assure basic human rights for all, including women, children, elderly, disabled, and cultural minorities.

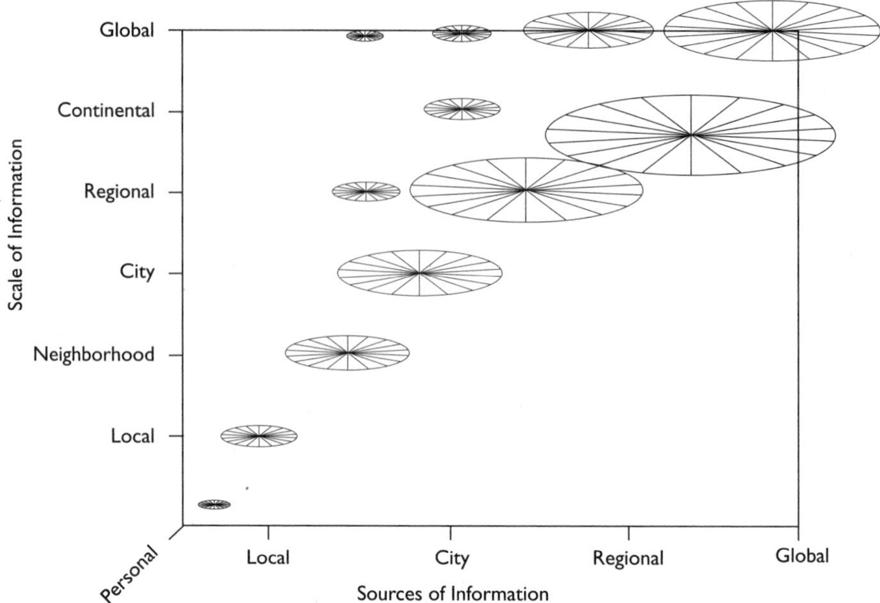

Figure 13.4 Scales of Information Transactions and Activity Spaces. *Source*: Stanley D. Brunn, "Human Rights and Welfare in the Electronic State," in *Information Tectonics*, edited by Mark I. Wilson and Kenneth E. Corey (New York: Wiley, 2000), 59. Reprinted with permission.

6. *Competitive K-economies.* "K" is for knowledge. The *K-economy* (or *information economy*) symbolizes the transition from *hardware* to *brainware* and the importance of images and symbols in product consumption. These *brain economies* will be of increasing significance in globally competitive and creative cities.
7. *Contested legal structures.* Increased volumes and densities of transborder urban networks and circulations will raise questions about the effectiveness of traditional city and state governments in daily life, including individual versus group rights and the legal and administrative structures affecting temporary and permanent urban residents. Additional fuzzy issues will include the rights of those without property and statehood, legal status of employees of international NGOs, and the ownership of natural resources and cultural properties.
8. *Redefining norms and abnorms.* Urban cultural and political clashes (subtle and violent) are likely to continue to emerge among groups: those calling for tolerance and diversity in work, living, lifestyle, and social spaces versus those seeking to retain traditional norms based on religious and rural values or the outdated modes of authority. Extremists may have a profound impact on urban life in many countries.

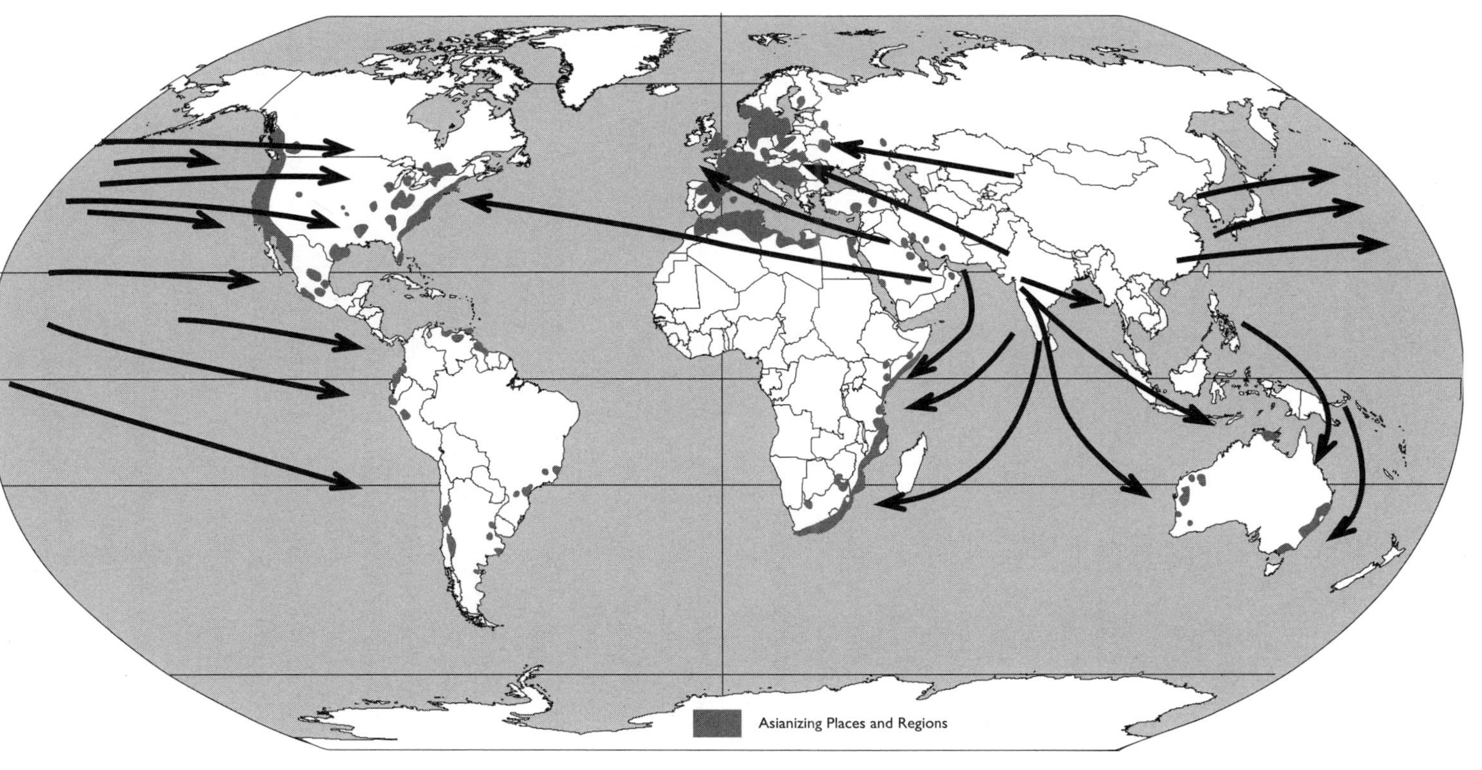

Figure 13.5 The "Asianization" of Europeanized Worlds. *Source*: Stanley Brunn

9. *Continued technological breakthroughs and limits.* Now that we have faster transportation and nearly instant ICTs (at least in MDCs), will there be constraints on the adoption and dissemination of new technologies because of adverse social impacts on a culture, high fixed costs, potential disasters, and government security concerns? Have space-adjusting technologies reached their limits? Will the technology "gaps" between *haves* and *have-nots* begin to narrow?
10. *Veneers of homogeneity amidst diversity.* The "McDonaldization of the World," or the creation of a consumer world dominated by major Western food, music, fashion, and entertainment, will reflect a certain visible sameness in many urban landscapes. But beneath these landscapes and icons of Western and American hegemony in LDCs will be the rich historical and cultural mosaics of enduring regional cultures existing alongside high-end Westernized consumerism.

Bearing these emerging futures in mind, we posit some distinguishing features of future cities and city life. Much of this thinking comes from professional social scientists, planners, and engineers in the MDCs, who dream solutions; design new architectures and technologies; plan urban infrastructures; collaborate with governments, transnational corporations, universities, and think-tanks; and serve as consultants with LDCs. Many MDC proposals then diffuse to LDCs and are adopted with regional and cultural modifications.

FUTURE CITIES: DESIGNS AND PLANS

Digital Technology and the City

Alongside the real (or ground-truth) city, a new city is emerging in MDCs. It is often called the digital (or *brain*) city, where digital technologies, especially *geographical information systems* (GIS), are used to plan, build, and manage the urban environment. Since the early 1970s, GIS use has become routine in urban planning tasks in North America, Western Europe, Japan, and Australia. Geographic information systems are also penetrating the cities of some LDCs, particularly such countries as India, China, South Africa, Senegal, Ghana, Brazil, and Mexico. GIS is the science and technology that integrates vast databases with georeferenced data (exact latitudinal/longitudinal coordinates) to prepare maps, satellite images, and aerial photographs. These data allow researchers and planners to perform a range of statistical and spatial analyses, including modeling, visualization, and simulation, to design, plan, and manage urban environments and devise future scenarios. GIS can be easily linked to GPS (global positioning system) units to ensure highly accurate spatial analysis. Also, mobile and hand-held GPS units integrated into GIS programs can be taken to remote areas to conduct real-time analysis. A common use of GIS in urban planning in MDCs is citizen participation, as it empowers citizens to obtain and access city records, increases their knowledge of neighborhood conditions, and provides a voice in decisions (box 13.2).

Box 13.2 GIS, Urban Planning, and Community Empowerment

The adoption of *geographic information systems* (GIS) in urban planning has grown steadily in North America and Europe since the 1960s, with applications in land use, zoning, transportation, site-suitability analysis, and economic development. Growing knowledge, awareness, and acceptance of GIS, coupled with lower costs of hardware and software, have assisted in implementation.

One recent sphere of activity is in neighborhood planning, a focus of major concern in cities seeking to combat continued deindustrialization and disinvestment. Both processes have severely affected many central-city neighborhoods of older and heavy-manufacturing cities in North America and Western Europe. These blighted neighborhoods suffer from high rates of poverty, unemployment, and crime and generally a degraded standard of living. To counter these trends, government agencies and nongovernmental organizations have implemented programs to revitalize declining neighborhoods. GIS greatly facilitates such neighborhood strategic planning and revitalization programs through an array of data-analysis techniques and visualization capabilities. Urban planners, citizens, and others are utilizing and analyzing a vast array of data in GIS, including data relating to demographics, housing quality, property ownership, tax assessment, land use, mortgage rates, transportation patterns, crime, health, and employment. By examining these data, constructing thematic maps showing trends, and applying spatial analysis techniques (such as overlaying and buffering), citizens' groups have persuaded authorities to take action against the problems of drug houses, vacant lots and boarded-up properties, absentee landlords, tax delinquencies, garbage pileup, inadequate sanitation, air and water pollution, soil contamination, and poor health conditions.

It is generally accepted in planning theory that citizen participation in neighborhood planning is highly significant and can make the planning process more effective. However, barriers remain, including the complexity of GIS and the high costs of gathering and importing data and attaining the necessary technology, and these barriers often severely limit citizen participation, effectively creating a *digital divide*. Based on the assumption that greater access to information leads to opportunities for citizens to participate in planning, a range of initiatives has been undertaken by various levels of government seeking to provide citizens with access to data and GIS. Both academic researchers and government officials applaud *public participation GIS* (PPGIS) efforts to empower community groups. The United States is a leader in the PPGIS movement, in which universities, nonprofit organizations, local government agencies, as well as federal agencies such as the Department of Housing and Urban Development establish PPGIS among marginalized groups. Similar movements exist in Western European cities. While numerous challenges remain in bridging the digital divide, unprecedented numbers of grassroots community organizations today are adopting and using GIS technology. U.S. cities include Milwaukee, Minneapolis, Detroit, Cleveland, Chicago, and Atlanta, while European cities include London and Sheffield. While PPGIS efforts occur mostly in MDCs, they have been introduced in Ghana, Senegal, China, and Nepal.

Internet Access

Another digital technology that is vital to urban economic growth and governance is Internet access. Many cities are being restructured as wired cities in order to compete for a vast array of ICT services to link businesses and households. San Francisco, Seattle, San Diego, San Jose, Los Angeles, New York, Washington, D.C., Chicago, Boston, and Miami are among the top U.S. cities in Internet penetration. Many of these cities are also identified as centers of technological innovation. The Internet is being utilized not only for luring capital and ICT firms, but also for security purposes. For example, web cameras monitor London's streets and its financial district. Internet penetration in LDCs is also significant and is a deliberate strategy to attract economic investment from the MDCs. In India, for instance, Delhi, Mumbai, and Bangalore have become significant wired cities that are part of a globalized economy.

Examples of countries making heavy investments in national and urban ITC economies are Singapore, Estonia, Slovenia, the Gulf States (as part of their postpetroleum economic planning), Hong Kong, Jamaica, and Trinidad. Digital cities invest in computer hardware and software design and support large and small companies performing various digital tasks, as well as the many *intergovernmental organizations* (IGOs), NGOs, and government institutions using digital services, including libraries, courts, and employment and environmental offices. Digital cities contain multiple cyber–land uses and cyberinstitutions, including:

- cyber-cafes, now a world-wide phenomenon;
- cyber-music, now downloadable in infinite varieties from the Web;
- cyber-photography, now posted and passed on via the Internet;
- cyber-education, now available no matter how close one is to a school or library;
- cyber-healing, which now links a person's vital signs with a distant doctor;
- cyber-conferencing, now with full visualization among participants; and
- cyber-tourism, where virtual reality tries to substitute for reality itself.

Location-Based Services

Location-based services (LBS) exist in Western Europe and Japan and are being introduced in North America. LBS delivers highly personalized mobile telecommunications services based on wireless technology or mobile/cellular phones using accurate locational information (available either through GPS or network-based positioning) to deliver a variety of services, ranging from real-time traffic information to airline, hotel, and restaurant reservations to information on specific restaurants, shops, cinemas, concierge services, and emergency services. LBS provides a range of applications related to trafficking. These include companies tracking vehicle and operator location. LBS works in tandem with GIS to generate mobility maps and answer navigation queries.

Smart Regions

Entry into the information or postindustrial economy has brought enormous changes to many MDC cities. While some have restructured and adopted new economies and are thriving, others remain blighted, poor, and unable to reindustrialize. The former are termed *smart regions,* while the latter are called *bypassed regions.* Smart regions are creative and innovative; they profit from financial support, patents, and imported talented labor pools, and from nearby universities and research labs for intellectual and product development. Not surprisingly, the top wired cities qualify as smart regions. *Silicon* is an adjective partnered with various features, including valleys, forests, plateaus, parks, suburbs, and polders, to define high-tech concentrations. In contrast, bypassed regions experience sustained out-migrations of youthful talent, contain outdated infrastructures, receive few monies for talent and product investment, show low university graduation rates, and have a poor quality of life and aging populations. These conditions reflect worn-out economies. Regions, such as rural Appalachia, that are dependent on dwindling and high-cost extractive industries and marginal industrial economies are good examples. Contrasts in development and investment exist in LDCs as well: Northeast China, a once-prominent industrial region that is experiencing decline, in contrast to the successful Special Economic Zones and prosperous cities (such as Shanghai or Guangzhou) along the east coast of China; the powerful state of Karnataka, India, which boasts the Silicon Plateau and the affluent, wired city of Bangalore, which are in sharp contrast to the once-prominent industrial and educational center of Kolkata.

Smart Cities

A new direction in the design and development of MDC cities is the *smart city.* The goal is to integrate knowledge from science, technology, and information systems and to create or recreate old cities as clean, secure, and efficient environments for living and working. Smart cities use advanced, integrated materials, sensors, electronics, and networks interfaced with information technologies to regulate and monitor their infrastructures, including transportation, energy, water, and emergency services, thereby making them safe and efficient. A smart city is like a wired "walled city" where smart sensors keep out intruders. Southampton, UK, is evolving into a smart city by using a "smart card," which will provide residents ready access to transportation, entertainment, services, and education. Many U.S. businesses and colleges also issue smart cards for parking. Collaboration between city government, the public, educational and health-care institutions, and businesses in Winnipeg and Kansas City contribute to these cities being heavily wired. These cities hope to establish a digital economy and to promote e-government.

Counterurbanization

While urbanization remains a prominent global process, there are some noteworthy countertrends, one of which is known as counterurbanization. Counterurbanization is the process in which people move from the central areas of cities to the urban fringe, even beyond the suburbs. It may occur simultaneously with greater urbanization (and suburbanization). Scenic amenities, historic architecture, recreational opportunities, and a strong place identity often determine the direction of counterurbanization. Counterurbanization forces in the Rocky Mountain region have seen sleepy little mountain towns being forced to address issues of sprawl and unplanned growth and adopt various growth-management strategies, including urban growth boundaries, in-fill, and cluster development. The American and British countrysides have also been the scenes of rural gentrification, that is, the process in which a new urban middle class leaves highly urbanized areas in search of picturesque countrysides within commuting distance of the cities. These processes may result in spiraling real estate costs in the countryside and the displacement of many original rural residents.

New Urbanism

In contrast to counterurbanization, MDCs are experiencing new urbanization—*New Urbanism*—alongside suburbanization. Suburban development, characterized by isolated, single-use residential neighborhoods, long has been criticized for its generic housing styles, contributions to the problems of sprawl, continued dependence on automobiles, long commutes, and endless traffic jams. New Urbanism seeks to reform the urban built environment by raising the quality of life and creating more livable cities with strong senses of identity. Conscious efforts are made to develop a sense of place through imaginative architecture, mixed-use neighborhoods with mixed-price housing, vibrant downtowns, and easily accessible public places. Cities are promoted that are both livable and sustainable. New Urbanism has become an alternative to single-use neighborhoods with cookie-cutter housing designs and to blighted and abandoned downtowns, suburbanization, unregulated sprawl, and sole reliance on automobiles and the continued expansion of roads and highways. There are more than 500 "New Urbanist" projects, half of which are in historic centers, planned or under construction in the United States alone.

Growth Management

Both smart-growth planning and growth management promote high-density living, in-fill development, cluster housing, mixed-use and mixed-price neighborhoods, pedestrian walkways, and mass transit. Portland, Oregon, is often used as a model in growth-management planning activities, as it has actively pursued various strategies for several decades. This type of planning has a strong regional focus in the United States, being associated primarily with small towns and cities in the Northwest (including Seattle) and Mountain West.

Gentrification

Another ongoing urban process in MDC regions is *gentrification,* which is a form of protest against suburban living. Gentrification reflects a desire for diversity, particularly in mixed-use urban neighborhoods containing historically prominent architecture. Gentrifiers in Europe and North America are predominantly white, middle class, well educated, and employed in professional occupations. They tend to be either single people—with or without children—or dual-income families. Gentrification is also popular in gay and lesbian communities. This process has revitalized many downtowns, but at the same time it has escalated housing prices and led to the displacement of poorer residents. Gentrification is a major trend in cities such as New York, San Francisco, Chicago, London, Paris, Amsterdam, and Sydney. It is often criticized as an elitist force that adversely affects low-income and mixed populations. In response, cities such as Chicago are trying to integrate gentrifying areas by requiring parts of such neighborhoods to maintain housing for the low-income population. Gentrification is largely missing in LDCs, because the central-city neighborhoods in LDCs tend to remain vibrant.

Brownfields

Another significant trend in some older industrial centers in the United States is termed brownfield development. *Brownfields* are abandoned or inactive rural or urban industrial sites that are contaminated with pollutants. Often, these unsightly derelict landscapes are situated near power plants, rail yards, docks, and cheap immigrant labor pools. There are estimated to be 450,000 brownfield sites in the United States, but developers are reluctant to recycle them because of the potential liabilities from environmental contamination. Such sites are numerous in older industrial areas of North America, Western and Eastern Europe, Russia, Central Asia, and Northeast China. In the former Soviet Union and Eastern Europe, the cities are places associated with human despair, including high unemployment, high rates of alcoholism and related diseases, poor health care, and domestic violence. Advocates of urban brownfield recycling often point to the potential benefits of redeveloping these sites, including creating jobs in regions of disinvestment, increasing local revenue, and revitalizing blighted areas. Brownfield redevelopment could curtail the decline of inner cities and reduce urban sprawl.

Gated Cities and Communities

Gated cities and communities directly reflect extreme socioeconomic inequities and ethnic/class intolerance. These can be independent cities, or portions thereof, that are separated from surrounding urban areas by defensive architecture, security gates, entrance codes, and even walls. Often the residents in these compounds are wealthy local residents or outsiders in positions of power and privilege. Los Angeles, a classic example, contains exclusive, wealthy neighborhoods (such as Beverly Hills) that are securely separated by high walls, sophisticated surveillance, and security systems. The southern California gated communities of Rolling Hills on the Palos Verdes Peninsula, Hidden Hills near Calabasas, and Canyon Lake boast expensive homes and an array of recreational facilities, such as lakes, pools, campgrounds, equestrian centers, ball fields, golf courses, and tennis courts. To maintain the exclusivity of these communities, access is restricted by security guards and imposing physical barriers. Some gated communities are literally on islands, while others are political and administrative islands in metropolitan areas. These communities have autonomous governments that distance themselves from the rest of the city; they have their own street maintenance and fire and police forces. These communities for the affluent, the retirees, workers in foreign embassies, and wealthy émigrés offer their residents segregation, safety, and security. They are often called *fortress cities* or examples of *urban apartheid;* they have been criticized as elitist, segregationist, and discriminatory. They are based on fear of the perceived chaotic, violent urban environment and the demand for highly controlled, secure, and private spaces separated from "others." These communities appear in large cities on all continents and in many ways are the antithesis of a positive movement in urban development, the sustainable city.

Sustainable Cities

These are cities with commitments to conservation, recycling, and practicing sustainable economies and ethics, that is, making wise use of resources for future generations. With continued urbanization a major worldwide trend, cities have become identified as major consumers of goods and resources, including the draining of many natural resources from surrounding regions. Among the ecological impacts of urbanization are rampant consumption rates for nonrenewable resources and a psychology of "out of sight, out of mind." Growing concerns surface about the negative ecological impacts of these tendencies, as well as associated large-scale social and economic inequities. These ecological concerns have led to movements for sustainable cities in both the MDCs and LDCs. A sustainable city is first and foremost accountable for its consumption patterns and their impacts on the human population and resource base.

These cities are also concerned with developing an ethic of recycling and reuse, as well as issues of social justice, gender equality, livable wages, affordable housing, and ready access for all members to education and health care. Integrating elements of ecology, economy, and community and social cohesion are thus the lynchpins of sustainable city development. Typical physical characteristics of sustainable cities include compact forms of residential development; mixed land use; use of mass transit as the major form of transportation, along with widespread use of pedestrian and bicycle paths; heavy use of wind and solar energy; protection of natural hydrologic systems; protection of wetlands, woodlands, natural open space, and habitats; use of natural fertilizers and integrated pest management; use of natural means of sewage treatment; reduction of waste; and recovery, reuse, and recycling of waste materials. These cities encourage strong citizen participation as well as coalitions with businesses. For example, sustainable cities in India aim to have controlled populations and sufficient employment opportunities; adequate government services in the cities; efficient basic civic amenities providing reliable supplies of electricity and water; planned housing communities with adequate infrastructure such as schools, parks, drainage systems, and medical establishments; efficient transportation planning with a range of choices; an effective environmental infrastructure to address issues of untreated sewage and polluted rivers and lakes; empowerment of women and their participation in the political, economic, and social aspects of the city; the development of an efficient private sector that generates more jobs and contributes to the elimination of poverty; and the development of efficient health care systems that address issues of nutrition, family planning, and sanitation systems. Initiatives leading to the development of sustainable cities are in progress on all continents.

The Sustainable Cities Programme enacted by the UN Habitat UNEP operates in 20 main demonstration and 25 replicating cities around the world. Countries hosting these programs include: China (Shenyang, Wuhan), Chile (Concepción), Egypt (Ismailia), Ghana (Accra), India (Chennai, formerly Madras), Kenya, Korea (Hanam), Malawi (Blantyre), Mozambique (Maputo, Nampula), Nigeria (Ibadan), the Philippines, Poland (Katowice Agglomeration), Russia (Kirshi), Senegal (Dakar), Sri Lanka, Tanzania (Dar es Salaam, Zanzibar, Moshi), Tunisia (Tunis), and Zambia (Lusaka). Similar projects have been undertaken by the International Centre for Sustainable Cities in Hat Yai and Udon Thani (Thailand); Iloilo and Bacolod (Philippines); Rantepao and Makale in the Tana Toraja Region, Sulawesi (Indonesia); Qingdao and Changzhou (China); Warsaw, Zabrze, and Katowice (Poland); Istanbul (Turkey); and Vancouver (Canada).

RANKING URBAN PROBLEMS

The catalog of urban problems presented in the regional chapters could well lead one to become a pessimist about the future of cities, as many cities have what seem to be irresolvable problems, many of which appear to be worsening. To gauge the severity of problems afflicting cities around the world, the regional authors of this text have rated their respective regions in regard to a number of persistent problems. They have used a scale of 1 to 5, with 1 indicating the problem is not serious and 5 indicating it is very serious (fig. 13.6). Although it is difficult to generalize about regions characterized by great internal variability, this snapshot illustrates that poverty is considered of greater concern in Central America and the Caribbean, South and Southeast Asia, and Sub-Saharan Africa than elsewhere. AIDS is seen as serious worldwide, but especially in Southeast Asia and Sub-Saharan Africa; ecological issues are of medium concern in most regions except Central America and the Caribbean; and gender issues are perceived as serious in the Greater Middle East, Southeast and South Asia, and Sub-Saharan Africa. The equity (rich-poor) gap is a concern in most regions. Oceania, East Asia, and Europe, followed by North America, consistently had the lowest rankings, in other words, they are considered to have the most livable cities.

WHAT IF? FUTURE SCENARIOS

One way to consider the severity of the problems depicted in figure 13.6 is to consider scenarios, that is, a series of "what if" events. When considering urban or regional futures, some events might easily be predicted, such as growing energy demands associated with population increases. But there also likely will be unanticipated events, such as the social impacts of inexpensive cures for HIV/AIDS, more women leading political parties, major environmental crises (the politics of water shortages), and the rise of maverick city mayors. Surprise events are also likely to occur in rich, industrialized, and democratically run cities as well as those that are poor and plagued with high disease, crime, and unemployment rates. Whether predicted or unexpected scenarios occur, their impact usually transcends the administrative limits of any city. Twelve overlapping "what if" problems and solutions are suggested below (in no particular order of importance).

The Natural Environment

From the monsoons of South Asia to the earthquakes of California, major natural disasters already bring death and destruction to urban areas around the world in both MDCs and LDCs. As the urban population grows, especially in hazard-prone areas, the potential for loss of life and property will only increase.

Global climate change as a result of human misuse of the environment could have devastating impacts on cities. Rising sea level threatens coastal cities everywhere and, as new weather patterns destroy crop and livestock economies, urban food supplies could be threatened as well. Megaengineering projects (airports, hydropower dams, irrigation systems) might also result in widespread environmental destruction.

Unknown and deadly human, plant, and animal diseases and viruses could be carried by humans, in food products, by pets, and through water and air and enter urban areas. The diffusion could come from residents

Problems \ Regions	U.S. and Canada	Middle America and Caribbean	South America	Europe	Russia	Greater Middle East	Sub-Saharan Africa	South Asia	Southeast Asia	East Asia	Australia/Pacific Islands
Level of Poverty	2	4	4	2	4	3	5	4.5	5	2	2
Equity (rich/poor gap)	5	4	5	3	5	4	5	4.5	5	3	3
Overall Quality of Life	3	3.5	3	2	3	3	4	3.5	4	1.5	2
Level of Unemployment & Underemployment	2	4	4	2	4	4	5	4	4	3.5	2
Level of HIV/AIDS	2	4	2	2	3	1	5	2	4	2.5	1
Population Fertility	4	2.7	2	4	3	5	3.5	3.5	3	1	1
Level of Aged (>65)	2	2.5	2	5	4	1	1.5	2	2	3.5	3
Ecosystem Quality	2	5	3	3	2	3	3	3	5	3.5	2
Physical Infrastructure (roads, bridges, etc.)	4	3.5	3	2	3	4	4	4	4	1.5	1
Sanitation/Housing	5	3.5	4	2	2	4	5	4.5	5	1.5	1
Levels of Pollution (air, water, soil)	3	4	3	2	2	3	2	4	5	2.5	2
Gender Equality	2	2.5	3	3	2	5	4	4.5	4	2.5	2
Quality/Levels of Education/Literacy	2	2.5	3	1	2	4	3.5	3	2	1	1
Quality/Effectiveness of Governments	3	3	4	1	4	5	4.5	3	1	2.5	2

1 ←——→ 5

(Not a serious problem) (A very serious problem)

Figure 13.6 Ranking of Problems in Major World Regions. *Source*: Regional chapter authors.

traveling anywhere for holidays, pilgrimages, sporting events, or military campaigns.

Cities dependent on various energy sources for their electricity, transportation, and communication could face unexpected disruptions and complete collapses in supplies, and thus rationing, because of heavy demands from anomalous weather, overloaded power sources, malfunctioning satellite systems, accidents at antiquated nuclear power facilities, or the spread of "deadly" computer viruses. These failures would likely affect public transportation, communication-dependent services and industries, stock markets, hospitals, schools, homes, and government services. Cities and urban regions anywhere could be affected.

The Social and Cultural Environment

Surprise military, biological, computer, and environmental terrorism could be directed against major cities by international, national, or local renegade groups that are networked. After 9–11 in the United States, the number and types of potential targets have increased. Likely targets include major political, military, and corporate headquarters (banking, media, medical, data processing), transportation and communication networks, high-rise office buildings, sites of major sporting events, water and energy supplies and delivery systems, cherished religious sites, national monuments, squatter and immigrant settlements, and wealthy gated communities.

Large-scale refugee populations could flee across political borders in South, Southeast, and East Asia or West, East, and Southern Africa in search of food, employment, safety, and political freedom. Areas where rich cities border the poor world, such as North Africa/Southern Europe and U.S. borders with Mexico and Caribbean countries, could be affected.

Civil unrest and violence would likely be accompanied by massive breakdowns in law and order. The causes would stem from large numbers of new rural migrants moving to the primate cities, rising unemployment and underemployment rates among new immigrants, and confrontations between old and new populations. These conditions favor the emergence of charismatic figures who may be anti-West, antitechnology, antidemocracy, anti–ruling establishment, or anti-immigrant.

Social and economic gaps could surface between the landless and propertied, the educated elite and illiterate, the favored few and marginalized masses, the new and old monied classes, and those who are or are not "wired." Cultural clashes could emerge based on differences in religious values, medical breakthroughs (cloning and euthanasia), changing gender roles in society, and values depicted in Western media. The clashes may result in frustration, hatred, and distrust of the powerful, plus the destruction of symbols of outside power and wealth.

The number and percentage of elders will continue to increase in MDC and LDC cities. Because of declining fertility rates, better nutrition, and better health care, people are living longer lives. With an increasing elderly population, there are increased problems of developing new welfare programs in societies with strong family traditions, single-child households, and stay-at-home women cultures.

The Economic Environment

The financial collapse of entire cities and metropolitan regions in older industrialized and urbanized parts of Europe, North America, Russia, and East Asia could occur because of capital investments and skilled labor moving to more prosperous cities and regions, and because of the failure of existing states to bail out troubled cities.

One consequence of the above could be investment being directed away from traditional centers of investment (Europe, North America, and East Asia) and to primate cities in Africa and Asia. Small city-states such as Brunei,

Bahrain, Kuwait, Barbados, Estonia, Slovenia, and Senegal might be among the new winners.

The Political Environment

New actors could appear on the political scene of MDC and LDC cities, including those who live transnational and peripatetic lives and hold multinational citizenships. They could face problems satisfying multistate requirements for citizenship, voting, property ownership, opening of bank accounts, and running for political office. These "stateless nomads" could include seasonal workers (in agriculture, tourism, and entertainment) and high-flying jet-setters.

POTENTIAL SOLUTIONS TO URBAN PROBLEMS

All problems have solutions, which range from easy fixes to those requiring major funding, new commitments of human resources, and imaginative thinking.

Solving Economic Problems

Investment in New Infrastructure

Investments by major international lending institutions and wealthy countries could help construct new transportation and telecommunication corridors linking cities not currently integrated into macroregional or continental systems. Examples include constructing fiber-optic cables and satellite relay stations across Amazonia, from West to East Africa, across Central Asia, or across Northeast Asia.

LDCs Investing in MDCs

Emerging rich, well-endowed, and powerful LDCs, including China, India, Brazil, Mexico, and South Africa, could use their incomes from natural resource extraction and a skilled labor sector to assist economically marginalized cities in Europe and elsewhere with loans and credit for economic restructuring. The "talent-drain" could be the reverse of previous generations; that is, traditionally rich MDCs could experience skilled labor shortages and welcome capital and talent coming from "emerging rich" LDCs.

Subsidizing Investment in Frontier Areas

To stimulate settlement and economic development in marginal, worn out, and new frontier areas considered environmentally unsafe or unhealthy, governments could provide subsidies and tax havens for companies, universities, individuals, and groups willing to commit themselves to long-term residence in these harsh lands. These new settlements could range from large gated communities to smart cities to subsistence villages.

Solving Social Problems

Empowerment of Women

This change will be evident in cities in all countries, but especially where there are strong commitments to eradicating illiteracy, HIV/AIDS, and child exploitation; to investing in local grassroots efforts; and to supporting political leadership.

Living with Alternative Structures

Rather than policies of rigid conformity, there could be groups and communities exploring alternative models of governance, policing, and administration. While some groups may choose very traditional and local forms of government and group participation, others may be a mix of local and global participatory processes. Still others may exhibit high degrees of nonconformity or even totalitarianism.

Using Government to Solve Problems

Mafia-Like Organizations

Criminal mafias and similar organized groups could replace traditional powerful or democratically elected elites. They could administer and finance bankrupt cities in parts of North America, Europe, and Russia and even new cities in Asia and Africa. These groups might appear as new owners/rulers of island states in the Mediterranean, Caribbean, and Pacific. Some gated communities may be run as dictatorships.

Greater Voice for New Communities

Two new groups could call for increased participation in urban governance: they are the new African and Asian diaspora communities in European, North American, and Australian cities and the dispossessed, poor, and recent rural migrants in LDC cities. Both groups could become sizable portions of the urban labor force in their new regions or cities and petition/protest for improved welfare programs, better housing and education, and political rights.

New Transborder Governing Systems

New types of coordinated city government and planning could emerge in those rich and poor world cities that straddle international boundaries. The separate government entities in such areas, already linked by thousands of daily commuters, could merge for cost effectiveness and to find more efficient solutions to mutual transportation, security, and environmental problems.

A World Organization of Cities

This organization could operate either separately or alongside the United Nations. If within the UN, it could be a separate chamber, for example, a permanent World Urban Cabinet comprising delegates from the largest agglomerations in each major world region. The body could address problems facing MDC and LDC agglomerations, including those that cross international borders.

Using Planning to Solve Problems

Corporate Ownership of Cities

A new class of owners could emerge on the world scene. Cities could be essentially bought and sold on international financial markets like food, energy supplies, industrial products, utilities, and transportation/communication products. Cities could be governed by transnational corporations rather than by traditional political parties or the state. This development would represent a further "hollowing out" of large territorial states and their replacement by city-state governments. Some cities might vote for separation from existing states, perhaps even if the alternative is control by corporations.

Triage Planning Strategies

Triage could be implemented by both rich and poor countries. Government officials might divide cities and city regions into three groups: (a) those worth saving to ensure healthy economies and societies, (b) those that might respond to short-term infusions of national and international human and financial resources, and (c) those to be left to fend for themselves.

Transnational "Urban Response Teams"

In much the same way that disaster-response teams are called on to aid communities facing disease outbreaks or experiencing major natural disasters, urban response teams could assist communities facing serious and unexpected problems: breakdowns in energy supplies, destruction of water systems, massive refugee populations, major industrial and transportation accidents, prolonged social conflicts, collapses of metropolitan governance, and massive failures in security systems. Response teams could draw on talent from around the world.

TYPOLOGIES OF EXISTING AND EMERGING SYSTEMS OF CITIES

Future cities and city systems in the world's regions will have some features similar to those of today, but also some new features. Realizing that many cities may exhibit more than one form, we suggest some snapshots of future urban systems (see fig. 13.7).

- *A single major urban cluster* that will increase in numbers, density, and territory. Frequently these are LDC primate cities.
- *Regional clusters* of small and large cities within the same state that will grow and gradually coalesce. Examples will include southeast Brazil, the lower Nile, and many parts of the United States (fig. 13.8).
- *Transborder regional systems* include cities of varying sizes that cross several international boundaries. Examples are the Malay peninsula, northern South America, and the Persian/Arabian Gulf states.
- *International gateway cities* that were formerly closed now have access to new water and land frontiers and present opportunities for investors and those seeking new jobs. Examples are cities in the Southern Cone of South America, Amazonia, and Northeast Asia.
- *Cross-border cities* exist side by side and will continue to experience either symmetrical or asymmetrical growth. Examples include Brazzaville and Kinshasa, Buenos Aires and Montevideo, San Diego and Tijuana, and Seattle and Vancouver.
- *Frontier cities* emerge with development of new natural (mineral) or human resources (tourism, retirement, etc.) or as foci for new transportation and communication networks. Examples are Dunedin for the Antarctic, Darwin for Southeast Asia, and Kashgar and Urumqi for Central Asia.
- *Corridor city systems* include cities spaced unevenly along railroads, highways, and rivers. These "beads on a string" experience asymmetrical growth. Examples include the Trans-Siberian railroad, the Trans-Amazonia highway, the revitalized Old Silk Road, and the proposed Trans-African highways from Dakar to Mombasa and Cairo to Cape Town.
- *Bypassed cities* experience persistent economic decline, an out-migration of youth, and an aging population and have dated infrastructures. They have lost their economic or political significance because of political shifts or declining demand for their services and goods. Examples include old mining and heavy-industrial centers in Eastern Europe, Western and Southern Russia, the Canadian Maritimes, and Appalachia.
- *Isolated cities* are at the termini of transportation and communications networks; they are often located in inaccessible and hostile environments. Examples include capital cities in the Sahara, the Eastern Caribbean, and the Pacific Islands.
- *Ephemeral cities* have populations with many residents who come and go, perhaps

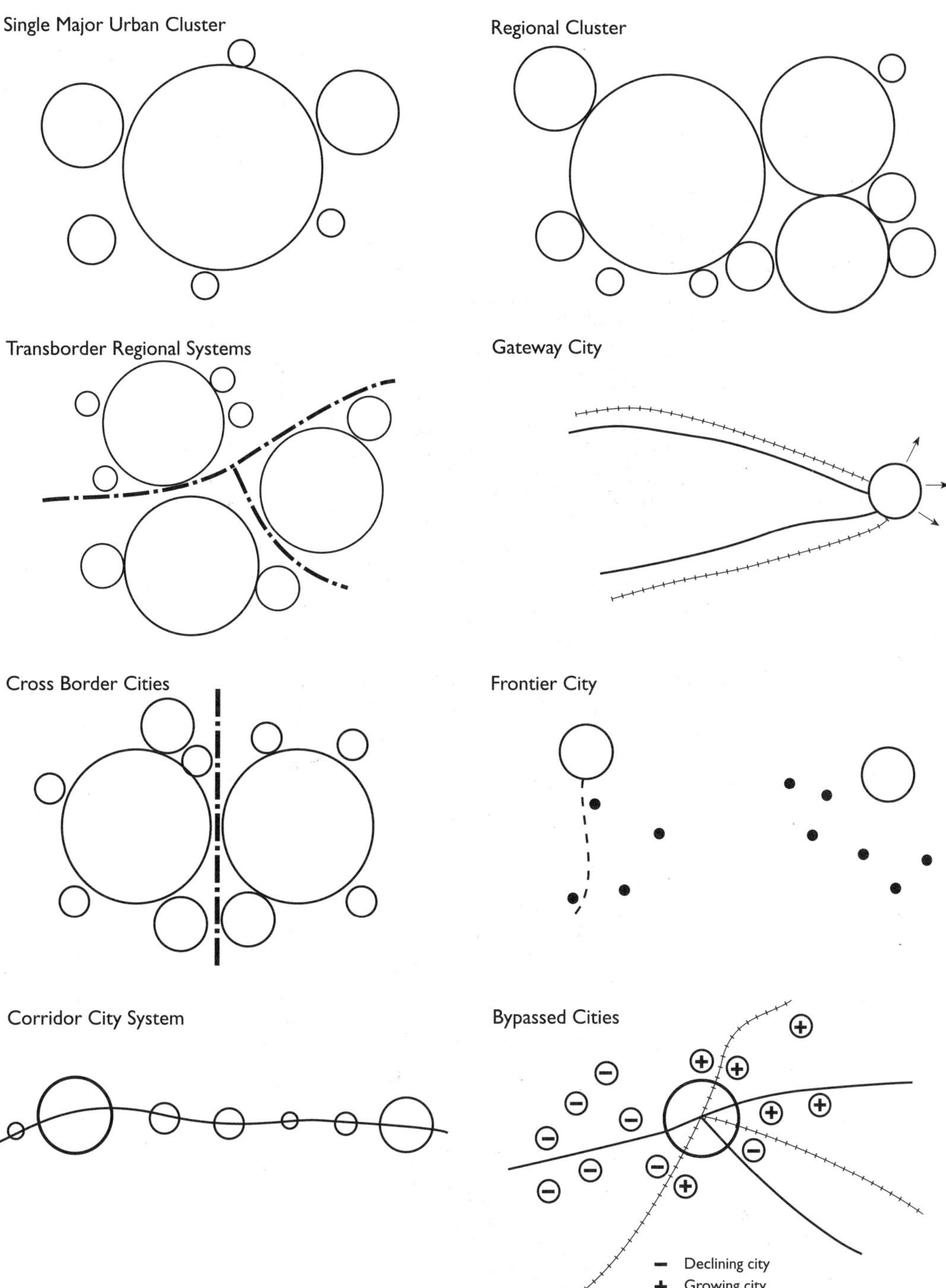

Figure 13.7 Systems of Cities: Existing and Emerging. *Source*: Stanley Brunn

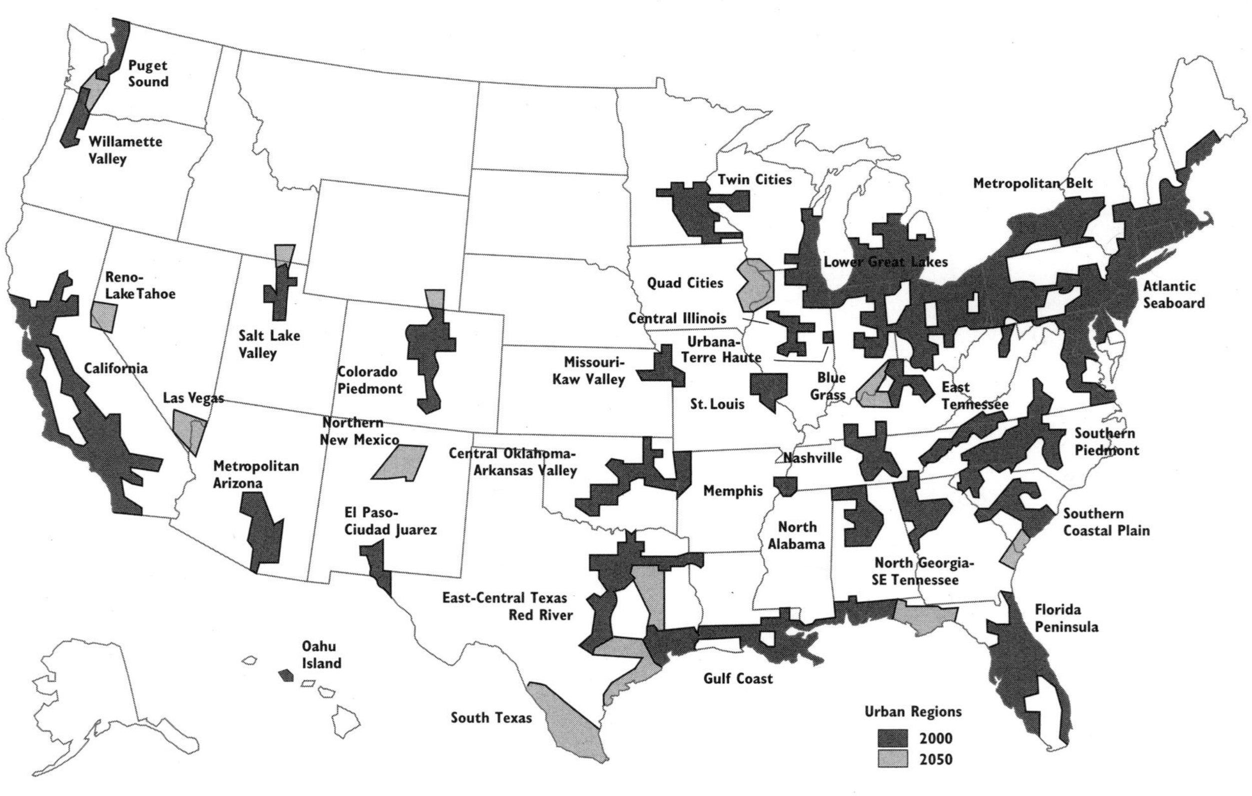

Figure 13.8 U.S. Urban Regions, 2050. *Source*: Stanley Brunn

staying for seasonal employment, or those regularly transferred to new locations by governments and corporations. Specialized university, military, health, and entertainment cities are prime examples.

- *Historic preservation cities* celebrate their pasts and use their heritage to generate income from tourism, retirees, and investments in historic preservation. Examples include Williamsburg, Vienna, and Fès. Some entire cities in Europe, North America, and elsewhere will become "museum," UNESCO, or national heritage sites.
- *Fun cities* are centers of hedonistic activities and have economies that thrive on the pursuit of entertainment and leisure. Examples include Orlando with Disney World, Las Vegas and Reno for casino gambling, and cities with major theme parks, regular sports events, or exotic and quasilegal forms of entertainment.
- *World cities* anchor dense commercial and cultural networks and include many cities that are recognized for their leading roles in finance, investment, and culture.
- *Global cities* are few and recognized for their pinnacle ranking in international organizations and networks. Tokyo, New York, and London are currently the only truly global cities (box 13.3).
- *Ecumenopolis*, a concept, developed by Constantin Doxiadis, the originator of the term *ekistics* (the science of human settlements), describes a vast urban system that links major populated areas on major transportation and communication corridors (fig. 13.9). While highly futuristic, this continental linking of future urban regions is not beyond the realm of possibility.

LOOKING FORWARD

Numerous questions arise about city size, functions, and organization when contemplating cities at 2050, 2100, 3000, and beyond. Will humans always have a need for cities, especially with faster and cheaper communication and connectedness? While diversity has long been a distinguishing feature of the urban fabric, might new forms of identity and social separation emerge that are based on new loyalty units and tribes, such as sports, lifestyles, and interests, more than on cultural traditions, ethnicity, and class? Might transurban loyalties replace those that are territorial based?

What will be the impacts of wireless communications on privacy and the lives of urban people? Will new behavioral norms evolve based on hypermobility and placelessness? Do these technologies promote gender and class equity? Will a voice and visual Internet world inhibit or resolve pressing urban social and political problems? Will fluidity in time more than space define the urban resident of the mid-21st century? What happens to the mosaic of the world's languages if international commerce is increasingly conducted in American English? What are the impacts of single-child households on urban population with growing numbers of elders? What are the long-term impacts of increased rates of HIV/AIDS on rural and urban residents in Africa and Asia?

As rural ways of life disappear, will "wilderness" rather than rural become the antithesis of urban? Will rural areas become "future museums" and fantasy places for the urban world to visit, the places where die-hard traditionalists reside, and places where societies' rejects and those with nonacceptable lifestyles live? Will the production of food (long considered vital in retaining rural livelihoods and for sup-

Box 13.3 Globalization and World Cities

Peter J. Taylor

Although there is a large literature on "world" or "global" cities, little evidence has been gathered on what actually makes such cities so important: their connections with other cities across the world. Thus, if world cities are indeed the crossroads of globalization, then we need to consider seriously how we measure intercity relations. It was just such thinking that led to the setting up of the Globalization and World Cities (GaWC) Study Group and Network at Loughborough University, United Kingdom, as a virtual center for world cities research.

GaWC currently carries out three strands of research:

- *Comparative City Connectivity Studies:* These focus on relations between chosen cities as they respond to particular events. In one study, Singapore, New York, and London were compared in the way in which their service sectors responded to the 1997 Asian financial crisis. In another study, relations between London and Frankfurt were studied in the wake of the launch of the euro currency. The generic finding of this work is that city competitive processes are generally much less important than cooperative processes carried out through office networks within the private sector.
- *Elite Labor Migrations between Cities:* Moving skilled labor around to different world cities is found to be a key globalization strategy for financial firms wanting to embed their businesses into the world-city network. For instance, London firms regularly send staff to Paris, Amsterdam, and Frankfurt to provide "seamless" service across European cities. The prime finding of this research is that a transnational space of flows is produced as a necessary prerequisite for firms accumulating financial knowledge.
- *Global Network Connectivity of Cities:* A world city network is specified as an amalgam of the office networks of financial and business service firms. This network has three levels: a network level of cities in the world economy level, a nodal level of cities as global service centers, and a subnodal level of global service firms that are the prime creators of the world city network. This specification directs a data collection that enables the global network connectivities of world cities to be calculated. These results are based on a uniquely large set of data for the year 2000 covering one hundred firms in 316 cities across the world.

GaWC research goes beyond world city formation to study world city network formation. The focus has been on this complex process within economic globalization. For a full global urban analysis, further research is required within other important strands of globalization. The Study Group's website is: www.lboro.ac.uk/gawc.

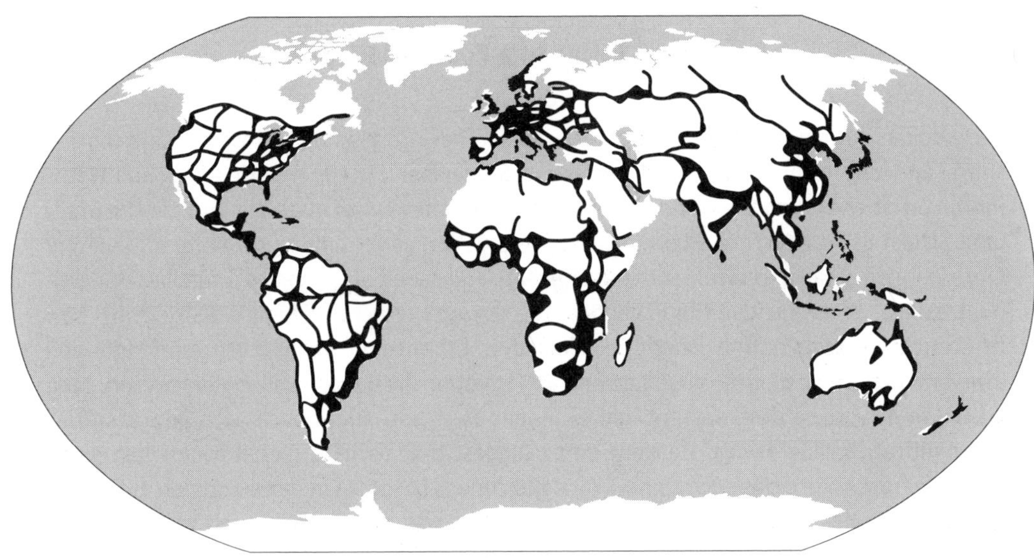

Figure 13.9 Ecumenopolis: The Global City. *Source*: Adapted from C.A. Doxiadis, "Man's Movements and His Settlements," *Ekistics* 29, no. 174 (1970), 318.

porting cities) by chemical and pharmaceutical factories signal the end of agrarian life?

How will cities and city life be affected by major events, such as September 11, 2001 (box 13.4)? Will people choose to work in different environments? Will urbanites become more supportive or less supportive of each other? Will skyscrapers, places of high density, and neighborhoods of new immigrants be the new urban landscapes of fear? Will the perception of domestic and international terrorism change lifestyles, modes of transportation, and discretionary spending? Will fantasy and exotic tourism be casualties of the leisure economy?

What new places and types of living might emerge? Some futurists foresee huge residential ocean liners or floating cities that circle the globe or ply major tourist rivers and the coastlines of wealthy megacities. Still others suggest using the "oil platform" model to build huge permanent or temporary residences anywhere. Might terratexture (underground) spaces become more popular? These alternative settings might be used to house the wealthy, the elites, and the powerful, but also the undesirable, unwanted, and unhealthy.

Will the world's future political agendas be dominated by cities rather than nation-states, by urban agglomerations in the present LDCs rather than the MDCs? Will the world's development divide be increasingly urban-rural rather than North-South? What will China's urban future look like as the population becomes more urban, globally aware, and wealthy? Will China, India, and Indonesia form the "Global Growth Triangle" of the late 21st century? Does the ethnic diversity in Sub-Saharan African cities make a cauldron for conflict or a model ripe for cooperation? Does urban homogeneity also contribute to conflict? Can cities of 10, 20, or 30 million be governed? Could the future megacity be composed of fifty rival "city governments," each competing for the best talent and most financial resources? Will territory

Box 13.4 Cities in a Post–9-11 World

Geographers, urban planners, architects, and engineers are among those considering the short- and long-term impacts of the events of September 11, 2001, in New York and Washington on cities around the world. Peter Marcuse, a professor in urban planning in the Graduate School of Architecture, Planning and Preservation at Columbia University in New York City, wrote an essay a week after the 9-11 events and called attention to a number of pertinent issues.* These include the impacts of the terrorist attacks on high-density cities, how personal travel (commuting) might be affected, whether employment patterns of high- and low-wage service employees might shrink, and whether the benefits of agglomeration, long crucial in downtown development and economic strength, might shift with new priorities and political considerations. He went on to suggest that perhaps global companies would shy away from huge cities such as New York and choose to locate in more outlying areas. The impact of the destruction of the World Trade Center was already being felt in other cities with what he called "trophy skyscrapers," including Frankfurt and Kuala Lumpur. His final comments were directed at security issues that "threaten the core of social and political life" of those living and working in cities. Public spaces, Marcuse added, will become less public and likely subject to more surveillance, while increased funding for police and law enforcement is expected, even though this will reduce the civil liberties of citizens. By contrast, controlled spaces such as malls will become more popular. In conclusion, Marcuse reflected on what the events of September 11 may mean to those in the academy who have devoted their careers to studying cities and the effects of globalization. He wrote: "Whatever we have thought and said and written up till now has been subjected to a major shock from 'outside the system' (although inside it in a terrible way), and will need significant reassessment."

In late 2001, a task force of the Association of American Geographers, composed of leading scholars with interests in urban technology and GIS, explored ways to collect and map data to aid in delivering vital services during and following emergencies, to rebuild infrastructures, and to support homeland security initiatives.

*Peter Marcuse, "All Cities Will Change," urbgeog@listserv.arizona.edu, September 17, 2001.

cease to be the basis for government and replaced by loyalty to transnational corporations, new diasporas, and regional sports?

While answering these questions is difficult, we anticipate the human settlement pattern will include preindustrial remnants existing alongside postmodern cities, smart (wired) cities alongside bypassed (little-wired) communities. There may even be governable and ungovernable places, segregated and integrated social structures, and innovative and laggard cities in the same region (fig. 13.10).

While pessimism about the future of cities might seem to be justified, based on the panoply of problems detailed in previous chapters, to succumb to this view is to give up

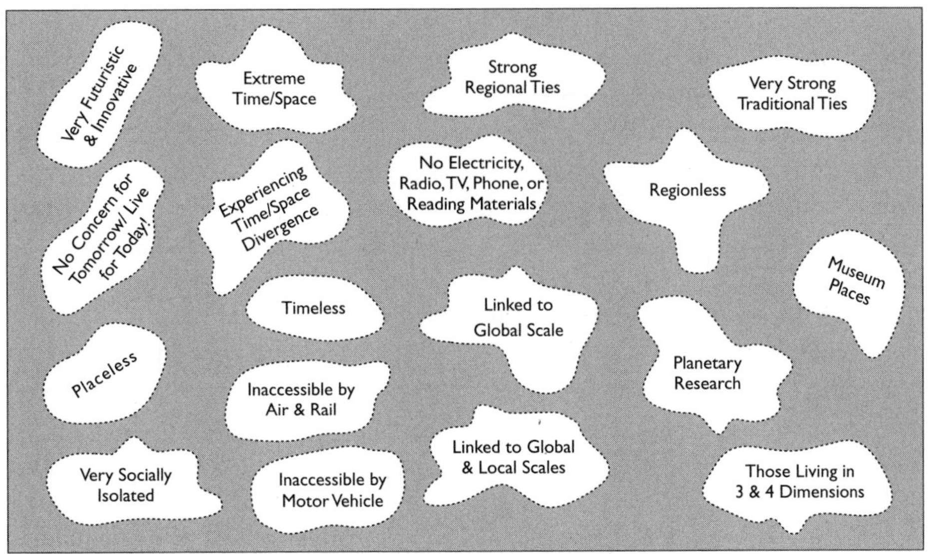

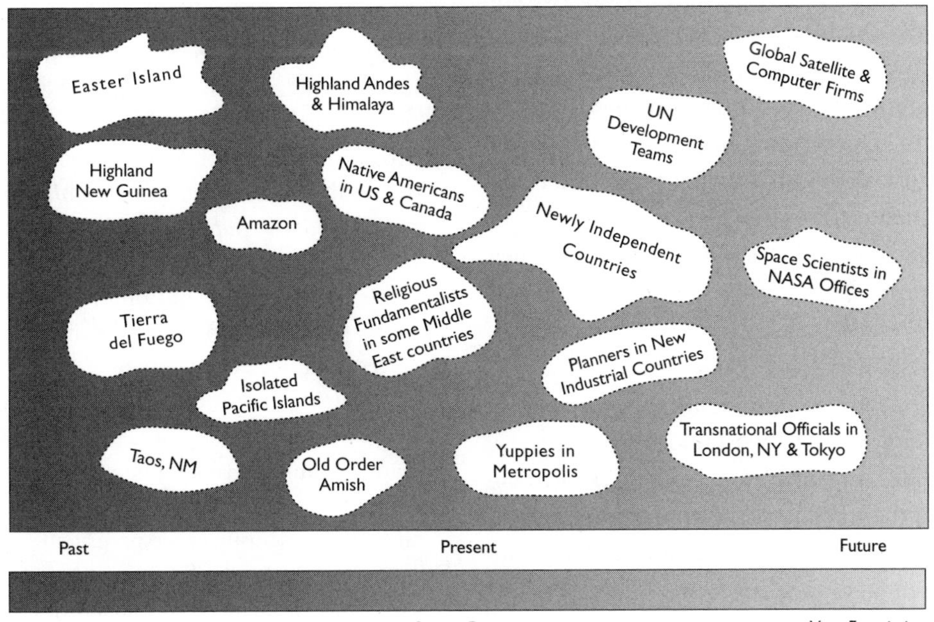

Figure 13.10 Future Time Regions. *Source*: Stanley Brunn, "Human Rights and Welfare in the Electronic State," in *Information Tectonics*, ed. Mark I. Wilson and Kenneth E. Corey (New York: Wiley, 2000), 60. Reprinted with permission.

hope. Humanity survives on hope, including hope in the future of cities. It is important to remember that cities continue to resonate with the very qualities that characterized the first cities in history. For thousands of years, humans have chosen to live in concentrated settlements of varying sizes around the world. Cities will always be:

- Tapestries of rich cultural diversity (religious, ethnic, lifestyle, etc.)
- Places where new identities transcend traditional social-class, local, and regional identities
- Centers of economic and social exchanges
- Opportunities for improving the quality of life for all ages
- Sources of alternative media, lifestyles, and counterculture
- Places to invest in human capital that accompanies economic growth
- Sites for investments in new goods and services (tourism, banking, entertainment, etc.)
- Incubators for designing and testing new products and ideas
- Nodes of political reform, often transregional and transnational
- "Action" places for political events, protests, and ad hoc demonstrations.
- Sites for international events (sports, entertainment, culture) and conferences
- Bases of untapped human resource potential to solve problems
- Symbols to revive the human spirit
- Sources of great architecture and art (old and new)
- Places that inspire human creativity, inventions, and innovations
- Homes of future leaders in society (intellectual, religious, scientific, political, arts, sports)

There never has been and never will be a single city anywhere in which all residents are happy, content, and peaceful. Utopia is unattainable. But among the new and old inhabitants in each city there can be a conscious effort to improve the human condition and to recognize that cities are special places that bring out the best of human qualities.

SUGGESTED READINGS

Abler, Ron, et al. *Human Geography in a Shrinking World.* North Scituate, Mass.: Duxbury, 1975. Chapters by fourteen geographers who discuss information and communications, future worlds, and futuristic planning.

Castells, Manuel. *The Internet Galaxy: Reflections on the Internet, Business, and Society.* New York: Oxford University Press, 2001. One of the leading scholars on Internet culture and commerce examines how the Internet is affecting urban and regional planning as well as society.

Craig, William J., et al., eds. *Community Participation and Geographic Information Systems.* London: Taylor and Francis, 2002. Includes numerous examples of community groups using GIS for empowerment and gaining voices in public policy.

Dodge, Martin, and Rob Kitchen. *Mapping Cyberspace.* New York: Routledge, 2000. This team of human geographers/cartographers explores, with many innovative graphics, issues of representing cyberspace at all scales.

Ducatel, Ken, et al., eds. *The Information Society: Work and Life in an Age of Globalization.* Lanham, Md.: Rowman & Littlefield, 2000. Social scientists, including geographers, consider issues about the impacts of information technologies on the workplace, gender, the household, education, and democracy.

Hall, Peter G. *Cities of Tomorrow. An Intellectual History of City Planning in the Twentieth Century.* Oxford, England: Blackwell, 1988. A history of the ideology and practice of urban planning, regarded by some as the successor to Lewis Mumford's *The City in History: Its Origins, Its Transformations, and Its Prospects* (New York: Harcourt, Brace and World, 1961).

Janelle, Donald G., and David C. Hodge, eds. *Information, Place, and Cyberspace: Issues of Accessibility.* New York: Springer, 2000. Explorations into the geographies of cyberspace and the information society, including transportation, accessibility, visualization, and representation.

Kotkin, Joel. *The New Geography: How the Digital Revolution Is Reshaping the American Landscape.* New York: Random House, 2000. An exploration of how the digital revolution is changing the way we live and work, including the essential role of cities in an information age.

Leinbach, Thomas R., and Stanley D. Brunn, eds. *The Worlds of E-Commerce: Economic, Geographical and Social Dimensions.* New York: Wiley, 2001. Discussions of theoretical and conceptual issues of e-commerce as well as developments in banking and finance, retailing, recruiting, government regulations, and international development.

Ruchelman, Leonard I. *Cities in the Third Wave: The Technological Transformation of Urban America.* Chicago: Burnham, 2000. Considers the impact of new space-adjusting computer technologies on cities, including a discussion of emerging city types.

Urban Land Institute (ULI). *ULI on the Future: Cities Post 9/11.* Washington, D.C.: ULI, 2002. Five articles on issues facing American cities, including security, immigration reform, corporate (re)location, housing, and civic leadership.

Wheeler, James O., et al. *Cities in the Telecommunications Age.* New York: Routledge, 2000. An interdisciplinary look at the impacts of recent developments in telecommunications on the economies, public policy, and society of urban regions.

Wilson, Mark, and Kenneth Corey, eds. *Information Tectonics: Spatial Organization in an Electronic Age.* New York: Wiley, 2000. The concept of electronic space is explored through analyses of commerce, finance, telecommunications, cybercommunities, governance, human rights and welfare, and urban and regional development.

Appendix: Populations of Urban Agglomerations with 750,000 Inhabitants or More in 2000, by Country, 1950, 1975, 2000, and projected for 2015

Country/Agglomeration	*Population (thousands)*			
	1950	*1975*	*2000*	*2015*
AFGHANISTAN				
Kabul	216	674	2,602	5,397
ALGERIA				
Algiers	469	1,507	2,761	4,142
ANGOLA				
Luanda	138	669	2,697	5,144
ARGENTINA				
Buenos Aires	5,042	9,144	12,024	13,185
Córdoba	416	878	1,368	1,613
Mendoza	248	534	934	1,165
Rosario	532	878	1,279	1,523
San Miguel de Tucumán	221	424	792	1,032
ARMENIA				
Yerevan	371	911	1,407	1,490
AUSTRALIA				
Adelaide	430	882	1,064	1,173
Brisbane	442	928	1,622	2,027
Melbourne	1,331	2,561	3,232	3,605
Perth	312	770	1,329	1,605
Sydney	1,896	2,960	3,907	4,467
AUSTRIA				
Vienna	1,787	2,001	2,065	2,069
AZERBAIJAN				
Baku	793	1,429	1,948	2,137
BANGLADESH				
Chittagong	290	969	361	6,360
Dhaka	417	2,173	12,519	22,766
Khulna	39	498	1,442	2,467
Rajshahi	39	150	1,035	2,003
BELARUS				
Minsk	323	1,120	1,667	1,667
BELGIUM				
Brussels	968	1,128	1,135	1,135

BOLIVIA				
La Paz	319	703	1,460	2,098
Santa Cruz	42	234	1,062	1,676
BRAZIL				
Belém	241	826	1,658	2,158
Belo Horizonte	385	2,095	4,224	5,395
Brasilia	39	826	2,016	2,667
Campinas	105	699	1,895	2,752
Campo Grande	33	204	821	1,437
Curitiba	149	1,117	2,562	3,457
Fortaleza	271	1,307	3,066	4,338
Goiânia	56	537	1,117	1,409
Maceió	123	331	886	1,359
Manaus	141	454	1,467	2,328
Natal	105	339	806	1,147
Porto Alegre	448	1,908	3,757	4,838
Recife	670	2,078	3,346	3,986
Rio de Janeiro	2,965	7,963	10,652	11,543
Salvador	406	1,454	3,238	4,436
Santos	245	786	1,270	1,506
São José dos Campos	58	300	972	1,560
São Luis	121	354	968	1,459
São Paulo	2,528	10,333	17,962	21,229
Teresina	93	296	848	1,310
BULGARIA				
Sofia	547	960	1,187	1,187
BURKINA FASO				
Ouagadougou	30	165	831	1,659
CAMBODIA				
Phnom Penh	364	397	1,070	1,766
CAMEROON				
Douala	101	380	1,642	2,607
Yaoundé	50	276	1,420	2,281
CANADA				
Calgary	132	457	953	1,228
Edmonton	163	543	944	1,101
Montreal	1,344	2,792	3,480	3,754
Ottawa	282	676	1,081	1,231
Toronto	1,068	2,770	4,752	5,679
Vancouver	556	1,150	2,049	2,513
CHILE				
Santiago	1,330	3,234	5,467	6,495
CHINA				
Anshan	479	1,082	1,453	1,592
Anshun	46	242	789	1,057
Baotou	97	918	1,319	1,554
Beijing	3,913	8,545	10,839	11,671
Benxi	414	713	957	1,065
Changchun	765	1,558	3,093	4,944
Changde	75	519	1,374	1,774
Changsha	623	942	1,775	2,674
Changzhou	111	360	886	1,202
Chengdu	725	2,076	3,294	4,030
Chifeng	133	343	1,087	1,318

Chongqing	1,680	2,439	4,900	7,440
Dalian	678	1,396	2,628	3,048
Daqing	264	605	1,076	1,275
Datong	165	877	1,165	1,210
Dongguan	224	805	1,319	1,250
Fushun	634	1,082	1,413	1,565
Fuxin	147	572	785	910
Fuyu	682	836	1,025	1,223
Fuzhou	492	1,012	1,397	1,519
Guangzhou	1,343	3,102	3,893	4,192
Guiyang	195	1,140	2,533	4,418
Handan	136	769	1,996	2,481
Hangzhou	638	1,097	1,780	2,388
Harbin	1,012	2,288	2,928	3,135
Hefei	256	637	1,242	1,550
Hengyang	167	410	799	1,008
Heze	381	780	1,600	2,406
Huaian	740	875	1,232	1,504
Huaibei	207	375	814	1,246
Huainan	498	980	1,354	1,643
Huhehaote	109	617	978	1,114
Hunjiang	553	653	772	907
Huzhou	678	879	1,077	1,235
Jiamusi	220	437	874	1,311
Jiaxing	448	613	791	928
Jilin	371	952	1,435	1,712
Jinan	598	1,236	2,568	2,996
Jingmen	447	747	1,153	1,445
Jining	68	335	1,019	1,323
Jinxi	226	583	1,821	2,775
Jinzhou	326	530	834	1,047
Jixi	157	656	949	1,194
Kaifeng	349	536	769	942
Kunming	641	1,223	1,701	1,962
Lanzhou	315	1,202	1,730	2,024
Leshan	604	863	1,137	1,324
Linqing	258	479	891	1,286
Linyi	411	1,013	2,498	4,076
Liuan	651	1,088	1,818	2,491
Liupanshui	1,275	1,606	2,023	2,435
Liuzhou	131	464	928	1,283
Luoyang	123	797	1,451	1,951
Mianyang	479	699	1,065	1,446
Mudanjiang	209	464	801	939
Nanchang	343	896	1,722	2,661
Nanchong	66	169	1,055	1,614
Nanjing	973	1,938	2,740	3,132
Nanning	157	659	1,311	1,639
Neijiang	83	214	1,393	1,653
Ningbo	470	819	1,173	1,313
Pingxiang	742	1,097	1,502	1,783
Qingdao	894	1,106	2,316	2,801
Qiqihar	265	1,090	1,435	1,601
Shanghai	5,333	11,143	12,887	13,598
Shantou	322	606	1,176	1,767
Shenyang	2,091	3,697	4,828	5,429
Shenzhen	105	270	1,131	1,645
Shijiazhuang	307	938	1,603	2,076

Suining	763	1,044	1,428	1,788
Suqian	519	811	1,189	1,470
Suzhou	457	619	1,183	1,813
Taian	829	1,157	1,503	1,749
Taiyuan	629	1,519	2,415	2,871
Tangshan	640	1,161	1,671	2,074
Tianjin	2,374	6,160	9,156	10,319
Tianmen	719	1,131	1,779	2,371
Tianshui	165	522	1,187	1,501
Tongliao	110	283	785	1,017
Wanxian	589	1,018	1,759	2,447
Weifang	183	472	1,287	1,586
Wenzhou	255	437	1,269	1,940
Wuhan	1,228	2,926	5,169	7,833
Wulumuqi (Urumqi)	102	715	1,415	1,924
Wuxi	572	730	1,127	1,391
Xi'an	650	1,939	3,123	3,714
Xiangxiang	664	777	908	1,061
Xiantao	689	1,054	1,614	2,126
Xianyang	103	353	896	1,218
Xiaoshan	1,070	1,097	1,124	1,236
Xinghua	1,282	1,412	1,556	1,766
Xintai	1,237	1,280	1,325	1,461
Xinju	600	764	973	1,182
Xinyi	195	397	808	1,216
Xuanzhou	586	695	823	968
Xuzhou	341	667	1,636	2,497
Yancheng	759	1,089	1,562	1,997
Yantai	114	295	1,681	2,564
Yichun (Heilongjiang)	554	741	904	1,012
Yichun (Jiangxi)	134	664	871	994
Yixing	911	1,004	1,108	1,259
Yiyang	397	734	1,343	1,904
Yangzhou	522	756	1,097	1,413
Yueyang	673	903	1,213	1,507
Yulin	688	1,036	1,558	2,037
Yuyao	611	720	848	995
Yuzhou	751	939	1,173	1,411
Zaoyang	522	765	1,121	1,450
Zaochuang	282	896	2,048	2,582
Zhangjiakou	304	521	880	1,204
Zhangjiangang	509	671	886	1,094
Zhanjiang	406	734	1,368	2,008
Zhaodong	615	723	851	998
Zhengzhou	521	1,227	2,070	2,711
Zibo	1,453	2,032	2,675	3,148
Zigong	564	795	1,072	1,295
CHINA, HONG KONG SAR				
Hong Kong	1,629	3,943	6,860	8,025
COLOMBIA				
Barranquilla	294	833	1,683	2,323
Bogotá	676	3,071	6,771	8,970
Bucaramanga	110	407	937	1,302
Cali	231	1,056	2,233	3,158
Cartagena	107	335	845	1,262
Cucata	70	264	772	1,080
Medellin	376	1,539	2,866	3,872

CONGO				
Brazzaville	216	340	1,306	2,259
CONGO, DEM. REPUBLIC OF THE				
Kinshasa	173	1,735	5,054	9,883
Lubumbashi	115	390	965	1,950
COSTA RICA				
San José	183	526	961	1,343
CROATIA				
Zaghreb	334	605	1,067	1,183
CUBA				
Havana	1,147	1,827	2,256	2,365
CZECH REPUBLIC				
Prague	1,002	1,125	1,203	1,203
DENMARK				
Copenhagen	1,212	1,381	1,332	1,330
DOMINICAN REPUBLIC				
Santiago de los Caballeros	89	350	804	1,064
Santo Domingo	219	1,094	2,563	3,397
ECUADOR				
Guayaquil	253	863	2,118	2,819
Quito	206	628	1,616	2,228
EGYPT				
Alexandria	1,038	2,241	3,506	4,330
Cairo	2,410	6,079	9,462	11,531
Shubra el Kheima	38	353	937	1,234
EL SALVADOR				
San Salvador	194	596	1,341	1,877
ETHIOPIA				
Addis Ababa	392	926	2,645	4,932
FINLAND				
Helsinki	365	582	937	937
FRANCE				
Lille	727	943	991	1,036
Lyon	572	1,185	1,353	1,446
Marseille	660	1,194	1,290	1,358
Paris	5,441	8,885	9,630	9,858
Toulouse	252	521	761	871
GEORGIA				
Tbilisi	574	993	1,406	1,406
GERMANY				
Aachen	710	951	1,060	1,070
Berlin	3,337	3,227	3,319	3,320
Bielefeld	941	1,127	1,294	1,310
Bremen	676	823	880	886
Hamburg	2,171	2,479	2,664	2,683
Hanover	990	1,210	1,283	1,291
Karlsruhe	632	861	977	988
Munich	1,258	1,957	2,291	2,317
Nuremberg	790	1,034	1,189	1,204
Rhine-Main (3)	2,295	3,215	3,681	3,718

Rhine-Neckar (4)	1,077	1,422	1,605	1,621
Rhine-Middle (5)	2,001	2,590	3,233	3,335
Rhine-Ruhr North (6)	5,296	6,448	6,531	6,554
Rhine-Ruhr South (7)	1,770	2,633	3,050	3,082
Saarland (8)	793	908	891	892
Stuttgart	1,483	2,300	2,672	2,703
GHANA				
Accra	250	869	1,868	2,890
GREECE				
Athens	1,783	2,738	3,116	3,138
Thessaloniki	292	617	789	825
GUATEMALA				
Guatemala City	428	715	3,242	5,268
GUINEA				
Conarky	39	561	1,232	2,073
HAITI				
Port-au-Prince	144	575	1,769	2,864
HONDURAS				
Tegucigalpa	74	298	949	1,492
HUNGARY				
Budapest	1,618	2,005	1,819	1,819
INDIA				
Agra	368	681	1,293	1,990
Ahmedabad	859	2,050	4,427	6,612
Allahabad	327	568	1,035	1,400
Amristar	332	512	955	1,452
Asansol	91	289	1,065	1,686
Aurangabad	65	218	868	1,461
Bangalore	764	2,111	5,567	8,391
Bhopal	97	488	1,425	2,148
Chandigarh	59	301	791	1,232
Chennai (Madras)	1,397	3,609	6,353	8,068
Coimbatore	265	810	1,420	2,044
Delhi	1,391	4,426	12,441	20,884
Dhanbad	69	526	1,046	1,497
Durg-Bhilainagar	18	330	906	1,337
Faridabad	49	232	1,018	1,977
Ghaziabad	42	181	928	2,027
Guwahati	151	347	797	1,230
Gwailor	238	465	855	1,120
Hubli-Dharwad	193	437	776	1,023
Hyderabad	1,122	2,086	5,445	7,513
Indore	306	663	1,597	2,626
Jabalpur	251	621	1,100	1,508
Jaipur	285	778	2,259	3,860
Jamshedpur	212	538	1,081	1,578
Jodhpur	178	388	833	1,157
Kolkata (Calcutta)	4,446	7,888	13,058	16,747
Kanpur	691	1,420	2,641	3,826
Kochi (Cochin)	187	532	1,340	1,721
Kozhikode (Calicut)	154	412	875	1,030
Lucknow	488	892	2,221	3,312
Ludhiana	149	479	1,368	2,011
Madurai	358	790	1,187	1,398
Meerut	230	432	1,143	1,733
Mumbai (Bombay)	2,981	7,347	16,086	22,577

Mysore	244	404	776	1,014
Nagpur	474	1,075	2,089	2,902
Nashik	154	330	1,117	1,997
Patna	279	643	1,658	2,883
Pune (Poona)	592	1,345	3,655	6,112
Rajkot	129	356	974	1,672
Ranchi	105	342	844	1,312
Solapur	273	445	853	1,330
Srinagar	248	494	954	1,374
Surat	219	642	2,699	5,715
Thiruvananthapuram	192	454	885	1,018
Tiruchchirapalli	217	522	837	1,080
Vadodara	207	571	1,465	2,127
Varanasi (Benares)	348	682	1,199	1,522
Vijayawada	157	419	999	1,294
Visakhapatnam	104	452	1,309	1,794
INDONESIA				
Bandar Lampung (Tanj)	28	228	915	1,595
Bandung	511	1,493	3,409	5,245
Jakarta	1,452	4,814	11,018	17,268
Malang	2,019	413	787	1,155
Medan	284	1,031	1,879	2,655
Palembang	277	597	1,422	2,200
Semarang	371	660	787	969
Surabaja	679	1,471	2,461	3,407
Tegal	30	266	762	1,186
Ujung Pandang	162	502	1,051	1,552
IRAN				
Ahväz	85	309	871	1,188
Esfahan	184	767	1,381	1,929
Karaj	22	126	1,044	1,538
Mashhad	173	685	1,990	2,498
Qom	78	228	888	1,428
Shiraz	128	418	1,124	1,471
Tabriz	235	662	1,274	1,674
Teheran	1,042	4,274	6,979	8,178
IRAQ				
Baghdad	579	2,815	4,865	6,549
Mosul	144	397	1,131	1,835
IRELAND				
Dublin	632	833	985	1,149
ISRAEL				
Tel Aviv-Jaffa	418	1,206	2,001	2,392
ITALY				
Florence	648	916	778	778
Genoa	908	1,086	890	890
Milan	3,633	5,529	4,251	4,251
Naples	2,750	3,624	3,012	3,012
Rome	1,566	2,998	2,649	2,649
Turin	880	1,641	1,294	1,294
IVORY COAST				
Abidjan	59	960	3,790	6,076
JAPAN				
Hiroshima	200	505	866	876
Kitakyushu	954	1,853	2,750	2,926
Kyoto	1,002	1,622	1,849	1,899

Nagoya	992	2,293	3,157	3,283
Osaka	4,147	9,844	11,013	11,013
Sapporo	254	978	1,813	2,002
Sendai	324	635	953	1,139
Tokyo	6,920	19,771	26,444	27,190
JORDAN				
Amman	90	500	1,148	1,654
KAZAKHSTAN				
Almaty	377	860	1,130	1,144
KENYA				
Nairobi	87	677	2,233	4,168
KOREA, NORTH (DEMOCRATIC PEOPLE'S REPUBLIC OF KOREA)				
Nampo	52	215	1,022	1,359
Pyongyang	516	1,348	3,124	3,580
KOREA, SOUTH (REPUBLIC OF KOREA)				
Ansan	53	140	984	2,230
Inch'on	258	791	2,884	3,270
Kwangju	174	601	1,379	1,395
P'ohang	43	154	790	1,275
Puch'on	51	108	900	929
Pusan	948	2,418	3,830	3,857
Seoul	1,021	6,808	9,888	9,918
Songnam	53	268	1,353	2,184
Suwon	74	220	876	907
Taegu	355	1,297	2,675	2,698
Taejon	131	501	1,522	1,624
Ulsan	29	246	1,340	1,800
KUWAIT				
Kuwait City	90	682	879	1,136
LATVIA				
Riga	490	789	761	761
LEBANON				
Beirut	327	1,062	2,070	2,500
LIBYA				
Benghazi	53	310	829	1,099
Tripoli	106	611	1,733	2,265
MADAGASCAR				
Antananarivo	180	408	1,603	3,190
MALAYSIA				
Kuala Lumpur	208	645	1,379	1,882
MALI				
Bamako	62	377	1,114	2,143
MEXICO				
Ciudad Juárez	123	474	1,239	1,781
Culiacán	49	230	750	892
Guadalajara	403	1,850	3,697	4,265
León	123	589	1,293	1,654
Mérida	143	351	849	1,038
Mexicali	66	302	771	954
Mexico City	2,883	10,691	18,066	20,434
Monterrey	356	1,590	3,267	3,906

Puebla	227	858	1,888	1,997
Querétaro	49	159	798	1,079
San Luis Potosí	132	378	857	1,046
Tijuana	60	355	1,297	1,937
Toluca	54	309	1,455	2,707
Torreón	189	556	1,012	1,157
MONGOLIA				
Ulan Bator	70	356	764	993
MOROCCO				
Casablanca	626	1,793	3,357	4,605
Fès	165	433	907	1,300
Marrakesh	209	367	822	1,210
Rabat	145	641	1,616	2,339
MOZAMBIQUE				
Maputo	92	456	1,094	1,899
MYANMAR				
Mandalay	168	442	770	1,134
Yangon	687	1,760	4,393	6,258
NETHERLANDS				
Amsterdam	855	989	1,105	1,115
Rotterdam	741	1,032	1,078	1,082
NEW ZEALAND				
Auckland	319	729	1,102	1,403
NICARAGUA				
Managua	110	443	1,009	1,529
NIGER				
Niamey	34	187	775	1,789
NIGERIA				
Ibadan	427	847	1,549	2,542
Lagos	288	1,890	8,665	15,966
Ogbomosho	113	432	809	1,356
NORWAY				
Oslo	492	634	779	836
PAKISTAN				
Faisalabad	169	907	2,142	3,526
Gujranwala	117	439	1,325	2,223
Hyderabad	233	667	1,221	1,891
Karachi	1,028	3,990	10,032	16,197
Lahore	826	2,399	5,452	8,721
Multan	182	599	1,263	2,000
Peshawar	148	347	1,066	1,750
Rawalpindi	232	670	1,521	2,500
PANAMA				
Panama City	171	528	1,173	1,543
PARAGUAY				
Asunción	223	551	1,262	1,959
PERU				
Lima	973	3,651	7,443	9,388
PHILIPPINES				
Davao	124	488	1,146	1,365
Metro Manila	1,544	5,000	9,950	12,579

POLAND				
Crakow	363	698	859	892
Gdansk	365	766	893	913
Katowice	1,689	3,019	3,494	3,547
Lodz	725	971	1,053	1,061
Warsaw	1,014	1,907	2,274	2,325
PORTUGAL				
Lisbon	778	1,168	3,861	4,544
Porto	362	500	1,940	2,400
PUERTO RICO				
San Juan	398	948	1,388	1,584
ROMANIA				
Bucharest	1,111	1,869	2,001	2,001
RUSSIA				
Chelyabinsk	573	966	1,045	1,008
Ekaterinburg	628	1,135	1,218	1,162
Kazan	514	942	1,063	1,051
Krasnoyarsk	290	734	840	811
Moscow	5,356	7,623	8,367	8,141
Nizhni Novgorod	796	1,273	1,332	1,290
Novosibirsk	719	1,250	1,321	1,276
Omsk	444	933	1,174	1,187
Perm	498	937	991	952
Rostov-on-Don	484	874	1,012	1,009
Saint Petersburg	2,903	4,326	4,635	4,488
Samara	658	1,146	1,132	1,083
Saratov	473	863	881	871
Tolyatti	27	382	771	899
Ufa	418	887	1,102	1,110
Ulyanovsk	136	416	864	1,144
Volgograd	461	884	1,000	1,000
Voronezh	332	732	918	934
SAUDI ARABIA				
Dammam	22	136	764	1,278
Jidda	119	594	3,192	5,183
Mecca	148	383	1,335	2,063
Medina	44	208	891	1,429
Riyadh	111	710	4,549	7,536
SENEGAL				
Dakar	223	768	2,078	3,481
SIERRA LEONE				
Freetown	52	288	800	1,506
SINGAPORE				
Singapore	1,022	2,263	4,018	4,756
SOMALIA				
Mogadishu	47	271	1,157	2,444
SOUTH AFRICA				
Cape Town	618	1,387	2,930	3,458
Durban	486	932	2,391	3,020
East Rand	546	997	1,552	1,703
Johannesburg	900	1,578	2,950	3,811
Port Elizabeth	192	575	1,006	1,150
Pretoria	275	667	1,590	2,152

SPAIN				
Barcelona	1,558	2,873	2,729	2,729
Madrid	1,550	3,823	3,976	3,976
SUDAN				
Khartoum	182	896	2,742	4,687
SWEDEN				
Göteborg	351	691	778	808
Stockholm	741	1,359	1,612	1,704
SWITZERLAND				
Zürich	494	713	939	947
SYRIA				
Aleppo	320	879	2,229	3,489
Damascus	367	1,122	2,144	3,170
Homs	101	312	811	1,291
TAIWAN				
Kaohsiung	255	986	1,463	1,697
Taichung	194	537	950	1,344
Taipei	604	2,024	2,550	2,678
TANZANIA				
Dar es Salaam	78	638	2,115	4,080
THAILAND				
Bangkok	1,360	3,842	7,372	9,816
TUNISIA				
Tunis	472	868	1,892	2,414
TURKEY				
Adana	138	471	1,091	1,288
Ankara	542	1,709	3,155	3,778
Bursa	148	345	1,186	1,551
Gaziantep	104	301	757	933
Istanbul	1,077	3,601	8,953	11,362
Izmir	480	1,046	2,214	2,704
UGANDA				
Kampala	53	399	1,213	2,706
UKRAINE				
Dnepropetrovsk	536	981	1,069	1,069
Donetsk	585	963	1,007	1,007
Kharkov	758	1,353	1,416	1,416
Kiev	815	1,926	2,499	2,499
Lvov	326	620	764	764
Odessa	532	982	931	931
Zaporozhye	315	730	813	813
UNITED ARAB EMIRATES				
Dubai	-	180	886	1,229
UNITED KINGDOM				
Birmingham	2,314	2,430	2,272	2,272
Leeds	1,414	1,508	1,433	1,433
Liverpool	981	818	915	951
London	8,733	8,169	7,640	7,640
Manchester	2,537	2,425	2,252	2,252
Tyneside (Newcastle)	909	838	981	1,026

UNITED STATES				
Atlanta	513	1,387	2,706	3,100
Austin	137	320	759	903
Baltimore	1,168	1,670	2,053	2,308
Boston	2,238	2,666	2,934	3,260
Buffalo-Niagara Falls	899	1,041	990	1,119
Chicago	4,945	6,749	6,989	7,603
Cincinnati	817	1,117	1,323	1,500
Cleveland	1,392	1,848	1,735	1,940
Columbus, Ohio	441	813	1,067	1,222
Dallas-Fort Worth	866	2,234	3,937	4,465
Denver	505	1,198	1,698	1,924
Detroit	2,769	3,885	3,809	4,193
Fort Lauderdale-Hollywood-Pampano Beach	67	797	1,471	1,689
Houston	709	2,030	3,386	3,816
Indianapolis	505	829	1,008	1,151
Jacksonville, Florida	246	564	883	1,025
Kansas City	703	1,100	1,460	1,667
Las Vegas	35	325	995	1,188
Los Angeles	4,046	8,926	13,213	14,494
Louisville	476	751	785	891
Memphis	409	720	894	1,020
Miami-Hialeah	466	1,410	2,224	2,524
Milwaukee	836	1,228	1,285	1,448
Minneapolis-St. Paul	996	1,748	2,378	2,688
New Orleans	664	1,021	1,079	1,217
New York	12,399	15,880	18,732	17,944
Norfolk-Virginia Beach-Newport News	388	720	1,963	2,329
Oklahoma City	278	628	901	1,039
Orlando	75	427	1,226	1,449
Philadelphia	2,939	4,069	4,427	4,873
Phoenix	221	1,117	2,623	3,029
Pittsburgh	1,539	1,827	1,735	1,939
Portland-Vancouver	516	925	1,328	1,516
Providence-Pawtucket	585	796	916	1,044
Riverside-San Bernadino	139	645	1,699	2,013
Sacramento	216	714	1,408	1,640
Salt Lake City	230	573	911	1,051
San Antonio	454	859	1,318	1,513
San Diego	440	1,442	3,002	3,445
San Francisco-Oakland	2,031	3,093	4,077	4,548
San Jose	182	1,135	1,635	1,860
Seattle	627	1,316	2,097	2,397
St. Louis	1,407	1,865	2,084	2,335
Tampa-St. Petersburg-Clearwater	300	1,094	2,064	2,362
Washington, D.C.	1,298	2,626	3,952	4,446
West Palm Beach-Boca Raton-Delray Beach	88	379	1,143	1,363
URUGUAY				
Montevideo	1,140	1,178	1,324	1,411
UZBEKISTAN				
Tashkent	659	1,612	2,148	2,428
VENEZUELA				
Barqusimeto	127	475	923	1,164
Caracas	676	2,342	3,153	3,587

Ciudad Guayana	5	201	799	1,223
Maracaibo	260	825	1,901	2,604
Maracay	89	435	1,100	1,498
Valencia	108	519	1,893	2,948
VIETNAM				
Hai Phong	168	968	1,676	2,269
Hanoi	280	1,884	3,751	5,227
Ho Chi Minh City	1,213	2,808	4,619	6,251
YEMEN				
Sana'a	46	142	1,327	3,028
YUGOSLAVIA				
Belgrade	432	991	1,673	1,680
ZAMBIA				
Lusaka	26	385	1,653	2,733
ZIMBABWE				
Bulawayo	77	323	824	1,314
Harare	84	529	1,791	3,013

Source: World Urbanization Prospects, 2001 Revision (UN Population Division).

Index to Cities

Pages covering representative cities in each region are in italics.

Index to Subjects

Some terms (such as "city") occur so frequently throughout the book that it would be impossible to list every mention. Therefore, only the first appearance is referenced below.

About the Contributors

Scott Baum is a research fellow at the Centre for Research into Sustainable and Regional Futures, University of Queensland. His teaching interests include urban sociology and social science research methods, and his current research considers the social impacts of cities and globalization, urban and regional development, and the home ownership aspirations of young Australians.

Stanley D. Brunn is professor of geography at the University of Kentucky. He teaches world regional geography, political geography, and geographies of information and communication. His research focuses on images of places, creative cartographies, disciplinary histories, the impacts of 9-11, and human geographies of the 21st century.

Kam Wing Chan is professor of geography at the University of Washington. His teaching interests are China, urban and economic geography, and population. His current research interests include migration, household registration system, and urban labor market and cities in China. He worked recently as a consultant on China for the UN and the World Bank.

Darrick Danta is professor of geography at California State University at Northridge, where he teaches the geography of Europe and urban geography. His current research involves monitoring changes in East Central European cities during the transition to market economies and the impacts of EU expansion.

Ashok K. Dutt is professor of geography, planning, and urban studies at the University of Akron, where he teaches urban geography, urban and regional planning, and Asia. His current research focuses on religion, language, crime, and medical geographies of Indian cities.

Gary S. Elbow is professor of geography at Texas Tech University. His major teaching interests include human ecology, urban geography, Latin America, and geographic education. His current research focuses on the role of secondary cities in Latin America and the changing view of regionalism.

Larry R. Ford is professor of geography at San Diego State University. He teaches comparative urban structure and design, especially on North America, Europe, and Asia, and the historical and cultural geography of cities. His current research examines American midtowns and downtowns, housing traditions and in-fill, new urbanism designs, and San Diego.

Rina Ghose is assistant professor of geography at the University of Wisconsin, Milwaukee. Her teaching interests include urban geography, South Asia, and geographic information systems (GIS). Her research focuses on public participation GIS, the role of GIS in local government planning, the social implications of GIS and digital technology, gentrification, and smart growth management.

Brian J. Godfrey is professor of geography at Vassar College. His major teaching interests are urban geography, Latin American studies, and urban studies. His research interests include global-city regions, community and neighborhood change, and sustainable development, especially in Brazil and the Amazon Basin.

Ellen Hamilton is an urban specialist at the World Bank in Washington, D.C. She conducts research on Eastern Europe and the former U.S.S.R., especially on poverty, housing and communal services, local economic development, and decentralization.

Maureen Hays-Mitchell is associate professor of geography at Colgate University. Her teaching interests include international development, gender and environment, and global change. Her current research includes fieldwork on the urban informal sector and microenterprise development in Peru and the role of grassroots women in the Peruvian civil war and reconstruction process.

Linda McCarthy is assistant professor of geography at the University of Wisconsin at Milwaukee. Her teaching interests are Europe, urban geography, land use planning, and the geography of the world economy. Her current interests related to Europe include comparative urban regional development, competition and cooperation among localities for private investment, and brownfield development.

Assefa Mehretu is professor of geography and director of the Center for Integrative Studies at Michigan State University. His teaching interests include economic geography, urban geography, location theory, and African development. His research focuses on questions of unequal development, including socioeconomic marginalization and African development.

Beth A. Mitchneck is associate professor of geography and regional development at the University of Arizona. Her major teaching interests are economic geography and regional development, research design, and the geography of the Former Soviet Union. Her current research focuses on local governance and economic development and internal migration in Russia.

Chris Mutambirwa is professor of geography and chair of environmental sciences at the University of Zimbabwe, Harare. He teaches courses on urban development, the geography of Africa, and quantitative methods. His current research focuses on a number of urban and regional development issues including gender, rural-urban migration, and rural development in Zimbabwe and Africa.

George M. Pomeroy is assistant professor of geography at Shippensburg University where he teaches courses on regional development and planning, urban geography, and Asia. His current research addresses questions about urban growth in South Asia and garden cities/new town planning in the U.S.

Lydia M. Pulsipher is professor of geography at the University of Tennessee, where she teaches cultural geography, qualitative research methods, national identity issues, and contemporary issues facing Middle America and the Caribbean. Among her current research projects are redefining and decolonizing Caribbean tourism.

Robert J. Stimson is professor of geographical sciences and planning and director of the Centre for Research into Sustainable Urban and Regional Futures at the University of Queensland. He teaches courses on human settlements, human spatial behavior, and regional economic development. His current research examines the socioeconomic performance of cities and regions, housing provision and policy, and human spatial behavior.

James Tyner is associate professor of geography at Kent State University, where he teaches East and Southeast Asia, urban geography, and population geography. His current research focuses on population movements in Asia, the spatial structure of overseas employment, and Manila as a global city.

Judy Walton is an independent scholar based in Portland, Oregon. Her teaching interests are urban and cultural geography, American cultural landscapes, and sustainable cities. Her research interests focus on new urbanism/urban design, downtown revitalization and economic development, urban tourism, theme towns, and American urban landscapes. She taught previously at Humboldt State University.

Jack F. Williams is professor of geography at Michigan State University. He teaches world regional geography, world urban development, geography of East Asia, and a multidisciplinary survey of Asia. His current research focuses on environmental problems and policies, especially in Taiwan and China, with an emphasis on urban areas.

Donald J. Zeigler is professor of geography at Old Dominion University. His teaching interests include the geography of the Middle East and political and cultural geography. His current research focuses on the changing geographies of religious minorities in Middle Eastern cities and the geographical basis of ancient history in the Mediterranean world.